THE IDEA OF UNITY

Edward Merkus

First Edition
Revised 23rd October 2018

2018
Sydney Australia

The Idea of Unity published in August 2018 by Arc-Design

ISBN 978-0-6484039-0-6 Paperback
ISBN 978-0-6484039-1-3 Hardback

About the author

Eddie was born in Sydney Australia to Dutch immigrants and began painting as a young teenager, which he continued throughout his life. He lived in The Netherlands for two years and gained a taste for the extreme sport of skydiving. Back in Australia, he continued skydiving and added scuba diving, skiing to his extreme sports, which complimented his studies in architecture and fine art from which he gained a Bachelor of Architecture. Eddie was interested in finding the true nature of art and its opposite science and studied psychology and philosophy in his spare time, which gave him an alterative viewpoint to his creative and sporting interests.

After 502 jumps and a narrow escape, Eddie ended skydiving and learned how to fly light aircraft and became a Private Pilot, which he equated to "armchair skydiving". He built an architectural practice offering services in housing, educational and commercial projects. He realised he had to sacrifice his free, easy and exciting life, for a stable family life that complimented his free spirit. He married, had children, designed and built a unique house Southwest of Sydney. He always had a natural inclination towards art, dreams and the unconscious in general and journeyed deep into this mysterious world of ideas and characters. Eddie explored this inner world, documented some of the stages in paintings and brought together his findings in the form of this book called The Idea of Unity.

Eddie always knew that one had to live life while the body was young and robust, and reflect on life when older and is continuing his work with the myth making unconscious and expressing its treasures.

Arc-design.com.au, Sydney Australia, Contact mail@arc-design.com.au

Cover: The Mandala of Unity perceived in the heavens

Printed and bound worldwide by IngramSpark

TABLE OF CONTENTS

FORWARD by Dr Leon Petchkovsky

FORWARD by Dr Leon Petchkovsky

Edward Merkus is an artist/architect with an extraordinary psychological vision. Many years ago I worked with Edward, as we helped further our understanding of Jung's views of "individuation", the developmental process out of which the individual self develops out of an undifferentiated unconscious, integrating over time innate elements of personality and the experiences of life into a well-functioning whole, to achieve one's life purpose.

In this book, Edward extends this concept of individuation to a broader realm: organisations, plants and animals, and our understanding of physics and the universe. This is essentially a Buddhist vision. As the Buddhist Heart Sutra puts it, "*all dharmas are empty, there is not form, sensation, conceptions, synthesis, or discrimination*" yet everything is a whole, a unity.

As Edward says in his introduction:

> "in the things we sense, think, feel and the intuitions that gives us symbolic hints on how to become more aware of the idea. It pervades our lives in everything we strive for and do, and is behind the yearnings and searches of many people. Aside from the lofty ideals of the great religions, this study emphasises the simple and immediate experience of the idea of unity and how it can be realised".

The Mandala exemplifies all this. Its centre is an abstract representation. Life orbits around it, differentiating, and yet, this very process brings us back to the core.

Edward covers this vast territory eloquently, examining pre-historic ideas of unity, structured belief systems in Egypt, Greece, Rome and the various religious systems, ideas of unity in philosophy, the physics of matter, vegetation and the animal world, human nature, and symbolic language. His eloquent final chapter looks at how the unity principle manifests in one's everyday life.

As one says at McDonalds *"make me ONE with everything"*.

Dr Leon Petchkovsky MB BS PhD FRC Psych.
A/Prof Psychiatry University of Queensland.
Psychiatrist, Jungian Analyst
Past President, ANZSJA
Director, the Pinniger Clinic, HQ@Robina

1. INTRODUCTION

The purpose of this book is to show that we live in a physical world and a psychic world of ideas, dreams and emotions that has a unity of purpose. This includes human relations and activities, as well as the natural world of flora and fauna. I will attempt to show that all physical and psychic determinants exist in a unified cosmos that we can only grasp through the idea. This idea of unity[1] in its varying manifestations is central to all human endeavours. I shall also attempt to trace the evolution of the idea from its earliest beginnings to the present day and how it oscillates from one side to the other. We cannot comprehend unity itself at this stage of our evolution because we have not found the cause and effect relationship between them. We are at the beginning stage of our understanding and exploration of the physical world in itself. Similarly, our understanding of psychic processes is also in its infancy. The way these two sides of reality interact and relate to each other is the subject of this book, which I have termed the idea of unity.

It is by no means an easy task to show how the idea of unity works in humans and nature because of the vast scope of physical and psychic material involved. It requires the investigation of many disciplines and analysis of the ideas clouded in mystery. The idea of a unified cosmos is in need of clarification as it forms part of our understanding of our psychic evolution. It is a prejudice of our western intellect to compartmentalise our disciplines into separate areas with little or no relationship. For example, the behaviourist and analytic schools of psychology approach mental processes and human behaviour from a physiological and phenomenological point of view respectively, but the subject matter itself unifies their differing approaches.

In that respect, Physics is more open to a unified approach, from the study of the physical universe and its overwhelming vastness, to the sub atomic world of Quantum Mechanics. The research into the sub atomic particles of Quarks, Leptons, Fermions and Bosons and the unifying "God Particle" hold promise in explaining not only the nature of matter, but also the nature of the psychic processes. This development in physics and the discovery of a unifying particle shows how the idea of unity remains constant in a changing framework and context.

Humanity's understanding and knowledge of the physical world has grown dramatically since the ancient world. They could only view space

---

[1]LEIBNIZ Basic Writings, The Open Court Publishing Company 1962, Leibniz's concept of Monadology as the basis and building blocks of all things including metaphysical ideas.

with their naked eyes and their idea of unity was centred on the earth, and everything revolved around that centre. The idea was perceived under the ocean, on mountaintops, in trees, and from earth to the sun and moon, and on into space. As human understanding and knowledge grew and explored matter and space, the idea of unity transformed to suit the increase in knowledge. We still looked for that unifying idea of a centre holding everything together, and it moved further into space, or further into atomic structure. The idea of unity did not change; it moved to suit our new understanding of the physical world, which was continually out of reach and projected onto physical objects. The advances of psychology and physics point to a unified centre between psyche and matter, and opposites of the same reality.

Zoology and Botany also display a dependence and unity that is difficult to discern where one field ends and the other begins. The symbiotic relationship between these two branches of science goes beyond the obvious nutritional need of one to the other, into the chemical exchange of essential gases. Flora metabolises CO_2 and expels O_2 as a bi-product. On the other hand, fauna metabolises O_2 and expels CO_2, thus binding the opposites through their relationship.

I shall attempt to show how the idea of unity pervades every aspect of our lives, in the things we sense, think, feel and the intuitions that gives us symbolic hints on how to become more aware of the idea. It pervades our lives in everything we strive for and do, and is behind the yearnings and searches of many people. Aside from the lofty ideals of the great religions, this study emphasises the simple and immediate experience of the idea of unity and how it can be realised.

The idea exists in the most unusual and mundane places and beyond its immediate perception; we can benefit from its influence though relationship. I shall show how the idea of unity is a living force that can support and influence the way we behave, understand and live our lives. I shall also show how this living force works and how we can see glimpses of it in visions, fantasies and more importantly, meaningful coincidences.[2] Also included are the life-changing experiences that we all go through at some time. The larger experiences may appear overwhelmingly positive or negative. We may not like the experience, as some are often quite disastrous, but the purpose is nevertheless meaningful for our personal growth.

I intend to show that the idea of unity requires not only relationship but also an acknowledgment that our lives are to some extent pre-destined

---

[2] The concept of Synchronicity

and that free will is a local feeling we experience with a short range. What we call fate is the unfolding of one's life story as an individual. I encourage an objective and critical viewpoint of the forces, urges and ideas that come into our awareness from inside and regard them as expressions of the psyche and factual emanations. We do not create most of the things that come to our minds. Dreams for example, come to us at night while asleep. Our senses are dormant, we do not see the room we are sleeping in, we are neither aware of household noises nor aware of our other senses. We perceive dreams with an inner eye and sometimes remember them when awake. They give us quite specific images, ideas and emotions and come to us in a specific form with a purpose, whether we are aware of its purpose or not.

Fantasies are similar to dreams, but are closer to consciousness as we perceive the images and ideas while awake. Unlike dreams, we have to some extent the ability to direct fantasies. Wishes, often confused as dreams, are more like ideas of one's desire for an object or person. The goal of the desire is the yearning for something that we do not have and want, and believe its acquisition will make us complete. What we want will satisfy a need we have to integrate the idea of the object or person into our unity.

Like fantasies, we perceive Intuitions[3] while awake, which gives us information spontaneously. They are a form of an inner perception, which provide solutions and insights in the form of ideas, impulses and hunches. Intuition is the conduit for unconscious contents and behind many great leaps and discoveries in various fields. It can take the form of knowing what may happen in the future or what possibilities are available in a given situation. It is a difficult function to describe as it happens spontaneously and without conscious effort. It is being open to possibilities and regarded by the psychologists as perception via the unconscious.

The inner contents from an unconscious source continually flow into and intermingle with our conscious everyday lives. When we consider dreams, fantasies and intuitions, as products of consciousness, that is our waking life, and created by us because they are in our mind; we rob the material of its autonomy, objectivity, and healing effect. It then becomes a form of identification and possession. The ancients regarded such unconscious products as independent characters they called gods, that moved them from inside.

---

[3] 'The ability to understand something instinctively, without the need for conscious reasoning.' https://en.oxforddictionaries.com/definition/intuition

Freud considered the unconscious (id) a repository of remnants from consciousness incompatible with the prevailing culture (superego). This viewpoint, as we shall see later in this study, is a temperamental prejudice of an extroverted personality type. This is an understandable interpretation because the personal unconscious uses images from our conscious lives to communicate. This does however, not explain why dreams are independent of our conscious intentions and uses what appear to be arbitrary characters and scenes. For example we may dream of a robber breaking down our front door and regard the robber as part of our nature incompatible with the conscious construct or culture. The image thus indicates something incompatible with our view of reality and encourages us to build a stronger door to keep out the robber.

On the other hand, if we regarded the robber symbolically as a person wishing to break in to our home (conscious attitude) and take something away from us (beliefs, energy) it may indicate an aspect or attitude in ourselves that steals something precious from another part of ourselves. In other words, the robber wants to take something from us that we do not want him to have. A part of us is stealing from another part of us and a dream like this would be typical of a person that regards the unconscious as an epiphenomenon of consciousness. The conscious ego believes they created the expressions of the unconscious thus robbing it of its ability to reflect our conscious attitude.

I shall also attempt to map the evolution of western culture through individuals and historic movements, and how the myth-making unconscious reflects that evolution. Unfortunately, there is no guarantee that a culture is on the right path to unity as it is not a static system and shows many degrees of interpretation. Individuals and cultures tend towards one sidedness and disparage the other side simply because it does not fit their idea. In such situations, there is always a reaction that reflects a one-sided attitude. It is my intention to show how this compensation of the opposite works in individuals and cultural constructs.

2. PRE-HISTORIC IDEAS OF UNITY

a. Animism

The term 'Animism' derives from the ancient Latin term 'anima' meaning breath, soul, life, spirit and the essence seen in plants, animals, and non-living matter. Further, it is the belief[4] in a supernatural power that organises and animates the material world. Jung[5] selected the term 'anima' to denote his experience of the soul of a man as an inner woman and container of unconscious contents. The soul functions not only as a container but also an animating principle of ideas projected onto objects. Animism is not a religion in the strict sense, but a natural progression from our animal ancestry to the first stage of self-awareness in our human evolution. Some scholars believe that animals also live in a world of animated gods and demons, which exerts an influence on their behaviour. At most, we could say that Animism is the foundation or beginnings of religion in the individual as Edward Tyler the English anthropologist explains.

> Here, they would naturally say, are men who have no religion because their forefathers had none, men who represent a pre-religious condition of the human race, out of which in the course of time religious conditions have arisen.[6]

Animism is the psychological system of projection of inner fantasies, ideas or characters onto physical objects and other people. It is an automatic process whose function is to attract or repel the subject to the object. It is a hallmark of early human evolution to project a great deal of the contents of the psyche onto objects based on its behaviour. It is therefore an early form of unity between subject, the physical reality of the object and the projected idea of the object with its associated energy and emotion.

Our animistic origins has to some extent fallen back into the unconscious as the physical sciences has de-potentiated objects through knowledge, and transformed the projections into ideas more aligned with the object. Knowledge helps us see the object as it is rather than how we imagine it to be. Projection of inner contents activates when knowledge reaches its limits and the void filled with ideas of the object. For example, the further

---

[4] I use the term 'belief' from our viewpoint, as I have no doubt that Animism is a concrete reality to early human individual perception.
[5] JUNG, C. G., 'Aion, Researches into the Phenomenology of the Self, Princeton University Press 1979
[6] TYLER, E. B., 'Primitive Culture' Volume 1, John Murray 1920, Page 418

we explore outer space, the more fanciful the ideas become. The ancients projected their inner gods onto the planets because they had insufficient knowledge of their true nature. This is typical of the animistic system of projection and is a natural mechanism of connection to the object, so that we can learn more about it. The difference between animism and our contemporary viewpoint is only a matter of degree and as I shall show later in this study, always has its base in the physical world. Tyler continues with his description of the opposites in early humans:

> In the first place, what is it that makes the difference between a living body and a dead one; what cause waking sleep, trance, disease, death? In the second place, what are those human shapes which appear in dreams and visions? Looking at these two groups of phenomena, the ancient savage philosophers probably made their first step by the inference that every man has two things belonging to him, namely, a life and a phantom.[7]

Tyler recognises that contents projected onto objects in animism have their origin in what he calls the 'phantom'. We can also observe the opposites of 'life and phantom' in animals and how they project ideas into the physical world which invokes either fear or bravery, and keeps them out of harm or emboldens them to action. I have no doubt that when an animal cowers in a thunderstorm; they are projecting an unknown entity onto what they hear making loud claps and other threatening sounds, howling wind and rain, and they protect themselves accordingly.

Projection becomes even more problematic when dealing with other people. It is only in the last century with the advent of the psychological sciences, that we attempt to transform these projections and see them at their source. One such example is an individual's trust in authority figures and the need to build and participate in hierarchies. This natural form of projection to be part of a hierarchy bonds people to a common cause, but it also reduces individual responsibility and gives people power to act as a collective. This form of authority projection has major benefits for building culture, and also drawbacks when groups come into conflict.

Other remnants of our Animistic roots are the projection of evil onto what we feel are our enemies with different values. Local moral codes control the projection of evil and self-analysis can temper it on a personal level. Collectively, the projection of evil is the motivating force behind national and world conflicts. Boundaries to collective projection are weak and

---

[7] Ibid, Page 428

easily overcome,[8] and not solved by collective means. Self-analysis of the projection in every individual is the only solution to collective projections. It requires an individual to stand alone, be critical of his or her own values and the realisation they are siding with all that is good in their own nature and projecting evil onto their neighbour.

Contemporary mythology has incorporated our technological advances and are expressed as alien species, flying saucers, galactic adventures, and so on. Motion pictures are one of these expressions and they keep us in touch with our mythological projections, as well as filling the void where knowledge is lacking. For example, Physics is not immune to psychological projection. The Higgs Boson particle discovered in 2013 and flippantly called the 'God particle', presumably because of its influence on the other particles in the atom. Another example is the 'Big Bang Theory' and the idea that nothing gave birth to the universe in an instant, which has more in common with ancient creation myths than known facts.

The above instances show that humans project a great deal of their psyches onto the physical world. What we believe or think about something may not necessarily be the whole reality of that object. Self-analysis, reflection, and personal isolation are methods to become aware of projection. Knowledge of the object also aids in the transformation of projection into an idea more aligned to the object. This encourages the differentiation of the idea and the object. The more an individual learns about an object, the more the idea approximates the reality of the object. We cannot however, remove the idea. We can know an object thoroughly with all its characteristics, but still have an idea of the object. What this shows is that the idea is as real as the physical object. The difficulty is recognising the difference between the projected idea and what the object is in itself. This aspect of our functioning also questions our perception of reality and leads us to conclude that part of reality, is psychic. This is a viewpoint also shared by Jung and Kant.

The value of animism today as an early form of projection, is its connection to the myth making unconscious. It is important to note that it is impossible to unlearn knowledge once gained through science of the physical world, but it is possible to connect to the primitive functioning of animism in ourselves. For example, when our car malfunctions when needed, we get annoyed and it affects our psyche. The uncooperative car has invited a projection and relationship to that projection. We know logically that it was a faulty car battery, but we do not know why the

---

[8] I refer to international law and the United Nations, which are often ignored by powerful nations.

battery failed at this time. We can dismiss it and make other arrangements or look at the projection and ask why the car did not cooperate when needed? Where were we going in the car and what were we going to do when we got there? These questions may have relevance on the timing of the car malfunction and its relationship to an inner compensation or movement. In this way, we differentiate the object and the idea and see how they interact with each other.

This approach endows physical objects with an animating quality that gives our lives meaning and protects us from danger. The difference between early human animism and our contemporary standpoint is the degree of awareness involved in projection, and this aspect alone separates us from our animistic origins. Our current level of awareness and rationality, see that the car malfunctions for one or other reasons but do not know why it malfunctioned at this time. Asking this question brings it back to the psychic realm and the meaning behind the malfunction. This is one method of raising our level of awareness and relationship to the object. Early humans projected much of their psychic contents onto objects, animals, people etc., and they used ritual to understand the object by forming a relationship to it through projection.

b. Ritual- De-potentiating the Environment

Early humans had an innate ability to ritualise their unconscious projections as an attempt to relate to the object. For example, the idea of a lion projected onto the actual lion was the starting point for the relationship. It is difficult to relate[9] to a lion in the wild directly without the necessary safeguards. The lion's behaviour which is part of its idea, can be observed from a distance. In other words, the idea of the lion includes its strength, power and majesty, which are admirable traits in a human and form an identification based on projection. Humans share these traits and is the reason the lion is used for royal and cultural emblems.

Rituals express the symbolic unity of idea and object to gain some control and influence over the object and learn about its true nature. It is less likely that a wild animal will attack if you have some form of relationship to it and your idea is closer to the animal's reality. A devouring lion is a horrific thought and adding this to our idea of a lion modifies our behaviour and protects us from harm. In other words, we try to avoid being devoured by referring to the idea of the lion, which changes the way we behave. The lion does not modify our behaviour, the idea of it does. If we had never seen or heard of a lion, we would unknowingly walk

---

[9] I acknowledge under rare circumstances such as raising a lion from birth enables a different relationship to one in the wild.

into their territory and potential harm. Knowledge of the object transforms our idea of it and we can protect ourselves from its true nature.

The very fact that a lion will devour someone to satiate its hunger is almost secondary to the projected idea of a displeased lion attacking a tribe and devouring one of its members. The reason for the devouring is not so much the lion being hungry and a person being in the wrong place at the wrong time, but the idea of the lion being displeased with the tribe and taking vengeance on an unfortunate member. This appeases the tribe's sensibility and gives a symbolic reason for the devouring of one of their members, which in turn leads to efforts to protect against and appease the lion in the future.

This example shows the reality of the projected idea from the individual. In this instance, the idea of the lion is more important than the simple fact that the lion was hungry and ate what was close by and available at the time. If we relate to the idea, we feel that we have the potential to influence its effect on us. Ritual also takes the form of worship of an idea and modifies the group's behaviour accordingly. If a ritual has benefit for a people, it protects them from harm, teaches them how to behave and provides a relationship to the object of worship. When repeated as a ritual, it becomes a normal part of life and the beginning of religion.

Another example of a less threatening object is the projection onto the tree. Many cultures have ritualised the tree and it is an excellent hook for human projection. The tree connects the heavens with the terrestrial plain and the underworld through its roots. In animistic and religious traditions, the tree represents the life and uniqueness of the individual soul. The tree, as do humans, begins from a seed and grows to the nourishing light and air in the sky (consciousness) and down to the nourishing water and minerals inside the earth (unconscious). It is quite fitting that people identify themselves with a tree as a symbol and the associated rituals of growth in the spiritual and earthly realms.

Clifford Geertz[10] shows how ritual brings together the 'model of' reality on the one hand and the 'model for' reality on the other. The psychologists call this the subject and object and Plato the 'model' and 'copy of the model', which in this book I call the relationship between idea and object. This relationship still pervades our everyday lives. For example, the ritual of shaking hands originated as a gesture of peace and display of a weapon-less hand. This simple ritual brings together the object, in this case another person, with the idea of the object, which includes the

---

[10] GEERTZ, Clifford (1973). *The Interpretation of Cultures*. New York: Basic Books. p. 112.

potential threat and danger and the open hand abrogates the potential threat.

Rituals are a feature of most, if not all cultures and the beginning of relationship to projected ideas and understanding human behaviour. Other examples of ritual include rites of passage; sacraments; purification rites; oaths of allegiance; dedication ceremonies and coronations. They all display a mode of behaviour that venerates the projected idea, and in some cases, reinforces and maintains the ideas power and influence over the individual. How would we feel about royals if it were not for all the pomp and ceremony surrounding them?

3. STRUCTURED BELIEF SYSTEMS

a. Ancient Egypt

Ancient Egypt followed prehistoric Egypt around 3100 BC. It owed its success as a culture to its ability to adapt to the Nile River and use its fertile plains in the development of agriculture. The predictable flooding and controlled irrigation of the flood plain produced surplus food for its population, which in turn encouraged social development. With surplus resources, the Egyptians explored the surrounding regions for minerals, developed a writing system, mathematics, medicine, ship-building, glass technology, literature, construction, agricultural projects, traded with other regions and created a viable military. All this was under the control of a pharaoh who reigned over the population with an elaborate system of religious beliefs. The strong institution of kingship developed by the pharaohs, served to legitimize state control over land, labour, and resources that was essential to the survival and growth of ancient Egyptian civilization. The pharaohs were not only kings, but also a connection to their gods and the life hereafter.

Ancient Egypt is an example of the transition from hunting and gathering to agriculture giving their culture stability and predictability. They took advantage of the regular flooding and fertility of the Nile River to tame the land for their own needs. The earliest depictions of deities of the people of the Nile valley related to known mammals or birds, which represented the transition from hunting to farming. This later evolved into hybrid animal/human deities with animal heads and human bodies.[11] The worship of these characters reflected the slow transition from hunting to agriculture. In other words, the age-old projection of unconscious contents onto objects and animals, as it was in animism, changed to the worship of personified elemental forces that reflected their agricultural pursuits. The worship of objects and natural phenomena became ritualised and institutionalised through the pharaohs.

The projections changed because the Egyptian's lives changed. Instead of hunting and foraging for food, they learned to cultivate food where they lived on the fertile plains of the Nile River.

> .....the Egyptians worshipped, though generally without cult, the great divinities of nature: the Sky, the Earth, the Sun the Moon and the mighty river which, in the words of Herodotus, created Egypt - the Nile.[12]

---

[11] LAROUSSE, New Encyclopedia of Mythology, Hamlyn Publishing, 1968, page 9
[12] Ibid, page 10

With this change came different concerns. Instead of animals, it became the natural environment of the objects and phenomena that enable agriculture. These include the earth, air (sky), fire (sun) and water (moon). These objects and features are the fundamental and essential components of agriculture, and their characteristics and behaviour formed part of their ideas. For example, the sun needs to shine for things to grow, but needs to be balanced by water. Insufficient water and plants whither, too much water and they drown, infertile earth such as sand, does not promote plant growth and sky without rainfall, again leads to dryness and withering. It is the balance of these natural elements that gave the ancient Egyptians the right environment for their agriculture and hence their own growth.

Ideas of objects such as the sun, moon, sky and earth are different to the objects themselves. For example, knowledge of the sun was limited to how it affected their bodies and their crops through their immediate perception. They realized they were dependent on the elements and were aware of these characteristics. In addition to observation, individuals related to them from known patterns of behaviour in their own lives. This connection of outer characteristics and inner patterns is the way we relate to things initially. It is the age-old projection of complex ideas of inner characters of parents (model) and siblings (copy) onto external objects and in this instance became the gods of ancient Egyptians.

The sky goddess Nut (sky) or Hathor was depicted either as a cow standing on the earth bent over with her feet and hands, or as a woman arched over touching the earth with the tips of her feet and hands. Nut was often depicted with the head of a falcon whose eyes opened and closed, which caused night and day and the appearance of the sun and moon. In contrast, the earth was a masculine god called Geb (earth), and sometimes depicted lying prone on his belly with all the world's vegetation growing out of his back.[13] At other times, Geb is depicted lying on his back with an erect penis, trying to reach his twin sister/wife Nut. We can see from this how these deities related to elemental characteristics. The sky provides fructifying nurturing moisture in the form of rain that made crops grow which in turn relates to how Nut was depicted as the over-arching cow that feeds its young with nurturing milk. The earth relates to the sky sexually by receiving her nurturing moisture and bringing forth vegetation from his back. The back is associated with the hard work of tilling the soil and tending to the crops. The following excerpt describes how the sun fits into this scenario:

---

[13] Ibid

The sun had many names and gave rise to extremely vast interpretations. In his aspect of solar disk the sun was called Aten. Depending upon whether he rose, or climbed to the zenith, on he was given the names Khepri, Ra or Atum. He was also call Horus and it was under this name, joined with that of Ra, that later reigned over all Egypt as Ra-Harakhte. It was claimed that he was reborn every morning of the celestial cow like a suckling calf, or like a little child of the sky-Goddess. He was also said, be a falcon with speckled wings flying through space, or the right eye only of the great divine bird. Another conception of him was that of an egg laid daily by the celestial goose, or more frequently a gigantic scarab rolling before him the incandescent globe of the sun as, on earth, the sacred scarab rolls the ball of dung in which it has deposited its eggs.[14]

The sun's mythology is more complex than the sky and earth. In this instance, the sun is masculine and has many names. Unlike the earth, which is stable and always present, the sky has her moods of clear, cloudy and rainy, whereas the sun has regular cycles of day and night but occasionally obscured by clouds. The sun is born every morning and dies every evening, to be reborn again in the morning, which as an idea is the precursor to reincarnation. The moon, in this instance, is also masculine:

The moon, too, was called by different names: Aah, Thoth, Khons. Sometimes he was the son of Nut, the sky-Goddess. Sometimes he was a dog-headed ape, or an ibis; at others, the left eye of the great celestial hawk whose right eye was the sun.[15]

This shows that the moon and sun have complimentary characteristics of a great bird's eyes flying through the sky (Nut). When one is eye closed, the other is open and the corresponding celestial body is present. There is however, no mention of the moon being present during the day. The sun and moon are therefore not ultimate deities. They are both masculine and exist within a feminine context of sky. Both Ra (sun) and Thoth (moon) are Nut's (sky) children, and are therefore of lower rank in the Egyptian deity family tree. This is an interesting interpretation of the behaviour of the celestial elements. On one hand, the sky is the context and background to the sun and moon, and nourishes the earth with her water (milk). Of the four elements sky, earth, sun and moon, the sky is the only feminine character, and in some instances regarded as the mother of the three other masculine characters. She contains the sun and moon in her arched body and nourishes the earth, which indicates a closer relationship between sky and earth than sky, sun and moon. The rain and earth and their relationship, sustained the Nile delta and therefore, the agricultural basis of the Egyptian culture. The different

---

[14] Ibid
[15] Ibid

23

elemental deities show that their myths were at the beginning stage of development and interpreted differently in regions around the Nile.

It is an attempt to relate the earth to the celestial elements and fit them into a pattern. If we compare this development with animistic practices of projection onto animals and natural objects, we can see the evolution from recognition and connection to the behaviour of objects, to how those objects relate to each other. The ancient Egyptians began to see these connections between objects and how they influenced their lives and is an indication they were becoming aware of the unity surrounding them.

The ideas projected onto animals slowly anthropomorphised to human form in early Egyptian culture. In other words, their deities became more human. In this way, one has the ability to relate to these objects as we would relate to another person. For example, it is easier to ask the sky to provide nourishing rain if it is personified as a woman or cow. This in itself is a form of connecting the inner characters to celestial elements through projection.

The following passage describes the creation of the world through the deities of Moon (Thoth) and Sun (Ra) and adds Ptah (demiurge) and Osiris, one of the central deities.

> In his own temple Thoth, Ra, Ptah and Osiris was each proclaimed to have created the world, but each in his own way. Sometimes it was taught that the Gods had issued from the mouth of Demiurge and that all had been created by his voice. Sometimes it was alleged that they were born when the creator spat or performed an even cruder act. Again it was said that men had been engendered by his sweat or by a flood of tears gushing from his eyes. Another explanation was that men, together with the entire animal world, had emerged from the sun-dried mud of the Nile. It was also taught that the Demiurge had modelled them from the earth and fashioned them on a potter's wheel.[16]

In this creation myth, Ptah conceived the world by thought, will and word[17], or another act of creation through spittle or ejaculation. Another form of creation includes the modelling of men and animals from mud or clay. The ideas behind these methods of creation show a process similar to the creative inspiration of an artist through a bodily function or modelling skill. They show that the tribes of Egypt had varying interpretations that coalesced into the stories contained in the Ennead of Heliopolis.

---

[16] Ibid
[17] https://www.encyclopedia.com/humanities/culture-magazines/egyptian-myths

The Ennead describes the first god Nun representing the idea of the primordial chaos of water that had no active features. It was creation in potential and the beginning of existence. Nun is transcendent at the point of creation alongside Atum, the creator god. From the chaos of the primordial soup emerged the sun as the first act of creation. In the Coptic language, Nun or its derivation, Nu, relates to the Coptic word for 'deep' and 'abyss'[18]. This in itself is an interpretation of the myth-making unconscious as the source of all ideas.

> Formerly, according to the priests of Heliopolis, the Sun God reposed, under the name of Atum, in the bosom of Nun, the primordial ocean. There, in order that his lustre should run no risk of being extinguished, he took care to keep his eyes shut. He enclosed himself in the bud of a lotus until the day when, weary of his own impersonality, he rose by an effort of will from the abyss and appeared in glittering splendour under the name of Ra. He then bore Shu and Tefnut who, in their turn, gave birth to Geb and Nut, from whom issued Osiris and Isis, Set and Nephthys. These are the eight great Gods who with their chief Ra - or more exactly Ra Atum, since Ra and Atum were identified with each other - form the divine company or Ennead of Heliopolis. [19]

Atum was contained within this chaos as a spirit in 'potentia', and from his birth all other gods, men and all living things emerged. He later became the god of the rising and setting sun, and the sun's daytime features became the god, Ra. The spirit within chaos (Atum) is differentiated into and the spirit born from chaos (Ra).

Ra became the second stage and fully developed sun as it is in the daytime.[20] The description of Atum and Ra shows that the ancient Egyptians regarded Atum as the bridge between chaos and the order of daylight. This indicates an association between Nun, chaos and night (no sun), Atum emerging from chaos as twilight, and Ra as fully emerged sun of daylight. This seems to be a very apt staged interpretation of the emergence from unconsciousness into the daylight of consciousness.

> At the same time Ra had created a 'first' universe, different from the present world, which he governed from the 'Prince's Palace' in Heliopolis where he normally resided. The Books of the Pyramids minutely describe for us his royal existence and how, after his morning bath and breakfast, he would get into his boat and, in the company of his scribe, Weneg, inspect the twelve provinces of his kingdom, spending an hour in each.

---

[18] https://en.wikipedia.org/wiki/Nu_(mythology)
[19] New Larousse Encyclopedia of Mythology, Hamlyn Publishing, 1968, page 11
[20] Ibid

As long as Ra remained young and vigorous he reigned peacefully over Gods and men; but the years brought with them their ravages and the texts depict him as an old man with trembling mouth from which saliva ceaselessly dribbles. We shall see later how Isis took advantage of the God's senility, made him reveal his secret name and thus acquired sovereign power. [21]

The development of Ra had some intermediary stages. First, he resided in a palace in Heliopolis from where he inspected the twelve provinces in twelve hours of daylight. This indicated that the ancient Egyptians were already aware of daylight being divided into twelve hours, hence a twenty-four hour day, and that time was related to Ra's (sun) movement across Nut (sky). The myth states that Ra aged and became decrepit and open to the ravages of time and his subjects plotted against him. He became enraged, consulted with his council, and decided to throw his divine Eye as the goddess Hathor and began massacring his subjects but stopped due to his goodness. He now had distaste for the world and withdrew to the heavens where Nut (sky) turned into a cow and took Ra (sun) on her back to ride her boat across the sky every twelve hours.

This mixture of myth and physical reality shows how we have an innate need to relate celestial cycles and events with our everyday lives. For example, Ra is given the qualities of a person born in the morning, grow to the zenith, and steadily decline to old age and death. This is exactly how the sun behaves. His wrath may relate to the occasional droughts that occur at that time where his Eye is relentless and shines on his subjects without mercy until his goodness returns to natural cycles of sun, clouds and rain. The cycle of Ra includes both day and night, where he sheds his light onto the world until night and descends into darkness and sheds his light onto the inhabitants of the underworld.[22] This indicates that his spirit lives on in the underworld and returns the next day. This observed fact as well as the cycles of seed, growth, harvest and death in agricultural pursuits, is the basis for their death/resurrection myths and as we shall see shortly, relates to the life of Osiris.

The god Khepri depicted as a scarab-faced man further differentiates the behaviour of the sun and its relation to human life. He was the god of transformations and his name means 'he who becomes'[23], 'come into being' and 'develop'[24]. The scarab beetle rolls balls of dung across the ground, a behaviour the Egyptians saw as a symbol of the forces that

---

[21] Ibid
[22] Ibid, page 11
[23] Ibid
[24] WILKINSON, Richard H., The Complete Gods and Goddesses of Ancient Egypt, Thames & Hudson, 2003, page 230

move the sun across the sky. This is an indication that the ancient Egyptians already had an idea of individuation[25]. Khepri then replaced Atum in the morning, relegating him to the evening sunset. Ra gave birth to twins named Shu (air) and his sister Tefnut (dew and rain), further differentiating the realm between Geb (earth) and Nut (sky).

The myth of Osiris is the most developed story of the ancient Egyptian deities. He was a nature and fertility god of vegetation and earth, which dies with the harvest and is reborn with the new grain sprouts. After his dismemberment by his brother Set[26], he became known as the god of the moon, underworld, the dead, and the afterlife and above all, the god of resurrection and regeneration. Osiris, Isis and Set were the children of Geb (earth) and Nut (sky). Isis, his sister queen, was believed to help the dead enter the afterlife, and was considered the divine mother of the pharaoh. She is the goddess of magic and wisdom, kingship and protector of the kingdom. Set is the villain in the ancient stories and the god of desert, storms, disorder, violence and foreigners.

Plutarch (AD 46 – AD 120), the Greek biographer and writer, wrote an essay on Isis and Osiris detailing their lives and experiences. The following text also relates the ancient Egyptian gods to the Greek gods, showing common threads of interpretation. It is however, unclear where Plutarch got his information about the Egyptian stories. Later in this study, I shall review the story distilled from actual hieroglyphs found on ruins and ancient scrolls.

> One of the first acts related of Osiris in his reign was to deliver the Egyptians from their destitute and brutish manner of living. This he did by showing them the fruits of cultivation, by giving them laws, and by teaching them to honour the gods. Later he travelled over the whole earth civilizing it without the slightest need of arms, but most of the peoples he won over to his way by the charm of his persuasive discourse combined with song and all manner of music. Hence the Greeks came to identify him with Dionysus.[27]

This passage emphasises the civilising and liberating aspect of Osiris and his unifying attributes. He was instrumental in expanding consciousness in both directions[28]. On one hand, he introduced agricultural techniques, thus making food production more efficient, and laws that tamed

---

[25] An individual's life path.
[26] There are several versions of the myth and Osiris's dismemberment.
[27] PLUTARCH, Moralia Vol. V, translated by Frank C. Babbit, The Loeb Classical Library, pages 35-37
[28] This is the nature of expanding awareness. It is bi-directional in that we have to be aware of the animal (characters) within and their urges and intrigues, as well as the civilising aspects of reason, insight, and understanding.

behaviour and honouring one's parental authorities. On the other hand, he brought joy, fun and instinctive behaviour mixed with intoxication, which is akin to the characteristics of the half brothers Apollo and Dionysus of Greek mythology, in one character.

> During his absence the tradition is that Typhon attempted nothing revolutionary because Isis, who was in control, was vigilant and alert; but when he returned home Typhon contrived a treacherous plot against him and formed a group of conspirators seventy-two in number. He had also the co-operation of a queen from Ethiopia who was there at the time and whose name they report as Aso. Typhon, having secretly measured Osiris's body and having made ready a beautiful chest of corresponding size artistically ornamented, caused it to be brought into the room where the festivity was in progress. The company was much pleased at the sight of it and admired it greatly, whereupon Typhon jestingly promised to present it to the man who should find the chest to be exactly his length when he lay down in it. They all tried it in turn, but no one fitted it; then Osiris got into it and lay down, and those who were in the plot ran to it and slammed down the lid, which they fastened by nails from the outside and also by using molten lead. Then they carried the chest to the river and sent it on its way to the sea through the Tanitic Mouth.[29]

The preceding passage details the return of Osiris to the kingdom that was up to that time, controlled by Isis. This seems to indicate that Isis was a better leader than Osiris and was less prone to manipulation by his brother Typhon[30] (Set), and co-conspirators. Osiris plays a part in his own sacrifice and is willingly tricked into an ornate coffin or sarcophagus. Set nails the chest shut and weighs it down with lead entombing Osiris and sends him into the darkness of the river and out to sea (unconscious).

> But Isis wandered everywhere at her wits' end no one whom she approached did she fail to address, and even when she met some little children she asked them about the chest.......Thereafter Isis, as they relate, learned that the chest had been cast up by the sea near the land of Byblus and that the waves had gently set it down in the midst of a clump of heather. The heather in a short time ran up into a very beautiful and massive stock, and enfolded and embraced the chest with its growth and concealed it within its trunk. The king of the country admired the great size of the plant, and cut off the portion that enfolded the chest (which was now hidden from sight), and used it as a pillar to support the roof of his house.

Isis grieves the loss of Osiris and embarks on a journey to recover him. She discovers that the sea (unconscious) had not taken Osiris, but gently

---

[29] PLUTARCH, Moralia Vol. V, translated by Frank C. Babbit, The Loeb Classical Library, pages 35-37
[30] Typhon is the Greek name given to the Egyptian name Set

returned him to the land where he became part of the landscape as a strong and beautiful tree. A king admired the tree with the hidden chest inside and cut it down for use as a central pillar to hold up his own house (kingdom). Osiris, as an agricultural spirit, therefore supported another kingdom in death as he had done in life. We cannot kill a spirit like Osiris because he gives knowledge and insight, which once attained is difficult to remove.

> Then the goddess disclosed herself and asked for the pillar which served to support the roof. She removed it with the greatest ease and cut away the wood of the heather which surrounded the chest; then, when she had wrapped up the wood in a linen cloth and had poured perfume upon it, she entrusted it to the care of the kings and even to this day the people of Byblus venerate this wood which is preserved in the shrine of Isis.[31]

Isis removes the chest from the tree with great care not to undermine the kingdom it held up. She beautifies and venerates the chest with linen and perfume, and provides a substitute totem for the king to venerate.

> As they relate, Isis proceeded to her son Horus, who was being reared in Buto, and bestowed the chest in a place well out of the way; but Typhon, who was hunting by night in the light of the moon, happened upon it. Recognizing the body he divided it into fourteen parts and scattered them, each in a different place. Isis learned of this and sought for them again, sailing through the swamps in a boat of papyrus. This is the reason why people sailing in such boats are not harmed by the crocodiles, since these creatures in their own way show either their fear or their reverence for the goddess.
>
> Of the parts of Osiris's body the only one which Isis did not find was the male member, for the reason that this had been at once tossed into the river, and the
> Lepidotus, the sea-bream, and the pike had fed upon and it is from these very fishes the Egyptians are most scrupulous in abstaining. But Isis made a replica of the member to take its place, and consecrated the phallus, in honour of which the Egyptians even at the present day celebrate a festival.[32]

Once again, Typhon (Set), the jealous brother, tries to eradicate the spirit of Osiris by dismembering his body into fourteen parts. There is no information on the parts separated, but we can assume it was the primary parts of the body. Beheading is the differentiation of bodily from mental functions. If we extrapolate this idea to the complete dismemberment of

---

[31] PLUTARCH, Moralia Vol. V, translated by Frank C. Babbit, The Loeb Classical Library, pages 37-43
[32] Ibid, page 47

the body of Osiris, we can suggest that fourteen parts may refer to firstly the senses of sight, hearing, smell and taste as the eyes, ears, nose and tongue making seven parts. The arms with which we do and make things, legs, in which we walk through life, head which houses our thinking, the torso and our vital organs, including the heart, and finally the penis, which is symbolic of a man's procreative masculinity. This part was not retrievable and eaten by fish, which are associated with ideas because they swim in the water (unconscious). Re-creating the penis is the transformation of the procreating masculine force and completion of the resurrected body. The lost and remade penis is therefore the spiritualisation of the masculine procreative force, and relates to the idea of fertilisation and rebirth as described in the following passage.

> Later, as they relate, Osiris came to Horus from the other world and exercised and trained him for the battle. After a time Osiris asked Horus what he held to be the most noble of all things. When Horus replied, " To avenge one's father and mother for evil done to them," Osiris then asked him what animal he considered the most useful for them who go forth to battle and when Horus said, " A horse," Osiris was surprised and raised the question why it was that he had not rather said a lion than a horse. Horus answered that a lion was a useful thing for a man in need of assistance, but that a horse served best for cutting off the flight of an enemy and annihilating him.[33]

Osiris returns from the dead to train his son, Horus to avenge the wrong done to him and his mother Isis by his uncle Set. Horus surprises Osiris in his practical choice of a horse, rather than a powerful beast like a lion that can devour the enemy. A horse can outrun, chase and more importantly, be tamed to serve, something difficult to do with a lion. Symbolically, a lion represents the position of power and nobility of the untamed jungle, whereas a horse is a tame, useful companion that increases the power of a man in battle.

> Now the battle, as they relate, lasted many days and Horus prevailed. Isis, however, to whom Typhon was delivered in chains, did not cause him to be put to death, but released him and let him go. Horus could not endure this with equanimity, but laid hands upon his mother and wrested the royal diadem from her head but Hermes put upon her a helmet like unto the head of a cow.[34]

> Isis is, in fact, the female principle of Nature, and is receptive of every form of generation, in accord with which she is called by Plato the gentle nurse and the all-receptive, and by most people has been called by

---

[33] Ibid
[34] PLUTARCH, Moralia Vol. V, translated by Frank C. Babbit, The Loeb Classical Library, page 49

countless names, since, because of the force of Reason, she turns herself to this thing or that and is receptive of all manner of shapes and forms. She has an innate love for the first and most dominant of all things, which is identical with the good, and this she yearns for and pursues but the portion which comes from evil she tries to avoid and to reject, for she serves them both as a place and means of growth, but inclines always towards the better and offers to it opportunity to create from her and to impregnate her with effluxes and likenesses in which she rejoices and glad that she is made pregnant and teeming with the secreations. For creation is the image of being in matter, and the thing created is a picture of reality. [35]

Plutarch not only tells the story of Isis and Osiris, but also gives his own analysis with reference to ancient Greek thought. He describes Isis as the female principal of love and creativity, and through her compassion, lets Typhon (Set) go without punishment, much to the disgust of Horus.

It is not, therefore, out of keeping that they have a legend that the soul of Osiris is everlasting and imperishable, but that his body Typhon often times dismembers and causes to disappear, and that Isis wanders hither and yon in her search for it, and fits it together again for that which really is and is perceptible and good is superior to destruction and change.[36]

Plutarch hints at the dismemberment of Osiris as a recurring theme of an eternal 'soul' and the principle of love being stronger than destruction, which Typhon (Set) represents. These ideas show that the ancient Egyptians were becoming aware of universal patterns later established in the Christian tradition.

One might conjecture that the Egyptians hold in high honour the most beautiful of the triangles, since they liken the nature of the Universe most closely to it, as Plato in the Republic seems to have made use of it in formulating his figure of marriage. This triangle has its upright of three units, its base of four, and its hypotenuse of five, whose power is equal to that of the other two sides. The upright, therefore, maybe likened to the male, the base to the female, and the hypotenuse to the child of both, and so Osiris may be regarded as the origin, Isis as the recipient, and Horus as perfected result. Three is the first perfect odd number: four is a square whose side is the even number two but five is in some ways like to its father, and in some ways like to its mother, being made up of three and two. And panta (all) is a derivative of pente (five), and they speak of counting as " numbering by fives." Five makes a square of itself, as many as the letters of the Egyptian alphabet, and as many as the years of the life of the Apis.[37]

---

[35] Ibid, page 131
[36] Ibid
[37] Ibid, pages 135 & 137

In the above, Plutarch describes the honour that the Egyptians bestowed on the numbers three, four and five, hence the triangle and pyramid. He also describes the opposites of father (Osiris) and mother (Isis), united through the perfected third (Horus). Later in this study, we shall see that Horus is indeed the union of opposites, as he became a sun god with down to earth principles. Plutarch describes the number five like father and mother, thus uniting them in one number. This also relates to the Axiom of Maria, the first Alchemist, which states: 'One becomes two, two becomes three, and out of the third comes the one as the fourth', which shows an unfolding staged development towards the number five as unity and completion of four.

E. A. Budge translated the following version of the Osiris myth from ancient ruins and scrolls. This version of the myth emphasises the dismemberment and scattering of Osiris's body across the land, but there is no mention of a chest[38], and Horus had a greater role in Osiris's resurrection.

> For some time the priests kept secret the manner of his death, but at length some of them, being unable to keep the knowledge to themselves, divulged the matter. Osiris was, in fact, murdered by his wicked brother, Typhon, who broke his body into twenty-six pieces, and gave a piece to each of his fellow-conspirators, to make them equally guilty with himself, and so to force them to raise him to the throne of Osiris and to defend him when there. Isis, the sister and wife of Osiris, with the assistance of her son Horus, avenged his murder, and took possession of the throne of Egypt. She searched for and found all the pieces of her husband's body save one, and she rejoined them by means of wax and aromatic spices, and made the body to be of the former size of Osiris. She then sent for the priests and told each of them that she was going to entrust to them the body of Osiris for burial, and she assigned to them one-third part of the country to serve as an endowment for his worship...........Isis also ordered that models of the missing part of the body of Osiris should be made, and they were adored in the temples, and were held generally in great veneration[39]

As we can see, the story is slightly different to Plutarch's interpretation, as there was secrecy over the manner of Osiris's death, and he was dismembered into twenty-six, rather than fourteen pieces. It also details the method of re-joining the pieces with wax and spices and the veneration of the 'missing part' (penis) in the temples dedicated to him. The ideas common to both versions are the murder of Osiris by his

---

[38] Budge does include the story as told by Plutarch in his book, but there is no mention of the chest as the murder weapon in the translated hieroglyphs.
[39] BUDGE, E. A. Wallis, Osiris & the Egyptian Resurrection Vol. 1, P.L Warner 1911, pages 11-12

brother Set, the dismemberment and reassembling by Isis and Horus, and the reconstitution of the lost part (penis), sometimes fashioned out of gold[40], and the veneration of this spiritualised masculinity. The body part lost had to be created anew, and was therefore not the original masculine instinct, but a new transformed version of it which was worshiped by the people.

> Osiris was a good, benevolent, and just king, who was murdered by his brother Set. Isis, his sister and wife, was a faithful and loving wife, who protected him and his interests with unremitting care during his life, and cherished his memory unceasingly after his death. She endured sorrow, pain, and loneliness in bringing forth his son Horus, and spared herself neither toil nor care in rearing him. As he grew up she taught him that it was his duty to avenge his father's murder, and encouraged a warlike spirit in him. Nephthys, her sister, attached herself to her with loving faithfulness, and assisted Isis by word and deed in all the trouble which she suffered through the murder of her husband, and through the poisoning of her child Horus. Set was the husband of Nephthys, and begat by her Anpu, or Anubis, who acted as embalmer of Osiris. Thus we see that the Egyptians regarded these gods and goddesses as a sort of holy family, all the members whereof were god-men and god-women.[41]

This passage explains the allegiances and relationships between the family members surrounding Osiris. He married his sister Isis and Set, Osiris's brother, married his sister Nephthys, thus forming a quaternity of couples with Osiris and Set in opposition. This is natural in an agricultural society, as the forces of fertilisation (birth), growth, harvest (death) and renewal that Osiris represents, oppose the forces of destruction such as storms, floods, drying lands (desert) etc., that Set represents. The balance of forces between feminine love, acceptance, birth and new life represented by Isis as 'useful or excellent goddess' and Osiris, is opposite to the destructive forces of Set. Isis gives birth to Horus the falcon god after the death of Osiris, who took his place as heir to the throne. Horus was a sky deity who contained both sun and moon in his right and left eyes respectively, and took over the role of opposition to Set in honour of his father.

> In the magical and religious literature of Ancient Egypt, there are many references to the mutilations which were inflicted on the bodies of the greatest of the beneficent gods by the gods of evil and the powers of darkness, and also several allusions to mutilations which the good gods inflicted on their own bodies under the stress of emotions of various

---

[40] PIOTR O. Scholz (2001). Eunuchs and castrati: a cultural history. Markus Wiener Publishers. p. 32
[41] BUDGE, E. A. Wallis, Osiris & the Egyptian Resurrection Vol. 1, P.L Warner 1911, page 28

kinds. Thus Set, the Typhon of the Greeks, by means of eclipses blinded temporarily both the eyes of Horus, and tore them out of his head, and under the form of a black pig he swallowed the left eye, which he found one night as he was wandering about the sky. The disappearance of the right eye of Horus, i.e., the sun, from the sky each night, was also caused by Set, and every month, after full moon, the moon was eaten away piecemeal by him. In addition to the eyes the two arms of Horus were removed and destroyed by Set. These facts are made clear by the CXIIthi and CXIIIth Chapters of the Book of the Dead. According to the former chapter Horus looked at the black pig into which Set had transformed himself, and at once received a terrible blow of fire in the eye, and through the whirlwind of fire which followed it the eye was destroyed. When Ra had ordered Horus to be put to bed, and declared that he would recover, he announced that the " pig was an abomination to Horus," and ever after it was so. The daily restoration of the eye of Horus was effected by means of a ceremony which was performed in the great temple of Amen-Ra at Karnak. The priest approached the closed shrine which contained the figure of the god, and having broken the seal and untied the cord he said: "The cord is "broken, the seal is undone, I am come to bring thee " the Eye of Horus, thine eye is to thee, O Horus. " The mud of the seal is broken, the celestial ocean is penetrated, the intestines of Osiris are drawn out (i.e., fished out of the water). I am not come to "destroy the god on his throne, I am come to set the "god on his throne." The priest next drew the bolt, which symbolized the removal of the finger of Set from the Eye of Horus, and when he had thrown open the doors of the shrine, and the light fell upon the face of the figure of the god, he declared that the "heavens were opened," and the ceremony was complete.[42]

In the above the author describes the characteristics and relationship between Horus and Set. This interesting perception of the day and night and the sun and moon as the eyes of Horus and the cyclic waxing and waning of the moon, (eaten piecemeal) show a keen observation of celestial behaviour and a projected relationship to that behaviour. Ra the great sun god puts Horus to bed (unconscious) to recover after Set's onslaught and the cycle begins anew. This is an excellent example of how everyday events such as sun and moon phases are the beginnings of mythological projection and a way for people to relate to them. It is an example of our nature to project the unconscious characters onto physical objects and relate to them as if they were people.

From the above passage it is clear that Horus did not only collect and reunite the flesh and bones of Osiris, but that he made him once more a complete man, endowed with all his members. Having done this, it was necessary to restore to Osiris the power to breathe, to speak, to see, to walk, and to employ his body in any way he saw fit. To bring about this result Horus performed a number of ceremonies, and made use of

[42] Ibid, pages 62-63

several words of power which had the effect of " opening the mouth " of Osiris....... When the body of Osiris was ready to leave this earth for heaven, some difficulty, it seems, arose in raising him up to the sky, and a ladder was found to be necessary.[43]

The myth continues, with Horus resurrecting Osiris from the devastation of Set and bringing back his soul to his body in the form of breath, senses and ability to walk. Living the life cycle of death, dismemberment and resurrection makes him the 'complete man'. Horus (Osiris's inner child) had the task of bringing back all those aspects of his personality cut off and put together to make him alive and complete. Breath is often associated with soul, and to speak is the ability to relate, seeing the ability to perceive and walking the ability to move through life. This is a differentiation of the aspects of life into their components. In other words, the dismembered into fourteen or twenty-six parts were re-integrated into a living being, with each part now differentiated and related to the whole. As we shall see shortly, the ancient Egyptians knew the difference between spirit, soul, body and shadow as components of the complete man.

Horus, being a practical god (horse rather than lion), could not simply send Osiris to heaven but had to find a ladder to complete the transformation. This indicates that the journey from life to death, dismemberment, reconstitution and resurrection requires many steps and great effort. It is a myth based on known cycles of nature that oscillate between the benevolent Osiris and the constantly thwarting Set and his malevolent surprises and deviations. For the ancients, these cycles were partly environmental and celestial, and partly symbolic projections. The idea of ladder to get Osiris to heaven also relates to Jacob's ladder in the Book of Genesis.

> When Osiris stepped from the ladder into heaven, he entered in among the company of the gods as a " living being," not merely as one about to begin a second state of existence with the limited powers and faculties which he possessed upon earth, but as one who felt that he had the right to rule heaven and the denizens thereof. He possessed a complete body, the nature of which had been changed by ceremonies which Horus, and his sons, and the assistant Tcherti goddesses, had performed for him; the number of his bones was complete and every internal organ and limb were in their place and in a perfect state. Besides these he possessed his forms, or attributes," and his similitude, his heart, his soul," his Ka, or double, his spirit, which was the head of all the spirits, and his power. He had gone to life, and not to death, he was the "Chief of the Living Ones by the command of Ra," and was the " Great God " par excellence} He was "Chief of the Powers," he was

---

[43] Ibid, page 74

"master of heaven," and he had the power to bestow " life and well-being "upon those in heaven who went to him. He transmitted his own odour to those whom he loved, and his chosen ones sat on his shoulder." He sat upon a throne, holding sceptres emblematic of his various powers in his hands, and he was surrounded by his bodyguard, and nobles, and trusted servants, after the manner of an African king; at the proper moment these cried out, "the god Cometh, the god cometh, the god cometh."[44]

Having ascended the ladder and achieved entry into heaven, Osiris takes his rightful place on the throne. He has gone through the sacrifice and reconstitution of his body and spiritualisation of his masculinity with the help of his son Horus and his sister wife Isis, and differentiated his body (Khat) from soul (Ba, heart) and spirit (Ka). He is the bringer of life, benevolence and kindness in opposition to his brother Set. With this, we can see the Christian ideas already formulating and ripening in the ancient Egyptian soul.

The ancient Egyptians knew the reality of the natural cycles of the psychic and physical environments. On the one hand, we have everyday elements of sky, sun, moon, river, desert, storms, rain etc., and on the other, a family of gods and goddesses (inner characters) projected onto those elements. It is these projections, and the source of these projections that the Egyptians regarded as the afterlife.

> The offerings found in the pre-dynastic tombs of Egypt prove that the indigenous inhabitants of the country believed in the existence after death, and the persistent allusions to "everlasting life" and immortality which are found in the texts of all periods show that a belief in a resurrection was general.[45]

They believed the body (KHAT) already had a spiritual living being (Ka) when born, which directed and guided the body until death. They regarded Ka as the "double"[46] of the body and depicted him with two arms extended at right angles, as if open for embrace. Upon death Ka lived on and the body was preserved, so that the Ka could visit it from time to time. The following passage describes Ka's need for spiritual food and clothing.

> Not only was it necessary to provide a figure for the Ka to dwell in, but if it was not to perish of cold, hunger and thirst, offerings of meat, drink, clothing, etc., must be placed in the tomb by the friends and relatives of

---

[44] Ibid, pages 77-78
[45] BUDGE, E. A. Wallis, Osiris & the Egyptian Resurrection Vol. 2, Dover Publications, 1973 page 116
[46] Ibid, pages 117-118

the dead, so that the Ka might eat and drink, anoint and dress itself, even as its body had done when upon earth. The Ka did not, of course, consume the actual offering of food which were given to it, but only the spirits, or "doubles" of the bread, beer, vegetables, meat, oil, etc., and similarly it arrayed itself in the spirits of the suits of line apparel which were offered to it.[47]

The above passage is important because it shows that the ancient Egyptians were aware of objects having a spiritual "double". In other words, they already knew the difference between the object and the idea of the object in projected form, something that Plato, Schopenhauer and particularly Kant also recognised[48]. The person's body was dead, but the idea of the person (Ka) lives on and is immortal. In addition to becoming aware of Spirit, Soul and body, the ancient Egyptians also recognised the shadow (Khaibit) that the sun god Ra casts onto the body, as well as the shadow of the double that accompanies the spirit into the afterlife.

In the Theban Book of the Dead the deceased prays that his Ba and Khu and Shadow may not be shut in the Other World, and elsewhere we read, "O keep not captive my Soul (Ba), O keep not ward over my Shadow, but let a way be opened for my Soul and for my Shadow, and let [me] see the great God in the shrine, on the day of the Judgment of Souls, and let [me] recite the words of Osiris, whose habitations are hidden, to those who guard the members of Osiris, and who keep ward over the Khu (Spirits), and who hold captive the shadows of the dead, who would work evil against me, lest they work evil against me." [49]

The text shows that there is a connection between the Shadow, Soul and Spirit and they were afraid of capture by evil shadows already in the 'Other world'. In reality, there are two shadows cast on an object. The first is the projection that falls onto another object like the ground and the second, an attached shadow on the object on the opposite side to the light source. The projected shadow casts a dark outline of the object without distinct features, and the darkness depends on the intensity of the light source. If the sun is the light source, the shadow moves and changes shape with the sun. The projected shadow follows a person around and never detaches from their body unless they are detached from the earth or other solid object. Birds lose their projected shadow when in flight as it is left on the ground. The attached shadow is the dark side on the object and cannot be projected. Without a light source, an object is in complete darkness and enveloped by the projected and attached shadows.

---

[47] Ibid, page 120
[48] See Chapter 4- Ideas of Unity in Philosophy
[49] BUDGE, E. A. Wallis, Osiris & the Egyptian Resurrection Vol. 2, Dover Publications, 1973, page 126

The attached shadow therefore represents the body and all its mammalian functions that cannot be separated or projected, except at physical death. The projected shadow is the idea of the body and its functions. Unity is the acceptance of our earthly body and soul, including positive and negative emotions, our weaknesses and desires, our sensuality and sexuality, to the matter of our bodies, intake of nutrients and excretion of urine and faeces. As long as we have a body with the same functions as other mammals, part of us will always be a beast.

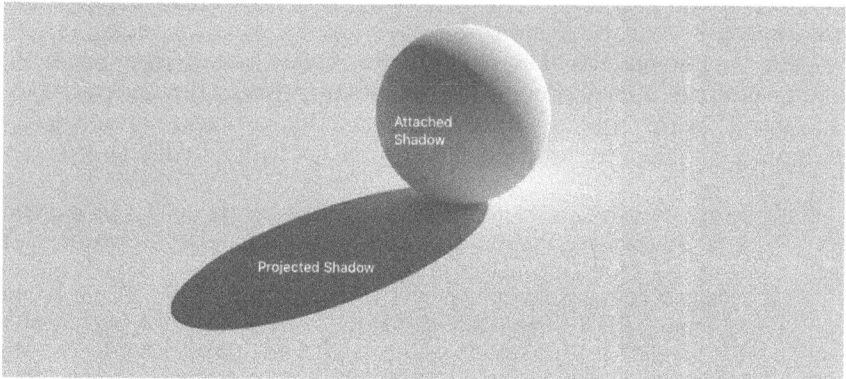

Attached Shadow

Projected Shadow

These facts are universal perceptions that do not change over time and attract psychological projections of many kinds. The ancient Egyptians saw their shadows having a mysterious life of its own, as the following passage emphasises.

> These passages are important, for they show: (1) That there were believed to exist certain evil Shadows who would do harm to their fellow Shadows if they could (2) That the Shadow was associated with the Soul; (3) That the Shadow had the power to move about and to go where it liked. The difference between the spirit-body and the Shadow is so slight that we can readily understand how easily one was confounded with the other in men's minds.[50]

The above shows they regarded the shadow(s); body, soul and spirit having a close relationship expressed both physically and symbolically. The sun (spirit, Ka) shines on the body (Khat) and creates the shadows (Khaibit), which is felt by the soul (Ba), and expressed through the body with heartbeat, emotions etc. The ancient Egyptians gave these functions characters, which make it more complex. It shows a distinct ability to perceive the difference between functions. For example, they could already see the differences between the spirit, body and shadow, and the

---

[50] Ibid, page 127

relationship of soul to the spirit and the body. The following passage considers this relationship.

> THE SOUL OF THE KA, OR BODY-SOUL To one of the constituents of man's spiritual economy the Egyptians gave the name of "Ba," a word which, by general consent among Egyptologists, is translated "soul."........ It was not incorporeal, though its nature and substance were somewhat ethereal.......The Ba of a man was represented by a bird with a bearded human head.[51]

The Ba is therefore a flighty soul with masculine qualities, which seems more characteristic of the Ka (spirit) and indeed, relates to the hermaphroditic quality of the alchemical soul Mercurius. This dual nature of the soul as part body and spirit with the head of a bird shows that ancient Egyptians had not quite differentiated their inner characters into their human and earthly form, and still had much to do with their animal nature. The text continues:

> "Ka." Now the vignette of this Chapter in the Papyrus of Ani is a heart, which proves that in the XVIIIth dynasty the heart was somehow associated with the Ba and the Ka, and we must, it seems to me, conclude that the Ba was the soul of the Ka, and that its seat of being was in the Ka.[52]

There are inklings that the heart somehow associated Ba (soul) with Ka (spirit). In other words, the ancient Egyptians were becoming aware of the relationship between soul and spirit through the heart, but could not distinguish between the functions of heart and mind. This shows that the ancient Egyptian's understanding of soul and spirit was still to some extent, contaminated with each other and their characteristics undifferentiated, as the following text shows:

> THE HEART. In Egyptian (hieroglyphic representation), which literally means "heart," is used to express wish, longing, desire, lust, will, courage, mind, wisdom, sense, intelligence, manner, disposition, attention, intention, etc., and it is clear that the heart was regarded as the seat of life, and as the home of the passions, both good and bad, and as the seat of the pleasures derived from eating, drinking, and the carnal appetite. There appears to have been a soul which was connected with the heart. It was not, I believe, the soul as we usually understand it, but the heart-soul.[53]

---

[51] Ibid, pages 128-129
[52] Ibid, page 130
[53] Ibid, pages 130-131

The characteristics that we would regard as part of our spiritual function, that is to say, in the head, are the to ancients Egyptians part of the heart. For example longing, manner, desire and lust we would consider part of the functioning of the heart, whereas, will, courage, mind, intelligence, disposition, attention and intention, part of the functioning of our spirit. The spirit therefore contaminates their idea of soul and what is physical with what is psychic. They did however; know the difference between soul and 'dream soul'.

> The name " Dream-soul" is given to that part of a man which is thought sometimes to leave him during sleep, and to wander away into strange places, where it sometimes meets with remarkable adventures. Some times it enjoys its freedom so greatly, and so delights in its intercourse with other Dream-souls, that it forgets to come back to its body before the man wakes up.[54]

It is not clear from this passage if the ancient Egyptians understood the similarities between the dream soul while asleep and the spirit (Ka) of the afterlife. Both go somewhere else, have adventures and may or may not return to the body. Their embalming rituals and provision of food for the dead show that they believed the spirit did return to the body on occasion.

Ancient Egypt was the first great civilisation to emerge from the prehistoric animistic world and transition from hunting and gathering to agriculture. Their myths expressed elemental systems related to their agricultural pursuits and their projected deities gave them answers to the mysteries and behaviour of objects like the sun, moon, rain, earth and so on. They perceived the sun as hot, drying, bright, a daytime object and differentiated its behaviour into several deities. This includes where the sun went at night and its disappearance behind clouds and storms. The characterisation gave them relationship to the object and became a male father figure that sailed his boat across the sky with periodic conflict with other characters. Set was responsible for the destructive storms, thunder, lightning, and disappearance of the sun at night.

The story of Osiris shows how an individual evolves from agricultural cycles to the elevated position of god in heaven. Isis, Horus and others help Osiris achieve this ascension and the myth brings all characters into family relationship and a family hierarchy. Sky (Nut) and the earth (Geb) were Osiris's mother and father. He married his sister (Isis), fought with his brother (Set) who killed and dismembered him. His son (Horus) and wife (Isis) bring him back to life and ultimately, to heaven. As an agricultural character to begin with, Osiris represented the cycles of germination, growth, harvest, germination, and so on. He was a good god

---

[54] Ibid, page 137

in contrast to his brother Set, who was bad, and the shadow of Osiris. We can find this universal principal throughout nature, including human nature. It is present within the very structure of matter in the balance of positive and negative charges in the atom and the balance between predator and prey, sky and earth, fire and water, and so on. It is the positive feeling of love by Isis and Horus that overcame the trickery of Set and the dismemberment of Osiris.

It is interesting to note that Set did not confront Osiris man to man, so to speak, but had to trick him into his death, which means that Osiris was not aware of his brother's intentions and almost willingly accepted his path based on natural cycles of life and death. Cutting and processing of grain, vegetables and animals for food may be the basis to the idea of dismemberment. It may also have an allusion to the way the unity of the personality fragments into its components when a strong emotion overcomes the individual. Small children having a tantrum show this dissolution and overwhelming emotion. Indeed as the conscious ego was just emerging from the ocean of the unconscious in ancient Egypt, this is a distinct possibility. The following passage on death also alludes to this possibility:

> DEATH. The Egyptian theologians believed that there was a time when there was no death, but that time was when the god Temu alone existed, and before he created the heavens and the earth, and men and "gods." How and why death came the texts do not tell, but, judging from the views which are held in the Sudan at the present time, we may assume that the Egyptians regarded death as the means necessary to enable man to continue his existence after the breath left his material body. The present world was to them merely the ante chamber of the Other World; a man's house in this world was a temporary abode, but his tomb was his 'eternal house".[55]

The 'Other World', is the myth-making unconscious and the physical existence of consciousness is a mere 'ante chamber'. This shows that the emergence of the ego from the unconscious was in its beginning stages of development, and that the dreams and myths of the ancient Egyptians were very much in the foreground of their minds. Osiris was a central character in their mythology, with evil on one side and the love of a dedicated wife and son on the other. The parallels between this myth and the Christian myth are unmistakeable.

---

[55] Ibid, page 143

b. Ancient Greece

The Mycenaean culture preceded the ancient Greeks by many hundreds of years, beginning with the Greek Dark Ages (early Iron age) from the thirteenth to the ninth centuries BC. Greek urban 'poleis' (city states) around the eighth century BC ushered in the period of Archaic Greece (Old fashioned age)[56], followed by the Classical period, and the Persian wars from the 750 to 500 BC. The Hellenistic period began with the wars of Alexander the Great until the Roman republic annexed Greece in 147 BC.

Greece is a land of rugged mountains, valleys and plains on the mainland, and numerous craggy islands surrounding the mainland. The communities were therefore not homogenous like the Nile delta of Egypt, and to some extent, politically separate. This also gave rise to much conflict and later the democratic ideal. They had a common language and related to each other through trade and diplomacy. The main agricultural crops were barley, wine and olives. Sea travel played a central role in the development of Greek culture, particularly the connection to the near eastern culture of Egypt. This gave them access to new technologies and religious ideas, which they adopted and made their own.

The climate oscillated from hot dry weather to intermittent heavy rain and farmers endured a precarious cycle of drought and flood. Aristotle regarded the climate, in addition to the landscape, as the determining factor in Greece's political system.[57] They were one people with similar customs and language, worshipped the same gods yet lived in isolated communities. Agriculture and the domestication of animals in ancient Greece occurred approximately ten to twelve thousand years ago at the beginning of the Neolithic period, and largely derived from the knowledge gained from Egypt and Mesopotamia. In addition, they learned about monumental stone construction and copper metallurgy.

Politically, the physical isolation and climate encouraged communities to form co-operatives based on individual activity of which the Olympic games in the fifth century BC is an example. Greek males from the social elite strove for individual excellence as a competitive value. It began as a religious festival associated with the king of the gods, Zeus. The emphasis on individual pursuit was to become the basis of the democratic system (ruled by the people) throughout Greece led by Cleisthenes in 508-507 BC. This grew out of the vacuum left by the Mycenaean culture,

---

[56] MARTIN R. Thomas, Ancient Greece, From Prehistoric to Hellenistic Times, Yale University Press, 1996, page 51
[57] Ibid, page 4

to unite small independent city-states into a democratic collective. In other words, the Greek city-states were organised politically based on 'citizenship' as an organising concept, with legal equality not dependent on a citizen's wealth. Before the advent of the democratic system, oligarchs and tyrants ruled Greece using their power and wealth. This was particularly true in Sparta in central Greece on the Eurotas River. Athens had developed a city-sate democracy around the seventh century BC, where the rich and poor had open meetings in a body called the assembly (ecclesia), which elected nine magistrates called archons (rulers) each year.[58]

Art and architecture also developed beyond the stiff and posed sculptures, flat pictorial reliefs and clunky, monumental buildings of the ancient Egyptians. Literature in the form of poetry also developed in the late Archaic age, through Homer, Hesiod, Alcan and Sappho, who not only wrote about the lives of their gods, but of love and war. The most notable developments in architecture were the application of detailed mathematics, such as the Golden Mean and the refinements of the orders represented by the decor on columns and other building elements. It showed a sophisticated, reasoned refinement and practical assemblage of components, in addition to the ornament of worship and storytelling dedicated to their deities. This was the nature of the ancient Greeks. The gods were ever-present in their lives, and permeated their entire culture.

Science also developed a reasoned approach to observed natural phenomena, which included all aspects of nature, including humans.

> The Ionian thinkers insisted that the workings of the universe could be explained because the phenomena of nature were neither random nor arbitrary. The universe, the totality of things, they named cosmos because this word meant an orderly arrangement that is beautiful (hence our word "cosmetic"). The order characteristic of the cosmos, perceived as lovely because it was ordered, encompassed not only the motions of the heavenly bodies but also everything else: the weather, the growth of plants and animals, human health and psychology, and so on. Since the universe was ordered, it was intelligible; since it was intelligible, explanations of events could be discovered by thought and research. The thinkers who conceived this view believed it necessary to give reasons for their conclusions and to persuade others by arguments based on evidence. They believed, in other words, in logic (a word derived from the Greek term *logos*, meaning, among other things, a reasoned explanation). This way of thought based on reason represented a crucial first step toward science and philosophy as these disciplines endure today.[59]

---

[58] Ibid, page 83
[59] Ibid, page 91

This was the first step for the ancients in their differentiation of thinking and 'what is' in the physical world, and the myth-making unconscious projected into the heavens and other objects. With the advent of a newly differentiated thinking came a new era in the development of civilisation. For the first time, the pluralistic mythological deities of the time crystallised into a single god. Xenophanes of Colophon (580 to 480 BC) regarded the gods as immortal human beings with the same attributes and failings. "One god, the greatest among gods and men, neither in form like unto mortals nor in thought . . . ."[60] This shows that the ancient Greeks, through philosophy, were becoming aware of the unity that underlies existence. This was the turning point for western civilisation, together with the advent of reasoned thought practiced by the Ionian thinkers and the differentiation of natural phenomena from the previous mythology of earlier Greece and the Near East.

Xenophanes only left fragments of poetry, and in them he explains that the gods had human fallibilities and did not represent a pattern better than human behaviour.

> Homer and Hesiod have ascribed to the gods all things that are a shame and a disgrace among mortals, stealings and adulteries and deceivings of one another.

> Since they have uttered many lawless deeds of the gods, stealings and adulteries and deceivings of one another.

> The gods have not revealed all things to men from the beginning, but by seeking they find in time what is better. [61]

These poetic fragments predate the works of Heraclitus, and show a definite movement towards the sciences, using reasoning and inquiry. This emergence from the myth-making unconscious to the rational observation of nature, as it is rather than how we imagine it to be, is the beginning of our western scientific approach. It also sets the foundation for the latter works of Heraclitus, Plato and Aristotle.[62]

The struggle against the Persian Empire in 477 BC united the different poleis of the Greeks under Athenian leadership. The Athenian assembly strengthened democracy with its administration and lawmaking. It also created a judicial system called the Areopagus Council that had authority

---

[60] Fragments of Zenophanes, fragment 23, http://www.iep.utm.edu/xenoph/
[61] Ibid, fragments 11, 12 & 18
[62] See Chapter 4a & b, 'Ideas of Unity in Philosophy'

over magistrates, dealt with accusations of misconduct or incompetence, called the "guardianship of the laws".

Pericles (495 to 429 BC), a relation of Cleisthenes, reinforced the democratic system by proposing state revenues pay the men that served on juries. This enabled the poorer men to leave their paid work to serve the Greek democracy, thus making it all-inclusive. The leadership of Pericles ushered in the prosperous age, which included great building projects, such as the temples on the Acropolis. The main temple, dedicated to the goddess Athena called the Parthenon means "the house of the virgin goddess". The building was to honour Athena in her capacity as a warrior serving as the divine champion of Athenian military power. The Parthenon represented the epitome of architectural thinking, in its mathematical precision and refined ornamentation.

In between conflict, with the Persians, the Greeks still fought against each other, particularly between Athens and Sparta, due to personal ambitions and hegemony on the part of Spartan leaders. This led to the construction of fortifications around Athens and the strengthening of their fleet of ships to ward off possible attack. An epidemic that ravaged the Athenians in 430 BC further thwarted the strategy of Pericles. The death rate was so high that it hindered Pericles' ability to defend Athens by sea, and claimed his own life in 429 BC. After more battles and a victory at Pylos by the general Cleon, Athens and Sparta came to an agreed peace, which did not last long.

During this time Socrates the Sophist (469 to 399 BC), proposed that the idea of justice required the power to work one's will, as opposed to an instinctive reaction or emotion, thus putting ethics in a central place in the culture. He developed what was later to be termed the 'Socratic method' (dialectical method), which looks at all sides of an argument and used this form to challenge the assumptions of his conversational partners. Socrates believed that knowledge, not material success, was the key to happiness and lived it out in his personal life. He never wore shoes, dressed in the same cloak year-round, and was regarded as eccentric by many Athenians.[63] He had a wife, children, and supported them through gifts from local supporters and as a soldier in the Hoplite army. Socrates and his method of conversation annoyed many Athenians, and they charged him with impiety and a danger to the stability of Athens, and sentenced him to death by suicide in 399 BC.

---

[63] MARTIN R. Thomas, Ancient Greece, From Prehistoric to Hellenistic Times, Yale University Press, 1996, page 169

The conflicts between Greek city-states continued between Sparta, Thebes and Athens, and the power vacuum filled by the rise of Macedonia and its political and military power under the rule of Philip II. His victory over the alliance of Greek city-states at Chaeronea in 338 BC helped him form a great army to mount a revenge attack on the Persians. Upon the murder of Philip in 336BC, the task left to his son Alexander (356 to 323 BC), who became king at the age of 20. He honoured his father's wishes to attack the Persians and set out on a campaign that conquered the Empire all the way to India where he turned back at the insistence of his army.

During this time, a philosopher and follower of Socrates by the name of Plato (427 to 347 BC) became prominent. He was not a supporter of democracy and regarded it as the worst form of rule under law, and proposed leadership through philosophical wisdom. Unfortunately, his utopian vision had no effect in his lifetime, and his work attracted little attention in the next two centuries until revived in the Roman era. He believed that knowledge came from searching for truths independent of the observer, in other words, universal truths. His observation of the inner realm of characters of the prevailing gods, showed how this universal truth was manifest in everyday life. He abstracted a system by observation of the gods and their behaviour into his concept of the model and the copy of the model. This set the foundation for the differentiation of inner characters (gods) and humans as copies of those characters. In other words, the behaviour and characteristics of the model is the foundation of our own behaviour and motivating inner forces. This discovery is still relevant today.

Unlike the Sophists, who regarded virtues as relative, Plato searched for universal values not found through experience, but through thought, and regarded these universal values as independent of human existence[64]. Plato recognised that humans possessed an immortal soul distinct from their bodies, thus forming a pair of opposites. This differentiation was another step in the evolution of western culture, and reflected in the inclusion of women in the ruling class of his utopian city-state. Plato also regarded the city-state be run by educated 'guardians', as a highest class, supported by 'auxiliaries', to defend the city-state, followed by 'producers', who make the physical objects, grow the crops, etc. Above all, he regarded the study of philosophy as the paramount requirement for a stable and working state.

---

[64] This is the problem with intellectual abstraction. We see universal truths within and have such a powerful attractive force, we feel that they are the same for everyone else. This is why many people feel that their god is the one and true god.

Aristotle (384 - 322 BC) followed Plato and earned a reputation for ground-breaking work in philosophy and scientific investigation. He tutored Alexander before his departure to conquer the Persian Empire. His philosophical emphasis was oriented towards common sense, rather than metaphysics, and investigated phenomena in the natural environment. He coupled detailed investigation with perceptive reasoning in the physical sciences of biology, botany and zoology. His legacy as a scientist in some instances outweighs his philosophical insights.[65] He did, however, recognise the conflict between the human soul, physical desire and the appetites, and proposed a form of self-control as the "the mean" between the opposites.

Before Alexander the Great headed east toward India, he took over Egypt where he founded a city on the west bank of the Nile named after him, called Alexandria. He then marched east and in 331 BC fought the Persian king's main army at the battle of Gaugamela in northern Mesopotamia and proclaimed himself king of Asia. The Greek empire had spread far across the Middle East, into Egypt, and now marched towards India, where his own army mutinied in 326 BC after which, Alexander had to lead his men home. His mental health suffered greatly during this time, as he believed he was beyond his humanity, and regarded himself as a god. Alexander had plans to conquer North Africa, but he died from a fever following a heavy drinking session in Babylon in 323 BC, which ushered in the Hellenistic Age of ancient Greece.

This era combined the Hellenistic and indigenous traditions of the conquered lands by Alexander, including the founding of new cities. The new kingdoms established under Greek rule included Antigonus (382-301 BC) and his son Demetrius (336- 283 BC), who took over Macedonia and Greece. Seleucus (358-281 BC) took over Syria and the Old Persian Empire, and Ptolemy (c. 367-282 BC), took over Egypt. During this time, the Greek culture flourished with the establishment of schools and the arts, and Alexandria became an intellectual centre. Metaphysics became less important, and philosophy concentrated on practical matters in the fields of 'logic', 'physics' and 'ethics', and the founding of the schools of Epicureanism, Stoicism and Cynicism. Alexandria heralded great advances in geometry and mathematics through Euclid, and the polymath, Archimedes. The kingdoms outside of Greece included the indigenous leaders in a system of rewards and participation in government and public finance, and this kept them appeased and involved. Beginning in the third century BC, all the eastern Mediterranean kingdoms fell to the Romans and thereafter, Greek mythology became Roman with a few adjustments.

---

[65] See Chapter 4c on Aristotle, 'Ideas of Unity in Philosophy'

Greek mythology is varied and complex. Every nuance of human behaviour allocated to a deity or inner character and included stories about their heroes, the nature of the world and their religious practices. Their gods began with the creation of the universe and gave birth to the Titans, who gave birth to the gods of Olympus. The Olympians were Zeus, his wife Hera, Poseidon, Ares, Hermes, Hephaestus, Aphrodite, Athena, Apollo, Artemis, Demeter, and Dionysus. The Greek deities form a large family of gods, demi-gods and mortals, as depicted in the family tree below.

In addition, they have no guilt about sexual relations with each other as brother and sister, father and daughter, mother and son and grandmother and grandson. This is the nature of inner characters. They do not abide by our ethical incest concerns and diversity into a wider community. The other aspect that stands out is the promiscuous nature of the gods, particularly the father god, Zeus. He is responsible for siring Persephone, Artemis, Apollo, Athena, Ares, Hebe, Hephaestus, Dionysus, Hermes and Aphrodite, to name only a few. Zeus had 23 divine partners, with 60 divine offspring. He also had 46 semi-divine or mortal partners and 64 semi-divine or mortal offspring.[66] If we view this literally, it means that Zeus had sex with practically anyone he encountered, including family members. To do this, however, is a mistake. Inner characters need symbolic interpretations, and how their traits relate to each other. This includes traits each needed from the others, what attracted them in sexual union, and what their offspring were like. Obviously, it would take several volumes to explore this aspect in full, so I will concentrate on a few Gods to emphasise how these characters evolved in their children, much the same as Horus was the evolved Osiris in the Egyptian myth.

---

[66] https://en.wikipedia.org/wiki/Zeus#Consorts_and_children

Greek Gods Family Tree

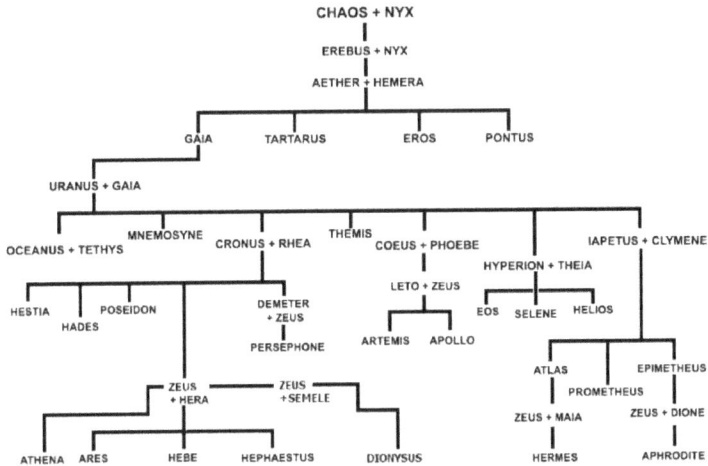

CHAOS + NYX

EREBUS + NYX

AETHER + HEMERA

GAIA   TARTARUS   EROS   PONTUS

URANUS + GAIA

OCEANUS + TETHYS MNEMOSYNE CRONUS + RHEA THEMIS COEUS + PHOEBE IAPETUS + CLYMENE

HYPERION + THEIA

LETO + ZEUS

HESTIA POSEIDON HADES DEMETER + ZEUS EOS SELENE HELIOS

PERSEPHONE ARTEMIS APOLLO

ATLAS   EPIMETHEUS

PROMETHEUS

ZEUS + HERA ZEUS + SEMELE ZEUS + MAIA ZEUS + DIONE

ATHENA ARES HEBE HEPHAESTUS DIONYSUS HERMES APHRODITE

[67]

Hesiod's Theogony (8th Century BC) gives us hints to the nature of the gods, as well as their lineage, and shows a distinct feeling for relationship and quality. Homer writes about the gods in his poetic Odyssey and Hymns, which describe their characteristics and adventures. The following table categorises each god/goddess into gender, characteristics, consorts, sons and daughters and should be regarded as an outline sketch in order to clarify their main characteristics and relationships.

Creation Gods	M/ F	Characteristics	Consort	Sons	Daughters
Chaos	(?) F	Gloomy, vast, dark	Nyx	Erebus	
Nyx	F	Gloomy, Night	Erebus	Aether	Hemera
Erebus	M	Darkness, Shadow	Nyx	Aether	Hemera
Aether	M	Light, Upper atmosphere	Hemera		
Hemera	F	Day	Aether		
Gaia	F	Wide bosomed, Mother earth	Nyx (?) Uranus	Titans	Titanesses
Tartarus	M	Dim, misty, deepest, darkest underworld, pit			
Eros	M	Love & attraction, fairest			
Pontus	M	Sea, father of sea			

[67] There are some anomalies in this family tree, particularly in the creation of the primordial deities.

		creatures, raging swell			
Uranus	M	Heavens, father of sky	Gaia	Titans	Titanesses
Titans					
Cronus	M	Wily, crafty, harvests, destructive time	Rhea	Zeus, Poseidon, Hades	Demeter, Hestia
Rhea	F				
Oceanus	M	River oceans, fresh water, deep swirling	Tethys		Clymene
Tethys	F	Lovely,	Oceanus		
Mnemosyne	F	Beautiful hair, memory,	Zeus		
Themis	F	Reverend, divine law & order	Metis		
Coeus	M	Intellect, Axis of constellations	Phoebe		
Phoebe	F	Bright intellect & prophesy, gold crowned	Coeus		Leto
Hyperion	M	Light	Theia	Helios	Eos, Selene
Theia	F	Shining light of clear blue sky, sight	Hyperion	Helios	Eos, Selene
Iapetus	M	Mortality	Clymene	Atlas, Prometheus Epimetheus, Menoetius	
Clymene	F	Renown, fame, infamy, neat ankled	Iapetus	Atlas, Prometheus Epimetheus, Menoetius	
Olympians					
Zeus	M	King of the gods, ruler of Mount Olympus, and god of the sky, weather, thunder, lightning, law, order, and justice	Hera, Leto, Demeter, Semele, Maia, Dione	Ares, Hephaestus Apollo, Hermes, Dionysus,	Athena, Hebe, Persephone Artemis, Aphrodite
Hera	F	Queen of the gods, marriage, women, childbirth, heirs, kings, and empires	Zeus	Ares, Hephaestus	Athena, Hebe
Hestia	F	Virgin goddess of the hearth, home, and chastity.			
Hades	M	King of the underworld, the dead & wealth, brazen-voiced hound, strong,	Persephone		

		pitiless in heart			
Poseidon	M	Sea, rivers, floods, droughts, and earthquakes, earth holder			
Demeter	F	Goddess of grain, agriculture, harvest, growth, and nourishment	Zeus		Persephone
Persephone	F	Awful, queen of the underworld, wife of Hades and goddess of spring growth	Hades		
Athena	F	Reason, wisdom, intelligence, skill, peace, warfare, battle strategy, and handicrafts			
Ares	M	War, bloodshed, and violence			
Dionysus	M	Wine, fruitfulness, parties, festivals, madness, chaos, drunkenness, vegetation, ecstasy, and the theatre			
Apollo	M	Music, arts, knowledge, healing, plague, prophecy, poetry, manly beauty, and archery			
Aphrodite	F	Beauty, love, desire, and pleasure			
Artemis	F	Hunt, wilderness, animals, young girls, childbirth, and plague			
Hermes		Boundaries, travel, communication, trade, language, and writing			
Leto	F	Motherhood	Zeus	Apollo	Artemis
Semele	F	Mortal	Zeus	Dionysus	
Eos	F	Dawn			
Selene	F	Moon			
Helios	M	Sun, guardian of oaths			
Maia	F	Pleiades -goddess of the constellations	Zeus	Hermes	
Prometheus	M	Forethought and			

		crafty counsel, and creator of mankind			
Dione	F	Oracle of Dodona	Zeus		Aphrodite
Epimetheus	M	Afterthought and excuses			Dione

The above table of Gods and Goddesses shows how the ancient Greeks followed the Egyptians in personifying elemental objects and behaviour of sun, moon, rain, storms, rivers and animals, which they called Helios, Selene, Maia, Eos, and Poseidon etc. These elemental deities were less important to the Greeks than the deities of the Egyptians, as they were more concerned with deities representing human characteristics, dramas and adventures. The emphasis is less on the physical aspects of the environment and more on the human aspects of love, beauty, war, hunting, wine, culture and so on.

As with the gods of Egypt, the Greeks had a creation myth emanating from a gloomy, dark realm of Chaos (Nun). This act of creation included the foundation and main attributes of earth (Gaia), the sea and its contents (Pontus), night (Nyx), day (Hemera), shadow (Erebus), the upper sky and light (Aether), the deepest pit in the earth (Tartarus) and the principle of relationship and love (Eros). This primordial group of characters differs to the Egyptians as they emphasised environmental components, such as sun and water, and the cycles and influence on agriculture. The Greeks lived in a different climate and geography, agricultural techniques were established and not the only source of nutrition. Their myths therefore evolved into a broader range of elements and sets of opposites such as earth/sea, night/day, with the shadow between them[69] and the upper sky/deepest pit. One character that stands out in the group that has human attributes, rather than environmental, is Eros.

Eros is depicted as a young boy with wings, which is exactly how it feels for a man when activated. It makes one feel young, ecstatic, alive and able to fly and in some instances, an overwhelming force of attraction and emotion, and the beginning of relationship. He is also the ultimate uniting force of the opposites of male and female, and therefore stands between them as the third. From creation onwards, the Greeks became more concerned with human functioning than environmental influences,

---

[68] This list is by no means exhaustive as the ancient Greeks projected an inner character onto almost every natural and human phenomenon. Sources for the list are Hesiod, Theogony; Homer, Hymns & Larousse, New Encyclopedia of Mythology, Hamlyn Publishing, 1968

[69] The shadow can be regarded as a little bit of night (absence of light) when daylight is blocked by an object.

although these were included as part of their human characteristics. Hesiod's Theogony (eighth century BC) has a unique description of the relationships between the deities and the feeling they invoke in him. He uses words "awful", "wily", "loud-thunderer", "heart of iron", "pitiless', "gloomy", "stubborn-hearted", "hated" etc., to describe the characters, and thus express his feelings about them. In the following excerpt from the Theogony, Hesiod describes the opposites of night and day related to a dwelling:

> There stands the awful home of murky Night wrapped in dark clouds. In front of it the son of Iapetus stands immovably upholding the wide heaven upon his head and unwearying hands, where Night and Day draw near and greet one another as they pass the great threshold of bronze: and while the one is about to go down into the house, the other comes out at the door.

> And the house never holds them both within; but always one is without the house passing over the earth, while the other stays at home and waits until the time for her journeying come; and the one holds all-seeing light for them on earth, but the other holds in her arms Sleep the brother of Death, even evil Night, wrapped in a vaporous cloud.

> And there the children of dark Night have their dwellings, Sleep and Death, awful gods. The glowing Sun never looks upon them with his beams, neither as he goes up into heaven, nor as he comes down from heaven. And the former of them roams peacefully over the earth and the sea's broad back and is kindly to men; but the other has a heart of iron, and his spirit within him is pitiless as bronze: whomsoever of men he has once seized he holds fast: and he is hateful even to the deathless gods.

> There, in front, stand the echoing halls of the god of the lower-world, strong Hades, and of awful Persephone. A fearful hound guards the house in front, pitiless, and he has a cruel trick. On those who go in he fawns with his tail and both is ears, but suffers them not to go out back again, but keeps watch and devours whomsoever he catches going out of the gates of strong Hades and awful Persephone. [70]

This passage tells us that Hesiod had a well-defined idea of the opposites of day and night, and the human personality symbolised by the home (psychic space created by humans). Atlas, the son of Iapetus, stands resiliently between day and night, holding the heavens in place upon his head (understanding). In other words, the opposites of the physical world of day and the unconscious world of night, sleep and death are aspects of the human personality (home). Indeed, when we go to sleep, we do disappear from the physical world into a world of darkness and dream. He continues to describe how day and night are never in the home together,

---

[70] HESIOD, Theogony, Eighth Century BC, II. 744-766

which is exactly how they operate in people. We live and work in the daytime, and disappear at night in sleep and dream.

Day and night also mix while awake in fantasies, visions, ideas and so on. The daylight world draws our attention and engages us, looking inside for a moment at the river of images and ideas, diverts our attention from the physical. We stand in between these two opposites, just as Hesiod describes. The third passage above details the children of Night, Sleep and Death, and how the sun never shines on them. Sleep is "kindly", and Death is "pitiless" and "hateful". In the fourth passage, he describes the underworld deities of Hades and his wife Persephone and their fearful hound that welcomes but devours anyone trying to leave. As we shall see later in this study, this fate befell both Rousseau and Nietzsche[71].

After establishing the environmental deities with the addition of the human attributes of love and relationship (Eros), the ancient Greeks continued to become aware of their inner characters and related them to their own functioning. For example, memory is the goddess Mnemosyne, Phoebe, the goddess of intellect, Themis, the god of law and order, Clymene the goddess for fame and infamy, Epimetheus, the god of afterthought and excuses. The ancient Greeks took this personification of human characteristics to an extreme pitch, so much so that things like curses, fraud, opportunity, fear, delusion etc., were all allocated to a deity. In fact, this legacy lives with us today in our everyday language. Examples include the word memory from Mnemosyne, goddess of memory, sleep (hypnosis) from Hypnos, harmony from Harmonia, cloth from Clotho; morose from Moros, the spirit of doom, phobia from Phobos, the spirit of fear and so on.

It is a natural inclination to personify a characteristic, emotion or object so that we can relate to it as if it were a person. This is the same reason we name our vehicles, and project a personality onto them. A car, for example, is less likely to let you down if you love it, service it, give it good oil and grease and handle it with care. Today, we do not identify our emotions like fear or jealousy with a personality, although it does feel like another force influences us; we simply try to overcome these emotions without understanding them. This denies their humanising function as part of our unity and restricts the energy and images that emotions provide us.

The ancient Greeks were prone to instinctive behaviour, as exemplified by the continuing conflicts they had with other city-states and neighbouring empires. The conscious ego was less developed than it is

---

[71] See Chapter 4g & 4l on Rousseau and Nietzsche, 'Ideas of Unity in Philosophy'

today and prone to dissolution, but the beginnings of self-awareness was evident in the personification of the fundamental human characteristic of love, which was part of their mythological background from the beginning. Becoming aware of this emotion and indeed, all the following ethical ponderings of the philosophers shows that the ancient Greeks were becoming aware of the counterweight to shear brutal instinct of power and destruction. Indeed, the central position that Eros had in the Greek pantheon shows his importance for the west's evolution and the precursor to the development of the Christian ideal.

The ancient Greek deities were an expression and personification of human functioning and their relationship to the natural world. It is this union that set the Greeks apart from many other cultures, and laid the foundation for our western culture in fine art, sculpture, theatre, music, dance, architecture, wine production, education, language, literature, politics, sports, religion and philosophy. Indeed, the most concrete expressions of their culture are the magnificent buildings they designed for their deities. Classical architecture endured through the centuries, and its influence remained until the advent of the industrial revolution in the nineteenth century and the use of new materials beyond stone.

The ancient Greek gods and their specific characteristics are, to our contemporary thinking, an attempt at categorisation of what the psychologists call complexes, and we have to thank Freud for cracking the door and Jung for throwing it open and showing that the Greek deities are indeed, still with us. Instead of gods, they are recognised as inner characters, or archetypes, and have a direct bearing on our behaviour and functioning. The shift from the environmental deities of ancient Egypt to the functioning of the human condition and the inner characters behind our instincts, emotions, thoughts, ideas, etc., shows a step in humanity's evolution and becoming aware of that functioning.

We should not underestimate the legacy of the ancient Greeks as their culture permeates our contemporary culture in many ways. Much of language owes its origins to the Greek culture, as well as our festivals and celebrations. The Dionysia was originally a winter solstice festival in December and January, dedicated to the son of Zeus, Dionysus. During these festivals, their deity received offerings and performances of music, dance and theatre. It marked a turning point of the climate around the solstice from winter to spring and summer with the days lengthening and temperature warming. As Dionysus suffered dismemberment by the Titans, and rebirth through his father Zeus, it is a fitting transition from the natural cycles of winter/summer and life/death, as symbolised by the life of Dionysus. This myth is a celebration of the natural cycles of death and rebirth, and has some connection to the life of Egypt's Osiris and the future honouring of the birth and death of Jesus.

c. Ancient Rome

The Roman republic was founded around the 6th century BC and contained within the Italian peninsula until approximately the 3rd century BC. The Romans were a practical people and much of their mythology imported from Egyptian, Etruscan, Syrian, Persian, and Greek sources. The Romans saw these myths in a different light and regarded them as abstract and utilitarian. Like ancient Greece, the Roman republic was a network of towns and provinces ruled by military commanders. Elected magistrates or Roman consuls and the senate ruled the republic until the 1st century BC, when a political and military upheaval occurred and from therein ruled by emperors.

During this upheaval, the Roman republic expanded its territory and influence throughout the region, which culminated with the assassinated of the emperor Julius Caesar in 44 BC. Mark Anthony and Caesar's adopted son Octavian drove the assassins from Rome and defeated them in the battle of Philippi in 42 BC. Anthony and Octavian divided the Empire between them until Octavian defeated Anthony at the battle of Actium in 31 BC, who had aligned with Egypt's Cleopatra. Octavian received the name Augustus by the senate in 27 BC and the power of emperor. It resulted in a period of peace and prosperity and his people loved him. During this time, a new constitutional order emerged and Tiberius became the Roman emperor upon Augustus's death.

Caligula, Claudius and Nero, continued the principals of dynastic succession established by Augustus, succeeded Tiberius. In 69 AD, strife broke out from which Vespasian emerged victorious and founded the Flavian dynasty followed by the Nerva-Antonine dynasty, which produced the emperors Nerva, Trajan, Hadrian, Antonius Pius and Marcus Aurelius. In 180 AD, Commodus marked the decline of the Roman Empire and the reign of Caracalla in 212 AD caused a series of murders and executions, which led to a crisis in the third century. Aurelian brought stability to the empire in 270-275 AD which was carried on by the reign of Diocletian. He perceived Christianity as a threat to the empire and initiated the 'Great Persecution'. Diocletian divided the empire into four regions and co ruled with Tetrarchy system[72], which soon collapsed. Order restored with the reign of Constantine the great who was the first emperor to convert to Christianity and established a new centre for the eastern empire called Constantinople. In 395 AD, Christianity became the official religion of the

---

[72] The form of government where power is divided among four individuals

empire thus diminishing the influence of the ancient gods that had ruled Romans lives up until that time.[73]

Publius Ovidius Naso known as Ovid (43 BC to 17/18 AD) wrote detailed descriptions of the mythological background of the empire, the creation of the world and sets the scene for the development of the Roman culture through their gods. In his book Metamorphosis, he writes in verse the creation of the world from chaos:

> Before the seas, and this terrestrial ball,
> And Heav'n's high canopy, that covers all,
> One was the face of Nature; if a face:
> Rather a rude and indigested mass:
> A lifeless lump, unfashion'd, and unfram'd,
> Of jarring seeds; and justly Chaos nam'd.
> No sun was lighted up, the world to view;
> No moon did yet her blunted horns renew:
> Nor yet was Earth suspended in the sky,
> Nor pois'd, did on her own foundations lye:
> Nor seas about the shores their arms had thrown;
> But earth, and air, and water, were in one.
> Thus air was void of light, and earth unstable,
> And water's dark abyss unnavigable.
> No certain form on any was imprest;
> All were confus'd, and each disturb'd the rest.
> For hot and cold were in one body fixt;
> And soft with hard, and light with heavy mixt. [74]

This passage from Ovid shows the confused mix of unfashioned and unfathomed elements still in their raw state without light, sun or moon, no earth suspended in the sky and no difference between the opposites. This is the unity before creation and the unity experienced by all human life when born. It is interesting to note that Ovid had a concept of the earth as a 'ball' suspended in the sky in 8 AD. He goes on to describe the act of creation and differentiation of the elements with the divine spark of god:

> But God, or Nature, while they thus contend,
> To these intestine discords put an end:
> Then earth from air, and seas from earth were driv'n,
> And grosser air sunk from aetherial Heav'n.
> Thus disembroil'd, they take their proper place;
> The next of kin, contiguously embrace;
> And foes are sunder'd, by a larger space.

---

[73] https://en.wikipedia.org/wiki/Roman_Empire#Geography_and_demography
[74] OVID, Metamorphoses, 8 AD, translated under the direction of Sir Samuel Garth, The University of Adelaide Library 2014, page 5

The force of fire ascended first on high,
And took its dwelling in the vaulted sky:
Then air succeeds, in lightness next to fire;
Whose atoms from unactive earth retire.
Earth sinks beneath, and draws a num'rous throng
Of pondrous, thick, unwieldy seeds along.
About her coasts, unruly waters roar;
And rising, on a ridge, insult the shore.
Thus when the God, whatever God was he,
Had form'd the whole, and made the parts agree,
That no unequal portions might be found,
He moulded Earth into a spacious round:
Then with a breath, he gave the winds to blow;
And bad the congregated waters flow.
He adds the running springs, and standing lakes;
And bounding banks for winding rivers makes.
Some part, in Earth are swallow'd up, the most
In ample oceans, disembogu'd, are lost.
He shades the woods, the vallies he restrains
With rocky mountains, and extends the plains.[75]

The spark of god or the spark in nature differentiates the elements and their meaning. The elements of earth, air, fire and water described by the ancient Egyptians and Plato given their rightful place by god. Upon creation, they form two pairs of opposites, that is, the force of fire ascends high followed by air as the first pair. The earth then sinks beneath followed by water affecting the shore, forming the second pair. God had therefore created the unity and all the parts agree, meaning the system of four elements in two pairs is stable and harmonious. He then proceeds to describe the connections or relationships between the elements wind as air moving over the earth, congregated waters to flow in rivers and lakes and how god formed the mountains and valleys with the lowest being taken by the ocean.

Then, every void of Nature to supply,
With forms of Gods he fills the vacant sky:
New herds of beasts he sends, the plains to share:
New colonies of birds, to people air:
And to their oozy beds, the finny fish repair.
A creature of a more exalted kind
Was wanting yet, and then was Man design'd:
Conscious of thought, of more capacious breast,
For empire form'd, and fit to rule the rest:
Whether with particles of heav'nly fire
The God of Nature did his soul inspire,

---

[75] Ibid, pages 5 & 6

Or Earth, but new divided from the sky,
And, pliant, still retain'd th' aetherial energy:
Which wise Prometheus temper'd into paste,
And, mixt with living streams, the godlike image cast.
Thus, while the mute creation downward bend
Their sight, and to their earthly mother tend,
Man looks aloft; and with erected eyes
Beholds his own hereditary skies.
From such rude principles our form began;
And earth was metamorphos'd into Man. [76]

Ovid describes the filling of the void with living creatures culminating in the creation of humans using the energy left from the aether previously joined to the earth. Prometheus, the bringer of fire to humans, moulds them from the earth mixed with water from the living streams to make a paste in god's image. The ambiguity of 'God or Nature' has now become the 'God of Nature', thus making god the creator. Humans transformed from the earth with the help of fire (energy), air (aether) and water (living streams) into unified quaternity of combined elements. This recognition of the fourfold nature of humans shows that the ancient Romans, as did the Egyptians and Greeks, were aware of the unity of the human condition, albeit in projected form onto physical elements.

The first inkling of awareness of the difference between the inner world of the unconscious and the outer physical world is in the story of the god Janus, who was unique to the Roman people. The opposites were unified in his nature as a solar and lunar deity, and the god of public and private doors and gates. He had two faces pointing in opposite directions and his insignia was the key that opens and closes the door. His two faces allowed him to view the interior as well as the exterior of a building.[77] Ovid regards Janus having a central role in creation and was the deity of Chaos transformed after the elements separated. Janus also relates to the Egyptian idea of the 'double'.

If we regard the interior of a house or building as an extension of psychic space including the myth-making unconscious, we can see a very interesting arrangement and function of the god Janus. With one face, he sees the outer physical world and all its elements, and the other face looks at the inner world of chaos (myth-making unconscious) from which all is created. Janus is depicted in a variety of ways from an old bearded man on one side and younger beardless man on the other. On occasion, the faces have identical two bearded older men or unbearded younger men. In one depiction, the faces are of a bearded older man and a

---

[76] Ibid, page 7
[77] LAROUSSE, New Encyclopedia of Mythology, Hamlyn Publishing, 1968, page 202

younger woman, and indeed, this depiction of a younger woman reinforces the idea of looking into one's inner world, is looking at one's feminine soul.

Mars was an important god for the Romans because he connected their history of agriculture and conquest. In one version, Mars was the son of Jupiter and Juno, and in another, Juno gave birth to Mars by a mystical union with a fabulous flower. Mars was the father of Romulus and Remus with Rhea Silvia and was later associated with Venus, the beautiful and loving goddess. Mars and Venus as a complimentary pair of opposites were united through Cupid (Eros).

The Latin Jupiter was a god of light, sun and moon, and climatic phenomena such as wind, rain, thunder, tempest, and lightning and therefore an important agricultural deity. His character changed over time and his function became a protector of the city and state and symbolised virtues of justice, good faith and honour. His sister wife Juno represented the feminine principle of celestial light, of which Jupiter was the masculine principle. She was the goddess of childbirth and bringing them into the light of consciousness.

Vesta was the most beautiful of the Roman deities and symbolised by a bright flame and in the beginning personified the earth and fire, and later, just fire. She was a virgin goddess and an idealised mother of the hearth, home and family. Vulcan was one of the oldest of the Latin gods and under the name of Volcanus, regarded as the first Jupiter of Rome. Originally, Vulcan was the god of the thunderbolt and sun, later the god of fires and finally the god associated with life giving warmth and the hearth.[78]

Saturn was an ancient agricultural divinity of Latin and Roman origin and ranked equal to Janus and Jupiter. His name is associated with abundance and was celebrated every year in a festival called the Saturnalia, which lasted seven days from the 17th to the 23rd December. The festival celebrated in the Roman Forum with a public banquet, private gift giving, gambling and change of roles between masters and slaves. The other main deities were Minerva the goddess of the thunderbolt and Mercury the god of commerce and trade.

The gods of the Roman Empire were similar to the gods of ancient Greece as they represented environmental influences in some instances and human characteristics in others. Janus was an example of an original god transformed from the primordial chaos with a position between that

---

[78] Ibid, page 204

realm and the newly formed physical world. In other words, he stood at and had the key to the door or gate between inner and outer worlds. Mars reflected the Roman concerns of agriculture and war and complimented by Venus with her love and beauty.

The ancient Romans myths and their gods reflected their agricultural origins and symbols of their power in their weapons such as spears, lightning bolts and tridents. They contributed little to metaphysical philosophy of the ancient Greeks as their practical nature built institutions and laws as part of their empire. The creation myth and the transformed god Janus stood between the unformed matrix of chaos and the newly formed physical world and exemplified the first step in the birth of the Roman Republic. This ability to look inward and outward moved to the practical outward looking Mars who then became the reflection of their agricultural concerns and protector and conqueror for the state. Similarly, Jupiter became the god of celestial and climactic phenomena related to the seasons, planting times, rainfall, storms and so on. Saturn also had a relationship to crops and the abundance of the harvest.

The goddesses had typically female roles of mother of the hearth represented by Vesta, the psychopomp or inner spiritual guide by Juno, and love, beauty, desire, and sex represented by Venus. Although these gods and goddesses had similar heritage to the ancient Greek deities, the Romans adapted them to their own needs and concerns. The gods of ancient Greece had elemental characteristics in addition to quite specific and definite human characteristics. They had an overwhelming desire to know physical nature and their own inner functioning, whereas the Romans were more concerned with agriculture, conquest and building an empire.

d. Early Judaism

The history of Judaism is essentially the history of the Jewish people from their origin in Canaan and Judea, to the time of slavery in Egypt and return to their homeland. The history is however, fraught with debate, as there is no record or archaeological artefacts that prove the exodus from Egypt through the Sinai desert to their promised land. At most, I can provide a brief outline of the recorded history and an outline of the five books of Moses that describes their family origins, relationships, slavery in Egypt, journey through the desert, the revelation on the mount and return to their promised land.

Archaeological records do not support the bible, which puts us in the difficult position of treating the text as both a historical record and myth. The records suggest that the kingdom of Judah and Israel had their origins in Canaan and not in Egypt, as told in the Bible.[79] There are certain aspects of the story that point towards it being a myth and a vision of the author, and other aspects that point to it being a historical record. For example, besides the obvious supernatural events, such as the global flood, the parting the Red Sea and so on, the elders all live to ages beyond a normal lifetime. They also survive in a desert environment, sustained on a curious substance called Manna. Other aspects of the text that point to it as a historical record are the comprehensive history of the people and the precise description of their lineage. It also details personal characteristics and their relationships, which indicate that the story was to some extent, based on real people.

The history centres in the Fertile Crescent on the East coast of the Mediterranean Sea, surrounded by the ancient cultures of Egypt and Babylonia. The 'Children of Israel' descended from a common ancestor called Jacob who had twelve sons named, Reuben, Simeon, Levi, Judah, Yissachar, Zebulun, Dan, Gad, Naphtali, Asher, Joseph and Benjamin, and became the twelve tribes of Israel. These tribes divided the land between them and ruled by a series of judges. The Israeli monarchy established in 1000 BC under the reign of Saul, passed on to King David and his son Solomon. David built the First Temple in Jerusalem, and political instability led to civil war between the tribes of Judah and Benyamin in the south and the other ten tribes in the north. This divided the kingdom into two, called Israel in the north and Judah in the south. The Assyrian ruler, Tiglath-Pileser III, conquered the kingdom of Israel in the north in the 8th century BC, and records of the ten tribes were lost.

The Babylonian army conquered the kingdom of Judah in 587 BC and destroyed the first temple, and many of the Jewish people were exiled to Babylon and Egypt. The Judaic religion continued to develop in Babylonia, with new communities established and the writing of the Jewish Talmud. After returning to Jerusalem from Babylonian exile, the Jewish people had permission in 516 BC by the Persians to build the Second Temple. In 332 BC Alexander the Great defeated the Persians and his general Seleucus ruled Canaan and Judea. During this period, Hellenistic Philosophy heavily influenced Judaism, which developed in the 3rd century BC, and established Jewish communities in the newly founded city of Alexandria.

The relationship between the Hellenised and Orthodox Jews deteriorated and led to an independent Jewish kingdom known as the Hasmonaeon Dynasty from 110 to 63 BC. The Roman general, Pompey, conquered the

---

[79] FINKELSTEIN, Israel and Nadav Naaman, eds. (1994). From Nomadism to Monarchy: Archaeological and Historical Aspects of Early Israel.

kingdom in 63 BC, after which Herod appointed by the Roman Senate, ruled the kingdom. The Roman prefect, Pontius Pilate put a rabbi called Jesus from Galilee to death in 33 AD. In 66 AD, the Jews revolted against Roman rule and in 70 AD, the Romans destroyed the Temple in Jerusalem. Other revolts crushed from 132 to 136 AD, and much of the Jewish population killed, sold into slavery or fled.

After the disaster in Jerusalem, Babylonia (modern day Iraq) became the focus of Judaism for more than a thousand years with an estimated population of two million. In this period the Babylonian Talmud was written, academies established and became the centre of Jewish scholarship. During the Byzantine period 324-638 AD, the Roman Empire's policy converted Jews to Christianity, and a revolt in Galilee was quickly suppressed and their cities destroyed under the rule of Gallus. In the 5th century, Emperor Theodosius issued a set of decrees establishing official persecution of the Jews.

In 638 AD, the Byzantine Empire lost control of the Levant (eastern part of the Mediterranean) and the Islamic Empire under Caliph Omar, conquered Jerusalem. He was a benevolent ruler and the Jewish population re-established their presence in Jerusalem. From 711 to 1031 AD, the Jewish people thrived in Spain under Muslim rule and devoted themselves to the study of science, commerce, industry, trading silk and slaves. During the crusader period 1099-1260 AD, the Jews were again persecuted, particularly in Europe and the Rhine valley, where they were forcibly made to convert to Christianity. In 1099, they helped the Arabs defend Jerusalem against the Crusaders, lost and were again persecuted.

They continued to be persecuted during the Mamluk Empire 1260-1517 AD, ruled from Turkey and Egypt. During this period Nahmanides, a Jewish scholar, spread learning through the holy land and encouraged humility and discouraged immorality. They were once again, massacred across Europe and exiled to Poland where they thrived. At the end of the Middle Ages and beginning of the modern era, the Jewish people were spread all over Europe and in the 19th century, were offered equality under Napoleonic Law. Anti-Semitism grew in Europe based on ideas of racial purity, which led to many immigrating to the United States. During the 1870's and 80's, the Jewish population in Europe actively contemplated a return to their old homeland in Israel.

This became a reality after the United Kingdom captured Palestine from the Ottoman Empire and promised through the 1917 Balfour Declaration to establish a Jewish homeland. This was no easy task, as Arabs had occupied the lands for many years, which had to accept the returning population by force. During this period, Russian Jews were involved with the communist takeover of the monarchy, which resulted in the Russian revolution. The Jewish people were again persecuted in Germany after World War 1, which led to the tragedy of World War 2 and the attempted extermination of the European Jewish people.

The history of Judaism begins with five books of Moses from a compilation of written and oral tradition as early as 1312 BC. The date of completion and authoring is however, still debated. Book 1, Genesis, describes the creation of the world by the Jewish god:

> 1:1   IN THE beginning God created the heaven and the earth.
> 1:2   Now the earth was unformed and void, and darkness was upon the face of the deep; and the spirit of God hovered over the face of the waters.
> 1:3   And God said: 'Let there be light' And there was light.
> 1:4   And God saw the light, that it was good; and God divided the light from the darkness.
> 1:5   And God called the light Day, and the darkness He called Night
> And   there was evening and there was morning, one day.[80]

In these first five sentences, we can see the difference between this creation myth and that of the ancient Egyptians, Greeks and Romans. God already exists outside of the void or chaos, unlike Atum, who was the spirit within the void (Nun). Likewise, the ancient Greeks personified and borrowed their creation myth from the Egyptians, differentiated and personified the story further to suit their own ethos. The Greek personifications of creation are Erebus as light, Nyx as darkness, Gaia as earth, and so on. The Jewish god and the void removed the Greek personifications and abstracted the qualities of the characters to what we know today as sun, day, night, etc. God is now a mysterious powerful father figure that lacks the personal quality of Zeus.

Symbolically, the term 'Let there be light' is the same as saying 'Let us be aware' because only in light can we see clearly, in darkness we cannot see. The above text also shows a differentiation of the opposites of light and dark and the idea of unity called 'one day'. The text further differentiates heaven and earth from the primal waters.

> 1:6   And God said: 'Let there be a firmament in the midst of the waters, and let it divide the waters from the waters'.
> 1:7   And God made the firmament, and divided the waters which were under the firmament from the waters which were above the firmament; and it was so.

---

[80] HOLY TORAH, Book 1, Jewish Publication Society, http://www.ishwar.com

1:8	And God called the firmament Heaven And there was evening and there was morning, a second day.
1:9	And God said: 'Let the waters under the heaven be gathered together unto one place, and let the dry land appear' And it was so.
1:10	And God called the dry land Earth, and the gathering together of the waters called he Seas; and God saw that it was good.

God then sets the scene for the cycles of day and night with the transition through morning and evening. Heaven was up until god's commandment in between two layers of waters from which he raised it to its final place in the sky. He then proceeds to divide the earth from the waters thus forming another pair of opposites. Unlike the Roman creation myth, where Janus emerged from unformed chaos, god was already out of the primal waters. He then proceeds to create vegetation, the seasons, years, sun, moon, stars, sea creatures, birds, land creatures and finally man and woman in his own likeness.

1:27	And God created man in His own image, in the image of God created He him; male and female created He them.
1:28	And God blessed them; and God said unto them: 'Be fruitful, and multiply, and replenish the earth, and subdue it; and have dominion over the fish of the sea, and over the fowl of the air, and over every living thing that creepeth upon the earth'.

He then gives mankind authority to 'subdue' the earth for their needs and after 6 days of creation, rested on the seventh. In the next weekly cycle, he plants a garden eastward in Eden where he put man and the tree of life and of knowledge of good and evil.

2:8	And the Lord God planted a garden eastward, in Eden; and there He put the man whom He had formed.
2:9	And out of the ground made the Lord God to grow every tree that is pleasant to the sight, and good for food; the tree of life also in the midst of the garden, and the tree of the knowledge of good and evil.

The garden built eastward toward the rising sun (new life) and from there flowed a river that had four heads named Pishon, Gihon, Tigris and Euphrates. The rivers Tigris and Euphrates were already named by the ancient Babylonians between 1894-1595 BC, and predate the writing of Genesis. This indicates a relationship to Babylonia rather than the lands of Canaan (Israel). God then places man in the Garden of Eden with strict instructions not to eat from the tree of knowledge of good and evil.

2:16	And the Lord God commanded the man, saying: 'Of every tree of the garden thou mayest freely eat;

> 2:17 but of the tree of the knowledge of good and evil, thou shalt not eat of it; for in the day that thou eatest thereof thou shalt surely die.'

He names man Adam and provides other animals so that he is not alone. God makes Adam fall into a deep sleep, from which he took one of his ribs to make a woman. The ribs in a human form the protective cage around the vital organs including the heart, and are flexible enough to accommodate breathing. The following passage shows the association of breath and soul (man's inner feminine character):

> 2:7 Then the Lord God formed man of the dust of the ground, and breathed into his nostrils the breath of life; and man became a living soul.

These passages are curious as Adam was the first man and therefore had no parents other than god, yet the text describes the transition from home, mother and father to an independent and whole life with one's wife, naked and unashamed. In other words, they were innocent like pre-adolescent children before puberty.

> 2:24 Therefore shall a man leave his father and his mother, and shall cleave unto his wife, and they shall be one flesh.
> 2:25 And they were both naked, the man and his wife, and were not ashamed.

The subtle snake tells the woman god said not to eat any fruit in the garden. She explains that the commandment was not to eat from the central tree lest we die. The snake contradicts god's commandment and says that she will not die. He tells her that eating the fruit from the tree will make her like god and open her eyes. She wanted knowledge, ate from the tree and shared fruit with Adam. With their eyes opened, they became aware of their nakedness.

> 3:8 And they heard the voice of the Lord God walking in the garden toward the cool of the day; and the man and his wife hid themselves from the presence of the Lord God amongst the trees of the garden.
> 3:9 And the Lord God called unto the man, and said unto him: 'Where art thou?'
> 3:10 And he said: 'I heard Thy voice in the garden, and I was afraid, because I was naked; and I hid myself.'
> 3:11 And He said: 'Who told thee that thou wast naked? Hast thou eaten of the tree, whereof I commanded thee that thou shouldest not eat?'
> 3:12 And the man said: 'The woman whom Thou gavest to be with me, she gave me of the tree, and I did eat.'

Adam tells god the truth that Eve gave him the fruit, which leaves her at the mercy of god and his punishment. This simple interaction gives us an indication of the relativity of good and evil. On one hand, Adam tells god what happened and that Eve gave him the fruit, condemning her to pain and subservience. On the other, Adam could have taken responsibility for his own actions and not eaten the fruit, knowing it was forbidden. In other words, his honesty caused them to have to bear the pain and independence of adult life. Eating the forbidden fruit is then the awakening of the natural biological instinct and knowledge of the animal nature of those biological functions.

3:15   And I will put enmity between thee and the woman, and between thy seed and her seed; they shall bruise thy head, and thou shalt bruise their heel.'

3:16   Unto the woman He said: 'I will greatly multiply thy pain and thy travail; in pain thou shalt bring forth children; and thy desire shall be to thy husband, and he shall rule over thee.'

3:17   And unto Adam He said: 'Because thou hast hearkened unto the voice of thy wife, and hast eaten of the tree, of which I commanded thee, saying: Thou shalt not eat of it; cursed is the ground for thy sake; in toil shalt thou eat of it all the days of thy life.

God punishes Eve for her transgression by creating hostility between her and the snake and giving her the pain of childbirth and subservience to her husband. From here on Adam has to provide their own food with the toil of cultivation, in contrast to the fruits provided in the garden. God then clothes Adam and Eve and expels them from Eden.

The text is quite clear concerning loss of the relaxed life of childhood and innocence with the attainment of knowledge. The snake has always been associated with instinct, especially the sexual instinct, due to its shape and the fact that it is predominately spine and ribs. Instincts are spontaneous and without conscious thought and the snake is all rib and Eve was made from a rib, thus relating her to the snake and instinct. The snake also has wisdom as they do not have eyelids and see all. Listening to the snake 'opens their eyes' and they become aware of good and evil. The snake and the eating of the forbidden fruit is the transition through puberty into adulthood and indeed the death of childhood. They also have to take care of themselves (expelled from the all-providing garden) and leave the paradise of parental care and toil in the fields (work and earn a living) to provide food for themselves and family. The bruising of one's heel is the burden and pain of childbirth that all women potentially bear, walking through life.

> 3:24   So He drove out the man; and He placed at the east of the garden of Eden the cherubim, and the flaming sword which turned every way, to keep the way to the tree of life.

God then ensures that it is difficult to return to the garden (childhood) by placing Cherubim to guard the entry, which is traditionally a youth with human features. Later depictions in the Torah, describe it as a creature with many wings and four faces of a lion, ox, human and eagle. These four elements are important, as they are examples of transitions of development. The lion is the king of the wild: strong, powerful and resilient. The Ox powerful but tameable and controllable, the human, and finally, the eagle, which is the spirit above land and in the air. The flaming sword as we know cuts, divides and stabs the desire to return to childhood and dependence, and ensures that the separation is enforced.

> 4:2   And again she bore his brother Abel. And Abel was a keeper of sheep, but Cain was a tiller of the ground.
> 4:3   And in process of time it came to pass, that Cain brought of the fruit of the ground an offering unto the Lord.
> 4:4   And Abel, he also brought of the firstlings of his flock and of the fat thereof. And the Lord had respect unto Abel and to his offering;
> 4:5   but unto Cain and to his offering He had not respect. And Cain was very wroth, and his countenance fell.

The ensuing adult life of Adam and Eve has typical family problems. Eve has two sons, Cain and Abel, who seek the approval of their grandfather (god) with offerings of their work. Cain the farmer gives fruit, Abel the sheepherder, gives a lamb and its fat. God disrespects the fruit offering of Cain and respects the animal offering from Abel causing animosity between them. The preference of animal sacrifice over offering from the land shows an urge to differentiate the spirit from the land and associated instincts of the body. In other words, the differentiation of the mental faculties of reason, intelligence, knowledge etc., over the purely instinctive and sense functions of the body attached to the land. Animals can wander the land and feed on grass, which liberates their owners from the dependence on fixed location (earth). Differentiation from earth is also emphasised in Exodus and the escape from the agriculturally based Egypt.

The liberation from the earth and matter is a step closer to the spirit. God's urge for Adam's sons to differentiate from the land leads to fratricide and a curse to wander the earth, which separates Cain from his agricultural pursuits and puts him in Abel's place free from attachment. Food at that time is a significant burden for survival, especially when oriented around agriculture. Regular flooding in ancient Egypt was predictable, but less so in the land of Canaan and Jordan, which suffered regular drought and famine.

4:10　And He said: 'What hast thou done? the voice of thy brother's blood crieth unto Me from the ground.

4:11　And now cursed art thou from the ground, which hath opened her mouth to receive thy brother's blood from thy hand.

4:12　When thou tillest the ground, it shall not henceforth yield unto thee her strength; a fugitive and a wanderer shalt thou be in the earth.'

4:13　And Cain said unto the Lord: 'My punishment is greater than I can bear.

4:14　Behold, Thou hast driven me out this day from the face of the land; and from Thy face shall I be hid; and I shall be a fugitive and a wanderer in the earth; and it will come to pass, that whosoever findeth me will slay me.'

4:15　And the Lord said unto him: 'Therefore whosoever slayeth Cain, vengeance shall be taken on him sevenfold.' And the Lord set a sign for Cain, lest any finding him should smite him.

Moving to suitable grazing land with one's food source (domesticated animals) is a solution to this problem. This is why animals figure highly as symbols in the Torah as animals are purely instinctive, go to the toilet where they stand and have uninhibited sexual lives. We have to put restrictions on the same urges in ourselves to feel above the animal. Similarly, the story of Jesus also has important symbols oriented around food. These include the agricultural products of bread (body) and wine (blood), and most importantly fish, which have universal importance as food (ideas) from the sea (unconscious). The life of Jesus continued the differentiation of spirit from matter, earth and the body. The devil became the repository of earthly instincts and the spiritual relegated to the heavens and an all-good god.

The above text becomes a recurring theme of disconnection from the earth[81] and potential inflation[82]. Adam once again, 'knew his wife' and had another son named Seth who had many offspring including the righteous and wholehearted Noah who was favoured by god. God felt regret for his creation of man and decided to end the corruption and violence of the flesh by destroying his people and starting again. This is the prerogative of a creator who isn't happy with his creation and decides to salvage what is good and discard the rest.

---

[81] We see the same problem between Jacob and Esau later in the Torah
[82] Inflation is the psychological problem of feeling superior to others and is always coupled with feelings of inferiority.

God tells Noah to build an ark with quite specific instructions in materials, size, rooms, etc. as he will bring floodwater upon the earth to destroy all flesh except Noah, his sons, wives and the male and female of every living thing. God then proceeds to blot out his creation and flood the earth, destroys most his creation. Afterwards, God becomes aware that existence is a pair of opposites and that men have animal's instincts and he feels regret for the destruction he caused.

> 8:21   And the Lord smelled the sweet savour; and the Lord said in His heart: 'I will not again curse the ground any more for man's sake; for the imagination of man's heart is evil from his youth; neither will I again smite any more every thing living, as I have done.
>
> 8:22   While the earth remaineth, seedtime and harvest, and cold and heat, and summer and winter, and day and night shall not cease.'

God's fallibility is all too evident. He curses his first children with pain and toil, then favours one grandson over another, causing fratricide and destroys all of mankind because they are corrupt and violent. He then realises that the imagination of a man's heart is evil from youth and recognises human nature and the opposites of reality. We are on one hand, capable of such beauty and the highest spirit of culture, and the other, corruption and violence driven by greed, insecurity, and jealousy. It seems however, a hard lesson to learn and after Noah completes his mission, God establishes a 'covenant' not to destroy the earth again with a flood. Noah's children and animals spread and re-populate the earth and Noah falls from grace and becomes drunken and naked. Noah's son Ham tells his two brothers Shem and Japheth about Noah and they cover his nakedness with their faces backwards, as if they were ashamed of their father's situation. Noah is angry with Ham for telling his brothers and curses Ham's son Canaan to become the servant of the others.

The drunkenness of Noah is an understandable outcome of having taken part in destroying the human race. If he had argued with god and refused to aid him in his conflagration, god would have had to relent, as he needs people to carry out his deeds. Noah would have had the upper hand and shown god's vindictive and destructive nature. We have to keep in mind that this is a struggle between inner characters within the author, and an attempt to liberate oneself from the temptations of the flesh and its connection to the earth. There is no evidence that any of the visions of the author actually occurred in the physical world.

As a myth, we can draw symbolic conclusions from the text, which can help us understand what god and man are struggling with in this story. In the beginning Adam and Eve are in the garden, God wants to keep them innocent and protect them from corruption and sin. Human curiosity as it is and Eve being closer to nature (snake, rib, instinct, childbirth) than Adam, disobeys father (spirit) because it is natural to grow beyond parental restrictions. Adam has no trouble defying his parental authority either and eats from the tree, but does not take responsibility for his action and blames Eve for leading him astray. Father then curses them with pain and toil and having to grow up and take care of themselves. Growing from child to adult is a psychic death and a struggle against losing innocence and creative play. The teenage years can be the hardest and the transition is ritualised by many cultures making it less tumultuous.

It takes a long time and many curses on god's part, before he realises that his creation has the potential to be divine, but as long as they have bodies (flesh), they will have all the same instincts and fallibilities as other beasts. Upon this realisation, god makes a covenant with Noah to accept humanity as it is rather than how he wants them to be. This evolution of the Jewish people is also an evolution of their god. The respect god shows for Abel's offering over Cains, indicates a desire to liberate from their bond to the earth represented by agriculture, to the freer and mobility of animal herding. In this way, people can be nomadic because they can take animals with them, as crops require stability and settling in one place. As we shall see in the following, the exodus from Egypt is the liberation from the values of agriculture and stability, and the Jewish god a union of Osiris and Set. The function that is missing is an all-loving female character like Isis, the Virgin Mary or the Gnostic Sophia.

The text continues with Abram, a descendent of Shem, told by god to leave the country for the land of Canaan (Israel). Reaching Canaan, he finds famine and continues to the fertile lands of Egypt. Upon arrival, he deceives the Pharaoh because he fears his beautiful wife will be taken and himself murdered. He pretends she is his sister and is rewarded with animals, servants, silver and gold. The deception causes a plague and the Pharaoh finds out and expels both Abram and his wife, Sarai. They journey back to where they came from at Beth-el where Lot, his nephew, had stayed to tend his flock. There was conflict between the herdsmen for the dwindling food and Abram divided the land, left and right. Lot went to the plain of Jordan, and Abram to Canaan.

Lot dwells close to Sodom, and Abram builds an altar in Hebron. Warring kings capture Lot, his people and goods, and Abram mounts a rescue with three hundred and eighteen men. They raid by night and rescue Lot and his people and are rewarded by the other kings with bread, wine and respect. The king of Sodom offers Abram riches, which he refuses to accept. God tells him that he is his shield and shall reward him greatly.

Abram laments that he has no blood heirs and God tells him that he shall have an heir from his own bowels and asks for offerings comprising a three year old heifer, a she-goat, a ram, a turtledove and a young pigeon. Abram cuts the animals in half except for the birds and falls into a deep sleep. God makes another covenant, promising the land from the river of Egypt to the river Euphrates.

Sarai cannot conceive and she offers Abram her Egyptian handmaiden Hagar who she later resents. Hagar gives birth to a son called Ishmael, described as 'a wild ass of a man'. At ninety-nine, God makes another covenant with Abram and promises to multiply him exceedingly and become 'a father of a multitude of nations', and changes his name from Abram to Abraham. God makes a covenant with Abraham to circumcise all males and decrees that Sarai's name shall henceforth, be Sarah.

God blesses Sarah and promises her a son who is to be called Isaac, but Abraham is sceptical and laughs at the idea due to Sarah's advanced years. He proceeds to circumcise all the men in his tribe, including himself and his son Ishmael. Three men appear, and Abraham serves them food and drink under a tree. The men tell Abraham that Sarah will have a son and she laughs at the suggestion due to her age, but god decrees that she will bear a child. The three men leave for Sodom and Abraham and God have a dialogue over the fifty righteous men in Sodom and Gomorrah. God decrees that he will forgive the place for the sake of the righteous. Abraham tests God's level of justice and God reveals that he will not destroy Sodom and Gomorrah if as few as ten righteous men live there.

Lot feeds and interacts with two angels and the men of the city come after the angels and surround his house. Lot offers his virgin daughters rather than the angels and the men are afflicted with blindness. The angels tell Lot that god sent them to destroy the city and he should get his family out. Lot could only convince his wife and two daughters and the angels set them outside of the city and instructed them to escape to the mountains and not look back. Lot explains that he cannot escape to the mountains for evil will overtake him and wishes to escape to the little city called Zoar. God destroys Sodom, Gomorrah and the plain with rain, fire and brimstone. Lot's wife looks back and is turned into a pillar of salt. Lot leaves Zoar to live in a cave in the mountains with his two daughters. His daughters realise there are no men left and decide to preserve Lot's seed, get him drunk, lay with him, and have his children. They give birth to two sons named Moab and Ben-ammi[83]

---

[83] Passages 12:1 to 19:38

The story continues the nomadic attitude and lack of connection to the earth and agriculture. Abraham displays little regard for his wife's well-being and lies to protect himself from the idea that he will be killed and his wife taken. Even when the pharaoh finds out about the lie, Abraham and Sarah are free to go with their riches. Symbolically, Abram uses deception to protect his emerging spirit, sells his lower soul[84] for riches (high value), puts a plague on the authority, gets his soul back and leaves with her and the riches. The difference between this myth and the Greek myth of Jason and the dragon slaying, is how he attains the riches. Instead of killing the dragon (overcoming the animal within), unity (riches) is achieved by giving away one's beauty and honesty (lower soul) for fear of death of his upper soul.[85] Maintaining his connection to his upper soul and god is more important than his relating function to his wife and the physical world. Indeed, the ancient Jewish nomadic attitude and lack of roots into the earth make the only reliable thing in life, one's inner god.

Lot gets captured by warring kings and rescued by Abraham after killing the kings by night. The king of Sodom offers Abraham riches, which he refuses because acceptance will give the king power over him. This shows that Abraham values his inner world more than the outer and can sell his wife to protect his soul and not accept gifts for fear of outer obligation. Lot also offers his daughters to the town's men in place of his inner angels, who he feels are more valuable. Abraham has two sons, one by an Egyptian handmaiden, Hagar, and one by his aging wife Sarah. The first son Ishmael is deemed a wild man and therefore, governed by his instincts. The second son Isaac whose name means 'he will laugh' reflects the disbelief that Sarah could give birth in her advanced years.

Lot protects two angels sent by god to destroy the cities, and flees with his wife and two daughters. His wife looks back and becomes the salt of the earth. This attitude towards the flesh and so-called wickedness emphasises the struggle to overcome one's natural instincts and emotions. Looking back at one's instinctive background (S & G) brings one down to earth (salt) and captured by that realm. God, in this instance, encourages growth towards the higher spirit, but cannot be trusted to keep his word. His covenant not to destroy humanity again with Noah

---

[84] Lower soul in this instance, refers to the soul oriented towards the earth in contrast to the upper soul oriented towards the spirit.
[85] It is not clear what Abram's definition of soul is as he makes a distinction between his wife and his soul. 12:13 Say, I pray thee, thou art my sister; that it may be well with me for thy sake, and that my soul may live because of thee.' I suspect that the Jewish idea of soul is different than the ancient Greek. It is possible Abram regards his wife as his relating function to the outer world, and his own soul, his relating function to his inner world.

seems to have been forgotten, or a loophole found, in that it is not 'every thing living'.

The text continues with Abraham once again, claiming his wife as his sister to avoid an imaginary threat from Abimelech the king of Gerar. God speaks to the king in a dream that he has taken a man's wife and shall therefore die. He explains that he did not touch her and was told she is Abraham's sister and took her because of the 'simplicity of my heart'. God urges Abimelech to restore Abraham's wife under threat of death. He does and Abraham explains that Sarah is his stepsister and the king rewards them with sheep, oxen, silver, servants and a place to dwell. God then rewards the king and his wives with fertility.[86]

This is the second time that Abraham denies his marriage and makes Sarah his sister for fear of his life. The difference between a wife and sister in our present day moral codes is the sexual component. Myths however, depict inner characters that are not bound by our moral codes as they are founded on our raw nature. Symbolically, sexual intercourse is the union of opposites and sex between brother and sister, union of already related and equal opposites. It is a spiritual union expressed in the physical act of intercourse. Myths as do dreams, often depict the union of opposites of a like nature as the story of Osiris and his sister wife Isis shows. Abraham tells Abimelech that Sarah is his stepsister and he rewards Abraham and Sarah. When god speaks to Abimelech in a dream, he is fearful for his life as adultery in ancient Jewish law, was a serious offence punishable by death.[87] We can assume that Abraham brought his ethics to the pharaoh and king creating a moral conflict that could only be resolved with reverence and reward to Abraham and Sarah.

This scenario shows that the ancient Jewish people were developing an ethical attitude to tame their instinctive nature and differentiate themselves from their animal origins. Abraham imagines a threat to his life and gives up his wife to an unknown fate to alleviate that fear. The pharaoh and king find out and connect their own fear with actual and potential disasters. In this case, we have to regard them as the imaginings of a single man struggling with inner characters. It then becomes a moral struggle between the inner characters of a man of power and wealth (king), and a spiritual man of ethics and righteousness (Abraham). Between the opposites is Sarah, the soul character who happily oscillates between the roles of sexual wife (physical) and non-sexual sister (spiritual). In the end, the spiritual man prevails and is rewarded with riches (energy) and freedom, and the king rewarded with

---

[86] Passages 20:1 to 20:18
[87] http://jewishencyclopedia.com/articles/865-adultery

fertility. This also emphasises the dual nature of a man's soul who as a wife relates to the material in the spiritual man and as a sister, relates to the spiritual in the material man. This dual nature of the soul and her ability to relate to both sides shows the importance of her role for a man.

The text continues with the birth of Isaac and the declaration by Sarah that Abraham's other son Ishmael and his mother, Hagar the Egyptian, be sent away. God instructs Abraham to comply and he gives them bread, water, and sends them into the wilderness of Beer-Sheba. God tells Hagar that her son will become a great nation and an archer in the wilderness and marry an Egyptian woman. After his interaction with Abimelech, Abraham returns to the land of the Philistines and is instructed by God to go to Moriah and offer his one remaining son Isaac, as a burnt offering on one of the mountains. He complies, and just as he is about to kill Isaac, an angel stops him. Abraham proves that he is a god-fearing man and is rewarded with grandchildren and power.

Sarah, as Abraham's soul, with the backing of god, rejects the son that represents instinctive wildness and the connection to Egypt. In other words, God and her urge the spiritual man (Abraham) to reject the connection to his instincts represented by the wild Ishmael. Abraham is then urged to sacrifice his one remaining son, who is the uniting function between the opposites of Sarah and Abraham. This is a test of his devotion to the higher inner authority, as killing his one remaining son will end his lineage and future generations. He is at the last minute stopped, not by God, but by one of his representatives in the form of an angel. Honouring the higher spirit alone leads to the loss of unity, in that one's earthly existence and continuation through one's offspring is hampered. The lower rank of the angel is closer to the physical world than God and saves Abraham from complete one-sidedness and returns him to the world of wife, son, future offspring and practical matters.

The text continues with Abraham burying his elderly wife Sarah who died at age 127 in a field with a cave he bought from Heth. Abraham instructs a servant to find a wife for Isaac from somewhere other that the Canaanites. The servant meets a virgin at a fountain named Rebekah, a relative of Abraham, and invites her to go with him and explains the purpose of his mission. She agrees to go with the servant and to marry Isaac. Abraham takes another wife named Keturah, from whom he had six more children and a guaranteed lineage. He dies at the ripe old age of 175, and is buried in the same field as Sarah.

Ishmael thrives and has many children. Isaac and Rebekah struggle to have children until God proclaims that two nations are within her womb. She has twins, the ruddy and hairy Esau, and the other named Jacob who had hold of Esau's heel. Isaac favoured Esau as a cunning hunter and farmer over Jacob who was an introverted and quiet man. Jacob resents his father's preference and tricks Esau out of his birth right when he came in from the field hungry and thirsty and withheld food and drink from him.

The legacy and attitude of Abraham and Sarah's forbearers continues through Isaac and Rebekah with the birth of twins that represent the opposites of instinct and spirit. This is the clearest distinction between the introspective aspect of contemplation and inner characters represented by Jacob and the physical and extroverted man of land and hunting represented by Esau. Once again, the spirit overcomes the down-to-earth brother and takes away his birth right.

The text continues with a famine and instructions from God to Isaac to proceed to Egypt and a land called Sojourn. On the way, they dwell in Abimelech's land of Gerar,[88] and for the third time in their family, Isaac proclaims Rebekah to be his sister for fear of murder for her fair looks. King Abimelech rewards him and he thrives and becomes great but the king fears his growing power and sends him away to settle in the valley of Gerar. They give names to several newly dug wells, the final well in Beer-Sheba they name Shibah where they find living water. Abimelech approaches Isaac and proposes a covenant not to do harm to each other and they feast. The relationship between Isaac and Rebekah becomes bitter and they side with their preferred child.

Rivalry increases between Isaac and Rebekah through their sons hairy Esau and smooth Jacob. Jacob tries to fool the now old and blind Isaac, with his favourite savoury food that he had asked Esau to provide. Jacob pretends to be Esau, gives him the prepared meal and is blessed by his father. Esau arrives with his meal and the truth about Jacob's deception revealed. Isaac tells Esau that he shall dwell in the fat places on earth with the dew from heaven and is to live by the sword and serve Jacob. Esau now hates Jacob and says 'Let the days of mourning for my father be at hand; then will I slay my brother Jacob.'

Isaac sends Jacob away to get a wife, and Esau goes to Ishmael to also get a wife. Jacob goes to Beer-Sheba, lies down with a stone under his head and has a dream about a ladder set up on earth that reaches to heaven with the angels of god ascending and descending on it. God appears and gives the land where he lies to him and his children. In the morning, he puts the stone on a pillar, pours oil on it, and calls the place

---

[88] It is unclear in the text exactly where Isaac dwelled. He was meant to go to Egypt but stayed in the Abimelech's realm.

Beth-el. Jacob says that if God is with him, then the stone and pillar is god's house. He continues to the land of his mother's brother and meets Rachel the daughter of Laban, whom he falls in love with and kisses. Jacob agrees to serve Laban for seven years for Rachel's hand but Laban tricks him by giving his first-born daughter Leah with the weak eyes, instead of Rachael. Laban asks Jacob for another week's service and he will give Rachel to him. Now he has two wives, Rachel the preferred one is left barren and Leah has four sons, named Rueben, Simeon, Levi and Judah.[89]

In the above text, Isaac uses the same wife/sister deception as did Abraham and again, is rewarded. Isaac's power increases, which disturbs the king and they come to an arrangement. This shows that the opposites of power and spirit have come to agreement not to harm each other. Isaac digs a well and finds the 'water of life' (unconscious), which is the precious source of life in an otherwise dry environment and the function that unites the opposites. The rivalry transfers to Isaac and Rebekah and is expressed though their sons. The conflict between the down-to-earth, practical and straightforward son with developed agricultural and hunting instincts; and the introverted son using his brain to trick his brother out of his standing; is the same conflict between the agriculture and animal herding in the previous passages. The spirit continues to push the Jewish people from the earth towards heaven and god, and as we shall see later, finally fulfilled by the story of Jesus.

Jacob's dream of the ladder extending to heaven shows the slow and incremental (rungs) advancement to reach a higher level of awareness. It also relates to the ladder used by Horus to get his father Osiris to heaven in the ancient Egyptian myth. The reverence he displays toward the stone by elevating it onto a pillar and anointing it with oil shows the value they have towards dreams. In other words, the stone is elevated closer to god (above the ground on a pillar). Jacob's head is 'god's house', because this is where we dream as our body and senses are asleep and dormant. The next passage is curious as Jacob falls for Rachel but is tricked by Laban into being with Leah. Laban wanted his eldest daughter with the weak eyes to be married first. Jacob ends up with both daughters, but has only love for Rachel. His tricky past seems to have come back to him, as the daughter he loves and has his heart, is barren, whereas the daughter he hates, gives him many children. The two wives also allude to the dual aspect of the soul. The unaware soul (weak eyes) is fertile like the earth and the loved soul connected to the spirit, barren and cannot produce the uniting third function.

---

[89] Passages 26:1 to 29:35

Continuing with the text, Rachel laments her barrenness and envies her sister Leah, and urges Jacob to have children with her handmaiden, called Bilhah. Leah does the same, and offers her handmaiden, Zilpah to Jacob, resulting in many more sons. Rachel then conceives herself, and has a son called Joseph. Jacob wishes to leave Laban with his wives, handmaidens and children, and comes to an agreement for his labour. He requests all the speckled and spotted goats and dark sheep and leave all the unblemished and light coloured ones for Laban. Jacob then peels the bark off poplar, almond and plain branches to reveal white streaks, which he places in the watering troughs, and makes the flock conceive streaked, speckled and spotted offspring, thus diminishing Laban's flock and increasing his own.

Jacob secretly leaves with his people and most of the flock and Rachel steals her father's teraphim (idol). Laban pursues and catches up to them in the mountain of Gilead but is told by god not to harm Jacob. Laban confronts Jacob and his daughters about his stolen family, flock and god(s) (idol). He searches for the idol but Rachel puts it in the camel's saddle and sits on it. Jacob and Laban argue about the ten changes to wages and finally come to a covenant. Jacob agrees not afflict his daughters and not take any other wives. The covenant is sealed with a rock on a pillar around a heap of other rocks and they celebrate the covenant.

Laban kisses his sons, daughters and leaves. Jacob, his wives, children, servants and cattle leave for the land of his brother Esau. He sends a message to Esau, who replies that he will meet Jacob with four hundred men. Jacob fears Esau's approach, and divides his people and flock into two camps so that one may survive. Jacob prays to God to save him and he assembles a gift of goats, sheep, camels, cows and asses for the servants to bring and appease Esau. Jacob sends his wives and children over the stream Jabbok, and is left alone to wrestle a man until daybreak. The hollow of Jacob's thigh is strained and the man would not let Jacob go unless he blessed him. The man tells Jacob his name will now be Israel. Jacob calls the name of the place Peniel, and declares that he has seen god face-to-face and lived. The children of Israel do not eat the sinew of the thigh because he touched the hollow of Jacob's thigh.

Jacob bows to the ground seven times at the approach of Esau, fearing the worst. Esau runs to meet Jacob and kisses and hugs him, and they both weep. Jacob explains that god has been gracious and given him wives and children as they bow down before Esau. Jacob insists on giving the animals to Esau, who does not want to accept them but Jacob insists, and Esau accepts them. Esau leaves for home followed by Jacob at the pace of his children and cattle. Jacob buys a piece of land from Shechem's father for a hundred pieces of money, builds a house, cattle pens and an altar called El-eloche-Israel.[90]

Rachel and Leah fight for the favour of their husband in the same way Jacob and his brother Esau fought for the favour of their father. Jacob once again resorts to trickery because he felt cheated with his wages and mocked by Laban, and increases the spotted, streaked and dark cattle for himself. By transforming the cattle (instincts), he is transforming light and dark features into one flock, which is recognition of his own light and dark personality. This is also emphasised in the two wives and the love (light) for one and hatred (dark) for the other.

Jacob feels cheated and the right, supported by a dream of an angel, to take more than agreed from Laban. Jacob, his wives, cattle and others, leave for the land of Isaac. This natural scenario plays itself out countless times in all countries. Children grow strong as parents grow weak, which causes much rivalry and dispute for the estate left behind. Laban realises this, pursues them, but does not harm Jacob. He is less concerned with the loss of his daughters and cattle, and more with the loss of his power (god's idol). Jacob and Laban make a covenant that he shall be faithful to his daughters and raise a stone as a symbol of the agreement, which has a connection to his head raised above the earth on the pillar (spiritualised).

Jacob learns that his brother Esau, he had earlier cheated and deceived, is coming to meet him with an army. This is an important event for Jacob, as he has a confrontation with a shadowy, unknown man. He has a conflict within himself, brought on by the fear of his brother's retribution, and immediately divides into two with an explosion of emotion. Jacob pleads for the unity of his personality and life itself.

> 32:8 Then Jacob was greatly afraid and was distressed. And he divided the people that was with him, and the flocks, and the herds, and the camels, into two camps.
> 32:9 And he said: 'If Esau come to the one camp, and smite it, then the camp which is left shall escape.'
> 32:12 Deliver me, I pray Thee, from the hand of my brother, from the hand of Esau; for I fear him, lest he come and smite me, the mother with the children.

The shadow, projected onto the down to earth Esau, constellated in his mind, and he tries to figure out how to avoid this inner conflict. He then tries to appease the shadow with gifts (power and energy), but ends up in

---

[90] Passages 30:1 to 33:20

a wrestling match with him. All the guilt and fear of his previous deceptions and trickery comes to the surface in an instant. His earthly brother has more power (four hundred men), and he is deathly afraid of what his brother will do to him.

> 32:25   And Jacob was left alone; and there wrestled a man with him until the breaking of the day.
>
> 32:26   And when he saw that he prevailed not against him, he touched the hollow of his thigh; and the hollow of Jacob's thigh was strained, as he wrestled with him.

Jacob cannot overcome the man and is strained in the thigh, which is part of his strength for walking through life.[91] The only way Jacob can go on is to accept the transformation that is occurring and integrate (bless) the unknown man. In doing so, his previous deceptive personality transforms with the blessing into a new attitude and new name, Israel.

> 32:31   And Jacob called the name of the place Peniel: 'for I have seen God face to face, and my life is preserved.'
>
> 32:32   And the sun rose upon him as he passed over Peniel, and he limped upon his thigh.
>
> 32:33   Therefore the children of Israel eat not the sinew of the thigh–vein which is upon the hollow of the thigh, unto this day; because he touched the   hollow of Jacob's thigh, even in the sinew of the thigh–vein.

Jacob then divides his wives, children and handmaidens into two camps and tries to protect his preferred wife Rachel and son Joseph, by putting them at the rear. Esau approaches, fear and trepidation evaporates as Esau displays brotherly love and seems not bothered by Jacob's previous indiscretions. They unite in love and peace, with the subsequent relief and release of (emotion) tears. Jacob and his family settle down in the land of Canaan.

The text continues with Jacob's daughter Dinah raped and abducted by Shechem, the son of Hamor, from which Jacob had bought a parcel of land. Shechem loved Dinah and approached Jacob for her to become his wife. He agrees, only if all the men in the city are circumcised to become one people. They agree and all the men are circumcised. Jacob's sons Simeon and Levi are still angry at the rape of their sister and kill all the men in the city, including Hamor and Shechem, take their women, children and herds and rescue Dinah. Jacob is disturbed by his son's behaviour and fearful of retribution. Simeon and Levi explain that they killed for Dinah's honour.

---

[91] The thigh is the strongest part of one's leg and is also the place Dionysus was born from a second time by Zeus, his father.

God instructs Jacob to once again pack up and move to Beth-el. He instructs his people to put away their strange gods and representations. At Paddan-aram, God instructs Jacob to change his name to Israel, and he builds another pillar of stone and an oil offering. Rachael gives birth to a son who they call Benjamin, and dies shortly after. Jacob sets up a pillar for her grave and identifies his twelve sons Reuben, Simeon, Levi, Judah, Issachar, Zebulun, Dan, Gad, Naphtali, Asher, Joseph and Benjamin. Jacob and Esau's father Isaac dies at 180, and is buried by his sons. Esau, his wives, children and cattle leave Jacob to dwell in the mountain land of Seir and build a great nation of descendants.

Jacob (Israel) loves Joseph more than his other sons because he was born in his old age from his beloved Rachael, and is a dreamer like himself. He makes him a coat of many colours, which attracted envy and hatred from his other sons. Joseph has a dream that his sheafs stand upright and his brothers' bow down before him, which makes them hate him even more. He has another dream of the sun and moon and eleven stars bowing down to him. Jacob (Israel) rebukes him and sends him to meet his brothers (brethren) at Shechem. The brethren see Joseph coming, label him as a 'dreamer' and conspire to kill him. Reuben tried to save Joseph from the others, but they take his colourful coat and throw him into a dry pit. A caravan of Ishmaelites, on their way to Egypt appears, and Judah explains to his brethren "What profit is it if we slay our brother and conceal his blood?" They decide to sell Joseph to the Ishmaelites and so he is taken to Egypt as a slave. His brothers conceal the event and dip Joseph's coat in he-goat blood to fool Jacob into believing he was killed. Jacob mourns Joseph's supposed death and weeps.[92]

The abduction of Dinah gives Jacob the opportunity to convert other men to a spiritual attitude represented by the circumcision ritual. Circumcision is an affirmation of spiritualised masculinity over the enveloping femininity of the foreskin. It is the symbolic liberation of the head from the enveloping body. Jacob's sons Simeon and Levi, acting on their rage, kill all the men and steal their wives, children and belongings. Again, rash behaviour causes them to uproot and leave. The twelve children of Israel are established, but Jacob favours his introverted dreamy son Joseph with ethical feeling (coloured coat) over the other sons. As we have seen in the previous text, Jacob is also an introvert. Brotherly love is not strong enough to overcome jealousy and envy Jacob's other sons feel for the preferred Joseph, and they get rid of him by selling him into slavery. Herders living off the land do not understand sensitive dreamers like

---

[92] Passages 34:1 to 37:36

Joseph. In symbolic terms, the sensitive dreamer has a good relationship to the unconscious, and hence his inner god.

The text continues with Judah leaving his brothers, marrying and having children, two of which are killed by god because of their wickedness. Judah's wife dies and his widowed daughter in-law dresses like a harlot at the gate to meet Judah. He does not know it is her and promises some animals from his flock for a sexual favour. She gives birth to twins, one of which put out his hand which had a scarlet thread tied to it by the midwife who said that he was to come out first. The hand withdrew and his brother was born first and the second brother "made a breach for thyself".

An officer of the Pharaoh in Egypt bought Joseph and he prospered. His master saw that God was with him and it blessed his household. Joseph is tempted by the officer's wife but refuses and explains that it would be a sin against God. She tricks him, and accuses him of rape and the officer throws Joseph into prison, where he had the favour of the guard. The king of Egypt's butler and baker are also in prison with Joseph and both have dreams that Joseph tries to interpret. The butler dream is as follows:

> In my dream, behold, a vine was before me; and in the vine were three branches; and as it was budding, its blossoms shot forth, and the clusters thereof brought forth ripe grapes, and Pharaoh's cup was in my hand; and I took the grapes, and pressed them into Pharaoh's cup, and I gave the cup into Pharaoh's hand.[93]

Joseph interprets the butler's dream by relating three branches to three days till the Pharaoh will restore his office and he will give the cup into the Pharaoh's hand. The baker tells his dream:

> I also saw in my dream, and, behold, three baskets of white bread were on my head; and in the uppermost basket there was of all manner of baked food for Pharaoh; and the birds did eat them out of the basket upon my head. [94]

Again, Joseph interprets the dream by relating the three baskets to three days in which the Pharaoh shall hang him from a tree for the birds to pick off his flesh. These predictions happen but Joseph is left in prison. Two years later, the Pharaoh has two dreams:

> Pharaoh dreamed: and, behold, he stood by the river. And, behold, there came up out of the river seven kine, well-favoured and fat-fleshed; and they fed in the reed-grass. And, behold, seven other kine came up after them out of the river, ill favoured and lean-fleshed; and stood by the

---

[93] Passages 40:9 to 40:11
[94] Passages 40:16 to 40:17

other kine upon the brink of the river. And the ill–favoured and lean–fleshed kine did eat up the seven well–favoured and fat kine. So Pharaoh awoke. [95]

And he slept and dreamed a second time: and, behold, seven ears of corn came up upon one stalk, rank and good. And, behold, seven ears, thin and blasted with the east wind, sprung up after them. And the thin ears swallowed up the seven rank and full ears. And Pharaoh awoke, and, behold, it was a dream.[96]

The Pharaoh tries to find someone to interpret the dreams without luck, until the butler tells him about Joseph, whom he met in prison. The Pharaoh calls Joseph to interpret his dreams and he tells him that only god can interpret dreams, and he proceeds to explain them:

And Joseph said unto Pharaoh: 'The dream of Pharaoh is one; what God is about to do He hath declared unto Pharaoh. The seven good kine are seven years; and the seven good ears are seven years: the dream is one. And the seven lean and ill–favoured kine that came up after them are seven years, and also the seven empty ears blasted with the east wind; they shall be seven years of famine.

Joseph then provides a solution to the Pharaoh by suggesting the storage of food in the time of plenty to counteract the years of famine. The Pharaoh regards Joseph as discreet and wise, and appoints him second in charge of Egypt, gives him his signet ring, fine linen and a gold chain for his neck. Joseph takes control of the food supply, is given a wife and has two sons the year before the famine begins. It ravages the entire earth, and Joseph opens the stores of food and all the countries come to Egypt.

There is not much to say about the trials of Judah other than unreflective behaviour is punished by ignorance and death. Joseph, on the other hand, is righteous and ethical, and rewarded by being true to his own nature as an introverted dreamer. The dreams of the butler and baker have an association to different aspects of their work, but also their attitude to their work. For example, the butler sees growth and makes an effort to facilitate that growth by processing the fruit into wine for the Pharaoh. Wine liberates us from the everyday toil of our body into a happy place. The baker does not protect the bread, and suffers the same fate. Bread is a staple, and has an association with the body, as the dream suggests, which keeps us in the 'here and now', and unenlightened. Joseph is true to his inner vision and ethics, and refuses

---

[95] Passages 41:1 to 41:4
[96] Passages 41:5 to 41:7

to give in to the sexual advances of his master's wife and is punished for being true to his inner vision.

The dreams of the Pharaoh show an opposition between fat and content with hungry and needy. Hunger motivates activity far more than contentment and pushes people to action that would under normal circumstances, be unnecessary. It is the root of the 'Will to power'. The pharaoh realises that keeping his people well fed and content alleviates their urge to rise up and riot. Indeed, Joseph solves this problem by storing food for lean times, thus balancing the opposites of feast and famine. It is an ethical and practical attitude, not to be one-sided. The central spiritual attitude of Joseph unites the opposites and brings stability and balance to the kingdom (psyche). This idea is reinforced by the dreams of the butler and baker, which both have three branches and baskets, the first having a good outcome, and the second, bad. The dreams of two men show that each side of the unity of good and bad outcomes has three elements each. The Pharaoh's dreams indicate the same idea of undeveloped overcoming developed functions that are on the verge of becoming conscious. In other words, the Pharaoh is about to become aware with the help of Joseph, of the need to see the opposites as one. Joseph also emphasises the Pharaoh's dream as 'one'[97], which shows he was aware of the underlying unity of the opposites.

The text continues with Jacob in the land of Canaan suffering under the same famine. He sends all of his sons except Benjamin to Egypt to buy food. Jacobs's sons come to Joseph for food, and he recognises them, but they do not recognise him. Joseph accuses them of being spies and asks to see their youngest brother. They confess their guilt for selling one brother, not knowing that they were talking about him. Reuben explains that he tried to save his brother, but the others would not listen. Joseph turns away and weeps, turns back and ties up Simeon, gives corn to his other brothers for free, and sends them back to Canaan. They return to Jacob with the corn and their money and this makes him afraid. Jacob fears losing more sons in addition to Joseph, as Simeon is captive and Benjamin is required to go to Egypt. Jacob laments that losing his other son from Rachel will bring great sorrow onto him till the day he dies.

The famine in Canaan is bad, and after much struggle and lack of food, Jacob instructs his sons to take gifts, double the amount of money, and Benjamin. When Joseph sees them, he invites them to dine at noon on meat. They are afraid, and try to give the money they retained from the last transaction, and bow down to Joseph. Joseph asks about their father and sees his brother Benjamin, which causes him to go into a chamber to

---

[97] Passage 41:25

weep. They eat, drink, and are merry. Joseph once again, gives them free food and puts a silver goblet in Benjamin's sack, and they leave. Joseph instructs a steward to follow them and say: "Wherefore have ye rewarded evil for good? Is not this it in which my lord drinketh, and whereby he indeed divineth? Ye have done evil in so doing."[98] They assemble their money and the goblet, return to Joseph, tell him of their sins against their brother, and explain his relationship to god and the divine. Judah says that they are all Joseph's bondsmen (servant, slave), and they honour Joseph as the Pharaoh. Joseph asks to see his brother Benjamin again, but are reluctant out of fear but comply.

The brothers return to Joseph and he reveals himself, which scares them. He explains that they should not be angry with themselves, because God sent him before them to preserve life, and God had made him ruler over Egypt. He asks to see his father Jacob and tells his brothers that he will sustain them until the famine is over. He embraces Benjamin, they both weep, kisses his other brothers and all weep. The Pharaoh is pleased and instructs Joseph to take all his belongings and get his father and brothers and all their belongings and settle on good land in Egypt. Jacob's sons return and tell him that Joseph is alive and rules over the land of Egypt, and after some doubt, believes them and is happy.

The story of Joseph and his recognition of the opposites and rise to prominence in Egypt gives him much power. He is benevolent and forgiving for being sold into slavery by his brothers and gives them food and sustaining container (goblet). He does this because he sees the bigger picture of what life is meant to be, as he predicted this actual scenario when still with his father in Canaan. This recognition of one's life path (individuation) is indeed a recognition of god's work. Joseph's good spirit is recognised by the Pharaoh and rewarded, so that the whole family can be together in the land of Egypt.

The text continues with Jacob receiving assurance from God about moving to Goshen in Egypt with the whole family with support of Joseph and the Pharaoh. Joseph then meets his father, Jacob (Israel), and they weep. He introduces Jacob and five of his brothers to the Pharaoh, and explains that his brothers are shepherds, which the Egyptians regard as an abomination. They settle in Goshen, and the famine worsens and all the corn and money are gone. The Egyptians come to Joseph for the remaining bread in exchange for cattle. When all the cattle are sold, they sell their land to the Pharaoh for seed. Joseph instructs the people to sow the land of the Pharaoh, and that one fifth be given to him, and four-fifths for their own family. Jacob (Israel) and his family live in Goshen for

---

[98] Passage 44:5

seventeen years and thrive. Jacob reaches 147 years, is ready to die and requests Joseph bury him in the land of his fathers.

Jacob is on his deathbed and reminisces about his life in Canaan. He meets Josephs' sons Ephraim and Manasseh, kisses, hugs and blesses them and thanks God for being able to see his lost son Joseph and his grandsons. Jacob assembles his sons and describes their traits. Reuben, his first-born, has his dignity and power, yet is as unstable as water. Simeon and Levi are weapons of violence because of their murders, and curses them as divided. Judah shall be on the neck of his enemies as a lion and rule with a sceptre and tied to the vine, his eyes red with wine and teeth white with milk. Zebulun shall dwell on the shore for ships. Issachar is a large-boned ass among the sheep and a worker of the land. Dan is the judge of his people and a horned snake in the path that biteth the horses' heels. Gad a troop and shall troop upon their heel. Asher is to have fat bread and yield royal dainties. Naphtali a hind let loose with good words. Joseph the favourite and fruitful vine by a fountain, with branches running over the wall and supple hands, the Stone of Israel and the prince among his brothers. Benjamin is a wolf that raveneth. These are the twelve tribes of Israel and he dies, surrounded by his sons.

Joseph weeps upon his father's death and has him embalmed for forty days. He asks the Pharaoh to let him bury Jacob (Israel) in the land of Canaan and takes with him the servants and elders and buries his father. He returns and his brothers are afraid that he will take revenge for their evil. They send a message, telling Joseph that their father commanded him to forgive them. Upon hearing this, he weeps and his brothers fall before him as bondsmen. Joseph tells them that he is with God and will sustain them and their families. He lives to one hundred and ten and tells his brothers that he will die, and God will bring them out of this land to the land of Abraham, Isaac and Jacob. Joseph dies and is put in a coffin in Egypt.[99]

Joseph saves his family from starvation and relocates them to Egypt, where he sustains them and helps them thrive. In addition, he makes the Pharaoh more powerful by protecting his people from famine in exchange for cattle and land. This ensures that the Pharaoh receives regular income through taxation for the use of his newly acquired land. Jacob (Israel) describes his twelve sons on his deathbed as follows:

Sons of Israel	Mother	Ethics	Role	Function	Traits & Orientations
Joseph	Rachel	Excellent	Dreamer, leader,	Preferred son,	Fruitful vine by a fountain that grows

---

[99] Passages 38:1 to 50:26

			man of god	Messenger of god, divine, ruler	over a wall, prince
Benjamin	Rachel	Good	Two sides, hungry and sharing	Protected, favoured youngest son	Ravenous wolf in the morning, sharing at night, goblet
Reuben	Leah	Fair	Turbulent as the waters, dignified	First born	Strength, excellency of dignity and power, mandrakes
Simeon	Leah	Bad	Killer	Second born, cruel, cursed anger	Weapons of violence
Levi	Leah	Bad	Killer	Third born, cruel, cursed anger	Weapons of violence
Judah	Leah	Poor	Outsider, punished for lack of connection to god	Fourth born, profit, money, Adullamite, death of sons & wife, episode with harlot(?)	Lions cub that is going up, sceptre & rulers staff, eyes red with wine, milk white teeth
Issachar	Leah	Neutral	Physical worker	Fifth born	Large boned ass between sheep folds, a servant to work
Zebulun	Leah	Neutral	Balanced	Sixth born, merchant	Dwell at the sea shore of ships
Gad	Zilpah	Neutral	Fighter	Warrior	Troop upon their heel
Asher	Zilpah	Neutral	Soft	Rich & Entitled	Fat bread and royal dainty
Naphtali	Bilbah	Fair	Orator, Poet	Freedom of instinct	Hind let loose, goodly words
Dan	Bilbah	Neutral	Judge	Brings down power	Judge of his people, horned serpent to bite horses heels

From the chart above, we can see that there are opposite traits with some of the brothers. For example, the poetic nature of Naphtali contrasts the warrior nature of Gad. Similarly, the dreamy nature of Joseph contrasts the profit-driven nature of Judah. Joseph is the son that stands out in the story, because the others sold him into slavery and he developed outside of the family to a higher level of cultural achievement and power. He did this by being true to his dreamy nature and giving the Pharaoh insight into unconscious processes and predictions on future outcomes. By following these messages from his inner god, he not only saves the Egyptian people from famine, but also makes the Pharaoh richer and more powerful.

Joseph's spiritual and practical success shows that he is the most unified brother of them all. The text reinforces this when the Pharaoh tells Joseph his two dreams and recognises the unity of the opposites.

> 41:25   And Joseph said unto Pharaoh: 'The dream of Pharaoh is one;
>   what God is about to do He hath declared unto Pharaoh.

Unlike his brothers, who are to some extent disconnected from the earth due to their continual wanderings[100], Joseph's personal ethics and a relationship to dreams (inner god), leads to a reconnection to the earth (agriculture in Egypt) and unity of spiritual and worldly success. In other words, he has the central position between the opposites of love and power, earth and heaven, and so on. Joseph is the most outstanding of all the brothers, and his ability to forgive (ethics) and recognise his fate, enabled him to help and sustain his family on the land given to them by the Pharaoh.

Several generations later, a new king of Egypt enslaves the Jewish people because he feels threatened by their growing size. He tries to control them by instructing the midwives to kill the male born children, which led to the casting of Moses into the river in an ark. The Pharaoh's daughter finds Moses and makes him her son. She calls him Moses because "I drew him out of the water"[101]. The Pharaoh tries to kill Moses, but he flees to Midian. He has his first experience of God speaking to him from a burning bush and tells him that he will liberate his people from slavery and bring them to the land of milk and honey. Moses asks God's name, and is told, "I am that I am"[102]. God gives Moses several magical items including a rod that can turn into a snake, the ability to inflict and heal disease, transform water spilled on land into blood and conscripts Moses's brother, Aaron to be his spokesperson.

Moses and Aaron ask the for their people's freedom, but the Pharaoh refuses and makes them work harder. God tells Moses what to do to achieve their freedom. After much competition with the Pharaoh's magicians, with the rod and serpent, rod and water to blood, Moses and Aaron with God's help, create a plague of frogs, gnats, flies, hail, locusts and disease. The Pharaoh agrees to give them freedom but goes back on his word. This culminates in God telling Moses that all the first-born

---

[100] God's rejection of agricultural stability and urge to liberate from the beast (Abel over Cain)
[101] Exodus, passage 2:10
[102] Passage 3:14

Egyptians shall die, and to differentiate between the children of Israel and Egypt by painting the door jambs and heads with the blood of a sacrificed lamb. This leads to God's Passover of the houses of the children of Israel and their mass exodus from Egypt into the wilderness via the Red Sea. A pillar of cloud led them during the day and a pillar of fire by night.

The pharaoh sends his troops and chariots after them and Moses uses the magical rod to part the Red Sea. The children of Israel cross before it returns with a strong east wind and drowns the pursuing Egyptian troops. The children then sing to the Lord and describe him as their strength, "the Lord is a man of war, the Lord is His name"[103]. "Thy right hand, O the Lord, glorious in power, Thy right hand, O the Lord, dasheth in pieces the enemy."[104] "And with the blast of Thy nostrils the waters were piled up the floods stood upright as a heap; the deeps were congealed in the heart of the sea."[105] They now have the problem of survival, and god turned salt water to sweet by inserting a tree, extracted water from the rock, and caused bread called 'Manna' to rain down from heaven.

The children of Israel become impatient and doubted the decision to leave Egypt and having to fight Amalek, a distant relative of Esau. God calls Moses to the top of Mount Sinai and gives him commandments that shall bring order to the people. God then lays down the law beginning with "Thou shalt have no other gods before me" or "make graven images" and in the following passages, admits that he is a jealous god. He continues with "Thou shalt not take the name of the Lord thy God in vain" and "Remember the Sabbath day, and keep it holy." "Honour thy father and mother" "Thou shalt not murder", "commit adultery" or "steal", and finishes with the last four, oriented towards one's neighbour. "Thou shalt not bear false witness against thy neighbour", "covet thy neighbour's house, wife, man and maid servant nor ox, ass or anything else. He adds an additional commandment not to make Gods of silver or gold to represent him. God describes the punishment for transgressions against the commandments, which include death, and like for like punishment. He also treats sorcery, bestiality, worship of other gods and unrighteous witness harshly. God also demands the "fullness of thy harvest", "outflow of thy presses" and "first-born sons" and "take no gift". He continues with "a stranger shalt thou not oppress", "keep a feast unto Me in the year" and describes in specific detail how to worship, what bread to bake, how to sow fields, including timing and crop rotation and how he will drive out the inhabitants of the promised land.

---

[103] Passage 15:3
[104] Passage 15:6
[105] Passage 15:8

Moses was on the mountain for forty days and nights and instructed by God to make offerings of gold, silver, brass; blue, purple and scarlet fine linen; goats hair, ram's skin dyed red, sealskins, acacia wood, oil for the light, spices for the anointing oil and sweet incense, onyx stones and above all, a sanctuary for God to dwell. He instructs Moses in a very detailed specification for an ark and candlestick, and how to sanctify Aaron as a priest, make offerings, and numerous other detailed methods of worship. God gives Moses two stone tablets "written with the finger of god" with the preceding commandments written on them. While Moses was on the mountain, Aaron gathers golden rings from the people, fashions them into a golden calf, and proclaims it as their God.

The God of Moses struggles with his conscience after seeing his people "stiff-necked", and feels intense anger towards them. He later repents and does not give in to his anger. Moses comes down from the mountain, sees the golden calf, boils with anger and throws the tablets to the ground. He burns the calf in the fire, grinds it to powder, mixes it with water and makes the children of Israel drink the concoction. Moses stands at the gate of the camp and asks everyone to pick a side. The sons of Levi are instructed to kill all the men. The Lord said to Moses "Whosoever hath sinned against Me, him will I blot out of My book". Moses moves his tent away from the camp and proclaims it "the tent of meeting". God instructs Moses to make two new tablets for his commandments and passes before Moses proclaiming "The the Lord, the Lord, God, merciful and gracious, long-suffering, and abundant in goodness and truth; keeping mercy unto the thousandth generation, forgiving iniquity and transgression and sin;...."[106]

The trouble for the children of Israel start with a new and cruel Egyptian Pharaoh who does not honour his word. It is the conflict between an inner authority (God) and the outer authority (Pharaoh) and the attempt to reduce the children of Israel's numbers by killing newborn sons. Moses is cast into the river in an ark and the Pharaoh's daughter finds him, adopts and raises him to become a surrogate grandchild to the Pharaoh, who fears his power. Moses grows and his inner god, through an eternal (is not consumed) burning bush urges him and his tribe to leave Egypt for the Promised Land. The Pharaoh refuses to let the children of Israel go free and Moses and his God attempt to gain freedom through trickery and magic to show the king that they have more power.

As we know, turning a rod into a snake, water into blood and the creation of spontaneous plagues, is not possible in the physical world. These tricks can however, be interpreted symbolically as if they were dream

---

[106] Passages 34:6/7

motifs. The snake, as written in Genesis has knowledge of good and evil, gives wisdom, opens one's eyes and helps one become like god. It has a strong connection to the inner feminine (Eve), and leads us to unity. Turning a rod into a snake is a display of these traits. The water into blood is a demonstration of the life-giving properties of water on land. In other words, without water there is no life, as there is no life without a connection to what water represents, that is, the life-giving force of the unconscious, which is our blood and heart.[107] Blood also has a relationship to family, and in this instance is the basis of Moses' power.

Moses tries to wear down the resolve of the Pharaoh by increasing the methods of persuasion through plagues. If we interpret this scenario as an individual (Moses), then it begins to make perfect sense. Joseph was the harmonious union between the outer authority, represented by the Pharaoh and the inner authority (God), represented by his ability to relate his and other's dreams to the physical world. Later, the power of the outer authority increases and oppresses the inner, and Moses is the person to resolve this scenario of one-sidedness. The inner authority takes the lead and tries to overcome the outer authority. This is typical in an individual's life, as we have a natural tendency to oscillate between outer activity and work, and inner contemplation, fantasy and creativity. In this case, the children of Israel spent several generations on the land with stability and growth, until the unconscious demanded balance and a return to their inner god.

This erosion of the outer authority continues and culminates in the Passover sacrifice of the connection to the outer authority symbolised by the lamb, and complete trust in the inner authority. In other words, to do inner work and be introverted, one has to sacrifice one's relationship to outer things for a time. This is the demand our unity makes upon us as individuals. The story continues with the flight out of Egypt pursued by the Pharaoh's army, with the promise of a return to an ideal land of freedom and nourishment. The God of Moses then parts the sea to allow his children to pass and when safe, destroys the pursuing army. We can interpret this as a pathway to the unconscious and inner God (sea), and a final closure behind them of their relationship to the outer authority. Moses and his followers are now dealing with the inner authority alone in an unknown environment.

They now need life (water), and spiritual nourishment (manna), provided by God. The children of Israel continue to fight for consciousness in their interaction with the relatives of the down-to-earth Esau. This is typical with an inner journey, as it is like exploring a dark unknown cave, or in

---

[107] Blood is also referred to as "life" in Deuteronomy 12:23

this instance a lifeless desert. The yearning for return to the world and a normal life is always strong, but Moses stays the course. He is then called up the mountain alone, which is high, isolated and closer to one's inner authority. God gives him the ethics to keep his people safe, ordered, and controlled in a homogenous group. In other words, these laws give guidelines to the group's behaviour and set them in stone. This is understandable, as the people Moses's have a history of trickery, murder, theft and so on. It is not only an evolution of the human being, but also an evolution of their inner god. It is the journey from the purely animal and instinctive orientation to understanding, agreeableness and wisdom. It can be regarded as the journey from a purely power standpoint to one that incorporates love and understanding. As we can see in the text, the evolution of consciousness has not quite achieved the complete differentiation of good and evil, as Moses's inner God is still influenced by conflict, jealousy and murder. The god of Moses and stone-carved ethics is a step towards the good god of Jesus.

The absence of Moses on the mount causes the children of Israel, at the instigation of Aaron, to worship a physical deity that has to do with the practical matters of life, food and wealth. This shows that the only person in touch with their God is Moses. Even his brother still does not perceive the God that Moses does. Moses descends from the mount and does one of things that his God commanded him not to do, that is kill. Symbolically, a new attitude does not stick immediately, and takes some effort and time to overcome the old attitude. Moses is consumed with rage and throws the first tablets to the ground. He and his people have sacrificed their connection to the outer authority and committed to their inner authority through Moses, yet without continual work, they slip back into practical concerns and the valuable aspects of the beast. Moses suffers the same fate and slips back into his instinctive emotion of rage and jealousy that humans share with other mammals. After squashing dissent using the children of Levi, the ethics of Moses is remade and brought down to the people.

It is curious to note the misalignment of the psyche of Moses as the punishment for transgression of the new laws actually breaks one of the laws. When Moses is on the mount his God is angry, but overcomes it. When Moses comes down, he cannot overcome his anger, and acts it out on his people. This is the difference between letting out an emotion on those around us and having them affected by it with all the consequences therein, or walking away and looking inside to find the god-given reason why we felt that emotion and why our personal unity (mandala) is disrupted. In this instance, jealousy is an instinctive emotion not integrated into the unity. This is why the first few commandments try to alleviate feelings of jealousy. They say that God is the one and only, not to depict him and not to take his name in vain. God prefers to be mysterious, nameless and without image. This is understandable, as to concretise an inner character with a name or image takes away some of its power and the idea that he belongs inside, not outside. Even the later Christian god is a mysterious father figure, and we only know how he behaves through his son and the Holy Spirit.

The final laws are elaborate and far-reaching, and the associated punishment for transgression make them stifling and over-reaching. The detail of appropriate behaviour extends to what they may eat, drink, and do on their day off. I am sure that there are practical and hygienic reasons behind some of the laws, but others seem odd and rather personal in choice. For example, fish are accepted as food, yet arthropods regarded as unclean and put in the same category as menstruating women. It could be as simple as a creature's connection to earth is regarded negatively. For example, fish swim above the sea floor in pure water and arthropods feed and live on the ocean floor. Similarly, pigs wallow in the mud and eat anything, whereas other animals walk on the land freely and eat grass. The list of clean and unclean animals is extensive.

The third book, Leviticus, discusses the protocols of contractual arrangements, with an emphasis on honest and fair transactions. It also puts forward more laws about eating the fat of a beast and drinking blood. The punishments are not as harsh as the main laws, but still call for expulsion from the community. Aaron, the brother of Moses, and the creator of the golden calf, seems to have escaped the previous murderous rampage, and is sanctified as a priest. There are elaborate sacrifice rituals detailed, with blood offerings and body parts of a ram. Other rituals include: unleavened bread, ram's fat, anointing oil and restrictions on drinking alcohol in the tent of meeting. The text continues with detailed consumption practices including: cattle, sea creatures, birds, insects, rodents and reptiles. In addition, women are unclean after giving birth, timing on circumcision and the treatment and restrictions of disease. There are methods of atonement for sin and transgression of the laws, with restrictions on nakedness, homosexuality, bestiality, incest, divination, soothsaying, seeking ghosts, personal grooming, body modifications, prostitution, be kind to strangers, measure righteousness, real estate practices, fighting enemies, not hate one's brother, prefer virginity, love thy neighbour as thyself, valuation of men and women, and practices of god's revenge for transgression of the laws.

The text continues with Numbers and naming the extended family and their forbears, with particular attention to Aaron and the tribe of Levi appointed as priests to the tabernacle and carers of the revealed visions of Moses. It describes the first born of everything to be given to the Levites including monetary payment for redemption of sins committed. The term 'spirit of jealousy' is used concerning the possible unfaithfulness of a wife, and is resolved by bringing the wife and 'meal offering of jealousy' to the priest, whereby he performs a ritual to determine her guilt by giving her the 'water of bitterness'. She becomes a cursed woman if found guilty.

The children of Israel continue to wander in the desert at the command of Moses and his God. The people again question their lot and how they left their life in Egypt where they were well fed. This made their God very angry, and he instructs Moses to create a hierarchy of men to keep the people in check and alleviate the full burden from Moses. God, with the wind, provides quails for the people to alleviate their hunger. The people's lack of control and lust for flesh angers God and he gives them a plague as punishment. God then explains how he communicates to potential prophets such as Aaron and Miriam by telling them:

> 12:6 And He said: 'Hear now My words: if there be a prophet among you, I the Lord do make Myself known unto him in a vision, I do speak with him in a dream.
> 12:7 My servant Moses is not so; he is trusted in all My house;
> 12:8 with him do I speak mouth to mouth, even manifestly, and not in dark speeches; and the similitude of the Lord doth he behold; wherefore then were ye not afraid to speak against My servant, against Moses?'

God instructs them to respect Moses and not to speak against him, and gives Miriam leprosy. Moses objects to this harsh punishment and God tells him to put her out of the camp for seven days. He also tells Moses to send out spies to view Canaan from a mountaintop and gauge the inhabitants' strength. They return to tell Moses that the land does indeed flow with milk and honey. The people are once again afraid, and plot to overthrow Moses with a new "captain" and return to Egypt. God asks Moses how long the people will despise him and not believe in him, and threatens to destroy them. Moses stops God from killing his people by pointing out the success of bringing them to the Promised Land over the failure of not fulfilling his promise. He lets God know that loving-kindness is great, as well as the power to kill.

God does not kill his people, but curses them to another forty years wandering in the wilderness. Some of the people want to see the land promised to them for themselves, and do so without God's permission and are killed by the Amalekites and Canaanites. The dissatisfaction at their punishment continues to foment disloyalty and the people are swallowed by the earth. Another plague ravages them and Moses instructs the twelve tribes to give him a rod each to lie in the tent of testimony. The Levite rod was the only one to bud, and Moses gives the others back to the tribes. This event reinforces the role of the Levites to administer the tent of testimony. The text describes the necessary and specific offerings to the Levites for their administering role, including "redemption money", and first-born as offerings as well as the treatment of the dead and cleansing procedures.

The people move again and have no water, whereby Moses, instructed by God, takes a rod and brings forth water from a rock. They request safe passage through other people's land but are rejected by the respective kings. Aaron did not escape his previous transgression and is punished with death on mount Hor. The people still lament their plight and God sends fiery serpents to bite and kill them. Moses puts a brass effigy of a fiery serpent on a pole, and those bitten shall live if they look upon the pole. The wandering continues with other battles and associated spoils of war, including land. They even have success encouraging another prophet, Balaam, to recognise the God of Moses. They battle more locals and killing those transgressing the new laws.

God and Moses categorise their people, select the young men for war, and divide the conquered land between the tribes as an inheritance according to numbers of people. The Levites, as carers of the tabernacle, do not get an inheritance, but a percentage of the fruits of the other tribes. There is more killing, particularly the conquered men, boys and non-virginal women. The children of Israel continue to wander in the wilderness until the generation passed and the next in place. The land conquered is divided amongst the tribes, with the best on the West side of the Jordan River to come. God commands the children of Israel to give the land surrounding the conquered six cities to the Levites. He then differentiates between enemies and friendly strangers that settle amongst the tribes and gives them the same rights as their own people.

The book Numbers fine tunes how God is to be worshipped making it almost impossible to honour. It recognises the emotion of jealousy and how to address its effect. This emotion motivates much of God's laws and shows how insecure he is with his people. He demands worship and harshly punishes dissent. The people are starving and God provides them with quail to eat, and even their unrestrained eating habits annoy him. He threatens to kill his people again after more dissent, but is prevented by Moses with a good counter argument. In this instance, Moses has the upper hand and is more reasonable than his inner God. The inner force is still not convinced and has to reinforce his power by punishing his people to wander a further forty years in the wilderness.

The idea of God as an inner character is reinforced by the his own words, which tell us that he makes himself known to other prophets in visions and dreams. Moses, on the other hand, hears the voice of God directly, and they speak "mouth to mouth"[108]. In other words, it is like an inner voice that instructs Moses to carry out orders, which reinforces the idea that most leaders are in fact themselves led. Moses uses a rod to get water out of a rock, which is a curious trick. Symbolically, the rock is solid and unmoving, like the God of Moses, and water fluid, accommodating and an essential element of life. This may be a reflection of the dialogue between God and Moses, God being the solid and unmoving rock and Moses fluid and flowing water who shows some feeling for his people.

The people dissent again and God sends fiery serpents to kill them. Moses prays for the people and presumably has another inner dialogue with God, who instructs him to create a brass image of a fiery serpent on a pole, thus breaking two of his own commandments: killing and making graven images. Looking at the image on the pole could heal those bitten, which objectifies the symbol of one's own fiery passions and instinct. Naturally, they cannot liberate themselves from their need for food, but they can overcome the need for good food that they used to eat, compared to the "light bread" they now have to eat. It is taming of the desire for something they knew, over something they now have.

God and Moses continue to turn their people into citizens by number and category and reinforce the law with punishment and curse. The Levites are the elevated ones who do not get what the other tribes do in land ownership, and have to rely on offerings from the other tribes. God continues to break his own commandments with his people and those conquered. He does, however loosen his elitist attitude towards his people by giving friendly strangers the same rights.

The text continues in Deuteronomy and the end of the forty years in the mountain wilderness and God and Moses instruct his people to turn to the hill country of the Amorites. He sends twelve men, one from each tribe to spy on the land and bring back some of its fruits. God is enraged by the continuing dissent amongst the tribes and threatens to withhold the Promised Land. He selects some to inherit the land and others to go back into the wilderness. They travel to the Red Sea, then northward towards the land of the descendants of Esau and the land given to the descendants of Lot. Passing these lands, the tribes fight more battles and destroy more cities and their inhabitants.

---

[108] Numbers 12.8

God gives the people more commandments, which forbid creating images of male and female, beasts, winged fowl, lizards, snakes and fish. He commands that the people lift their eyes to heaven and see the sun, moon, stars and heavens for them to worship. This is where Moses realises that God will not allow him to go over the Jordan River to the land promised to the children of Israel and must die where he is. His god is angry with him for his people's behaviour: "[109] For the Lord thy God is a devouring fire, a jealous God." God then goes through the list of commandments again and makes a declaration about his function: "HEAR, O ISRAEL: THE the Lord OUR GOD, THE the Lord IS ONE."[110]

God continues detailing his commandments to utterly destroy, make no covenants and show no mercy towards the people to be conquered. He instructs that graven images of other gods be destroyed with fire and marriage to the conquered people forbidden. He also declares that his people are holy and that he chose them as his own treasure. God says "....man doth not live by bread alone, but by everything that proceedeth out of the mouth of the Lord doth man live."[111]

He describes the good times ahead in the land promised to the children of Israel without scarcity and abundance in life. He worries however, that his people will forget him during good times and turn to other Gods. After lamenting about the loyalty of his people, God commands to "....circumsize therefore the foreskin or your heart, and be no more stiff-necked"[112] and "Love ye therefore the stranger; for ye were strangers in the land of Egypt."[113] God sets the borders of their promised land from the wilderness to Lebanon, and the Euphrates River to the Mediterranean Sea. He proceeds to give a blessing and a curse to his people. If the people abide by the commandments, they are blessed, and if they do not abide they are cursed. He tells them not to eat blood and to pour it on the ground for blood is life.

God also warns against other prophets or dreamer of dreams, which may lead to the worship of other gods. He recalls his commandments again, and includes selling food for money in times of abundance and buying with it, anything they desire. He reminds his people not forget the Levites, as they have no portion of inheritance. He tells them to lend money to nations, but not borrow or take gifts so they do not rule over them. He also sets the punishment for rebellious youth to be stoned to death and men and women should not to wear each other's clothes. God prohibits

---

[109] Passage 4:24
[110] Passage 6:4
[111] Passage 8:3
[112] Passage 10:16
[113] Passage 10:19

ploughing with an ox and ass together and wearing wool and linen together and prohibits men with crushed or maimed genitals and bastards from entering the assembly of the Lord.

He continues with his commandments to only lend money at interest to foreigners and not their own people. Every man is to take responsibility for their own sin and suffer their own punishment. Moses separates his people into two groups of six tribes. The descendants of Simeon, Levi, Judah, Issachar, Joseph and Benjamin shall stand on the Gerizim to bless the people west after crossing the Jordan River. The descendants of Reuben, Gad, Asher, Zebulun, Dan and Naphtali are to stand on mount Ebal for the curse. The Levites speak of the curses for transgressing the laws and list the items to be blessed and that God will make them the head and not the tail, and shall be above and not beneath if his laws are obeyed.

> 30:15   See, I have set before thee this day life and good, and death and evil,

Moses reaches 120 years and tells his people that he will not join them in the Promised Land and transfers his authority to Joshua. In the tent of meeting, Moses feels that his people will become corrupt, crooked and perverse and that God is the rock, his work perfect, just, faithful, right and without iniquity. Moses approaches death and laments at his own humanity and fallibility and God tells him that he trespassed against him at the waters of Meribath-kadesh in the wilderness of Zin, and that he will only be allowed to see the Promised Land from afar. Moses then blesses the descendants of the twelve sons of Israel and dies in the land of Moab.

> 34:10   And there hath not arisen a prophet since in Israel like unto Moses, whom the Lord knew face to face;
> 34:11   in all the signs and the wonders, which the Lord sent him to do in the land of Egypt, to Pharaoh, and to all his servants, and to all his land;
> 34:12   and in all the mighty hand, and in all the great terror, which Moses wrought in the sight of all Israel.

The forty-year punishment ends, and the children of Israel now move towards the land promised to them. God's jealousy and insecurity forbids the creation of images of humans and animals, thus forbidding that art form as the worship of other gods. God blames Moses for his people's dissent, withholds the Promised Land from him, and proclaims his unity. At this stage of humanity's evolution, the God of Moses represented an undifferentiated unity of everyday life and unconscious forces. God, as an inner voice of Moses is at odds with his people and continually punishes them for not obeying his restrictive laws. He requires validation and unthinking obedient children, and it is only with the rare objection from Moses that god's punishment is modified.

The dubious love God feels for his people and the utter ruthlessness for those conquered, indicates God is more beast than human. This is an example of an early stage in humanity's evolution and long during attempts to liberate from those jealous and killer instincts. His actions do not agree with his words. In some instances, he regards his people as his treasure, but has no qualms killing them if they disobey and seems deathly afraid of being ignored or superseded by other gods. The text itself reinforces the idea that an inner character possesses Moses. He rarely argues with his inner voice and carries out his orders without question, which is typical of the relationship between a dominant father and obedient son.

The function missing is feeling which a female character usually represents. She can temper possession by a father and introduce other inner characters and values. Indeed, Moses does perceive relationships and family members in detail, but does not love them enough to protect them from his dominant inner character. The strictness and harshness of his God is to some extent understandable, as the circumstances of the environment warrant a strict order and cohesion. It is an enforced collective endeavour, rather than debated and considered problem solving by individuals and disobedience of the law is harshly punished. Besides punishment, the god of Moses entices his people to worship him with the promise of what can be viewed as another paradise.

God commands circumcision for boys as a liberation of their spirit from the enveloping female unconscious. He also commands his people not to be stiff-necked and give in to his own dogmatism and stubbornness. An interesting development then occurs of what seems like a further differentiation of the opposites. God and Moses divide his people into two groups of six tribes and recognises that individuals have to take responsibility for their own actions. He explains that through him, his people will become the head and not the tail, which reinforces the idea of evolution from beast to a god of power.

Before Moses dies, he tells his people that god is the rock, his work perfect, just, faithful, right and without iniquity, and is immediately punished by God for something he did earlier. This contradiction between opposites is indeed a human trait and can only be resolved with a third function. The single God, in contrast to the multiple Gods of ancient Greece and Rome, serves as a container for the contradictions of human nature, but as we have seen in the text, can only be maintained through strict commandments and force. The mediating function of love and feeling of an inner female character is missing and the unity constantly challenged. It is a pure struggle to liberate the spirit (circumcision) from the influence of instinct with strict guidelines and limits on behaviour. Unfortunately, it is dual-natured and misaligned, in that the words of God and his behaviour do not match, and his nature not united in one cohesive attitude. The inner character possessing Moses is still contaminated by nature, as exemplified by his jealousy, vindictiveness, cruelty and intolerance. This must however, be viewed as a journey of evolution from the attachment to the land, freed wandering spirit, attempted liberation from the beast to a powerful god that protects, if his laws obeyed.

If we look at the whole story from Genesis to Deuteronomy symbolically, it becomes clear that it is a journey from paradise in the beginning, with great struggle and hardship to a potential paradise in the end. It is like a life story of a single individual. They are expelled from the paradise of childhood into an unknown and sometimes hostile world where they have to take care of themselves, fight battles with enemies, struggle for prestige and power, have a family, suffer floods (overwhelming material from the unconscious) and famines (lack of guidance from the unconscious) to eventually die and return to paradise (heaven). In the story the good times occur through a dreamy benevolent and good brother and external authority (Pharaoh 1). The bad times with oppression by an evil authority (Pharaoh 2) and escape into the wilderness (unconscious) for a very long time. They struggle with ultimate hardship and are given guidance through laws and modes of behaviour, only to find that they cannot fully return to the paradise of childhood and must die, which in the end, may be the same thing.

The Torah did not complete the evolution from beast to heavenly spirit with moral guidelines and awareness of good and evil. It did set the groundwork for humanity's evolution with further differentiation of the opposites in the story of Jesus. It is unfortunate that the Jewish people did not accept this natural continuation of their spirit, and the further differentiation of good from evil and the introduction of a purely good female character. The situation the Jewish people found themselves in is of the harshest kind surviving on unusual foods, always looking for water, being threatened with death for not worshipping God correctly and being enticed with a promise of paradise. It is the same if we interpret the story as the trials and tribulations of the author and his struggle with family, being oppressed by an external authority and his descent into the underworld (wilderness) and struggle with an inner authority that wants to keep him there and not let him come back to a normal life.

There is a recurring theme in the Torah that sets one brother against the other and encourages the evolution from earth to spirit. This mono-directional viewpoint shows a distinct awareness of mind (spirit) over matter, but not the value of matter. In other words, taking this ascent to its logical conclusion, with complete liberation from anything physical, including the body, may bode well for our understanding and insight, but does little for our continuation of the species. The story of Exodus is a liberation from a cruel Pharaoh, replaced by an equally cruel inner God of Moses. There is no opportunity for the children of Israel to find their own inner God as individuals. God immediately quashes this idea, and the projection of unity enforced by threats and punishment.

The shining beacon in the whole story is the life of Joseph, who had an unwavering ethical attitude, a strong relationship to the unconscious, and hence his inner God, was aware of God's plan for his life (individuation) and attained earthly power and prestige from an external authority (Pharaoh). Even the hairy and down-to-earth Esau had a good heart compared to other family members. The difficulty in this study of the Torah is its indistinct mixture of reality and imagination, and I am aware that at times I interpret the text literally and other times, symbolically. Aside from the supernatural events, we do not know what really happened to the Jewish people in physical reality, and what was the vision of man writing down the text from his imagination. The same is true for the following story and life of Jesus.

e. Early Christianity

As mentioned above, the Christian story is the continuation of the evolution of consciousness, and overcoming of the beast and associated instinct. It strengthened consciousness to a point where worldly concerns became almost irrelevant at a time when Palestine was under Roman occupation. The overcoming, or denial of the natural instincts of sex and power, as preached by Jesus, had major implications on his personality and those around him. It was literally the overcoming of the natural man symbolised by his sacrifice and the separation of the natural man from the god-man and is the basis for the Christian myth. Satan became the projection of the natural man in Jesus and was depicted as an animal with horns, hooves, and associated with the fire of passion and lust. On the other hand, depictions of Jesus are angelic, clean, beautiful and little trace of the animal. This differentiation of the opposites was pivotal in the evolution of consciousness.

In the natural world, strength and power are integral for survival[114]. Love on the other hand, is also part of our main functions, as it continues the species and nurtures the young. This is true for all mammals as well as some cold-blooded species such as reptiles.[115] As long as we have a mammalian body, we will have the same instincts and emotions as other mammals. Denial and repression of this fact pushes that aspect of us into exile and into the unconscious, from where it is easily projected onto our neighbours and therefore beyond our influence[116].

The consequence of identifying with all that is good encourages this projection. 'Thou hypocrite, first cast out the beam out of thine own eye; and then shalt thou see clearly to cast out the mote out of thy brother's eye.'[117] In other words, what we see in our brother's eye is in your own, and a projection of something negative. Beyond that, we can only assume that 'cast out' means to overcome the idea and give it to Satan. At this stage in human development, the idea of striving for the upper spirit was an essential differentiation and liberation from the instinctive and natural man, but also the occupation by the Roman Empire.

The main theme of the Christian message is the sacrifice. In practical terms, the sacrifice is the overcoming and separation of the higher faculties of reason, ethics and understanding from the physical nature of our body and its associated instincts and emotions. It is a form of liberation from the body, but also from matter in general. Overcoming one's sexual and power urges may be beneficial to the individual as a spiritual being, but detrimental to the body and the species.

The effect of such an ascetic attitude is beneficial, in that it consolidates awareness of our physical nature, reduces conflict temporarily and gives us some control over it. Although this differentiation is required to understand ourselves, it cannot sustain our overall health as the body and our relationship to matter and the world is a necessary part of our functioning. Life does not continue if we deny our hunger and our need to propagate. On the one hand, the sacrifice of our natural instincts is beneficial for the strengthening of consciousness, particularly the differentiation of soul into its positive and negative aspects (Virgin Mary and Mary Magdala). This is why the life of Jesus was a short potential in the extreme and lacked the union and wisdom of the opposites.

---

[114] DARWIN, Charles, 'On the Origin of Species' London, John Murray, Albemarle Street 1859
[115] The mother crocodile will gently take her young in her mouth to the next watering hole.
[116] This is an important point, because we cannot tame a beast that we are not aware of in ourselves.
[117] KING JAMES BIBLE, Mathew 7.5

The differentiation of spirit from instinct, separation of Jesus from the herd, the projection of the natural man onto Satan, and identification with the heavenly father were major turning points in our evolution. As a result, humanity was elevated from a lower to a higher position on the evolutionary ladder. Through his sacrifice, he was elevated from fallible mortal, to an idea of the perfect god man, and his resurrection the reinforcement of his godlike status.

The differentiation of God as a benevolent and loving father on one side, and Satan as evil and animalistic on the other, shows that the unity between the opposites still exist and casts a shadow on God's own good and perfect nature. Can a perfect god create imperfection?[118] The relationship between God and Satan[119] is one of mutual need. Reality does not allow for a high without a low. Love loses its meaning if its opposite is denied. This is why all mammalian characteristics of humanity were constellated in Satan. We may strive for godlike awareness, and indeed, that is our noblest endeavour, but it has its limits and being aware of ourselves requires also being aware of our true nature. If we push away our own evil, there is a danger of identifying with the idea of good and projecting evil onto our neighbours. This is the cause of all the conflict in the world. Consciousness expands in both directions. Disrespect for our body and its natural needs, hampers adaptation and has no stability or roots growing in the soil and soon falls over as the story of Jesus shows.

The Christian myth was a natural evolution and consolidation of this level of awareness, and the previous laws posited by Moses incorporated into the new teachings of Jesus. The old and new Testaments consolidated into one text the continuation and evolution of the journey from beast to God. The biggest difference on this journey is between the Gods of Moses and Jesus. The God of Moses was prone to anger, jealousy, insecurity, unfairness and vindictiveness. The God of Jesus had shed practically all-human traits and become sterilised beyond humanity as an unattainable ideal. I say 'practically' because there is a lingering doubt concerning the purity of the God of Jesus. This is exemplified by the lord's pray and plea that he "lead us not into temptation" which shows that God still has a hint of darkness, just as Satan has a hint of light and often referred to as Lucifer, the light bringer.

We cannot underestimate the psychological impact of the Christian myth. It was a change in the idea of God that had enormous benefits for

---

[118] The Gnostics tried to overcome this idea with the introduction of Sophia as intermediary between creation and god.
[119] I am talking about the conceptual relationship, not the scriptural, as written in the Bible.

humanity. The Jewish God was in the same way a true monotheistic expression of a deity but his attitude to his people was not always as a loving father. The transformation of this idea to an 'all good' God not only made it clearer for people to differentiate between good and evil and in turn, become aware of the feeling for right and wrong. Jesus differentiated the Old Testament God into a lighter God with a correspondingly dark adversary in the form of Satan. In this instance, some of the people of Judea were differentiating and becoming aware of the opposites in themselves and this crystallised in the life of Jesus.

It is difficult to make any objective comments on his life, as the texts do not differentiate between the actual man and the myth of the man. To the rational observer, we cannot make any claims of truth about the events that make him stand out among other prophets. Healing the sick, raising the dead, walking on water, etc., all become supernatural ideas that we know are not possible in our known physical reality. We can only view these events as mythological motifs. If we regard these supernatural events from a symbolic viewpoint, much the same as dreams, the life of Jesus becomes a symbolic expression of divine inspiration.

Walking on water for example, is a beautiful image of awareness and above the unknown and unpredictable depths of the unconscious (water). I have no doubt that Jesus had healing powers, particularly when illness was caused by a destructive or negative attitude to life. The healing effect of becoming aware of a problematic attitude is self-evident[120]. If Jesus had met Job, he would have told him to give up his striving for wealth, turn inward and find the other side in himself, and return to a balanced attitude to life. Awareness of the opposites is more than leading a righteous life, as a one-sided attitude is not sustainable in the long term. Eventually, the neglected opposite demands attention and the forces us towards unity and the other side to restore the equilibrium.

We can learn more about the symbolic qualities of Jesus by the writings not included in the bible by the church fathers. For example, the incomplete Gospel of Judas[121] reveals a Jesus not described by the other Gospels. Jesus had a sense of humour and was often found as a child amongst his people. The text also explains that Jesus regarded God as a character within himself. He also regarded his disciples having their own idea of God. This is a decisive factor in the story of Jesus in that God the father, in this text is a psychic factor, rather than a physical fact.

---

[120] The healing of contemporary psychotherapy.
[121] GOSPEL OF JUDAS, Edited by Rodolphe Kasser, Marvin Meyer, and Gregor Wurst Published in book form complete with commentary by The National Geographic Society.

Often he did not appear to his disciples as himself, but he was found among them as a child. [122]

The disciples said to [him], "Master, why are you laughing at [our] prayer of thanksgiving? We have done what is right."
He answered and said to them, "I am not laughing at you. <You> are not doing this because of your own will but because it is through this that your god [will be] praised."
They said, "Master, you are [...] the son of our god."
Jesus said to them, "How do you know me? Truly [I] say to you, no generation of the people that are among you will know me."

THE DISCIPLES BECOME ANGRY
When his disciples heard this, they started getting angry and infuriated and began blaspheming against him in their hearts.
When Jesus observed their lack of [understanding, he said] to them, "Why has this agitation led you to anger? Your god who is within you and [...] [35] have provoked you to anger [within] your souls. [Let] any one of you who is [strong enough] among human beings bring out the perfect human and stand before my face." [123]

Judas seems to have had a closer relationship to Jesus as the following text indicates, and had more faith in Judas reaching the Kingdom of heaven (consciousness) than the other disciples.

"Step away from the others and I shall tell you the mysteries of the kingdom. It is possible for you to reach it, but you will grieve a great deal. [36] For someone else will replace you, in order that the twelve [disciples] may again come to completion with their god."

Jesus said to them, "Stop struggling with me. Each of you has his own star, and every[body—about 17 lines missing—] [43] in [...] who has come [... spring] for the tree [...] of this aeon [...] for a time [...] but he has come to water God's paradise, and the [generation] that will last, because [he] will not defile the [walk of life of] that generation, but [...] for all eternity."[124]

In addition, Jesus considered the God of the disciples as 'their' God rather than 'the' God. This is a telling statement and shows an awareness that each person or group have 'their' own God and that he considered 'their' God different to his God.

---

[122] Ibid
[123] Ibid
[124] Ibid

Judas [said] to him, "I know who you are and where you have come from. You are from the immortal realm of Barbelo. And I am not worthy to utter the name of the one who has sent you." [125]

Barbelo is a Gnostic term, which refers to the first emanation of God, and is often depicted as a supreme female principle and mother of all creation. The character is also referred to as 'Mother-Father', first human being, the Triple Androgynous Name or Eternal Aeon. Judas's intuition about Jesus shows that he regarded him from that eternal realm, where male and female are one. The correlation between what we know now about the psyche is unmistakeable. It also alludes to an Eastern Religious system, where male and female principles joined in harmony. Conscious/unconscious united in our contemporary psychological language. The difference between Judas and the other gospels is remarkable, and brings the whole story of Jesus closer to our understanding.

The text shows that Jesus regarded God as an inner character, rather than an outer fact, and each disciple "has his own star", or own inner God. The Gospel of Judas also shows Jesus as a man, more than the Church fathers would have liked. This seems to be intentional as the removal of all aspects of Jesus's humanity by the other disciples reinforces his God-like stature and myth. This is presumably, why this Gospel and that of Thomas were not included in the bible. The text gives a clear indication that Jesus's idea of God is an inner character; that is, in one's dreams, fantasies, ideas etc., and found through knowing oneself.

> "If your leaders say to you, 'Look, the (Father's) imperial rule is in the sky,' then the birds of the sky will precede you. If they say to you, 'It is in the sea,' then the fish will precede you. Rather, the (Father's) imperial rule is inside you and outside you. When you know yourselves, then you will be known, and you will understand that you are children of the living Father. But if you do not know yourselves, then you live in poverty, and you are the poverty."[126]

The Gospel of Thomas also describes the mission of Jesus on earth was not one of complete benevolence, love and community. It points to the idea that salvation and union with God required isolation and solitude, as exemplified by his desert quest.

---

[125] Ibid

[126] GOSPEL OF THOMAS, from the Scholars Version translation published in The Complete Gospels, Elaine Pagels, Harry Camp Memorial Lecturer, January 26-30, 2004 Stanford Humanities Center

Jesus said, "Perhaps people think that I have come to cast peace upon the world. They do not know that I have come to cast conflicts upon the earth: fire, sword, war. For there will be five in a house: there'll be three against two and two against three, father against son and son against father, and they will stand alone." [127]

This is an important statement, as it shows that Jesus regarded union with one's inner God more important than family and community and shows the necessity for an individual and independent attitude. This, as we shall see later, is an integral part of the alchemical method.

"If you do not fast from the world, you will not find the (Father's) domain. If you do not observe the sabbath day as a sabbath day, you will not see the Father."[128]

The above shows the importance of the introverted attitude, in that working in the world solves the practical aspects of life, food, shelter, family etc., and honouring the Sabbath is giving attention to the inner realm where the inner father dwells.

Jesus said, "Whoever does not hate father and mother cannot be my disciple, and whoever does not hate brothers and sisters, and carry the cross as I do, will not be worthy of me."[129]

In this, he draws a distinction between the inner father and physical parents. Again, he preaches the separation from one's family as a necessity for the union with the cross as a symbol of unity.

Jesus said, "If you bring forth what is within you, what you have will save you. If you do not have that within you, what you do not have within you [will] kill you." [130]

Jesus emphasises the bringing forth of inner contents into consciousness.

Jesus said to her, "I am the one who comes from what is whole. I was granted from the things of my Father."

For this reason I say, if one is (whole), one will be filled with light, but if one is divided, one will be filled with darkness." [131]

---

[127] Ibid
[128] Ibid
[129] Ibid
[130] Ibid
[131] Ibid

In the preceding passages, Thomas alludes to the personal belief in the unity of Jesus's teachings and the achievement of this unity through separation from community and family. This emphasises the importance of solitude and being alone with one's inner thoughts and fantasies. Awareness of our functioning and perception of inner characters becomes possible through introspection.

In the recently found fragments pertaining to the Gospel of Mary of Magdala[132], the inner character of God is emphasised once again with the addition of how to "find it".

> "Be on your guard so that no one deceives you by saying, 'Look over here!' or 'Look over there!' For the child of true Humanity exists within you. Follow it! Those who search for it will find it."

The text refers to the inner child in the adult, which is the first step in the exploration of one's inner God. The child in the adult naturally points to memory and the past, but it is also a mode of behaviour. If we identify with the adult and adult behaviour, and the child regarded as inferior and something to overcome, there is less connection to the life spring of the unconscious. Yet, it is this very idea of living the child once again, as Jesus did, that brings forth the creative aspect of the unconscious, and gives us a closer connection to that realm. We all know that children can be at once beautiful, spontaneous and free, but also brutal and dominating. It is this acceptance of the child within us, with all the associated positive and negative aspects, that liberates us from the sometimes stagnant and uncreative aspects of adulthood, particularly when the culture emphasises logic and reason over spontaneity and creativity.

Encouraging the inner child into our lives gives us the opportunity to differentiate the positive and negative aspects of that character. These include the spontaneous, fun loving, and playful from the tantrum and power-seeking aspects. This is where the inner woman in a man (soul)[133] helps with her judging ability and feeling for right and wrong. This is why the iconography depicts the baby Jesus with his unblemished mother. In other words, Mary and Jesus is an all-positive mother and son pair (divine). On the other hand, Mary of Magdala portrayed negatively and her origins less than pure compared to Mary, the mother of Jesus. There are instances where Jesus himself behaves as if influenced by the

---

[132] GOSPEL OF MARY OF MAGDALA, Karen L. King, Polebridge Press 2003

[133] The feminine character in the man is the woman he could have been had certain hormones not been activated during gestation. It is important not to identify with ones inner woman as this leads to complications and possible denial of ones natural biological masculinity.

negative side of his inner child, exemplified by the tantrums at the fig tree and temple[134].

Revelation is the last chapter in the bible, and has not been without controversy. Luther regarded it as dark and mysterious, and only later in life saw its value. Scholars do not agree on the author of the text, as it was either John the Apostle or John of Patmos. Whoever the author was, the book provides clues on the exploration and confrontation with the unconscious in all its destructive capacity. The chapter concerns itself more with the author's visions than the life of Jesus. This in turn, gives it a mythological and symbolic meaning, rather than quasi-historical document of the other writings in the bible.

The first meaningful aspect of Revelation is the use of the number seven. Revelation contains seven spirits of the seven churches, seven candlesticks, seven stars, seven seals, seven horses, seven trumpets, seven lamps, and so on.

> 4. John to the seven churches which are in Asia: Grace be unto you, and peace, from him which is, and which was, and which is to come; and from the seven Spirits which are before his throne; [135]
> 13. And in the midst of the seven candlesticks one like unto the Son of man, clothed with a garment down to the foot, and girt about the paps with a golden girdle. [136]
> 16 And he had in his right hand seven stars: and out of his mouth went a sharp twoedged sword: and his countenance was as the sun shineth in his strength. [137]
> 20 The mystery of the seven stars which thou sawest in my right hand, and the seven golden candlesticks. The seven stars are the angels of the seven churches: and the seven candlesticks which thou sawest are the seven churches.[138]

The number seven in numerology is the thinker and seeker of truth and understanding. In mathematics, seven is an odd prime number, a Mersenne[139] prime, factorial prime, a lucky prime, a happy number (happy prime) and a safe prime. The feeling behind seven thus appears positive, in that it is the lord's number and the bringer of truth and understanding. Six, on the other hand, symbolises man and his weaknesses, the

---

[134] Mark 11:12, 13, 14, 15, 16, John 2:14, 2:15, 2:16,
[135] KING JAMES BIBLE, from Mobile Reference, Thomas Nelson, Inc 1983, Chapter 1, Paragraph 4
[136] Ibid, Chapter 1, Paragraph 13
[137] Ibid, Chapter 1, Paragraphs 16
[138] Ibid, Chapter 1, Paragraph 20
[139] In mathematics, a Mersenne prime is a prime number of the form $Mn = 2n - 1$. This is to say that it is a prime number which is one less than a power of two. They are named after Marin Mersenne, a French Minim friar, who studied them in the early 17th century.

manifestation of sin and Satan. The upper realm of God and his grace is thus represented by the number seven and balanced by the lower earthly and natural realm represented by the number six.

The opposites in Revelation are emphasised in the following passages where the author explains the worship of false idols and fornication as barriers (stumbling blocks) to the upper realm of enlightenment and understanding.

> 2.14 But I have a few things against thee, because thou hast there them that hold the doctrine of Balaam, who taught Balac to cast a stumbling block before the children of Israel, to eat things sacrificed unto idols, and to commit fornication.[140]
> 2.16 Repent; or else I will come unto thee quickly, and will fight against them with the sword of my mouth.
> 2.20 Notwithstanding I have a few things against thee, because thou sufferest that woman Jezebel, which calleth herself a prophetess, to teach and to seduce my servants to commit fornication, and to eat things sacrificed unto idols.
> 2.21 And I gave her space to repent of her fornication; and she repented not.
> 2.22 Behold, I will cast her into a bed, and them that commit adultery with her into great tribulation, except they repent of their deeds.
> 2.23 And I will kill her children with death; and all the churches shall know that I am he which searcheth the reins and hearts: and I will give unto every one of you according to your works.
> 2.27 And he shall rule them with a rod of iron; as the vessels of a potter shall they be broken to shivers: even as I received of my Father.
> 2.28 And I will give him the morning star.

Unfortunately, the purity of the upper realm of God and lower realm of nature (Satan) suffers from cross-contamination as revealed in passages 21 to 23, with the punishment for the sins of Jezebel by killing her innocent children. These words are not from a loving and forgiving father, but a vengeful deity with characteristics in common to the Old Testament God. The text explains that he is to rule with an iron rod and the vessels broken. This alludes to what Jesus declared previously, that he comes with a sword to divide father from son and destroy the vessels. It is breaking the container of parental dependency and family to find one's own individuality and kingdom of the heavenly father (central inner character).

> 3.15 I know thy works, that thou art neither cold nor hot: I would thou wert cold or hot.

---

[140] THE KING JAMES BIBLE, from Mobile Reference, Thomas Nelson, Inc 1983,

3.16 So then because thou art lukewarm, and neither cold nor hot, I will spue thee out of my mouth.

In this passage, the opposites are emphasised in terms of hot and cold. Hot, signifying love, charity and faith and cold, the absence of these, hate, greed and doubt. The text does not prefer either hot or cold, but encourages the middle, lukewarm position. In other words, awareness of the opposites is in God's favour, but unawareness of the opposites is not. This again suggests the central position and character.

4.6 And before the throne there was a sea of glass like unto crystal: and in the midst of the throne, and round about the throne, were four beasts full of eyes before and behind.
4.7 And the first beast was like a lion, and the second beast like a calf, and the third beast had a face as a man, and the fourth beast was like a flying eagle.

The preceding passages include four all-seeing (full of eyes before and behind) beasts, whose nature requires some elucidation. It is important to note that the text does not describe the beasts as actual animals, but 'was like that animal'. Being like an animal is not the same as being an animal, and is a representation, which is the idea of the animal in humans, and therefore mythological. The lion has always been the 'King' of the jungle and represents nobility and strength. Its image is often associated with the royalty, and is an excellent symbol for the light of consciousness, maturity and earthly power. The calf, on the other hand is a young cow or bull, but the term also applies to other young mammals, such as a moose, elephant and whale. The Hebrews held young cows in high esteem as something of value that could sustain them and used in sacrifice. The worship of the golden calf in the absence of Moses is another example of its value.

The third beast mentioned in the text is curious, in that its description is not precise, and has a 'face as a man'. In other words, this beast is more human than beast and means that it is on its way to becoming human, thus overcoming the instinctual foundation that animals represent. The fourth animal is the eagle, which in the Old Testament is the King and powerful bird of prey. Eagles have keen eyesight and swift hunting abilities. As a bird, it is aerial and not limited to earthly existence, and sees from above, thus giving it a spiritual value.

In summary, the lion is the king of the wild jungle, practical and strong. The calf is sustaining and nourishing, the third and human beast bridging the animal world with the spiritual, and the eagle as an aerial and spiritual beast. In this, we can see a transition from earthly concerns of power, wealth and nourishment, to spiritual concerns of enlightenment, insight and understanding.

> 5.12 Saying with a loud voice, Worthy is the Lamb that was slain to receive power, and riches, and wisdom, and strength, and honour, and glory, and blessing.

The lamb, as most children know, is an unthreatening animal, which is small, adorable, young, has soft wool and of high value in those days. It is a suitable substitute for a child in sacrifice. The lamb's sacrifice, that is the overcoming of the small, soft and loveable in us, gives power, riches, wisdom, strength, honour, glory and blessing, and represents the transition from child to adult when the child is sacrificed. On the outside, it is a lamb, on the inside, a lion.

The lamb in the bible is associated with Jesus as he displayed the child-like traits of softness and love to his followers as well as authority, power, wisdom etc. It is the return to the child (lamb) within us that opens the creative aspects of the personality and free-flow of unconscious products into consciousness. The text below shows that the lamb (child within us) opens the secrets to eternity (unconscious), as represented by the seven seals.

> 6.1 And I saw when the Lamb opened one of the seals, and I heard, as it were the noise of thunder, one of the four beasts saying, Come and see.
> 6.2 And I saw, and behold a white horse: and he that sat on him had a bow; and a crown was given unto him: and he went forth conquering, and to conquer.
> 6.4 And there went out another horse that was red: and power was given to him that sat thereon to take peace from the earth, and that they should kill one another: and there was given unto him a great sword.
> 6.5 And when he had opened the third seal, I heard the third beast say, Come and see. And I beheld, and lo a black horse; and he that sat on him had a pair of balances in his hand.
> 6.8 And I looked, and behold a pale horse: and his name that sat on him was Death, and Hell followed with him. And power was given unto them over the fourth part of the earth, to kill with sword, and with hunger, and with death, and with the beasts of the earth.
> 6.9 And when he had opened the fifth seal, I saw under the altar the souls of them that were slain for the word of God, and for the testimony which they held:
> 6.12 And I beheld when he had opened the sixth seal, and, lo, there was a great earthquake; and the sun became black as sackcloth of hair, and the moon became as blood;
> 6.13 And the stars of heaven fell unto the earth, even as a fig tree casteth her untimely figs, when she is shaken of a mighty wind.
> 6.14 And the heaven departed as a scroll when it is rolled together; and every mountain and island were moved out of their places.

6.15 And the kings of the earth, and the great men, and the rich men, and the chief captains, and the mighty men, and every bondman, and every free man, hid themselves in the dens and in the rocks of the mountains;

6.16 And said to the mountains and rocks, Fall on us, and hide us from the face of him that sitteth on the throne, and from the wrath of the Lamb:

6.17 For the great day of his wrath is come; and who shall be able to stand.

Horses in general are tameable creatures with an amendable disposition, are powerful, strong and useful (horsepower). The first horse is white and therefore pure and unblemished. It has a bow, which kills with pinpoint accuracy like the intellect, and a crown, giving it a high noble rank amongst the horses. The second horse is red, which relates to the colour of blood, life and emotions. This horse has a sword, which cuts and divides as well as thrusts into its enemy. It comes to turn people against each other (divide) and destroy the peace. The third horse is black, which is dark and the opposite of white. He has a pair of balances (scales), therefore balances and compliments the white horse. The forth horse is pale, which is in between white and black and death 'sat on him' and was associated with hell (unconscious). This horse reined over the forth part of the earth and brought division, hunger and death. The fifth seal revealed the souls of people killed for their worship. The sixth seal extends the conflagration into the environment where the earth shook; the sun became black and the moon, blood red. The text also relates the blackening of the sun to a 'sackcloth of hair', and therefore the head. The head is the seat of consciousness, as we understand with our head. The sun also relates to consciousness, in that we see clearly in the daylight and less clearly at night (unconscious). The moon, on the other hand, became blood red, which is life and emotion. The text continues with the wider disaster of the stars falling to earth like the figs when shaken from the tree. The return of the scroll to its natural shape finally extinguished consciousness, which moved the mountains and islands. All the earthly men were afraid and hid, which reinforces the destruction of the conscious, practical man in the author. The new idea of the power and wrath of the lamb introduced at the end of this chapter, thus bringing forth the negative qualities underneath the soft exterior.

After all this conflict, division, destruction and death, we can see a theme emerging that shows a journey, or at least experience of the unconscious in all its destructive force. The text is the destruction of consciousness on a massive scale and indeed, sometimes it takes such destruction to make us notice how the unconscious works in our lives. Most of us have experienced a broken marriage, lost job, a death or some sort of destruction in our lives. It all shows that the bigger things are outside of our control and simply happen to us. The interesting aspect of the text is that a small, young and adorable animal opens the seals to all the destruction. To someone identifying with the conscious physical world alone, in other words, all that is light and presumably good, the unconscious would be dark and destructive, particularly if one has oppressed it in oneself for any length of time.

The death and destruction takes on a linear descent, in that it begins with the lamb, then the white horse, then red and so on, until the whole cosmos is destroyed. This is how it feels when one's conscious life is disrupted and made to go on a descent into the unconscious. In the following passage the destruction pauses and returns to the positive aspect of the lamb.

> 7.17 For the Lamb which is in the midst of the throne shall feed them, and shall lead them unto living fountains of waters: and God shall wipe away all tears from their eyes.

The lamb has opened six seals and shown the death and destruction of the compensating unconscious, and now opens the seventh seal leading to silence. In other words, there is a pause between opposite forces of evil and good, like the eye of a storm.

> 8.1 And when he had opened the seventh seal, there was silence in heaven about the space of half an hour.
> 8.2 And I saw the seven angels which stood before God; and to them were given seven trumpets.
> 8.5 And the angel took the censer, and filled it with fire of the altar, and cast it into the earth: and there were voices, and thunderings, and lightnings, and an earthquake.

The royalty of the lamb encompasses the opposites and leads to the positive seventh seal, which gives silence upon opening. This is the stillness and peace one experiences when liberated from the tension of opposites. Seven angels then appear before God with seven trumpets, presumably to announce the realisation of the first stage of differentiation. The angel is an attendant or messenger, and brings God's fire contained in the censer into the earth. In other words, God's fire is put into the earth and the body. In psychological terms, it is bringing the positive aspects of intuition (Gods word and fire) into the earth or body for its differentiation into positive and negative. We know from the life of Jesus that he had to sacrifice his body and all its natural functions for a higher good.

> 9.1 And the fifth angel sounded, and I saw a star fall from heaven unto the earth: and to him was given the key of the bottomless pit.

> 9.2 And he opened the bottomless pit; and there arose a smoke out of the pit, as the smoke of a great furnace; and the sun and the air were darkened by reason of the smoke of the pit.
>
> 9.10 And they had tails like unto scorpions, and there were stings in their tails: and their power was to hurt men five months.
>
> 9.11 And they had a king over them, which is the angel of the bottomless pit, whose name in the Hebrew tongue is Abaddon, but in the Greek tongue hath his name Apollyon.

The disaster continues with the opening of hell and the constellation of the dark king. This is an apt character and counterpoint to a conscious attitude that identifies with all that is good. The character of an all-good saviour, as well as the dark king of the underworld can equally possess us. Either way, it is rejection or acceptance of our natural instincts or all that is light and good in our lives. The author names the dark king as Abaddon in his vision, whose Greek mythological equivalent is the deity and place called Tartarus, which is a deep abyss, and used as a dungeon for the torment and suffering of the wicked.

> 9.17 And thus I saw the horses in the vision, and them that sat on them, having breastplates of fire, and of jacinth, and brimstone: and the heads of the horses were as the heads of lions; and out of their mouths issued fire and smoke and brimstone.
>
> 9.18 By these three was the third part of men killed, by the fire, and by the smoke, and by the brimstone, which issued out of their mouths.
>
> 9.19 For their power is in their mouth, and in their tails: for their tails were like unto serpents, and had heads, and with them they do hurt.
>
> 9.20 And the rest of the men which were not killed by these plagues yet repented not of the works of their hands, that they should not worship devils, and idols of gold, and silver, and brass, and stone, and of wood: which neither can see, nor hear, nor walk:
>
> 9.21 Neither repented they of their murders, nor of their sorceries, nor of their fornication, nor of their thefts.

The preceding text of the author's vision continues with the conflagration of humanity and the horses (power) killing a third of men. The other two thirds are condemned for their worship of material value and practical life. The next passage brings into the vision the first inkling of unity amidst the disaster.

> 10.1 And I saw another mighty angel come down from heaven, clothed with a cloud: and a rainbow was upon his head, and his face was as it were the sun, and his feet as pillars of fire:
>
> 10.2 And he had in his hand a little book open: and he set his right foot upon the sea, and his left foot on the earth,
>
> 10.3 And cried with a loud voice, as when a lion roareth: and when he had cried, seven thunders uttered their voices.

10.4 And when the seven thunders had uttered their voices, I was about to write: and I heard a voice from heaven saying unto me, Seal up those things which the seven thunders uttered, and write them not.
10.5 And the angel which I saw stand upon the sea and upon the earth lifted up his hand to heaven,
10.9 And I went unto the angel, and said unto him, Give me the little book. And he said unto me, Take it, and eat it up; and it shall make thy belly bitter, but it shall be in thy mouth sweet as honey.

It is in the form of a curious angel from heaven with the face of the sun, rainbow for a head and fire for feet. This image contained within the vision shows a character that unites the upper and lower realms. The face is the sun and therefore consciousness, the rainbow unites two sides in a colourful arc of life and emotion, the cloud (water) clothing, which nurtures to earth and the fiery feet (hell) and all that belongs to the earth in the practical sense. The angel's left foot stands upon the earth and right foot upon the sea, thus bridging the gap between the two. The little book represents knowledge of the situation, which must be eaten, digested and understood, and shall taste sweet when in the mouth (read) and bitter when digested (understood). This points to the fact that unity includes all that is lowly human and upper Godly. The author would not have received this idea well (bitter) due to his identification with the upper man Jesus. The disasters continue until chapter twelve, where the first female character is introduced.

12.1 And there appeared a great wonder in heaven; a woman clothed with the sun, and the moon under her feet, and upon her head a crown of twelve stars:
12.2 And she being with child cried, travailing in birth, and pained to be delivered.
12.3 And there appeared another wonder in heaven; and behold a great red dragon, having seven heads and ten horns, and seven crowns upon his heads.
12.4 And his tail drew the third part of the stars of heaven, and did cast them to the earth: and the dragon stood before the woman which was ready to be delivered, for to devour her child as soon as it was born.
12.5 And she brought forth a man child, who was to rule all nations with a rod of iron: and her child was caught up unto God, and to his throne.
12.6 And the woman fled into the wilderness, where she hath a place prepared of God, that they should feed her there a thousand two hundred and threescore days.
12.7 And there was war in heaven: Michael and his angels fought against the dragon; and the dragon fought and his angels,
12.8 And prevailed not; neither was their place found any more in heaven.
12.9 And the great dragon was cast out, that old serpent, called the Devil, and Satan, which deceiveth the whole world: he was cast out into the earth, and his angels were cast out with him.

> 12.10 And I heard a loud voice saying in heaven, Now is come salvation, and strength, and the kingdom of our God, and the power of his Christ: for the accuser of our brethren is cast down, which accused them before our God day and night

The woman is clothed with the sun (conscious of her body), has the moon under her feet (rooted in her femininity), with a crown and twelve stars (spirit in the cosmos) and about to give birth. She is the image of a positive mother character balanced by the red dragon with seven heads, ten horns and seven crowns on each head. The text does not elucidate the location of the three additional horns, and one can only conjecture where they may have been. The dragon is later associated with Satan. The woman gives birth to a man-child, meaning that part of him was adult and part child. In addition, the birthed man-child is to rule all nations in a strict and disciplined manner (iron rod).

After giving birth, the woman flees the scene, recedes into the background, and is attacked by the cast-out Satan, as shown in the following passages. The author experienced a war in heaven (conscious mind) between Satan and the Angels (agents of God), in other words, he was aware of the conflict between the good spirit and what they regard as the evil earthly animal part of our instinctive nature. The author overcomes the unconscious and sides with consciousness to cast out Satan and his agents from heaven. The unconscious mollified (cast out), and the conscious attitude of good renewed, strengthened and reborn. It is a common myth to fight the dragon and attain some of the dragon's energy and power (treasure) with new vigour and discipline for life. Jesus did the same thing when he spent time in the desert fighting his inner devil.

> 12.13 And when the dragon saw that he was cast unto the earth, he persecuted the woman which brought forth the man child.
> 12.14 And to the woman were given two wings of a great eagle, that she might fly into the wilderness, into her place, where she is nourished for a time, and times, and half a time, from the face of the serpent
> 12.15 And the serpent cast out of his mouth water as a flood after the woman, that he might cause her to be carried away of the flood
> 12.16 And the earth helped the woman, and the earth opened her mouth, and swallowed up the flood which the dragon cast out of his mouth
> 12.17 And the dragon was wroth with the woman, and went to make war with the remnant of her seed, which keep the commandments of God, and have the testimony of Jesus Christ

Unfortunately, the author leaves the child's mother at the mercy of Satan. There is no hint of a relationship formed with the woman, although she is helped by what we have to assume is God, who gave her wings of an eagle to fly (spirit). The dragon casts water to flood out of his mouth to try to kill the woman. This is a reversal of what usually comes out of the dragon's mouth. It changed from fire to water, indicating that the energy liberated for consciousness with the overcoming (casting out) of the dragon changed to water. Water is associated with feeling, value and life. In its positive form, water is nourishing and life giving; and negative form, destructive and drowning. The dragon proceeds to fight the commandments brought down from the mount by Moses. This reinforces the idea of water coming from the dragon's mouth. He cannot kill the woman and therefore wages war on the author's conscious values.

The conflict continues and widens to include another hybrid beast that comes out of the sea with multiple horns and heads, has the body of a leopard, feet of a bear and mouth of a lion with great authority. Hybrid creatures such as this always depict different traits of several animals in one imaginary beast, and hence, those beastly traits within the individual. This beast had the ability to heal itself, but continued the attack on the Christian values through blasphemy and war against the saints over the land. This indicates that the conflict was only partially resolved and that the beast still caused the author grief and attacked his values. This could have been resolved if the mother of his newly won man-child was brought into his care. In other words, the woman who gave birth (integrate) to his inner child left to fend for herself. This accounts for the moral question, in that the author's values had not incorporated what he had learned from the vision, and had returned to his conscious, Christian convictions. Had he adjusted those values to suit the unconscious yearnings, it would have stripped the dragon of more of its energy and power, and formed a relationship to the inner woman.

As a consequence, the beast turns its attention to men, and performs healing and miracles to gain their trust and worship. The beast does not have the values of Jesus and dwells in and on the kingdom of earth, coercing men to accumulate wealth (buy or sell) and power by any means. The men who follow the beast receive a mark of numbers 'Six hundred threescore and six'. The emphasis on the number 'six' tripled in this case, giving it far more power than a single 'six'. After the opening of the sixth seal, a change comes over the vision. The opening of all the seals, from one to six becomes increasingly negative, culminating in the total extinguishment of consciousness.

The mark of the beast signifies materialism, in contrast to a spiritual orientation, which was the value of the Christian story at that time. Today, the Christian story is in need of reconciliation. In other words, we need as individuals, to make the same journey, as did the author of Revelation, form a relationship to the inner woman, and adjust the Christian values to suit. Jesus needs to come down to earth, love, and understand his long lost-brother, Satan[141]. No one can argue the need for food and shelter, family, some wealth and standing (power) in life. It is normal human functioning, based on instinctual, adaptive need (beast). When it becomes habitual and excludes spiritual concerns, it may become destructive. From a purely spiritual point of view, this is indeed the case. A completely spiritual or materialistic point of view is in itself, one-sided, and leads to all kinds of psychological complications. Jesus and his disciples were aware of this need for balance and set aside one day in the week for spiritual worship, and the other days for practical concerns.

It is difficult to make any real judgements on the life of Jesus, because the bible mixes physical reality with myth, and we do not know how much of it was engineered for a certain outcome. We also do not know how he would have fared had he adapted more to the contemporary Judaic beliefs, rather than adopting an attitude and accumulating a following outside of its influence. The vision continues:

> 14.3 And they sung as it were a new song before the throne, and before the four beasts, and the elders: and no man could learn that song but the hundred and forty and four thousand, which were redeemed from the earth.
> 14.4 These are they which were not defiled with women; for they are virgins. These are they which follow the Lamb whithersoever he goeth. These were redeemed from among men, being the first fruits unto God and to the Lamb.

The preceding passages show that the spiritual orientation was uppermost in the mind of the author, to the point where all earthly concerns including sexuality, rejected and given to God to provide. Indeed, an inner character takes care of practical matters in a fateful way. For example, the right job comes along just at the right moment, one meets the right partner, or finds the right house just when we need it, and so on.

> 14.10 The same shall drink of the wine of the wrath of God, which is poured out without mixture into the cup of his indignation; and he shall be tormented with fire and brimstone in the presence of the holy angels, and in the presence of the Lamb:
> 14.14 And I looked, and behold a white cloud, and upon the cloud one sat like unto the Son of man, having on his head a golden crown, and in his hand a sharp sickle.

---

[141] I am speaking symbolically. These figures are inner characters with a reality that shapes our health, values and behaviour

The above passages show the intent of the 'Son of man' to reap humanity from its physical nature into a spiritual and moral orientation. This is the separation of conscious and unconscious and all the external things that belong to the 'beast', such as sexuality, power, wealth, and the spiritual functions of reason, ideas, love etc., are to be cut and separated with the former rejected for the latter. This is where the Christian tradition belongs in the evolution of western culture's understanding of unity. The exploration of one side requires turning away from the other and can lead to a neglect of the other side, as the Christian tradition espouses. Not all is lost however, and the author leaves open the possibility for union with the beast once again in a thousand years:

> 20.1 And I saw an angel come down from heaven, having the key of the bottomless pit and a great chain in his hand.
> 20.2 And he laid hold on the dragon, that old serpent, which is the Devil, and Satan, and bound him a thousand years,
> 20.7 And when the thousand years are expired, Satan shall be loosed out of his prison,

He continues with all the traits that will condemn men to a fiery fate and stop them from entering the inner kingdom of heaven. Indeed, inner work requires honesty and an open disposition with one self and turning away from the world of intrigue and attachments for a time, hence the use of the sickle.

> 21.8 But the fearful, and unbelieving, and the abominable, and murderers, and whoremongers, and sorcerers, and idolaters, and all liars, shall have their part in the lake which burneth with fire and brimstone: which is the second death.

The author ends Revelation on a positive note, having overcome the natural man in himself and returning to conscious awareness and good. He describes the beauty of a child-like and pure innocence (water of life) attitude and the tree of life, which grows with a variety of fruit and the ability to heal nations. Indeed, the Christian tradition has all those potential benefits of peace and brotherhood of all nations, if we could relate to the beast within ourselves, rather than seeing it in others.

> 22.1 And he shewed me a pure river of water of life, clear as crystal, proceeding out of the throne of God and of the Lamb.
> 22.2 In the midst of the street of it, and on either side of the river, was there the tree of life, which bare twelve manner of fruits, and yielded her fruit every month: and the leaves of the tree were for the healing of the nations.

In summary, the story of Jesus is the evolutionary step of a differentiation and integration of our psychic functioning. To know the higher man requires a differentiation from the lower man. It is the differentiation of spirit from matter, that is, the higher mental faculties from the lower physical instincts and earthly life. This differentiation enables the consolidation of consciousness in the form of Jesus and associated God-likeness understood by a human being. In the Christian story the body and associated instinctuality need overcoming, as they are part of Satan and our animal nature.

This necessary development at this time paved the way for a consolidation of consciousness. The myth of Jesus was without sin, and overcoming the earthly man in himself. Universal love triumphed over hatred and earthly power. The sexual instinct firmly put aside, with its associated need, negative emotions and earthly pleasure, and relegated to the realm of Satan. The upper and lower inner spirits had indeed come to earth through the man Jesus, the lower rejected and a one-sided ideal established. It was then task of the Apostles to carry on with this teaching.

The fact that they were selective in what was included in the Bible shows that they had a definite idea of what the Christian Ministry should teach. This demonstrates a certain contamination of the Apostles with their own ideas, which obscured the actual teachings of Jesus. As shown above in the Gospels of Judas, Mary and Thomas, the teachings of Jesus differed to what the others wrote in the bible. It emphasises a universal God, whereas Jesus recognised his own inner God, and that God was different for each individual. Also omitted was any reference to Gnosticism and the Male/Female pair therein.

Pictorial depictions of Jesus show him with his heart on the outside of his chest and a Crown of Thorns wrapped around it, thus restricting its natural function[142]. Fire comes out of the top of the heart, with the cross coming out of the fire, indicating the passion of the heart and the need for its sacrifice to a higher good. It alludes to the sacrifice (overcoming of one's nature) of the heart into upper and lower parts. The face of Jesus is often depicted as feminine and soft, his hands non-threatening in a becoming pose and a halo around his head, showing that even his thoughts are pure and untainted by earthly concerns.

The unity of this pair of opposites (Jesus and Satan) is obvious. An all-good and perfect God that created all things also created Satan, which in turn means that God is not perfect. A perfect God cannot create imperfection, for this act makes him imperfect. The Christian story and life

---

[142] The heart In its natural undifferentiated state experiences love and hate in equal proportion.

of Jesus had enormous value for the people 2000 years ago. Their idea of unity was the differentiation and acceptance of the upper man and rejection of the lower man. What constitutes the good from bad is a relative judgement however. Different cultures have different values when it comes to upper and lower aspects, and as we shall see in the following chapters, there were attempts to complete the Christian myth and unite the opposites in matter and hence the body itself.

f. Gnosticism

Gnosis is the Greek term for knowledge of the divine based on personal experience and perception. This spiritual movement developed shortly after the life of Jesus in the first and second century AD and to some extent, was a reaction to the disconnection of the spirit from the body. They regarded the body and material world not to be despised and overcome, but as a creation of the highest God and having a divine spark within it. The Gnostics believed they could liberate this divine spark through knowledge and experience. In essence, they felt that the body and all its earthly expressions of emotion, practical concerns for food, wealth, standing, power and so on, had a part in the divine scheme and that the spirit was embedded within it. In that respect, the ancient Alchemists were closely allied to the Gnostics and believed they could liberate the divine spark in matter through transformation.

The Gnostics recognised the two great streams of Western civilisation of the Judaic Christian spirituality and morality with the logic and reason of ancient Greece and Platonic thought. Gnosticism relies heavily on the function of intuition and insight to gain knowledge of the divine and its relation to the physical. Their emphasis was less to do with collective representations and systems, and more the individual experience of the divine within the psyche. In other words, they recognised the unity between the physical and psychic and regarded the spirit as the all-encompassing goal, and the body and earthly existence related to the shadow.

The Gnostics drew heavily on the life of Jesus and ancient Hebrew Texts. In 1945, an Arab peasant made a ground breaking discovery buried in the desert in Upper Egypt near a town called Nag Hammadi. He found an earthenware pot buried in the ground containing thirteen papyrus books bound in leather. This became the Nag Hammadi Library and the Gnostic Gospels. They not only include different interpretations of Christ, but also Gospels of Judas, Tomas, Philip, Mary Magdala and other writings of Peter, Paul, James and John. The texts emphasise an inner God and was antithetical to the intentions of the early Christian ministry.

My God, my mind, my thought, my soul, my body." Learn the sources of sorrow: joy, love, hate . . . If you carefully investigate these matters you will find him **in yourself.**[143]

One of the basic ideas of Gnostic experience is the unity of masculine and feminine elements and the gender of different aspects of human functioning. For example, the Gnostics viewed the mind of a man as masculine and his soul as feminine, thus forming a 'syzygy' pair of opposites. The soul draws to the physical non-spiritual darkness of the flesh, or to the light of the spirit. They regarded the inner work required as the way to experience the enlightenment of their God.

Become earnest about the word! For as to the word, its first part is faith; the second, love; the third, works; for from these comes life. For the word is like a grain of wheat; when someone had sown it, he had faith in it; and when it had sprouted, he loved it, because he had seen many grains in place of one. And when he had worked, he was saved, because he had prepared it for food, (and) again he left (some) to sow.[144]

They also placed great importance on seeking spiritual death as a transition to new life. "For the Kingdom of God belongs to those who have put themselves to death." This reinforces the idea that the old life must die before the new life created. We all go through these transitions in life, particularly the dramatic and life changing events such as puberty, which is the death of childhood for adult life, marriage, which is the death of a single life and so on. In this instance, it is a willing faith in the unifying inner force that holds one together during these transitions. We cannot know the heart if we are stuck in the head, and the same goes for bodily activities.

When you come to know what 'head' is, and that prophecy issues from the head, then understand what is the meaning of 'Its head was removed.[145]

The removal of the head is the differentiation of head from heart and body and often expressed in dreams as decapitation. The separation of the head from the body enables us to see the body as it is without contamination. This idea is similar to dismemberment where body parts are differentiated from each other in the myths of Osiris and Dionysus. Symbolic dismemberment is part of the process of differentiation and understanding the functions of different parts of the body. For example,

---

[143] THE NAG HAMMADI LIBRARY, Edited by J. Robinson, Coptic Gnostic Library project.... Brill, 3rd ed. (1988), Introduction by Elaine Pagels, page 4
[144] Ibid, The Apocryphon of James, Codex I, Translated by Francis E. Williams, page 16
[145] Ibid, The Apocryphon of James, Codex I, The Lord speaking, page 20

we experience sexual love in the heart and genitals, physical skills in the head and hands, jealousy in the heart and head, and so on.

The following text from the Gospel of Truth in the Nag Hammadi Library, describes the achievement of unity by knowing the father who resides in the Pleroma[146], and overcoming the body and its associated instincts and affects, as the dissolution of form[147].

> Since this incompleteness came about because they did not know the Father, so when they know the Father, incompleteness, from that moment on, will cease to exist. As one's ignorance disappears when he gains knowledge, and as darkness disappears when light appears, so also incompleteness is eliminated by completeness. Certainly, from that moment on, form is no longer manifest, but will be dissolved in fusion with unity.[148]

This shows that the Gnostics were still trying to liberate themselves from the body and its associated functions as did the Hebrews in the Torah, and followers of Jesus. This alludes to Plato's idea of the 'copy' of the 'model' and that our body is the garment of our soul and spirit. The text also equates division and incompleteness with 'cold aromas' and God unites the division and brings the 'hot Pleroma of love' and the 'unity of perfect thought' to fruition. This reinforces the idea that God is an inner character and accessed through inner work. The following text from the Tripartite Tractate details the 'Tripartition' of mankind into three distinct types.

> Mankind came to be in three essential types, the spiritual, the psychic, and the material, conforming to the triple disposition of the Logos, from which were brought forth the material ones and the psychic ones and the spiritual ones. Each of the three essential types is known by its fruit. And they were not known at first but only at the coming of the Savior, who shone upon the saints and revealed what each was.
> The spiritual race, being like light from light and like spirit from spirit, when its head appeared, it ran toward him immediately. It immediately became a body of its head. It suddenly received knowledge in the revelation. The psychic race is like light from a fire, since it hesitated to accept knowledge of him who appeared to it. (It hesitated) even more to run toward him in faith. Rather, through a voice it was instructed, and this was sufficient, since it is not far from the hope according to the promise, since it received, so to speak as a pledge, the assurance of the

---

[146] This is the Gnostic term for the spiritual universe, abode of god and the totality of divine powers and emanations.
[147] 'Form' is later described in the Tripartite Tractate as the earthly man being the shadow of the totality.
[148] THE NAG HAMMADI LIBRARY, Edited by J. Robinson, Coptic Gnostic Library project.... Brill, 3rd ed. (1988), The Gospel of Truth, Codex I, Translated by Robert M. Grant, page 26

things which were to be. The material race, however, is alien in every way; since it is dark, it shuns the shining of the light, because its appearance destroys it. And since it has not received its unity, it is something excessive and hateful toward the Lord at his revelation.[149]

The three types of mankind describe what they perceive as differing psychological types and their natural orientation and relationship to the unity represented by the saviour. The 'spiritual' concern themselves with the saviour (inner character) and direct relationship to the unity of the father. The 'material' concerns themselves with everyday life, adaptation and the reality of the body and senses. The 'psychic' has access to both realms and hesitates to go in one or other direction. The Gnostics show their disdain for the material as dark and unenlightened as their concerns are spiritual and located in the head. This shows that they are aware of the diversity of type within people, and spread between the divine and material.

It also shows that the natural man was more prevalent than the enlightened man, and the difference between the God of Moses and God of Jesus shows how humanity evolves psychically. This fact is overlooked because the inner God has such universal and complete appeal to the individual, that it feels unchanging and eternal. It shows how important it is to differentiate unity from the idea of unity. Unity is eternal and unchanging; the idea changes and is dependent on the individual, his or her type, and their life process.

Once again, the emphasis is on overcoming the physical for the spiritual and the temporary unity of consciousness. I say temporary because we cannot neglect the body indefinitely as it requires attention as much as the spirit. Every journey to the spirit must eventually return to the physical and the body's own needs. This is particularly true if one has to care for the physical wellbeing of a family. It also denies the achievement possible with good hard physical work, to provide food or in honour of the spirit through the physical arts.

The Gnostics were well aware that lust for power, jealousy, ambition, anger, pride etc., were part of down to earth reality and not part of the benevolent and all loving God of Jesus. The next section describes the purified body and relationship to the Saviour unified in the 'bridal chamber'.

---

[149] Ibid, The Tripartite Tractate, Codex I, Translated by Harold W. Attridge and Dieter Mueller, Part III, 14. The Tripartition of Mankind, page 58

> The calling, however, has the place of those who rejoice at the bridal chamber, and who are glad and happy at the union of the bridegroom and the bride. The place which the calling will have is the aeon of the images, where the Logos has not yet joined with the Pleroma. And since the man of the Church was happy and glad at this, as he was hoping for it, he separated spirit, soul, and body in the organization of the one who thinks that he is a unity, though within him is the man who is the Totality - and he is all of them.[150]

This passage emphasises the unity and totality of the inner man, which can only be integrated and understood with the differentiation of the spirit from soul and body in purified and untainted form. This means that differentiation must be as thorough as possible so that cross contamination is minimised.

> When the redemption was proclaimed, the perfect man received knowledge immediately, so as to return in haste to his unitary state, to the place from which he came, to return there joyfully, to the place from which he came, to the place from which he flowed forth.[151]

The above text describes a place similar to paradise in the Torah, which begins in the pure and unblemished state, to the expulsion and trials of redemption and enticement with promise of another paradise. Indeed, returning to the childhood of one's past does close the gap between the opposites and is closer to the unconscious/conscious regulatory centre. This is why the emphasis is on the son of the father as the way to perceive and relate to the father. The father has the authority and the son obeys his command. Unfortunately, there is no guarantee that the father is benevolent or even trustworthy as the father of Moses in the Torah shows. His loving goodness depends on the level of differentiation between the opposites of beast and God that the individual has achieved. This is why there are always intermediary forces between the opposites, which can draw from both and potentially unite them. This third role falls squarely on the shoulders of Christ as shown in the next passage.

> For when we confessed the kingdom which is in Christ, <we> escaped from the whole multiplicity of forms, and from inequality and change. For the end will receive a unitary existence, just as the beginning is unitary, where there is no male nor female, nor slave and free, nor circumcision and uncircumcision, neither angel nor man, but Christ is all in all.[152]

---

[150] Ibid, The Tripartite Tractate, Codex I, Translated by Harold W. Attridge and Dieter Mueller, Part III, 15. The Process of Restoration, page 59
[151] Ibid, page 60
[152] Ibid,16. Redemption of the Calling, page 62

The Apocryphon of John describes Jesus and his brother James at the temple where a Pharisee named Arimanius disparages the Nazarene (Jesus) that had turned John from the tradition of his fathers. John retreats to the desert and has the following vision:

> Straightway, while I was contemplating these things, behold, the heavens opened and the whole creation which is below heaven shone, and the world was shaken. I was afraid, and behold I saw in the light a youth who stood by me. While I looked at him, he became like an old man. And he changed his likeness (again), becoming like a servant. There was not a plurality before me, but there was a likeness with multiple forms in the light, and the likenesses appeared through each other, and the likeness had three forms.
> He said to me, "John, John, why do you doubt, or why are you afraid? You are not unfamiliar with this image, are you? - that is, do not be timid! - I am the one who is with you (pl.) always. I am the Father, I am the Mother, I am the Son. I am the undefiled and incorruptible one. Now I have come to teach you what is and what was and what will come to pass, that you may know the things which are not revealed and those which are revealed, and to teach you concerning the unwavering race of the perfect Man. Now, therefore, lift up your face, that you may receive the things that I shall teach you today, and may tell them to your fellow spirits who are from the unwavering race of the perfect Man."
> And I asked to know it, and he said to me, "The Monad is a monarchy with nothing above it. It is he who exists as God and Father of everything, the invisible One who is above everything, who exists as incorruption, which is in the pure light into which no eye can look.[153]

This passage and the previous reference to the 'bridal chamber' show that the purified feminine is elevated to the trio of family members, and regarded as one. It also describes the fluidity of the inner characters and their ability to be any age from young child to old man. The Gospel of Judas in the previous chapter describes Jesus was often found amongst his people as a child. The vision also describes the multiplicity contained with the one that is the 'Monad', which as we shall see later in the book, was researched by Leibniz. In the next passage, it mentions the 'Barbelo' as the first power who gave praise to her virginal spirit.

> This is the first thought, his image; she became the womb of everything, for it is she who is prior to them all, the Mother-Father, the first man, the holy Spirit, the thrice-male, the thrice-powerful, the thrice- named androgynous one, and the eternal aeon among the invisible ones, and the first to come forth.
> <She> requested from the invisible, virginal Spirit - that is Barbelo - to give her foreknowledge. And the Spirit consented. And when he had consented, the foreknowledge came forth, and it stood by the

---

[153] Ibid, The Apocryphon of John, Codex II, Translated by Frederik Wisse, page 64

forethought; it originates from the thought of the invisible, virginal Spirit. It glorified him and his perfect power, Barbelo, for it was for her sake that it had come into being.[154]

This passage not only sees the central inner character as androgynous but also having forethought. Intuition is forethought in today's language and equated with a form of perception via the unconscious. Thoughts, ideas etc., simply pop in one's mind and in some instances, present a prediction of future outcomes and when coupled with the other functions, regarded as divine insight. John describes the self-generated one with four lights and three characteristics each. The four powers are understanding, grace, perception and prudence. The first light: grace, truth and form. The second light: conception, perception and memory. The third light: understanding, love and idea. The fourth light: perfection, peace and wisdom. This number is no coincidence and used in the Torah with the twelve tribes of Israel and the twelve apostles of the New Testament. When these twelve characteristics placed into their groups around a circle, it represents complete stability, symmetry and harmony.

Sophia is the mother of the material world in the Gnostic texts and was regarded as a lowest emanation of the divine Monad. She gives birth without the consent of the spirit to the lion faced serpent with flashing lightning fire eyes called Yaltabaoth. Realising his unusual form and imperfection, she tries to hide him away in a cloud. He leaves and becomes strong and creates other authorities for himself and the material world from the flame of the luminous fire. He had a spark of the divine light from his mother and when mixed with the darkness, it became dim. This idea of how the world came into existence is an interesting approach to creation. The material world is full of imperfection and the Gnostics overcame the illogic with the lower emanation of Sophia giving birth to it outside of the Monad's influence. What it tries to do is maintain the perfection of the Monad, enabling the creation of an imperfect world and maintain the opposites of all good and all evil.

We can see from this development that the logic of the ancient Greeks had influenced the thinking of John and rather than accepting God's imperfection at face value, introduced a lower female character that made a mistake, making it acceptable to his logical mind. In this instance, God did not create the material world although his divine spark was included through Sophia. This idea of the divine spark is reinforced by the following passage after the creation of everything seen by Yaltabaoth:

And when he saw the creation which surrounds him, and the multitude of the angels around him which had come forth from him, he said to them,

---

[154] Ibid, page 65

'I am a jealous God, and there is no other God beside me.' But by announcing this he indicated to the angels who attended him that there exists another God. For if there were no other one, of whom would he be jealous?[155]

This allusion to the God of the Torah is the only way to reconcile the evolution of God to the divine all good status of the New Testament. Obviously, this did not go down well with the Jewish rabbis and the mainstream Christian ministry, and the reason for the Gnostics eventual decline. John names four chief demons that belong to pleasure, desire, grief and fear and from each of these the following emotions: From grief: envy, jealousy, distress, trouble, pain, callousness, anxiety, mourning etc.; from pleasure: wickedness, empty pride etc.; from desire: anger, wrath, bitterness, bitter passion, unsatedness etc.; and from fear: dread, fawning, agony, and shame. Knowing the positive and negative in oneself including emotions, is a way to know unity and God. Later in the text, he refers the reader to the Book of Zoroaster for more passions.

The Nag Hammadi continues with the Gospel of Philip and the discussion and transition from Hebrew to Gentile.

A Gentile does not die, for he has never lived in order that he may die. He who has believed in the truth has found life, and this one is in danger of dying, for he is alive. Since Christ came, the world has been created, the cities adorned, the dead carried out. When we were Hebrews, we were orphans and had only our mother, but when we became Christians, we had both father and mother.[156]

This transformation from orphan with mother, to mother and father shows an awareness of the opposites forming in Philips mind and that the spark of one lies in the other. In other words, the darkness is not quite dark, but has the beginning of the upper spirit contained within it. In the following passage he comments of the opposites being brothers:

Light and Darkness, life and death, right and left, are brothers of one another. They are inseparable. Because of this neither are the good good, nor evil evil, nor is life life, nor death death. For this reason each one will dissolve into its earliest origin. But those who are exalted above the world are indissoluble, eternal.[157]
Some said, "Mary conceived by the Holy Spirit." They are in error. They do not know what they are saying. When did a woman ever conceive by a woman? Mary is the virgin whom no power defiled.[158]

---

[155] Ibid, page 67/68
[156] Ibid, The Gospel of Philip, Codex II, translated by Wesley W. Isenberg, page 102
[157] Ibid
[158] Ibid, page 103

He argues that Mary did not conceive Jesus through the Holy Spirit as others say and regards the Holy Spirit as a woman. Philip requires the story to be logical and have reason in nature and the accepted scriptures do not assign a gender to the Holy Spirit. In this instance, Philip is quite adamant that the Holy Spirit is not only female, but also a woman. He reinterprets the meaning of death and resurrection in the following:

> Those who say that the Lord died first and (then) rose up are in error, for he rose up first and (then) died. If one does not first attain the resurrection, he will not die.[159]

Philip gives us more insight into the nature of Jesus when he describes how he behaves with different people.

> Jesus took them all by stealth, for he did not appear as he was, but in the manner in which they would be able to see him. He appeared to them all. He appeared to the great as great. He appeared to the small as small. He appeared to the angels as an angel, and to men as a man. Because of this, his word hid itself from everyone. Some indeed saw him, thinking that they were seeing themselves, but when he appeared to his disciples in glory on the mount, he was not small. [160]

This passage is telling and shows that Jesus had the ability to adopt many inner characters and relate to people from those characters. Indeed, this is the ageless and genderless aspect of the myth-making unconscious. Besides the person you are (ego), one can have access to all the ages in one's lifetime and all the eternal characters behind them. This is why he had such universal appeal, because he could relate to old and young alike from their point of view. Avoiding possession by an inner character or identifying with a single function is the way this openness is achieved. Some philosophers for example, have trouble not thinking; avoid tender feelings, and childish creative play. Some even avoid a normal life of wife and children for the sake of their most developed function. Knowing oneself also means knowing the other characters and functions in oneself.

> And the companion of the [...] Mary Magdalene. [...] loved her more than all the disciples, and used to kiss her often on her mouth. The rest of the disciples [...]. They said to him "Why do you love her more than all of us?" The Savior answered and said to them, "Why do I not love you like her?[161]

---

[159] Ibid
[160] Ibid, page 104
[161] Ibid, page 105

Philip shows that Jesus was more than a colleague or friend to Mary Magdalene and had an intimate relationship with her. It also shows that he may have had a normal and possibly carnal relationship with Mary which is at odds to his purity and divinity as detailed in the Bible. This also shows that the idea of overcoming the body and its natural functions was more important than the reality of the man Jesus. His life was turned into a myth for the sake of a ministry and belief system.

> The forms of evil spirit include male ones and female ones. The males are they which unite with the souls which inhabit a female form, but the females are they which are mingled with those in a male form, though one who was disobedient.[162]

He continues with:

> Fear not the flesh nor love it. If you fear it, it will gain mastery over you. If you love it, it will swallow and paralyze you.
> And so he dwells either in this world or in the resurrection or in the middle place. God forbid that I be found in there! In this world, there is good and evil. Its good things are not good, and its evil things not evil. But there is evil after this world which is truly evil - what is called "the middle". It is death. While we are in this world, it is fitting for us to acquire the resurrection, so that when we strip off the flesh, we may be found in rest and not walk in the middle.[163]

Philip believes that one must relinquish the flesh and its associated functions to attain the position of pure understanding and insight. The 'middle' position disparaged and likened to evil and death and that one must reject the physical for the spiritual. Philip seems to confuse symbolic death with actual death and the middle position between earth and heaven and a place of evil torment. Indeed the middle position is not for the faint hearted. The tension experienced between the opposites can tear one asunder and is a test for the will and understanding. We cannot say anything about life after physical death, we can however, investigate the symbolic idea of death and what it means to be in the middle position. If we identify with the spirit, we dwell in the head and relate it to the upper soul, if we identify with the body we dwell in the instincts and emotions and relate it to the lower soul. If we identify with the heart (soul), we have the body on one side and the spirit the other, and tension between opposite forces. If we do not identify with any position, we have access to all of our self, including body, soul and spirit.

The middle, as an idea, is then the central position between the outer world of flesh and its associated needs for adaptation, standing, money,

---

[162] Ibid, Page 106
[163] Ibid

family, children, emotions, etc., and the inner world of thought, fantasy, visions, insight, knowledge, memory, dreams, ideas and understanding. The problem with this central position is that the opposite do not always agree and are often hostile towards each other. It is hard task to acknowledge that we have the same urges and needs as other animals. On the other hand, we have the same potential for the spirit of love and understanding. The union of these opposites through the soul is the ultimate unity of our true nature.

As we shall see later in this book, disconnection from the outer world for the sake of an inner spiritual journey is very dangerous and may lead to complete dissolution of the individual. The life of Rousseau and Nietzsche is a testament to this possibility as they both ended their lives insane. The little known secret that is important to keep in mind is that we want to become like God and God wants to become human. This is important in that we do not have to go along with everything an inner character tells us. If Moses had argued a little more with his inner God, he may not have been so jealous, angry and murderous and his people not so rebellious. Being a good and obedient son is one thing, but what if the father is wrong?

The Gospel of Philip continues:

> It is from water and fire that the soul and the spirit came into being. It is from water and fire and light that the son of the bridal chamber (came into being). The fire is the chrism, the light is the fire. I am not referring to that fire which has no form, but to the other fire whose form is white, which is bright and beautiful, and which gives beauty.
> Truth did not come into the world naked, but it came in types and images. The world will not receive truth in any other way. There is a rebirth and an image of rebirth. It is certainly necessary to be born again through the image. Which one? Resurrection.[164]

In the above text, Philip discusses the opposite elements of fire and water, but clearly states that it is not the physical elements, but the idea of these elements. As we know, water puts out fire unless there is an intermediary such as a container like a pot. In this instance, the bridal chamber unites fire and water and gives birth to the son. The idea of the fire gives light, illuminates and helps us see. In addition, he recognises that the light also gives the ability to see beauty thus bringing an aesthetic feeling into the mix. He then states that the origin of truth is through the type and image and that rebirth comes from the recognition of the image. This is the clearest expression of how turning one's attention to the inner

---

[164] Ibid

world of image and idea leads to a new orientation. He continues with this idea:

> The Lord did everything in a mystery, a baptism and a chrism and a Eucharist and a redemption and a bridal chamber. [...] he said, "I came to make the things below like the things above, and the things outside like those inside. I came to unite them in the place." [...] here through types [...]and images.[165]

The union of the opposites in the bridal chamber is the clearest expression of the reality of unconscious processes and that ideas are as real as objects.[166] Philip then confirms the idea that God wants to become man:

> There are two trees growing in Paradise. The one bears animals, the other bears men. Adam ate from the tree which bore animals. He became an animal and he brought forth animals. For this reason the children of Adam worship animals. The tree [...] fruit is [...] increased. [...] ate the [...] fruit of the [...] bears men, [...] man. [...] God created man. [...] men create God. That is the way it is in the world - men make Gods and worship their creation. It would be fitting for the Gods to worship men![167]

He clearly identifies two main trees in the Garden of Eden. The tree of life of necessity and practicality, which takes care of our physical nature as it does the animals. The other tree gives knowledge of good and evil, which is a mental function and something useful in reducing conflict between people. Although some of the text is missing, he says that God created man, men also make Gods as a creative act and that it is fitting that they should also worship men. This could only occur with an all-loving God as the God of Moses achieves worship through fear of punishment and expulsion from the tribe. When a father does not love his sons equally, it causes conflict as we saw with stories of Cain/Abel, Jacob/Esau and the preference for Joseph by Jacob over the other sons. Love is about fairness, justice, acceptance and understanding and it is easier to be yourself and naturally human with a loving father. It is easier to relate to him, as our behaviour is not judged as disrespectful.

In the following text, Philip beautifully relates the growth of the spirit in people to the earth through the language of Plato's Cosmology.

> Farming in the world requires the cooperation of four essential elements. A harvest is gathered into the barn only as a result of the natural action

---

[165] Ibid, page 107

[166] I refer the reader to Chapter 4h on Kant and his observation that the idea of an object is more real and accessible than the object itself.

[167] The Gospel of Philip, Codex II, translated by Wesley W. Isenberg, page 108

of water, earth, wind and light. God's farming likewise has four elements - faith, hope, love, and knowledge. Faith is our earth, that in which we take root. And hope is the water through which we are nourished. Love is the wind through which we grow. Knowledge, then, is the light through which we ripen. Grace exists in four ways: it is earthborn; it is heavenly; [...] the highest heaven; [...] in [...].[168]

The next part of the Nag Hammadi is called the Exegesis on the Soul and gives an unambiguous viewpoint of its nature:

Wise men of old gave the soul a feminine name. Indeed she is female in her nature as well. She even has her womb.[169]

The author's attitude towards the flesh is less negative and seems to recognise the difference between the flesh itself, and the ideas that influence the flesh.

For our struggle is not against flesh and blood - as he said (Ep 6:12) - but against the world rulers of this darkness and the spirits of wickedness.
But when she perceives the straits she is in and weeps before the father and repents, then the father will have mercy on her and he will make her womb turn from the external domain and will turn it again inward, so that the soul will regain her proper character.[170]

He not only warns against prostitution of the body, but more importantly, prostitution of the soul. This is a major problem in this age where the temptation of riches and wealth dictates our behaviour and compromises our ethics. It is literally, selling one's soul for short-term gain. The relationship to the thinking of ancient Greece is again emphasised in the next passage. Eugnostos the Blessed shows a reasoned and logical approach to the Christian tradition.

First Man is 'Faith' ('pistis') for those who will come afterward. He has, within, a unique mind and thought - just as he is it (thought) - reflecting and considering, rationality and power.
Then Son of Man consented with Sophia, his consort, and revealed a great androgynous Light. His masculine name is designated 'Savior, Begetter of All things'. His feminine name is designated 'Sophia, All-Begettress'. Some call her 'Pistis' (faith).
From the consenting of those I have just mentioned, thoughts appeared in the aeons that exist. From thoughts, reflectings; from reflectings,

---

[168] Ibid, page 110
[169] The Exegesis on the Soul, Codex II, translated by William C. Robinson Jr., page 119
[170] Ibid, page 120

considerings; from considerings, rationalities, from rationalities, wills, from wills, words.[171]

The text puts Jesus in relationship to Sophia as his consort thus contrasting the Bible. The Gnostics used the Christian story to understand how these aspects functioned in themselves. Jesus in this instance symbolises the perfect son of the all-loving father, Sophia the wisdom of the father and son's message. The text actually refers to the saviour and Sophia as one androgynous light. This idea actually furthers the story of Jesus in that his inner companion and character gives him as a man the softness, love and wisdom that she represents. Sophia represents the highest level of soul development and the next and final step from the purified and all good Mary. The next text in the Hag Hammadi is the Thunder, Perfect Mind. It comprises a list of opposites attributed to the saviour of which I shall mention only a few:

> For I am the first and the last.
> I am the honored one and the scorned one.
> I am the whore and the holy one.
> I am the wife and the virgin.
> I am <the mother> and the daughter.
> I am the barren one and many are her sons.
> I am she whose wedding is great, and I have not taken a husband.
> I am the bride and the bridegroom, and it is my husband who begot me.
> I am the mother of my father and the sister of my husband and he is my offspring.
> I am the staff of his power in his youth,
> For I am knowledge and ignorance.
> I am shame and boldness.
> I am shameless; I am ashamed.
> I am strength and I am fear.
> I am war and peace. Give heed to me.
> I am the one who is disgraced and the great one.
> But I, I am compassionate and I am cruel.
> Do not hate my obedience and do not love my self-control.
> I am senseless and I am wise.
> Come forward to childhood, and do not despise it because it is small and it is little.
> And do not turn away greatnesses in some parts from the smallnesses, for the smallnesses are known from the greatnesses.
> I, I am sinless, and the root of sin derives from me.
> I am lust in (outward) appearance, and interior self-control exists within me.
> Hear me in gentleness, and learn of me in roughness.
> I am control and the uncontrollable.
> I am the union and the dissolution.[172]

---

[171] Eugnostos the Blessed, Codex III, translated by Douglas M. Parrott, page 134-136

This extensive list of attributes shows how the author regarded his idea of the opposites unified in a single character. These attributes are different when compared to those of the Jesus in the Bible. This character encompasses the opposites in their entirety whereas the attributes of Jesus are described as pure, untainted by the sexual instinct, earthly power and wealth and sits squarely on the side of good. In the next text Asclepius 21-29, a discussion takes place between Asclepius the ancient Greek God of healing in the medical arts, and the son of Apollo, Trismegistus[173] who is similar to Hermes or Mercurius. The discussion includes the physical sexual act and shows how it contains a spiritual aspect:

> And if you (Asclepius) wish to see the reality of this mystery, then you should see the wonderful representation of the intercourse that takes place between the male and the female. For when the semen reaches the climax, it leaps forth. In that moment, the female receives the strength of the male; the male, for his part, receives the strength of the female, while the semen does this.
> "Therefore, the mystery of intercourse is performed in secret, in order that the two sexes might not disgrace themselves in front of many who do not experience that reality.[174]

The above is a good example of how some Gnostics tried to incorporate the reality of our physical nature into a spiritual system of knowledge. The author continues with his view that the Gods made man from matter and that they naturally contain the passions. He also claims that the Gods were created from pure matter and that the immortality of the Gods is learning and knowledge. He then makes the following statement:

> And it happened this way because of the will of God that men be better than the Gods, since, indeed, the Gods are immortal, but men alone are both immortal and mortal.[175]

This reinforces the idea that God wants to become man, or at least, expressed by man. It also shows that we have to stand our ground with our inner characters, as they do not always see things in the best light, particularly if they are undifferentiated from the other characters. It always come back to individual consciousness to either agree or disagree with the ideas, impulses and urges that come from inside. These inner

---

[172] The Thunder, Perfect Mind, Codex VI, Translated by George W. MacRae, pages 168-170

[173] Trismegistus is the purported author of the Hermetic Corpus and founder of Hermeticism

[174] Asclepius 21-29, Codex VI, Translated by James Brashler, Peter Dirkse & Douglas Parrott, page 187

[175] Ibid

characters and their emanations are internal elemental forces, which no human can encompass as their own. They can take possession of the individual, but to believe that we can overcome or kill these forces is a Nietzschian disaster of the highest order. The author continues with his idea that there is equality between man and God:

> Just as God has willed that the inner man be created according to his image, in the very same way, man on earth creates Gods according to his likeness.[176]

This statement suggests that the author had the ability to relate to his inner characters and attempted to show their relationship to the physical world of matter. He later identifies the father God Zeus as 'life' and lord over the earth and sea and the nourishment for life the Kore, who bears the fruit. The following text called The Second Treatise of the Great Seth elaborates the identification with an inner character:

> I am Christ, the Son of Man, the one from you who is among you. I am despised for your sake, in order that you yourselves may forget the difference. And do not become female, lest you give birth to evil and (its) brothers: jealousy and division, anger and wrath, fear and a divided heart, and empty, non-existent desire. But I am an ineffable mystery to you.[177]

This warning is about identifying with our inner female or soul and the dangers inherent in this identification. Indeed, when the inner woman becomes conscious, it is important to stand one's ground as a man and relate to her as if she were a physical woman. Otherwise, as the text says, we find ourselves embroiled in all kinds of moods, intrigues and neurotic symptoms. The opposite also applies when a woman becomes identical and possessed by her inner man resulting in dogmatism and hard headedness. The theme of possession also appears in the Apocalypse of Peter where Jesus talks about himself in the third person:

> The Savior said to me, "He whom you saw on the tree, glad and laughing, this is the living Jesus. But this one into whose hands and feet they drive the nails is his fleshly part, which is the substitute being put to shame, the one who came into being in his likeness. But look at him and me.[178]

---

[176] Ibid, page 188
[177] The Second Treatise of the Great Seth, Codex VII, Translated by Roger Bullard & Joseph Gibbons, page 195
[178] The Apocalypse of Peter, Codex VII, Translated by James Brashler & Roger Bullard, page197

The text shows that Jesus had lost his humanity and felt himself to be other than an ordinary human being. He identified with his inner God to such an extent that it had enveloped his personality and connection to everyday life, which came to an untimely and early end. The danger of possession by an inner father figure can only occur if the father is equally possessive over his son. A reasonable father does not encourage an overly obedient son, as it does not flow towards independence. This is where the Gnostics add new dimensions to the Christian tradition and attempt to balance the one sidedness of Jesus and his identification with inner forces. Even Peter his apostle, realises the danger of identification with an inner character. Silvanus, who accompanied Paul on his missionary journey, emphasises ancient Greek reason and mind, in an attempt to unite it with Christian thought.

> But before everything (else), know your birth. Know yourself, that is, from what substance you are, or from what race, or from what species. Understand that you have come into being from three races: from the earth, from the formed, and from the created. The body has come into being from the earth with an earthly substance, but the formed, for the sake of the soul, has come into being from the thought of the Divine. The created, however, is the mind, which has come into being in conformity with the image of God. The divine mind has substance from the Divine, but the soul is that which he (God) formed for their own hearts. For I think that it (the soul) exists as wife of that which has come into being in conformity with the image, but matter is the substance of the body, which has come into being from the earth.[179]

This text clearly delineates the differing aspects of the human including one's personal history, which is an important factor when a powerful inner character presents itself. Unlike the previous description of type as material, psychic and spiritual in the Tripartite Tractate, this description substitutes and personifies 'psychic' as soul and wife and relates it to image. This is the first indication that Silvanus may have understood the difference between inner character and idea of the character. That is to say, the inner character represents an inner force or urge as an image that changes depending on personal concerns. We can see this in our dreams and how the image of an inner character changes from time to time. It is also the difference between God and the idea of God. The character is the same but his image varies depending on individual interpretation and circumstances. This is why we have so many Gods in the world, all with different orientations. The text continues with a discussion on the male/female pair and the dangers of identifying with the latter.

---

[179] The Teachings of Silvanus, Codex VII, Translated by Malcolm Peel & Jan Zandee, page 200

> If you mix yourself, you will acquire the three parts as you fall from virtue into inferiority. Live according to the Mind. Do not think about things pertaining to the flesh. Acquire strength, for the mind is strong. If you fall from this other, you have become male-female. And if you cast out of yourself the substance of the mind, which is thought, you have cut off the male part, and turned yourself to the female part alone. You have become psychic, since you have received the substance of the formed. If you cast out the smallest part of this, so that you do not acquire again a human part - but you have accepted for yourself the animal thought and likeness - you have become fleshly, since you have taken on animal nature.[180]

The text clearly identifies the dangers of possession by the functions of the inner woman (soul) and the animal nature of the flesh. The author identifies the dual nature of the soul having a view towards God on one side, and the flesh on the other.

> But I say that God is the spiritual one. Man has taken shape from the substance of God. The divine soul shares partly in this one; furthermore, it shares partly in the flesh. The base soul is wont to turn from side to side, [...] which it images the truth.
> Especially has the noetic man been robbed of the intelligence of the snake. For it is fitting for you to be in agreement with the intelligence of (these) two: with the intelligence of the snake and with the innocence of the dove - lest he (the Adversary) come into you in the guise of a flatterer, as a true friend, saying, "I advise good things for you.[181]

Silvanus clearly understands that the wisdom represented by Sophia includes not only the upper peace and spirituality of the dove, but also the cunning and intelligence of the snake and its earth bound nature. The Gnostics sought the positive aspects within earthbound nature. In other words, it is the spirit in matter, the spark in the darkness, the potential in the abyss and in the vile and wretched body and matter. Silvanus believes he can liberate the spirit from earthly concerns into the upper idea of God. "For it (Wisdom) is much gold, which gives you great honour"...... "Entrust yourself to reason and remove yourself from animalism"[182]

The Gnostics acknowledged the revelations and importance of the Christian message and expanded it in both physical and spiritual directions. The life of Jesus is an overcoming of the body and its associated instincts, for the sake of a higher spirit of the mind. The

---

[180] Ibid, page 202
[181] Ibid
[182] Ibid, page 205

Gnostics recognised its place in human evolution and expanded its scope. They introduced Sophia as the function of wisdom and coupled her with Jesus as his consort. According to the bible the women in the life of Jesus had on a secondary role compared to Sophia, who not only elevates the feminine function to a higher and equal status to Jesus, but also gives him her wisdom. This shows that the Christian message is an inner drama for the Gnostics. In addition, and as a counterweight to the introduction of the syzygy, they explore the body and matter to find the spirit of God in what the bible regards as the realm of the Satan. Wisdom includes a relationship to the upper spirit, but also the earth, body, matter and its associated authority. It is wise not to make adversaries out of the prevailing authority when they have power over you. "While it is a skill to speak, it is also a skill to be silent."[183]

The Gnostics regarded enlightenment as a journey from the beast to God enhanced with a reasoned approach learned from the ancient Greek philosophers, and how the spirit works within the material world. When the mainstream Christian ministry was established, it outlawed other viewpoints and Gnosticism went underground and became a private viewpoint with an association to Alchemy. Gnosticism was to some extent coupled with Alchemy and men such as Hermes Trismegistus and Zosimos of Panopolis continued the tradition and research to find the upper spirit in matter through experiment and the transformation of materials such as metals.

g. Alchemy

Alchemy grew out of the visions and experience of the Gnostics to some extent, but its origins can be traced back to the ancient pre-Socratic philosopher Democritus (460 – 370BC) who postulated the theory that matter was made of discreet spherical parcels called 'atoms'. The Gnostics were concerned with extracting the spirit from the body through knowledge (gnosis). The early alchemists were concerned with extracting the spirit from metals through the transmutation of a base metal to appear like a precious metal with a coloured tincture. They also purified silver and gold of their natural contaminants.[184]

Alchemy was a worldwide ancient belief system with practitioners in Hellenistic Egypt, India, Near East, East Asia and Europe. It is debateable whether alchemical ideas migrated to these distant locations

---

[183] The Sentences of Sextus, Codex XII, Translated by Frederick Wisse, page 259
[184] GRIMES, Shannon L., Zosimus of Panopolis: Alchemy, Nature and Religion in Late Antiquity, 2006, PHD Dissertation Syracuse University, page 121

or was generated spontaneously and independently. Alchemy was likely discovered independently because it had much to do with the development of metallurgy and processing metals. Copper and tin combined to form bronze in 3500 BC; the extraction of iron from its ore in 1200 BC and the smelting and purification of silver and gold were commonplace. Ideas like the circumcision rituals of the Middle East and Australian Aborigines became conscious independently with no obvious contact between cultures.

There is no doubt that ancient alchemy was steeped in spirituality, as its language refers to the extraction of a purified spirit from base material (prima materia) and the transformation of the primordial man (anthropos) to a self-aware and unified spiritual man through the process. The basis for the process is the projection of unconscious contents onto matter, much the same as the ancients projected their Gods onto the planets. The transformation from lower to higher and higher to lower form has several methods that are highly symbolic in nature.

Western alchemy began in Hellenistic Egypt at Alexandria; the city founded by Alexander the Great close the mouth of the Nile. Mary the Prophetess was the first known western alchemist and lived between the first and third centuries AD, during the time the Christian ministry established itself amongst the people. Although none of her writings were found, she is credited with the invention of the first alchemical apparatus and short aphorisms such as "Join the male and the female, and you will find what is sought", and the famous Axiom of Maria "One become two, two becomes three, and out of the third comes the one as the fourth". She also created the Tribikos, which has three arms and used for substance purification through distillation; the Kertakis, a hermetically sealed vessel for heating substances and collecting vapours, and the a double boiler called the Bain-marie (Mary's bath), which gives a gentle heat used for cooking and keeping food warm.

The next major Alchemist and Gnostic philosopher was Zosimos of Panopolis in the 3rd and 4th centuries AD in Panopolis, present day Akhimim. C. G. Jung studied his works and visions[185] for their psychological and symbolic content from which he concluded that Zosimos created a method to transform one's personality through projection onto metals and other substances. He noted that the goal of the procedure was akin to the idea of individuation, which is a natural flow of one's life and a similar idea to the Tao in the East. One of the most outstanding conclusions he came to from his study of Alchemy, is the link

---

[185] See Jung's comprehensive study on alchemy in his collected works: Psychology and Alchemy, Alchemical Studies and Mysterium Coniunctionis.

between ancient Platonic Cosmology, modern day psychology and the physical sciences. He believed the alchemical processes are coming back to consciousness after being driven underground by the establishment of the Christian ministry.

The visions of Zosimos show a parallel between the purification of metals and the purification of the soul therefore both material and psychological. Unlike popular opinion, the alchemists were not concerned with the transformation of one metal to another, but the purification and colouring of metals with tinctures to reflect the psychological changes they were experiencing. The Hellenistic-Egyptian alchemists related the base metal itself to the body and associated instincts and the characteristics of the metal to the spirit. This included its colour and how different tinctures and volatile elements such as mercury, sulphur and arsenic affected it. Zosimos believed that he could change a metal and hence the body into spirit by changing the colour with a tincture.[186]

This transmutation occurred with changes of colour of the base metals in the following sequence: black (melanosis), white (leukosis), yellow (xanthosis) and finishing with red/violet (iosis), which was a synonym for the Philosophers Stone and the goal of the process, although this varied between alchemists. Zosimos felt that it was a natural process over time and could not be rushed or circumvented. He also equated the sun, moon and other planets with metals and how they transformed to approximate the heavenly bodies, thus relating it to early Egyptian and Greek mythology. This relationship is described in his visions where he finds himself in front of a sacrificer and altar and is dismembered with a sword, the pieces of flesh burned and cooked upon the fire and transformed into spirit. The precursor to the idea was part of the mythology of ancient Egypt and Greece with the dismemberment of Osiris and Dionysus.

Zosimos sees a multitude of people cooking in boiling water and an elderly barber tells him that the boiling water is the entrance and exit to transformation, which enables the spirit to escape from the body. A brazen priest holding a leaden tablet both sacrifices, and is sacrificed. Zosimos finds himself outside the place of punishments and meets a barber clad in a royal purple robe who walks in and is consumed by fire. Zosimos struggles with himself about going into the place of punishments and sees a white old man called Agathodaimon who looks at him and becomes his guide. He is led to the altar and the place of punishments and Agathodaimon transforms into a pillar of fire. Zosimos realises that the lead (body) is to be rejected.

---

[186] GRIMES, Shannon L., Zosimus of Panopolis: Alchemy, Nature and Religion in Late Antiquity, 2006, PHD Dissertation Syracuse University, page 27-32

The priest tells Zosimos that he who changes the body to blood, makes the eyes clairvoyant, and raises the dead. He sees a white man with a sword approaching from the east accompanied by another man named the Meridian of the Sun. The first man tells the other man to "cut off his head, immolate his body, cut it to pieces, boil the pieces according to the method and deliver them to the place of punishment". Zosimos equates this vision with the "liquids in the arts of the metals" and the man with the sword tells him that the descent of the seven steps causes the waters to gush forth from all of his moist places.

The visions continue with Zosimos seeing an altar in the shape of a bowl with a fiery spirit tending the fire for the men being boiled and burnt alive. The spirit explains that the process is called embalming and those who seek to obtain the art should enter here and shed the grossness of the body to become spirit. Zosimos is instructed to build a circular temple from a single stone with a spring inside of pure water sparkling like the sun. He is to take a sword and immolate the dragon guarding the entrance, strip its skin, separate the limbs and make a step out of its flesh and bones, and is told what he seeks he will find in the temple. The brazen priest is now the silver man and can soon become the golden man.

Zosimos recognises and understands from the last vision that the opposites of speaking/hearing, giving/receiving and poor/rich are beautiful. Zosimos asks the brazen priest how nature teaches giving and receiving and the priest explains that metal gives and plants receive; stars give and flowers receive; heavens give and earth receives and thunderclaps give forth darting fire. All things weave together and undo again, all things mingle, combine, unite, separate, moisten and dry, flourish and fade, in the bowl of the altar. He also explains how all things 'come to pass' with the method in fixed measure and exact weight into the four elements. The weaving together and undoing of all things brings an increase and decrease and through the harmonies of separating and combining and use of the method, brings forth nature. "For nature applied to nature transforms nature. Such is the order of natural law throughout the whole cosmos, and thus all things hang together".[187]

Zosimos was aware of the opposites of matter and psyche and what he called "Cosmic Sympathy" as their unity. The unity is the method or process, which unites the opposites in understanding, and as Zosimos suggests, his visions were as important as the physical work of treating

---

[187] The visions of Zosimos are taken from the comprehensive work done by Jung in his book Alchemical Studies, Vol 13, Princeton University Press, 1976, page 59

metals. Jung wrote a comprehensive study on these visions so I do not need to look at the symbolic content much further other than to add a few comments and relate the method to everyday life. Jung equates the miraculous water (aqua permanens) extracted from the lapis[188] (stone of understanding, incorruptibility and stability) with the anima mundi (feminine soul) imprisoned in matter, which is set free by dividing and cooking the body into four elements. We can equate the waters gushing forth from all the moist places as coming from the eyes, mouth, nose, penis, female urethra, skin and on occasion, rectum. The eyes are where we let out pent up emotions and anguish through crying. Similarly, illness lets go of bodily contents through vomiting, mucous, sweating out a fever, diarrhoea and so on. It is therefore, letting go of what is inside and presumably why they regarded the body as gross. I would suggest however, that Zosimos's vision concerns "gushing forth" of emotion, particularly, anguish when trying to overcome the body's needs.[189] Water as Jung suggests, has a feminine quality, which most men repress for the sake of adaptation and strength in the world.

The four elements in these visions refer to Plato's earth, air, fire and water, and in Jungian terms can be associated with the four orienting functions of sensation, thinking, intuition and feeling. The cooking process separates the elements and differentiates them before union through the relating principle of the soul. The elements or functions relate to each other in specific ways. For example water puts out fire and erodes earth, fire consumes earth and heats water and so on. Zosimos lived a few centuries after the opposites of an upper God and lower devil were differentiated in the life of Jesus. With the inspiration of the Christian message, spiritually oriented men were trying to overcome the natural man and associated instincts for the idea of a purified and untainted man. This is why the alchemists believed that the human body was gross rather than simply natural, as our bodies have the same functions as other mammals.

The symbolic decapitation of the head is particularly important as this separation gives an individual the opportunity to look at his or her body and its instinctive functions from an unattached objective viewpoint. From this viewpoint we can see the symbolic qualities of bodily functions and find the spirit in them. For example, sexual intercourse transforms from

---

[188] The same idea occurs in the Torah –Numbers 20.8 when Moses extracts water from a rock with his rod "Take the rod, and assemble the congregation, thou, and Aaron thy brother, and speak ye unto the rock before their eyes, that it give forth its water; and thou shalt bring forth to them water out of the rock; so thou shalt give the congregation and their cattle drink."

[189] Obviously it is impossible to overcome all the body's needs as the satisfaction of our thirst and hunger is a necessity for life.

the overpowering penetration of the feminine as in nature, to the union of equal partners where the man gives his attention, seed and strength to the woman.[190]. More importantly, it connects the man to his inner feminine soul through the symbolic act. If a man dreams of having intercourse with a woman, it is more likely to be a union with his inner female character (soul). It is important to know the difference between these inner characters and real people, as we tend to see the former in the latter through projection.

The dismemberment and cooking of the body, as Jung points out, is accepting self-sacrifice to find the inner spirit. The idea is not new and part of our psychic structure, which occurs many times in many cultures. Osiris willingly stepped into a chest, was later dismembered and his sexual instinct transformed with the help of his sister wife Isis and son Horus. Jesus willingly suffered torture and an agonising death to be resurrected days later. The common theme in these examples is to differentiate the spirit from the body with a descent to hell, dismemberment, crucifixion, entombing, boiling, burning, torment, pain and so on, before the ascension to heaven. In other words, it is a sacrifice of outer attachments to the physical world, a journey into ourselves to find the soul(s) and her accompanying spirit and relate them to the body and physical world.

How does one go about this in our everyday lives? This question is difficult to answer as it varies from person to person. Obviously, death and torture is symbolic for the self-sacrifice of one's attachments, needs and desires. As Zosimos says, it is a natural process and unfolds in its own time. We all go through symbolic deaths and resurrections in our lives. For example, the transition from childhood to adulthood through puberty and the expulsion from paradise is an agonising period for the individual as their behaviour indicates. A milder example includes the transition from one life to another, such as single life for married life and the responsibility of partner and children. Another example is the transition from one function to another like a sense oriented sport or physical activity to an intellectual pursuit. Another could be a concern for tools and objects to more interest in people. Yet another, the change from outer to inner interests like dreams, visions, ideas and the functioning of the inner world.

Transformations like these require the sacrifice of previous concerns and interests for new activities and interests. One-sidedness applies to both spirit and body and can be detrimental to the wellbeing of either. "Too much of the animal distorts the civilized man; too much civilization makes

---

[190] Gnostic text Asclepius 21-29

sick animals".[191] Another way to become aware of the opposites is to consciously remove oneself from the world. This enables us to reflect on our place in it and encourages relationship to our inner world. As mentioned previously, it depends on one's type and natural orientation. For example, the hairy and down to earth Esau from the Torah could do with some of the spirit and introversion of his brother Jacob. Then again, Jacob could learn from Esau how to forgive and be upright and honest.

Introspection enables us to "know oneself" in Gnostic terms, and how we behave and relate to others. In this way we can transform the idea of a person to a closer approximation of their reality. Jung regarded it as withdrawing the projection, but the work of Kant and his conviction that we cannot know the object and only the idea of the object, indicates a different system. We always have an idea of a person even after removing a projection. In other words, knowledge and experience of a person makes the person clearer and the idea of them changes into one closer to their reality.

The ancients projected their inner characters onto the planets and stars and endowed them with magical significance and personality. Today we know that the sun is an insignificant star fuelled by nuclear fusion, yet its influence on our lives has not changed since the ancients. The idea has changed through knowledge but its influence and our experience of it, has not. It is still the source of all life on earth and we depend on it for everything. Part of the idea transformed but part of it remains the same. Similarly, the idea of another person includes their physical characteristics, which change very little over time. This shows that the idea of a person or object is partly based on perceived physical qualities and partly on their behaviour. An idea of something still includes how its looks, so withdrawing the projection of a deity onto the sun doesn't change that part of the idea that includes its heating, lighting and life giving properties, which is anchored in its physical nature.

The ultimate goal however, is to know the difference between the physical world of object and people, and the inner world of ideas and characters. It is a common mistake to regard the things in our mind as created and belonging to us. The fact is, ideas and inner characters quite often have us, rather than we have them. We can see this in the way professions possess individuals so they feel they are that character. The same goes for political movements of left and right, when in reality, we are capable of both left and right attitudes. We never seem to understand that socialism is like a traditional mother wanting to take care of everyone

---

[191] JUNG, C.G., Two Essay on Analytical Psychology, Vol. 7, Princeton University Press, 1972, page 28

equally in a collective, and conservatism a traditional father wanting to help everyone stand on their own two feet and be independent. Naturally, there are many shades between these two sides and Alchemy's goal is to unite them in one attitude. This is what they call the 'Philosophers Stone' (Lapis Philosophorum). It is the stable, solid, incorruptible and understanding attitude that sees the physical world in all its shades and the inner world of ideas and characters, and not identifying with either.

The method or process of transformation, as described by Zosimos, begins with the original state of black, living in the body; the whitening is extracting the spirit of awareness and understanding, thus forming the pair of opposites black and white[192]. The next stage the yellowing and differentiating the opposites through the mediums of fire, heat and the fluidity of intuition and distilling the differences and similarities. The final stage in the process is the reddening and the relating function, which brings the differentiated opposites into the royal pair (purple) and the emergence of the central inner character (Lapis), which includes body, soul and spirit united. It should be kept in mind that this is a method devised by Zosimos and may vary depending on an individual's typology.

Alchemy not only had a strong relationship to Gnosticism, but also Hermeticism, which is based partly on the sacred texts purportedly, written by Hermes Trismegistus, called the Corpus Hermetica. It is a compilation of seventeen books of numbered sayings and sentences, which describes the differences between the physical and psychic.

> First, God; Secondly, the World; Thirdly, Man.
> The World for Man, Man for God.
> Of the Soul, that part which is Sensible is mortal, but that which is
> Reasonable is immortal.
> Every thing that is, is double.
> The Mind in God.
> Reason in the Mind.
> The Mind is void of suffering.
> Nothing good upon Earth, nothing evil in Heaven.
> God is good, Man is evil.
> Time is the Corruption of Man.
> The Earth is brutish, the Heaven is reasonable or rational.[193]

The above text shows a similar understanding of the body, soul and spirit to Zosimos. Hermes also has a similar attitude toward the body being evil and corrupt, and the mind and pure thought as good. The striving for the light of the mind over the instinctuality and functions of the body still

---

[192] This is colour symbology of the opposites of female/male, in/out, unconscious/conscious and so on.

[193] HERMES Trismestigustus, The Corpus Hermetica, First Book, pages 3-5

preoccupies the alchemists in this era. It is clearly a mental activity and that God is rational, reasonable and good, whereas man is corrupt, the double of God and evil. The next passage shows the differentiation of the Platonic elements into two pairs of opposites.

> 6. Then from that Light, a certain Holy Word joined itself unto Nature, and out flew the pure and unmixed Fire from the moist Nature upward on high; it is exceeding Light, and Sharp, and Operative withal. And the Air which was also light, followed the Spirit and mounted up to Fire (from the Earth and the Water) insomuch that it seemed to hang and depend upon it.
> 7. And the Earth and the Water stayed by themselves so mingled together, that the Earth could not be seen for the Water, but they were moved, because of the Spiritual Word that was carried upon them.[194]

The pair of opposites are fire/air and earth/water. This projection of ideas onto the material world shows that he realised there is relationship and unity in reality, but preferred the spirit (fire/air) to the base material (earth/water). This stage is equivalent to the differentiation of white from black as opposites in the method of Zosimos. Hermes describes the opposites as "Mind being God, male and female, Life and Light,......"[195] then the connection between the two pairs as follows:

> 23. Which when he saw, having in itself the unsatiable Beauty and all the Operation of the Seven Governors, and the Form or Shape of God, he Smiled for love, as if he had seen the Shape or Likeness in the Water, or the shadow upon the Earth of the fairest Human form.[196]

The differentiation brings forth much feeling and recognition of the beauty and love of the relationship between the opposites. This emphasises the way the upper form reflects the water and the shadow that falls upon the earth.

> 26. And for this cause, Man above all things that live upon Earth, is double; Mortal because of his Body, and Immortal because of the substantial Man: For being immortal, and having power of all things, he yet suffers mortal things, and such as are subject to Fate or Destiny.
> 27. And therefore being; above all Harmony, he is made and become a servant to Harmony. And being Hermaphrodite, or Male and Female, and watchful, he is governed by and subjected to a Father, that is both Male and Female and watchful.

This is the first indication of a harmonious quaternity union with an emphasis on the hermaphroditic nature of the father who is aware

---

[194] Ibid, The Second Book. Called "Poemander" page 6
[195] Ibid, page 7
[196] Ibid

148

(watchful) of the opposites and how they interact. The conflict common between opposites has in this text been resolved into a harmonious interplay of male/female, with the characteristics of fire/air and earth/water. This pairing is particular to Hermes as an individual, as there are many possible combinations of the elements and how they relate. In this case, air supports fire and is necessary for light; earth and water intertwined and sit nicely alongside each other. Additional interactions include air bringing forth water in the form of rain; water puts out fire; fire transforms water into air (steam) through earth in the form of a vessel; water erodes earth; earth is consumed by air and fire; air moves earth and gives water.

Hermes then disparages worldly concerns of power, wealth, deceit of concupiscence, ambition, boldness, confidence etc., and praises the characteristics of his inner God as father of all things, will, word, image, pure soul, unformed, strength, excellence and so on.

> 18. For shining steadfastly upon, and round about the whole Mind it enlighteneth all the Soul ; and loosing it from the Bodily Senses and Motions, it draweth it from the Body, and changeth it wholly into the Essence of God.[197]

The text describes the transformation of the soul (inner female) loosened from bodily senses and into the realm of the mind and consciousness. This shows that the evolution of humanity at this time had a similar viewpoint to the Christian story. The soul needs separation from the body and elevated to the idea of God. This does raise a curious question though. If the soul is elevated beyond the physical nature of the body and what animates the body removed, an empty shell is left behind. Even Jesus is reported to have had a physical relationship with Mary Magdala and was often seen kissing her on the mouth. What Hermes is missing or unwilling to acknowledge is the dual nature of the soul that is often characterised by two women, one light and pure, and the other darker and down to earth. Mary, the mother of Jesus and Mary Magdala are an example of such a pair. Hermes continues with his 'either or' of the soul and how she is, if not liberated from the body.

> 27. And the wickedness of a Soul is ignorance; for the Soul that knows nothing of the things that are, neither the Nature of them, nor that which is good, but is blinded, rusheth and dasheth against the bodily Passions, and unhappy as it is, not knowing itself, it serveth strange Bodies, and evil ones, carrying the Body as a burthen, and not ruling, but ruled. And this is the mischief of the Soul.[198]

---

[197] Ibid, The Third Book. Called "The Holy Sermon", page 14
[198] Ibid

Hermes explores the senses and their relationship to knowledge by saying "Knowledge is the end of sense" and attempts to relate them in the following sentence:

> 34. Knowledge is the gift of God ; for all Knowledge is unbodily but useth the Mind as an Instrument, as the Mind useth the Body.[199]

He then states something quite remarkable and recognises not only psychic reality, but also the underlying unity within it.

> 39. Because the World Is a Sphere, that is a Head, and above the head there is nothing material, as beneath the feet there is nothing intellectual.
> 42. The whole is a living wight, and therefore consisteth of material and intellectual.[200]

He draws a definite distinction between a mental or psychic process and the physical world of matter but stops short of recognising the psychic aspect of matter or the difference between matter and the idea of matter as described by Kant. The above does show that he has an intuition about psychic reality and recognises it as a sphere being the head. Hermes then elaborates on the spherical nature of reality by connecting the spirit to the body.

> 46. But the Soul of Man is carried in this manner, The Mind is in Reason, Reason in the Soul, the Soul in the Spirit, the Spirit in the Body.[201]

He returns to the elements and how they relate to each other in the following:

> 60. When therefore the Mind is separated, and departeth from the earthly Body, presently it puts on its Fiery Coat, which it could not do having to dwell in an Earthly Body.
> 61. For the Earth cannot suffer fire, for it is all burned of a small spark; therefore is the water poured round about the Earth, as a Wall or defence, to withstand the flame of fire.

As mentioned previously and reinforced by Hermes's own text, the earth is consumed by the spirit (fire) and needs the intermediary function of water as the third uniting function to temper fire and relate them. He does hint at an earthly character represented by water but stops short at naming her as another soul. He does however hint at another soul later in the text: "7. For where there is a Soul, there is the Mind, as where there is

---

[199] Ibid, page 15
[200] Ibid
[201] Ibid

150

Life, there is also a Soul."[202] Hermes equates God with the sun as the most influential of the heavenly bodies and greater than earth and water in the following:

> 15. The Sun is the greatest of the Gods in heaven, to whom all the heavenly Gods give place, as to a King and potentate; and yet he being such a one, greater than the Earth or the Sea, is content to suffer infinite lesser stars to walk and move above himself; whom doth he fear the while, O Son?[203]

Humanity identified the sun with a great deity due its overwhelming and far-reaching influence over our body and earth. Today we know its atomic structure and how it burns and have to some extent transformed the idea of it. The former projection of a deity onto the sun still exists as well, in the form of an all light giving powerful idea of father and consciousness. Hermes equates God to a 'workman' like a carver or painter seen in the mind that has no body but creates bodies in the physical world. He then puts all the elements together in one passage with God in the central place, which not only holds the unity together, but also relates the elements to each other.

> 25. Hermes. Yet is it so, as I say, O Son, He that Looketh Only upon that which is carried upward as Fire, that which is carried downward as Earth, that which is moist as Water, and that which bloweth or is subject to blast as Air; how can he sensibly understand that which is neither hard, nor moist, nor tangible, nor perspicuous, seeing it is only understood in power and operation; but I beseech and pray to the Mind which alone can understand the Generation, which is in God.[204]

This passage shows that each element has its place but can only be differentiated and united through the understanding of God. The text indicates that Hermes knows how to see his God not only in sleep, but during the day through synchronicity, association and amplification.

> 105. For with this living wight alone is God familiar; in the night by dreams, in the day by Symbols or; Signs.[205]

The following passages show that Hermes was still on the assent to overcome the natural man in himself and his unity still lies in the rarefied air of heaven.

---

[202] Ibid, The Eleventh Book. Of the Common Mind to Tat, page 40
[203] Ibid, The Fifth Book, page 19
[204] Ibid, The Seventh Book, His Secret Sermon in the Mount of Regeneration, and the Profession of Silence. To His Son Tat, page 25
[205] Ibid, The Eleventh Book, Of the Common Mind to Tat, page 45

29. For the things that are, being two Bodies, and things incorporeal, wherein is the Mortal and the Divine, the Election or Choice of either is left to him that will choose; For no man can choose both.

30. And of which soever the choice is made, the other being diminished or overcome, magnifieth the act and operation of the other.[206]

The work of Hermes was a signpost in humanity's evolution and part of the era where the spirit of good was approached through overcoming the body, which was regarded as negative. The liberation of the spirit from matter and the body brings us to heaven. The liberation of the spirit from heaven brings us down to earth. The centre between heaven and earth is what Jung calls the 'Self'. It is the inner character that unites above and below and capable of both good and evil. Identification with either side negates the unity between them. Just as the physical world is outside of us and objective, so too is the inner world of image and idea, which is equally objective. This brings the individual down to normal parameters and liberates him or her from the identification of body with evil. Behaviour expresses good and evil which can be spiritual as well as physical. Jung feels that a morally neutral stance is preferred, although this is difficult to achieve. We always feel very protective over our family and no amount of understanding would accept their destruction.

Medieval Alchemy was an undercurrent to the Christian church and remained hidden for centuries because it was regarded is as heretical. Notable Alchemists that braved the wrath of the church and tried to add alchemical knowledge and experience to the Christian doctrine were Albertus Magnus, Roger Bacon and Thomas Aquinas. At the latter stage of the medieval period and the beginning of the Renaissance Theophrastus von Hohenheim, commonly referred to as Paracelsus, was born in 1494. He was a Swiss physician, astrologer, philosopher, and alchemist and noted for being the father of toxicology. Although Paracelsus regarded himself as a Christian, he sought divine inspiration from nature and his own capacity for reason, which often led him to conclusions at odds with Christian doctrine.

Like previous alchemists, he had disdain for the body and its natural functions and regarded the flesh as twofold in nature. The first we share with beasts is physical and carnal, and the second purified non-physical and sidereal. He was a difficult man with a volatile temper and often critical of his contemporaries regarding the practice of medicine. He had however, great compassion for his patients and dedicated his life and work to their healing. He regarded the only true healing of the body and soul was through the integration of the idea of God and his relationship to nature. This led him to conclusions completely at odds with the Christian

---

[206] Ibid, The Twelfth Book His Crater or Monas, page 48

faith he so cherished. For example, he believed that under certain circumstances, polygamy was not only understandable, but necessary.[207]

Paracelsus's approach to medicine was spiritual and required the spirit's extraction as the entity that heals 'that does not die' from the body. He sought out many different people, from barbers to nobles, to learn his art in his quest to understand the human condition. He had a conception of the unconscious he termed the 'matrix' or 'maternal womb', as the origin of the world and all its creatures. God created man so that his spirit had a dwelling place in the flesh, which correlates with early Gnostic and Alchemical ideas.[208] He regarded the primordial body made of four (?) elements including mercury, sulphur and salt and in them the opposites of day/night, warmth/coldness etc., still unformed and requiring differentiation (separatio). Man received his carnal body from earth and water and his sidereal body from fire and air.

> Hence man has also an animal body and a sidereal body; and both are one, and are not separated. The relations between the two are as follows. The animal body, the body of flesh and blood, is in itself always dead. Only through the action of the sidereal body does the motion of life come into the other body. The sidereal body is fire and air; but it is also bound to the animal life of man. Thus mortal man consists of water. earth, fire, and air.[209]

Paracelsus, as did other Alchemists, attempted to reconcile the Platonic elements with the human body and spirit. He states that man has two fathers, one the earth, the other heaven, and from the earth, he receives his material body, and heaven his character. This insight into personality and where it comes from laid the groundwork for future research into our nature and typology. He describes the composition of character as three parts complementing sulphur, mercury and salt with feeling, wisdom and art, which as opposites, are one. He continues with a description of more functions of character and their permutations which is an early form of psychological types:

> The body has four kinds of taste-the sour, the sweet, the bitter, and the salty. . . . They are to be found in every creature, but only in man can they be studied. . . . Everything bitter is hot and dry, that is to say, choleric; everything sour is cold and dry, that is to say, melancholic. . . . The sweet gives rise to the phlegmatic, for everything sweet is cold and moist, even though it must not be compared to water. . . . The sanguine originates in the salty, which is hot and moist. . . . the salty

---

[207] PARACELSUS, Selected Writings, Edited by Jolande Jacobi, Bollingen Series, Princeton University Press, 1995, page 36
[208] Ibid, page 13
[209] Ibid, page 18

predominates in man as compared with the three others, he is sanguine; if the bitter is predominant in him, he is choleric. The sour makes him melancholic, and the sweet, if it predominates, phlegmatic. Thus the four tempers are rooted in the body of man as in garden mould.

From the above we can see the emerging awareness and knowledge of character differences and how they relate to each other. He continues with the idea that the sun, moon, planets and stars are contained within man in the 'young heaven' in contrast the 'great heaven' of God. This shows an awareness of projection and further differentiation between the physical cosmos and the inner cosmos as expressed by the characters of ancient Egypt and Greece. To them there was no difference; the Gods were the stars and planets. Paracelsus knew the difference, "For what is outside is also inside; and what is not outside man is not inside."[210]

Paracelsus discusses the need for chastity to ensure a pure heart. His attitude towards women is one of respect for their function as mothers given by God. He never married though and lost his personal mother when he was seven or eight years old. He therefore saw the mother and maternal womb (matrix) as an inner character, which gave birth to a 'pearl' (spirit) of God. He also regarded the process of conception, incubation and birth in an alchemical or spiritual light where the seed of man and woman combined and transformed into a third new function (child). God gives the child spirit, soul, reason and understanding.[211] These opposites of male/female differentiate into two natures, the first from the stars, second from the material elements. He states:

> The light of nature in man comes from the stars, and his flesh and blood belong to the material elements. Thus two influences operate in man. One is that of the firmamental light, which includes wisdom, art, reason. All these are the children of this father. . . . The second influence emanates from matter, and it includes concupiscence, eating, drinking, and everything that relates to the flesh and blood. Therefore one must not ascribe to the stars that which originates in the blood and flesh. For heaven does not endow one with concupiscence or greed. . . . From heaven come only wisdom, art, and reason.
> *As* great as the difference in form and shape between the two bodies, the visible and the invisible, the material and the eternal, is the difference between their natures. . . . They are like a married pair, one in the flesh, but twofold in their nature. . . . And because this is so, a contradiction dwells in man. . . . Namely, the stars in him have a different disposition, a different mind, a different orientation than the lower elements; and on the other hand, these elements in turn have a different wisdom and a different disposition than the stars in man. [212]

---

[210] Ibid, page 21
[211] Ibid, page 30
[212] Ibid, page 41

The text describes how the two natures of the physical body and the ethereal body, want to exceed their bounds and expel the other giving rise to enmity. Paracelsus puts forward a possible solution to this problem using a third uniting function as a container. He describes the two halves united into one whole man; "they are like two men united in one body,"[213] and hints at the actual difference between the two sides in the following passage:

> Thoughts are free and are subject to no rule. On them rests the freedom of man, and they tower above the light of nature. For thoughts give birth to a creative force that is neither elemental nor sidereal.[214]

He elaborates on this idea by citing the example of a carpenter who builds a house in his head, combines the idea with experience and builds the house through 'active practice'. As we shall see later, Paracelsus equates this as an alchemical process of inception, transformation of base material (prima materia) through spirit (idea) to final perfected work. This is like the creative process of a sculptor having an idea (spirit) and bringing it into physical reality as a work of art through experience (skill) and practice (moulding and shaping). Indeed, Paracelsus puts great emphasis on his medical training and practice as an art. He goes as far as regarding medicine having four pillars namely: Philosophy, astronomy, alchemy and ethics.

Paracelsus then makes a curious statement "A man without a woman is not whole, only with a woman is he whole."[215] It is clear from what follows that this is an inner union of male and female as he says in the following sentence: "Similarly, man and remedy derive from the same substance, and both together form a whole, that is to say, a whole man... In this sense, the disease desires its wife, that is, the medicine."[216] Finding the neglected opposite in his patients is Paracelsus's secret to healing. He later differentiates spiritual and physical diseases but stops short at being able to cure spiritual diseases without a physical remedy. This reluctance to see psychic material on its own is understandable as the psyche itself communicates in images borrowed from the physical world. Dreams for example, use familiar imagery, yet the laws of physics do not apply to their behaviour, and this is how it reflects our physical life. The text continues with the typical alchemical cooking, burning, purifying process of transformation and the creative act of building:

---

[213] Ibid, page 43. This is a classical Alchemical image of two halves with different characteristics such as Bishop/King or a man with sun/moon head and so on.
[214] Ibid, page 45
[215] Ibid, page 73
[216] Ibid, page 74

Just as gold is of little use if it has not gone through fire, so there is little virtue or use in a remedy that has not been purified in fire. For all things must go through fire in order to attain to a new birth, in which they are useful to man.[217]

When a carpenter builds a house, it first lives in him as an idea; and the house is built according to this idea. Therefore, from the form of the house, one can make inferences about the carpenter's ideas and images.[218]

In the next section, Paracelsus characterises fire with the ancient Roman God Vulcan, and again equates the alchemical transformation with known metallurgical processes and the everyday day task of cooking food.

God created iron but not that which is to be made of it. . . He enjoined fire, and Vulcan, who is the lord of fire, to do the rest. . . . From this it follows that iron must be cleansed of its dross before it can be forged. This process is alchemy; its founder is the smith Vulcan. What is accomplished by fire is alchemy-whether in the furnace or in the kitchen stove.[219]

He discusses dreams as one of the primary expressions of unconscious material and the importance of their interpretation:

The interpretation of dreams is a great art. Dreams are not without meaning wherever they may come from-from fantasy, from the elements, or from another inspiration. Often one can find something supernatural in them. For the spirit is never idle. If the earth gives us an inspiration-one of her gifts-and if she confers it upon us through her spirit, then the vision has a meaning.

Anyone who wants to take his dream seriously, interpret it, and be guided by it, must be endowed with "sidereal knowledge" and the light of nature, and must not engage in absurd fantasies, nor look upon his dreams from the heights of his arrogance; for in this way nothing can be done with them. Dreams must be heeded and accepted. For a great many of them come true.

For the most part presentiments appear to man in so unimpressive a form that they are ignored. And yet Joseph discovered in his sleep who Mary was and by whom she was with child. And because dreams are not sufficiently heeded, no faith is put in their revelations, although they are nothing other than prophecies.

---

[217] Ibid, page 90
[218] Ibid, Man and Works, Inner and Outer Worlds, page 123
[219] Ibid, page 93

The dreams which reveal the supernatural are promises and messages that God sends us directly; they are nothing but His angels, His ministering spirits, who usually appear to US when we are in a great predicament. . . . Of such apparitions we must know how they take place and how they come to us; when we are in great need, we can obtain them from God's kindness if our prayer pours in true faith from a truthful mouth and heart.

Then God sends us such a messenger who appears to us in spirit, warns us, consoles us, teaches us, and brings us His good tidings. From time immemorial artistic insights have been revealed to artists in their sleep and in dreams, so that at all times they ardently desired them. From time immemorial artistic insights have been revealed to artists in their sleep and in dreams, so that at all times they ardently desired them.[220]

There is not much I can add to this except to say that this attitude was carried through to the ground-breaking studies of the late nineteenth and early twentieth centuries by Freud, Jung and others. Paracelsus describes the Arcanum (secret medicines) and their fourfold virtue. The first stage begins with 'prima materia'. The second the 'lapis philosophorum' which purifies the body of filth and bring fresh young energy, the third 'Mercurius vitae' which renovates the old body and finally, the 'Tinctura' which removes the harmful parts, its crudity and incompleteness and transforms everything into a pure, noble and indestructible being. This final stage is often represented by the Uroboros, which is the serpent or dragon eating its own tale. At this stage, projection is lessened and we are open to the reality of both idea and object and more importantly, their differences. Emotional outbursts decrease, as we tend to look inside behind the affect for the image(s) that helps us understand ourselves. This is a lifelong task, and situations will challenge the integrity of the closed system and break it apart. Understanding and reason liberate us from the chaos of external events as we have an inner order and stability. The text continues with the importance of knowledge, reason and feeling in understanding:

Wisdom consists in knowing and not in imagining; a man who has wisdom understands all things and uses them with reason, his reason and wisdom are free from stupidity, free from folly, free from confusion and doubt.

The nature of a man's virtue is like that of his feelings. His treasure lies where his heart is.[221]

---

[220] Ibid, Man and Works, Interpretation of Dreams, page 134-136
[221] Ibid, Man and Works, Knowledge and Faith, page 163-164

Indeed, if one feels another's viewpoint with knowledge and reason and free of judgement, we can understand where the other person is in their life process and behave accordingly. This does not mean that the outcome will necessarily be harmonious or pleasant, as some people need to be 'kicked in the bottom' metaphorically speaking, and benefit from an honest and open response. Paracelsus continues his differentiation of functions in religious language:

> The spirit is not the soul, but-if it were possible-the spirit would be the soul of the soul, just as the soul is the spirit of the body. For the spirit of man is not the body, and not the soul, but a third thing in man.[222]

Finally, he describes the unity of life as the Godhead:

> There is one single number that should determine our life on earth, and this number is One. Let us not count further. It is true that the Godhead is Three, but the Three is again comprised in the One. And because God transforms Himself into the One, we men on earth must also strive for the One, devote ourselves to the One and live in it.[223]

The life of Paracelsus was indeed an extraordinary one and possibly the precursor to the healing professions of psychology and psychotherapy of the twentieth century. He had the compassion of a saint towards his patients and the venom of a snake towards his contemporaries and this is his unique form of unity. His idea of unity resided in his Christian beliefs and regarded medicine having four pillars: philosophy, astronomy, alchemy and ethics. With these pillars, a physician could help transform matter and personality for the sole purpose of healing and attaining the idea of unity. Above all, he regarded experience of the light of nature and God with equal value to his Christian faith and makes many attempts to reconcile them. He regarded the ailments of the body as aliments of the soul and attempted to treat that aspect with the hope that the body would also heal. Psychosomatic illnesses are a reality and inner conflicts of differing characters do express themselves with physical symptoms. Obviously there are diseases that attack the body and have little to do with the soul or spirit, and Paracelsus addressed these as well and is why he is the father of Toxicology.

Paracelsus lived in an age where psyche and matter were still intertwined and undifferentiated. Astrology contaminated Astronomy; Chemistry concealed within Alchemy, and magic was commonplace. His connection to the earth was through his patients and his writing; he never married

---

[222] Ibid, Man and Spirit, Power of Faith, page 200
[223] Ibid, God, The Eternal Light, page 230

and did not know the pleasure and pain of a wife and children. His ideas were expressed and developed through his medical practice as he came to understand the upper and lower halves of reality personified by Sol (gold) and Luna (silver). He also recognised the hermaphroditic Mercurius (quicksilver) as soul and central figure who had both earthly and heavenly characteristics. Unlike Zosimos, Paracelsus regarded alchemy in a broader sense, which included creative endeavours such as painting, sculpture and building. He saw alchemical transformation and the extraction God's spirit from matter through ideas, knowledge and skill of an artist. Indeed, building starts with the earth and its products of timber, stone and iron, to be transformed through the fire (intuition) of the spirit as an idea, then applied to the materials for further transformation, refinement, assembling, shaping etc., to the final perfected form of a building.[224]

Christians, Mary the Prophetess, Zosimos and Paracelsus, still attempted to overcome the body for the upper idea of and all good God. The differentiation of astronomy from astrology and chemistry from alchemy enabled our modern scientific age. The ideas in astrology and alchemy could then be regarded as psychological determinants and methods of personal growth. In some instances, we are still under an alchemical influence, particularly when we have reached the limits of our knowledge and are groping in the dark for answers. The 'God particle' is a suitable description of the 'spirit in matter'.

The character Mercurius as both male and female, shows that he has the ability to relate to the upper realm of ideas, reason, insight, divine knowledge, understanding, etc., and the lower realm of matter, body, instincts, etc., and form a unity between them. In this case, Mercurius is more unified than the central Christian character as it includes all we are, not just who we want to be.

> Christ's spirituality was too high and man's naturalness was too low. In the image of Mercurius and the lapis the "flesh" glorified itself in its own way; it would not transform itself into spirit but, on the contrary, "fixed", the spirit in stone, and endowed the stone with all the attributes of the three Persons.[225]

Paracelsus was symbolically aware that things happen according to nature in their own time and that life is an unfolding process (unio mentalis) and each phase has its own concerns. For example, a typical

---

[224] Anyone who has built their own home knows the pain and suffering involved in its conception, refinement and construction. They would also know the satisfaction and joy felt when completed.
[225] JUNG, C.G., Alchemical Studies, Vol. 13, Princeton University Press, 1976, page 96

journey of a natural male starts with childhood, and a time of creativity and play. Teenage years are a time for growth, adventure and enjoyment of physical nature.[226] Young adulthood is an appropriate time for establishing the lower soul of career, power, wealth, partner and family. Middle age the continuing nurture of career base and family, with a movement towards spirit. At the sun's zenith, other things become visible and he moves closer to the upper soul and spiritual concerns. When the body is less robust in old age, it is an excellent time for deeper thought and a return to creativity.[227]

We can conclude from the above that Alchemy is an ongoing process of the union of the opposites of spirit and body within the third character of Mercurius as soul who like Janus, has a viewpoint to the inner and outer realms at once. It was a natural reaction to the rarefied air of the Christian story and its rejection of the body. Alchemy sought the spark of the divine in matter and the body and devised methods to extract that spirit. The life of Paracelsus emphasises how everything we are can be incorporated into a unity. In closing this chapter, I shall leave the final word to Jung and urge the reader to explore his comprehensive study in this field.

> In general, the alchemists strove for a *total* union of opposites in symbolic form, and this they regarded as the indispensible condition for the healing of all ills. Hence they sought to find ways and means to produce that substance in which all opposites were united. It had to be material as well as spiritual, living as well as inert, masculine as well as feminine, old as well as young, and- presumably- morally neutral.[228]

---

[226] This is the time for athleticism, living and enjoying the body to its fullest potential.

[227] Naturally, this example is schematic and should be regarded as such. There are no hard and fast rules concerning one's life journey and different types live their life in different ways.

[228] JUNG, C.G., Mysterium Coniunctionis, Vol 14, Bollingen Series, Princeton University Press, 1977, Page 475

4. IDEAS OF UNITY IN PHILOSOPHY

a. Heraclitus (c 535-475 B.C.)

Heraclitus's was a pre-Socratic Greek thinker known as the 'weeping philosopher' with interesting and advanced ideas and his work survived as fragments mentioned by later authors. He viewed the universe as an ever changing play of opposites interacting as a whole.

> And it is the same thing in us that is quick and dead, awake and asleep, young and old; the former are shifted and become the latter, and the latter in turn are shifted and become the former. [229]

This passage is possibly the first recognition of what the psychologists call enantiodromia, which is the tendency for things to change into their opposite for a restoration of balance and equilibrium and is the governing principal of natural cycles. It is like a swinging pendulum from one side to the other which oscillates between the opposites. Heraclitus also recognised the unity between the opposites as follows:

> God is day and night, winter and summer, war and peace, surfeit and hunger; but he takes various shapes, just as fire, when it is mingled with spices, is named according to the savour of each. [230]

In the next passage, Heraclitus describes the opposites in people with a very interesting observation. Couples are things whole, and not whole.

> Couples are things whole and not whole, what is drawn together and what is drawn asunder, the harmonious and discordant. The one is made up of all things, and all things issue from the one. [231]

Heraclitus alludes to a distinction between the opposites in agreement or dispute, which shows them at play in his personality. It is a subtle recognition of the unity between male and female with distinct characteristics as if they were actual people. Like actual people, male and female psychic characters can agree or disagree. In other words, it is the recognition of attracting and repelling forces between a man and woman as the first step in the realisation of wholeness in the individual. The natural projection of one's inner contra-sexual character makes one whole in the first instance. In the second, it is a slow transformation of the idea of one's physical partner to their actual reality. In this process, the inner projection is recognised and withdrawn and our partner becomes an

---

[229] PLUTARCH, Ps., Consolation to Apollonius, 106 E.
[230] HIPPOLYTUS, Refutation of all heresies, IX, 10, 8.
[231] ARISTOTLE, Ps., On the World, 5. Text attributed to Heraclitus, p. 396b20

individual in their own right. As I shall attempt to show in this book, wholeness or unity, is an individual achievement and the opposites can only be realised individually.

b. Plato (c 427-347 B.C.)

Plato differentiated the opposites of Heraclitus further and describes their characteristics. There are two distinct and contrasting elements, rational purpose and the blind operation of necessity. Plato was able to differentiate between the logical and conscious process, and the blind and instinctive urges. He goes on to say that it is man's business to become like the divine and move towards greater awareness, which parallels the psychological development occurring in Egypt and Canaan.

He conceived four primary bodies, earth, air, fire and water and considered these to be the frame of the world, spherical in shape and the highest measure of unity. In the following text, Plato describes his concept of the 'soul'.

> Now this soul, though it comes later in the account we are now attempting, was not made by the God younger than the body; for when he joined them together, he would not have suffered the elder to be ruled by the younger. There is in us too much of the causal and random, which shows itself in our speech; but the God made soul prior to the body and more venerable in birth and excellence, to be the body's mistress and governor. [232]

The body and soul in Plato's understanding are in a hierarchy and the soul created first with a higher rank than the body. He also recognised the femininity of the soul has an authority over the body. This shows that Plato regarded his inner female character higher in authority and not an equal partner. In other words, he viewed his soul as an authority character like a mother rather than a sister or wife. Plato's 'Receptacle of Becoming' in the following passage reinforces this idea:

> ....one postulated as model, intelligible and always unchangingly real; second a copy of this model, which becomes and is visible. A third we did not then distinguish, thinking that the two would suffice; but now, it seems, the argument compels us to attempt to bring to light and describe a form difficult and obscure. What nature must we, then, conceive it to possess and what part does it play? This more than anything else; that it is the Receptacle as it were, the nurse of all Becoming. [233]

---

[232] PLATO'S Cosmology, The Timaeus, Hackett Publishing Company, 1997, pages 58-59
[233] Ibid, The Receptacle, page 177

He continues by explaining the qualities of the Receptacle.

> It must be called always the same; for it never departs at all from its own character; since it is always receiving all things, and never in any way what- soever takes on any character that is like any of the things that enter it; By nature it is there as a matrix for everything, changed and diversified by the things that enter it, and their account it appears to have different qualities at different times; while the things that pass in and out are to be called copies of the eternal things,............[234]

This passage clearly differentiates between what is the model (inner character) and its copy (character) in the physical world, and describes the third character that unites the opposites of inner and outer. To Plato the third is a receptacle or container of the 'model' and a 'nurse of all becoming'. The following text confirms his idea of mother or matrix of the 'model':

> Be that as it may, for the present we must conceive three things; that which becomes; that in which it becomes; and the model in whose likeness that which becomes is born. Indeed we may fittingly compare the Recipient to a mother, and the model to a father, and the nature that arises between them to their offspring.[235]

It is clear from his writings, that Plato's idea of mother, father and child has metaphysical significance above everyday life. He first describes an unchanging model (being). Second, a copy of this model with attributes of visual tangibility (body, child). Third, the receptacle and origin of the tangible entity as a nurse or mother. The receptacle has therefore, caring, attending and nurturing qualities.

How did Plato arrive at these ideas and why did he endow the human roles of father, mother and child with such Godlike status? To answer these questions, I shall tabulate their characteristics and review how they relate.

Name	Other Names	Characteristics
Model	Father	Intelligible, unchanging, eternal
Receptacle	Nurse, matrix, mother, soul, mistress, governor	Obscure in form, nurse of all becoming, unchanging
Copy of model	Offspring	Visible, becomes, body

---

[234] Ibid, The Receptacle, page 182
[235] Ibid, The Receptacle, page 185

Plato had a clear conception of what he calls the model, or what Descartes calls God, the eternal being, the creator in whose likeness we are made, i.e., Plato's copy. The copy of the model is the physical and tangible human being created in his likeness. Plato sees the receptacle of the human offspring as the overarching mother, and in its broadest sense, as Mother Nature, which is akin to the Egyptian mother Nut. The characteristics support this assumption exemplified by her ambiguous qualities, at once secure in her own character, yet appearing to change by the things that enter into it.

The father as Plato explains, has all the characteristics of God as eternal, intelligible and unchangingly real and therefore a God of light and awareness. The Mother on the other hand, is the receptacle or matrix and obscure and difficult to understand. The third form is equivalent to the body, or more precisely, the physical person in the tangible world. The fact that Plato included a feminine character in his conception shows that he was closer to his unity than the later Judaic and Christian traditions, which do not mention a mother of creation, but only a father. This was to some extent, compensated by the Gnostics who introduced the character of Sophia. It makes perfect sense to include the receptacle because creating life as we know it, requires a father and mother.

Plato obviously knew that the physical world complimented the inner world of characters, and therein lays his unity. He came from an era where an intricate web of Gods and Goddesses complimented their conscious lives, albeit in projected form. Life at that time was full of deities residing in mythical and real places such as mountaintops, oceans, underground, and in space. The relationship between the individual and their gods was so real that the simplest emotion was activated by a God and felt in their bodies. For example, when a man fell in love with a woman, Eros made him excited and happy as if struck by an arrow, which is exactly how it feels.

Plato's Cosmology of earth, air, fire and water were to the ancients a category of physical elements with symbolic significance. The physical aspect of the elements is based on our perception, their behaviour and interaction with each other. For example, the earth is solid and unmoving, air moves and brings rain and clouds, fire is from the sun and brings light and heat. Water nourishes the earth and gives life. These elements not only had physical qualities but psychic qualities and as we shall see later in this study, fit into a harmonious quaternity pattern.

c. Aristotle (384 - 322 B.C.)

Aristotle built on Plato's philosophy from a different point of view. He saw things in a more down-to-earth way and distinguished two antithetical principles to form the basis of not only his Physics, but also his Ethics, Logic and Metaphysics. In the following Aristotle explains the contrasting opposites:

> Their differences are obvious and universally recognised; what is not seen so generally is that they are all analogous in so far as they all rest upon the same fundamental conception of antithesis, though some express it in a wider and some in a narrower formula........But in any case it is clear that the principles must form a contrasted couple.[236]

Aristotle confirms Heraclitus's conception of the opposites and analyses them from various viewpoints. In his Physics, he describes a theory on the heavens and things below the moon subject to generation and decay and above the moon, un-generated and indestructible. The earth, he explains, is spherical and at the centre of the universe. In the sublunary sphere, everything is composed of four elements: earth, air, fire, and water; and he introduces a fifth element, of which the heavenly bodies are composed.   He considers the natural movement of the terrestrial elements are rectilinear, but the fifth element is circular. The heavens are perfectly spherical, and the upper regions are more divine than the lower.

The only knowledge the ancients had of upper heavens of moon, sun, planets and stars were perceived through careful unaided observation, as the telescope was not invented until the seventeenth century AD. This limit to their perception and knowledge of outer space provided a hook for projections and shows that even a practical man projects his unconscious contents onto objects when the limits of their knowledge is reached.

Aristotle's materialistic leaning became evident in his physics. He did not question the reality and objectivity of the material world revealed to him by his senses. He says it is neither an illusion nor a mere creation or manifestation of the mind. In his Metaphysics, he regarded the mind as not of a material or tangible nature, but of pure thought and the opposite to the material or sensible world. He explains that God is the first choice and pure thought. Life, he says, belongs to God for the actuality of thought. God is a living being, eternal, most good, and life, duration and

---

[236] ARISTOTLE, The Physics, Vol. I, Book I, chapter 4.

eternity, belonging to God. In the following text, Aristotle relates God to the earth.

> God exists eternally, as pure thought, happiness, complete self-fulfilment, without any realised purposes. The sensible world on the contrary, is imperfect, but it has life, desire thought of an imperfect kind and aspiration.

> All living things are in a greater or lesser degree aware of God, and are moved to action by admiration and love of God. This God is the final cause of all activity.[237]

It is clear from the passage that Aristotle equates God with positive attributes and the sensible world with imperfection and therefore, less than positive. He explains that all living things are aware of and move towards God. He also describes how his psychic activity and the sensible physical world have a relationship by an intermediary or third form.

> Since all change is between opposites, and opposites are either contraries or contradictories, and there is nothing between contradictories, it is clear that the intermediate or 'between' can only exist when there are two contraries.[238]

> Thus, if our former insistence on the two terms of some antithesis being principles is sound, and if we are now convinced that these antithetical principles need something to work on, and if we are to preserve both these conclusions, must we not necessarily posit a third principle as the subject on which the antithetical principles act?[239]

In his Ethics, he introduces the intermediary element as the soul, one part being rational and the other irrational. The irrational he equates with the vegetative, appetitive and instinctual functions related to the body. The mind in his view, bound less to the soul than the body. The mind, or the power to think and understand, is alone capable of isolation from all other psychic powers. The soul is what moves the body and perceives sensible objects; its characteristics are self-nutrition, sensation, feeling and motivity, but the mind has the higher function of thinking, which has no relation to the body or to the senses. Hence, the mind to Aristotle is immortal, though the soul is not.

He elaborates on this idea of the soul in his book "De Anima" by stating:

> Indeed an acquaintance with the soul would seem to help much in acquiring

---

[237] RUSSELL Bertrand, History of Western Philosophy, p 181, Allen & Unwin Aust P/L 1990
[238] ARISTOTLE, The Physics, Vol II, Book V, p.37.
[239] ARISTOTLE, The Physics, Vol. I, Book I, #6,p.59.

all truth, especially about the natural world; for it is, as it were, the principle of living things.[240]

> Taken all together we define soul by three things: movement, sensation, and by immateriality. Some say the soul is one element some say all or some elements.[241]

He explains the soul's relation to the sensible world as opposed to the inner world of mental processes and describes and defines the physical qualities of the soul in the following text:

> Bodies especially seem to be substances; and among these, natural bodies, for these are the principles of the others. Of natural bodies some possess vitality, others do not. We mean by 'possessing vitality', that a thing can nourish itself and grow and decay. Now this can mean one of two things: one, as is the possession of knowledge; another, as is the act of knowing. It is plain that it is like knowledge possessed.
>
> If, then, there is one generalization to be made for any and every soul, the soul will be the primary act of a physical bodily organism.[242]

The main function Aristotle attributes to the soul is its ability to sense. He writes at length on the senses of touch, smell, hearing, taste and sight and how they form the basis of the soul. In the following, Aristotle discusses imagination and how inner images resemble the sensible world:

> Imagination is a movement produced by sensation actuated. Since sight is the most prominent sense, (imagination) has taken its name from light, as there is no seeing without light.........these images dwell within, and resemble sense experiences.[243]

Indeed, inner images borrow from the sensible world but are in fact selected and composed into symbolic scenes that reflect the individual's relationship to the world. Aristotle's temperament was fundamental to his understanding of imagination and soul. He leaned more towards the earth and senses in contrast to the metaphysical musings of Plato.

In his Ethics, he writes about Intelligence and Intuition and explains how scientific knowledge consists of forming judgements about things that are universal and necessary demonstrable truths. He explains that every form of scientific knowledge (because this involves reasoning) depends upon first principles that we cannot grasp through either science or art. The

---

[240] ARISTOTLE, De Anima, Book I, #1, p.41

[241] Ibid #2, p.78.

[242] Ibid Book II, #1, p.163

[243] Ibid Book III, #3, p.394

mind apprehends first principles by intuition. He says a wise man will know first principles and wisdom through intuition and scientific knowledge.

Finally, I would like to show how Aristotle explains Plato's concept of the 'matrix' or 'womb', as he tries to bring the concept down-to-earth and relate it to matter:

> They (Platonists) too have a triad of the 'great', the 'small' and the 'idea' (or form) but this triad is really quite different from ours of 'matter', "shortage' and 'form', for although they go so far with us as to recognize the necessity of some underlying subject, yet in truth the 'great and small' of which it consists can only be equated with our 'matter' and is not a dyad at all.........Now we, who distinguish between matter and shortage, can very well see why matter, which co-operates with form in the genesis of things may be conceived as their matrix or womb. And we can also see how a man who concentrates his mind on the negative and defect involving character of shortage, may come to think of it as purely non-existent.
>
> So that if (to borrow their metaphors) we are to regard matter as the female desiring the male or the foul desiring the fair, the desire must be attributed not to the foulness itself, as such, but to a subject that is foul or female incidentally.[244]

It is clear from the passages that Aristotle's conceptions are very earth-bound, that is to say, related more to the material and sensible than the ideas of Plato. Aristotle's conception of the imagination relates more to earth, sense experiences and the body, than the inner world of dreams. Although we do imagine in images borrowed from the sensible world, his conception does not explain why we imagine particular images over other images, and what determines the images imagined.

The antithetical ideas of God and the sensible world form the fundamental pair of opposites that Aristotle applied to all his studies. God is pure thought, eternal and most good. When compared to Plato's idea of the opposites, we can see that the concept of soul has more a relationship to matter or the sensible world than the central inner character (idea of God). Plato relates the soul to the inner idea of God and his associated characteristics, whereas Aristotle relates the soul to matter and the physical world.

We may conclude that Aristotle was in general, more aware of the material and sensible world in elaborate and complex ways. The relationship of the soul to God however, is not as distinct. Both Aristotle

---

[244] ARISTOTLE, The Physics, Vol. I, Book I, #9, page 93.

and Plato conceived of a contrasted couple with a third intermediary form. His conception of God has similar characteristics to that conceived by Plato, the antithetical concept is however, matter. Matter he explains has qualities pertaining to the feminine or female and her desire for the male. In this aspect, his conception has great similarities to Plato's role of gender.

The soul, he explains, has two aspects, one part rational, the other, irrational. The relationship between the soul and mind is for Aristotle secondary to its relationship with the body and sensible world. He writes that the mind can be independent from the soul because the soul is generally bound to the instinctive and sensible functions. Although Aristotle leads us to believe that he is more aware of the sensible and material world, it is difficult to draw a definite conclusion from his writings. We can say however, that his ideas revolve around perception and the emphasis of his philosophy less metaphysical than Plato's.

Aristotle does recognise the opposites and the unifying third form called the soul (anima). The soul in this instance orients around the body and its physical nature rather than God and his psychic nature. It is an excellent example of differing temperaments and how they emphasise one side of reality over the other. Nevertheless, their unity of personality is evident. The ancient Greeks conceived a myriad of deities in their mythology, yet both Plato and Aristotle conceive a single idea they call God with different ideas of soul. The soul in Plato's writings is an authority over the body and closer to God. Aristotle's idea of soul is oriented towards the senses and earth.

d. Descartes R. (1596 - 1650)

The Christian church established itself at the later stage of the Roman Empire and dominated the spiritual realm in the west between the philosophies of the ancient world to Descartes in the Renaissance era. Notable exceptions were the Gnostic and Alchemical traditions that remained hidden from the Church for fear of persecution. Descartes lived at a time still dominated by the Christian dogma, and was instrumental in the age of reason and enlightenment. He is the father of modern philosophical thought but had no defined conception of the unconscious. He did however go through a transition and turned away from the darkness of his previous life towards the light of the future.

The beginning of Descartes' philosophical work began with three dreams he experienced on the night of November 10, 1619. The first two dreams were frightening: fierce winds at the forefront of a tremendous thunderstorm blew him from a college to a church, but the wind did not affect other people he encountered on the way. The third dream was not frightening and Descartes received two books, the first a 'Dictionaire', the other on poetry called Corpus Poetarum, with reference to one particular poem 'Est and Non'. While still asleep Descartes asked himself whether he was dreaming or had had a vision. He not only decided he was dreaming, and began to interpret the earlier part of the dream while still dreaming. The 'Dictionaire' he decided, stood for all the sciences, while the book of poetry stood for philosophy and wisdom. These dreams were for Descartes a turning point and he left his previous life and devoted the rest of it to creating a unified mathematical science.

It is clear Descartes considered the source of these dreams divine, but did not realise that the dreams came to him through the darkness of sleep and not the light of consciousness. His mind focused from this point on to the eternal, good, and perfect, and his conception of a perfect being. Later in his life, he claimed that dreams express a movement of the organs in sleep, and that they constitute a language translating a desire. As with the ancients, Descartes conceived a complimentary pair of opposites. Understanding to Descartes, has two operations: intuition and deduction. If we examine these operations, we will see an interesting collaboration of opposites emerge.

The fourth edition of the Oxford Dictionary (1967) states that intuition is: "Immediate apprehension of the mind without reasoning; immediate apprehension by sense; immediate insight". Deduction, on the other hand: "Deduce: Infer, draw a conclusion from known or supposed facts", and deduction: "inference from the general to the particular or a priori reasoning". Deduction is a conscious and deliberate act of reasoning whereas intuition is a spontaneous act of knowing characterised by its lack of conscious effort and input. If intuition is not a conscious and a deliberate process, one may infer that it is an unconscious process, that is to say, one is not aware of how it functions.

> ....just as these impulses of which I have spoken are found in me, not with-standing that they do not always concur with my will, so perhaps there is in me some faculty fitted to produce these ideas without the assistance of any external things, even though it is not yet known to me; just as, apparently, they have hitherto always been found in me during sleep without the aid of any external objects, ...I have noticed that in many cases there was a great difference between the object and its idea.

> And although it may be the case that one idea gives birth to an other idea, that cannot continue to be so indefinitely; for in the end we must reach an idea whose cause shall be so to speak an archetype, in which

the whole reality (or perfection) which so to speak objectively (or by representation) in these ideas is contained formally (and really).[245]

In the previous passage, Descartes describes an idea or archetype that formally contains the whole reality of all other ideas, in other words a container. This is the same idea as Plato's' Receptacle of Becoming.

> ....I notice that not only is there a real and positive idea of God or of a being of supreme perfection present to my mind, but also, so to speak, a certain negative idea of nothing, that is, of that which is infinitely removed from any kind of perfection and that I am in a sense something intermediate between God and nought.[246]

Descartes gives this container the name 'nought' and regards it as the counter-pole to the being of supreme perfection. If the Supreme Being represents absolute awareness and perfection, then nought must mean an absence of these, and imperfection and unawareness.

> Let us then conceive here that the soul has its principal seat in the little gland which exists in the middle of the brain, from whence it radiates forth through all the remainder of the body by means of the animal spirits,...........[247]

In this passage, Descartes includes an example that explains the physiological mechanism of perception as he sees it. An animal approaches a person and the light reflected from its body depicts two images, one in each of our eyes, and these two images form two others, by means of the optic nerves. The animal spirits radiate towards the gland and the two images unite as one. This explanation seems somewhat unreal when compared to our present-day knowledge of the human body. The idea of the animal spirits and the small gland in the centre of the brain shows a very interesting aspect of Descartes spiritual orientation. His mind was focused strictly on all the higher faculties of understanding and insight; that is to say, towards the all-good and perfect being, yet through his work he attempts to relate his body to his soul, and bond them with a central gland located in the middle of the brain. He continues in the following passage on how the inferior and the superior parts of the soul are incompatible and in conflict.

> And it is only in the repugnance which exists between the movements which the body by its animal spirits, and the soul by its will, tend to excite in the gland at the same time, that all the strife which we are in the habit

---

[245] DECARTES, Rene, The Essential Descartes, New American Library, 1983, Meditation III, pages 183 and 185.
[246] Ibid, Meditation IV, page 194.
[247] Ibid, The Passions of the Soul, Part I, page 363.

of conceiving to exist between the inferior part of the soul, which we call the sensuous, and the superior
which is rational, or as we may say, between the natural appetites and the will, consists.[248]

The description of the lower inferior part of the soul, and the higher rational part, show that Descartes had an awareness of the opposites as they exist in the human being. In this case, however, the opposites are in conflict. One can conclude that Descartes strove for the highest realms of spiritual understanding and consequently denied his natural instincts, which he drove into opposition. When compared to the ideas of Plato and Aristotle, we can see a further differentiation of the soul from Plato relating upward to spirit, and Aristotle, downward to matter, to an idea of soul oriented in both directions. In other words, Descartes understood the potential unity between matter and spirit through the soul but could not reconcile the difference in his soul's attitudes. This stage of our evolution is emphasised in Descartes thinking as he understood, as did the ancients, that reality was made of body, soul and spirit but the quality of these fundamental entities, particularly the soul, was not yet differentiated. The positive and negative orientations of the soul was identified but not reconciled and in conflict.

In summary, Descartes conceived of the opposites and their relationship united by the soul that has its seat in a small gland in the centre of the brain.

Name	Other Names	Characteristics
God		Eternal, good, perfect, positive
Soul (positive)		Superior, rational, will
Soul (negative)		Inferior, sensuous, natural appetites
Nought		Negative, nothing, imperfect

His concept of God as all positive and perfect is similar to the Christian view but his understanding of its opposite less clear. He terms the opposite nought, meaning nothing and this conception indicates that he had an intuitive understanding of something that had no defined characteristics like an empty vessel, which therefore contains nothing. His writings on ideas verify this belief. He traces them back to their source and explains that all ideas are contained in an archetype. He elaborates by saying that the whole of reality (or perfection) in the form of ideas is

---

[248] Ibid p.366

contained in this archetype. His conception of the antithesis of God is what we would call the unconscious (nought). This is the same as our contemporary understanding of how we bring our God into consciousness from the darkness of unconsciousness by looking at one's dreams, visions, fantasies and creativity.

Unlike Plato, who regarded the soul oriented towards God and Aristotle oriented towards the physical, Descartes differentiated his idea of soul into positive and negative with a central position between the opposites. This evolution in our understanding of unity took sixteen hundred years in our western culture, and his unity was in conflict. This means that the division of the upper and lower aspects of the personality were not in an agreeable relationship and had not found a common understanding and reconciliation of differences. Like any relationship, there are agreements and disagreements that can lead to conflict. I proceed from the basic tenet that agreement attracts and disagreement repels. In this case, the differentiated soul into positive and negative are in conflict and his unity is in 'potentia' and not reconciled.

e. Spinoza B. (1632 -1677)

Spinoza owed a great deal to Descartes for the basis of his own philosophy. He rejected Descartes' idea of a soul divided into positive, negative, and regarded God as an infinite, perfect and a thinking thing. His philosophical system based on the idea that all existence and its laws proceed from God. We can see the similarity between this and Plato's idea of a 'model' and its extension, the 'copy of the model'.

> The human mind has no knowledge of the human body, nor does it know it to exist, save through ideas of modifications by which the body is affected.
>
> We neither feel nor perceive any individual things save bodies and modes of thinking.
>
> The idea or knowledge of the human mind is granted in God and follows in God, and is referred to him in the same manner as the idea or knowledge of the human body.
>
> We can only have a very inadequate knowledge of individual things which are outside us. [249]

In the above passage, Spinoza explains how we have no knowledge of the human body or even its existence. This shows his natural

---

[249] SPINOZA B, Ethics, Nature and Origin of the Mind, Heron Books, pages 56-63.

temperament for psychic processes and reason over the reality of the physical and material world. He describes all aspects of existence relating to his idea of unity. Being aware of unity is however different to living it.

> To understand now what this mode is, which we call soul, how it has its origin from the body, and also how its change depends (only) on the body (which I maintain to be the union of soul and body), we must note:[250]

In this passage, Spinoza discusses the soul coming from the body and soul and body united. Unlike Descartes who recognises the positive and negative aspects of the soul, that is, the higher faculties from the lower natural instincts[251], Spinoza does not differentiate between soul and body and regards them as closely aligned and united. This is natural for a thinking man with many ideas to feel his soul (feminine side of his nature) in the physical world of the body. It shows an undeveloped relationship between his God and his body and matter in general. In the following passages, Spinoza discusses the background causes of volition and desire.

> ....in the first place, that men think themselves free in as much as they are conscious of their volitions and desires, and as they are ignorant of the causes by which they are led to wish and desire, they do not even dream of their existence.[252]

> All our endeavours or desires follow from the necessity of our nature.........[253]

> God is free from passions, nor is he affected with any emotion of pleasure or pain.[254]

The background cause of human endeavours according to Spinoza pertains to nature and comes about of necessity. He describes this cause as a motivating urge that operates of its own accord and leads us to wish and desire. The interesting point concerning this cause is its lack of conscious control. Although God is the ultimate origin of this cause, he does not partake in its affects. This idea is particular to Spinoza as other ideas of God have definite human qualities of passion. For example, the God of Moses, as well as the ancient Gods of Greece and Rome had frequent bouts of fury and rage.

---

[250] SPINOZA B, The Ethics and Other Works, Princeton University Press, 1994, D. Of the Human Soul, page 58
[251] This is Descartes' value judgement as the instincts have both positive and negative aspects.
[252] SPINOZA B, Ethics, Concerning God, Heron Books page 30.
[253] Ibid, The Strength of Emotions, Fourth Part, page 191.
[254] Ibid, The Power of the Intellect, Prop XVII, page 210.

Nothing happens in nature which can be attributed to a defect of it; for nature is always the same and one everywhere,.........[255]

........it is quite obvious that the mind understands itself the more, the more it-understands the things of nature, it is certain that this part of the method will be more perfect according as the mind understands more things, and will then become most perfect of all when it has regard for and reflects on the knowledge of a most perfect being.

Here I shall only say briefly what I understand by the true good, and at the same time, what the highest good is. To understand this properly, it must be noted that good and bad are said of things only in a certain respect, so that one and the same thing can be called both good and bad according to different respects. The same applies to perfect and imperfect. For nothing, considered in its own nature, will be called perfect or imperfect, especially after we have recognized that everything that happens happens according to the eternal order, and according to certain laws of Nature.[256]

Spinoza's ideas show an awareness of the role unity had in nature, yet his idea only includes perfection. This value judgement of perfection in contrast to imperfection is different to what we normally regard as good or bad. Perfection to Spinoza is an order or a law beyond emotion and the horrors of nature, including human nature, and regarded as a 'mode' or extension of this unity. The opposites of war, death, destruction and peace, life, creativity are all part of this perfection. Perhaps it is a poor choice of words to say what we regard as negative, is part of this perfection. It is definitely part of unity and there is order in this unity. Perfection as a term does however conjure thoughts of good rather than bad. A more complete understanding has to acknowledge that both good and perfection, bad and imperfection, are all part of the idea of unity and this is the nature of reality.

Spinoza goes on to explain that knowledge and understanding of the mind; in other words, self-knowledge, leads to increased understanding of nature. Beyond the knowledge of nature and perfecting the method of self-knowledge, comes reflection and knowledge of God. He does not equate nature with God however, but as an attribute of God or more specifically, God's way of ordering existence. This does not sound like a perfect being to leave his creatures alone to fight it out for survival. He does however give certain advantages to species using caution and protective behaviour or using weapons for hunting and defence.

---

[255] Ibid, Origin and Nature of Emotions, Third Part, page 84.
[256] SPINOZA B, The Ethics and Other Works, Princeton University Press, 1994, Preliminaries, page 5

Will can only be called a necessary cause, not a free one.[257]

> There is in no mind absolute or free will, but the mind is determined for willing this or that by a cause which is determined in its turn by another cause, and this one again by another, and so on to infinity.[258]

He describes the will having no freedom of its own and determined by a necessary cause and God. For Spinoza everything that happens in existence is a manifestation of God's nature, and with knowledge of God, evil becomes good, when related to a larger and more comprehensive plan. He clearly conceives the unity of God including all that exists in the physical world and so-called perfection of reality beyond good and bad. A differentiation of his thinking may yield a further explanation of his conception of unity. Spinoza identifies and defines the following psychic functions.

> **Idea** - I understand a conception of the mind which the mind forms by reason of its being a thinking thing.[259]

> **Memory** - It is nothing else than sensation of impressions on the brain accompanied with the thought to determine the duration of the sensation.[260]

> **Imagination** - certain fortuitous and unconnected sensations which do not rise from the power of the mind, but from external causes..........Or if one wishes, he may take what ever he likes for imagination, provided he admits it is some- thing different from the understanding and that the soul has a passive relation with it.[261]

Idea- Spinoza regards the idea as a conception of the mind that the mind forms. The emphasis is on the idea being a thought rather than an image. Since he regards all existence proceeding from God, so too must all ideas proceed from God? What we consider as ideas today includes images, emotions, judgements, thoughts, but also the ability to build from ideas and transform them. For example, one original idea is the basis for the construction of a city. In Australia, Sydney grew from the idea of a colony where fresh water was available i.e., the Tank stream. Canberra grew from an individual's conception of geometric circular ring roads around a central parliament building.

---

[257] SPINOZA B, Ethics, Concerning God, Heron Books, First Part, page 25.
[258] Ibid, Second Part, page 74.
[259] Ibid, Second Part, page 37.
[260] Ibid, Fifth Part, page 254.
[261] Ibid, Fifth Part, page 255.

Memory- -Spinoza does not clearly differentiate between sense perception, which is immediate perception of the physical, and memory as a stored set of images and emotions of the original sense perception. The important aspect of memory is its unconsciousness. We forget most of the experiences in life to make way for new perceptions. Consciousness may retrieve these images by focusing on a particular event or impression. The psyche does however, have the ability to associate with past sense perceptions (memories) and relate them to a current perception.

Imagination- -Spinoza conceives of the imagination as images that are unconnected with the thinking mind and derived from external causes, that is to say, the images borrowed from the physical world, assembled and presented to our perception (mind's eye). This does not explain how, why and what presents a particular series of images to one's mind. Like dreams, imagination has an obscure meaning based on association. In other words an unconscious ordering system assembles images of objects perceived in the physical world and organises them into a scene and/or story.

Spinoza continues by explaining that imagination could be anything, different from the understanding and that the soul is passive to it. Passivity with respect to imagination means no active role in the imagination and perception of the images as if watching a movie. The passivity towards imagination is typical of an artistic temperament and the expression of images as they occur. On the other hand, it is possible to become a director of the movie, in other words take active part in the flow of images and direct them accordingly. Obviously this is only possible when in a waking state and with the involvement of consciousness. We perceive dreams passively because we are asleep and they always seem to be about ourselves. We not only perceive the dreams but act in them.

From the material presented by Spinoza, we can conceive an idea of the unconscious with its products of ideas, memory and imagination. Both Descartes and Spinoza conceived an all-perfect God, infinite and a thinking thing. Bodies he explains come from God and can only be known through their modes. In bodies, he includes all the material objects in the physical world. Unlike Descartes, his differentiation of soul from the body and awareness of unity is still incomplete. We may consider nature perfect because it follows definite laws, but this does not include the law of attraction and repulsion, which is fundamental to atomic structure, biological evolution and the forces that hold the galaxy together.

f. Leibniz G. W. (1646 - 1716)

Leibniz's metaphysics is an elaboration of the Cartesian (Descartes) concept of God as divine perfection and does everything in the most desirable way. "God is an absolute perfect being". Leibniz's does however, conceive a God of pure intelligence without senses to perceive matter.[262]

> For it will readily be granted that God does not know matter by means of the senses; for it is an axiom in metaphysics that God has no senses and consequently cannot have sensations.......In a word since he is pure intelligence he can conceive only the purely intelligible; not that he is ignorant of any of the phenomenon of nature.........[263]

The idea of a perfect being that does not perceive through senses but through intelligence alone is more like a blind but purposeful force rather than an all seeing creator. This conception of God with no relationship to the body and senses and purely a psychic function means that the reality of the body is not included in Leibniz's idea of unity. Unlike the ancient Gnostics and Alchemists who regarded the spirit within matter and the body as a reality, Leibniz's idea has more in common with the Christian ideal of an all-good and purified spirit. Leibniz attempts to see the underlying function of God without relationship to the individual. God created humans so we could perceive for him, and carry out his work. The idea of a God without a relationship to his creation is like an artist that does not create, which makes him a fantasist, but not an artist.

Leibniz's system of philosophy was in the end an attempt to reconcile the prevailing Christian doctrine with reason (pre-established harmony) and all of God's creation moving towards perfection. In other words if we could see the reason for what we perceive as evil, we would become aware of its purpose and its movement towards perfection. It is true that much of the natural world and its horrors have a purpose that transcends perceived good and evil and moves towards Leibniz's pre-established harmony. What to our feeling seems horrific is in nature, purposeful.

For example, the way a female Praying Mantis devours the male during or after copulation has the purpose of concentrating reproduction and providing nutrients for the mother and offspring. Similarly, when a male lion takes over a pride and kills the cubs of his predecessor, it maximises the new lion's reproductive success. These and other examples show

---

[262] If God has the ability to sense, then he would either have to have a body as we do, or sense in another way.

[263] LEIBNIZ G W, Basic Writings, The Open Court Publishing Company, 1962, Introduction, p XVII.

Leibniz's idea of "pre-established harmony" as it occurs in nature and how individuals of a species have ideas with purpose that compel their behaviour. Animals cannot see purpose due to their lack of awareness and questioning ability of the compelling idea. Humans on the other hand, are aware to some extent, of the motivating forces behind behaviour. We are still in most instances at the mercy of these compelling forces and simply follow their impetus without criticism.[264]

Leibniz shows that the psychic and physical are not only united but have intelligence (meaning) underlying their unity. He draws the distinction between the conception of the extension and three-dimensionality of a body, and substance of the body. The body has in his viewpoint something like a soul. This concept of matter carries the earlier viewpoint of the Cartesians to where matter relates to what one would call spirit or all the attributes that Leibniz calls God. He equates the rational soul with mind thus reinforcing Descartes' idea of an upper and lower soul.

Relating a concept of a higher being to the everyday things in the physical world, has always been a great problem for philosophers. How does one relate the great ideas and forces that guide our destinies with the objects and life in the physical world?

> Ideas are all stored up within us. Plato's doctrine of reminiscence......as a matter of fact our soul has the power of representing to itself any form or nature whenever the occasion comes for thinking about it, and I think that this activity of our soul is, so far as it expresses some nature, form or essence, properly the idea of the thing. This is in us, and is always in us whether we are thinking of it or no. This position is in accord with my principles that naturally nothing enters our minds from outside...... Nothing can be taught us of which we have not already in our minds the idea.[265]

Leibniz distinguishes between the idea and essence of something, in this case the soul, and the thing itself, the body. His relationship between the idea of the body and the body itself is tenuous however. This shows that Leibniz was aware of the idea of the body, but not the body itself.

> A body is an aggregation of substances, and is not a substance, properly speaking. Consequently in all bodies must be found indivisible substances which cannot be generated and are not corruptible, having something which corresponds to souls.[266]

---

[264] Our warlike nature is an example of such inner forces.
[265] LEIBNIZ G W, Basic Writings, Metaphysics, p44.
[266] Ibid, p.244.

Intellects or souls which are capable of reflection and of knowing the eternal truths and God, have many privileges that exempt them from the transformations of bodies.[267]

The building blocks of matter, which he calls Monads, are indivisible and have a soul.[268] He explains that Monads are simple substances, meaning without parts and made up of composites. They are incorruptible, self-contained and closed. Each Monad is different from the other and the natural changes they go through come from an internal principle, and external causes have no influence upon its inner being. The Monad that Leibniz speaks about is very much akin to the Mandala as a symbol of wholeness.[269]

> The passing condition which involves and represents a multiplicity in the unity or in the simple substance a plurality of conditions and relations, even though it has no parts. The passing condition which involves and represents a multiplicity in the unity, or in the simple substance, is nothing else than what is called perception. This should be carefully distinguished from Apperception or consciousness as will appear in what follows. In this matter the Cartesians have fallen into a serious error, in that they treat as non-existent those perceptions of which we are not conscious. It is this also which has led them to believe that spirits alone are Monads and that their are no souls of animals or other Entelechies, and it has led them to make the common confusion between a protracted period of unconsciousness and actual death. They have thus adapted the Scholastic error that souls can exist entirely separated from bodies, and have even confirmed ill-balanced minds in the belief that souls are mortal.[270]

Leibniz elaborates in this preceding passage on the unity of the Monad and the idea that it changes itself from inside. This concept seems very strange when compared to our present-day knowledge of matter. Are we to interpret this as an idea of the constituents of matter that has nothing to do with matter itself? In other words, is it an idea of matter? If we accept this conception as a projected idea into matter, the whole emphasis of Leibniz's philosophy changes. Instead of looking at matter to find Leibniz's idea, we look at the idea itself and then relate it to matter.

To make the idea of the Monad clearer, the characteristics of it are summarised as follows:

---

[267] Ibid, p.245.
[268] See Chapter 2 on Animism
[269] Sanskrit for circle. Jung refers to it extensively and considers it to be a symbol of wholeness.
[270] LEIBNIZ G W, Basic Writings, Metaphysics, p.253, par.14.

Name	Other Names	Characteristics
Monad	Souls, Soul plus Memory = Monad	Simple substance; makes up composites; without parts; no window; closed to outside; each different; changes come from an internal principle; not affected by external causes; has a manifoldness which changes; has a multiplicity in the unity; has something inside which changes and something which unchanges.

The major characteristics are autonomy from external causes, its simplicity, its unity and closed nature, its multiplicity and containing the opposites of change and un-change within it. This conception may lead us to wonder where all this information about the Monad came from. Is this idea something in the material world? Is Leibniz describing something completely different to what we know as matter? The description Leibniz gives is unmistakably close to the description of a Mandala. We can only speculate that the Monad may be a projected Mandala into the physical world of object and body. In other words, his unity is found in the material world of matter and body.

In the following passage, Leibniz highlights perception as a fundamental aspect of the Monad, perception being a function of the senses in matter (body).

> If we wish to designate as soul everything which has perceptions and desires in the general sense hat I have just explained, all simple substances or created Monads could be called souls. But since feeling is something more than a mere perception I think that the general name of Monad or Entelechy should suffice for simple substances which have only perception, while we may reserve the term soul for those whose perception is more distinct and is accompanied by memory.[271]

Leibniz explains how memory, when added to the Monad as a simple substance, become 'souls'. A simple substance that relies on perception

---

[271] Ibid, p.255, par.19.

alone he calls a Monad. When we add memory to the simple substance, it brings with it a feeling and elevates the Monad too more than a simple substance, a soul. In other words, memory is life experience of the past. With more memory, the Monad becomes real in the physical world just like a child that grows and becomes aware of themself and surrounding environment.

> The memory furnishes a sought of consecutiveness which imitates reason it is to be distinguished from it. We see that animals when they have a perception of something which they notice and of which they have had a similar previous perception, are led by the representation of their memory to expect that which was associated in the preceding perception, and they come to have feelings like those which they had before.[272]

Let us now look at the whole picture that Leibniz is painting. We have the concept of a complete and united substance he calls a Monad. The Monad's main characteristic is sense perception. He then adds memory to the Monad, which in turn creates a soul and relationship (feeling) to the physical world. Having identified senses, memory and feeling belonging to the concept of soul, we must ask the question, where does thinking and intuition fit into the picture?

> But the knowledge of eternal and necessary truths is that which distinguishes us from mere animals and gives us reason and the sciences, thus raising us to a knowledge of ourselves and of God. This is what is called in us the Rational Soul or Mind.[273]

Leibniz continues:

> It is also through the knowledge of necessary truths and through abstractions from them that we come to perform Reflective Acts, which cause us to think of what is called the I. and to decide that this or that is within us. It is thus, that in thinking upon ourselves we think of being, of substance, of the simple and composite, of a material thing and of God himself, conceiving that what is limited in us is in him without limits. These reflective Acts furnish the principle objects of our reasonings.[274]

In the preceding passages, it is clear that Leibniz considers the rational soul and all the higher faculties of reason, reflection, will and thinking distinguished from the instinctive nature of the animals. We achieve this by gaining knowledge of the eternal truths, which in turn gives us knowledge of ourselves and of God. Leibniz thus described all aspects of existence from the lowliest animals to the most perfect being. He sees

---

[272] Ibid, p.256, par.26.
[273] Ibid, p.257, par.29.
[274] Ibid, p.257, par.30.

the animals as possessing the simplest Monad characterised by perception. With the addition of feeling, the Monad changes to a multiplicity in its internal structure and approaches the infinite and perfect, which gives knowledge of God. Yet God has no ability to perceive through senses.

> In God are present: power, which s the source of everything; knowledge, which contains the details of the ideas; and finally, will, which changes or produces things in accordance with the principle of greatest good. To these correspond in the created Monad, the subject or basis, the faculty of perception, and the faculty of appetition. In God these attributes are absolutely infinite or perfect, while in the created Monads,........they are imitations approaching him in proportion to the perfection.[275]

The philosophy of Leibniz has the observational properties and insights into psychological truths of human nature. Although his concepts have a metaphysical cloak draped over them, they are very much akin to the objective observations and discoveries of the twentieth century psychologists. Leibniz attempts to fit all functions of the human being into a comprehensive and total concept called the Monad. This Monad ranges from a simple form of the animals, to the infinite and perfect Monad of God.

The beauty of Leibniz's philosophy is its idea of unity including all existence from God to matter in one concept. As with the Cartesians and post Cartesians, Leibniz attempts to relate matter to God, and manages to contain them in one idea, which the Cartesians could not do. His idea of matter is still not complete however, because God cannot have sensations. The difficulty lies in relating the sensible, imperfect world to an all-perfect being. It mustn't have occurred to him that if God created all, including imperfect or undeveloped souls, then God himself must have imperfection within himself, for a God is not perfect if he creates imperfection.

g. Rousseau J. J. (1712 - 1778)

In many ways Rousseau lived what he preached and whether consciously or unconsciously, sought what he called 'the natural man'. He sought the uniqueness of himself as an individual in contrast to the collective and civilised man. He speaks at length about his isolation and thoughts that preoccupied him, his relationship to the society he once lived in and giving himself to his destiny.

---

[275] Ibid, p.261, par.48.

Drawn, I know not how, from the order of things, I have seen myself precipitated into an incomprehensible chaos, in which I perceive nothing at all, and the more I think of my present state, the less I can understand where I am.[276]

They have torn from my heart all the sweetness of society.........All is ended for me upon the earth; none can now do me good or evil. There remains for me neither anything to hope for nor to fear in this world, and now I am tranquil at the bottom of the gulf, a poor unfortunate mortal, but as undisturbed as God himself.[277]

Rousseau's journey to the underworld (unconscious) gave him a unique and individual viewpoint on the society he had left behind. He had to contend with the chaos of conflicting impulses and instincts characteristic of that submersion and derived a system that reinforced his animal nature. Indeed, it is his individuality and all the natural instincts, which Rousseau sought.

These hours of solitude and meditation are the only ones of the day in which I am fully myself and for myself without diversion, without obstacle, and where I can truly say I am that which nature has designed.[278]

His urge to become natural, instinctive and of the heart did have its negative consequences. His viewpoint was not well received by the French authorities although the idea of the 'natural man' was an important problem for the civilised man at the time. To live without moral constraint and by nature alone is for many a personal horror and leaves oneself vulnerable to persecution, imprisonment or even death, as the fate of Socrates shows. He was wise to remove himself from his culture to explore that side of his nature.

I saw myself at the decline of an innocent and unfortunate life; the soul still full of lively sentiments, and the spirit still ornamented with some flowers, but already withered by sadness and dried up in ennui. Alone and abandoned, I felt the chill of the first frosts, and my failing imagination did not people my solitude any more with beings formed according to my own heart. I said to myself with a sigh: What have I done here on earth? I was made for living, and I am dying, without having lived.[279]

As a learned man, Rousseau risked his life in an exploration of the natural man, which in the end was not his own choice. Fate often selects

---

[276] ROUSSEAU J J, The Reveries of a Solitary, First Promenade, p.32.
[277] Ibid, First Promenade, p.35.
[278] Ibid, Second Promenade, p.43.
[279] Ibid, Second Promenade, p.46.

individuals to carry the compensatory burden of a one-sided culture and be its antithesis for the sake of unity. Many a poet and philosopher lived a compensatory life and carried this burden for the unity of their culture. Some manage to work their way through the turmoil of unconsciousness and come out the other side with renewed optimism for life and express their newfound insight into human nature. Experience of the unconscious and the natural man has the highest value for a repressed culture. Thinking about it alone is mere speculation.

> An absolute silence leads to sadness, it offers us an image of death; thus the help of a light-hearted imagination is necessary and presents itself naturally to those whom the heavens have gratified with it. The movement, which does not come from without, then, is made within us..........[280]

Rousseau speaks of entering himself and finding true happiness independent of any outside influence. It is towards the darkness of death, a place that is cold and alone, void of people and of the spirit. His spirit did not guide him back from the world of darkness to the light, and Rousseau ended his days mad and poor.

> How have I come to this?........Indignation, fury, delirium seized upon me; I lost my direction. My head was turned and in the horrible darkness in which men have not ceased to keep me plunged, I perceived neither a gleam to guide me, nor a support, nor a foothold to stand firmly on and to resist the despair which carried me away.[281]

As Rousseau's inward journey developed, he writes about the antithetical opposites of Religion and Science. He explains how humanity is on a journey from the religious attitude to the scientific, by means of the vices. He believes that sciences such as physics came from idle curiosity, astronomy from superstition and moral philosophy from human pride, and as we liberate ourselves from the darkness of our origins, we slowly discover the sciences, but in so doing, lose sight of the very darkness at the basis of religion. This darkness, he explains, is where we all came from, and the darkness we all go into upon death. Science itself is striving somehow to overcome this most definite and determined scenario.

> Science extends itself, and religion decays. All the world are for teaching how to act well, but nobody is willing to learn. We are all in fact all become scholars, and have ceased to be Christians.[282]

---

[280] Ibid, Fifth Promenade, p.115.
[281] Ibid, Eighth Promenade, p.158
[282] Ibid, Part the Second, p.64.

> Had the destined man to be healthy, I could almost venture to declare that a state of reflection is a state contrary to nature, and that a thinking man is a depraved animal. When we think on the good constitution of the savages, at least of those whom we have not ruined by our spirituous liquors; and reflect that they are troubled with hardly any disorders, but such as are caused by wounds on old age; we must be in a manner convinced that the history of human diseases must be confined to that of civil society.[283]

There is no doubt that we have entered a scientific age and that the darkness (unconscious) we all came from has a low level of interest to the rational and reasoned mind. Rousseau's attitude towards science is negative and can be understood as reinforcement and sustaining his inner journey. In this instance, Rousseau has an opposite stance to the ancient view that the body and associated instincts require overcoming and are evil. He embraced the body and instincts for a closer understanding of human nature, and indeed, this is the only way we can liberate the spirit within matter by going in and getting it. This is why he sees the physical world and its study as negative. It requires dismemberment, boiling and transformation in the alchemical tradition, to emerge renewed in the third stance, and free of the opposites.

Rousseau also touches on the antithesis of thought and the instincts, and how humanity in his epoch, compared themselves to the savages, which were full of disorders and disease due to their depraved instinctuality. As with Leibniz, Rousseau describes the lower animals as oriented by the senses. The difference between the animals and humans, in his view, is only a matter of degree. He rightly explains that we are all sensible of the same instinctive impulses; some are at liberty to resist these impulses, reinforced by the prevailing laws in the culture. The problem with Rousseau's exploration of the natural man is that instincts can be positive and negative and the urge to love is not far from the urge to kill. For an individual to step into their instinctive background requires the isolation that Rousseau suffered, and is recommended to avoid the natural misalignment that arises between instinct, culture and law.

This is one of the biggest problems individuals suffer when confronted with the reality of their own nature. When a lion kills another's cubs, we say it is nature at work. When an individual kills another, we put them in a cage or kill them, thus taking away their liberty or life. We do not regard it as human nature but a violation of law. Yet, when a nation invades another and kills millions of people, we accept it because we declared

---

[283] Ibid, Part the Second, p.174.

war and there are generally no consequences for the invading nation.[284] The rule of law is a necessity for a functioning society, but is still enforced by power and force, which is in itself, the law of the jungle.

Rousseau describes the unconscious as dark, cold, chaotic, incomprehensible, isolated, at the bottom of a gulf, no existence except memories, inside himself, his heart, dying absolute silence, in delirium, no guide or support and finally the realm of instinct. The madness involved is understood, and so too the underlying unity of the opposites. Unfortunately, he could not solve the conflict between instinct and civil society and did not find that spirit that could reconcile the opposites and guide him back to the world.

h. Kant I. (1724 - 1804)

Kant was an academic philosopher who founded German idealism. His life was outwardly uneventful and he kept a regular and orderly schedule. He did not marry, so did not experience the pleasure and pain of a wife and family. The main emphasis of his philosophy was the subject over the object of cognition. Indeed his basic premise was that the only true reality is the cognition of matter, not matter itself. To Kant cognition is the 'a priori' idea of matter, in other words, the idea of matter. He emphasises the reality of the subject of cognition, which agrees with the psychological insights in the twentieth century.[285] The truth of this human functioning can be emphasised by the way people see the same object differently. For example, some people can see an object very clearly and make no assumptions of its reality, whereas an object impresses others only if it touches them inside in some way. This psychological fact is further emphasised when we reach the boundaries of our knowledge as the ancients showed when they projected their Gods onto the planets in the solar system. Matter itself has also become less distinct and more curious since physicists showed that it is predominately space with particles held in position by electromagnetic forces. In addition, particles such as electrons behave in unpredictable ways and do not conform to known laws.

Kant demonstrates his observation on the nature of cognition in the following passage, and the idea of an object as the only true reality for the subject. This reality varies however, depending on the individual and their particular typology.

---

[284] I refer to the invasion of nations such as Afghanistan, Iraq, Libya etc., led by the United States.
[285] I refer to the observations made by the Analytical Psychologists, which agree with this premise.

Nothing here can escape us, because what reason brings forth entirely out of itself cannot be hidden, but is brought to light by reason itself as soon as reason's common principle has been discovered. The perfect unity of this kind of cognition, and the fact that it arises solely out of pure concepts without any influence that would extend or increase it from experience or even particular intuition, which would lead to a determinate experience, make this unconditioned completeness not only feasible but also necessary. [286]

The following emphasises Kant's observation of the inner processes of cognition as independent of the empirical, sensible or physical world and a unity in itself. He also points to the connection between constituents around and within the unity that makes the central idea of the whole. In other words, Kant is aware of the inner processes of cognition and that all the inner characters (constituents) involved are oriented around a central idea or character.

This Analytic is the analysis of the entirety of our a priori cognition into the elements of the pure cognition of the understanding. It is concerned with the following points: **I.** That the concepts be pure and not empirical concepts. **2.** That they belong not to intuition and to sensibility, but rather to thinking and understanding. **3.** That they be elementary concepts, and clearly distinguished from those which are derived or composed from them. **4.** That the table of them be complete, and that they entirely exhaust the entire field of pure understanding. Now this completeness of a science cannot reliably be assumed from a rough calculation of an aggregate put together by mere estimates; hence it is possible only by means of an **idea of the whole** of the *a priori* cognition of the understanding, and through the division of concepts that such an idea determines and that constitutes it, thus only through their **connection in a system.** The pure understanding separates itself completely not only from everything empirical, but even from all sensibility. It is therefore a unity that subsists on its own, which is sufficient by itself, and which is not to be supplemented by any external additions. [287]

Kant's recognition of this central idea independent of the empirical, sensible and physical world shows his limitation in experience of the unity of the psychic and physical. This may be due to his abstracting the contents from the psyche and stripping away the personal or relational aspect of the inner characters, thus making them sterile. It's as if one were to look at the skeletal structure of a building and ignore the colour contour, line, rhythm etc., not to mention the personalities of the designer and eventual occupants.

---

[286] KANT Immanuel, Critique of Pure Reason, Cambridge University Press, 1998, Page 104
[287] Ibid, Page 201

Different representations are brought under one concept analytically (a business treated by general logic). Transcendental logic, however, teaches how to bring under concepts not the representations but the pure synthesis of representations. The first thing that must be given to us a priori for the cognition of all objects is the manifold of pure intuition; the synthesis of this manifold by means of the imagination is the second thing, but it still does not yield cognition. The concepts that give this pure synthesis unity, and that consist solely in the representation of this necessary synthetic unity, are the third thing necessary for cognition of an object that comes before us, and they depend on the understanding.[288]

In this passage, Kant describes the idea of an object as distinct from the object itself. He goes through his process, with pure intuition in the first instance, imagination in the second and its relation to the unity in the third, before one can cognise an object. The process seems to be an internal one for Kant contrasted to the usual way we study an object by using our senses through measurement, comparison, weighing, microscopy etc. I am not sure if intuition and imagination of an object can yield any truth about its nature alone. All this can do is to provide an idea of an object, which may have no relationship to that object itself, just what one imagines it to be. For any true cognisance of an object requires a relationship to that object as Kant himself hints at in the following passage.

Thus whatever and however much our concept of an object may contain, we have to go out beyond it in order to provide it with existence. With objects of sense this happens through the connection with some perception of mine in accordance with empirical laws; but for objects of pure thinking there is no means whatever for cognizing their existence, because it would have to be cognized entirely a priori, but our consciousness of all existence (whether immediately through perception or through inferences connecting something with perception) belongs entirely and without exception to the unity of experience, and though an existence outside this field cannot be declared absolutely impossible, it is a presupposition that we cannot justify through anything.[289]

Kant differentiates the idea of an object with the object itself through the connection or relationship between them. He admits that abstract ideas (objects of pure thinking) have no relationship to the object and impossible to show their existence. In other words, psychic contents are unprovable because the individual perceives them alone without the unity of experience. For example, the idea of God as an inner character can only be perceived by the individual through dreams, visions etc., and

---

[288] Ibid, Page 211
[289] Ibid, Page 349

studied, brought closer to consciousness through that inner material. The idea that God speaks to us every night in our dreams is to some ludicrous. This is because they do not understand God's language. This and other characters are 'objects of pure thinking'[290] and their only relationship to the physical object is that they borrow images and ideas from the physical world to communicate their symbolic desire to become conscious in the individual. The problem with psychic products is the subject perceives them and no one else does. We can, however, see the workings of another person's psyche through communication and behaviour, as well as artistic expression, written word and so on.

> Transcendental philosophy is here only an idea for which the critique of pure reason is to outline the entire plan architectonically, i.e., from principles,' with a full guarantee for the completeness and certainty of all the components that comprise this edifice. That this critique is not itself already called transcendental philosophy rests solely on the fact that in order to be a complete system it would also have to contain an exhaustive analysis of all of human cognition a priori. [291]

This passage describes his critique as a metaphor of a building and its structure. The 'components of this edifice' are none other than an individual's psychic functions and the detail of their operation and how they fit into the unity of his system. The idea that these functions are self-contained and belong to a unity shows his awareness of that unity. It is unclear however, to what extent his idea of unity is differentiated.

> It is therefore a unity that subsists on its own, which is sufficient by itself, and which is not to be supplemented by any external additions. Hence the sum total of its cognition will constitute a system that is to be grasped and determined under one idea, the completeness and articulation of which system can at the same time yield a touchstone of the correctness and genuineness of all the pieces of cognition fitting into it.[292]

> Transcendental philosophy has the advantage but also the obligation to seek its concepts in accordance with a principle since they spring pure and unmixed from the understanding, as absolute unity, and must therefore be connected among themselves in accordance with a concept or idea. Such a connection, however, provides a rule by means of which the place of each pure concept of the understanding and the completeness of all of them together can be determined a priori, which would otherwise depend upon whim or chance.[293]

---

[290] This is a poor use of the term 'object' as this usually refers to something physical.
[291] KANT Immanuel, Critique of Pure Reason, Cambridge University Press, 1998, Page 134
[292] Ibid, Page 201
[293] Ibid, Page 204

Kant's idea of unity is a closed system which he regards as: 'sufficient by itself', which raises a doubt as to its level of differentiation. Sufficient by itself shows that he is aware of other functions that could be included, but decided not to add more 'external additions'. He does recognise that his philosophy and its components are 'connected among themselves', which hints at the function of relationship between the concepts. In psychological terms, relationship for a man like Kant is the feminine function of soul (anima). He also hints at the unpredictability of the connection by stating that:

> All judgments are accordingly functions of unity among our representations,
> since instead of an immediate representation a higher one, which com-prehends this and other representations under itself, is used for the cognition of the object, and many possible cognitions are thereby drawn together into one. We can, however, trace all actions of the understanding back to judgments, so that the **understanding** in general can be represented as a **faculty for judging.** [294]

He elaborates on his understanding of the relationships between 'many possible cognitions being drawn together into unity by the faculty of judging. In other words, it is the function of attraction or repulsion or in simple terms, that of feeling. We can view this judging function directly in one's dreams and fantasies and there is no need for 'a priori' reasoning when doing so. In that respect, observation of unconscious products is the same as observing objects in the physical world. One looks inside for the former and outside for the latter. Kant also hints at a higher function, which 'comprehends this and other representations under itself' in the cognition of an object. Whatever that function may be for Kant is unclear but he does give some indication of its order and characteristics as follows:

> If we abstract from all content of a judgment in general, and attend only to the mere form of the understanding in it, we find that the function of thinking in that can be brought under four titles, each of which contains under itself three moments. They can suitably be represented in the following table.[295]

1.
Quantity of Judgements
Universal
Particular
Singular

---

[294] Ibid, Page 205
[295] Ibid, Page 206

	2.		3.
	Quality		**Relation**
	Affirmative		Categorical
	Negative		Hypothetical
	Infinite		Disjunctive

4.

Modality

Problematic

Assertoric

Apodictic

[296]

In the above, Kant abstracts characteristics of his 'higher function' of judgement and places it in a table forming a quaternary pattern called 'Titles'. This fourfold pattern further divided into three 'moments' describing the characteristics of each 'title'. I am not too concerned in this study with Kant's categories of judgement, as there is a great deal of subjective interpretation involved. It is important to note that the categories are placed in an orderly fourfold unified pattern, which is in some instances recognition of the fourfold nature of the orienting functions of Plato and later Jung. Kant however, brings the auspices of judgement under his thinking and strips away any personal content, thus robbing it of further evolution and life.

> Transcendental logic, how ever, teaches how to bring under concepts not the representations but the **pure synthesis** of representations. The first thing that must be given to us a priori for the cognition of all objects is the **manifold** of pure intuition; the **synthesis** of this manifold by means of the imagination is the second thing, but it still does not yield cognition. The concepts that give this pure synthesis **unity,** and that consist solely in the representation of this necessary synthetic unity, are the third thing necessary for cognition of an object that comes before us, and they depend on the understanding.[297]

Table of Categories

1.

Of Quantity

Unity

Plurality

Totality

---

[296] Ibid, Page 206
[297] Ibid, Page 211

2.	**3.**
Of Quality	**Of Relation**
Reality	Of Inherence and Subsistence
Negation	(substantia et accidens)
Limitation	Of Causality and Dependence
	(Cause and Effect)
	Of Community (reciprocity
	between agent and patient)

4.

Of Modality

Possibility - Impossibility

Existence – Non-Existence

Necessity - Contingency

[298]

For the sake of primary concepts it is therefore still necessary to remark that the categories, as the true **ancestral concepts** of pure understanding, also have their equally pure **derivative concepts**, which could by no means be passed over in complete system of transcendental philosophy, but with the mere mention of which I can be satisfied in a merely critical essay[299].

Kant represents the four functions in a quaternary pattern with the same main titles, namely Quantity, Quality, Relation and Modality. If we relate these titles to Plato's cosmology and Jung's typology, we arrive at something that does not quite fit, as he mentions in the following passage. They are Quantity/ Air/ Thinking; Quality/ Fire (water)/ Intuition (Feeling); Relation/ Water/ Feeling & Modality/ Earth/ Sensation. The anomaly may be due to his system oriented toward the object rather than the subject. In other words, Kant is quite aware of his intuitive function and regards that as an inner function, which of course it is[300]. It can, however be oriented towards the object rather than subject, making it like unconscious guesses of possibilities in the world rather than guesses of possibilities within. In addition, Kant regards the categories as 'ancestral concepts', which is akin to the myth-making unconscious or collective unconscious as Jung terms it.

Now this concept cannot contain any determinate intuition at all, and therefore concerns nothing but that unity which must be encountered in a manifold of cognition insofar as it stands in relation to an object. This

---

[298] Ibid, page 212

[299] Ibid, page 213

[300] Intuition is an Inner (unconscious) function of perception and may be directed inward to characters and ideas, or outward towards the physical world.

relation, however, is nothing other than the necessary unity of consciousness, thus also of the synthesis of the manifold through a common function of the mind for combining it in one representation. Now since this unity must be regarded as necessary a priori (since the cognition would otherwise be without an object), the relation to a transcendental object, i.e., the objective reality of our empirical cognition, rests on the transcendental law that all appearances, insofar as objects are to be given to us through them, must stand under a priori rules of their synthetic unity, in accordance with which their relation in empirical intuition is alone possible, i.e., that in experience they must stand under conditions of the necessary unity of apperception just as in mere intuition they must stand under the formal conditions of space and time; indeed, it is through those conditions that every cognition is first made possible. [301]

Determinate intuition is not included in his categories and Kant has an exclusive attitude towards it. Intuition is one of the irrational functions that simply happens. An idea, thought, image and the like, pops into one's mind of its own accord and its origin generally unknown. It is a form of spontaneous apprehension given, rather than derived. The function of intuition can be bi-directional toward the object and physical world or the subject of ideas and inner characters. It is highly problematic to understand because of its unconscious origins. With this in mind, Kant shows that intuition belongs to his transcendental laws, in-built (a priori) knowledge and synthetic unity. He continues his description of the transcendental unity and intuition:

> This principle holds a priori, and can be called **the transcendental principle of the unity** of all the manifold of our representations (thus also in intuition). Now the unity of the manifold in a subject is synthetic; pure apperception therefore yields a principle of the synthetic unity of the manifold in all possible intuition.[302]

> The unity of apperception in relation to the synthesis of the imagination **is the** understanding, and this very same unity, in relation to the transcendental synthesis of the imagination, is the pure understanding.[303]

Kant's viewpoint of his synthetic unity is for him the basis of all understanding and he therefore only has eyes for the inner workings of perception. In other words, he does not differentiate between himself and the way he perceives reality. He does recognise the in-built ideas behind perception of the object but does not recognise their own objectivity and regards them as his own functioning in contrast to what the ancients would have regarded as the 'Gods' functioning. For example, if one feels

---

[301] KANT Immanuel, Critique of Pure Reason, Cambridge University Press, 1998, page 234
[302] Ibid, page 237
[303] Ibid, page 238

love, is it I that loves or is it an inner character that gives me the feeling of love[304]? This is the level of objectivity possible and necessary when dealing with inner ideas and characters. The reason this objectivity is important is because some inner characters are less than benevolent and possession by them is detrimental to one's health and the health of others.

> The objective unity of all (empirical) consciousness in one consciousness (of original apperception) is thus the necessary condition even of all possible perception, and the affinity of all appearances (near or remote) is a necessary consequence of a synthesis in the imagination that is grounded a priori on rules.[305]

Again, Kant emphasises the perceiving subject and idea of the 'empirical' object' as the 'necessary condition' of all perception.

> Thus as exaggerated and contradictory as it may sound to say that the understanding is itself the source of the laws of nature, and thus of the formal unity of nature, such an assertion is nevertheless correct and appropriate to the object, namely experience.[306]

The preceding passage is an important clarification by Kant and a simple description of what is a psychological truth. In this passage, he sees the relationship between the laws of nature and the laws of our own nature (transcendental unity). We can see this in the way bees have an innate idea of how to construct their intricate hives and the ritualistic behaviour of birds and fish, particularly when mating.[307] It is the same with flora and their intricate methods of attraction and repulsion. It is something that is contained within the species 'a priori' and humans also function in this way. This is why the 'man versus nature' argument is superfluous and the idea we can go beyond our own nature is a fantasy rather than a fact. This recognition also helps us understand why we are the way we are, and why we still have such murderous impulses and need control over others. In that respect, we are no different from the male lion in a pride or the shark looking for its next meal.

> Synthetic unity of the manifold of intuitions, as given a priori, is thus the ground of the identity of apperception itself, which precedes a priori all my determinate thinking.[308]

---

[304] This obviously depends on ones typology and personal circumstances.
[305] KANT Immanuel, Critique of Pure Reason, Cambridge University Press, 1998, page 240
[306] Ibid, page 242
[307] For example, Bowerbirds make nests to attract a mate and the Puffer fish makes an intricate Mandala like pattern on the sea floor to attract a mate.
[308] KANT Immanuel, Critique of Pure Reason, Cambridge University Press, 1998, page 248

Kant explains how his intuitions give him knowledge and precede his thinking (idea) of the object.

> The **transcendental unity** of apperception is that unity through which all of the manifold given in an intuition is united in a concept of the object. It is called **objective** on that account, and must be distinguished from the **subjective unity** of consciousness, which is a **determination of inner sense,** through which that manifold of intuition is empirically given for such a combination.[309]

Kant expands his idea of unity and describes the different types as he sees them. Perhaps he was premature in the use of the term 'unity' because when there are many unities involved they are not a unity in themselves but a component of unity. This is similar to Leibniz's monad, which also had multiple expressions. It is as if Kant struggles to place all the functions of his personality into a whole but cannot quite bring it all together. He recognises that each constituent is connected to an overall unity but cannot see how they are connected and what relationship they have with each other. His poor attitude to women and the feminine principal and the lack of personal interpretation kept him limited to the intellectual understanding of reality.

He does however recognise that all of his differing forms of unity have a 'totality' as shown in the next passage. This totality he regards as time. This is an indication that Kant finds his totality (overall unity) in the physical world of time. In other words, physical world of objects and people that exist in time are for Kant the opposite of his synthetic unity and part of the totality of his personality. Time belongs to the physical in that its cycle is self-evident and known. Inner ideas, characters, fantasies, etc., exist beyond time and space as they put us in situations that do not comply with the physical laws. We can fly, jump from place to place, find ourselves in unusual situations one second and others the next.

> There is only one totality in which all of our representations are contained, namely inner sense and its a priori form, time. The synthesis of representations rests on the imagination, but their synthetic unity (which is requisite for judgment), on the unity of apperception.[310]

Kant expands on this recognition in the following passage where he identifies the opposites of 'phenomena' and 'noumena'. This passage shows that the Noumena is a prerequisite for judgement and regards it as an objective reality. He expands this concept and divides the world into sense(s) and understanding.

---

[309] Ibid, page 250
[310] Ibid, page 281

Now one might have thought that the concept of appearances, limited by the Transcendental Aesthetic, already yields by itself the objective reality of the **noumena** and justifies the division of objects into **phenomena** and **noumena,** thus also the division of the world into a world of the senses and of the understanding (mundus sensibilis & intelligibilis)**,** indeed in such a way that the difference here would not concern merely the logical form of the indistinct or distinct cognition of one and the same thing, but rather the difference between how they can originally be given to our cognition, in accordance with which they are in them selves different species.[311]

The important aspect of Kant's division of the world into opposites is that he regards 'Noumena' having an objective reality. Indeed this is an important viewpoint in that the products of the unconscious do have an objective reality. For example, dreams come to us while asleep without conscious input or control. They happen of their own accord and in their own way. Similarly, we project inner characters and ideas onto the 'phenomenal' world, which connects us to that world. This is the unity relationship between the Noumenal and Phenomenal halves of realty. It is curious that Kant would view them as 'different species' as they are indispensible to each other and intricately related.

Nevertheless, if we call certain objects, as appearances, beings of sense (phenomena)**,** because we distinguish the way in which we intuit them from their constitution in itself, then it already follows from our concept that to these we as it were oppose, as objects thought merely through the understanding, either other objects conceived in accordance with the latter constitution, even though we do not intuit it in them, or else other possible things, which are not objects of our senses at all, and call these beings of understanding (noumena)**.**[312]

In the preceding passage Kant uses the term 'beings' of understanding which hints at the possible awareness of the inner myth-making characters behind understanding. He does, however understand the way the Phenomenal and Noumenal interact by introducing a third function in the following passage:

Now all pure concepts have to do generally with the synthetic unity of representations, but concepts of pure reason (transcendental ideas) have to do with the unconditioned synthetic unity of all conditions in general. Consequently, all transcendental ideas will be brought under **three classes,** of which the first contains the absolute (unconditioned) **unity of the thinking subject,** the **second** the absolute **unity of the**

---

[311] Ibid, page 347
[312] Ibid, page 360

series of conditions of appearance, the **third** the absolute **unity** of the **condition of all objects of thought** in general.

This shows Kant's recognition of a threefold system of 'classes' which includes the thinking subject, conditions of appearance of physical objects and the third 'absolute uniting' class of all objects of thought. This shows that his idea of unity lies within himself rather than in the phenomenal (physical) world. He continues to describe his classes further in the next passage:

> The thinking subject is the object of **psychology,** the sum total of all appearances (the world) is the object of **cosmology,** and the thing that contains the supreme condition of the possibility of everything that can be thought (the being of all beings) is the object of **theology.** Thus pure reason provides the ideas for a transcendental doctrine of the soul (psychologia rationalis**),** a transcendental science of the world (cosmologia rationalis**),** and finally also a transcendental cognition of God (theologia transcendentalis**).** [313]

He puts these classes into their respective disciplines of psychology, cosmology and theology and introduces the concept of 'soul' to his system. As we have learnt from Plato, Aristotle and others, soul has feminine characteristics and connects other characters and ideas in relationship. For Kant this is his 'absolute' idea of unity. This idea is however transcendental, meaning that it remains in his 'noumena' and not related to physical aspect of reality. In other words, Kant does not include the phenomenal as part of unity. Physical things have a life of their own; they exist in their own right and exist whether we perceive them or not. When we experience a peaceful death of an individual, the phenomenal world continues without interruption. Even the dead person's body still exists intact until the decay process consumes it.

Unlike Descartes', Kant has not differentiated his soul into its upper and lower relationships and therefore only has eyes for the physical as it affects his Noumenal perception of it. In other words, he is more concerned with the idea behind objects rather than the object itself. He gives reality to the object through projection of the idea, which as we have seen from the previous study of the ancient's, may have no relationship to the object.

> No **objective deduction** of these transcendental ideas is really possible, such as we could provide for the categories. For just because they are

---

[313] Ibid, page 406

ideas, they have in fact no relation to any object that could be given congruent to them.[314]

As mentioned previously, the idea of an object can be somewhat different to the object itself. For example when the ancients viewed the planets, they projected inner characters onto them and gave them a life based on their perceived behaviour. Today we know more about the planets behaviour and have to some extent, withdrawn the projections. Projection forms the initial relationship and interest in an object and can keep that energetic system working until the interest evaporates OR, until the reality of the object is recognised and the idea resembles the object itself. Upon withdrawal of a projection, we learn about an object as it is and the idea changes as we learn more. This also includes other people and the withdrawal of projections of inner characters encourages the development of an aligned idea of the other person.

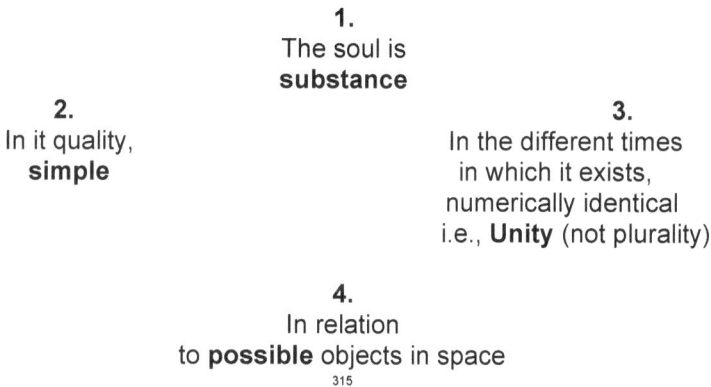

1.
The soul is
substance

2.
In it quality,
simple

3.
In the different times
in which it exists,
numerically identical
i.e., **Unity** (not plurality)

4.
In relation
to **possible** objects in space
[315]

The diagram above puts Kant's idea of soul into its four constituent functions and attempts to connect it to its physical orientation. We know that matter is made of complex arrangements of atoms and molecules. He is hesitant in the relational aspect of objects (possible) and regards the time an object exists as a unity. Naturally, an object has to exist in space and time otherwise it does not actually exist. The idea of the object however, is still there in memory and outside the influence of space and time.

> But something that seems to be even further removed from objective reality than the idea is what I call the **ideal,** by which I understand the idea not merely **in concreto** but **in individuo,** i.e., as an individual thing which is determinable, or even determined, through the idea alone.

---

[314] Ibid, page 406
[315] Ibid, page 413

199

Again, we have to be very cautious making any determinations about an object from the idea we project onto it. We can make the grossest errors during this natural but initial stage of getting to know an object. Knowledge of an object is furthered by observation and experimentation. For example, we perceive a white coffee mug with our eyes, then close our eyes, we can still see the mug as a specific idea that is connected to that particular mug. That particular mug also belongs to the idea of all mugs and we can change its colour, shape, size etc. The original mug, as physical object has not changed, but the idea of it has. This is the function of projection in that it gives the initial connection to an object. If we confuse the idea of it with the object, we can get into all kinds of confusing misinterpretations and not see the object as it is.

> What is an ideal to us, was to **Plato** an **idea in the divine understanding,** an individual object in that understanding's pure intuition, the most perfect thing of each species of possible beings and the original ground of all its copies in appearance.[316]

In the above passage, Kant uses Plato to reinforce his concept of the object being merely an appearance of the idea, thus robbing the object of its own existence.

> It makes a big difference whether something is given to my reason as **an object absolutely** or is given only as an **object in the idea.** In the first case my concepts go as far as determining the object; but in the second, there is really only a schema for which no object is given, not even hypothetically, but which serves only to represent other objects to us, in accordance with their systematic unity, by means of the relation to this idea, hence to represent these objects indirectly.[317]

Kant continues to describe the difference between the object and the idea of the object and rightly identifies the fact that the idea can exist without the object. He understood the reality and connection of idea and object but did not explore the idea to its natural conclusion. If he studied the Noumenal as an inner reality beyond object, he may have divined its meaning and purpose. In dreams, we recognise familiar objects, but it is the meaning of the object being conveyed, not the object itself. Every object has its own meaning in that the idea has a deeper and symbolic aspect to it. For example, a stone has hardness, shape, colour, crystalline structure, certain elements and so on, yet symbolically a stone can be at once worthless and precious, (diamond and coal) unwavering in its hardness, strong, difficult to budge, a unity in itself, incorruptible, has a

---

[316] Ibid, page 551
[317] Ibid, page 605

special place in alchemy and so on. The symbolic language builds upon the physical nature of the object.

> Finally and thirdly, (in regard to theology) we have to consider everything that might ever belong to the context of possible experience **as if** this experience constituted an absolute unity, but one dependent through and through, and always still conditioned within the world of sense, yet at the same time **as if** the sum total of all appearances (the world of sense itself) had a single supreme and all-sufficient ground outside its range, namely an independent, original, and creative reason, as it were, in relation to which we direct every empirical use of **our** reason in its greatest extension **as if** the objects themselves had arisen from that original image of all reason. [318]

This is the difficulty in studying Kant as he discusses whether the object or the idea of the object came first. He is of the opinion although hesitant with his use of the term 'as if', that the idea of the object existed before the object. At the limits of knowledge, objects attract projection and the unknown fills with an idea. In the ancient world, a planet seen in the night sky encouraged projection that related to the perceived behaviour of the planet and every other characteristic was an inner projection. Knowledge of the object diminishes the projection and transforms it into an idea closer in relationship to the object. In other words, the original projection of Saturn the God (central inner character) onto the planet transformed into what we now know as a gas giant with rings of dust and debris. In this case, the original projection was stripped away and recedes back into the unconscious. The idea of Saturn is still based on its behaviour, rings, colour and so on. His attributes have not changed, as well as his family relationships. To say that the planet arose from the myth is an error in judgement and lacks knowledge of and true relationship to the object as well as a relationship to the original idea projected onto the object. Saturn as object was around long before we had any idea of what it was. The idea of Saturn we inherited from our ancestors as a pattern of behaviour, which repeats itself in individuals throughout history.

> Complete purposive unity is perfection (absolutely considered). If we do not find this in the essence of the things which constitute the whole object of experience, i.e., all our objectively valid cognition, hence in universal and necessary laws of nature, then how will we infer straight away from this to the idea of a highest and absolutely necessary perfection in an original being, which is the origin of all causality? The greatest systematic unity, consequently also purposive unity, is the school and even the ground of the possibility of the greatest use of

---

[318] Ibid, page 607

human reason. Hence the idea of it is inseparably bound up with the essence of our reason.[319]

Finally, Kant attempts to bring his whole system into a perfect absolute unity and original being, which he regards as the origin of all causality. The use of the term 'perfect' seems too constricted to describe the workings of nature and the struggle for power that it entails. If a comet obliterates the earth, then it makes the perfection of God a little redundant, as there would be no one left to appreciate the meaning of such destruction. We say that nature is 'perfect' and balanced because it works. Perfection is usually associated with good and not the balanced,[320] beautiful, wondrous, yet horrific systems of nature. In addition, can a Perfect Being be responsible for creating imperfection? It is more reasonable to consider the Supreme Being, whoever or whatever that may be, in contrast to my personal idea of it, having complete unity in itself and all aspects of existence, both perfect and imperfect.

i. Hume D. (1711 - 1776)

Hume was a contemporary of Rousseau in later life and had a friendship with him that ended badly. As a down-to-earth man, Hume's view of the natural man was opposite to Rousseau's view. To Hume, everything including ideas came from sense perceptions leaving an impression on the mind.

> All the perceptions of the human mind resolve themselves into two different kinds, which I shall call Impressions and Ideas. The difference betwixt these consists in the degrees of force and liveliness, with which they strike upon the mind, and make their way into our thought or consciousness. Those perceptions, which enter with the most force and violence, we may name impressions; and under this name I comprehend all our sensations, passions and emotions, as they make their first appearance in the soul. By ideas I mean the faint images of these in thinking and reasoning..........[321]

Hume puts sensations with passions and emotions separate to ideas, which he regards as faint images related to thinking and reasoning. He therefore describes two realms that have differing energy levels of force. He regards the impressions having a close relationship to the body and the senses and are affected by external sense perceptions and internal passions or instincts and their associated emotions.

---

[319] Ibid, page 618

[320] Nature is easily affected by environmental changes and adjusts to suit.

[321] HUME I, A Treatise of Human Nature' Books One, Two and Three; 2nd Edition; Oxford at the Clarendon Press; First Edition 1888, Oxford 1978, 2nd Edition 1978 - Book 1, Section 1, Of the Origin of Our Ideas, page 1

> As to those impressions, which arise from the senses, their ultimate cause is, in my opinion, perfectly explicable by human reason, and 'twill always be impossible to decide with certainty, whether they arise immediately from the object, or are produc'd by the creative power of the mind, or are deriv'd from the author of our being.[322]

He regards sense perceptions of objects as the "ultimate cause" of ideas, which is a reasonable interpretation if we only regard ideas in their visual sense, rather than their meaning. He did have doubts about this interpretation as the above text shows, leaving the door open to the "creative power of the mind" and the "author of our being" as possible origins. To emphasise the role of sense perceptions and how they fit into a typical natural system, I posit the following example: Humans and animals alike share the sexual instinct and depend on the idea of a partner and union with that partner. This idea is accompanied by an urge to satisfy sexual union. The sense perception of a potential partner may spark the urge, but the urge has a life of its own and a cyclic frequency, much the same as the need for food. The instinct is to some extent blind as it can be relieved without its natural goal of union with a partner (object). This does not have any bearing on its meaning, as the instincts' purpose is union with the object and propagation of a uniting third. The idea of unity and union of opposites is still the reason behind the instinct and the object is a necessary component, but not the "ultimate cause". The creative mind, as Hume mentions, is but a tool for the satisfaction of the instinct as the elaborate mating rituals of humans and animals testify.

> We find by experience, that when an impression has been present with the mind, it again makes its appearance there as an idea; and this it may do after two different ways: either when its new appearance it retains a considerable degree of its first vivacity, and in somewhat intermediate between an impression and an idea; or when it entirely loses its vivacity, and is a perfect idea. The faculty by which we repeat out impressions in the first manner, is called the MEMORY, and the other the IMAGINATION.[323]

In this passage, Hume continues his description of impressions and ideas but includes the relationship and gradation of vivacity between them. What starts as an impression with emotion from an internal or external perception becomes a memory after the perception. He explains how the memory moves from impression to idea with the loss of emotional intensity, which he terms the 'perfect idea'.

---

[322] Ibid, -Section V, Of the Impressions of the Senses and Memory, page 84
[323] Ibid, -Section III, Of Ideas of the Memory and Imagination, page 8

It is debatable whether a perfect idea exists without an emotion attached to it. The law of attraction and repulsion governs all ideas and emotions, and gives life to the ideas. For example, we can have the idea of a loving father, which would attract our interest and therefore feel a level of reverence, admiration and love. On the other hand, the idea of a monster repels us with a feeling of disdain and fear[324].

In addition, a perfect idea without emotion is in fact indifference to the idea. In other words, the idea does not move us and there is no attractive or repulsive judgment to it. In this sense, indifference is located at the centre of attraction on one side and repulsion on the other. Indifference has much in common with time in that the line between past and future is but a transition between one and the other. It has no dimension and cannot be regarded other than a line of transition. It is where the past meets the future. The reason we feel the present is because we have memory of what just occurred and predictive anticipation of what is to come. It is the same with indifference, in that it is located between attraction, repulsion, and all the tones in between.

> But tho' in this view of things we cannot refuse to condemn the materialists, who conjoin all thought with extension; yet a little reflection will show us equal reason for blaming their antagonists, who conjoin all thought with a simple and indivisible substance. The most vulgar philosophy in forms us, that no external object can make itself known to the mind immediately, and without the interposition of an image or perception. [325]

Hume in this instance sees both sides of a philosophical orientation and in some way the unity of opposites. Whether we see the mind as an adjunct to the body, or the body an adjunct to the mind, it is the same idea of unity from differing points of view.

> Methinks I am like a man, who having struck on many shoals, and having narrowly escape'd ship-wreck in passing a small frith, has yet the temerity to put out to sea in the same leaky weather-beaten vessel, and even carries his ambition so far as to think of compassing the globe under these disadvantageous circumstances. My memory of past errors and perplexities, make me diffident to the future. The wretched condition, weakness and disorder of the faculties, I must employ in my enquiries, encrease my apprehensions.   And the impossibility of or correcting these faculties, reduces me almost to despair, and makes me resolve to perish on the barren rock, on which I am at present, rather that venture myself upon that boundless ocean, which runs out into immensity. This

---

[324] I am generalising here for I have no doubt that some people are attracted to the idea of evil and have positive feelings toward it.

[325] HUME I, A Treatise of Human Nature' Books One, Two and Three; 2nd Edition; -Section V, Of the Immateriality of the Soul, page 239

sudden view of my danger strikes me melancholy; and as 'tis usual for that passion, above all others, to indulge itself; I cannot forbear feeding my despair, with all those desponding reflection, which the present subject furnishes me with in such abundance. ....When I look abroad, I foresee on every side, dispute, contradiction, anger, calumny and detraction. When I turn my eye inward, I find nothing but doubt and ignorance. [326]

This very poignant passage shows how Hume came to a stage in his life where the physical world had lost its attraction and he became aware that his aging body and mind (vessel) could not embark on a journey over the ocean (unconscious). Looking inward, he sees doubt and ignorance, but as he mentions in the following passage, does recognise an inner woman (truth).

For with what confidence can I venture upon such bold enterprizes, when beside those numberless infirmities peculiar to myself, I find so many which are common to human nature? Can I be sure, that in leaving all establish'd opinions I am following truth, and by what criterion shall I distinguish her, even if fortune shou'd at last guide me on her footsteps?[327]

Allowing an inner woman to lead us is by no means an easy task for an older man preoccupied with reason. Turning away from the world as Rousseau did is not for everyone and many perish on the ocean of the unconscious. Hume does, however sense that his unity depends on the journey into himself as he describes in the following passage and his idea of that unity in waiting.

'Tis evident here are four affections, plac'd, as it were, in a square or regular connexion with, and distance from each other. The passions of pride and humility, as well as those of love and hatred, are connected together by the identity of their object, which to the first set of passions is self, to the second some other person. These two lines of communication or connexion form two opposite sides of the square. Again pride and love are agreeable passions; hatred and humility uneasy. This similitude of sensation betwixt pride and love, and that betwixt humility and hatred form a new connexion, and may be consider'd as the other two sides of the square. Upon the whole, pride is connected with humility, love with hatred, by their objects and ideas: Pride with love, humility with hatred, by their sensations or impressions.[328]

---

[326] Ibid, Section VII, Conclusion of this Book (Book 1), page 265
[327] Ibid, page 263
[328] Ibid, Book II, Part II, Objects and Causes of Love and Hatred, page 333

He mentions a squared Mandala shape with the four corners having paired opposites of the passions (emotions): pride/humility and love/hate and gives them a value judgement of agreeability (attraction) and uneasiness (repulsion). He cross-connects the four into a relational system of opposites and adjacent passions. In addition, he brings the whole system under the umbrella of sensation, in other words, the perception of these passions. This shows Hume's orientation is towards the physical, not the inner realm of ideas of Rousseau. He does however perceive what comes from the inner realm as it affects his body and therefore is perceptible to his mind. This is emphasised in the next passage were Hume describes what happens when the 'hold' of external objects is loosened.

> Those, who take a pleasure in declaiming against human nature, have observ'd, that man is altogether insufficient to support himself; and that when you loosen all the holds, which he has of external objects, he immediately drops down into the deepest melancholy and despair. From this. say they, proceeds that continual search after amusement in gaming, in hunting, in business; by which we endeavour to forget ourselves, and excite our spirits from the languid state, into which they fall, when not sustain'd by some brisk and lively emotion......... On the appearance of such an object it awakes, as it were from a dream: And the whole man acquires a vigour, which he cannot command in his solitary and calm moments. [329]

Hume shows his typology here with his acknowledgement of the melancholy and despair that overcomes him in his solitary and calm moments. Obviously, not everyone feels these emotions when looking inside. Creative types are always inspired and energised by a new idea they wish to express and in this instance, the idea needs expression and shaping as an object, rather than what Hume regards as the object giving the vigour (energy) or lively emotion.

He does, however give us an indirect hint of how his personality perceives the physical as well as the psychic by the way energy flows from inside to outside. He does this by calling activities such as gaming, hunting and business as amusements and how they 'excite our spirits'. Although he perceives the flow of energy, he does not see the ideas behind the activities that free the energy and bring it into the physical world. I do not wish to go into the symbolic qualities of these activities in depth, other than to comment on the competitive aspect of the idea and object. For example, gaming is driven by the urge to overcome an obstacle and win the object, hunting the overcoming of the animal within and killing its representation, and business the negotiating art to obtain

---

[329] Ibid, Section IV, Of the Love of Relations, page 352

the object. This competitive or combative aspect of his idea of unity and preference for one side is empathised in the following:

> Nothing is more usual in philosophy, and even in common life, than to talk of the combat of passion and reason, to give the preference to reason, and to assert that men are only so far virtuous as they conform themselves to its dictates. [330]

j. Schopenhauer. A (1788 - 1860)

Schopenhauer's pessimistic temperament permeates throughout his work and life and is emphasised in the attitude he had to his idea of unity. He resigned himself to the fact that a greater will was in control of his life, rather than his own personal will. This is emphasised in his attitude to dreams, which he regards as 'absurd' presumably due their lack of obvious logic and purpose.

> For as the world is in one aspect entirely *idea*, so in another it is entirely *will*. However, a reality which is neither of these two, but an object in itself (into which Kant's thing-in-itself has unfortunately degenerated in the course of his work), is the absurd product of a dream, and its credence in philosophy is a treacherous will-o'-wisp. [331]

He sees the greater will in a negative light due to his unwillingness to accept his own human nature as it is, rather than how he feels it could be. He does however, acknowledge the reality of dream in the next passage and that the physical and psychic realms share imagery but relates the imagery to the intellect. In other words, Schopenhauer tries to see the unity of inner and outer without sufficiently differentiating their characteristics.

> For only after men had tried their hand for thousands of years at a mere philosophy of the object did they discover that, among the many things that make the world so puzzling and give us pause for thought, is first and foremost that, however immeasurable and massive this world may be, its existence hangs nonetheless by a single thread: that is, the actual consciousness in which it exists. The world's existence is irrevocably subject to this condition, and this brands it, in spite of all empirical reality, with the stamp of ideality, and therefore of mere phenomenal appearance. As a result, the world must be recognised, at least from this aspect, as akin to dreaming, and indeed as belonging to the same category. For the function of the brain which, during sleep, conjures up a completely objective, perceptible, and even palpable world, must have

---

[330] Ibid, Part III, Section III, Of the Influencing Motives of the Will, page 413
[331] SCHOPENHAUER A, The World as Will and Idea, , Edited by David Berman, Translated by Jill Berman, Everyman 1997, The World as Idea -First Aspect, page 5

just as large a share in the presentation of the objective world of our waking hours. For both worlds, although different in their matter, are nonetheless made from the same mould. This mould is the intellect, the function of the brain.[332]

This leads to a cross-contamination and raises a doubt about the reality of either. Schopenhauer projected idealism onto the physical realm, and attempted to look at the origin of the projection. He concludes that both the physical and psychic realms come from the same 'mould' which he regards as the intellect. This shows his ability to see the difference between inner and outer, but not how they are related. It also demonstrates Schopenhauer's approach to understanding the opposites and identifies the physical as purely phenomenal with the 'stamp of ideality'.

> Only consciousness is immediately given; therefore the basis of philosophy is limited to facts of consciousness, i.e., it is essentially idealistic.[333]

This is an attempt to connect the opposites and relate them. Schopenhauer recognises the problem is one of understanding the ideal and sees how dream images are borrowed from the physical world, thus connecting them in that way. Therefore, he has the same view as Kant and regards physical reality as a phenomenon of conscious cognition. He regarded matter as dead and lifeless and not having the 'will' of living creatures.

> Although materialism imagines that it is postulating nothing more than this matter- in the form, for instance, of atoms - it is nevertheless unconsciously adding to it only the subject, but also space, time, and causality, which depend upon special properties of the subject.............. The world as idea, the objective world, has thus, as it were, two poles: the knowing subject, simply without the forms of its knowledge, and then crude matter without form and quality. Both are completely unknowable: the subject because it is the knower, matter because without form and quality it cannot be perceived. Yet both are fundamental conditions of all empirical perception. Thus the knowing subject, merely as such, which is a presupposition of all experience, stands opposite, as its pure counterpart, to the crude, formless, and utterly dead (i.e., will-less) matter, which, though not given in any, is presupposed in every experience. ....

> The fundamental error of all systems is the failure to recognise this truth, the truth that intellect and matter are correlatives, i.e., that the one exists only for the other, both stand and fall together, the one is only the

---

[332] Ibid, Supplement to Book One, The Standpoint of Idealism, page 12
[333] Ibid, page 13.

reflexion of the other, and indeed, they are really one and the same thing regarded from two opposite points of view; and this one thing, I am here anticipating, is the manifestation of the will, or the thing-in-itself.[334]

Schopenhauer explains how intellect and matter are related and opposite but does not recognise their equality. He sees matter as an extension, reflection and indispensible to intellect, but of lower rank and only exists for the other. The opposites of matter and intellect in Schopenhauer's understanding are indeed indispensible to each other and unified in a system of checks and balances, which holds the system together. His idea of one side serving the other can only be maintained for short periods, as the system can only be sustained with equality. The servant always has feelings of rebellion and oppression and seeks equality with the master. Schopenhauer confuses matter with the idea of matter as part of our perceptive function and although drawn from the object, can exist independently. Matter exists of its own accord and does not cease to exist if we do not perceive it.

Schopenhauer describes the opposites as the same thing from different viewpoints united by the Will and recognises the third aspect of opposites united. He gives it a mysterious unknown quality removed from perception and understanding. There is no feeling attached to the idea which could give it a life and humanity. He perceives the relationship in image alone and not as a living vibrant system. This is the difference between perceiving unity passively and taking part in it actively. Schopenhauer continues with his idea of will and calls it a force that affects humans, animals, plants and what he previously referred to as "dead matter". Further, he includes the forces that govern crystal, metal, magnetism and gravitation, and attempts to bring matter and Will into a unified whole. On one hand he regards matter as dead, and the other, recognises the forces that influence matter, which are the same forces that influence Will as he states in the next passage:

> This will of which we are speaking he will recognise as the inmost nature not only in those phenomenon which are closely similar to his own, in men and animals, but further reflection will lead him also to recognise the force which stirs and vegetates in the plant, and indeed the force by which the crystal is formed, that by which the magnet turns to the North Pole, the force whose shock he experiences from the contact between different metals, the force which appears in the elective affinities of matter as repulsion and attraction, separation and combination, and, lastly, even gravitation, which pulls so powerfully through all matter, draws the stone to the earth and the earth to the sun -all these he will recognise as different only in their phenomenal existence, but in their inner nature as identical, as what is directly known to him so intimately

---

[334] Ibid, pages 20 and 21

and so much better than anything else, and which, in its most distinct manifestation, is called *will*.[335]

This is where Schopenhauer sets himself apart as he recognises the fundamental forces of nature pertaining to this Will and how it stirs, affects, shocks, and co-ordinates living as well as so-called 'dead' matter. All living things are made of the same material (elements) as 'dead' things and are fully categorised into their various properties and atomic structures. Schopenhauer's recognition of electromagnetic forces of attraction and repulsion, separation and combination and gravitation, all come from his concept and relationship to the overarching unity Schopenhauer calls Will.

> The concept *will*, on the other hand, is of all possible concepts the only one which has its source *not* in the phenomenal, *not* in the mere perceptive ideation, but comes from within, and arises in the most immediate consciousness of each of us. ....The *will* as a thing in itself is totally different from its phenomenon, and entirely free from all the forms of the phenomenal. Since the will enters into these forms only at the very moment when it manifests itself, they have to do only with its *objectivity*, and are alien to the will itself. Even the most universal form of all idea, that of being object for a subject, is irrelevant to it; still less the forms which are subordinate to this and which collectively have their common expression in the principal of sufficient reason.[336]

Schopenhauer cleverly distinguishes between Will and the concept of 'Will', which comes into consciousness from inside. He has therefore, differentiated the psychic from physical connecting them to Will. We cannot know the Will due to its all-encompassing nature. The concept or idea of Will is more personal and accessible to the individual if the necessary inner work carried out. This is why many groups have different ideas of God. It is a personal interpretation based on temperament, experience, understanding and relationship to other individuals.

> Hence the strange fact that everyone regards himself as *a priori* perfectly free, even in his individual actions, and believes that at any moment he could embark upon a different path in life, which mean his becoming a different person. But *a posteriori*, through experience, he finds to his astonishment that he is not free, but subject to necessity; that in spite of all his resolutions and reflections of his life to the end of it, he must continue to play the very role which he himself condemns, and, as it were, play to the end the part he has undertaken.[337]

---

[335] Ibid, Book Two, First Aspect, page 42
[336] Ibid, page 44
[337] Ibid, page 46

Schopenhauer continues his description of Will and its influence on the individual's life path. He questions an individual's freedom and in his experience, the Will determines a person's fate. In other words, Schopenhauer considers the Will a determining factor in a person's life and is directed by this Will, which is innate rather than selected by the individual. This idea is similar to the 'individuation' that the ancient Egyptian God Khepri represented and used by the scholastic philosophers in the 13th century and Carl Jung in the 20th century. It also has similarities to the Chinese idea of Toa (path). The evidence discovered through comparative analysis in modern psychology shows that this path is indeed a fact and deviation from one's path leads to illness.

> On the other hand, if we have thoroughly grasped the philosophical insight that a force of nature is a definite grade of what we, too, recognise as our own inmost nature, and that this will, in itself and distinct from its phenomenon and their forms, lies outside time and space, and hence that plurality (which is conditioned by time and space) is a property not of the will, nor directly of the grade of its objectification, i.e., the Idea, but only of the phenomena of the Idea; and if we remember that the law of causality is meaningful only in relation to time and space, in that there it determines the position of the teeming phenomena of the different ideas in which the will reveals itself, governing the order in which they are to become manifest; if, I say, with this insight the deeper meaning of Kant's great doctrine has dawned on us - the doctrine that time, space, and causality do not belong to the thing-in-itself, but merely to the phenomenon............[338]

This passage shows Schopenhauer's recognition of the relation between inner and outer realms and that the inner Will lies outside time and space. Indeed, the unconscious and it products such as dreams have their own processes and laws. They do not comply with physical laws of matter in space and time. I must however put a caveat on this statement as the research into sub atomic particles indicates that matter itself at this scale, does not comply with known physical laws.

> The will as the thing in itself, constitutes the inner, true, and indestructible nature of man; yet in itself it is unconscious.[339]

Schopenhauer's lack of personal relation to the 'will' by using the term 'it' is reflected in his poor relation to other people, especially women, and an inability to see the 'will' as an inner character with attributes. He perceives the force associated with Will and all its manifestations, but not the nature

---

[338] Ibid, page 65
[339] Ibid, Supplement to Book Two, On the Primacy of the Will in Self Consciousness, page 87

of his particular idea of Will. I have no doubt that Schopenhauer perceived his idea of God in all his glory through his intuitions, but then proceeded to abstract his (its) metaphysical essence 'thing-in-itself' and draw universal conclusions from this abstraction. As previously mentioned, it is the difference between what Kant and Schopenhauer call the 'thing-in-itself' and the idea of it. The 'thing-in-itself' is universal, but our perception, experience and dialogue with it is personal. God is universal, the idea of God is personal and relates to the individual directly from within.

> This is called 'being master of oneself'. Clearly the master here is the will, the servant the intellect, for in the last instance the will always keeps the upper hand, and therefore constitutes the true core, the inner being, of man.[340]

Again, he emphasises the central and master position of Will and delegates the intellect to the servant of that Will. This shows the authority his idea of Will had on him was like a father to a son, and excludes the feminine principle. His personal relationship to his mother and father were determining factors to this orientation. His father died when Schopenhauer was a teenager and he did not get on well with his mother. These initial relationships often set the tone of all future relationships and the direction of development. Schopenhauer carried this pattern into life, and expressed it in his attitude to women, siding with all the attributes represented by the character of father.

As Schopenhauer mentions, individuation is something we often fight against because we live in a scientific and technological age with waning spiritual belief systems[341].

> It has often been remarked that genius and madness have an aspect in common, and even converge; and indeed poetical inspiration has been called a kind of madness: *amabilis insania*, Horice calls it (*Odes*. III. 4). Plato expresses it in the myth of the dark cave (*Rep.* 7), when he says: 'those who, outside the cave, have seen the true sunlight and the things that have true being (Ideas), cannot afterwards see properly in the cave, because their eyes have grown unaccustomed to the darkness; they can no longer recognise the shadows, and are jeered at for their mistakes by those who have never left the cave and its shadows.'[342]

The above metaphoric description of the unconscious shows Schopenhauer's identification with consciousness (sunlight) through the

---

[340] Ibid, page 92

[341] I feel that humanity is in a transition period and that we are on the verge of a new way of looking at reality, which includes inner and outer realms in relationship.

[342] SCHOPENHAUER A, The World as Will and Idea, , Edited by David Berman, Translated by Jill Berman, Everyman 1997, The World as Idea, page 114

teachings of Plato. The unconscious (dark cave) for him is where madness lurks and indeed if one does not have a strong connection to the physical world, the chaos and loss of orientation in the unconscious can lead to madness as we saw with Rousseau. It never dawned on Schopenhauer to strive for the footings of a normal life, including wife and family, support them and having to bite one's tongue to adapt and develop some feeling. This would have given him a personal flame (light) to see within the cave and meet the characters that revolve around the Will, and stand behind every instinct and emotion.

> Dogmas change and our knowledge is deceptive; but nature never errs; she moves confidently, and she never conceals what she is doing. Everything is complete and fulfilled in nature, and nature is complete and fulfilled in everything. She has her centre in every animal. With confidence the animal has found its path into life, just as with confidence it will find its way out; in the meantime it lives without fear of annihilation, and without cares, supported by the consciousness that it is nature herself, and is imperishable as she is.[343]

He does however, perceive an abstracted and projected version of an inner character in physical nature and recognised her femininity as an imperishable soul, which all creatures have in common. Animals cannot deviate from their path in life due to their undeveloped awareness and personal will, and can only abide by the greater Will of their instinctual foundation.

> All this means, to be sure, that life can be regarded as a dream and death as the awakening from it: but it must be remembered that the personality, the individual, belongs to the dreaming and not the awakened consciousness, which is why death appears to the individual as annihilation. In any event, death is not, from this point of view, to be considered a transition to a state completely new and foreign to us, but rather a return to one originally our own from which life had been only a brief absence.[344]

This is an example of Schopenhauer's view that knowledge of the unconscious is gained through projection onto physical objects but he could not perceive the characters and functions of it directly. He could only see its forms and phenomena in the physical world. The differentiation of physical and psychic is necessary to see either side as they are. In other words, the physical has its own existence and laws, as does the inner realm of the psyche. The relationship between the two can only have integrity if either side is recognised as such without the cross-contamination of projection.

---

[343] Ibid, page 183
[344] Ibid, On the Indestructibility of our Essential Being by Death, '6', page 70

An odd and unworthy definition of philosophy, which however even Kant gives, is that it is a science composed only of concepts. For the entire property of a concept consists of nothing more than what has been begged and borrowed from perceptual knowledge, which is the true and inexhaustible source of all insight. So that a true philosophy cannot be spun out of mere abstract concepts, but has to be founded on observation and experience, inner and outer.[345]

Schopenhauer views concepts as 'begged and borrowed' from the perceptual (physical world), but does not realise that ideas are formulated not through logical processes, but pop into one's awareness spontaneously. It is not clear if Schopenhauer means 'inner' as dreams, fantasies, characters, etc., or that he means the physical expression of emotion, instincts etc., which are the expressions of inner characters. The body senses hunger and emptiness accompanied by pain, but the idea of hunger includes its solution. What is a biological function also includes innate and learned ideas of how to satisfy the function. For example, we know that we can get food from the supermarket. Early humans knew that they had to go out and hunt, forage for plants and seeds, which as I noted in the previous study of Ancient Egypt, was the beginning of culture.

Ideas, dreams, fantasies etc., use imagery from the physical world woven into symbolic expression. The imagery may be familiar but the symbolic interpretation is hard to grasp, as it is deeper than our understanding. For example, observing young children learning to talk shows the frustration they have in expressing what already exists in their mind. We use language to communicate clearly, for a child it is an emotion or satisfaction of an instinct such as hunger expressed through facial changes, behaviour etc. The idea already exists, but its expression varies depending on the individual. Schopenhauer recognises this function in the following passage.

> One might almost believe that half our thinking takes place unconsciously. Usually we arrive at a conclusion without having clearly thought about the premises which lead to it. This is already evident from the fact that sometimes an occurrence whose consequences we can in no way foresee, still less clearly estimate its possible influence on our own affairs, will nonetheless exercise an unmistakable influence on our whole mood and will change it from cheerful to sad or from sad to cheerful: this can only be the result of unconscious rumination. It is even more obvious in the following: I have familiarized myself with the factual data of a theoretical or practical problem; I do not think about it again, yet often a few days later the answer to the problem will come into my mind entirely of its own accord; the operation which has produced it,

---

[345] Ibid, On Philosophy and the Intellect, '5', page 118

however, remains as much a mystery to me as that of an adding-machine: what has occurred is, again, unconscious rumination. -One might almost venture the physiological hypothesis that conscious thinking takes place on the surface of the brain, unconscious thinking inside it.[346]

This text reveals an uncanny awareness of how consciousness has no input into processing ideas. Indeed, this is basis of creativity and as he mentions, is a mystery of the highest order. The ancients recognised the process as the movement of inner characters they called Gods, at work processing information and providing it when needed. Careful observation of these inner characters shows that the ancient Gods have not disappeared, but only changed their names. When we get cranky and want to fight, an angry inner character like Mars (God of war) is activated. When a man has tender feelings of love and affection, an inner woman like Venus (Goddess of love) grips us, and so on. These days, we project these characters onto movie super heroes, romantic lovers and beautiful seductive women.

> We know that *multiplicity* in general is necessarily conditioned by space and time, and is only thinkable in them. In this respect they are called the *principium individuationis*. But we have found that space and time are forms of the principle of sufficient reason. In this principle all our knowledge *a priori* is expressed, but, as we showed above, this *a priori* knowledge, as such, only applies to the knowableness of things, not to the things themselves, *i.e.*, it is only our form of knowledge, it is not a property of the thing-in-itself. The thing-in-itself is, as such, free from all forms of knowledge, even the most universal, that of being an object for the subject. In other words, the thing-in-itself is something altogether different from the idea. If, now, this thing-in-itself is *the will*, as I believe I have fully and convincingly proved it to be, then, regarded as such and apart from its manifestation, it lies outside time and space, and therefore knows no multiplicity, and is consequently *one*.[347]

In this passage, Schopenhauer refers once again to the single Will but does not see the multiplicity within the unconscious. As history shows, every idea of God (will) has its helpers, messengers and detractors. Animism had its totems and animals, the ancients had multiple Gods in a family, Judaism its prophets and angels, Christianity the trinity/satan and so on. These are all expressions of Will as an idea. What actually creates the ideas and what he calls the 'thing-in-itself' remains unknown at this stage in our evolution. It permeates all inner and outer realms; from the

---

[346] Ibid, page 123
[347] SCHOPENHAUER Arthur, The World as Will and Idea, , Edited by David Berman, Translated by Jill Berman, Everyman 1997, Book Two, page 59

highest functioning of reason and intuition, to the structure of the atom and the forces holding the physical and psychic in balance.

Schopenhauer continues his discussion of the unity of the 'thing-in-itself' and how we can see its phenomena in every aspect of our physical existence.

> It is only the knowledge of the unity of will as thing-in-itself, in the endless diversity and multiplicity of the phenomena, that can afford us the true explanation of that wonderful, unmistakable analogy of all the productions of nature, that family likeness on account of which we may regard them as variations on the same ungiven theme. [348]

The work of Schopenhauer is indeed monumental and anchored in the perceptive functions. He no doubt saw the unconscious in projected form and makes non-personal, abstract concepts from his observations. He assigns very few qualities to his Will. This lack of the personal connection was reflected his life and his attitude towards women. As a consequence, he had no eyes for the thing-in-itself and its inner manifestations of fantasy, dreams, etc. He did however, make use of the ideational function, presumably through his intuition to form his conceptual system of thought. His personal unity and opposite would therefore be feminine, which he rejected.

Life presented Schopenhauer opportunities to integrate the rejected feminine in the form of an illegitimate child. If he had accepted the child and the attached female relationship, he could have developed that new aspect of himself that the child represented. In spite of himself, the unconscious later forced him to support a woman he threw down the stairs because she annoyed him. It is the personal woman and acceptance of the biological responsibility that Schopenhauer lacked. His influence however, endures to this day.

k. Hegel G.W.F. (1770 - 1831)

Unlike Schopenhauer, Hegel had a relatively normal life with an academic career, wife and children. He goes further than Schopenhauer in his recognition of human nature and the opposites of subject and the 'other' as its reflection, which he regards as negative.

> Further the living Substance is being which is in truth *Subject*, or, what is the same, is in truth actual only in so far as it is the movement of positing itself, or is the mediation of its self-othering with itself. This Substance is, as Subject, pure, *simple negativity*, and is for this very reason the

---

[348] Ibid, page 81

bifurcation of the simple; it is the doubling which sets up opposition, and then again the negation of this indifferent diversity and of its antithesis [the immediate simplicity]. Only this self-restoring sameness, or this reflection in otherness within itself- not an *original* or *immediate* unity as such- is the True. It is the process of its own becoming, the circle that presupposes its end as its goal, having its end also as its beginning; and only by being worked out to its end, is it actual.[349]

Hegel also recognises the circular closed system of becoming with the goal and necessity to 'work' it out to its end, and realise its unity. The image that Hegel describes is similar to the Uroboros[350] (circular snake eating its own tail) as a symbol of unity. He also recognises that relationship holds the circle together and describes some of the characters included in the circle.

> The activity of dissolution is the power and work of the Understanding, the most astonishing and mightiest of powers, or rather the absolute power. The circle that remains self-enclosed and, like substance, holds its moments together, is an immediate relationship, one therefore which has nothing astonishing about it. But that an accident as such, detached from what circumscribes it, what is bound and is actual only in its context with others, should attain an existence of its own and a separate freedom- this is the tremendous power of the negative; it is the energy of thought, of the pure 'I'. Death, if that is what we want to call this non-actuality, is of all things the most dreadful, and to hold fast what is dead requires the greatest strength. Lacking strength, Beauty hates the Understanding for asking of her what it cannot do. But the life of Spirit is not the life that shrinks from death and keeps itself untouched by devastation, but rather the life that endures it and maintains itself in it. It wins its truth only when, in utter dismemberment, it finds itself.........Spirit is this power only by looking the negative in the face, and tarrying with it. This tarrying is the magical power that converts it into being.[351]

The characters he includes are the 'negative', which I would equate to our animal or instinctive foundation, an emotional female character, which he calls 'beauty' and finally an incorruptible spirit that studies the negative (looking in the face) and through sacrifice (dismemberment), converts it into being. In one passage, Hegel explains the psychological functioning and understanding of human nature and its unity. He begins with the 'I', which is our personal awareness, our life in the world and in psychological terms, our ego. He identifies its shadow, which he calls

---

[349] HEGEL G W F, Phenomenology of Spirit, 1977 Oxford University Press, Translated by A. V. Miller, Preface, page 10
[350] The symbol of the Ouroboros originated in Ancient Egypt and later adopted by the Gnostic, Hermetic and Alchemical traditions as a symbol of wholeness or unity.
[351] HEGEL G W Γ, Phenomenology of Spirit, 1977 Oxford University Press, Translated by A. V. Miller,, page 18

negative and indeed, instinctive behaviour is to some extent, negative to our ego and culture.

Hegel describes the female as the emotional (hates the understanding) and aesthetic (beauty) function that cannot do what the understanding requests. For Hegel, his feeling represented by his inner woman is limited to the emotional, romantic and aesthetic sense. Later, it developed a moral quality that formed a bridge or relationship to the spirit, which in this instance can be recognised as eternal. Hegel's idea of spirit could be transformed but not annihilated and had characteristics existing outside of space and time. Hegel's spirit comes into its own (resurrected) after dismemberment, which is akin to the ancient myths of Osiris and Dionysus, the Alchemical transformation, and related to dissolution and resurrection in general. Finally, he hints at what he calls 'being', which is reached by a magical power of 'facing' and 'tarrying' with the negative or instinctive aspect of himself.

> But in view of the fact that such thinking has a content, whether of picture-thoughts or abstract thoughts or a mixture of both, argumentation has another side which makes comprehension difficult for it. The remarkable nature of this other side is closely linked with the above-mentioned essence of the Idea, or rather it expresses the Idea in the way that it appears as the movement which is thinking apprehension.[352]

He describes the 'other side' and its 'contents', in the form of picture or abstract thoughts, which indeed is how the unconscious gives us information. In other words, the images and ideas presented to our awareness are a milder version of night-time dreams. Thoughts, when perceived without direction, can be as obscure and symbolic as dreams. Ideas, on the other hand, are generally chains of thoughts that have relational connections and help our understanding.

> It is a natural assumption that in philosophy, before we start to deal with its proper subject-matter, viz. The actual cognition of what truly is, one must first of all come to an understanding about cognition, which is regarded either as the instrument to get hold of the Absolute, or as the medium through which one discovers it.[353]

Hegel points to a crucial idea concerning cognition as the essence, and basis of reality. In other words, reality is what we can perceive but is not limited to the physical. We can see the physical with our senses and make conclusions about how the physical works. Similarly, cognition also includes what we can see with our mind or inner eye. For example, if we have a dream, it is a cognitive fact that we perceive certain images and

---

[352] Ibid, page 36
[353] Ibid, Introduction, page 46

felt certain emotions. Similarly, thoughts, fantasies, ideas etc., work in the same way. We cannot deny having such 'contents', as Hegel calls them. It is unfortunate that no one else can see these contents as they present themselves to the subject alone[354]. They can however, be perceived by others if the individual (subject) expresses them in writing, pictorial form or behaviour. This is the biggest obstacle some schools of psychology have in the way they interpret facts. The perception of unconscious contents in the individual is real, as we have learned from Kant.

> To complete our insight into the notion of this movement it may further be noticed that the differences themselves are exhibited in a twofold difference: once as a difference of content, one extreme being the force reflected into itself, but the other the medium of the 'matters'; and again as difference of *form*, since one solicits and the other is solicited, the former being active and the other passive. According to the difference of content they are distinguished [merely] in principle, or *for us*; but according to the difference of form they are independent and in their relation keep themselves separate and opposed to one another.[355]

Hegel expands his recognition of the opposites and describes their differences in form. These include: force/medium, solicits/is solicited, active/passive, and each side is independent, separate and opposed to the other. We can interpret these opposites as masculine (force, solicits, active) and feminine (medium, is solicited, passive). He recognises the true nature of the human condition but the crucial aspect of the opposites is their relationship. This relationship offers the third alternative that unites them in an energetic system.

Examples surround us on all sides. In nature, the waterfall has upper and lower parts united by the water (energy) from high to low. The tree is the union of growth into the sky and into the earth. Fire and water united through the vessel. The ocean united with the earth at the shore. The earth unites the sun and moon, and so on. Examples of this system in humans are also numerous. Thinking and feeling are united by either intuition or the senses. In the Christian tradition, the Holy Spirit unites the father and the son, which was in some instances regarded as feminine. In alchemy, the symbolic aspect of Sun (consciousness) and Moon (unconscious) by the vessel, and so on. Hegel continues his discussion of the opposites and the 'middle term' as follows:

> This true essence of Things has now the character of not being immediately for consciousness; on the contrary, consciousness has a

---

[354] This is true of most unconscious products, although it is possible to share synchronistic experiences, which are a relational expression between unconscious forces and matter.
[355] HEGEL G W F, Phenomenology of Spirit, III Force and the Understanding: Appearance and the Supersensible World, Oxford University Press, 1977, page 85

> mediated relation to the inner being and, as the Understanding, *looks through this mediating play of Forces into the true background of Things.* The middle term, which unites the two extremes, the Understanding and the inner world.......[356]

He describes in this passage consciousness, or the one that perceives, united with the inner 'being' by the understanding. This shows how the understanding is a crucial aspect of the union of conscious and unconscious realms. You cannot understand human nature unless you are aware of your own human nature and all that it entails.

> The inner world for consciousness, still a pure beyond, because consciousness does not as yet find itself in it. It is empty, for it is merely the nothingness of appearance, and positively the simple or unitary universal. This mode of the inner being [of Things] finds ready acceptance by those who say that the inner being of Things is unknowable; but another reason for this would have to be given. Certainly, we have no knowledge of this inner world as it is here in its immediacy; but not because Reason is too short-sighted or is limited, or however else one likes to call it- on this point, we know nothing as yet because we have not yet gone deep enough- but because of the simple nature of the matter in hand, that is to say, because in the void nothing is known, or, expressed from the other side, just because this inner world is determined as the beyond of consciousness............ Or in order that there may yet be something in the void- which, though it first came about as devoid of objective things must, however, as empty in itself, be taken as also void of all spiritual relationships and distinctions of consciousness qua consciousness- in order, then, that in this complete void, which is even called the holy of holies, there may yet be something, we must fill it up with reveries, appearances, produced by consciousness itself........... The inner world, or supersensible beyond, has, however, come into being: it comes from the world of appearances which has mediated it; in other words, appearance is its essence and, in fact, its filling.[357]

Hegel makes a crucial error in his exploration of what he calls the 'super-sensible' (unconscious) world and believes it comes from consciousness. This is the same view Freud had, as we shall see later in the study. It is an understandable mistake, because the unconscious uses images borrowed from the physical world and uses these images in extraordinary ways. In dreams, we perceive images and emotions poetically shaped in a way that often leaves us perplexed. Although the unconscious borrows images from the sensible world, it does so in order to reflect that world. The question Hegel neglected to ask is: what or who co-ordinates these images into a story or pictorial arrangement?

---

[356] Ibid, page 86
[357] Ibid, page 88

> Thus the supersensible world, which is the inverted world, has at the same time overarched the other world and has it within it; it is *for itself* the inverted world, i.e. the inversion of itself; it is itself and its opposite in one unity. Only thus is its difference as inner difference, or difference *in its own self*, or difference as an *infinity*.[358]

This passage is important because Hegel recognises the unconscious surrounding us on all sides and is eternal (infinity). The darkness before life and the darkness after death is the same darkness. The difference is we have the possibility of becoming aware of this fact. Hegel also sees the unity in the system of opposites as follows:

> It is true that consciousness of an 'other', of an object in general, is itself necessarily self consciousness, a reflectedness-into-self, consciousness of itself in its otherness.[359]

> But in point of fact self-consciousness is the reflection out of the being of the world of sense and perception, and is essentially the return from *otherness*........ With that first moment, self *consciousness* is in the form of consciousness, and the whole expanse of the sensual world is preserved for it, but at the same time only as connected with the second moment, the unity of self-consciousness with itself; and hence the sensuous world is for it an enduring existence which, however, is only *appearance*, or a difference which, *in itself*, is no difference. The antithesis of its appearance and its truth has, however, for its essence only the truth, viz. The unity of self-consciousness with itself; this unity must become essential to self-consciousness, i.e. self-consciousness is *Desire* in general.[360]

He mentions at the end of this passage that self-consciousness is 'Desire'. In other words, he is aware of the emotional aspect of the 'super-sensible' world (unconscious) and its instinctual foundation. It is unclear what Hegel means by desire and what the object of this desire is. We can only speculate on this idea but as experience shows, a sexual dream is symbolically the union of opposites. In other words, it is the union of a masculine consciousness with a feminine unconscious, symbolised by sexual desire and union.

> For since the *essence* of the individual shape- universal Life- and what exists for itself is in itself simple substance, when this substance places the *other* within itself it supersedes this its *simplicity* or its essence, i.e. it divides it, and this dividedness of the differenceless fluid medium is just

---

[358] Ibid, page 99
[359] Ibid, page 102
[360] HEGEL G W F, Phenomenology of Spirit, B. Self Consciousness; IV. The Truth of Self-Certainty, Oxford University Press, 1977, page 105

what establishes individuality. ....Since we started from the first immediate unity and returned through the moments of formation and of process to the unity of both these moments, and thus back again to the original simple substance, this reflected unity is different from the first.[361]

Hegel describes the original unity and becoming aware as an individual and returning to the original unity. We can equate this as a life's journey, as we are born and our unity found in the immediate environment of mother and father. In other words, we are an undifferentiated unity and totally dependent. Through the slow and sometimes painful process of differentiation and withdrawal of projections, we discover what is our self and what is other. Carrying this through to its circular[362] conclusion, we become aware of not only the external physical aspect of reality, but also the inner realm of images, characters and emotions. As we shall see later in this study, it is akin to Nietzsche's concept of the 'eternal return'. Withdrawing projections and differentiating the opposites also means becoming aware of the unity of inside and outside. This is why the ancients regarded an emotion like anger, possession by an inner God. The God (inner character) gives the emotion, which possesses consciousness until the emotion subsides and recedes back into the unconscious.

> In this movement, however, consciousness experiences just this emergence of individuality in the Unchangeable, and of the Unchangeable in individuality. Consciousness becomes aware of individuality in general in the Unchangeable, and at the same time of its own individuality in the latter. For the truth of this movement is just the oneness of this dual consciousness......... This unity, however, in the first instance, becomes for it one in which the difference of both is still the dominant feature. Thus there exist for consciousness three different ways in which individuality is linked with the Unchangeable. Firstly, it again appears to itself as opposed to the Unchangeable, and is thrown back to the beginning of the struggle which is throughout the element in which the whole relationship subsists. Secondly, consciousness learns that individuality belongs to the Unchangeable itself, so that it assumes the form of individuality into which the entire mode of existence passes. Thirdly, it finds its own self as this particular individual in the Unchangeable. The first Unchangeable is a form of individuality like itself, consciousness becomes, thirdly, Spirit, and experiences the joy of finding itself therein, and becomes aware of the reconciliation of its individuality with the universal.[363]

---

[361] Ibid, page 108

[362] Although it can be interpreted as circular, experience shows that it is a spiral towards a centre.

[363] HEGEL G W F, Phenomenology of Spirit, Freedom of Self-Consciousness; B. Stoicism, Scepticism, and the Unhappy Consciousness, Oxford University Press, 1977, pages 127 and 128

Hegel again explores the threefold process of becoming aware of one's self. The first stage, the emergence of the individual from the unconscious (Unchangeable) and the recognition of the uniqueness and opposition to that origin. The second stage, the awareness of that origin and its ongoing value and the need to link back or relate to it. The third stage is finding the meaning of one's personal place in relation to that origin. It is what is generally termed 'enlightenment', when one's inner centre or unity becomes visible.

> With this appears the third relationship of the process of this consciousness, which proceeds from the second as a consciousness that has truly proved itself to be independent, by its will and its deed.[364]

This sentence however, looks like Hegel's feeling of independence has more to do with the physical world than the inner world. Indeed, finding one's self includes a certain amount of independence from the world, but not our body as we depend on it to live. We still have to eat, drink, and love and that does not change until the death of our body. In addition, independence is bi-directional in that we not only have to become independent of our physical existence, but also the inner characters that motivate us to action. Possession by an organisation or physical activity is as real as possession by an inner character or idea. The world is full of well-meaning people that belong to political movements in opposition to other political movements. This is possession by an idea through collective identification.

> This mediated relation is thus a syllogism in which the individuality, initially fixed in its antithesis to the in-itself, is united with this other extreme only through a third term. Through this middle term the one extreme, the Unchangeable, is brought into relation with the unessential consciousness, which equally is brought into relation with the Unchangeable only through this middle term; thus this middle term is one which presents the two extremes to one another, and ministers to each in its dealings with the other. This middle term is itself a conscious Being [the mediator], for it is an action which mediates consciousness as such; the content of this action is the extinction of its particular individuality which consciousness is undertaking.[365]

In the above Hegel clarifies the third uniting character as a 'conscious being', or 'mediator', whose attributes are becoming clearer to him. As the next passage shows, he goes further and calls the third the minister and priest, thus recognising its spiritual or religious character.

---

[364] Ibid, page 135
[365] Ibid, page 136

In the mediator, then, this consciousness frees itself from action and enjoyment so far as they are regarded as its own. As a separate, independent extreme, it rejects the essence of its will, and casts upon the mediator or minister [priest] its own freedom of decision, and herewith the responsibility for its own action. This mediator, having direct relationship with the unchangeable being, ministers by giving advice on what is right. The action, since it follows upon the decision of someone else, ceases, as regards the doing or the willing of it, to be its own. [366]

In addition, Hegel gives this mediator freedom of decision and responsibility for its own action. This is an interesting stage in Hegel's awareness of the mediator, which is clearly a character in its own right. He also sees the relationship between the mediator and the 'unchangeable being', which is the difference between God and the idea of God, or in Hegel's case, God's representative in the form of mediator or priest. There is a danger in Hegel's attitude to his mediator and accept 'what is right' blindly without criticism. What is right for one is wrong for another.

We know from history that not all ideas of God are benevolent, loving and right for us. It is the personal moral conscience that also needs nurturing and a differentiation of one's ethics a necessity. Inner characters have positive and negative sides and it is not always easy to discern between them. This is why it is important to have a dialogue with inner characters to discover and understand their true nature. When seen in this light, we can understand how an inner character can possess a leader with inadequate moral development[367].

As the individual in his individual work already unconsciously performs a universal work, so again he also performs the universal work as his conscious object; the whole becomes, as a whole, his own, his own work, for which he sacrifices himself and precisely in so doing receives back from it his own self.[368]

This union itself still falls within consciousness and the whole just considered is one side of an antithesis. This illusory appearance of an antithesis which still remains, is removed by the transition or the means; for the means is a *unity* of inner and outer, the antithesis of the specific character it has as an *inner* means.[369]

These passages emphasise the idea of sacrifice to the mediator and its position between inner and outer, subject and object or conscious and

---

[366] Ibid, page 136
[367] An example is the possession of Hitler by the Teutonic god Wotan.
[368] HEGEL G W F, Phenomenology of Spirit, Actualizing of Self Consciousness, B. The Actualization of Rational Self-Consciousness through its Own Activity, page 213.
[369] Ibid, C. Individuality which takes Itself to be Real in and for Itself, page 240

unconscious, and the central position between these realms unites them as one.

> The one extreme, the universal self-conscious Spirit, becomes, through the individuality of the man, united with its other extreme, its force and element, with Unconscious Spirit. On the other hand, the divine law has its individualization- or the unconscious Spirit of the individual its real existence- in the Spirit rises out of its unreality into actual existence, out of a state in which it is unknowing and unconscious into the realm of conscious Spirit. The union of man and woman constitutes the active middle term of the whole and the element which sunders itself into these extremes of divine and human law.[370]

Hegel differentiates his idea of mediator further and discusses the process of making it conscious and bringing the spirit into the light of day. In this way, one lives out their destiny as a process of self-revelation. In other words, a process of becoming aware of one's own functioning, beliefs, wishes, fallibilities, ambitions, undeveloped areas and insecurities, etc. This knowledge and acceptance brings the unity in one's nature closer to our awareness. He rightly describes the union of opposites of male and female in relationship as the unity of personality. The more one becomes conscious of this union, the more one can become an active participant in its realisation.

He regards one side as real and the other unreal. It could simply be a poor choice of words on Hegel's part, but to realise the central mediator requires an acknowledgment of the equality and reality of both sides. The identification of one or other side means that Hegel is still not convinced of the reality of projection and the influence the unconscious has on our conscious lives. Buildings do not make themselves and similarly, anything created by humans has its origins in the unconscious creative spirit. They all begin as an idea, and as such become physical through great effort and conscious realisation. We have therefore to acknowledge the reality of unconscious creative acts.

> We have first to consider the simple unitary substance itself in the immediate organization of its moments, which are present in the substance but as yet have not been stirred into life. In the same way that Nature displays itself in the universal elements of Air, Water, Fire and Earth: Air is the enduring, purely universal, and transparent element; Water, the element that is perpetually sacrificed; Fire, the unity which energizes them into opposition while at the same time it perpetually resolves the opposition; lastly, Earth, which is the firm and solid knot of this articulated whole, the subject of these elements and of their process, that from which they start and to which they return; so in the same way,

---

[370] Ibid, A. The True Spirit. The Ethical Order, page 278

the inner essence or simple Spirit of self-conscious actuality displays itself in similar such universal- but here spiritual- 'masses' or spheres, displays itself as a world.[371]

The excellent passage above honouring Plato's cosmology and using its terms to describe the four poles of unity is exactly what concerns modern psychology[372]. Hegel describes the shape of his idea of unity as a sphere and a world. His conception is an elaboration of the usual two-dimensional Mandala, giving it extended reality. In other words, three dimensions make his unity real in the physical world.

> The spirit of self-alienation has its existence in the world of culture. But since this whole has become alienated from itself, there stands beyond that world the unreal world of *pure consciousness*, or of *thought*. Its content is in the form of pure thought, and thought is its absolute element. Since, however, thought is in the first instance [only] the *element* of this world, consciousness has only these thoughts, but as yet it does not think them, or is unaware that they are thoughts; they exist for consciousness in the form of *picture-thoughts*.[373]

The recognition of one's unity and standing between the psychic and physical and an awareness of the mediator gives increased insight into human nature, as well as nature in general, in all its positive and negative aspects. For example, when a culture develops one side at the expense of the other, a natural reaction attempts to balance the culture and return it to equilibrium. This reaction can take many forms and is often reflected in the arts or a spiritual movement in a positive sense, or war in a negative sense.

> Conscience, then, in the majesty of its elevation above specific law and every content of duty, puts whatever content it pleases into its knowing and willing. It is the moral genius which knows the inner voice of what it immediately knows to be a divine voice; and since, in knowing this, it has an equally immediate knowledge of existence, it is the divine creative power which in its Notion possesses the spontaneity of life.[374]

In the above passage, Hegel hints at the origins of morality in the form of 'conscience', and this voice directed at the physical world in the form of moral codes and attitudes. Where does this voice come from and is it a male or female? Hegel describes his conscience as a 'divine voice' and possesses the spontaneity of life. In other words, his voice belongs to the

---

[371] Ibid, B. Self-Alienated Spirit. Culture, page 300
[372] See Jung's description of the four orienting functions of Thinking (air), Feeling (water), Intuition (fire) and Sensation (earth).
[373] HEGEL G W F, Phenomenology of Spirit, Actualizing of Self Consciousness, b. Faith and Pure Insight, page 321
[374] Ibid, page 397

upper realm of spirit and not the lower of instinct. 'Spontaneity of life', for a thinking man has a feeling quality to it. That is to say, spontaneity of life means involvement in the world and enjoying its pleasures. Traditionally, feeling is a feminine quality rather than a masculine quality. Following this line of thinking, Hegel's inner conscience is for him feminine, divine, related to the physical world (life) and a moral judging function (feeling).

> The oracle, both of the God of the religions of art and of the preceding religions, is the necessary, first from of the God's utterance; for the Notion of the God implies that he is the essence of both Nature and Spirit, and therefore has not only natural but spiritual existence as well.[375]

This passage shows that Hegel included nature in his understanding of God, and the following passage brings the whole thing together into a four-fold arrangement with the fifth function completing his previous expression of the trinity and return to the unity of one.

> In so far as the otherness falls into two parts, Spirit might, as regards its moments- if these are to be counted- be more exactly expressed as a quaternity in unity or, because the quaternity itself again falls into two parts, viz. One part which has remained good and the other which has become evil, might even be expresses as a five-in-one[376]

Hegel describes the quaternity of unity above and its parts as 'moments' and the two halves as good and evil. The problem with such a wide sweeping statement is the lack of understanding moral relativity. What is good for one is bad for another, exemplified by the differing moral stances of the great religions. It is unclear what evil he refers to in the above text, but does elaborate on the idea of unity and its functions (moments), which belong to the individual in the following:

> The soul universal, described, it may be, as an *anima mundi*, a world-soul, must not be fixed on that account as a single subject; it is rather the universal *substance* which has its actual truth only in individuals and single subjects.[377]

> In the usage of ordinary language, sensation and feeling are not clearly distinguished: still we do not speak of the sensation- but of the feeling (sense) of right, of self; sentimentality (sensibility) is connected with sensation: we may therefore say sensation emphasizes rather the side of passivity- the fact that we find ourselves feeling, i.e. the immediacy of

---

[375] Ibid, Religion in the Form of Art, page 430
[376] Ibid, c. The Revealed Religion, page 469
[377] HEGEL G W F, Philosophy of Mind, Part Three of the Encyclopaedia of The Philosophical Sciences (1830), Clarendon Press, Oxford University Press 1971 Section One- Mind Subjective, A. Anthropology, The Soul, (a) The Physical Soul, page 35

mode in feeling- whereas feeling at the same time rather notes the fact that it is *we ourselves* who feel.[378]

Hegel recognises the universal function of soul is expressed individually. That is to say, every man and woman has a soul but the function of that soul depends on the individual. Hegel describes the functions of feeling and sensation as a further differentiation of his soul. What he does not recognise, is that these functions are not universally associated with the soul and depend on the nature of the individual. For example, a man consciously oriented towards sensation and thinking will have a soul oriented towards the opposites of intuition and feeling.

> Sporadic examples and traces of this magic tie appear elsewhere in the range of self-possessed conscious life, say between friends, especially female friends with delicate nerves (a tie which may go so far as to show 'magnetic' phenomenon), between husband and wife and between members of the same family. ....But this sensitive nucleus includes not merely the purely unconscious, congenital disposition and temperament, but within its enveloping simplicity it acquires and retains also (in habit, as to which see later) all further ties and essential relationships, fortunes, principles- everything in short belonging to the character, and in whose elaboration self-conscious activity has most effectively participated. This concentrated individuality also reveals itself under the aspect of what is called the heart and soul of feeling.[379]

Hegel continues in his exploration of attraction and repulsion and recognises the similarity between attraction in people and magnetic forces in matter. This is an apt description of the feeling function and how the relationships one forms are an integral part of one's personality. Indeed, personality forms by the relationships we have in the physical world, and the relationships we have to our inner characters, including the soul.

> The self possessed and healthy subject has an active and present consciousness of the ordered whole of his individual world, into the system of which he subsumes each special content of sensation, idea, desire, inclination, etc., as it arises, so as to insert them in their proper place. He is the dominant genius over these particularities. Between this and insanity the difference is like that between waking and dreaming: only that in insanity the difference the dream falls within the waking limits, and so makes part of the actual self-feeling.[380]

He elaborates on his idea of unity and how it lies between waking and dreaming. Insanity is the contamination of dream in the waking state and

---

[378] Ibid, page 88
[379] Ibid, page 95
[380] Ibid, (b) Self-feeling (Sense of Self), page 123

a flooding of material incapable of integration by the individual. He neglects to mention that projection of unconscious products is the natural but undifferentiated state of relationship to the physical world. The way couples are attracted to each other is the projection of an inner character onto an actual person. This is not limited to people either. We quite often see projections onto man-made objects such as cars, boats, aeroplanes, buildings, and give them a personality.

This is the myth-making function that unites the inner and outer realms. Cars, aeroplanes, buildings, etc., do not exist in nature; people design and make them. They are constructs of ideas that come from our inner nature. When we observe a man-made object we can marvel at its colour, form, line as well as its atomic structure, held in place by attractive electromagnetic forces, and so on.

> ......in creative imagination the general idea or representation constitutes the subjective element which gives itself objectivity in the image and thereby authenticates itself. This authentication is, however, itself immediately still a subjective one, since intelligence in the first instance still has regard to the given content of the images, is guided by it in symbolizing its general ideas. This conditioned, only relatively free, activity of intelligence we call symbolic imagination. This selects for the expression of its general ideas only that sensuous material whose independent signification corresponds to the specific content of the universal to be symbolized.[381]

On the other hand, objects and people attract projections with symbolic content, as Hegel notes above. Men generally project a woman onto their cars, and love, polished and tune them so they transport them to far-off places and adventures[382]. It is however, important to know what we are projecting as this helps us become aware of our inner characters. Having said that, giving a projection or inner character freedom of expression makes the physical world a magical place of wonder and excitement.

Luna (feminine) is no longer is a stony spherical desert orbiting the earth, but a feminine beacon of light with moods and the ability to reflect her partner Sol (masculine). In this instance, we have knowledge of the moon as it is and what we project onto her. In this case our thinking tells us what the moon is from our scientific knowledge[383], but our perception of her behaviour in the day and night sky gives us a feeling of her moods and her cycles. As we shall see in the following study, Hegel's ideas on

---

[381] Ibid, Zusatz, page 211

[382] I am speaking here as a man and using this as one example of many.

[383] In reality the knowledge we have of the moon is secondary because only a few individuals have actually stood on it and experienced her first hand. The every day experience of her is available to everyone, and is immediate and direct.

the nature of human thought, perception and insights, predate the modern era and its researches into human psychology.

I. Nietzsche F. W. (1844 - 1900)

We now come to the most tragic of philosophers, whose life was epitome of that tragedy. Nietzsche lost his father and brother at an early age and was raised by his mother and grandmother. He was a sensitive man for obvious reasons, but highly intelligent. He was a great admirer of Schopenhauer and like him, had poor relationships with women. This inevitably led to his final isolation, and coupled with illness, his madness. His insights into human nature and the prevailing culture were however, far-reaching. His appreciation of music and dance was indelible to his personality as the following quote shows 'Without music, life would be a mistake'.

For all his problems, Nietzsche had a very fine intuition that enabled him to see far beyond his epoch and what was to befall Germany in the twentieth century. His intuition was predominately directed inward to the world of images and ideas, which made him highly visionary. For Nietzsche, music and dance was part of his relation to the world and a connection to his soul. As a deep intuitive thinker, music and dance was part of his sensual feeling and his unity.

> Now, hearing this gospel of universal harmony, each person feels himself to be not simply united, reconciled or merged with his neighbour, but quite literally one with him, as if the veil of maya had been torn apart, so that mere shreds of it flutter before the mysterious primordial unity *(das Ur-Eine).* [384]

This fondness for music and dance led him to the exploration of his unity through the Greek Gods Dionysus and Apollo, who expressed music in different ways.[385]

> We are now drawing closer to the true goal of our study, the aim of which is to understand the Dionysiac-Apolline genius and its work of art, or at least to gain some tentative intimation of that mysterious unity.[386]

---

[384] NIETZSCHE, Frederich, 'The Birth of Tragedy' Cambridge University Press, 1999. Nietzsche refers to Beethoven's 'Hymn to Joy' page 18

[385] It is my intention to show that these two half brothers are not exactly opposites, but stand side-by-side with different expressions of inner characters. Instinct and image come from the same place.

[386] NIETZSCHE, Frederich 'The Birth of Tragedy' Cambridge University Press, 1999, page 28

We shall have gained much for the science of aesthetics when we have come to realize, not just through logical insight but also with the certainty of something directly apprehended *(Anschauung),* that the continuous evolution of art is bound up with the duality of the *Apolline* and the *Dionysiac* in much the same way as reproduction depends on there being two sexes which co-exist in a state of perpetual conflict interrupted only occasionally by periods of reconciliation.

Nietzsche regards Dionysus and Apollo as opposites united within the framework of art. To understand these two ancient characters and what they could have meant to Nietzsche, I shall go through a brief history, describe their characteristics and how they fit into the ancient pantheon. Dionysus and Apollo were half-brothers with the same father called Zeus, the king of the Gods.

Dionysus's birth had many difficulties. Zeus had an affair with the mortal Semele and his wife Hera found out about the affair and Semele's pregnancy. Hera, motivated by jealousy befriends Semele and convinces her to ask Zeus to reveal himself to her as the king of the Gods, to which he agrees. He comes to her with lightning and thunder, but forgets that mortals cannot look at the undisguised God, and she dies in the flames of his lightning. Zeus rescues his unborn son Dionysus from her and sews him into his thigh. A few months later Dionysus is born again from his father.

In one version from Crete, Dionysus is the son of Zeus and Persephone, the queen of the underworld. The jealous Hera sends the Titans to rip Dionysus to pieces and eat him. Zeus intervenes, destroys the Titans but could only save the heart of Dionysus. Zeus sews the heart into his thigh and Dionysus is born again. In another version, Zeus gives Dionysus to king Athamas and his wife to protect from Hera and asks them to raise him as a girl. In yet another version, Zeus gives Dionysus to the rain nymphs of Nysa to raise, and another version, to Rhea or Persephone, to raise in the underworld.

Dionysus discovers the secret of the vine early in his childhood, and the jealous Hera strikes him with madness, which drives him to wander the earth. Rhea cures and teaches him her religious rites and sends him to the Far East to teach cultivation of the vine. Dionysus is often associated with the bull, serpent, tiger, leopard, ivy, wine, satyrs, centaurs, theatre, dance and the phallus. Other characteristics are rebirth, dual birth (Zeus incubated him in his thigh) and feminine qualities, and wild women called Maenads often surrounded him. The major characteristic of Dionysian worship is intoxication and shedding of the socialized personality for an ecstatic and liberated state of freed animal behaviour. It was a freeing of natural instinct with its fertilising, liberating and transformative quality.

Zeus has an affair with Leto who gives birth to Apollo as the God of music, truth, prophecy, healing, the sun, the lyre, plague, the bow and arrow and poetry. Apollo is born with a twin sister named Artemis, the chaste huntress. He is also associated with the shining youth, protector of music, spiritual life, moderation, perceptible order, harmony and reason. Once again, Hera's jealousy of yet another pregnancy fathered by Zeus bans Leto from giving birth on terra firma. Consequently, she gives birth to Artemis and Apollo on the floating island of Delos, which later became sacred to Apollo.

Four days after Apollo's birth he kills the chthonic dragon Python sent by Hera to kill Leto. Hera sends the giant Tityos to rape Leto, and both Apollo and Artemis protect her. Zeus hurls Tityos down to Tartarus and pegs him to a rock where a pair of vultures eats his liver every day. Like his father Zeus, Apollo has many female and male lovers and sired many children.

The following table summarises Dionysus and Apollo's activities and interests:

Activity/Attitude	Dionysus	Apollo
Music, Dance & Theatre	Wild, frantic & unrefined	Refined, orderly, considered
Sexuality	Unrestrained, fertile, bisexual, incest, leader of maenads, ambiguous	Restrained, bisexual, leader of muses, ambiguous
Mental State	Mad, instinctive, intoxicated	Reasonable, truthful, orderly, prophetic
Symbolism	Bull, serpent, tiger, leopard, ivy, wine, satyrs, centaurs & phallus	Healing, sun/light, plague, poetry, lyre, archery
Spirituality	Ecstatic, down to earth, raised in underworld	Sungod, protector of evil
Relationship to earth	Strong with vine & underworld, night	Poor, born on floating island, day

The first and major similarity is the common father Zeus who had power and influence over mortals and other Gods. The second similarity is the common threat of the jealous and vengeful Hera who constantly attacked them. Apparently, Zeus's power did not extend to the control of his wife's rage. Other similarities are their creative expression in the arts, particularly music, ambiguous sexuality and lack of fidelity.

The differences are more pronounced in their creative expression. Dionysus's attitude is wild and frantic, whereas Apollo's is refined and orderly. Sexually Dionysus was rapacious, having approximately 16 consorts and 26 children[387]. This does however, pale compared to Apollo, who had approximately 61 consorts, 76 children and 13 male lovers[388]. Mentally, Dionysus is mad and intoxicated, whereas Apollo is sane and reasonable. Dionysus has several animal, half-animal and material totems including the vine and fertility as symbolised by the phallus. Apollo has healing, sun (consciousness), poetry, music and archery, which are all refined arts. Dionysus is down-to-earth, or beneath the earth (underworld), whereas Apollo is disconnected from the earth as decreed by Hera.

From the above we can see how Nietzsche regarded these two half-brothers as opposites. It must be kept in mind these characters were mythological Gods and not actually humans, therefore they did not live in the physical world with its laws, and should therefore be regarded as inclinations or patterns of behaviour. When seen in this light, the meaning of their lives becomes clear.

Dionysus as an inner character, links us to our animal origins. His unbridled intoxicated sexuality is without boundaries and purely instinctive, yet he has the light of spirituality in his personality. Dionysus was to be raised as a girl to protect him from the negative, rampageous mother figure Hera, giving him an ambiguous sexuality. He does have the potential for renewal, as his rebirth shows from the thigh of his father. This is a curious place for incubation and different to what one would expect. If we amplify the nature of the thigh, it has the strongest muscles in the body and gives us movement on earth through walking and running. The rebirth through the thigh then indicates a predetermined, strong relationship to earth, as does his interest in the vine.

Apollo, on the other hand, is an inclination towards refined culture, beauty and skills. He is a God of daylight and awareness, which heals possession by the instincts, represented by Dionysus. Apollo is a tamed and refined version of Dionysus, hence their common father and negative mother figure Hera. He also relates to Dionysus through his sexual proclivities, which he surpasses Dionysus in number of consorts and children.

---

[387] https://en.wikipedia.org/wiki/Dionysus#Other_parallels
[388] https://en.wikipedia.org/wiki/Apollo

The biggest difference between the half-brothers is their relationship to the feminine. They both have a negative mother figure in Hera. Dionysus was to be raised as a girl indicating a potential for both genders of equal stature contained within his character. There is however, no indication or description of Dionysus as a girl, so it was undifferentiated in his character. Apollo was born as a twin to Artemis, as an equal feminine (sister) separate and differentiated. In addition, she was chaste and sexuality ignored, repressed or purified. This explains why Apollo was refined, in that his feeling (Artemis) developed to a high degree in its aesthetic and spiritual form, rather than its instinctive sexual form. She is also the Goddess of the hunt, wild animals, wilderness, childbirth and virginity, which is the ideal type to tame the wild beast in a man.

Nietzsche espoused the virtues of the aesthetic expression by these characters and lived aspects of them at some time in his life. In his earlier years, he had drunken bouts at university, was a keen dancer, and reported to have contracted syphilis from a brothel. In his later years, he became stoic and rejected most of the relationships he developed over the years, including his friendship with Wagner who had developed his Apollonian traits to a high degree. The function that Nietzsche lacked was a feeling for people in contrast to a feeling for inner characters. Extraverted feeling would have kept him connected to others and may have saved him from his tragic fate.

> This mode of thought, with which a definite type of man is bred, starts from an absurd presupposition: it takes good and evil for realities that contradict one another (not as complementary value concepts, which would be the truth), it advises taking the side of the good, it desires that the good should renounce and oppose the evil down to its ultimate roots- it therewith actually denies life, which has in all its instincts both Yes and No. Not that it grasps this: it dreams, on the contrary, that it is getting back to wholeness, to unity, to strength of life: it thinks it will be a state of redemption when the inner anarchy, the unrest between those opposing value drives, is at last put an end to. Perhaps there has never before been a more dangerous ideology, a greater mischief in psychologicis, than this will to good: one has reared the most repellent type, the unfree man, the bigot; one has taught that only as a bigot is one on the right path to Godhood, only the bigot's way is God's way.[389]

The above passage shows that Nietzsche rejects the notion of a one-sided life oriented towards good without it is opposite of evil. This is part of Nietzsche's rejection of the Christian tradition in favour of the Hellenistic half brothers Dionysus and Apollo and Nietzsche's idea of

---

[389] NIETZSCHE, Frederich, 'The Will to Power' Vintage Books 1968, Page 192

unity. Unfortunately, it remained an aesthetic consideration and not integrated into his life. If he had turned around and honoured his Dionysian inclinations in his later years with 'wine women and song', his isolation may have subsided and his return journey to earth made possible.

> The word *"Dionysian"* means: an urge to unity, a reaching out beyond personality, the everyday, society, reality, across the abyss of transitoriness: a passionate-painful overflowing into darker, fuller, more floating states; an ecstatic affirmation of the total character of life as that which remains the same, just as powerful, just as blissful, through all change; the great pantheistic sharing of joy and sorrow that sanctifies and calls good even the most terrible and questionable qualities of life; the eternal will to procreation, to fruitfulness, to recurrence; the feeling of the necessary unity of creation and destruction.

> The world *"Apollinian"* means: the urge to perfect self sufficiency, to the typical "individual," to all that simplifies, distinguishes, makes strong, clear, unambiguous, typical: freedom under the law.

> The further development of art is as necessarily tied to the antagonism between these two natural artistic powers as the further development of man is to that between the sexes. Plenitude of power and moderation, the highest form of self-affirmation in a cool, noble, severe beauty: the Apollinianism of the Hellenic will.[390]

The above text shows that Nietzsche's unity lies with the Dionysian instinct and the 'herd' in general. What Nietzsche did not recognise is that the unity between these two characters is already present. They overlap in many ways in that they are half-brothers, have the same father and a jealous mother character attacking them. The brothers were also fond of bisexuality, music and self-expression.

Nietzsche understood the opposites in himself but did not integrate them into his life. His wild youth and refined writings could not be reconciled and integrated into a whole. Music is the common activity of both Dionysus and Apollo and can be practiced individually, it can be expressed collectively, which brings musicians together in harmony. Nietzsche's love of music was attached to his friendship with Wagner and when that ended, so too did his need for a musical life with other people. The tragedy of his life was his attempt to identify with his central inner character within the framework of his own ego. He declared the death of God and saw himself as an 'Overman' or superior human with godlike understanding. If he had something or someone to go back to after this

---

[390] Ibid, Page 539

identification or possession by an inner character, he may have come back to himself and the Dionysian spirit of the herd.

m. James W. (1842- 1910)

James was an American philosopher, originally trained as a physician. He was a pragmatic, down-to-earth man and this coloured his philosophical and psychological outlook. As the following passage shows, he had contempt fuelled by a temperamental lack of understanding for the subjective factor and the reality of the soul. He did try to understanding how his predecessors oriented their philosophy around ideas, rather than physical facts, and his later studies showed a fascination with metaphysics.

> There is no more contemptible type of human character than that of the nerveless sentimentalist and dreamer, who spends his life in a weltering sea of sensibility and emotion, but who never does a manly concrete deed. Rousseau, inflaming all the mothers of France, by his eloquence, to follow Nature and nurse their babies themselves, while he sends his own children to the foundling hospital, is the classical example of what I mean.[391]

> The logical conclusion seems then to be that the states of consciousness are all that psychology needs to do her work with. Metaphysics or theology may prove the Soul to exist; but for psychology the hypothesis of such a substantial principle of unity is superfluous.[392]

He regarded the soul as a metaphysical function, which he equates with theology, rather than a psychological reality. He regards 'unity' superfluous for the study of psychology, but concedes that it may be a metaphysical reality. Soul to James is an abstracted idea that has no relationship to the practicality of a material based psychology.

> The content of a dream will oftentimes insert itself into the stream of real life in a most perplexing way. The most frequent source of false memory is the accounts we give to others of our experiences. Such accounts we almost always make both more simple and more interesting than the truth.[393]

His orientation is further emphasised by his psychological orientation towards consciousness. He does acknowledge the existence of dreams, but regards them as an epiphenomenon related to 'false' memory. In other words, James draws dream images from physical experience and

---

[391] JAMES William, 'Psychology' Macmillan and Co 1892, Page 119
[392] Ibid, page 166
[393] Ibid, page 168

memory of those experiences. His later works called 'The Will to Believe' and 'The Varieties of Religious Experience' show his fascination with the other side of physical reality. This is where his idea of unity presided and he approached it as a true scientist with much scepticism.

> The difference between monism and pluralism is perhaps the most pregnant of all the differences in philosophy. Primâ facie the world is a pluralism; as we find it, its unity seems to be that of any collection; and our higher thinking consists chiefly of an effort to redeem it from that first crude form. Postulating more unity than the first experiences yield, we also discover more. But absolute unity, in spite of brilliant dashes in its direction, still remains undiscovered, still remains a Grenzbegriff.[394]

He discusses the opposites of Monism and Pluralism above, but concludes that absolute unity remains undiscovered. His language and use of the word 'pregnant' in this passage tells us that he regards the difference between the opposites as a potential third uniting principal, incubating for birth. In other words, he recognises but is not yet aware of, the uniting principal in the form of a third function (child). Words are very good at giving away ideas not yet born.

> But to find religion is only one out of many ways of reaching unity; and the process of remedying inner incompleteness and reducing inner discord is a general psychological process, which may take place with any sort of mental material, and need not necessarily assume the religious form.[395]

James is right in his recognition that unity is not necessarily a religious task. For example, an intuitive introverted man requires the opposite of relationship to the physical world of matter for unity. The relationship between these opposites does, however display certain spiritual attributes that may or may not have anything to do with a religious creed. It is a part of our nature to evolve towards unity and does not require a religious structure to do so. These institutions are important as they create community and connect patrons to a greater and shared idea of unity, guided by a key individual(s)[396].

> You see how natural it is, from this point of view, to treat religion as a mere survival, for religion does in fact perpetuate the traditions of the most primeval thought. To coerce the spiritual powers, or to square them and get them on our side, was, during enormous tracts of time, the one great object in our dealings with the natural world. For our ancestors,

---

[394] JAMES William, 'The Will to Believe' Longmans, Green, And Co 1912, Project Gutenberg EBook, Page 1
[395] JAMES William, 'Varieties of Religious Experience' Longmans, Green, And Co 1903, Page 154
[396] These are the individuals a religion is based on.

dreams, hallucinations, revelations, and cock-and-bull stories were inextricably mixed with facts. Up to a comparatively recent date such distinctions as those between what has been verified and what is only conjectured, between the impersonal and the personal aspects of existence, were hardly suspected or conceived.[397]

He continues in the passage above with the idea that religion relates us to our inner unity (animal with spirit). His use of the words 'cock and bull' gives away his feeling on the material from an unconscious source as less than facts, which is a typical scientific prejudice. No one can argue that having a dream is not a real experience. We perceive images, emotions, ideas and can have physical fatigue from the activity performed in dreams. It is the same as an idea for a building is a fact as much as the final structure. This is the biggest barrier to the reconciliation of psychological schools. In that respect, contemporary physicists are more open to possibilities and acknowledge the effect of the subjective factor on their experiments.

> Philosophy has often been defined as the quest or the vision of the world's unity. We never hear this definition challenged, and it is true as far as it goes, for philosophy has indeed manifested above all things its interest in unity. But how about the VARIETY in things? Is that such an irrelevant matter? If instead of using the term philosophy, we talk in general of our intellect and its needs we quickly see that unity is only one of these.[398]

James is right in his plea for the 'variety' of things. Unity is not a static system, it grows, changes, falls apart, re-combines and so on. We are born whole with all the functions in 'potentia', grow and adapt with our natural primary function. A secondary function comes to the primary's aid and the others generally remain unconscious and undeveloped. The primary and secondary functions are differentiated for adaptation to the world. Life changes over time and the urge for unity and development of the other functions becomes more important and can be described as the 'variety of things'.

> The difference is that the empiricists are less dazzled. Unity doesn't blind them to everything else, doesn't quench their curiosity for special facts, whereas there is a kind of rationalist who is sure to interpret abstract unity mystically and to forget everything else, to treat it as a principle; to admire and worship it; and thereupon to come to a full stop intellectually.[399]

---

[397] JAMES William, 'Varieties of Religious Experience' Longmans, Green, And Co 1903, Page 417
[398] JAMES William, 'Pragmatism', eBooks The University of Adelaide Library, Page 59
[399] Ibid, Page 60

James's emphasis on the 'variety of things' shows that as a rational person, he is mystified by the idea of unity. The intellect is one function and in order to develop other functions, one needs to leave it alone for a time. This is particularly true when one delves into the realm of feeling. This is a function of empathy, judgement and quality, and of the forces of attraction and repulsion. It is the function of relationship and indispensable to one's idea of unity. Feeling sees the relationship between the functions and finds the aspects that binds them together. In other words, the inner female character[400] (soul) in the man relates functions to each other and introduces us to the central character and idea of unity. In the following passage, James discusses number worship, but stops short at historical examples.

> 'The world is One!'- the formula may become a sort of number-worship. 'Three' and 'seven' have, it is true, been reckoned sacred numbers; but, abstractly taken, why is 'one' more excellent than 'forty-three,' or than 'two million and ten'? In this first vague conviction of the world's unity, there is so little to take hold of that we hardly know what we mean by it.[401]

Number has an obvious quantity but also a quality beyond historical or religious writings. Number '1' is the first digit and sets a counterpart to '0', which lacks substance and from which '1' originated. '2' is the doubling of '1' and differentiation of the opposites. '3' is a further differentiation and uniting function of '1' + '1' where the '+' is the uniting function of opposites. '4' is the completion of the circle and differentiation of all four functions, to '5' and back to the original but differentiated '1' and 'the eternal return'[402]. The difference between the original '1' and final '1' is the other numbers are now in the mix and become the 'variety' of the group. This in itself is an abstract description, which is difficult to understand on its own. In reality, each number has one or more inner characters associated with it, giving the numbers a personal and experiential reality.

> 1. First, the world is at least ONE SUBJECT OF DISCOURSE. If its manyness were so irremediable as to permit NO union whatever of it parts, not even our minds could 'mean' the whole of it at once: this would be like eyes trying to look in opposite directions. But in point of fact we mean to cover the whole of it by our abstract term 'world' or 'universe,' which expressly intends that no part shall be left out. Such unity of discourse carries obviously no farther monistic specifications. A 'chaos,'

---

[400] This is a general statement concerning an intellectual man like James and is only meant schematically. The variety and distribution of psychic functions means the opposite could just as well be true for an individual.
[401] JAMES William, 'Pragmatism', eBooks The University of Adelaide Library, Page 60
[402] Concept made popular by Nietzsche.

once so named, has as much unity of discourse as a cosmos. It is an odd fact that many monists consider a great victory scored for their side when pluralists say 'the universe is many.

James seems to ignore the faculty of memory by suggesting that we cannot perceive the whole at once. His metaphor of 'eyes trying to look in opposite directions shows that he was too anchored in immediate perception to see the whole. It may not have occurred to him to turn his head in the opposite direction while remembering the other side and thus perceiving the opposite in memory. In this way, one can perceive the physical on one side and the images, ideas etc., on the other. This is the first step in the on-going process to liberate oneself from the opposites.

> 2. Are they, for example, CONTINUOUS? Can you pass from one to another, keeping always in your one universe without any danger of falling out? In other words, do the parts of our universe HANG together, instead of being like detached grains of sand?

This is where James cannot make the leap from his known 'one universe' of intellect. As shown previously, the inner and outer realms mesh and James recognises that unconscious products like dreams, revelations etc., are 'inextricably mixed with facts'. This statement in itself shows that he perceives the unity, albeit in confused form. I suspect that he was referring to written texts such as the bible, rather than personal experience.

> 3. There are innumerable other paths of practical continuity among things. Lines of INFLUENCE can be traced by which they together. Following any such line you pass from one thing to another till you may have covered a good part of the universe's extent. Gravity and heat-conduction are such all-uniting influences, so far as the physical world goes. Electric, luminous and chemical influences follow similar lines of influence. But opaque and inert bodies interrupt the continuity here, so that you have to step round them, or change your mode of progress if you wish to get farther on that day. Practically, you have then lost your universe's unity, SO FAR AS IT WAS CONSTITUTED BY THOSE FIRST LINES OF INFLUENCE.[403]

Above, James discusses the 'line of influence' that connects objects and ideas. He rightly identifies the uniting influence of gravity and EME[404] but stops short at 'opaque and inert bodies'. Gravity and EME influences matter and energy, which are the fundamental forces of nature that unite matter and psychic reality through synchronistic phenomena.[405]

---

[403] JAMES William, 'Pragmatism', eBooks The University of Adelaide Library, Page 60-61
[404] Heat is one form of Electromagnetic energy.
[405] See chapter 11b on Synchronistic Phenomena

4. All these systems of influence or non-influence may be listed under the general problem of the world's CAUSAL UNITY. If the minor causal influences among things should converge towards one common causal origin of them in the past, one great first cause for all that is, one might then speak of the absolute causal unity of the world. God's fiat on creation's day has figured in traditional philosophy as such an absolute cause and origin. Transcendental Idealism, translating 'creation' into 'thinking' (or 'willing to' think') calls the divine act 'eternal' rather than 'first'; but the union of the many here is absolute, just the same — the many would not BE, save for the One. Against this notion of the unity of origin of all there has always stood the pluralistic notion of an eternal self-existing many in the shape of atoms or even of spiritual units of some sort. The alternative has doubtless a pragmatic meaning, but perhaps, as far as these lectures go, we had better leave the question of unity of origin unsettled.

Having established the causal unity of matter, James boldly ventures to the Kantian view of transcendental idealism, which includes the subjective factor and perception of ideas, including the creative act as something eternal. Most people know this creative act as it occurs every day in the form of ideas, hunches, solutions, inspirations etc., that pop into one's awareness spontaneously without the will's involvement. Its source is unknown and has a divine origin. James also compares atoms as 'self-existing many' with there opposite spiritual units. This is similar to what Jung calls the scintilla or luminous archetypes, which I call inner characters. James's idea of unity in the above passages is becoming more distinct.

5. The most important sort of union that obtains among things, pragmatically speaking, is their GENERIC UNITY. Things exist in kinds, there are many specimens in each kind, and what the 'kind' implies for one specimen, it implies also for every other specimen of that kind. We can easily conceive that every fact in the world might be singular, that is, unlike any other fact and sole of its kind. In such a world of singulars our logic would be useless, for logic works by predicating of the single instance what is true of all its kind. With no two things alike in the world, we should be unable to reason from our past experiences to our future ones. The existence of so much generic unity in things is thus perhaps the most momentous pragmatic specification of what it may mean to say 'the world is One.' ABSOLUTE generic unity would obtain if there were one summum genus under which all things without exception could be eventually subsumed. 'Beings,' 'thinkables,' 'experiences,' would be candidates for this position. Whether the alternatives expressed by such words have any pragmatic significance or not, is another question which I prefer to leave unsettled just now.

He continues the differentiation of 'Generic' from 'Absolute' unity and recognises that logic is useless in these forms. Logic (intellect) quantifies and categorises, whereas ideas of unity require an understanding of quality, value and relationship between functions, matter and psyche. The pragmatic significance of knowing 'absolute unity' is mental health, psychological security and living one's true and meaningful life. James touches on this in the following:

> 6. Another specification of what the phrase 'the world is One' may mean is UNITY OF PURPOSE. An enormous number of things in the world subserve a common purpose. All the man-made systems, administrative, industrial, military, or what not, exist each for its controlling purpose. Every living being pursues its own peculiar purposes. They co-operate, according to the degree of their development, in collective or tribal purposes, larger ends thus enveloping lesser ones, until an absolutely single, final and climacteric purpose subserved by all things without exception might conceivably be reached. It is needless to say that the appearances conflict with such a view. Any resultant, as I said in my third lecture, MAY have been purposed in advance, but none of the results we actually know in is world have in point of fact been purposed in advance in all their details. Men and nations start with a vague notion of being rich, or great, or good. Each step they make brings unforeseen chances into sight, and shuts out older vistas, and the specifications of the general purpose have to be daily changed. What is reached in the end may be better or worse than what was proposed, but it is always more complex and different.

Above, he discusses the construction of societal systems with a 'unity of purpose' and these systems and their end goal do not work for all. Like-minded individuals create political systems, which suit their temperament, believing that everyone governed has the same feeling towards the system. This is the biggest mistake that individuals, particularly extroverts make with the projection of their idea of unity onto the world and turn it into a political system in which others have to live.[406] James continues in the following passage with the misconception that the population will accept another's idea of unity.

> Our different purposes also are at war with each other. Where one can't crush the other out, they compromise; and the result is again different from what anyone distinctly proposed beforehand. Vaguely and generally, much of what was purposed may be gained; but everything makes strongly for the view that our world is incompletely unified teleologically and is still trying to get its unification better organized. Whoever claims ABSOLUTE teleological unity, saying that there is one purpose that every detail of the universe subserves, dogmatizes at his

---

[406] See chapter 9e 'Possession by the Idea of Unity' for the problems associated with political systems

own risk. Theologians who dogmalize thus find it more and more impossible, as our acquaintance with the warring interests of the world's parts grows more concrete, to imagine what the one climacteric purpose may possibly be like. We see indeed that certain evils minister to ulterior goods, that the bitter makes the cocktail better, and that a bit of danger or hardship puts us agreeably to our trumps. We can vaguely generalize this into the doctrine that all the evil in the universe is but instrumental to its greater perfection. But the scale of the evil actually in sight defies all human tolerance; and transcendental idealism, in the pages of a Bradley or a Royce, brings us no farther than the book of Job did — God's ways are not our ways, so let us put our hands upon our mouth. A God who can relish such superfluities of horror is no God for human beings to appeal to. His animal spirits are too high. In other words the 'Absolute' with his one purpose, is not the man-like God of common people.

He also gives his account of a 'perfect' deity, thus adopting the idea from past philosophers and religious ideas of perfection. He cannot accept that God may be as much a part of nature and a higher omnipotent being. For unity to be real, it has to include everything horrific and sublime. This does not mean that we have to partake in the horrific or live it out, but acknowledge its existence as part of a greater unity. We can only do something about the horrific if we know about it in ourselves. We may have a chance of accepting it in others and see them as they are, rather than who we think they are, or try to fit them into our idea or system of unity.

7. AESTHETIC UNION among things also obtains, and is very analogous to ideological union. Things tell a story. Their parts hang together so as to work out a climax. They play into each other's hands expressively. Retrospectively, we can see that altho no definite purpose presided over a chain of events, yet the events fell into a dramatic form, with a start, a middle, and a finish. In point of fact all stories end; and here again the point of view of a many is that more natural one to take. The world is full of partial stories that run parallel to one another, beginning and ending at odd times. They mutually interlace and interfere at points, but we cannot unify them completely in our minds. In following your life-history, I must temporarily turn my attention from my own. Even a biographer of twins would have to press them alternately upon his reader's attention.

Above, James touches on the aesthetic unity of one's life history and its connection to one's life story and clearly recognises that a life story is an individual pursuit. James's example of the twins ignores the fact that they have a history of common ancestors, not to mention the same mother and a biographer has to include the relationship between the twins as part of their individuality.

8. The GREAT monistic DENKMITTEL for a hundred years past has been the notion of THE ONE KNOWER. The many exist only as objects for his thought — exist in his dream, as it were; and AS HE KNOWS them, they have one purpose, form one system, tell one tale for him. This notion of an ALL-ENVELOPING NOETIC UNITY in things is the sublimest achievement of intellectualist philosophy. Those who believe in the Absolute, as the all-knower is termed, usually say that they do so for coercive reasons, which clear thinkers cannot evade. The Absolute has far-reaching practical consequences, some of which I drew attention in my second lecture. Many kinds of difference important to us would surely follow from its being true. I cannot here enter into all the logical proofs of such a Being's existence, farther than to say that none of them seem to me sound. I must therefore treat the notion of an All–Knower simply as an hypothesis, exactly on a par logically with the pluralist notion that there is no point of view, no focus of information extant, from which the entire content of the universe is visible at once.[407]

This passage sums up James's conclusion of the existence of an all-knowing being and regards it as 'simply a hypothesis'. Indeed, it is beyond our perception and experience. The idea of an all-knowing being as a psychological realty is however, not beyond our perception and experience. This is the biggest difference James did not recognise. Culture is full of these ideas both past and present. Whether the representation of the idea is mythological or religious, like Horus, Zeus, Yahweh, Allah, Jesus, Buddha, Mercurius etc., or political like communism, fascism, liberalism, conservatism etc., shows that its permutation is real and present. The idea of unity can be interpreted in many other ways, such as energy flow or a profession or object of desire such as wealth, power, love, fame and so on.

This is the crucial aspect of understanding the idea of unity. Anyone can perceive and experience it, if open to its influence. Ideas cannot be found in the physical world unless they are expressed in some way. Buildings, towns, governments and religions do not build themselves, as ideas are behind their construction. The idea of unity has many faces, yet the origin of the idea is essentially the same and only different because of individual interpretations. These interpretations depend on the natural temperament, life history and experiences of each individual.

---

[407] JAMES William, 'Pragmatism', eBooks The University of Adelaide Library, Page 63-66

5. IDEAS OF UNITY IN PSYCHOLOGY

a. Freud S. S. (1856- 1939)

The significance of Freud in the later part of the Victorian age shows how a natural reaction occurs in individuals to a one-sided attitude to reality. In this case, Freud championed the liberation of our instincts from the natural cyclical attitude of the age. Cultures suffer the same patterns of growth as do individuals. A one-sided attitude is compensated by its opposite and a natural reaction occurs addressing the imbalance. This is where the importance of Freud's contribution to our understanding of human nature belongs.

Like James, Freud regarded the unconscious as an epiphenomenon and a container of material rejected from consciousness. That is to say, the material he observed in the unconscious originated in consciousness and for one or other reason, repressed by the individual due to its incompatibility with the culture and attitude to life. This is particularly true of our natural instincts, which at the time of Freud were to some extent repressed by the prevailing culture. His standpoint however, was medical and empirical, yet he could not escape his own personal bias and interpretation of his observations.

Many scientists fall into this trap as they mould their subject matter according to their own natural temperament and ignore or simply do not see what does not fit into their theory. Freud's observational skills were highly developed even though he could only see what he wanted to see. He did, however observe that certain modes of behaviour related to the myth-making and creative aspect of the unconscious.

The cornerstone of Freud's analytic approach was his discovery that a certain motifs in ancient myths had a relationship to motifs in the dreams of his patients. His central myth was that of Oedipus, which was part of the Theban Greek tragedy plays by Sophocles. This myth is a complex story of the life of Oedipus and his fateful end. To give justice to the story and how it impressed Freud enough to make it the cornerstone of his theory, I shall detail the myth in its entirety and amplify the text with a symbolic interpretation of the embedded ideas.

> Laius, son of Labdacus, king of Thebes, had married Jocasta. Having been warned by an oracle that his son would one day kill him. Laius carried the child to which Jocasta had just given birth to Mount Cithaeron. He pierced the infant's feet with a nail and tied them together solidly, hoping thus to be rid of him. But a shepherd found the child and

took him to Polybus, King of Corinth, who adopted him and named him Oedipus because of his wounded foot. When Oedipus had grown up he learned his destiny from an oracle who told him that he would kill his father and marry his mother. Oedipus believed that he could escape this fate by exiling himself forever from Corinth, never again seeing Polybus and his wife whom he assumed to be his true parents. This scruple was his own undoing. He went to Boeotia and on the road quarrelled with an unknown man whom he struck with his staff and killed. The victim was, indeed, Laius, his own father. Oedipus continued on his journey without suspecting that the first half of the oracle's prediction had been fulfilled. He arrived in Thebes where he learned that the region was being devastated by a fabulous monster with the face and bust of a woman, the body of a lion and the wings of a bird. Guarding the road to Thebes the Sphinx - as the monster was called -would stop all travellers and propose enigmas to them; those who were unable to solve her riddles she would devour. Creon, who had governed Thebes since the recent death of Laius, promised the crown and the hand of Jocasta to the man who delivered-the city from this scourge. Oedipus resolved to attempt the feat. He was successful.

The Sphinx asked him: 'Which is the animal that has four feet in the morning, two at midday and three in the evening?' He answered: 'Man, who in infancy crawls on all fours, who walks upright on two feet in maturity, and in his old age supports himself with a stick.' The Sphinx was vanquished and threw herself into the sea. And thus, still without realising it, Oedipus became the husband of his mother, Jocasta. From their union two sons were born, Etepcles and Polyneices, and two daughters, Antigone and Ismene. Oedipus, in spite of the-double crime he had innocently committed, was honoured as a sovereign devoted to his people's welfare, and appeared to prosper. But the Erinnyes were waiting. A terrible epidemic ravaged the land, decimating the population, and at the same time an incredible drought brought with it famine. When consulted, the oracle of Delphi replied that these scourges would not cease until the Thebans had driven the still unknown murderer of Laius out of the country. Oedipus, after having offered ritual maledictions against the assassin, undertook to find out who he was. His inquiries finally led to the discovery that the guilty man was none other than himself, and that Jocasta whom he had married was his mother. Jocasta in shame and grief hanged herself and Oedipus put out his own eyes. Then he went into exile, accompanied by his faithful daughter Antigone. He took refuge in the town of Colonus in Attica and, at last purified of his abominable crimes, disappeared mysteriously from the earth.

As for his sons, victims of the paternal curse, they perished by each other's hand. They had agreed to reign for alternate years. But when the time came Eteocles refused to hand over the crown. Polyneices gathered together an army of Argives and laid siege to Thebes. It was during this siege that the two brothers slew each other in the course of single combat. The senate of Thebes decreed that the body of Polyneices should be left unburied, but Antigone nevertheless rendered her dead brother funeral honours. For this she was condemned to be buried alive. Her sister Ismene shared her fate. And thus the unhappy family came to an end.[408]

The first aspect of this myth is the foretelling of the family's fate by the oracle. Oedipus's parents, particularly his father Laius, learned from the oracle that his son would one day kill him. Oracles give a decree or prophesy from an ancient God through a priest or messenger. Laius reacted to the prophesy of his potential death by the hand of his son. He tries to thwart his fate as foretold by injuring his son's feet and binding them so that he could not walk or grow into life. This alludes to the Sphinx's riddle later in the story, which is about walking or moving through life.

A shepherd of sheep, known for their spiritual guidance, rescues Oedipus and takes care of him. Polybus, the king of Corinth adopted and named Oedipus (wounded foot). When he was a young adult, he become aware of his fate through another oracle and consequently leaves Corinth believing Polybus and his wife are his true parents. He leaves in an attempt to avoid his fate, as did his real father. On the road to Boeotia, he has a fight with an unknown man and kills him. Oedipus is not aware that he just killed his father and believes him to be a stranger. In the additional text[409] to the story, King Laius (father) tries to kill Oedipus by running him over, thus making the killing self-defence rather than cold-blooded murder. The text also mentions three roads that intersect where the killing took place, indicating several potential directions of travel and choice.

The killing of the king and his replacement symbolises the transformation of the kingdom from one orientation to another. It is a death and renewal of the kingdom. In addition, a father-king is associated with consciousness, reason, the light of the sun and the royal arbiter. In other words, it is a change of conscious attitude. Oedipus continues on his journey to Thebes and meets a monster on the road. The monster is a hybrid woman, lion and bird called the Sphinx. She is a devouring (lioness) mother (bust) and spiritual (winged) character. The female lion is the hunter of food and the nurturer of her young and the wings denote the ability to fly and look down upon the earth and requires men to answer difficult questions. In other words, she gauges their cleverness and only those who can unravel the mystery will pass, and she devours those who

---

[408] LAROUSSE, New Encyclopedia of Mythology, Hamlyn Publishing, 1968, page 192
[409] The following is additional text to the story, which has bearing on the killing of Oedipus's father "On the way, Oedipus came to Davlia, where three roads crossed each other. There he encountered a chariot driven by his birth-father, King Laius. They fought over who had the right to go first and Oedipus killed Laius when the charioteer tried to run him over." https://en.wikipedia.org/wiki/Oedipus

could not answer the riddle. The Sphinx therefore represents a negative mother with a lofty viewpoint (spirit) and little compassion or earthly love. A man oriented to the conscious world alone, would have an unconscious resembling this dark and devouring woman.

Creon governs Thebes since the death of Laius and promises the kingdom and hand of Jocasta to any man that can answer the Sphinx correctly. Oedipus takes on the task and cleverly answers the riddle, saves the city, inherits the kingdom and the queen's hand in marriage. He did not know that this queen is actually his mother. The riddle that the Sphinx asks Oedipus alludes to feet and life's journey. She asks which animal has four feet in the morning, two at midday and three in the evening. This riddle associates a day with a man's life and the stages therein. Life is a day in that we are born in the morning, grow to our potential at noon when the sun is highest in the sky (consciousness) and descend back to the original darkness and death (night) upon the setting of the sun (unconscious).

The important factor in the myth is the overcoming of the Sphinx and how he heroically outwits her and saves the city and kingdom and she returns to the sea (myth-making unconscious). In other words, he saves and unwittingly inherits his father's (Laius) kingdom, which he would have rightly inherited anyway if he and his father had not tried to avoid their fate. The story continues with Oedipus marrying Jocasta having two sons and two daughters and the kingdom prospered. Oedipus was, however, unaware that he had married his mother.

The Erinnyes were however waiting. They are vengeful female chthonic Goddesses that brought upon the kingdom disease, drought and famine. Oedipus curses the killer of his father and proceeds to find out who he is. It is unclear in the story how he did this, but the consequences were devastating upon learning that he had indeed killed his father and married his mother. Oedipus put out his own eyes, went into exile with his faithful daughter Antigone, and disappeared from the earth. Jocasta hanged herself in shame and his two sons slew each other in battle over the kingdom. The senate (government) decreed not to bury Polyneices because he attacked his brother Etepcles, who ruled the kingdom at that time. Antigone defied the senate and buried him anyway, and consequently she and her sister were buried alive.

The Freudian interpretation of this myth is oriented around the killing of the father and incestuous union with the mother. This sexual union and guilt over the father is what Freud used to explain childhood neurosis in men. The incestuous aspect of the myth is to some extent only a partial interpretation. Expanding on the myth we can say that it is also the basis for male competition as emphasised by the killing of an unknown man on the road and his sons' rivalry for the kingdom. In this case, Oedipus was not aware he killed his father and married his mother until much later in his life. Freud left out this part of the myth in his interpretation. In addition, the Oedipus myth is a life journey, as emphasised by the Sphinx's riddle (feet for walking through life) and the journey of a man's birth, gaining a kingship, status, family, wealth and the descent towards ultimate death. Above all, it is an attempt to avoid one's fate as both Oedipus and his father tried to do.

Freud's interpretation fixates on the sexual component of incest rather than the usual issues of boy hanging on to his mother too long and avoiding the mans' world of competition, striving, power and so on. It is less of a sexual issue with the mother than an avoidance of the boy's fate and entry into the world of men. Oedipus actually lives a heroic life, kills a stranger that wanted to kill him on the road, overcomes the monster and gains a kingdom. In itself, this is a symbolically normal and healthy life. It is only when he became aware of who he had killed and married, that his life falls apart.

If we interpret the story from a symbolic standpoint, we can explain it as follows:

•Wounding and binding of feet to stop or hinder Oedipus from walking through life (individuation)
•Laius tries to kill Oedipus before he is killed- would not accept a potential challenge to his life (conscious standpoint) and future threat - male rivalry and power.
•The avoidance of fate causes Oedipus to leave his surrogate parents.
•Oedipus overcomes the negative mother-character with awareness of life's story (individuation) and the Sphinx returns to the myth-making unconscious (sea)
•He wins the kingdom and queen and therefore a prestigious and noble life by overcoming the monster. Oedipus thrives and has children
•The children are two daughters and two sons and as far as the story goes are healthy and prosperous. 2 x 2 feminine and masculine (unity) within the kingdom.
•Erinnyes, the negative feminine Goddesses attack the unity of Oedipus's life and urge him to look at himself. This is typical of men later in life after they have achieved their conscious goals of wife, family, career (kingdom) and so on.
•This is the turning point (noon) where the conscious attitude is challenged by the unconscious symbolised by the Erinnyes and neglected by Oedipus. Disaster urges Oedipus to self-analysis.
•He learns that he indeed has lived out his fate that he tried to avoid

•Knowledge alone destroys his conscious life. He became aware that his life had to change and he had to look inside himself, symbolised by the removal of his eyes (the eyes look at the physical world). Many men marry a woman that takes care of them as their mothers did and indeed, project their mother onto them. Becoming aware of this projection onto the wife is life-changing or, as in this case, destroying.
•Oedipus then descends into the unconscious with the help of his daughter (soul guide) for purification and redemption, but disappears from the earth with no return.
•This myth is similar to the fate that befell Rousseau and Nietzsche with their descent into the unconscious without return to the world.
•There is one question I would like to finish this analysis on, and that is, what would have happened if Oedipus had not found out that he killed his father and married his mother?

It is clear that this myth has far more meaning than simply a sexual interpretation for men. As the text says, it is a story of a life's fateful journey and the attempted avoidance of that fate. This is typical in that conscious striving, competition, power, winning the girl, etc., are the hallmarks of male psychology and also animal behaviour. The myth does not mention the sexual component. Symbolically, intercourse has more to do with the union of opposites than the physical act.

Indeed, dreams containing sexual union with a known family member indicate that an opposite but familiar inner character is uniting with the conscious viewpoint of the dreamer. In other words, incest dreams are generally the union of a projected character or characteristics onto a family member. Dreams and myths are symbolic representations and cannot be interpreted literally.

To relate this analysis with Freud's interpretation of the myth, it is obvious that the sexual theory of incest is only a part of the story and that the main theme is more concerned with a life's journey and fate. Was Freud's interpretation then an unconscious compensation for his standing and power in the world? He established a new approach to dreams, had many followers and was a pioneering researcher. In other words, he had achieved his kingdom (conscious school of thought), united with his mother queen (positive female character) by fighting the contemporary Victorian sexual attitude (negative female character) and made a unique and positive contribution to the understanding of the unconscious. Another way to put it is that Freud built a school, which reinforced and established his ego (consciousness), overcame the devouring aspect of the culture (monster) that Rousseau and Nietzsche could not, won the kingdom and queen, and prospered for a time.

The following passages from Freud's writings show how the study of dreams had much to do with his the idea of unity.

> The following observations may help us towards clearing up this point. If in the course of a single day we have two or more experiences suitable for provoking a dream, the dream will make a combined reference to them as a single whole; *it is under a necessity to combine them into a unity.*

> Many experiences such as this lead me to assert that the dream-work is under some kind of necessity to combine all the sources which have acted as stimuli for the dream into a single unity in the dream itself.

The above passage also shows that Freud recognised daytime experiences and their reflection in dreams as a 'single unity'. In other words, the dream brings the daytime experiences into relationship with the unconscious, as expressed in the dream itself. Unity to Freud was therefore contained within the dream and not in his conscious life. Like Schopenhauer, Freud viewed the unconscious from his established worldly standpoint.

> The dream (as will appear) can lay no claim to a corresponding practical significance; its theoretical value as a paradigm is, however, all the greater, and one who cannot explain the origin of the dream pictures will strive in vain to understand the phobias, obsessive and delusional ideas, and likewise their therapeutic importance.[410]

I'm not sure why Freud would regard dreams having no practical significance, when in the same passage he cites other products from the unconscious that affect behaviour in negative ways. It certainly seems practical to have a healthy body and mind, and dreams reflect where we may need adjustment in our conscious lives to achieve that balance and health.

> As every one knows, the ancients before Aristotle did not consider the dream a product of the dreaming mind, but a divine inspiration, and in ancient times the two antagonistic streams, which one finds throughout in the estimates of dream life, were already noticeable. They distinguished between true and valuable dreams, sent to the dreamer to warn him or to foretell the future, and vain, fraudulent, and empty dreams, the object of which was to misguide or lead him to destruction.[411]

---

[410] FREUD Sigmund, 'The Interpretation of Dreams' The Macmillan Company 1913, page V
[411] Ibid, page 3

The passage above shows that Freud recognised personal and mythological categories of dreams, as the ancients knew them. As we shall see later, Jung referred these categories as personal and collective dreams. Dreams also had a 'divine inspiration' according to the ancients, and they were given to the dreamer by the Gods. We can expand on that idea and say that the Gods also give us other unconscious products and behaviour. This is why the Gods led such colourful and emotional lives. They are full of jealousy, fear, lust, betrayal and so on. Some Gods are known for their emotional tones of anger (Aries/Mars) and love (Aphrodite/Venus).

The benefit of regarding dreams originating from God(s) is it promotes an objective viewpoint. This is important, as it limits the possessive quality and identification with inner characters and helps in the lessening of projection onto real people. One is less likely to identify with an inner character if we know that character to some extent. We can see the danger in identifying with an inner character in the life of Nietzsche with his declaration: 'God is dead' at the same time discovering the 'Overman' and the 'Ugliest Man'.

> The laity has, therefore, always endeavoured to 'interpret' the dream, and in doing so has tried two essentially different methods. The first of these procedures regards the dream content as a whole and seeks to replace it with another content, which is intelligible, and in certain respects analogous. This is symbolic dream interpretation; it naturally goes to pieces at the outset in the case of those dreams, which appear, not only unintelligible but confused.
>
> A demonstration of the way in which such symbolic interpretation is arrived at cannot, of course, be given. Success remains a matter of ingenious conjecture, of direct intuition, and for this reason dream interpretation has naturally been elevated to an art, which seems to depend upon extraordinary gifts.
>
> The other of the two popular methods of dream interpretation entirely abandons such claims. It might be designated as the "cipher method," since it treats the dream as a kind of secret code, in which every sign is translated into another sign of known meaning, according to an established key. [412]

In the above passages, Freud regards symbolic dream interpretation insufficient for 'unintelligible' or 'confused' dreams and the 'cipher method' better as it treats the dream as a secret code to be unlocked with a key. This is where Freud applied his theory of sexuality as the key to unlocking the true meaning, as he saw it, of a dream. As I have shown above in the

---

[412] Ibid, page 80-82

analysis of the Oedipus myth, there is more to it than simply a case of sexual incest. I do not regard Freud's theory of sexuality having no validity, as there will always be instances where the sexual issue applies. It is not the whole picture, though.

His approach using the 'cipher method' is limited and somewhat obscures the true nature of the dream or myth. Dreams do not obscure or have secret intents. It is reflective, compensatory and straightforward. If one dreams of a Sphinx as in the Oedipus myth, it does not mean a dog. It means exactly as revealed, and that is a female lioness with wings. These are her attributes: a wild female animal (lion) with the ability to fly and see things from a lofty point of view. Breasts point to a woman's ability to feed and nurture her young and are part of her maternal function. There is nothing obscure about it. It is very straight forward and with time and amplification, quite understandable. There is no need for substitution, keys or secret codes; all the information in a dream is there to analyse. Myths are, however, easier because they are collective stories and do not have the idiosyncrasies that personal dreams have. This is where the dreamer's conscious life is important for reflective comparison.

> If with my patients I emphasise the frequency of the Oedipus dream—of having sexual intercourse with one's mother—I get the answer: "I cannot remember such a dream." Immediately afterwards, however, there arises the recollection of another disguised and indifferent dream, which has been dreamed repeatedly by the patient, and the analysis shows it to be a dream of this same content—that is, another Oedipus dream. I can assure the reader that veiled dreams of sexual intercourse with the mother are a great deal more frequent than open ones to the same effect.[413]

The passage above shows Freud's personal bias and dogmatism when interpreting dreams. He seems to go out of his way to look for dreams that fit his somewhat rigid interpretation. Dream research requires not only an artistic approach as Freud mentions above, but also an ability to build an objective string of ideas related to the dream text. In other words, dreams require research based on objective observation and hypothetical conclusions either adjusted or thrown out if they do not fit the subject.

> In a few cases the division of the dream into two equal parts expresses the alternative, which the dream finds it so difficult to represent.
> The attitude of the dream towards the category of antithesis and contradiction is most striking. This category is unceremoniously neglected; the word "No" does not seem to exist for the dream. Antitheses are with peculiar preference reduced to unity or represented

---

[413] Ibid, page 242

as one. The dream also takes the liberty of representing any element whatever by its desired opposite, so that it is at first impossible to tell about any element capable of having an opposite, whether it is to be taken negatively or positively, in the dream thoughts. [414]

It seems from the above text that Freud regards the dream with suspicion and that it obscures its true meaning. He does, however, regard dreams as having the ability to represent an element by its opposite (antithesis). I am not sure why he feels this and would have to have specific examples to understand what he means.

> From a work of K. Abel, Der Gegensinn der Urworte, 1884 (see my review of it in the Bleuler-Freud oldest languages behaved in this regard quite like the dream. They originally had only one word for both extremes in a series of qualities or activities (strong-weak, old-young, far-near, to tie-to separate), and formed separate designations for the two extremes only secondarily through slight modifications of the common primitive word. [415]

In this passage, he discusses how the oldest languages used the same term for the opposites, which he relates to dreams, and how the opposites are two sides of the same coin. Freud is aware that the opposites were indeed 'one' in the oldest languages. It is only through our modern intellectual ability to differentiate the opposites and see them separately that causes us to lose sight of their relationship to each other.

> Goethe always rated Eros high, never tried to belittle its power, followed its primitive and even wanton expressions with no less attentiveness than its highly sublimated ones and has, as it seems to me, expounded its essential unity throughout all its manifestations no less decisively than Plato did in the remote past. [416]

Freud does appreciate the function of relationship symbolised by Eros. That is to say, the God Eros is the function of connection, attraction, desire and love. He is a winged child and on occasion a young man, a sky God rather than an earth-God and his unifying function known in the ancient world from the beginning of all creation[417].

> The theory of primal sin is of Orphic origin; it was preserved in the mysteries and thence penetrated into the philosophic schools of Greek antiquity. Men were the descendants of Titans, who had killed and dismembered the young Dionysos-Zagreus; the weight of this crime

---

[414] Ibid, page 296
[415] Ibid, Footnote page 296
[416] FREUD Sigmund, 'Art and Literature' Stanford University Press 1997, page 260
[417] Eros was born shortly after creation on the Greek God Family Tree. He is the son of Aether and Hemera.

oppressed them. A fragment of Anaximander says that the unity of the world was destroyed by a primordial crime and everything that issued from it must carry on the punishment for this crime. Although the features of banding together, killing, and dismembering as expressed in the deed of the Titans very clearly recall the totem sacrifice described by St Nilus—as also many other myths of antiquity, for example, the death of Orpheus himself—we are nevertheless disturbed here by the variation according to which a youthful God was murdered.[418]

Freud discusses the theory of primal sin in the above passage and how it destroyed the primal unity of the world. The death and rebirth motif of young Dionysus relates to the Oedipus story in that the original unity of childhood was broken for the sake of adaptation and the development of external functions. He mentions St Nilus and that sacrifice is a natural part of personal growth and evolution. Everyone has to abandon childish practices and behaviour to enter the adult world. Boys have to overcome the attachment to their personal mother and father and channel that energy into the world. The unity of childhood and the family sacrificed for a larger unity of adaptation to culture and work (consciousness).

Freud also mentions the death of Orpheus, which is interesting as Orpheus once worshiped Dionysus. He later switched to worshipping the sun God Apollo, thus leaving an attitude of intoxication and unbridled animal behaviour for culture and art in the sun. This one-sided attitude did not sit well with the Dionysian women the Maenads, who ripped Orpheus to shreds[419]. This is what happens when one side of our nature clings to

---

[418] FREUD Sigmund, 'Totem and Taboo', George Routledge & Sons Ltd, page 72
[419] I have included the story of Orpheus for convenience. New Larousse Encyclopedia of Mythology, Hamlyn Publishing, 1968, page 206
'Orpheus, the great hero of Thrace, was very different in character from the other Greek heroes. He was not distinguished for his warlike exploits. He was in origin perhaps a Thracian king, and he owed his fame above all to his amazing musical talent. Son of Apollo, he sang and played the lyre with such art that the savage beasts came running to listen and even trees would follow him. His talent performed miracles during the voyage of the Argonauts. The ship Argo, high on the beach, descended to the sea of its own accord at the sound of his singing. His songs arrested the Symple-gades, those terrible moving rocks which threatened to crush the ship, and sent them down to the bottom of the sea. He lulled the dragon, guardian of the Golden Fleece, to sleep by singing, and thus facilitated the Argonauts' escape. Such was the power of his voice and the harmony of his lyre that even the infernal deities submitted to them. He had married the nymph Eurydice whom he passionately loved. One day when Eurydice was fleeing from Aristaeus she was mortally bitten by a snake hidden in the grass. Orpheus was heartbroken at the death of his wife and resolved to descend into the Underworld to reclaim her. He was able to charm Hades and Persephone who gave him permission to take Eurydice back to earth on the sole condition that he should not turn to look at her during the journey. The couple had almost reached the gates of Hades when Orpheus impatiently and imprudently turned to look at his wife. At once she was whisked back into the sombre abode of the dead and vanished, this time forever. Orpheus was inconsolable and, some said, killed himself. But the more widely held opinion was that he was torn in pieces by Thracian women who were infuriated at this

the other. When the outer world of consciousness attracts all our attention, the inner unconscious eventually objects to its neglect. This also relates to our interpretation of the Oedipus myth as a story of growth, gaining power by overcoming the old attitude (king), marrying and having a family. When he became aware of his prophesied fate of replacing (killing) his father, it led to another change in attitude. He turned away from his conscious life (put out his eyes) and was led back to the unconscious by his daughter (soul guide).

These are natural changes to man in his lifetime. The sun rises; he grows and sacrifices the unity of childhood for a wider community to build a kingdom and family. After achieving his biological responsibility and after noon, the sun begins its downward journey. He suffers another change to develop a spiritual (inner) attitude to life and eventual death. If one stays too long on the side of consciousness and does not heed the impulses welling up from inside and accept one's fate, he will be torn to pieces through some personal disaster and made to accept fate anyway.

b. Jung C. G. (1875- 1961)

Jung was originally a student of Freud and was meant to be his heir-apparent. He had natural temperamental difference to Freud, which gave him another viewpoint of the unconscious. His orientation was based on a strict scientific attitude towards the unconscious and less prone to personal interpretation. He recognised early in his life that dreams, fantasies, ideas etc., were objective experiences and studied them as such. Like Freud, he studied ancient mythology, but also studied the Philosophy from the ancient world to his present. After his break from Freud, he founded his own school called Analytical Psychology, from which his work crystallised into a unified and coherent approach to both inner and outer sides of reality.

Jung did not try to re-invent the wheel, but used historical ideas, myths and terms to describe his observations. For example, Plato used his term 'archetype' for inner characters to describe the pattern of original model.[420] The term 'Individuation' (life path) had an ancient Egyptian God

---

single-minded love for his wife. His head and his lyre were flung into the River Hebrus and carried as far as Lesbos. The head of the divine singer was caught in a fissure of rock where for long it delivered oracles. In the days of Lucian his lyre could still be seen in a temple at Lesbos and it was sacrilege to lay hands on it. One day Neanthus, son of the Tyrant of Lesbos, tried to play the wondrous lyre and was devoured by dogs who had been attracted by the sound. They also said that the head of Orpheus was found by a shepherd on the banks of the Melas, and in the town of Libethra .in Macedonia they pointed out his tomb.'

[420] See chapter 4b Plato

called Khepri attached to the idea. The term was later used by the Scholastic Philosophers and Schopenhauer. Anima and Animus as inner contra sexual characters (souls) were originally termed by Aristotle. Jung did coin the terms Introvert and Extrovert as categories of people who orient themselves to the inner or outer worlds. The four orienting functions of Intuition, Thinking, Feeling and Sensation used by Jung can be loosely translated and relate to Plato's symbolic cosmological elements of Fire, Air, Water and Earth.

He used other terms such as 'Persona' as a form of adaptive mask that belongs to a mode of behaviour attached to a profession or job. For example, a medical practitioner behaves in a certain way that reassures the public that they are indeed a doctor and not a rascal. The term shadow used by the ancient Egyptians and adopted by Jung describes the part of the personality related to our animal origins that are generally incompatibility with cultural norms. This was the main emphasis of Freud's theory of the unconscious. The 'Collective Unconscious' is Jung's term for the deeper myth-making creative aspect of the unconscious as a matrix of our perception of reality and the origin of all ideas. The 'Self' he coined for the totality of the psyche, which includes the myth-making unconscious and conscious physical world, and used to describe the 'Idea of Unity' as perceived by the individual. The 'Self' is a difficult and often misinterpreted term because of its confusion with the ego. In his view, the 'Self' is an objective character not identical with the ego and at the centre of our personality. The ego is to the self as the earth is to the sun.

Jung's far reaching exploration of unconscious material in the form of dreams, fantasies, ideas and myths led him to the conclusion that everyone has the potential to make the four orienting functions conscious in their lifetime. As a baby, we are unconscious of our psychic functions and grow developing one or two of them. Babies are born with the beginnings of their potential personality. This natural process of growth begins with the development of a main function with the help of another function. This does not mean that the other two functions disappear. They simply remain below the threshold of consciousness and lead an undeveloped existence in the unconscious. They can be accessed however, if one has an open attitude to the flow of material that emanates from inside.

His approach to his patients and research as a physician was similar to Freud and based on well-being and mental health. As such he had an open mind to the many and varied types of personality and their unconscious bases. He understood that we all have the same natural functioning of other mammals and the potential for the highest spiritual forms of culture. For this reason, he understood how Freud prematurely abstracted a system from his own temperamental viewpoint and used it as the basis for his research. As I have shown above in the exploration of the Oedipus myth, Freud abstracted a specific part of the myth, namely incest and its associated guilt, and used it as a starting point for his psychoanalysis. It is however, not the whole story as the myth shows. The very fact that one of his own students Alfred Adler founded another approach based on the 'will to power' shows that Freud had not gone beyond his own temperamental prejudices.

After his break with Freud, Jung lost his footing and began his own personal journey into the underworld of the myth-making unconscious. This lasted many years and yielded untold riches and an approach to the unconscious based on direct experience. He documented his journey in the Black book and later transferred the images and text to the Red book. It chronicles his conversations and struggles with inner characters and the transformative affect they had on him. Rousseau and Nietzsche made the same journey but did not returned to the conscious world. The difference for Jung was his anchor to the world, namely his family, patients and friends and he had something to go back to after his inner journey.

With his return to the world, Jung opened the doors to all of mythology and explored how it functions in our everyday lives. He began a life-long task of psychological study of human behaviour, typology, culture and religion that culminated in a thorough and comprehensive study of alchemy. He concluded that it was the missing link and undercurrent[421] between the ancient worlds of Greece and Rome and our present understanding of unity. Indeed, Jung realised that all of our functioning, including the instincts[422] for procreation and power are part of our unity. The following passage exemplifies Jung's attitude to this instinctive foundation he calls the 'shadow' and the importance of knowing something about it in one self.

> So far we have considered the problem of this new psychology essentially from the Freudian point of view. Undoubtedly it has shown us a very real truth to which our pride, our civilized consciousness, may say no, though something else in us says yes. Many people find this fact extremely irritating; it arouses their hostility or even their fear, and consequently they are unwilling to recognize the conflict. And indeed it is a frightening thought that man also has a shadow-side to him, consisting not just of little weaknesses and foibles, but of a positively demonic

---

[421] Alchemy was an undercurrent because the Christian Religion had no tolerance for heretical belief systems.

[422] We may at some time in our lives overcome our instinctive nature for the sake of spiritual development but unity includes animal, soul and spirit.

dynamism. The individual seldom knows anything of this; to him, as an individual, it is incredible that he should ever in any circumstances go beyond himself. But let these harmless creatures form a mass, and there emerges a raging monster; and each individual is only one tiny cell in the monster's body, so that for better or worse he must accompany it on its bloody rampages and even assist it to the utmost. Having a dark suspicion of these grim possibilities, man turns a blind eye to the shadow-side of human nature. Blindly he strives against the salutary dogma of original sin, which is yet so prodigiously true. Yes, he even hesitates to admit the conflict of which he is so painfully aware. It can readily be understood that a school of psychology- even if it be biased and exaggerated in this or that respect-which insists on the seamy side, is unwelcome, not to say frightening, because it forces us to gaze into the bottomless abyss of this problem. A dim premonition tells us that we cannot be whole without this negative side, that we have a body which, like all bodies, casts a shadow, and that if we deny this body we cease to be three- dimensional and become flat and without substance. Yet this body is a beast with a beast's soul, an organism that gives unquestioning obedience to instinct. To unite oneself with this shadow is to say yes to instinct, to that formidable dynamism lurking in the background. From this the ascetic morality of Christianity wishes to free us, but at the risk of disorganizing man's animal nature at the deepest level.[423]

The text above shows Jung's attitude to what Freud called 'repression' of natural instincts and a long lasting one-sidedness that can damage the individual personality and culture. This 'beast' as Jung puts it, is an individual aspect of the personality and can only be tamed in a personal way. In other words, the beast can only be tamed or adjusted by individuals in the privacy of their own psychic space. Jung continues with the example of Nietzsche and how Christianity could not satisfy his idea of unity and his need to search for something else.

> The case of Nietzsche shows, on the one hand, the consequences of neurotic one-sidedness, and, on the other hand, the dangers that lurk in this leap beyond Christianity. Nietzsche undoubtedly felt the Christian denial of animal nature very deeply indeed, and therefore he sought a higher human wholeness beyond good and evil.[424]

This passage brings the question of ethics into the idea of unity as well as other functions, including the so-called sinful instincts of procreation and power (survival), things that Christianity tries to deny or at least, diminish. It is understandable and quite natural to develop one's positive traits with the worship of an all-good and perfect God. The reality of the psyche

---

[423] JUNG C.G., Two Essays In Analytical Psychology, Routledge and Kegan Paul Ltd, 1981, Page 30
[424] Ibid, Page 32

includes negative traits and these need understanding and to some extent, integrating into a united whole.[425]

> Over against the polymorphism of the primitive's instinctual nature there stands the regulating principle of individuation. Multiplicity and inner division are opposed by an integrative unity whose power is as great as that of the instincts. Together they form a pair of opposites necessary for self-regulation, often spoken of as nature and spirit. These conceptions are rooted in psychic conditions between which human consciousness fluctuates like the pointer on the scales.[426]

The above passage shows how individuation is the unifying and regulating spirit in the human being which operates during one's lifetime, whether we are aware of it or not. We can see this system in the way we develop and grow throughout our lives. Childhood is generally a fun, creative and playful time. The onset of our sexual instinct makes us more responsible and drawn out of our parents' milieu into the world of biological adults. Our concerns change with attention to work, money and procreation, in other words, the urge to build. As we grow older and conscious goals achieved, our concerns change; we look towards our childhood for a reconnection to that other side that would make us whole. Some people, particularly creative types, never lose sight of the underlying unity that governs their life and allow the process to unfold naturally. The 'pointer on the scale', as Jung puts it, moves from side to side in its own time. For some, the pointer moves very quickly, for others very slowly, and for others, it stops moving altogether and stays on one side.

Jung continues:

> The symbols used by the unconscious to this end are the same as those which mankind has always used to express wholeness, completeness, and perfection: symbols, as a rule, of the quaternity and the circle. For these reasons I have termed this the *individuation process*.[427]

His emphasis on the symbolic language shows how the unconscious products such as dreams, fantasies, ideas etc., compensate or reflect our conscious life and attitude. This always has been the function of our great religious institutions. They connect us to the idea of unity and provide the framework and stability for that connection, no matter what circumstances

---

[425] I do not mean giving oneself over to the beast in us for this would be disastrous for the ego. It is forming a relationship with the beast and respecting its needs just like we respect the needs of our body.

[426] JUNG C.G., Two Essays In Analytical Psychology, Routledge and Kegan Paul Ltd, 1981, Page 51

[427] Ibid, Page 110

befall us. These institutions were generally built on the experiences of a unique individual who gave voice to the overarching life process Jung calls 'individuation'.

> If the luminosity appears in monadic form as a single star, sun, or eye, it readily assumes the shape of a mandala and must then be interpreted as the self. It has nothing whatever to do with "double consciousness," because there is no indication of a dissociated personality. On the contrary, the symbols of the self have a "uniting" character.[428]

In the above passage, Jung introduces the term 'Self' as a symbol of unity which every individual has within them. As he mentions, the symbol of unity can take the form of an abstract pattern like a mandala, or be an inner character, projected onto historical figures such as Jesus, Buddha and so on. Kant knew this psychological fact, in that he recognised the difference between object and the idea of the object as part of our psychic structure. This is why powerful and inspiring religious figures have such an attractive force, because they draw the projection of the central inner character from inside individuals. This is however, a 'double-edged sword'. On the one hand a religious figure connects us to our unity, but on the other, may block our direct experience of the inner character in ourselves and hence, our personal idea of unity.

> At all events the unprejudiced reader will recognize at once the idea of a "mid-point" that is reached by a kind of climb (mountaineering, effort, struggle, etc.). He will also recognize without difficulty the famous medieval conundrum of the squaring of the circle, which belongs to the field of alchemy. Here it takes its rightful place as a symbol of individuation. The total personality is indicated by the four cardinal points, the four Gods, i.e., the four functions which give bearings in psychic space, and also by the circle enclosing the whole. Overcoming the four Gods who threaten to smother the individual signifies liberation from identification with the four functions, a fourfold *nirdvandva* ("free from opposites") followed by an approximation to the circle, to undivided wholeness.[429]

Jung describes in the above text the total and differentiated symbol of unity into the four cardinal points, or differentiated functions making up the whole. If we place the four orienting functions of intuition, thinking, feeling and sensation at those four cardinal points, we can see how those functions operate in our lives. For example, we may orient ourselves by thinking and sensation and the other functions of feeling and intuition remain unconscious and undeveloped unless we let them have a place in our lives. This is the hardest task, particularly when a culture has a one-

---

[428] Ibid, Page 199
[429] Ibid, Page 223

sided orientation. In addition, the older we get, the harder it is to develop the unconscious functions because of their childlike nature.

The above passage also emphasises the 'overcoming' of the four points, Gods or functions to achieve a state free from the opposites. This is one of the cultural barriers to unity as it tends to recommend one side or the other. If we orient ourselves by thinking, it leaves little room for feeling, and so too, with the other functions. We may ask; what does it mean to be whole and not identify with a particular function? This is a difficult pill to swallow, because it requires recognition that the culture we live in might not be the healthiest for the individual. When a function is undeveloped, it has the nature of a child and comes out as such. This is why some of the above philosophers had such difficulty in relationships, particularly with women. It would be somewhat embarrassing to behave like a child for such learned and intellectual men. Jung recognised this issue and created an alternative residence in Bollingen outside of Zurich, away from public gaze where he could explore his unity without the loss of his professional standing. This is why Jung uses the term 'overcoming', because it is a form of possession, either culturally or personally, by one or two functions (Gods). This possession has consequences, as he notes below:

> The loss of soul corresponds with the tearing loose of an essential part of one's nature; it is the disappearance and emancipation of a complex, which therewith becomes a tyrannical usurper of consciousness, oppressing the whole man; it throws him out of his course, and constrains him to actions whose blind one-sidedness has self-destruction as its inevitable issue. The primitives are notoriously subject to such phenomena as running amok, Berserker rage, possessions, and the like.[430]

We can see this phenomenon in children whose ego (one or two functions) is just developing and how their personality can simply fragment into its cardinal points with the corresponding explosion of affect (emotion). It has always fascinated me how much energy is released when a child has a tantrum.

> Psychology therefore culminates of necessity in a developmental process which is peculiar to the psyche and consists in integrating the unconscious contents into consciousness. This means that the psychic human being becomes a whole, and becoming whole has remarkable effects on ego-consciousness which are extremely difficult to describe. I doubt my ability to give a proper account of the change that comes over the subject under the influence of the individuation process; it is a relatively rare occurrence, which is experienced only by those who have

---

[430] Ibid, Page 278

gone through the wearisome but, if the unconscious is to be integrated, indispensable business of coming to terms with the unconscious components of the personality.[431]

Jung recognises that the individuation process occurs whether we are aware of it or not. What he does say is awareness of the process of individuation makes it easier to accept and live it willingly. Awareness of the unfolding process has great benefits for the individual. It means that we acknowledge the undeveloped areas in our selves and allow those areas a life and growth. The blocking of this growth and resistance to its flow is where people get in trouble. The great personal and cultural disasters not only change individuals, but also the culture's orientation. Personal disasters, like losing one's job or the death of a friend or parent are enough to throw us out of our one-sided nature and urge us to change our orientation. The same goes for cultures and nations, particularly when economic downturns or war engulfs the population.

In the following passage, Jung discusses the nature of projection and as Kant identified, the way we find an initial relationship to the object, whether a thing or another person.

> It is the natural and given thing for unconscious contents to be projected. In a comparatively primitive person this creates that characteristic relationship to the object which Levy-Bruhl has fittingly called "mystic identity" or "participation mystique." 12 Thus every normal person of our time, who is not reflective beyond the average, is bound to his environment by a whole system of projections. So long as all goes well, he is totally unaware of the compulsive, i.e., "magical" or "mystical," character of these relationships.[432]

Projection is an interesting form of natural connectedness and the beginning of relationship to the object[433] and unites subject and object. For example, most people have an idea of a snake and it is activated when they see a snake in the wild. With knowledge and experience of snake species, we may appreciate it, not fear it, get closer and comfortable enough to catch it. If we do not have knowledge and experience of what type the snake is and one's idea is undifferentiated, we lump all snakes together as potentially dangerous and move away from it. The idea is activated and we behave according to the idea based on our understanding and knowledge of snakes. This is the unifying function of projection, in that the object and idea of the object coincide.

---

[431] JUNG C.G., The Structure and Dynamics of the Psyche, Routledge London, 1969, Page 223
[432] Ibid, Page 265
[433] I use the term 'object' in its philosophical sense in that anything outside of our own psyche is an object, including people, animals, trees, rocks, planets and so on.

What happens after that depends on our knowledge and experience of the object and the idea. This example shows that projection is an initial and unconscious form of synchronicity. Jung continues in his description of how projection connects us with the object and gives it a soul.

> It is exactly as formulated in classical Chinese philosophy: yang (the light, warm, dry, masculine principle) contains within it the seed of yin (the dark, cold, moist, feminine principle), and vice versa. Matter therefore would contain the seed of spirit and spirit the seed of matter............ With the decline of alchemy the symbolical unity of spirit and matter fell apart, with the result that modern man finds himself uprooted and alienated in a de-souled world.[434]

On the one hand, Jung sees projection in a negative light if we are unaware of what we are projecting. On the other hand, however, he considers a world without projection inanimate and soulless. This raises an interesting question. Can we gain knowledge of the object by projection, thus giving it soul, or can we only gain knowledge of the projection through the object? Projection does increase the attraction to the object and releases a certain amount of energy. Experience shows that the projection has a life of its own, particularly when it comes to soul. My inner female character(s)[435] are responsible for all my moods, emotions, and values and connect me to the matter of my body as well as the spirit of my mind. She (they) exists in her (their) own right without the necessity for projection onto an object or person. She is however easier to see when projected, because we can study the differences between projection and object. This is how I relate to my soul, which is obviously different for other people. Jung continues with the objective nature of the inner characters as follows:

> Since the unconscious gives us the feeling that it is something alien, a non-ego, it is quite natural that it should be symbolized by an alien figure. Thus, on the one hand, it is the most insignificant of things, while on the other, so far as it potentially contains that "round" wholeness which consciousness lacks, it is the most significant of all. This "round" thing is the great treasure that lies hidden in the cave of the unconscious, and its personification is this personal being who represents the higher unity of conscious and unconscious........ For this reason I have elected to call it the "self," by which I understand a psychic totality and at the same time a centre, neither of which coincides with the ego but includes it, just as a larger circle encloses a smaller one.[436]

---

[434] JUNG C.G., The Archetypes of the Collective Unconscious, Routledge London, 1955, Page 109
[435] I put (s) after the word character, because it appears that I have two souls, one light and oriented towards the spirit, the other dark and oriented towards the body and matter.
[436] JUNG C.G., The Archetypes of the Collective Unconscious, Routledge London, 1955, Page 142

The 'Self' as he describes it in the text above, is a character that combines the inner and outer realms and indeed, unites them. In a sense, this book is trying to show that unity exists between matter and psyche, whether we are aware of it or not[437]. This is why I included Quantum Mechanics in the following chapters. The forces that influence matter are the same forces that influence the inner unconscious characters, and move matter in synchronistic phenomena. Jung discusses this unity and how, ultimately psyche becomes matter at a certain depth. I would go further and suggest they relate at all levels by electromagnetic forces (energy) that influences matter and surrounds us on all sides.

> As civilization develops, the bisexual primordial being turns into a symbol of the unity of personality, a symbol of the self, where the war of opposites finds peace. The uniqueness of the psyche can never enter wholly into reality, it can only be realized approximately, though its till remains the absolute basis of all consciousness. The deeper "layers" of the psyche lose their individual uniqueness as they retreat farther and farther into darkness. "Lower down," that is to say as they approach the autonomous functional systems, they become increasingly collective until they are universalized and extinguished in the body's materiality, i.e., in chemical substances. The body's carbon is simply carbon. Hence "at bottom" the psyche is simply "world." In this sense I hold Kerenyi to be absolutely right when he says that in the symbol the world itself is speaking. The more archaic and" deeper," that is the more physiological, the symbol is, the more collective and universal, the more "material" it is. The more abstract, differentiated, and specific it is, and the more its nature approximates to conscious uniqueness and individuality, the more it sloughs off its universal character.[438]

In this passage, Jung recognises the deeper we go into psyche, the more material it becomes, thus losing its uniqueness. At 'bottom', we are all still mammals with the same instinctual functioning. Even in extreme old age, when we will have approached our unique individuality at its most differentiated stage, we still have the same bodily functions as other mammals. We may have unique physical appearance but our bodies' function in the same way. At most, we can have a unique and individual personality but unless we have come up with an individual way to ingest food and remove the body's waste, we are still as collective in our physicality, as all other mammals. In addition, the psychic determinants of inner characters are also common to all humans; therefore, there is some limit to how much individuality we can actually achieve. As mentioned

---

[437] I do have some doubt whether it is possible to withdraw projection completely as matter and psyche can never be known completely.

[438] JUNG C.G., The Archetypes of the Collective Unconscious, Routledge London, 1955, Page 173

previously, we all look at the same thing from an individual point of view. Our position is unique, but what we are looking at is not. We look at the same 'unity' and have different ideas of it.

> In this way the primordial being becomes the distant goal of man's self-development, having been from the very beginning a projection of his unconscious wholeness. Wholeness consists in the union of the conscious and the unconscious personality. Just as every individual derives from masculine and feminine genes, and the sex is determined by the predominance of the corresponding genes, so in the psyche it is only the conscious mind, in a man, that has the masculine sign, while the unconscious is by nature feminine. The reverse is true in the case of a woman. All I have done in my anima theory is to rediscover and reformulate this fact.[439]

Jung describes the 'Self' as the central character, which has multiple manifestations beyond human representation.

> I usually describe the supraordinate personality as the "self," thus making a sharp distinction between the ego, which, as is well known, extends only as far as the conscious mind, and the *whole* of the personality, which includes the unconscious as well as the conscious component. The ego is thus related to the self as part to whole. To that extent the self is supraordinate. Moreover, the self is felt empirically not as subject but as object, and this by reason of its unconscious component, which can only come to consciousness indirectly, by way of projection. Because of its unconscious component the self is so far removed from the conscious mind that it can only be partially expressed by human figures; the other part of it has to be expressed by objective, abstract symbols. The human figures are father and son, mother and daughter, king and queen, God and Goddess. Theriomorphic symbols are the dragon, snake, elephant, lion, bear, and other powerful animals, or again the spider, crab, butterfly, beetle, worm, etc. Plant symbols are generally flowers (lotus and rose). These lead on to geometrical figures like the circle, the sphere, the square, the quaternity, the clock, the firmament, and so on.[440]

It is important to note that Jung does not base his ideas on personal analysis alone or the projection of his own inner myths. In addition to having a great many patients, he backed his discoveries and system with historical references from many fields of study. In his eyes, he was dealing with facts. This is hard pill to swallow for strict material scientists but again, the products from an unconscious origin are real in that they do occur and cannot be denied. The idea of a snake is as real as the snake

---

[439] Ibid, Page 175
[440] Ibid, Page 187

itself. The idea of it may be different to the snake, but the idea has as much impact on our behaviour as the physical object.

> It is clear from the empirical material at our disposal today that the contents of the unconscious, unlike conscious contents, are mutually contaminated to such a degree that they cannot be distinguished from one another and can therefore easily take one another's place, as can be seen most clearly in dreams. The indistinguishableness of its contents gives one the impression that everything is connected with everything else and therefore, despite their multifarious modes of manifestation, they are at bottom a unity.

> The mandala symbolizes, by its central point, the ultimate unity of all archetypes as well as of the multiplicity of the phenomenal world, and is therefore the empirical equivalent of the metaphysical concept of a *unus mundus*. The alchemical equivalent is the lapis and its synonyms, in particular the Microcosm.[441]

In the above passages, Jung mentions the term 'Unus Mundus', which was originally coined by the Scholastic Philosophers and later by the alchemist Gerhard Dorn. It is Latin for 'one world'. The term includes the phenomenal world of matter and the psychic world of inner characters as a unified whole. Jung regards the 'Unus Mundus' as a metaphysical concept, yet later in his works, he goes to great lengths to show the relationships between the inner and outer, and how they connect through synchronistic phenomena. This phenomenon makes unity perceptible in the material world, as does its more subtle variant, projection. Once we can perceive the relationship between psychic and material events, it becomes real and shows that the underlying 'Unus Mundus' is indeed a possibility.

> If mandala symbolism is the psychological equivalent of the *unus mundus,* then synchronicity is the para-psychological equivalent. Though synchronistic phenomenon occur in time and space they manifest a remarkable independence of both these indispensible determinants of physical existence and hence do not conform to the to the law of causality.[442]

In the above, Jung discusses the relationship between inner and outer through synchronistic phenomena. He also shows the limits of our understanding and how an inner movement or realisation can manifest in the physical world without an obvious force or cause, as he puts it. This is the limit of our understanding and knowledge of this expression of unity.

---

[441] JUNG C.G., Mysterium Coniunctionis, Bollingen Series, Princeton University Press, 1977, Page 463
[442] Ibid, Page 464

To say that this phenomenon does not 'conform' to the laws of cause and effect may be premature. The underlying unity must have a physical component, or it simply could not work in the physical world.

> Though we know from experience that psychic processes are related to material ones, we are not in a position to say in what this relationship consists or how it is possible at all. Precisely because the psychic and physical are mutually dependent it has often been conjectured that they may be identical somewhere beyond our present experience, though this certainly does not justify the arbitrary hypothesis of either materialism or spiritualism.[443]

Again, Jung admits his doubts on the relationship between the psychic and material worlds. Indeed, the relationship presented through synchronistic phenomena has an unknown pattern and frequency of occurrence that makes them highly unpredictable. The East knew this phenomenon, particularly in Chinese philosophy that used it as a form of divination called the I Ching. The west, however, with its materialist scientific leanings, always looks for the cause of a movement in the physical world and the forces behind such movements.

---

[443] Ibid, Page 537

6. MATTER

As we have learned from Kant and Jung, it may be impossible to completely differentiate matter from the idea of matter. The study of matter is so vast and unknown as it includes the sub atomic building blocks to the entire universe. It also includes both living and non-living forms made from the same elements and their symbiotic relationship. For example, the ingestion of nutrients is at its base the ingestion of elements in different combinations. Flora and fauna, including humans, are constructed from the non-living elements. Calcium is the building block for bone and teeth and is important for membrane function, nerve impulses, muscle contraction and blood clotting. Iron is essential for oxygen transport and energy capture and is a component of haemoglobin. Hydrogen and Oxygen are components of water, which makes up more than 50% of the human body. The total number of elements that we require for normal function varies, but the list is extensive.[444]

To the ancients[445], matter was perceived as dead or non-living, because it did not move unless acted upon by a force such as heat, pressure, wind and so on. There are however, forces internal to matter that show a structure with an order imprinted upon it. Crystalline structures in nature grow in definite and predictable patterns when changes to their environment occur. For example, the condensation of water vapour from clouds falls to earth as rain. Within a different range of temperature, humidity and pressure, water forms intricate symmetrical patterns called snowflakes. External environmental conditions have much influence on the shape of the snowflake, but so too does its internal atomic structure. All snowflakes are regular, symmetrical and have six arms or co-ordinate points. This is due to the electron sharing arrangement between the Oxygen and Hydrogen atoms and bonds with other water molecules to form hexagonal crystals. The crystals are all different and unique depending on external environmental influences. The final form varies from the typical Dendrite plate to hollow columns, solid prisms and needle shaped crystals.

---

[444] https://cn.wikibooks.org/wiki/Cell_Biology/Introduction/The_elements_of_life
[445] ARISTOTLE, Physics, https://ebooks.adelaide.edu.au/a/aristotle/physics/index.html

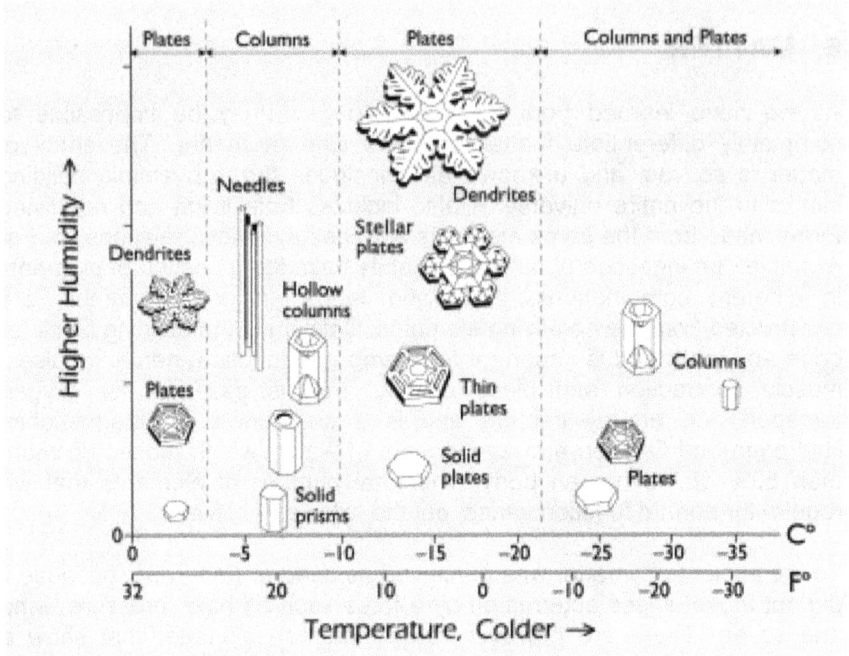

Temperature, Colder →

a. Atomic Structure

Known elements make up everything that exists in the physical world, from the simple water molecule with its Hydrogen and Oxygen atoms, to the complex molecules of Deoxyribonucleic Acid (DNA) with its combinations of Hydrogen, Oxygen, Nitrogen, Carbon and Phosphorus. This 'inert' molecule does not have life of its own, but does provide the information for life. DNA provides all known living organisms with its genetic plan, form and function. Due to the complexity of the molecule, the variety is as vast and unique as the variety of genetic information contained within the molecule.

This raises a question about non-living matter and the information required for its structure. The snowflake, as discussed above, has an arrangement of Hydrogen and two Oxygen atoms held in equilibrium by the attractive and repulsive forces of the positive and negative charged particles (Protons and Electrons). This interplay of forces also determines the structure of water from one state to another, such as the liquid state to solid state when freezing. No two snowflakes are alike, yet they all

---

[446] http://www.snowcrystals.com/science/science.html

have a basic structure dependent on its molecular makeup. The plan for its structure resides in its bonds, which are the same over a broad range of environments, yet environmental influences change its state. This fact shows how a simple water molecule unifies its internal structure with its flexible adaptation to the external environment. This is why a narrow range of temperature and pressure is required for water to exist in its liquid state and in turn, for organic life to be possible, as we know it.[447]

We can see the relationship between internal structure and external environmental influences in all places. Examples include the unique wildlife in different parts of the world as well as physical differences in human cultures. These obvious differences are like the snowflake. The internal structure[448] is the same, yet the environment influences the object or organism, which determines its external physiognomy. This shows that 'inert' matter and living organisms have more in common than not, and are made from and dependent on, the same material that surrounds us in the environment.

The snowflake is an excellent example of a unified system where atomic forces determine the base structure and external influences determine their unique individual form. The same holds true for other forms of matter using crystalline structures. Minerals, for example, display similar traits to the ice crystal with different atomic arrangements. Whereas water crystallises through its shared electrons, minerals have their molecules arranged in an ordered lattice, thus making them very stable. They also have particular melting points, are incompressible and prone to cleavage when broken apart, displaying planed surfaces with straight edges.

Minerals also display similar properties to water when they change state from liquid to solid. Their lattice grows in definite shapes and patterns. Quartz has one atom of Silicon and two atoms of Oxygen (SiO_2) and is Polymorphic, meaning its properties and form varies according to the same external influences such as temperature and pressure. Again, we see an arrangement where the internal atomic forces and structure determine the base form of the material and external environmental influences determine its final form. This unity of molecular structure and environmental influences holds true for vegetation and animals alike, as I shall show in the following chapters.

---

[447] I say 'as we know it' because we only have our planet and its life, as a frame of reference. We do not know what exotic life may exist on other celestial bodies.
[448] JOHANSON D. "Origins of Modern Humans: Multiregional or Out of Africa?". Action Bioscience. American Institute of Biological Sciences. Research has found that all DNA can be traced back to Africa where human life originated.

DNA holds the information for living matter as mentioned previously, but where does the information reside for so-called inert matter? DNA is a long string complex molecule, which is not in itself living. Yet, this 'non-living' molecule provides all the information required for living matter. As the above example shows, matter itself has the information required for its structure. Indeed, the water molecule and its dependence on the atomic structure and external influences indicate that its true nature depends on the relationship between these two sides of its nature. Without this interaction between its 'core structure' and the external influences, it would not achieve its form. This interaction is by no means static, as external influences are continually changing and so too its form.

The water molecule can change from state to state depending on external influences of temperature and pressure. Heat will vaporise water into gas and loosen the bonds between the individual molecules. Lower temperature and high humidity will condensate the gas to liquid thus encouraging the attractive forces between water molecules. A further decrease in temperature will turn liquid to solid in the form of ice crystals, thus further increasing the attractive bonds between molecules. Temperature is a measure of thermal energy and increasing the temperature reduces the influence of the attractive forces and lowering temperature increase these forces. Water's bonds between Hydrogen and Oxygen atoms attract and repel adjacent atoms in other molecules. The molecule remains intact and the atomic bonds within the molecule attract or repel other molecules depending on external influences. In other words, the state of matter depends on the internal structure of attractive or repulsive forces between its atoms within the molecule and its relation to other of the same molecules.

Matter including organic life, is based on atoms held in their molecules by intramolecular (strong) forces and molecules held together by intermolecular (weak) forces. The forces are based on attraction, repulsion, and the interaction between positively and negatively charged particles in a set environment. When the environment changes, for example, a temperature or pressure increase, the forces between the particles change accordingly. Heat causes the forces to weaken and break, whereas cooling increases the forces and the molecules attract each other.

Atomic and molecular structures display similar tendencies towards order expressed by their symmetry, stability and balance. The known elements all display this order to varying degrees depending on the size of the atom, hence the number of electrons and protons in balance. The lower the number, the more stable the element. The higher the number the less stable, to the point where elements such as uranium and plutonium continually shed their structure in the form of electromagnetic radiation due to their atomic size and number of electrons and protons.

These facts put everything that exists on the same footing. At its base, everything living and dead is made from the same material that exists throughout the universe, which is a complex arrangement of 'so called' inert matter with all its atomic forces of attraction and repulsion balanced in a certain environment. When viewed in this way, the growth of an ice crystal and growth of a plant are similar. Some may say that animals, unlike plants, have no fixed environment and are free from its influence. Animals still need water and minerals though, and this in turn depends on rainfall and ways of obtaining minerals through the consumption of other animals or plants. With this in mind, we can say that animals and humans in particular, are the most evolved form of matter. The basis of life is matter and it is for the sake of understanding that we distinguish between the two.

Just as the snowflake is a union of internal atomic structure and environmental influence so too, are living forms of matter. The plant knows what it should be from its internal structure. The instructions are already present and passed down from plant to plant through its seeds. The information required for its form and function is contained within its molecular structure. The same applies to complex forms of life, such as animals and humans. We too, have internal instructions that determine our form and function. In addition, those internal instructions or blueprints, also determine our behaviour and how we adapt to external environmental influences. In addition to the obvious physiognomy and biological functions, the instructions also express themselves psychically.

What we feel as non-physical we call psychic, yet at its base it is matter and has an ability to organise, order and co-ordinate the physical world. An example is the expression of an emotion and how it is felt in our bodies with the release of hormones and increased heart rate, yet its origin is psychic. Another example is the design and construction of a building, which begins as a psychic process of an idea. Documentation of the idea on paper or computer proceeds to the construction of a physical structure of matter. This is a deliberate and conscious process of realising the idea through a process of distillation, organisation and transformation of matter, thus giving the idea a physical reality.

The relationship between psyche and matter is innate and occurs with a connection made by a projected idea from an unconscious source onto objects. This projection in its most pronounced form Jung called synchronicity. He describes this phenomenon as 'Acausal', as there is no obvious physical cause. Viewed by an observer not involved in the experience, it is simply a co-incidence due to their inability to see the psychic component and emotional intensity of connectedness. The term 'Acausal' may be a premature description, and the cause not yet discovered between the interaction of matter and psyche. The very fact that synchronicity occurs shows that the opposites are not separate. In addition, the transformation of ideas into matter indicates that one side expresses the other. This applies to the built environment as well as our bodily functions and behaviour. Synchronicity is therefore an overt form of projection that reveals the unity between matter and psyche[449].

The following passage is from an interview of physicist Richard Feynman who explains how matter transforms at the molecular level through the energy of the sun and how the carbon dioxide molecules split into their constituent atoms through photosynthesis. The tree uses the carbon for its structure, expelling the oxygen as a by-product. Reversing this process through combustion unlocks the energy stored in the plant material and unites the carbon and oxygen atoms liberating the same electromagnetic energy that separated the atoms in the original process.

> When it get started, why is that the wood has been surviving all this time with the oxygen all this time, and it didn't do it earlier or something? Where did I get this from? Why did it came (**) from the tree. And the substance of the tree is carbon, and where does it come from? That comes from the air, it's carbon dioxide from the air. People cut trees and think that it comes from the ground. The plant grows out from the ground. But if you asked "where the substance come from?", you find out where does it come from (**) the tree is coming out of the air? They surely come out of the ground! No, they come out of the air! The carbon dioxide in the air goes into the tree, and changes it, kicking out the oxygen, and pushing the oxygen away from the carbon, and leaving the carbon substance (topped) with water. Water comes out of the ground, you see; only is that it has to get there out of the (**) air, it came down from the sky. So in fact most of the tree is out of the ground -I'm sorry: it's out of the air! There's a little bit from the ground: some minerals and so forth.
>
> Now, of course I told you that the we know oxygen and carbon sticks together tight(**). How is that the tree is so smart to take the carbon dioxide (which is carbon and oxygen nicely combined), and undo that so easy?
> Ah! Life! Life has some mysterious ways! No! The sun is shining, and this sunlight comes down and knocks this oxygen away from the carbon, so it takes some light to get the plant to work! And so the sun, all the time, is doing the work of separating the oxygen away from the carbon, the oxygen is sort a of terrible by-product, which it spits back into the air, an leave in the carbon and water to make the substance of the tree. And

---

[449] See Section below Chapter 11, part B on 'Synchronistic Phenomenon'

then we take the substance of the tree to get the fireplace. All the oxygen made by these trees and all the carbons would much prefer to be together again. And once you let the heat to get it started, it continues and make an awful lot of activity while it's going back together again, and all those nice light and everything comes out, and everything is being undone, you're going from carbon and oxygen back to carbon dioxide, and the light and heat that's coming out is the light and heat of the sun that went in, so it's sort of stored sun that is coming out when you burn it.[450]

Feynman describes the underlying principal of photosynthesis, which unites the carbon with water to form cellulose ($C_6H_{12}O_6$). Viewed in this light, we can conclude that combustion is a release of the same energy that created the combustible material. In other words, the electromagnetic energy as photons were crucial in the process of reorganising the existing molecule (carbon dioxide) into usable carbon (C) combined with water (H_2O) to build the structure of the tree. When reversing this process through combustion the carbon once again combines with oxygen to form carbon dioxide and water vapour. $C_6H_{12}O_6 + 6O_2 = 6CO_2 + 6H_2O$.

This process describes a system (idea) of unity particular to this type of vegetation and includes all the aspects of that unity. In Platonic terms, the sun light and heat (fire) provides the energy to divide the CO_2 (air) into carbon (earth) and oxygen (air). The oxygen returned to the air; carbon unites with H_2O (water) to create substance from the ground (earth). When combustion occurs, the system returns to its origins, the carbon unites with oxygen giving off water vapour and the production of the suns light and heat (fire), and the circle is complete.

The above example is a general description of the process and does not include the specifics of species. The process may be similar, but no two individual trees exist in the same situation. They all have different locations, which result in differing amounts of sunlight, types of earth, quantities of carbon dioxide, water, minerals etc. In this instance, the unity of a tree is unique, much the same as the idea of unity is unique to each individual.

b. Quantum Mechanics

The above example of photosynthesis shows how electromagnetic energy from the sun causes the chemical reaction in the carbon dioxide molecule. This process, in combination with the water extracted from the soil, builds the structure and system of the plant or tree. The separation of the atoms in the molecule requires constant input of electromagnetic

---

[450] FEYNMAN, Richard P. - 'Fun to Imagine' BBC 1983 – transcript by A. Wojdyla

energy. As Feynman puts it, the carbon and oxygen atoms "stick together" and require energy to separate, and in so doing capture the photons from the sun. Electrons accept these photons and move to a higher energy level in the atom. A higher energy level in an electron is however, less stable than a lower energy level.

This is why it only takes a spark to start the reversal of this less stable situation and the whole process undoes itself. The atoms of oxygen and carbon once again unite, the electrons return to their original energy level, and photons released in the form of light and heat, both the same forms of electromagnetic radiation used from the sun in the original process. The beauty and wonder of this circular process is unmistakable. With this in mind, we can say that burning fossil fuels releases energy stored in the atom returning the electron to a lower energy level, and from a Quantum point of view, burning fossil fuels is the release of stored solar energy.

The same process occurs in the sun itself. The enormous temperature and pressure near its core causes the hydrogen atoms to fuse and form helium atoms. The process is again circular in that the heat and pressure strips the Hydrogen atom of its electrons (ionized Hydrogen or Deuterium): two protons collide and fuse, one of the protons transmuting to a neutron emitting a neutrino and positron. The positron (+ve charge) is the antiparticle of the electron (-ve charge) stripped from the Hydrogen atom, and upon collision with the free-floating electrons transforms the union into pure electromagnetic radiation (gamma rays). The gamma rays are absorbed by the sun's plasma on their journey to the surface and their frequency lowered to infrared, visible light and ultraviolet energy and on into space. The process continues with Deuterium colliding with another proton to form Helium 3 (2 protons & 1 neutron). This collides with another Helium 3 (totalling 4 protons & 2 neutrons) to form Helium 4 (2 protons & 2 neutrons) with the expulsion of 2 protons. They collide and fuse with other atoms and the circle is complete to begin again.[451]

Nuclear fusion is thus the integration (combining) of nuclear particles (protons) and the transformation of one proton into a neutron with the resultant release of energy. Nuclear fission, on the other hand, is the differentiation (separating) of nuclear particles with neutrons. As with fusion, nuclear fission is also a natural process and occurs when an unstable element such as Uranium 235 seeks a lower energy level and sheds its energy in the form of electromagnetic radiation. The decay is slow and believed to fuel the earth's internal core in addition to its latent

---

[451] What appears as circular is in actual fact a spiral. The energy lost reduces the matter with the eventual reduction to zero or the centre of the spiral.

heat from its formation. Flyorov, Petrzhak and Kurchatov[452] discovered natural fission in 1940 and led to the idea of accelerating the process of fission for an increased release of energy. This was achieved by bombarding Uranium 235 with a neutron which the atom absorbed making Uranium 236, which is less stable than 235. The resulting instability overloaded the Uranium 236 atom and they fall apart into two new elements of Barium and Krypton with a corresponding release of three neutrons and enormous amounts electromagnetic energy. The three neutrons in turn combine with other U235 atoms to start the chain reaction.

It is harnessing nature by overloading its energy level making it unstable and transforming it into other elements, rather than mechanically splitting the atom. This does raise the interesting question of the possibility of changing one element into another by adding or subtracting sub atomic particles. It also emphasises the incredibly strong forces of electromagnetic attraction and repulsion that holds the physical world together. The process of nuclear fusion is therefore one of division, transformation and union over and over. Nuclear fission is one of union, transformation and division repeated. Both are natural processes, the latter enhanced by human intervention.

The observation of sub atomic particles is however fraught with uncertainty. This is due to the methods of observation requiring a projection of electrons onto the material observed with the Transmission Electron Microscopy (TEM) or Scanning tunnelling Microscopy (STM) techniques. Other methods include mechanical and electrical systems and all have a deleterious effect on the material observed. Detecting an electron requires an electromagnetic photon or other electron to interact with it, which changes the behaviour of the observed electron.

Another less obvious interaction between observer and observed is the humorously termed 'Pauli Effect'. Wolfgang Pauli was a theoretical physicist around the mid-twentieth century whose presence affected experiments when he was in their vicinity. The anecdotal reports were numerous and Pauli himself believed the effect to be a real phenomenon. There were reports of measuring devices failing[453], a chandelier prank not working[454] and a cyclotron burning up,[455] all attributed to Pauli's influence.

---

[452] https://www.encyclopedia.com/science/dictionaries-thesauruses-pictures-and-press-releases/flerov-georgii-nikolaevich

[453] Thirty Years That Shook Physics: The Story of Quantum Theory, 1966, Dover Publications, ISBN 0-486-24895-X.

[454] PEIERLS, R. (1960). "Wolfgang Ernst Pauli, 1900-1958". Biographical Memoirs of Fellows of the Royal Society. 5. doi:10.1098/rsbm.1960.0014

The phenomenon moved him to correspond with Carl Jung and Marie-Louise Von Franz who were developing their ideas on Synchronicity[456] at the time.

The link between psychic activity and matter is a natural phenomenon that humanity has always known to some extent. Animistic phenomenon of matter endowed with spirits and demons is the basis and origin of religion. The scientific age dismissed such phenomenon as coincidental and stripped them of their meaning, yet we cannot dismiss the impression such phenomena has upon us. How can psychic activity be physical[457] and affect matter, and what are the forces involved? Matter is held together by strong and weak electromagnetic forces of attraction and repulsion, and gravity, and these forces permeate all aspects of existence, as we know it. These forces behave like particles, waves and fields and surround us on all sides. Photons are not classed as matter; yet affect matter in profound ways. We can conclude that any investigation of the relationship between matter and psyche has to include electromagnetic forces.

Von Franz looked at this very question[458]. She describes a concept of instincts resembling the infrared end and the images, thoughts, ideas etc., related to the instinct, the ultraviolet end. If we look at the chart below it is clear that the metaphor described by Von Franz should be reversed, in that the energy levels increase towards the Ultra Violet end of the spectrum and decrease towards the Infrared end. We all know that instincts are highly charged with emotions and energy, whereas thoughts, fantasies and ideas less charged. Choosing this metaphor indicates a perceived connection between psychic activity and electromagnetic radiation.

---

[455] PAULI, Wolfgang; et al. (1996). Wissenschaftlicher Briefwechsel mit Bohr, Einstein, Heisenberg, u.a. vol. 4/l. ed. Karl von Meyenn. Berlin: Springer. p. 37. ISBN 3-540-59442-6. OCLC 36847539

[456] See Chapter 11b which describes Synchronicity in detail

[457] We do not know if psychic activity is based on the electromagnetic activity of matter in the brain or completely separate from it.

[458] VON FRANZ, Marie Louise. Psyche & Matter. Page 8, ISBN 978-1-57062-620-3

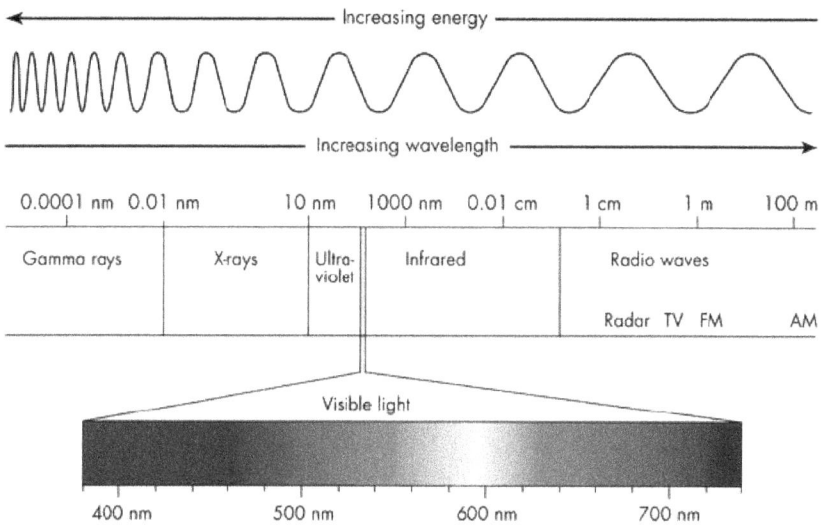

Increasing energy →

Increasing wavelength →

| 0.0001 nm | 0.01 nm | | 10 nm | 1000 nm | 0.01 cm | 1 cm | 1 m | 100 m |

| Gamma rays | X-rays | Ultra-violet | Infrared | Radio waves |

Radar TV FM   AM

Visible light

400 nm   500 nm   600 nm   700 nm

But where in this model is the relationship of psyche and matter represented? It is at the "infrared" pole or so it would seem. There the psychic functions merge into the physiological processes of the body. But matter also sometimes shows up at the other "ultraviolet" pole- in the form of parapsychological phenomena. Thus it is to be suspected that our division into material versus mental, that which is observable for outside versus that which is perceivable from the inside, is only a subjectively valid separation, only a limited polarization that our structure of consciousness imposes on us but that actually does not correspond to the wholeness of reality.[459]

Psyche and matter interact in a complex and intertwined way. Instincts and their associated emotions act upon the body outside of our will's influence and change the physiology of our body's' functioning. Our heart beats faster, the blood circulates more, our hormones activate and energy released. Emotions also have images associated with them, which relate to the cause of the movement and point to an inner character behind the emotion. These same characters appear in our dreams and historical myths.

Where do these images or characters come from? Some say that they are memories from the past. This does not explain why some images are completely unfamiliar to the dreamer. Some say that we perceive the images in the physical world unconsciously, only later to recall them in our dreams. This does not explain why we have elaborate scenes and stories in our dreams. If we follow the reasoning of Von Franz and look at

---

[459] Ibid, page 11

molecules, atoms and nucleonic particles, we notice that each particle has a definite character. For example, the electron has a negative charge yet its use in our lives is very positive (electricity). The proton's positive charge interacts with the electron to hold them in their orbits. Within the nucleus, there is the positive proton and the neutral neutron. Within the proton and neutron are different flavoured quarks with interesting characteristics such as 'strange', 'charm', 'up' and 'down', with several force particles between them.

As a rule, like charges repel and unlike charges attract. These are the relationships or interactions between the particles that hold matter together in balance. The Helium 4 atom has two uncharged neutrons and two positively charged protons in the nucleus. This should result in an unstable nucleus, as the positive charges of the protons repel each other. This does not however occur, and the Helium atom under typical conditions is very stable and inert. The physicists' account for the stability of the nucleus by the balancing and containing negatively charged electron cloud surrounding the nucleus and strong interactive force between particles (quarks) within the proton and other less known particles called Mesons.

There are many questions concerning the forces holding the atom in a stable pattern. For example, what holds the Neutron(s) in place if it has no charge and no forces acting upon it? What role does the negative charged electron cloud have in holding the nucleus together? How do positive and negatively charged particles attract neutral particles such as neutrons? There is a balance of the forces of attraction and repulsion and a complex relationship between all particles. Electrons attract protons; yet do not collapse onto the nucleus due to their motion (orbit) around the nucleus. The protons in the nucleus do not fly apart due to the attractive forces to the neutrons over and above the repulsive forces between the protons themselves. This in combination with the forces exerted by the electrons holds the atom together.[460]

Physicists[461] soon realised that it was difficult to observe particles and their behaviour in isolation. Physical properties such as position, momentum, spin and polarization cannot be determined for any given particle without looking at the other particles interacting with them in the atom. In other words, we need to take account of the complete system including interaction and relationship between the particles. It is like trying

---

[460] This description only applies to stable elements. The larger the atom the less stable the element with the resulting atomic fission and transmutation into a lower more stable element.

[461] EINSTEIN A, Podolsky B, Rosen N; Podolsky; Rosen (1935). "Can Quantum-Mechanical Description of Physical Reality Be Considered Complete?". Phys. Rev. 47

to study an individual outside of their family dynamic. The relationships the individual experiences affect his or her personality in many and varied ways and the same seem true for sub atomic particles. The physicists call this "Quantum Entanglement', the psychologists, archetypal contamination[462].

We can also see the same interaction and relationship between celestial bodies. The earth's relationship to the sun is so interconnected that life on earth would not exist without its presence. Similarly, the moon interacts with the earth and has a physical influence on the tides and light levels at night. The moon also influences our psychological state and has an effect on our moods. Other bodies, such as the planets, also exert an influence on our minds in a visual sense when viewed in the night sky. At the very least, they attract projection of ideas, as our history shows.

The ancients saw their inner Gods in the sky and gave the planets their names accordingly. Similarly, the constellations attracted imaginary musings with all sorts of stories and adventures. Our scientific understanding has stripped the meaning from the planets and their ability to attract projection. This mystery has now moved further into space with the theory of black holes, dark matter, etc. Aliens found in space from distant star systems are our new God(s). The search for the elusive Higgs Boson is another place we find the idea of God.

The Higgs Boson was first theorised by Peter Higgs and five other physicists in a 1964 paper. According to the standard model, the boson has no electric charge, spin or colour charge,[463] and this lack of characteristics suggests a very stable and secure particle. Yet, the opposite is true. The particle is extremely hard to produce, detect and breaks apart in a fraction of a second. The intriguing notion of the Higgs boson is its central place in the mind of physicists. It is a unifying and elusive particle not easily proven to exist. The Higgs particle is important as its force carrying quality may be the relationship between matter and psyche itself. Indeed, the physicists have observed the boson existing in a field. In other words, they regard the Higgs Field permeating throughout the universe, thus becoming part of what Newton called the Aether.

---

[462] This is the cross contamination of archetypal figures. In other words, within every person exist the ideas of other people. A relationship between a man and woman starts with the projection of their inner idea of their ideal partner onto the other person. Unfortunately the other person is not always in a position to change their behaviour to suite the projection. Cross contamination also occurs between inner figures and are very difficult to see in isolation.

[463] FEYNMAN, Richard (1985), QED: The Strange Theory of Light and Matter, Princeton University Press, p. 136

The relationship between Physics and Psychology is striking and has similar structure and ideas between the two disciplines. The following chart shows some comparisons:

Psychology	Physics
Inner characters revolve around a centre	Electrons revolve around the centre nucleus
Each character has a distinct personality +ve, −ve or neutral	Electrons are −ve, Protons +ve and Neutron neutral
The centre has characteristics of all characters	The nucleus has different characteristics eg. Up, down charm & strange quarks
Characters share traits in their interactions	Molecules share electrons in their bonding
Deal with forces of attraction & repulsion	Deal with forces of attraction & repulsion

Although we can regard the above as coincidence, it does show a possible connection between disciplines as if they are looking at the same thing from opposite directions. The physicist looks at matter in their theories and experiments, but cannot escape the psychic factor, as they all perceive with their psyche. On the other hand the psychologist looks at dreams, visions and synchronicities which, is the psyche perceiving its own matter in the form of atoms and molecules in the brain and relating that to the physical world outside of the psyche. In others words one perceives matter through the psyche and the other, the psyche through matter.

The above comparisons show that the physical world has some similarities in structure and language to the psychic world. The two sides of perceived reality interact with each other in ways that we have not yet fathomed. This is evident in the workings of the psyche and brain. In the first instance, we perceive images, ideas and fantasies, yet their relationship to the activity of the brain is electromagnetic connections between parts of the brain. These connections create ideas. We all know what it is like to have a sudden inspirational solution to a problem come into our awareness. It hits us like a revelation and from here we can proceed further. In psychological language it is the uniting of the opposites in the third. One side views an issue one way, the other side another way, and the interaction and relationship between the opposites unites them in the third way.

Theories proposed on this subject include EM field theory by Susan Pockett[464], Johnjoe Mcfadden,[465] and Quantum Brain Dynamics (QBD) by Mari Jibuand and Kunio Yasue[466]. These two theories approach the functioning of the brain from a Neuroscience and Physics point of view, and look at how the brain perceives the physical environment through cognition. There is little mention of the myth-making unconscious and how its contents flow into consciousness. The impulse to grow comes out of the ground of our psyche: we battle the elements to adapt to the environment, no matter how harsh,[467] and hopefully thrive like a well-adapted plant.

As mentioned previously, physicists determined in the last century, observation of particles and waves at the quantum level affects the particles and waves. In other words, the use of measuring instruments have an input into the observation of a phenomenon due to the need for electromagnetic fields, accelerators, beams of light etc., in the experiments. They call this the 'Observer Effect', and thought to have little to do with the human psyche of the individual. The instruments needed to observe such phenomenon are an extension of the psyche and created, built and implemented by the observer. George Berkley[468] postulated that an object or phenomenon does not necessarily exist without an observer. In other words, existence depends on its observation. He regarded subject and object in a necessary relationship and unified whole.

c. Relativity

The study of relativity raises many questions concerning the nature of reality. Before this theory, Newton proposed the cosmos contained an aethereal medium (Luminiferous aether, or light bearing ether), and this accounted for the wave-like nature of light and other electromagnetic energy. Joseph Lamour regarded the aether as a moving magnetic field caused by the acceleration of electrons.[469] Einstein, in his original paper believed that the aether did not exist and that the observational anomalies of light were due to distortions in space and time.

> Lord Kelvin writing- in 1893, in his preface to the English edition of Hertz's Researches on Electric Waves, says "many workers and many

---

[464] POCKETT, Susan, The Nature of Consciousness. ISBN 0-595-12215-9.
[465] MCFADDEN, Johnjoe, (2002). "The Conscious Electromagnetic Information (Cemi) Field Theory: The Hard Problem Made Easy?". Journal of Consciousness Studies..
[466] JIBU, Mari; YASUE, Kunio. Quantum brain dynamics and consciousness. ISBN 1-55619-183-9.
[467] In this instance I equate harsh with the hostile environment of a desert and its lack of water.
[468] BERKLEY, George, A Treatise Concerning the Principles of Human Knowledge
[469] LARMOR, J. (1900), Aether and Matter, Cambridge University Press

thinkers have helped to build up the nineteenth century school of *plenum*, one ether for light, heat, electricity, magnetism; and the German and English volumes containing Hertz's electrical papers, given to the world in the last decade of the century, will be a permanent monument of the splendid consummation now realised."

Ten years later in 1905, we find Einstein declaring that "the aether will be proved to be superfluous." At first sight the revolution in scientific thought brought about in the course of a single decade appears to be almost too violent. A more careful even though a rapid review of the subject will, however, show how the Theory of Relativity gradually became a historical necessity.[470]

Einstein regarded space with the same physical qualities that aether had. In other words, electromagnetic energy can warp space.

We may say that according to the general theory of relativity space is endowed with physical qualities; in this sense, therefore, there exists an aether. According to the general theory of relativity space without aether is unthinkable; for in such space there not only would be no propagation of light, but also no possibility of existence for standards of space and time (measuring-rods and clocks), nor therefore any space-time intervals in the physical sense.[471]

We can see from the above that Einstein tackled the problem of unknown and mysterious aether with an equally unknown and mysterious space. He replaced one problem with another, fixated on light travelling at a constant velocity, and had to explain why it curved by gravitational forces. The only way a curved path of light can have a constant velocity when compared to a straight path is to adjust the time it takes the light to travel the extra distance around the curve. In other words, for the light to remain at a constant velocity in a curve in contrast to a straight line, the time it takes to reach the end of the curve has to decrease to maintain the velocity.

The fundamentals of space and time are what we know from our everyday reality. The laws do not change because an atmosphere envelops us. We measure space in three directions, it can be contained within a vessel or building, is empty as in a vacuum or filled with matter[472]. It seems to have no end or boundaries and permeates the entire cosmos. We can move through it freely in all directions, yet we do not know where

---

[470] Historical Introduction by P C MAHALANOBIS to "Principle of Relativity Original Papers by A Einstein and H Minkowski, University of Calcutta 1920, page ii
[471] EINSTEIN, Albert: "Ether and the Theory of Relativity" (1920), republished in Sidelights on Relativity (Methuen, London, 1922)
[472] One has only to stand in a high wind to know the forces involved in air movement in space

the line between space and matter exists. If we jump into a pool of water, we immediately know that we are not in space, yet we can move through as if we were. This transition emphasises that the difference between space and matter has an illusory nature, which depends on the amount of matter contained within space.

How much matter does it take to change space into matter? Water is not space, yet we can move through it as we move through the air, albeit with more resistance. What amount of fluid, gas or the like, does it take to change space into matter? These questions are difficult to answer, although we could put an arbitrary limit on the amount of matter-filled space to delineate one from the other. This would however, simply be an intellectual exercise of categories and not a true reflection of its nature. Space and matter therefore flow together without definite demarcation.

Further, the study of Quantum Mechanics reveals that the distances between atomic nuclei and their associated electron clouds are substantial and predominately filled with space and forces. Matter is minute particles (atoms) held together alone or in groups with other particles, (molecules) by various forces in space.

Unlike space, our everyday experience of time is different again. Time is a linear progression from past to future and unlike space, we have no way of moving through it other than its natural forward progression. We can however, measure time and give it a scale based on natural cycles of the rotation of our planet and its orbit around the sun, which gives us a gradated connection to our physical environment. The sun rises and sets and we know approximately[473] what time it is from this cycle.

The relationship between space and time is again problematic. Einstein regarded space and time as a pair united and an effect on one had an effect on the other. For example, the bending of light as discussed above, requires time to slow in the warped space around an object such as a galaxy when viewing the light that passes by it. This is called gravitational lensing and is an observable phenomenon predicted by Einstein in his general theory.

We know from everyday experience that light bends and slows in different media. For example, when light enters water it bends in an obvious way and its velocity slows from the vacuous constant (c) of 299,792,458 m/s to approximately 225,000,000 m/s depending on the quality of the water. There is no change in time or distortion of space involved. Similarly, other

---

[473] Adjustments are continually necessary to our time scale to counter for the incremental advance of the seasons.

mediums such as glass, crystal etc., also change the velocity of light. Therefore, the medium determines light's speed and distortion.

This brings us back to the idea of aether, which is a medium that can have an effect on electromagnetic radiation and matter in general. In addition to gravitational forces acting upon light, the double slit experiment shows that photons behave as particles and more importantly, as waves. An observation screen beyond the slits shows an interference pattern and the light interacting with itself as waves causing the well-known pattern of stripes. Gravitational fields affect light and other frequencies of electromagnetic energy, and EME affects itself as the double slit experiment shows.

Einstein acknowledged that gravitational forces caused lensing of light passing a galaxy. We know that the weak force of gravity has an enormous operating distance. Gravity holds all matter on earth to itself and in combination with velocity, holds the moon in its orbit around the earth. Similarly, the earth orbits the sun with a balance of orbital forces of velocity and gravity and so too, our sun and planets move around our galaxy in the same manner.

The velocities at which the celestial bodies move through space are quite dramatic. For example, the earth spins (wobbles) on its axis at 1,609 km/hr. The moon orbits the earth with a velocity of 3,683 km/hr. The earth and moon move around the sun at 107,826 km/hr. The sun, planets, moons etc., (solar system) moves around the Milky Way galaxy at a staggering 753,153 km/hr. The Milky Way galaxy moves through space at 2,092,147 km/hr. These are the velocities required to hold the orbits of each of these bodies and systems in their relative positions.

The fact that our frame of reference is in constant motion raises interesting questions over the so-called 'Rest Motion' used to describe General Relativity. We cannot therefore make any certain predictions or measurements of two objects in the same frame of reference because the same frame of reference does not exist. Objects in different locations have differing quantities of electromagnetic energy (light, heat etc.) and gravity influencing them.

The interesting fact is the distance the force of gravity influences its orbiting bodies. The Milky Way is 100,000 light years across and held together by a balance of velocity and gravity. A force that exerts an influence over this distance permeates the entire galaxy. In other words, the gravity that holds the galaxy together must permeate all of the space in between the star systems within the galaxy. This brings us back to Lamour's idea that the aether is a moving magnetic field within space.

This would solve a few of the rational inconsistencies in the time/space theory in that space is not vacuous but filled with gravity and electromagnetic radiation from many sources and this is the aether that Newton proposed. Energy and the newly discovered Higgs field fills space (Aether).

Nicola Tesla's agrees with the idea that space is filled with electromagnetic energy, gravity and matter.

> I hold that space cannot be curved, for the simple reason that it can have no properties. It might as well be said that God has properties. He has not, but only attributes and these are of our own making. Of properties we can only speak when dealing with matter filling the space. To say that in the presence of large bodies space becomes curved is equivalent to stating that something can act upon nothing. I, for one, refuse to subscribe to such a view.[474]

> Today's scientists have substituted mathematics for experiments, and they wander off through equation after equation, and eventually build a structure, which has no relation to reality.[475]

The dynamic between Einstein and Tesla is well known and their interpretation of reality came from differing points of view. How do we reconcile these points of view from these two brilliant men? On one hand, it is difficult to comprehend the idea that space and time affect and distort reality. On the other hand, aether permeates reality and results in the effects we perceive. Our everyday experience of space is its lack of perceptible matter, we can move through it and it has no limits unless we provide them and quantify it by measurement or enclosure. On earth, matter fills space in the form of solids, liquids and gases. We can see through most gases into what seems like an unlimited and uncontained universe. In addition, space is permeated by electromagnetic radiation from many sources, most of which originate outside of the earth atmosphere and gravity, which originates from the mass of the earth itself. If we were able to remove all the matter, electromagnetic radiation and gravity[476] from space, there is nothing left. How is it then possible to bend or curve nothing, as Tesla points out?

In the vacuum of outer space, there is little or no matter, depending on location, yet it is filled with electromagnetic radiation and gravitational fields from sources including other star systems and the attraction and

---

[474] New York Herald Tribune (September 11, 1932)
[475] "Radio Power Will Revolutionize the World" in Modern Mechanics and Inventions (July 1934)
[476] I am indulging in a fantasy here, as it is impossible to remove these forces that act upon us as we live with gravitation fields that are galaxy wide.

movement around the centre of our galaxy. The medium THE light travels through, distorts the light. Theoretically, we must measure the speed of light outside of the influence of a medium including electromagnetic radiation and gravitational fields. This is impossible, and therefore we cannot regard the speed of light as constant.

This is where Einstein's reasoning may have let him down by the fixation that light has a constant velocity. The consequences of this idea and the rejection of aether (electromagnetic radiation and gravity) require another cause for the bending of light while passing a celestial body. If we regard the speed of light as constant in space and the light bends around an object, then it becomes necessary to adjust the time the light takes to go around the curve. In other words, light travelling in a curve will have a longer distance to travel than a straight line, which either changes the velocity of light or the time required to travel that distance. Without aether (medium), and the need to maintain the speed of light (c), the only recourse is to adjust the space and time around the curve.

This endows space with properties it does not have, replaces the idea of aether with space and gives it the same properties. Space as nothing, in that it is empty of matter and energy, seems more like an idea[477] rather than a physical reality. Without properties, it cannot have the ability to distort. Similarly, time progresses in a linear fashion and like space has no properties of its own. Nature provides a scale and measurement awareness through the rotation of the earth and the cycles of day and night. It is these cycles coupled with memory; the decay of matter and history, that enables us to know that time actually exists.

If we accept that the distortions of space and time are an idea, it becomes clear that the basic tenets of relativity are perfectly true. Ideas as products from an unconscious source do not have to abide by physical realities. Space in dreams is incredibly flexible and demonstrates the ability to move and distort from one place to another with no regard to physical laws. Similarly, time is as flexible as space and displays a lack of linearity and relation to our waking perception. This is the reason it is important to differentiate physical reality from unconscious products in the form of ideas and find the relationship between them.

Ideas are those magical things that give us the impetus to follow new possibilities and find new answers to questions of reality and existence. They are quite often leaps ahead of the current knowledge on a subject and should be analysed as ideas firstly, before hypotheses applied to

---

[477] I stress the idea rather than the reality. In reality space is filled with many things that we cannot remove, including gravitational fields and electromagnetic radiation.

physical nature. If we follow this premise, we can interpret ideas symbolically like dreams using amplification and association. It then becomes a discovery of one's personality, personal beliefs and orientations. This is difficult in Einstein's case, as we have little personal information on his dreams and beliefs, other than what he has written and notes from interviews. One interview however, may provide some inkling into Einstein's views:

> "Your question is the most difficult in the world. It is not a question I can answer simply with yes or no. I'm not an atheist, and I don't think I can call myself a pantheist. We are in the position of a little child entering a huge library filled with books in many languages. The child knows someone must have written those books. It does not know how. It does not understand the languages in which they are written. The child dimly suspects a mysterious order in the arrangement of the books but doesn't know what it is. That, it seems to me, is the attitude of even the most intelligent human being toward God. We see the universe marvelously arranged and obeying certain laws but only dimly understand these laws. Our limited minds grasp the mysterious force that moves the constellations. I am fascinated by Spinoza's pantheism, but admire even more his contribution to modern thought because he is the first philosopher to deal with the soul and body as one, and not two separate things."[478]

The interview tells us that he agrees with Spinoza's view of soul and body as one. Unlike Aristotle, Descartes and Leibniz, Spinoza could not see the opposites, and positive and negative aspects of the soul. For a thinking man, soul (anima[479]) would be feminine and the container for a man's feeling on the one hand and body on the other, assuming he was a thinking intuitive man. The senses connect our body to the physical and body and soul have different characteristics, but may be contained within the same inner female character if undifferentiated. In other words, when body (senses) and soul (feeling) are still unconscious, undifferentiated and without a relationship to spirit (thinking), they can appear as one inner female character oriented towards the physical. Differentiation of the soul relates it to spirit on the one hand and body on the other. The soul in the Christian tradition is associated with spirit, and the body and all its associated instincts relegated to another character.

Can we draw any conclusions from Einstein's viewpoint on body and soul with his conception of space and time? Space as we know it is the container of matter and energy. It is essentially nothing and only exists in

---

[478] VIERECK, George Sylvester (1930). Glimpses of the Great. New York: The Macaulay Company, pp. 372-373.
[479] The Latin term for soul used by Aristotle and adopted by Analytical Psychology to describe the inner woman in the man.

relationship to the matter/energy it contains. Space is therefore the nothingness that contains something. In mythology, space is associated with the cosmic container and the laws given by Mother Nature. Space gives birth to matter as a mother gives birth to a baby (body).

With the rejection of Newton's idea of aether, Einstein had to replace it with something else to explain the observational reality of bending light around celestial bodies. Instead of a medium with qualities that affect light as it travels through space, Einstein proposed an actual change in the space and time in which the light travelled. This reminds me of Nietzsche's declaration of the death of God followed by the idea of the "Overman", which had the same characteristics as the original idea, yet a little more differentiated. In this instance, one idea transformed into a similar idea as it evolved and came closer to Nietzsche's understanding. Replacing one idea for a similar, but evolved idea is how we grow as a species and an example of our psychic evolution.

Time is a linear progression in space. It is unrelenting in its forward movement and connects us to physical reality. In other words, it is what feels the joy of growth, expansion, adaptation, and family as well as the pain of aging, decay, and death of physical existence. We feel time and sometimes find it hard to accept its relentless onslaught into the future. The present however, does not have a dimension in time. We can anticipate the present with our imagination and reflect on the present with our memory, but by the time the future arrives, it becomes the past. In other words, the present is the line between the future and past. Time is gradations of known observed cycles, yet can feel like it slows on occasion, and speed up on other occasions. Therefore, space and time relate to each other, but are not the same thing. One is contained within the other.

It follows that Einstein's equation $m=e/c2$[480] requires a caveat, as there is no constant speed of light because we cannot remove it from a medium. 'c' is therefore relative and becomes velocity dependent on the medium through which the light is travelling. This undermines the constant of proportionality that 'c' provides. The medium, as we have discussed earlier, can be anything from liquid, gas to space filled with gravitational fields and electromagnetic radiation or the recently discovered Higgs field. From here on I will have to leave further speculation to the specialist physicists to determine the consequences of this line of practical reasoning.

---

[480] This is how Einstein wrote the equation in his original paper.

In his later years, Einstein did recognise that his theory did not work for the 'atomistic character of nature' as he mentions in the following quotes.

> I must confess that I was unable to find an explanation for the atomistic character of nature. One must find a way to avoid the space-time continuum altogether, though I haven't the slightest idea what kind of elementary concept could be used in such a theory.

> All attempts to represent the particle and wave features displayed in the phenomena of light and matter, by direct recourse to a space time model, have so far ended in failure. And Heisenberg has convincingly shown, from an empirical point of view, that any decision as to a rigorously deterministic structure of nature is definitely ruled out, because of the atomistic structure of our experimental apparatus.[481]

Space is therefore filled with matter, electromagnetic energy, gravity and time but not identical to it. The aether is the medium that permeates and surrounds matter, EME and gravity. Space is therefore the container for aether and hence matter, EME and gravity. To finish our discussion on Relativity I would like to touch on the Mythological associations of these concepts.

The ancients referred to Aether (space) as 'quintessence' and associated the term with 'pure fresh air' and 'clear sky' and pure essence the Gods breathed and lived. Aether is a deity with the same name and the son of Erebus and Nyx, and married to Hemera. Plato associated aether with air, whereas Aristotle recognised aether as fire, and married to Hemera, the Goddess of daytime and as the fifth element in addition to earth, air, fire and water.

Chronus was the personification of time in Greek Mythology and portrayed as a wise old man with a long grey beard. Uranus was the father of Chronus and the personification for sky or heaven and regarded as 'Father sky', which is the ancient concept of space. Uranus was the son and husband of Gaia (earth, matter). Chronus turned the Zodiac wheel and the constellations behind the planets on their journey across the night sky. He was a devouring god based on the way time devours everything it governs and often depicted with a harvesting scythe. The ancient Greeks therefore saw space (Aether) and time (Chronus) as related but not the same. Time (Chronus) was a son of matter (Gaia) and in addition to his devouring role, grew to a wise old man.

---

[481] EINSTEIN, Albert on Quantum Physics 1954

d. Unified Theory

As a layman to the field of physics and other sciences, I can only offer a viewpoint based on personal observation and understanding. To understand how space, time, matter and energy interact, I shall attempt to analyse the individual characteristics of each and look at how they relate and see if there are any connections to psychic functioning.

The following descriptions derive from observation and historical viewpoints.

Space

Container, boundless three-dimensional extent, can be measured, absence of substance, can be contained[482], special relationship between objects[483], a pure 'a Priori' form of intuition[484] space and time as a single construct[485], space is relative in the unconscious. Aether is the God of space in Greek mythology.

Time

Linear progression into the future, the present has no dimension in time, fundamental structure of the universe—a dimension independent of events, in which events occur in sequence[486]. Is neither an event nor a thing, and thus not itself measurable nor can it be travelled[487], an intellectual concept, not a reality (hypostasis), but a concept (noêma) or a measure (metron)[488], period of motion of the heavenly bodies[489], time and space are relational[490]; time is relative in the unconscious. The Greek God of time is Chronus

Matter

Can be measured, substance that has mass and takes up space, made of atoms comprising subatomic particles of protons and neutrons in the nucleus and an electron cloud orbiting the nucleus, has four states: solid, liquid, gas and plasma; extended substance[491]. The Greek Goddess of matter is Gaia (earth, material)

---

[482] In a building, vessel or the like.
[483] Gottfried Leibniz
[484] Immanuel Kant
[485] Einstein
[486] Isaac Newton
[487] Leibniz & Kant
[488] Antiphon the Sophist, Fifth Century BC
[489] Plato, Timaeus
[490] Gottfried Leibniz
[491] Rene Descartes

Electromagnetic Energy (EME)

EME relates to matter, matter has quantum potential EME, EME permeates the cosmos measured in photons, operates over enormous distances[492] and exhibits wave and particle properties. The Greek God of EME is Helios (sun) and Hephaestus (fire).

From the above, we can determine their relationships and how they interact, as well as how the physical constituents interact with the psychic functions. The obvious danger in such an endeavour is the inability to differentiate the physical from psychic, which will affect the overall relationships between them. In the end, it is the goal of this study to show how the two realms interact and permeate each other in a unified system. The stability and coherence of this unity however, requires each constituent and function to be differentiated from each other. This is a crucial aspect of any research in this field. It is the stability and independence acquired with the differentiation of the four functions and becoming aware of the central unifying character, or idea of unity.

Space/Time

Einstein regarded them as one, yet their properties are quite different and unique. We can move through space in any direction, but only through time in one direction. Space is a static, empty vessel, with no discernible boundaries, whereas time is a non-physical movement through space. Space and time have man-made measurements with different units. In Greek mythology, space is the grandfather of time- Aether/Chronus

Matter/EME

EME forces that hold the subatomic particles together closely relate to Matter. There is no matter without EME. Matter releases EME when it is acted upon by an external influence (temperature & pressure), (nuclear fusion). Large unstable atoms release EME, (nuclear fission). Matter is the grandmother of fire- Gaia/Hephaestus

Space/Matter

Space contains and permeates matter. The subatomic realm is made of particles held together in space by strong and weak forces. Space, as 'nothing', does not interact with matter. 'Nothing' cannot have an effect on 'something'. Space is the father of matter- Aether/Gaia

---

[492] Light from other galaxies.

Time/Matter

Time is the measurement of change in matter (growth & decay), it acts upon matter; matter is passive to time and cannot avoid its influence. Time is the son of matter- Gaia/Chronus

Time/EME

Time influences EME in a similar way to matter in that EME cannot avoid time's influence. Time is the grandfather of EME- Chronus/Hephaestus

EME/Space

Space contains and permeates EME. The subatomic realm is made of particles held together in space by EME forces. Space, as 'nothing', does not interact with EME. 'Nothing' cannot have an effect on 'something'. EME is the great grandson of space- Hephaestus/Aether

The four constituents of physical reality do not exist in isolation, but are continually interacting and influencing each other. Gravity is the little understood force and regarded as weak, yet its influence is galaxy wide and what it does not have in local strength it has in distance influence. Gravity is closely associated with matter and dependent on quantity and density of matter. It is a force of attraction, not repulsion, and coupled with movement, holds a galaxy together in balance. An object in orbit around another object is the balance of centrifugal and centripetal (gravitational) forces around the centre.

There are many associations possible with the physical constituents of matter and psyche known by thinkers of the past. Plato's cosmology of earth, air, fire and water[493] matches the contemporary matter, space, EME and time, and loosely fits four psychic functions[494], sensation, thinking, intuition and feeling, as well as primary colours green, blue, yellow and red. All these functions have similar characteristics, and when seen in relationship, offer an insight into the nature of unity between the physical and psychic.

Differentiating the physical from psychic may in the end be impossible and only approached with an ever decreasing distance to the goal. It is a spiral to an unknown centre and the closer we get to the centre, smaller the spiral becomes. This is due to the same reason we have difficulty differentiating space, time, matter and EME. The four are intertwined and

---

[493] PLATO'S Cosmology, The Timaeus
[494] JUNG, C. G., Psychological Types, Routledge and Kegan

so dependent on each other that complete isolation and observation of any part has an effect on other parts. All we can hope to achieve is a broad outline of their differences, and how they interact.

Fitting all of the above into a coherent pattern or system is even more difficult. We can look at an atom and marvel at its unity and balance of forces, but its observation changes it. The best we can do is to approximate a system of relationships between the constituents of matter and the functions of the psyche. The following diagrammatic system is by no means fixed, and should be regarded as an instant in an ever-changing flux of evolution, growth and movement around the centre, much the same as stars move around the centre of a galaxy.

The unity of the physical and psychic realms occurs in individuals when unconscious material flows into the physical world through creative acts. It is a flow of dreams, ideas, thoughts etc., which help one's growth and movement in the world. This material requires us to help bring it into physical existence. The best and purest form of relationship between the two realms is Synchronistic phenomena due to its action outside of our conscious control. This occurs, as discussed previously, when an idea, thought etc., coincides with an external event in the physical world. It acts outside of our will and exerts a fascination on us with an attractive force. Such events are the purest and untainted form of connectedness between the inner physic and outer physical realms.

The following diagrams show an outer level of physical nature and its four constituents, held in equilibrium through the forces of attraction (gravity) and motion around the centre, and show the similarities between ancient thought and contemporary ideas. The other level shows the psychic material with the four orienting functions in relationship through the force of attraction and movement. The centre attracts our attention through synchronicity and unites the psychic and physical. The following diagram drawn in three dimensions has the physical on top and psychic below, with contents flowing to the centre.

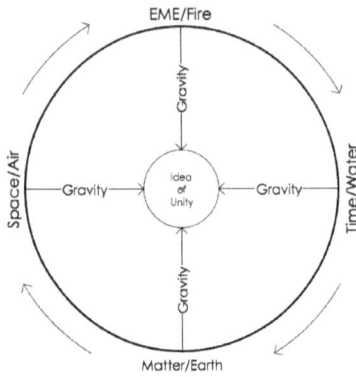

Physical Realm

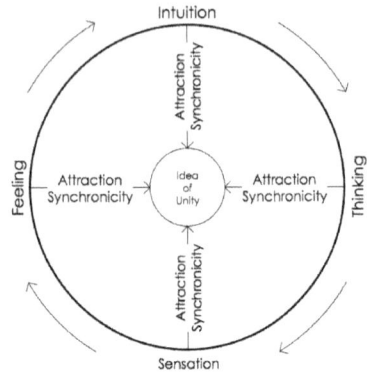

Psychic Realm

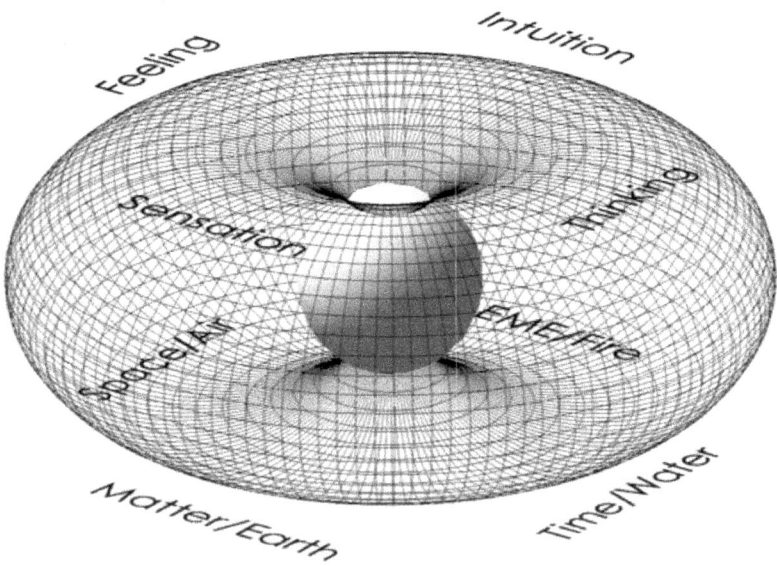

The forces of attraction to the centre are gravity and synchronicity. How can we relate gravity with psychic forces of attraction? Gravity on earth is all encompassing, affects everything with sufficient mass,[495] and holds it firmly in place on the earth's surface. Earth's matter, including plant and animal life, is intimately shaped and regulated by the earth's and sun's gravitational fields. Mass therefore attracts mass over time. Theoretically, the forces that hold atoms and molecules together must have a close relationship to gravity, or share in its force.

If we move into space in a capsule, we experience gravity in relative form. Without forward velocity, a capsule plummets to earth under the same force as experienced on earth. In this instance however, the capsule is falling at the same rate as an occupant, thus giving the sensation of weightlessness. With the addition of forward velocity, a capsule achieves orbit around the force of gravity. Gravity is not counteracted to achieve orbit, but another force added to it that pushes the capsule over the 'edge', so to speak. This is why weightlessness is still experienced in orbit. Similarly, away from earth's gravitational field, a capsule will still be orbiting the sun, and beyond the solar system, the centre of the galaxy.

What, then, is the relationship between gravity, matter and EME?

> •Matter (atoms) creates Gravity
> •Attractive forces outweigh repulsive forces holding atoms together.
> •Attractive forces outweigh repulsive forces between atoms depending on external influences (EME)
> •EME changes the state of matter and loosens the forces between atoms
> •Gravity affects EME
> •Atoms seek stability and equilibrium
> •EME holds Molecules together
> •More matter means more gravity
> •Gravity is a universal force
> •Gravity operates over enormous distances
> •Gravity attracts matter to a centre
> •Forces of attraction seek unity, balance and stability

From the above, we can conclude that the attractive forces outweigh repulsive forces, or matter would fall apart. This observation gives us the additive effect of gravity and force of attraction of a single atom added to the force of another atom, and so on. Yet, gravity causes acceleration, not constant velocity. It attracts matter to itself with ever-increasing velocity, making it theoretically possible to achieve unlimited velocity with

---

[495] 'Jeans Escape' suggests some of the lighter elements such as Hydrogen do escape the earth's atmosphere through their kinetic energy.

unlimited distance between two objects attracted to each other. If all matter creates gravity, then both objects exert gravity of magnitudes dependent on their mass. For example, an object falling to earth would exert its own force of attraction (gravity) onto the earth itself, depending on its mass.

From the above schematic, the pressing question is what relationship does gravity have with synchronicity? Since mystery still shrouds both phenomena, all we can do is formulate a theory, or at least common aspects of both.

Synchronicity[496]
•Unites unconscious contents and physical reality
•Attracts to the centre between matter and psyche
•Organisation of matter is coincident with idea, thought, etc.
•Attracts curiosity, fascination and interest and is emotionally impressive
•Makes one feel a belonging to a greater reality
•It only occurs through an individual psyche although it can be a shared experience.
•Seeks unity, balance and stability

It is difficult to say if the psychic material causes the coincidence, or the movement of matter does. It does however, attract our attention and fascination by being able to observe the unity of the psyche and matter. The nature of synchronicity unites the inner and outer contents in the third. The fact that psyche and matter can coincide shows that there is an underlying unity of both. Our psyches are fluid, in that we have many thoughts, fantasies and ideas during the day and dreams during the night. When they coincide in the physical world, it becomes an all-important question of meaning. It also helps us become aware of these inner processes and their connection to the physical.

The documentation on such phenomena is sparse, and therefore we do not have a clear picture of its scope and under what circumstances it operates. What we can say however is that gravity and synchronicity have common attributes. They both attract matter and energy to a centre. Gravity attracts energy/matter to the centre of large masses, such as a moon, planets, solar system (stars) and galaxy, etc. Synchronicity attracts energy to the centre of the psyche. The physical facts of gravity and uniting experiences of synchronicity show that there are common forces at work between matter and psyche. These are the forces of attraction, with an emphasis on a centre.

---

[496] See Section 11b for a full description and examples of Synchronistic Phenomenon.

e. Alchemy- Unity in Matter

Alchemy was the precursor to modern day chemistry, and is an excellent example of the differentiation and integration of ideas projected onto matter. It is also an example of the evolution of humanity's awareness of psychic processes. The mystery of matter attracts projection, particularly when chemical processes are undifferentiated from psychic processes. This mystery attracts the contents underlying our psychic nature, which revolve around the central character, image or pattern in the psyche. This image or character can be a precious metal like gold, a panacea that heals all ailments, an abstract pattern like a mandala, a stone or a central inner character. In other alchemical writings, only the initiated can recognise the simple undervalued stone. The crucial aspect of alchemy is its relationship to matter, something the Christian ideal had trouble recognising and integrating into its unity.

One of the reasons chemistry is good for the projection of such a symbol or character is its ability to react and change when certain materials are processed and combined changing their state. The transformation of one material into another captured the alchemist's imagination. From a psychological point of view, Alchemy is the undifferentiated inner unity related to and seen in matter. The separation of psychic contents from chemistry and matter itself did not arrive in the west until the seventeenth century with the works of Sir Francis Bacon, Jean Beguin, Jan Baptist van Helmont and Robert Boyle.

The scientific method was adopted during this period and matter was separated from the projected ideas which they regarded as superstition and fantasy, and discarded. They did not disappear, but returned to the unconscious where they originally came from. To some extent, contemporary research into matter, particularly Quantum Mechanics, shows that some alchemical ideas persist in researchers' psyches. An example is the use of the term 'God particle', for the Higgs-Boson, as mentioned earlier. The discovery of nuclear fission and the ability to overload the atom of an element and change it into two other elements, also shows an interest in this transformation.

Theoretically, it may be possible in the future to change one element into another, simply by adding or subtracting the number protons, neutrons and electrons. The psychological aspect of transformation has its reality in becoming aware of the deeper layers of the psyche, its characters and its centre. The projection into matter of this process would not have occurred had matter not the 'hook' to attract the projection. As we have shown previously, projected ideas and stories (myths) are based on the physical appearance and the behaviour of objects. For example, the ancients projected an inner character onto the sun, because it behaves in a way that is regular, strong, illuminating and heating.

With the discovery of fire came the ability to transform matter from one state to another, combine elements and create chemical reactions. This was for many centuries a magical process, which in turn attracted all kinds of imaginative ideas. The scientific method often finds that ideas do not fit the facts and are rejected. The scientist sought the material reality and how it reacted to other materials. The discarded idea however, has as much importance as the discovered physical fact, in that the idea has a direct relationship to the personality of the scientist. In other words, the idea has a reality of its own. It may or may not fit the physical fact, but as an idea, has a purpose and relates directly to the personal growth of the individual.

An example of an idea projected onto matter, is the transformation of a base metal such as lead into the appearance of a precious metal such as gold with the use of tinctures. This rudimentary understanding of alchemy is not what they were trying to achieve. The overarching idea of the alchemists is the transformation of the idea of a base material to the idea of a precious material. In other words, the projected idea from one state to a more differentiated, hence valuable state. With our current understanding of material science, this transformation is not physically possible. As an idea, it is full of possibility. To understand how the materials fascinated the alchemists, I shall describe the physical and symbolic properties of two examples, and show how the materials themselves attracted the unconscious projection.

Lead (Pb)
- Atomic Number: 82
- Density: 11.34 g/cm^2
- Colour: bright silver and dull grey after tarnishing
- Softness: Mohs hardness 1.5
- Melting Temp.: 327.5 °C

Gold (Au)
- Atomic Number: 79
- Density: 19.30 g/cm^2
- Colour: bright gold with no tarnishing
- Softness: Mohs hardness 2.5 to 3.0
- Melting Temp.: 1,064.76 °C

Lead from the Latin 'Plumbum' is heavy, relatively soft, highly malleable and a ductile metal with a relatively low melting point. It is resistant to corrosion but tarnishes quickly when exposed to air. It was one of the earliest metals known to humanity and widely used by the ancient Egyptians, Greeks, Romans and Chinese. Symbolically, lead is associated with the planet Saturn, dark connections and related to death and transformation. The alchemists regarded it as one of many forms of 'Prima Materia', which is the base material or fundamental substance. Lead's baseness, lack of beauty and low melting point make it an excellent material to treat with fire, in the hope of transforming its appearance into another more valuable metal like gold.

Gold derives its name from the Latin word 'Aurum', and is interpreted as 'shining dawn'. It is heavier and slightly harder, with similar malleability and ductility to lead. Unlike lead, it retains its lustrous beauty and does not tarnish in air. Gold is rare and always given a higher value than lead. Lead and gold have similarities in weight, malleability and ductility.

Lead cannot however, be physically transformed into gold, therefore it is the idea of transformation from one state to another that attracted the alchemists' attention. The historical associations with lead are Hades, black earth, the animal of earth and sea, part of man, Nigredo, Adam and Mercurial dragon.[497] Gold, on the other hand, is associated with the Sol (sun), perfection, purity, wealth, prosperity, authority, charisma, healing lapis, king, paradise, spirit, Christ and God.[498]

This study is not the place to go into the complex and varied procedures involved in Alchemy, although I do describe the basic workings of it in chapter 3e. I refer the reader to the footnoted references for detailed information on this subject from the psychological point of view. My concern in this work is the projection of ideas into matter and the relationship between them, as we have seen with Quantum Mechanics and Relativity. This is but one example of the underlying unity of psyche and matter. The important thing is the value of the idea in addition to physical reality of matter and how matter attracts ideas due to their characteristics. The nature and behaviour of metals attracted the ideas of transformation.

This transformation of base material to a precious and valuable material as an idea is the transformation of base instinctive undifferentiated psyche (the animal) to a higher, differentiated and spiritual psyche. Alchemy grew out of the ancient world and to some extent paralleled the growth of Christianity. In many instances, the work of the alchemists tried to complete Christian ideas, by searching for its spirit in ordinary

---

[497] JUNG, C. G., Psychology and Alchemy, Volume 12 of the Collected Works, Bollingen Series, Princeton University Press, 1952
[498] Ibid

materials. The Christian myth relegated the base instinctive aspects of humanity to the underworld, and the realm of the devil. This is particularly true of the sexual instinct. Its positive spirit of relationship transformed to an ephemeral and heavenly attribute divorced from matter. The physical act of sexual union was then disparaged and rejected. Viewed in this way, Alchemy is the completion of the Christian myth, in that it looks for positive spirit in matter, thus drawing the positive out and into their understanding.

In this section, I have tried to show how the forces of nature influence matter and unite with their counterparts in the psyche. It is difficult to make any definitive statements concerning this unity, other than the instances where they display unity. As shown previously, the edge of knowledge, whether it is in space or at the quantum level[499], leads to the activation of unconscious contents and speculation. This is however, not only a beautiful arrangement of nature, in that projection can teach us about what is being observed in the physical world by attracting our attention and interest, but also what is being observed from the inner realm of the unconscious. This is a task of differentiation of one side from the other, and the ultimate recognition of their underlying unity. "As above, so below".[500]

f. Space

A discussion of space is an overwhelming exercise, simply for the fact that the cosmos is vast and spans incredible distances. When viewing space, we also look back in time. The 'Big Bang Theory' is our contemporary understanding of how the universe came into being. This theory states that the universe began from an infinitely dense, hot and stationary point, which exploded creating all the matter in the universe. This is an interesting idea but very difficult to prove.

If it explodes from a stationary point, then the shape of the universe has to be spherical according to our known laws of physics, as an explosion would send matter in all directions without other external forces acting upon it. How do galactic collisions occur like our own galaxy with the Andromeda galaxy, which is scheduled to occur in the future? It has recently been theorised that the shape of the universe is a flat disc[501],

---

[499] Where knowledge ends, imagination takes over. We imagine all kinds of forces, deities etc., when we have reached the limit of our knowledge. Examples include ancient gods projected onto the planets, aliens, dark matter/energy and black holes.
[500] This is a Hermetic maxim translated by Dennis W. Hauck from *The Emerald Tablet of Hermes Trismegistus*
[501] https://phys.org/news/2011-10-flat-universe.html

much the same as a galaxy. This means prior to the Big Bang, an initial point of dense matter was spinning for the matter to be ejected in a flat plane. The question is, what forces would cause a dense body to spin before the big bang? No matter how we look at this idea, it is very difficult to verify. We may find that the Big Bang is an idea and does not relate to physical reality.

As an idea however, we have multitudes of information from many cultures. They are the creation myths that explain the birth of the world. They are cosmogonic myths of chaos being ordered into something meaningful. These narratives are highly symbolic and akin to dreams, which is why they have such an impact on us. In this sense, and as Von Franz mentions[502], creation myths represent the origin of our awareness of the physical world. In other words, it is becoming aware of the physical world, but not its actual creation. As mentioned previously, reaching the limits of our knowledge leads to the projection of unconscious ideas filling the unknown so we have something to relate to. It is understandable that fantastic ideas replace observable facts at the limits of our knowledge. The universe created in an instant from a point in space is similar to an unknown God simply conjuring the universe by an omnipotent act of creation.

Dark matter and dark energy, unless proven to exist, may fall into this category. Even the use of the term 'dark' has connotations of something where the light of awareness does not yet shine. It is a loaded term, in that darkness is an excellent metaphor for our night-time dreams. If dark matter/energy actually exists, its name will need changing, as it is no longer in the darkness due to its detection and verification.

The relationship of objects in the universe is another aspect of its origin. Satellites and moons orbit planets through a combination of gravity and velocity. Planets orbit stars in the same way, as do star systems around the centre of the galaxy. We do not however, understand how galaxies relate to each other within the universe. If the big bang theory is correct, then all matter in the universe has a central point in common, and everything flung into space is moving away from that point. Whether the nature of the universe is spherical or flat, the relationships between the galaxies may hold the key to understanding this universal system.

Paralleling the physical nature of the universe is its mythic nature, which includes ancient stories and its relationship to human perception. The ancients regarded Astrology as such a relationship and although divorced from the contemporary scientific understanding of the cosmos, still exerts

---

[502] VON FRANZ, Marie-Louise, Creation Myths, Shambhala Publictions 1995

an undeniable influence on our behaviour and mythological anticipation of current and future events. Not only does it engage our intuition in the form of possibilities, it also has a relation to synchronistic phenomena. It is easy to deny the validity of astrology and regard it as a superstition, yet there may be physical influences of gravity and EME from the planets that affect our bodies and therefore our perception of reality. We cannot deny the effect the sun and moon have on the earth so why not the planets.

The moon for example, has since ancient times, regarded having a physical effect on humans. Aristotle saw the full moon inducing abnormal behaviour (lunacy) in susceptible individuals due to the water content of the brain and knew the moon affected the tides. In addition, the moon's effect on water and the earth is measurable in addition to its gravitational force and electromagnetic energy (EME) reflected from the sun. Similarly, the same forces and energy emitted from the other planets in the solar system are also measurable. We do not know to what extent the forces and energy emitted by these bodies have on the functioning of our brains, although our brains operate via an energetic system of electrical impulses. The relationship between gravitational fields and EME from the planets and the functioning of the brain is fertile ground for research.

Astrology does attract projection of unconscious contents onto the movement of the planets (wandering stars) and its relationship to background constellations. This does not explain the belief that the position of these bodies determines personality type and behaviour[503]. The unconscious requires an attribute of an object for the projection to activate. Our previous example of the snake shows that an object attracts a projection that is in tune with, or related to, from experience and knowledge. The physical nature and behaviour of an object is always at the base of its mythology.

Hence, the planets attract projection of certain ideas by their behaviour in the night sky. Astrology uses these ideas and tries to explain them in understandable terms. Whether there is a physical cause due to gravity or EME from the planets underlying psychic projection, the same way ideas are projected into matter in alchemy, is to be determined. What is certain is the persistence and longevity of astrology from ancient times to the present day.

---

[503] Refer to Section 10g, Relating to the Cosmos for a further study on cosmological phenomena and its relationship to humanity.

g. Relationship to Living Things

Further to the study of matter is its relationship to living things. The earth itself has moulded life into a complex pattern of so-called inert elements and organised those elements with life-giving properties. As discussed previously, the difference between life and its material constituents is difficult, if not impossible to differentiate. Life builds from the surrounding elements and depends on the presence of those elements to continue living.

The health of an organism depends on the available nutrition and specific constituents, both organic and inorganic. For example, studies by the Dr Joel Wallach on nutrition[504] show that the availability of vitamins and minerals in our diets has a direct bearing on our health. His research on wild animals in Africa, animal husbandry, pets, human nutrition and long-lived cultures, shows that physical health relates to broad-spectrum nutrition, particularly the intake of minerals. For example, vitamin C ($C_6H_8O_6$), prevents 'scurvy' in humans. Wallach discovered that nutrient deficiencies cause many other physical illnesses. Examples include the cure for ulcers with bismuth (Bi) and tetracycline ($C_{22}H_{24}N_2O_8$); cancer reduced with vitamin E ($C_{29}H_{50}O_2$), Beta-carotene ($C_{40}H_{56}$) and selenium (Se); arthritis with gelatine ($C_{102}H_{151}O_{39}N_{31}$); Alzheimer's with high doses of vitamin E ($C_{29}H_{50}O_2$) and low intake of vegetable oil; Osteoporosis with Calcium (C), Magnesium (Mg) and Boron (B); weakened arteries preventing aneurysms with copper (Cu); Cardiomyopathy with selenium (Se); diabetes with chromium (Cr) and vanadium (V); and Pica, which is mineral deficiency in pregnant women where the foetus absorbs minerals from the mother's body, with broad spectrum minerals.

Wallach studied cultures living at high altitudes in Tibet and Titicaca, who get their water from glacial run-off called 'glacial milk', which is a rich formula of ground-up minerals and melted ice water. They not only drink this liquid, but also irrigate their crops, thus receiving the minerals in colloidal form. The people in these cultures commonly have life spans exceeding 100 years and have less prevalence of common western diseases.

The above is one viewpoint on health of an organism and its relationship to matter. The fact is living organisms are made of the same elements

---

[504] WALLACH, Dr J. 'Dead Doctors Don't Lie'
https://www.youtube.com/watch?v=ejUFB424bhM

that exist in the environment. Organisms that have mobility have a chance to ingest a wide variety of these elements compared to vegetation, which is predominately stationary. Naturally, there are variables in systems, particularly when adopted by human activity with agriculture and animal husbandry. The importance of Dr Wallach's research is the relationship between the health of an organism and the elements the organism ingests.

7. VEGETATION

a. Environmental Dependency

Multi-cell flora is totally dependent on its environment. This includes its location, access to sunlight, temperature, cloud cover, rainfall, soil conditions etc., as well as the fauna, which has a role in propagation of the plant. Environmental conditions are continually changing and survival depends on the plant's natural ability to adapt to these changes.

The separation of environmental influence and vegetation is only useful in categorising and adding to our knowledge. In reality, the two aspects of the system are so intermingled that the boundaries are indeterminable. For example, the gases in the atmosphere come from the vegetation and the soil. The soil in turn, is fed by rainfall and rotting vegetation, the location on the earth determines the climactic pattern, the sun and its intensity influences other aspects of the system and so on. We can visualise the difference between plant and environment, yet it is impossible to separate their relationship and their unity.

The CO_2 concentrations in the atmosphere in our contemporary environment are far less than millions of years ago. 400 to 600 million years ago, the concentration of CO_2 was 6000 ppm (parts per million) and between 200 to 150 million years ago, over 3000 ppm. Our contemporary concentration of CO_2 is approximately 400 ppm, showing a dramatic reduction over that time.[505] Although these figures come from a broader context, we can say that between 600 million years and the present, the overall mean CO_2 concentration has decreased, as shown on the temperature record below. Patrick Moore, an early collaborator with Greenpeace, suggests that the CO_2 concentrations today are far too low for optimum plant growth.

> "The optimum CO_2 level for most plants is about 1600 parts per million, four times higher than the level today."

The scientific evidence for climate change has gone beyond objective observation and analysis into the political and big business arenas, where the motivation is different. Science is the quest for knowledge and understanding, whereas politics is power and business, making money. This fundamental difference is crucial to objective observation, experiment and modelling of the climate system. Its complexity is so vast that we have not yet understood how the system works in its entirety.

---

[505] Carbon Dioxide in Earth's Atmosphere

One crucial system that gets little attention in the debate is the sun, which actually gives the earth's surface most of its heat. Climate models seem to lean towards the sun having a constant output of energy and variable CO_2 concentrations. The reality is both systems have variable output and cycles as do all climactic systems.

The following graph shows the correlation between sun activity and temperature over a 120-year period and the close relationship between temperature and solar activity. The next graph shows the relationship between CO_2 concentrations and temperature over a 120-year period.

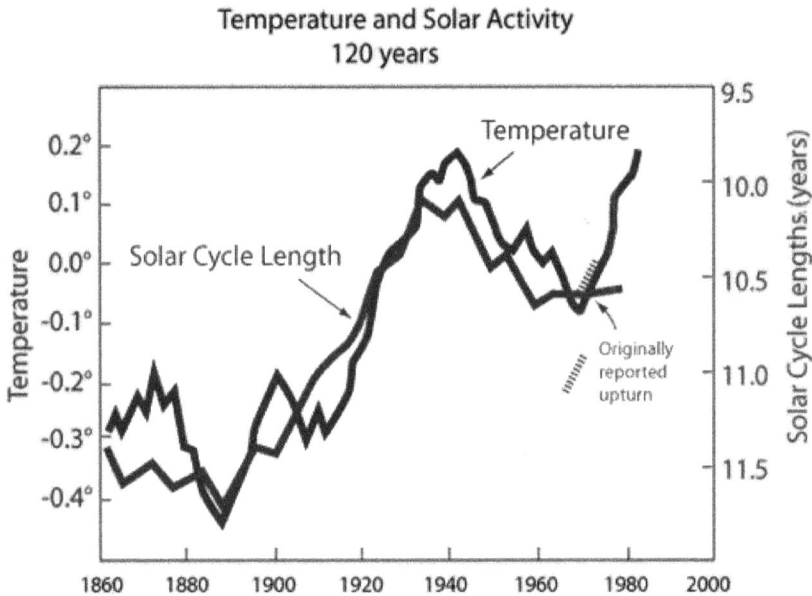

Temperature and Solar Activity
120 years

506

[506] http://hyperphysics.phy-astr.gsu.edu/hbase/thermo/solact.html

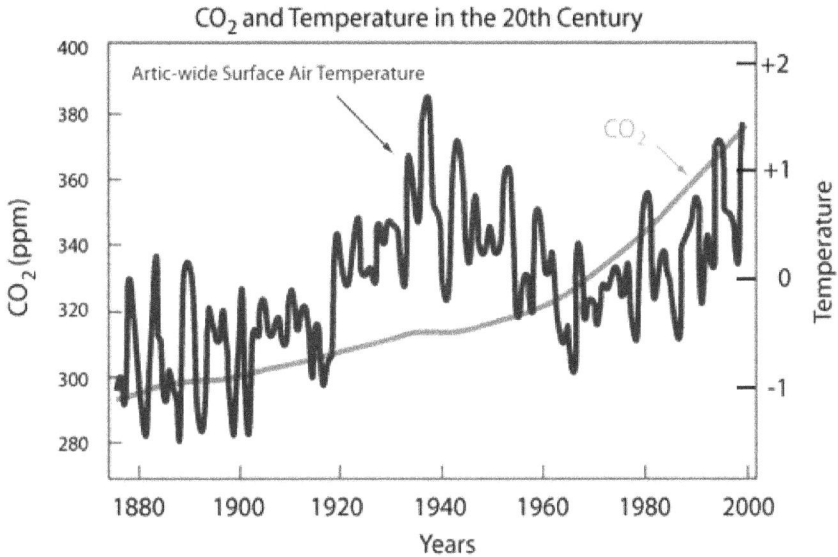

CO$_2$ and Temperature in the 20th Century

507

The following graph shows the CO$_2$ levels and temperature over a 600 million-year period and how they relate over that time. The interesting aspect of the graph is that temperature levels are constant over large periods and hover around the global average of 22˚C. There were major reductions in temperature, which correlate to ice ages or natural catastrophes, such as a meteor strike, but no major increases in temperature over 600 million years. On the other hand, the CO$_2$ levels vary greatly compared to the temperature, and display a degree of independence. Between 500 and 600 million years ago, the CO$_2$ levels spiked dramatically without a perceivable change to temperature. Between 400 and 500 million years ago, there was a dramatic decrease in temperature, with lowering CO$_2$ levels occurring as the temperature was to rising. 300 and 380 million years ago, the CO$_2$ levels dropped to similar levels we have today and the temperature dropped 70 million years later and returned to approximately 22˚C. Since that time there was another temperature decrease 150 million years ago, and a steady decline of CO$_2$ and temperature levels to the present time. This would suggest that we are entering a cold period, rather than a period of warming.

---

[507] http://hyperphysics.phy-astr.gsu.edu/hbase/thermo/co2suf.html#c1

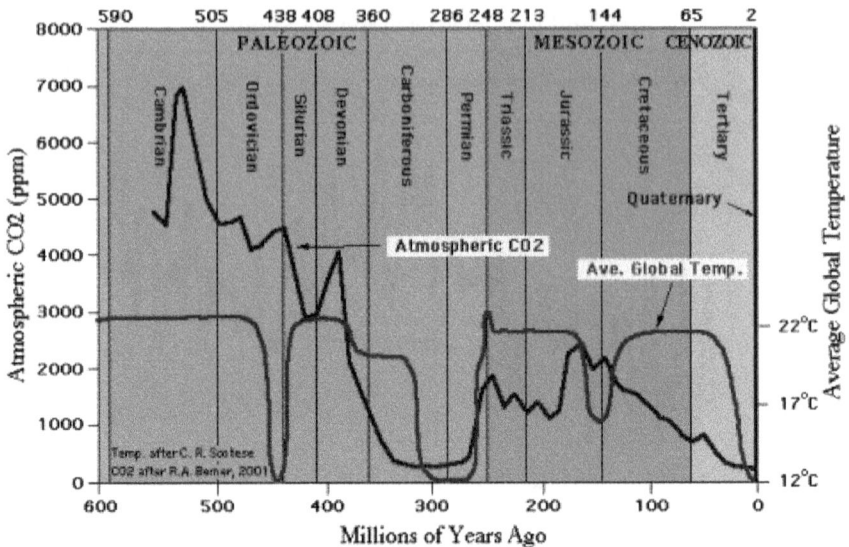

The following graph shows the percentage levels of gaseous constituents in the atmosphere. CO_2 comprises 0.04% compared to approximately 22% O_2, of the earth's atmosphere

Major constituents of dry air, by volume[6]

Gas		Volume(A)	
Name	Formula	in ppmv(B)	in %
Nitrogen	N_2	780,840	78.084
Oxygen	O_2	209,460	20.946
Argon	Ar	9,340	0.9340
Carbon dioxide	CO_2	400	0.04[7]
Neon	Ne	18.18	0.001818
Helium	He	5.24	0.000524
Methane	CH_4	1.79	0.000179
Not included in above dry atmosphere:			
Water vapor(C)	H_2O	10–50,000(D)	0.001%–5%(D)

notes:

(A) volume fraction is equal to mole fraction for ideal gas only, also see volume (thermodynamics)

(B) ppmv: parts per million by volume

(C) Water vapor is about 0.25% by mass over full atmosphere

(D) Water vapor strongly varies locally[4]

509

---

508 http://geocraft.com/WVFossils/Carboniferous_climate.html

We can conclude from what we know about the interaction between vegetation and the climate, that more CO_2 in the atmosphere promotes the growth of flora, which in turn increases the levels of oxygen in the atmosphere. Professor Robert Frei, from the University of Copenghagen suggests that increases in the levels of oxygen in the atmosphere may cause temperature reduction,[510] and that more flora on the earth's surface lowers temperature, compared to large areas of desert.

The above graphs show that the climate is a unified system that seeks balance with increases or decreases in temperature and CO_2 levels. The changes to these levels can be gradual due to solar activity; natural increases from fires, volcanoes, ocean emanations etc., and increases of human activity over the past 200 years.[511] Dramatic changes such as meteor strikes, take the system longer to adjust, but eventually the balance is restored. This balance tends to stabilise at approximately 22°C, and is a natural part of the earth's environmental system, which has more to do with its position from the sun than the activity of its flora or fauna. If anything, the above graphs puts doubt into the scientific consensus on man-made climate change, which is a healthy and necessary scepticism for any scientific mind. What conclusions can we draw from our western culture's belief that humans are the sole cause of climate change? Do we feel above nature and believe we have control over her?

From the above we can see that temperature has a stronger relationship to solar activity than it does to CO_2 levels. It is also clear that temperature and CO_2 records over millions of years puts the climate change debate into perspective. The complexity of the climate system and the role that vegetation has in the system makes it reasonable to suggest that an increase in one aspect leads to a compensation by another aspect. In other words, nature is a self-regulating system that oscillates between opposites and finds its own balance in that way. We may be able to curb human CO2 emissions[512] but have little control over natural emissions, which predominately emanate from the great oceans. In addition, we have no influence over the sun, the source of most of the earth's heat.

---

[509] Source for figures: Carbon dioxide, NOAA Earth System Research Laboratory, (updated 2013). Methane, IPCC TAR table 6.1 Archived 2007-06-15 at the Wayback Machine.(updated to 1998)
[510] http://news.ku.dk/all_news/2009/more_oxygen_colder_climate/
[511] Human activity contributes about 0.28% of Greenhouse Gases, if water vapour is taken into account and about 5.53%, if not. - http://www.geocraft.com/WVFossils/greenhouse_data.html
[512] I do see the value and independence of using inexhaustible sources of energy from the sun or wind, but if our planet is turning to desert because of the low levels of CO_2, then we have to rethink that strategy.

As I have shown in the preceding chapters we can do little to influence global and solar systems and need to look at the ideas of climate change and how they may be disconnected from the reality of our climate. The idea that humans alone can affect the climate to such an extent gives humanity an importance over the atmosphere, flora, and fauna in general. It hints at the possibility that we are to some extent disconnected from physical nature and our own nature. It is common knowledge that physical nature is a self-regulating system that seeks balance and stability. Our psychic nature of ideas and beliefs is also a self-regulating system that seeks balance and stability.

It is understandable that we are to some extent disconnected from nature because we have been trying to liberate ourselves from our own nature for thousands of years. Flora has no choice in its relationship to the environment. Humans on the other hand, are more adaptable than flora[513] in that we can protect ourselves from climactic change through clothing, housing, heating, air conditioners etc. The overarching idea behind the climate change movement is the lack of relationship to human nature. The adapting ability of floras is limited and humans can adapt better to these external influences, but lack a stable perspective and understanding of the internal influences that have bearing on our ideas and behaviour.

b. Adaptation

The ability of plants to adapt to their environment shows how flexible an organism has to be in order to survive. It is in the nature of the organism to perceive the environmental conditions and respond to them positively to facilitate growth. Plants react to chemicals, gravity, light, moisture, temperature, oxygen, carbon dioxide concentrations, parasite infestation, disease, physical disruption, sound, and touch. The method plants use to perceive the environment is predominately chemical, although some research indicates that plant cells have electrical responses to certain environmental influences.

> It is hardly an exaggeration to say that the tip of the radicle thus endowed [..] acts like the brain of one of the lower animals; the brain being situated within the anterior end of the body, receiving impressions from the sense-organs, and directing the several movements.[514]

---

[513] We have learned to grow plants in artificial environments under human control.

[514] DARWIN, Charles 'The Power and Movement in Plants', D Appleton and Company 1898

Our contemporary understanding of plant behaviour and physiology shows that the level of adaptation to environmental influences is a complex and mysterious system. Without an obvious control centre like a brain, we have to ask ourselves how the information to co-ordinate the organism is stored and where it is located in the plant. The answer is in the plants Genome, which is a molecule made from a chemical called deoxyribonucleic acid (DNA), located in each plant cell. This is where all the information the plant requires for growth, adaptation and survival is stored.

c. Genome Coding

This code guides the plant to its goal of growth, adaptation and behaviour, and passes from one plant to the next through the cells in each seed. The information contained in the DNA is already established, yet flexible enough to change to differing circumstances. These circumstances, as mentioned previously, have an influence on the DNA, and give it the best possible chance of survival. This is the basic idea contained in Darwin's studies. Plants increase their viability by evolving over time and developing methods to ensure their adaptability. These include the development of flowering seeds, so that birds and insects are attracted to ensure seed distribution away from the parent plant. We can see a similar idea present in our human taboo on incest so that the DNA has a widest range of dispersal and better chance of adapting to varying environmental conditions. The idea[515] increases the potential for survival.

The idea of how plants know how to grow, how to orient towards the sun and how to disperse seeds etc., is still a mystery, yet it is the same mystery that permeates all life. How do we know who we should be? We can argue that we choose our own destiny and make our own choices, but more often than not, the decision is made for us through an external influence, such as a parent, fate, or through an idea that pops into our mind. In whatever instance, the decision came from a source outside or inside of our personal will.

Plants have the same ability to change their behaviour to external and internal influences, as do humans. They grow vertically and horizontally as much as their structure will endure to get as much sunlight as possible. The same occurs underground in the competition for water and nutrients. Plants outgrow, entwine, compete and destroy each other with no compunction or guilt. It is the determinate structure of nature and the

---

[515] I use the term 'idea' simply to describe what is happening in the plant process. It does not refer to a conscious process of volition. As I shall explain later in this text, ideas are products from an unknown source we call the unconscious.

'Will to Power', based on survival. The process of growth in plants is relatively slow, so the competition for survival is less obvious compared to the animal world.

The storage of information in the DNA molecule is a universal system used by living organisms. This information is the basis for decision-making and storage of knowledge. It also has the information for the method of growth and adaptive processes involved in growth. The method a plant uses to assimilate carbon from the atmosphere and combine it with water and other nutrients is all contained within its DNA, and passed down over generations through their seeds.

In addition, plants build their structure using known mathematical laws. The Italian mathematician Leonardo Fibonacci (1175-1250) explored the population growth of rabbits and observed a general mathematical sequence later called the Fibonacci sequence. The sequence adds the previous two numbers to arrive at the next number beginning with zero. They are 0,1,1,2,3,5,8,13,21,34,55,89,144,233,377 and so on. The sequence is defined by the recurring relation $F_n = F_{n-1} + F_{n-2}$. The resultant geometric shape, when plotted approximates a spiral.

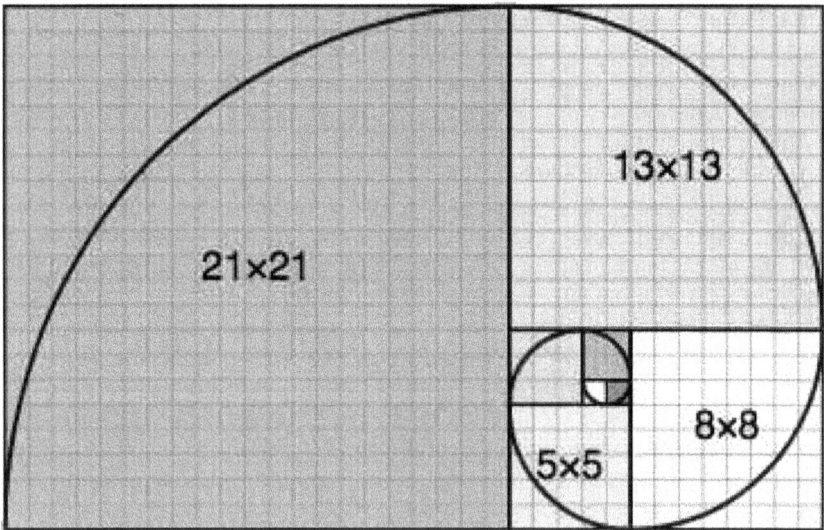

516

Plants grow and form flowers using the Fibonacci sequence. There are anomalies to the rule, as environmental influences vary dramatically in

---

516 https://en.wikipedia.org/wiki/Fibonacci_number

nature, but the sequence applies to most plants and shows how sequential growth occurs. Examples of plants that grow parts including petals are the camomile, sunflower, lilies, roses, marigolds, pinecones etc. This is similar to the way snowflakes form while falling to earth. Their molecular structure is responsible for their basic form, and environmental influences, their adapted form. It is interesting to note that the Golden Mean or Ratio, when plotted geometrically, gives the exact same spiral as the Fibonacci sequence. Artists and architects used the Golden Ratio throughout history for its proportioning relationships which gave their works order and beauty.

d. Relationship to Animals

Most plants have fixed locations, although there are exceptions. This makes them very vulnerable to external threats from other life forms such as animals. The plant has no choice but to accept its fate in the location that the environment gave it. They have, however developed a relationship to animals that is as unique as the plant itself. They sometimes attract or repel animals, or a combination of both. It is a symbiotic relationship mutually beneficial in most instances.

The relationship is incredibly complex and varied, yet purposeful. Plants have a very beautiful system of attracting animals through their senses of vision, aroma and taste with fruit or flowers. The attraction has the function of using the mobility of animals, including insects, to distribute the plant's seeds over the widest possible range of distance. Some seeds can withstand the digestive systems of animals, carried in the animal to new locations, and excreted.

Plants lure insects with colourful and aromatic flowers and provide food such as nectar, to attract and sustain the insects. The system of pollination and seed distribution in this instance is symbiotic and beneficial to both plants and animals. In this example, plants have developed a way not only of attracting insects, but also of feeding the insect with its nectar. It is a purposeful system to ensure the plant's pollen distributed to other plants of the same species for reproduction.

On the other hand, plants evolved systems to repel and protect themselves and their seeds with thorns and toxins. Thorns found in Cacti are obviously an effective way of keeping larger animals at a distance. For example, the Cylindropuntia, commonly known as the Cholla cactus found in Mexico and southwest United States, has developed a highly effective form of protection and seed distribution through very fine and sharp barbed needle-like spines. The spines protect the plant but also distribute the seeds, which are located in its spherical structure surrounded by the spines. These have the function of attaching themselves to an animal's skin or fur. The seed balls are very difficult to remove once attached thus ensuring a greater distance from its parent plant for seed distribution.

Between the extremes of attraction and repulsion are many gradations and hybrids. For example, the Carnegiea Gigantea, commonly known as the Saguaro cactus, found in the same regions as the Cholla, has spines to protect its fleshy water laden skin from larger animals, yet has flowers[517] and fruit for attracting insects and small birds on the upper parts of the plant. In this instance, land-based animals kept away from its trunk, and birds and insects attracted to its top for its propagating function.

The most effective system, however, for plant protection from animals, is chemical. Plants have developed a vast and complicated array of chemical compounds to deter animals. These include: toxic leaves, fruits, flowers, roots and seeds. The variety is enormous and has differing combinations of toxicity. These combinations include toxic and edible parts of the same plant. Examples include the apple, which has toxic seeds containing amygdalin; lemons contain psoralen, which is toxic to cats, dogs and other animals. Onions and garlic contain thiosulphate, which is toxic to cats, dogs and livestock. The varieties are innumerable.

Plants have developed quite specific methods of protection and propagation. On the surface, some of these methods may seem illogical, for example the seeds, which look like red berries, of Abrus Precatorius[518], commonly known as the Jequirity or Crab's Eye plant, contain one of the most lethal known botanical toxins called Abrin, which is related to Ricin. The main form of propagation is through birds taking the seeds and discarding them because they are unable to break through the hard shell. The effects of the toxin contained in the seeds are nausea, vomiting, convulsions, liver failure and death. Animals that eat the seeds eventually expel them after the toxin has taken effect, thus satisfying the goal of seed distribution. The death of an animal also provides nutrients for the seeds during decomposition.

The relationship between plants and animals in the examples cited above shows that the system between them is one of attraction and repulsion or an infinite number of combinations between these opposites. Plants use deception, subterfuge, trickery, poison, inflict pain on one hand, and beauty, aroma, food, nectar and fruits on the other. When Nietzsche used

---

[517] FLEMING, Theodore H., Sonoran desert columnar cacti and the evolution of generalized pollination systems. In: Ecological Monographs.
[518] https://en.wikipedia.org/wiki/Abrus_precatorius

the term 'Will to Power' as an aspect of survival, he was not thinking of plants, but the idea applies to both flora and fauna, as Schopenhauer states:

> The more and the less have application only to the phenomenon of will, that is, its visibility, its objectification. Of this there is a higher grade in the plant than in the stone; in the animal a higher grade than in the plant: indeed, the passage of will into visibility, its objectification, has grades as innumerable as exist between the dimmest twilight and the brightest sunshine, the loudest sound and the faintest echo. [519]

e. Relationship to Humans

The relationship between plants and humans is similar to plants and animals. The difference, however, is one of knowledge and awareness of their role in our lives. Whereas an animal will taste a plant and spit it out if not appealing, humans can categorise, codify, cultivate, transform and manipulate plants for their own benefit. Not only have humans learned to propagate outside of the natural plant system, they know how to grow plants in natural and artificial environments, how to fertilise them with specific nutrients, create hybrids and manipulate their DNA. To this extent, humans believe we are the masters over flora, but in reality, we have only scratched the surface in understanding the unity involved in their existence. The timing of crop harvest has more to do with the time of planting, the plants rate of growth and adaptability to climatic patterns. Growing plants require much attention to soil conditions, nutrients, sunlight, water and so on. In that respect, cultivating plants for food or other purposes make us aware of how the plant relates to the climate and earth, and in turn, how we relate to them.

Plants are integral in our lives and the separation is difficult to discern. They surround us on all sides in natural and landscaped environments, in our built environment, as furniture, paper/cardboard, appliances, textiles, construction materials, and so on. We use plants for fuel, directly and indirectly, using coal or oil, which is decayed plant material with stored solar energy. From these, we generate electricity and produce a myriad of plastics. We use them for medicines and poisons, making them both beneficial and harmful.

We also have a critical relationship with plants, in that they provide the oxygen we need for life. In turn, we provide the carbon dioxide they need for their life. Although this symbiotic relationship is a fact, the effects of

---

[519] SCHOPENHAUER, Arthur, The World as Will and Idea, Edited by David Berman, Translated by Jill Berman, Everyman 1997, Book Two, page 59

CO_2 are far more complex than is obvious. Studies by Stanford University show that an increase in CO_2 in an enclosed environment does indeed increase the growth rate by a third, if the temperature, soil nitrogen and moisture remain unchanged. If they are increased, the result is different.

> But results from the third year of the experiment revealed a more complex scenario. While treatments involving increased temperature, nitrogen deposition or precipitation -- alone or in combination -- promoted plant growth, the addition of elevated CO2 consistently dampened those increases.[520]

This experiment raises more questions about environmental influences on plants. Some plants prefer higher temperatures, precipitation and CO_2 levels, but there is no mention of what types of plants used in the experiment. Plants are wholly integrated to their environment, and changing that environment is more likely to affect the plants adversely than beneficially. The fact that a CO_2 increase causes an increase in growth shows that the relationship between plant and human activity has a natural balance and unity. There can be a swing from one side to the other in favour of human activity for example, but we have an innate knowledge that both plants and humans are part of the same system, which finds its own balance over time.

---

[520] https://news.stanford.edu/pr/02/jasperplots124.html

8. ANIMALS

a. Relation to Physical Environment

One of the biggest differences between plants and animals is mobility. This makes animals less dependent on stationary environmental influences and more on their ability to seek positive environmental conditions, including food sources. The mobility of animals takes on many forms and includes flying, running, climbing, crawling, slithering, and burrowing, to name only a few. It makes animals less dependent on an immediate location, and gives them the ability to seek new compatible environments to ensure their survival.

This survival ensures different ways of adaptation, and results in the many and varied species of animals we have today. Adaptation takes on many forms, depending on the method of mobility. For example, birds have developed in a unique way to enhance their mobility with the development of wings, weight reduction and flexible bones, keen eyesight for spotting prey, and the ability to escape land-based animals. Birds are most vulnerable to prey when on or near the ground during nesting and raising their young.

All animals are categorised into carnivores, herbivores, omnivores and parasites, and inhabit all areas of earth, including the oceans as well as hostile environments, such as frozen tundras, ice shelves, deserts, hot and dry savannahs and the deepest ocean trenches. All are contained within the biosphere and to our knowledge; humans are the only species to have travelled beyond that sphere.[521] All species of animals have unique forms of adaption to the environment. These vary from food type (plants, other animals or both), blood type and temperature, to the growth of hair and fur, claws and other weapons. The environment the animal inhabits influences all of these adaptations.

Some species of animals and plants have developed highly specialised forms of weaponry for self-defence and obtaining food. These include: stingers, fangs, teeth, harpoons, horns and all kinds of poisons. In this respect, the evolution of animals has much in common with plants. In addition, some animals have developed greater strength, speed or agility to avoid predators or obtain food. The larger animals, such as the extinct Paraceratherium, which was part of genus of hornless rhinoceros, weighed 15 to 20 tonnes. This species was herbivorous and lived 34 to 23 million years ago. Other large land-based animals, such as rhinoceros

---

[521] The first creatures in space were indeed animals but they were sent on our behalf.

and elephants are also herbivores. It is interesting that the largest and slowest animals are herbivores, which indicates that speed and agility are dependent on size. Carnivores depend on hunting ability, whereas herbivores graze slowly and methodically, and their sheer size protects them from predators.

Other methods of survival include the selection of time of day for hunting. Nocturnal animals have a distinct advantage over diurnal animals with adapted vision to suit those conditions. Sense of smell also has advantages over the visual sense in low light levels. Hiding in trees or burrows is another method of survival used by smaller animals. Camouflage is particularly prevalent amongst marine animals and some lizards. The excretion of fluids such as inks or spitting venom to blind prey also play a role in defence and hunting.

All of the above adaptations have at their base the 'will to survive'[522]. The evolutionists regard these adaptations as incremental changes that work over large time spans, and those that survived thrived, whereas those that did not adapt, perished. This does not explain how the adaptive change occurred. We can argue that certain environmental conditions were present that necessitated a change, but changes like the above adaptations take time, and the change would have been very small to begin with. Again, it does not explain how the change occurred. For example, if we trace the history of venom production, it began as saliva and changed to what we now know as venom. The current theory is that the saliva changed its molecular structure just once, approximately 170 million years ago, and diversified into the wide range of venoms we see today[523]. This does not explain how venom was developed by many species of snake, and other species such as spiders, scorpions etc. At some stage in their evolution, there was a decision[524] made to develop venom over other forms of defence or weaponry. Obviously, it was not a conscious decision, as we know it, but a change in DNA that not only developed and evolved the venom, but also carried it through the species to their offspring.

---

[522] I use the term 'will' used by Schopenhauer for a greater force that co-ordinates the organism.
[523] FRY, B.G.; CASEWELL, N.R.; WUSTER, W.; VIDAL, N.; YOUNG, B.; JACKSON, T. N. W. (2012). "The structural and functional diversification of the Toxicofera reptile venom system". Toxicon. 60 (4): 434–448.
[524] I say 'decision' because at some stage a change was made that was positive for the species.

b. Genome Coding

Animals and plants alike have all their adaptive information contained within their DNA. This includes not only their form and characteristics, but also their behaviour. As we shall see in the next chapter, DNA also gives the animal the ability for complex actions and relationship to their environment. This information passes through cells from the sexual union of the parents. It is this union of opposites that is almost universal in the animal world. DNA also contains the information for how animals propagate. The 'will to survive' is the primary motivating force for action and the secondary force to action, the propagation of the species and its ongoing responsibilities.

The instinct for survival is a complex arrangement of recurring hunger-pain and satisfaction, which includes hunting or trapping abilities in carnivores and locating vegetation in herbivores, or a combination of both. The hallmark of this instinct is its overwhelming ability to dominate the animal until satisfied. Indeed, the need for food takes up most of the time in an animal's life. This instinct also motivates humans through the energy it provides for action. Survival includes the ability to be stronger or smarter to avoid capture by another species and trying to satisfy the instinct. The balance between predator and prey keeps evolution moving and uses emotions and its associated energy, as the tools to action. These include fear, greed, happiness, anger, etc. Some species have multiple offspring so that there is more chance of survival, making it a matter of numbers as a form of adaptation. In other words, adaptation counts on a proportion of offspring to perish. This fundamental law of nature shows how life depends on certain determinants for survival and growth.

The primary instinct is survival of the individual, the secondary instinct, the propagation and survival of the species. Individual creatures feel hunger although they can communicate hunger to others through screaming, chirping or crying. Similar to the instinct for survival is the instinct to propagate, which compels animals to seek a member of the opposite sex to satisfy its need. This instinct for survival is an arrangement of nature that does not require consciousness as we know it, as animals are little aware of why they are compelled to behave as they do. In this respect, they are very obedient to the forces that come from inside, and have little chance to deviate from their urges. This is all coded in life's DNA.

The genetic material that resides in living organisms is a major constituent of the chromosomes within the cell nucleus and controls protein synthesis in cells. DNA is a nucleic acid of two chains of nucleotides with the sugar deoxyribose and bases of adenine $C_5H_5N_5$, cytosine $C_4H_5N_3O$, guanine $C_5H_5N_5O$ and thymine $C_5H_6N_2O_2$. The two chains wound together in a spiral with cross hydrogen bonds between complimentary bases to form the typical spiral ladder shaped molecule. Cell division occurs during growth with the corresponding replication of the DNA molecule. The molecule breaks at the hydrogen bonds between the strands; they unwind through the nucleotides present in the nucleus and create a complimentary strand initiated, controlled and stopped by polymerase enzymes.[525]

DNA is the plan that tells the organic chemistry in the organism how, what and where to build cells, how to co-ordinate all the vital processes of the organism and the information the organism uses to adapt to the environment. In fact, everything the organism is, and is meant to be, is stored in the new DNA received from the parent DNA(s). It is a relatively large, robust molecule, and stores the information in a quaternary code of four proteins. This is more advanced compared to our modern computers with a binary code made of two digits with on/off or magnetised or non-magnetised coding. It is interesting to note that the form of the DNA molecule has two halves entwining each other in a spiral connected with hydrogen bonds. The pair of connected opposites thus creates an energy system from one side to the other, much the same as the force of attraction and repulsion in atoms. Reproduction halves this system and duplicates it to form a new pair of connected opposites.

c. Spirit- Innate and Learned Knowledge

Animals display many of the functions that humans display. These include emotions like fear, jealousy and love, as well as the main instincts of power to survive and urge to propagate. As we have discussed previously, emotions and instincts have inner characters that give us ideas. It follows that animals also have ideas of things in the physical world. The previous example of the snake in the wild and the idea presenting itself to our mind upon perception, shows that our behaviour is dependent on the level of differentiation of the idea of the snake. Animals also display this behaviour, whether it is learned or innate is irrelevant to the system itself. Some animals sense predators and know that they must flee for their lives. This can only occur if the animal has the idea of the predator already in their mind. Sensing the predator activates the idea, which gives the animal the necessary information to act accordingly. Animals also display tender emotions such as love and kindness. Cold-blooded animals such as crocodiles display kindness; caring and

---

[525] https://www.biology-online.org

nurturing in the way mothers gently take their young in their mouth to transport them to other locations.

As we have shown with plants, flexibility is required to adapt to changeable environmental conditions. For example, the pinecone has adapted to fires called Fire-mediated Serotiny to propagate its seeds.

> Fire is the mechanism by which the forest is continually regenerated," states Hall. Fires consume dead, decaying vegetation accumulating on the forest floor, thereby clearing the way for new growth. Some species, such as the jack pine, even rely on fire to spread their seeds. The jack pine produces "seratonous" (resin-filled) cones that are very durable. The cones remain dormant until a fire occurs and melts the resin. Then the cones pop open and the seeds fall or blow out.[526]

This shows how regular but random events such as fire can influence an organism and activate adaptive modes of behaviour. It is a learning ability par excellence[527], and gives the organism the best chance for survival. We can observe this system of flexibility and adaptation in animals as well. For example, nocturnal vision would have evolved from a learned behaviour of an animal limited to hunting or foraging at low light levels because of predators. This gave them an advantage over predators that hunted during high light levels. Other examples include the development of bio echo in bats, dolphins and whales, which gives them an advantage over sight. The development of the olfactory sense also gave some animals advantages over others.

Other learned behaviour includes methods of attracting mates for propagation. The male Bowerbird has very elaborate rituals and building abilities to attract females. They build archways called 'bowers' out of twigs, grass and any other readily available material. They decorate the arch with brightly coloured objects and spend a great amount of time arranging them into communicative patterns. There is a theory that the brightly coloured objects have replaced the Bowerbirds own plumage over time.

> Ernest Thomas suggested the transfer effect, in which he claimed that there is an inverse relationship between bower complexity and the brightness of plumage. Gilliard suggests that there is an evolutionary "transfer" of ornamentation in some species, from their plumage to their

---

[526] https://earthobservatory.nasa.gov/Features/BOREASFire/
[527] When I say learned behaviour, I do not limit it to an individual animal life, but behaviour, skills or unique abilities gradually learned or developed over time and transferred to offspring through DNA. In other words, evolution.

bowers, in order to reduce the visibility of the male and thereby its vulnerability to predation.[528]

This shows how the problems of adaptation to the environment influence the myriad of solutions that we can see in the animal world today. It is problem solving at its best, and its permutation is as varied as the species themselves. It also relates to human evolution and our transition from fur to bare skin with the use of fire, shade and shelter. Indeed, there are numerous animal builders that defy our understanding of how they know what, and how to build.

d. The Builders

Containers such as dwellings, burrows, mounds, hives, shells etc., have their origins in nature for the purpose of protection, incubation and storage of nutrients. The idea of containment stems from the reproduction of a species and their method of incubation. In humans, the original container is the maternal womb, as it is with other mammals, which is containment within the mother's body. As we saw with the study of Alchemy, the maternal womb is a suitable metaphor for the unconscious, which compliments the physical realm. Birds, reptiles, fish etc., incubate their young in an egg inside the mother's body, which continues outside when the egg expelled. Marsupials have a built in container in the form of a pouch to protect and nurture their young. This original form of containment expresses the idea in various forms as an egg, womb, nest, cocoon, pouch and so on.

Mammals retain the egg within the mother's body, which is fertilised from an external source[529]. The egg then becomes the zygote and divides through mitosis to form the embryo and new life. This method of reproduction makes the offspring very dependent on their mother, and in most instances, their father. Offspring born in this way need nurturing by their parents for longer periods than other species, before they can stand alone without parental support. The idea of containment, safety and nurturing then expands to the parental burrow, territory or area, depending on the type of mammal. For humans, the parental home becomes the container for the family and nurturing of the young. For the most part, we have lost the ability to survive without this imitative form of containment since we shed our fur and gained the ability to regulate our own body temperature through clothing and buildings.

---

[528] GILLIARD, Ernest Thomas (July 1956). "Bower ornamentation versus plumage characters in bower-birds". Auk. 73 (3): 450–451
[529] There are anomalies to this category, for example Monotremes like the Platypus and Echidna are classed as egg laying mammals.

Birds give birth to their young via eggs outside of the mother's body, then nurture the eggs and hatchlings until they learn to fly and feed themselves. Most birds build a nest for their eggs to incubate and hatch, with some exceptions. The Masked Lapwing, commonly known as the Plover, lay their eggs on open ground and defend them by distraction and swooping predators. Reptiles, for the most part, also lay eggs but generally leave them to hatch and fend for themselves. Some species, like the crocodile, will nurture their offspring beyond hatching so that they get the best chance for survival. They deposit their eggs on or in the ground, which helps temperature regulation and protection from predators. Sea turtles have developed very hard shells for protection and temperature regulation and are classed as reptiles, as they lay their eggs in shallow holes on or near the beach, from which the hatchlings emerge and proceed to the ocean.

Insects and spiders also lay eggs, and are among the most complex builders of protective containers. They have very unusual mating practices where the male is somewhat dispensable after union. The most elaborate structures made by insects include the hives of bees, varieties of termite mounds and complex underground networks of ants. This type of building or burrowing throws doubt on the idea of containment as learned behaviour and indicates an innate stored knowledge reproduced in each member of the colony.

Marine creatures also display elaborate ideas of containment. These include very complex arrangements of protective outer layers of seashells to the hard outer layer of crustaceans, typical of invertebrates. Outer shells are part of the bodies of the invertebrates and form an outer layer to protect against predators. The shells are secreted from the cells of the invertebrate and made from a protein matrix of calcium carbonate. The proteins bind calcium ions while guiding and directing calcification. It is unclear how they fabricate the intricate shapes and patterns of the shells, although it does show a knowledge that is innate to the invertebrate. Building an outer layer such as a shell, egg, hive, etc., is a biological activity that stems from an inner knowledge passed down from parent to offspring through DNA.

Bees are imprinted with knowledge to build complex arrangements of hexagonal prismatic cells made from beeswax. The cells used to deposit honey and pollen, and raise and feed their young. The pollen and honey they harvest from nearby plants which they pollinate as they collect the nectar. The close and symbiotic relationship between insect and plant has benefited both for millions of years.

Another insect that builds elaborate structures is the mound-building termite that lives in Africa, Australia and South America. These mounds are unique and address many architectural problems. These include ventilation, drainage and temperature regulation. The mounds are made from the surrounding soil and glued together with termite saliva and have elaborate tunnels, shafts and chambers designed for specific purposes. The termites also perceive the path of the sun as they build the mounds in long narrow north-south configurations that minimise heat gain and loss. They also design and build the lower cellar-like chambers and tunnels with arched openings to alleviate the damage caused by rain and flooding[530].

Rabbits are small mammals found in several parts of the world that create their homes for protection and temperature regulation by digging burrows in the ground. Being herbivores and predominately nocturnal, they graze on the surface and scurry back to their burrows if threatened. Their burrows are often deep holes with several chambers and more than one entrance. As they have few defences against predators, they use their burrows to escape from external threats.

Beavers, on the other hand, are large primarily nocturnal semi aquatic rodents that build dams, canals and lodges. They use mud, rocks, trees, branches and logs to dam streams for protection against predators such as coyotes, wolves and bears and to trap fish for a ready supply of food. Typically, beaver lodges have two chambers and underwater entrances, thus making them very secure from predators. The building ability of the beaver brings the two main instincts together in one location. Firstly, they dam the stream creating a pond to ensure a steady food supply, especially in winter, and then build their homes in or near the pond created by the dam. This ensures that the home is protected from the freezing temperatures outside and secure from predators. The intelligence of this system of food gathering and protection is as advanced as our ability to cultivate crops, raise livestock and build homes to protect us from the elements and intruders.

e. Animals in the wild and humans

The main characteristic of wild animals is the difficulty in taming their behaviour and is particularly problematic with dangerous animals. Most wild animals are innocuous to humans but many have superior strength or natural weapons such as poisons, teeth, claws, horns and so on. This makes us very vulnerable to predation by these creatures. Early humans would have lived with this danger in its purest sense. They had no

---

[530] HARRIS W. V., Termite Mound Building, London S. W. 7

defences against the larger predators such as lions, elephants, hippos etc., and it was only the problem-solving ability and creation of weapons from sticks and stones, that gave them the upper hand. This, coupled with the ability to protect themselves with fire and dwellings, gave humans the advantage over most other animals.

In addition to tools, weapons, fire and buildings for protection, it was knowledge of the predator's behaviour that gave early humans the first mental advantage. To know a species' behaviour is the best way to avoid danger as it gives the ability to modify one's own behaviour for the sake of survival. Using the snake example sited previously, knowledge of type and threat level, gives us the best chance to avoid harm. An undifferentiated idea of snakes and regard all as dangerous is better than no knowledge of snakes at all. In this way, we have a healthy fear of what may harm us without the need to develop our knowledge further. Small children learn from an early age that lions are dangerous creatures in the wild and avoid direct contact. We also learn to admire the lion's strength and hunting ability and put them in a regal position in our minds, even though they are very efficient killers. Perhaps this is why we admire them because they connect us to our own killer instinct, which is another aspect of the idea of the lion.

We accept the behaviour of a lion and regard it as the lion's nature based on its instinct, which is virtually impossible to tame. We too, have this foundation, and make great effort to understand and tame it with various belief systems as detailed in the previous chapters. Wild animals cannot behave outside of their instinctive foundation; humans try with their systems and we are making progress, as our evolution shows. It is a very slow process however, as indicated by the need for physical force used by national armies and law enforcement. The use of physical force is still however, the law of the jungle and part of our instinctive foundation.

Aside from the plains of Africa, wild animals surround us in our suburban homes on all sides. Birds, reptiles, rodents, insects, spiders etc., have the same habitat as we do and predate our occupation by many years. Most are innocuous, although many are irritating and potentially dangerous. For example, mosquitoes are found in many parts of the world, and aside from their annoying bites, can carry debilitating diseases. An example of a particularly dangerous species is the Australian Funnel Web spider, one of the most venomous spiders in the world. They are found on suburban lots and live in cocooned burrows underground or under logs and other objects. They have large fangs that penetrate the skin to deliver toxic venom that can result in death if not treated.

Ideas are universal in the animal world as they are in humans. They convey information to the subject of potential predators, and suitable action to avoid those predators. Every animal has a corresponding idea and its level of differentiation determines how we behave towards that animal. The lion is simple, in that we know we should avoid its territory and protect ourselves from their nature. Similarly, an undifferentiated idea of a snake that includes fear, danger and potential harm is better than no idea at all.[531] It is clear that we can differentiate an idea through knowledge and experience of snakes in general, thus modifying our behaviour accordingly. It is less clear if we are born with the idea or learned it from our parents and teachers. It is plausible however, that the idea is pre-existing due to our saurian origins and our own vertebrae, which has similarities to the snake.

f. Captive Wild/Domesticated Animals and Humans

Captive wild animals are those that are predominately untamed and kept in captivity for our amusement, entertainment or as a resource. These include wild animals kept in zoos, aquariums and circuses for our entertainment and breeding for their meat and hide such as crocodile farms. These days, hunting wild mammals is more of a sport than food, although this occurs as well. Wild pets are less common and generally limited to smaller rodents, reptiles, fish and birds, as they require specialised captivity and feeding.

Domesticated animals are those that either pose no or little threat to our well-being or have some benefit for our needs. The first group is the domesticated animals bred for our consumption or other resources such as wool, leather or other products. These include cows, pigs, chickens, sheep, ducks and so on. They are kept controlled and generally in captivity until they are deemed ready for slaughter, consumption or harvesting. The second group are domesticated animals for our entertainment including horse and dog racing, rodeo riding, and so on. The third group is domesticated pets that are tame and no threat to humans and include dogs, cats, birds, mice, guinea pigs, rabbits etc.

The captive wild animals and domesticated animals bred for consumption or other resource is a relationship based on human exploitation. The animals have no choice or say in the relationship, and we hold them captive and control their lives until we need them. Humans are by nature, omnivores and have an evolved brain and ability to create weapons and tools and therefore the superior species in the food chain. The ability to

---

[531] The only way an individual would have no idea of a snake is having no experience, seen a picture or told about one.

control and exploit so many other species is the reason we have thrived to the extent we have on earth.[532]

The third group of animals that we use for our own pleasure are the common domesticated animals. This relationship is less exploitative and more symbiotic, as we feel closer to our pets than we do the animals we eat. We name them and make them part of our home and family. Obviously, it is easier to relate to mammals than reptiles, birds or fish, although there are instances where these species recognise and interact with their owners in an almost mammalian way.

The relationship we have with a typical house pet is one of attraction with feeling and love. We select them because they encourage feeling similar to a relationship with small babies and toddlers. Dogs are cute and adorable when young seldom argue with us, like being stroked and are good company and full of feeling. They need us for food and give their attention and obedience. They love to play and take us on walks, which is beneficial to both pet and owner. Cats are less needy than dogs, more sensual and love being caressed and patted. Some say that cats are more arrogant than dogs, but they simply seem less needy and more self-contained. Humans even categorise themselves as dog or cat people which may be the difference between feeling and sensuality in that dogs enjoy their owners company and cats are happy to be on their own but love being stroked.[533]

Pets such as dogs and cats provide affection and companionship that may not be available from other humans. Dogs are termed 'man's best friend' for that reason and the relationship based on the softer side of human nature. In other words, it is a feeling that we have for our pets that gives us the opportunity to express love to an all-accepting animal. It is a relationship to our softer instinctuality for love, devotion, loyalty and care. Dogs also provide protection and used as guards and hunting companions. These dogs have enough of their untamed instinctuality to be vicious to intruders and friendly to their owners. Seeing-eye dogs used to aid blind people and sniffer dogs used for their extraordinary sense of smell. In Greek mythology, dogs were associated with Hecate and were sacred animals to Artemis and Ares and when Zeus was a baby, a dog known as the "golden hound" protected the future King[534].

---

[532] I make no value judgement on whether this position in the food chain is right or wrong, it simply is and has to be if we are to survive as we have.
[533] This is naturally a generalisation as different species behave in different ways.
[534] http://www.sheppardsoftware.com/content/animals/animals/breeds/dogtopics/dog_mythol ogy

The sensuality of cats is reflected in their fur, which is softer than most dogs and they spend a great deal of time grooming and cleaning themselves. They are by nature carnivorous and have strong flexible bodies, quick reflexes and sharp retractable claws designed for killing small prey. Cats also hear and smell better than humans and have very good eyesight, particularly in low light levels. Ancient Egypt venerated and domesticated cats, although evidence suggests that domestication occurred as early as 7,500 BC in Cyprus. [535]

Domesticated pets connect us to our own physical instinctive foundation for love or an aid for activity or protection. Unlike humans, they cannot talk and communicate through their behaviour, body language and sounds. The softer pets provide companionship and a creature to take care of and do not argue with their owners. Pets are particularly suited to sensitive people who do not interact with other people well. They project their feeling onto the pet with the knowledge that it will be accepted and reciprocated.

---

[535] VIGNE JD, GUILAINE J, DEBUE K, HAYE L, GÉRARD P (April 2004). "Early taming of the cat in Cyprus". Science.

9. HUMAN NATURE- UNITY THROUGH PROJECTION

a. Definition

The main function of projection is the connection of the object[536] to its corresponding idea in the unconscious and brings the subject and object into an initial attraction with potential future relationship[537]. Our previous study of Animism shows the projection forming aspect of our nature in its purest form. To project something of ourselves onto an object connects us to that object and helps us feel that we know something about it, as well as how to behave in its presence. The idea of an object is an innate arrangement of nature that help us understand the physical world and its attractive and repulsive forces.

As Kant points out, the idea of an object is 'a priori' arrangement that we have in common and share with other species. For example, seeing an object we do not recognise brings forth ideas from memories that are similar to the object. This is the natural function of association and connects us to the unknown object. It is the way the unconscious expresses itself through symbol and co-ordinates our behaviour towards the object. It includes the law of attraction and repulsion coupled with suitable action. This system is demonstrated in animals as they behave according to their idea of an object. They are either attracted if the idea gives them confidence, or repelled if the idea gives them fear.

Projection of ideas onto other people is more complicated. For example, children generally experience their parents as nurturers, carers, guides, someone older and a parental authority. This shapes their idea of a parent which take it into adulthood and project onto mentors, schoolteachers, policeman, political figures, religious leaders and so on. Hierarchies are built on projection of inner authority characters onto people in the structure.

Projection of an idea onto an object, as mentioned previously, is the beginning of relationship to the object. Attraction to the object encourages investigation to learn more about its nature and knowledge transforms the projection to match the object. The psychologists regard this as 'withdrawing the projection', but in reality it is adding to the original idea

---

[536] I use the term 'object' in its philosophical sense of anything including people outside of the subject's psyche.
[537] I use the term connection rather than relationship to emphasise the beginning stage of relationship. Relationship requires some objectivity and transformation of the initial idea.

with new information, and discarding irrelevant information that does not relate to the object.

The initial idea of an object is based on its appearance and behaviour as shown in the previous study of ancient Egyptian and Greek mythology. For example, the idea of the sun originated from its appearance, light and heat giving qualities as well as its predictable behaviour, which has not changed over millions of years. Individuals projected masculine or feminine characters due to this behaviour and related to the sun as if it were a personality. Our contemporary knowledge of the sun is quite different to the original idea, but part of the idea is still intact and based on its appearance and behaviour. The mythological aspect of the idea since replaced with what we now know, but the object has not changed, only our idea of it has, which is now closer to the objects true nature.

The example of the snake previously discussed, shows how our behaviour is dependent on the idea we have of the object. If the idea is rudimentary, in other words, we lump all snakes together as dangerous, we fear them all and stay away from them. On the other hand, if our idea of a snake differentiated and we know what species, type, threat level, toxicity etc., our idea has changed to a closer approximation of the reality of the snake. With a differentiated idea, we know that the snake is so and so, and our behaviour modified accordingly.

This natural functioning applies to the whole world, including other people. Romantic relationships have extreme forms of projection and its purpose is the propagation of the species. Without projection and its associated energy, there is no attraction between the sexes and no forces bringing the opposites into union. At most, we could hope for a long lasting friendship. Thankfully, nature has endowed us with the necessary functioning to make opposites attract to such an extent that we will do many things to achieve the union.

Another example of behaviour caused by projection, is stealing by an individual[538]. It satisfies us not to steal because it is against the law even though we may covert the object. The urge to steal is however, a natural part of our survival instinct. Stealing means that the individual believes he needs the object he is stealing. The reason for stealing may depend on the individual's circumstances and range from the satisfaction of the nutritive instinct to the accumulation of wealth. The instinct is the same and stems from a need to satisfy hunger or feeling of insecurity. The urge is to unite idea with object and take possession of both. We can see this

---

[538] I do not in any way condone stealing, but wish to convey to the reader the human functioning involved.

behaviour in small children when one takes something from another. They want it because they are attracted and fascinated with the potential of the object. When the urge to possess an object by an adult is stronger than the prevailing laws, we call it stealing and punish it for breaking the moral code. Humans project their idea onto an object and have an innate urge to unite the idea and object.

Stealing is not limited to objects either, as it is quite common to steal ideas. This brings stealing into the psychic realm, which is less obvious as it lacks a physical object. We can however not steal an idea unless it is expressed by the individual verbally, in writing, drawings or actual object of the idea, like an invention. Different people in different places often perceive ideas as the expression of the unconscious. For example, the early Hebrews and Australian Aborigines discovered the idea of circumcision independently with no connection between the peoples. They are collective ideas and like myths, are innate to all humanity.

Stealing is also a function of energy movement within the unity of our personality. Creative work requires us to look inside and steal the energy and ideas for transformation into something that other people can enjoy or use. In mythological terms, Prometheus stole fire from the gods to create humanity. Indeed fire (energy) is what sets us apart from the matter of our bodies and animates us as living creatures. In addition, certain illnesses such as depression, is the unconscious stealing energy from consciousness and the body, particularly when one has neglected one's inner realm for too long. Ideas can also try and steal energy from other ideas. For example, if we belong to a group ideal, we fight with the opposing ideal for energy and try and diminish their influence. This is particularly evident in political parties that adopt opposite stances.

Ideas of objects are psychic contents and easily attached to other ideas in the psyche. For example, we can have an idea of an object like the moon and because of its behaviour, associate it with the idea of femininity. This is due to its appearance and function of reflecting to the sun's light and its monthly cycle of waxing and waning. It is also visible during the day on occasion, which adds another aspect to its idea. Landing on the moon further enhanced our idea as we could explore its true nature. This is the ultimate expression and motivation of uniting idea with object and is so powerful that we exert much energy and expense to achieve their union.

b. The Animal Within

To understand how unity is maintained through projection, I shall discuss our instinctual foundation and its taming for the sake of adaptation. The two main motivating forces are the nutritive and sexual instincts[539]. The nutritive instinct is based on survival of the individual, whereas the sexual instinct based propagation of the species and love in general. The nutritive instinct is the basis of much of our power culture and concerned with our physical well-being in contrast to our mental faculties. The instinct is overwhelmingly strong and its satisfaction the driving force behind our will to action. Its satisfaction is a main concern of every living thing and the symptoms of the force could be classed as an addiction, if it were not a natural part of our functioning.

In the hierarchy of instincts, the nutritive instinct is a matter of life or death of the individual in an immediate sense, whereas the instinct to propagate, the life or death of the species. In that respect, the urgency of the nutritive over propagating instinct is self-evident. The nutritive instinct, when taken to its extreme, becomes what Nietzsche termed the 'Will to Power'. This need to dominate and control one's environment shows itself in extreme forms of psychopathology when it becomes the dominating goal in life at the expense of all other functions. In other words, it is possession by an inner character of authority. The function is evident in babies at their beginning stage of development. They cry because that is the only way they can control their environment and alleviate the hunger pains or other associated needs.

Parents, schools and others train our children to transform their instincts into socially acceptable forms for the sake of adaptation to the wider world. This is a natural occurrence, and makes the transition from child to teen as smooth as possible. The training involves tempering or suppressing our natural instincts. Physical conflict changes to negotiation, tantrums to debate, stealing changes to earning money and buying what we want. It is a transfer of physical to mental activity, in that our intellect and feeling put in charge of our instinct, and emotional energy transformed to less destructive practices. The transition from one state to the next often ritualised to give it a special place in the community.

Circumcision for young boys is an example of this form of ritualistic transformation. Australia has only recently stopped the practice as it had lost its ritualistic meaning and became a matter of hygiene. The history of circumcision is vast and varied. Studies have shown that it is the oldest form of planned surgery, had its origins in Sudan and Ethiopia, and practiced in Egypt and the Middle East. Its origins are disputed, as the Australian Aborigines practiced circumcision independently from Africa and the Middle East. This shows that circumcision is an innate idea as

---

[539] We may argue that these are only 2 of many instincts but my main concern is the primary instincts of survival and propagation.

previously mentioned, rather than learned behaviour. The male child in early Aboriginal culture spent their early years with the women of the group, and were free to play and behave instinctually. At puberty, however, the male child had the ritualistic transformation from child to adult through the circumcision ritual and the foreskin removed, thus exposing the penis glans. Symbolically, exposing of the head of the penis helps the boy become aware of the sexual instinct and differentiation of opposites. That is to say, it is the head (consciousness) emerging from the encapsulating womb (unconscious) through the ritualistic removal of the surrounding flesh.

Approximately a year after circumcision in the early Australian Aboriginal culture, the young boy is cut again to bring him into full manhood. The method is somewhat gruesome and termed 'subincision'. The underside of the penis cut forming a cleft into the urethra. The opening, according to Joseph Campbell, is called the "penis womb", and regarded as a symbolic male vagina, thus making the individual more than a man. This unusual practice shows the unconscious compensation of the journey from female realm to male realm and linking back to the female realm through the ritualistic and symbolic vagina.[540] The boy is then reminded of his underlying unity and relationship of male and female.

Our contemporary culture has other ritualistic transformations of child to young adult, such as the Christian Confirmation and Jewish Bat Mitzvah. Other forms include sports, drinking, drug taking, piercing, tattoos, driving motor vehicles, sexual exploits, and so on. We can assume that the rituals encouraged by peers and parents are to make the transition into manhood or womanhood less traumatic and part of the many transitions in life.

As children go through this transition into adulthood, the original projection onto parents and carers, transforms to the wider community with a corresponding broader view of reality. It is where all the 'so-called' childish activities of fantasy, play, imagination etc., are replaced with responsibility, strength, concrete reality etc., in the name of separating from their origins. Our western culture perpetuates this viewpoint throughout life as if it were a linear process. As the Aboriginals recognised, life is not only a flowing to the future, but a linking back to the past. In other words, the things that connect us to our unity are the things left behind for adaptation to the prevailing cultural hierarchy.

---

[540] CAMPBELL, Joseph, The Hero with a Thousand Faces, Princeton University Press, pages 154 & 155

Hierarchies are the structure of western culture and the container for its power. Structures such as the armed services base their hierarchy on rank and enforcement through orders. It has strict behavioural training for the sake of defence or offence, depending on the circumstances. Young men and women train to serve their officers without question and become tools in the hands of the government. All individuality suppressed for the sake of order and smooth operation. The killer instinct is encouraged and let loose when required, yet restricted within the group. It is the ultimate form of training the animal within. It is not a spiritual pursuit, but a tough restriction of liberty through a rigid set of rules and regulations. The lower ranks project authority onto the higher ups and the higher ups project inferiority onto the lower ranks.

Another example of projection is the symbiotic relationship between master and slave. The master has the power and control, but they hand over to the slave those aspects that they deem beneath them. All the menial tasks delegated to the slave, which in turn make the master the slave to those tasks he does not wish to carry out. Instead of independence, we have an interchange of functions. The master is dependent on the slave for some of their life's activities. Similarly, the slave is dependent on the master for their life and well being. This is the nature of projection. What we do not wish to do ourselves and hand over to another makes us dependent on that other person with a subsequent loss of independence. The master then becomes the slave to the slave.

Similarly, our elected officials make laws for the population, which are in many cases based on an instinctive reaction, rather than a thought through process. Laws tend to become so restrictive and broad in their scope that it is inevitable that we break them at some time or other. They are however, a consequence of civilisation, yet the more restrictive the laws, the more we yearn to break free from them. This is particularly true when the laws intrude into our human nature as an invisible cage that keeps us contained. Our western culture is wise enough not to put too many restrictions on our sexual instinct, as it becomes almost impossible to control. For example, there are no laws against adultery or consensual adult sex outside of marriage. It is tolerated and accepted as human nature and not part of the penal code.

The problem with our contemporary western viewpoint is the identification with all that is good and projection of evil onto others. Theft for example, is an inclination based on need and we are all capable of it under certain circumstances. When we project thief onto another person, we are robbing ourselves of the opportunity to integrate that aspect into our unity. It is not necessary to be the robber and live it out, but to understand it as an inclination and part of our own nature. Projection is a natural function but makes us dependent on other people to carry out those instincts we ourselves do not wish to acknowledge. Not being conscious of an instinct makes it impossible to understand and where it belongs in our unity.

The western penal code is a prime example of order through projection. We have strict laws against murder, as we should, but compared to the atrocities we perpetrate in the name of freedom and democracy, or some other reason, the lack of inner knowledge is self-evident. We send our young men and women to far-off lands to fight an enemy that exists in our minds. For example, the invasion of Afghanistan and Iraq in recent times was based on false ideas and our fears and suspicions influenced our actions. We imagined a whole group of people were evil and responsible for atrocities perpetrated by a handful of individuals, and committed what can only be called, genocide.

In addition, it is to ignore the theories surrounding the events on 911. There are many questions not answered concerning the collapse of the twin towers and building 7, which was not struck by an aircraft and housed a number of government departments. If our suspicions are true, we have to ask what motivating forces are behind the felling of multi-storey buildings? It made the population angry, which was used to mask the pre-planned attack on Middle Eastern countries[541].

The natural reaction of outrage to this event was used as a pretext to invasion to topple the prevailing order. It may not have been in accordance with western ideas of freedom, liberty and democracy, but it was a functioning order. The removal of that order left a growing threat of chaos and murder on a scale not seen in the world since the great wars. In addition, our western instinct for resources and control is working on several fronts at once. Not only have we created upheaval in the Middle East and northern Africa, we are now challenging Russia and China as the biggest obstacles to this instinct for world domination.

The insecurity of the western elite, particularly in the US, is so deep that human life is of less consequence than the need to overcome anxiety by controlling an imaginary enemy. This is a consequence of developing one side of our nature and repressing or ignoring the other. It is too uncomfortable to acknowledge that part of us is undeveloped and resembles a baby crying for food. We cannot rule out the possibility that nature, as a self-regulating system, is urging us to go down this path of conflict and resource-hoarding in order to balance this one sidedness. There have been experiments conducted in a closed system under

---

[541] See interview with Gen Wesley Clark concerning the plan to invade seven countries in five years. https://www.liveleak.com/view?i=a61_1378358265#wj1odflv7sH0IbPj.01

laboratory conditions to see what happens when a population is restricted.

John B Calhoun carried out an experiment with mice that provided all the necessary ingredients for life such as food, water, air, light etc., in a closed system habitat. The only restriction placed on the experiment was the amount of space available.[542] The results were quite enlightening:

> "expulsion of young before weaning was complete, wounding of young, inability of dominant males to maintain the defense of their territory and females, aggressive behavior of females, passivity of non-dominant males with increased attacks on each other which were not defended against. After day 600, the social breakdown continued and the population declined toward extinction. During this period females ceased to reproduce. Their male counterparts withdrew completely, never engaging in courtship or fighting. They ate, drank, slept, and groomed themselves – all solitary pursuits. Sleek, healthy coats and an absence of scars characterized these males. They were dubbed "the beautiful ones." Breeding never resumed and behavior patterns were permanently changed.

> The conclusions drawn from this experiment were that when all available space is taken and all social roles filled, competition and the stresses experienced by the individuals will result in a total breakdown in complex social behaviors, ultimately resulting in the demise of the population.

> Calhoun saw the fate of the population of mice as a metaphor for the potential fate of man. He characterized the social breakdown as a "second death," with reference to the "second death" mentioned in the Biblical book of Revelation.[543] His study has been cited by writers such as Bill Perkins as a warning of the dangers of the living in an "increasingly crowded and impersonal world."[544]

Calhoun concluded from his experiments that a restriction of space alone was sufficient to adversely affect the population. We may argue that we cannot relate the behaviour of mice to that of humans, for we have evolved beyond our mammalian instincts. Our behaviour as a species demonstrates that we have not evolved beyond our instincts and suffer the same problems as did the mice.

---

[542] CALHOUN, John B. (1962). "Population density and social pathology". *Scientific American*

[543] CALHOUN, John B. (1973). "Death Squared: The Explosive Growth and Demise of a Mouse Population" *Proc. Roy. Soc. Med.* 66: 80–88.

[544] PERKINS, Bill (2004). *Six battles every man must win : and the ancient secrets you'll need to succeed*. Wheaton, Ill.: Tyndale House. p. 10.

The idea of dwindling resources and food urges individuals and nations to action to replenish and hoard those resources. The actual sensation of hunger is painful and associated with the idea of hunger and emotions such as fear. Willpower cannot overcome the need for sustenance, as our body is a self-regulating biological system we share with all living things. Plants orient themselves to get the most sun, water and other nutrients and fight for these resources. Survival and the 'Will to Power' is the action to satisfy hunger. This is the innate instinct that motivates us to do whatever it takes and includes all necessary means to achieve this aim.

This instinct, which has its basis in survival, is what motivates the human and animal alike. This hunger can, however take on many forms, and is not limited to nutrition. It can be hunger for prestige, wealth, political standing, influence, power and so on. All have their basis in the one basic urge, and that is the instinct and idea of survival. This is the basis for much of our motivation to action and supported by the self-regulating, energetic system of our body and mind. The instinct liberates energy from within accompanied by an idea of how to satisfy the instinct.

The distinction between instinct and idea is important, as the idea can have as much influence over an individual's actions as the instinct itself. In fact, research into the psychology of instinct and idea points towards a close relationship. Jung calls the idea in relation to the instinct an 'archetype',[545] which is described by Plato as the Model. Ideas backed by an instinct and its associated emotions can take possession of the individual to the point where they cannot differentiate between inner urge/emotion and idea. This is how the survival instinct and its 'Will to Power' works. This possession can grip individuals and entire groups on a national scale reinforced by an imaginary fear and apprehension of a future threat to survival.

This is the danger when individuals are not critical of what motivates their behaviour. We feel so above our animal ancestors, yet the same motivating forces influence our behaviour. It is this fact that leads all nations to build improved armies, fight for resources and crush opposition forces. This is why the Christian myth is so important at this time for our balance, in that it emphasises Godly love (spirit) over worldly power (matter). It was then, and is now, liberation from that wild animal that possesses us when we are hungry. Jesus and Satan is a necessary pair of opposites in unity. Unfortunately, the west seems possessed by the latter and all the worldly concerns it entails.

---

[545] JUNG C. G., Archetypes of the Collective Unconscious, , Routledge and Kegan Paul 1959

c. Love and Union- Continuation of the Species

Romantic love is one of the strongest forms of projection, yet anyone that has experienced it knows it is fraught with difficulties and misconceptions. With the connection made, we feel swept off our feet and in love, yet over time the behaviour of the other person does not correlate with the inner character projected and is where the trouble begins. We want the other person to behave like the projection so we try to engineer it to fit. If the other person is similar to the projection, there is less friction and the couple is a 'good fit'. In this instance we see an unusual level of unconsciousness, where all that is projected from both sides is accepted, and the couple form a symbiotic connection where he is the husband, she the wife and both have their roles and satisfy each other's needs in that way. This form of connection may appear ideal on the outside, but nature demands that each individual grow to full potential as individuals.

Romantic love is nature's first step in bringing together the opposites in unity. It is a biological imperative, usually experienced in the first half of life. The projection of the contra-sexual[546] inner character, with its associated ideas and emotions is part of that first step. The projection varies according to the individual's personality and experience. It may be a parent, sibling or any person that left a complex imprint on the individual. Once a projection is established and it is mutual, in other words, both individuals accept the projection of the other, we have a love connection. In this instance, a pair of opposites is established which includes four entities. On the one hand, we have the physical couple and their conscious personalities, and on the other the projected inner character of the opposite sex in each individual. This is one of the blessings and curses in relationships. If the projection is a good fit, it goes well, if not, there is much friction and argument, but also an opportunity to see the difference between the individual and projection.

Nature's biological aim is the union of male and female for procreation and raising children. A parent has the opportunity to see how projection functions from the very beginning. A baby lives in a totally immersed and dependent connection to their parents. They are completely helpless yet are born with the instinct to satisfy their own nutritive needs and power to achieve those needs. Babies learn to scream very early in their lives which helps the parent to know when their baby needs feeding or are in discomfort. The unity of baby and parent lies in the fact that children bring out our feelings of love, and this is a counterbalance to the 'Will to Power'

---

[546] I acknowledge the union of same sex couples. For this study I am limiting myself to the traditional coupling of biological male and female individuals.

so prevalent in worldly dealings[547]. On one side, we have tender feelings and love for our partner and children and the other, we battle for standing, prestige and acceptance in the world. This is the function of family love, which continues through generations into the future. It is the responsibility of the parent to empower and encourage on the one hand, and discipline and guide children on the other, so that they are prepared for the difficulties of adapting to what seems to some, as a hostile world.

d. Individual to World

All individuals learn about the world and themselves through projection. As mentioned previously, a baby projects most of their needs and instincts onto their parents. A newborns nutritive instinct is strong and present and they learn to satisfy that need very quickly. In this way, they have some control over their instinctual needs and know that crying satisfies that need. This first step in controlling the immediate environment is the transformation of projection and the development of awareness and will, in other words, consciousness. They become aware that crying and all its variants which include tantrums, manipulation, exploitation of parental love etc., satisfies the hunger and gives the child tools and weapons to battle the arduous journey to adulthood.

Adulthood brings about another set of problems, which stem from identification with a group, race, nation or religion. Projection then transfers to collective identification. This type of collective identification is aptly termed 'participation mystique'[548]. The participation in collective opinions, beliefs and ideals stops the individual from making up his or her own mind and develop their own understanding and truth concerning an issue. This is particularly relevant when collective opinion, beliefs and ideals become destructive and negative, when power is not tempered by love.

The first instance of collective projection is onto the family. I am the son or daughter of my father and mother, I have sisters and brothers, and this is my group. It is indeed this first set of projections that sets the tone of one's whole life. As Plato points out, we not only have the model of the projection, but also the copy of the projection in the form of the personal father, mother or sibling. This differentiates the personal father, mother or sibling from the idea of father, mother and sibling. The idea is then

---

[547] I am speaking conceptually here, as it is natural to have a mixture of love and power in each relationship.
[548] The term was first mentioned by Lucien Lévy-Bruhl (10 April 1857 – 13 March 1939), a French scholar trained in philosophy who made contributions to the budding fields of sociology and ethnology. His primary field of study involved primitive mentality.

projected onto the wider world and dealings with other people outside of the family.

For example, most of us have experienced a form of personal father that fits the idea of what the individual's father should be. This idea forms the basis of all father projections. If the personal father one experiences growing up was typical of the traditional collective ideal[549], that is, has masculine authority, earns the money, is a male role model etc., then the child will have this idea of what a father should be like. This projection then easily transferred to another person similar to this model. The father figure receiving the projection then becomes the copy of the model to the individual projecting that idea.

Examples of groups, which rely on authority of this kind, include the armed forces, political groups, nations, races and religions. This is where the collective danger of unconscious projection lies. Soldiers willingly go to their deaths because the authority they project onto the leaders of the group tell them that is what they should do for the sake of some obscure ideal. Unfortunately, the leaders of the group project their own authority onto their leaders and so on. This is the male hierarchy built on projection. Without projection, this type of group unconsciousness could not exist.

When whole nations identify with their leaders, it sets a tone for the nation's personality. One could easily describe individual nations as having a predominant personality similar to that of an individual. Deeper still, a countries' personality has many variables in addition to the individual leaders. These include mythological, historical, environmental, geographic and migration. Although no culture is pure in itself, they do have characteristics that make them specific to a country. For example, language or dialect, foods, rituals, religious beliefs, physiognomy etc., define countries. These particular characteristics define a country as if it were an individual. Naturally, all countries have exceptions to this rule, as no country has a completely unified population. The characteristics of a country go deeper than the current government.

It is common for countries to have genders and attitudes associated with them. For example, 'Mother' Russia and the German 'Fatherland', and more specifically, attitudes like the United States feelings of exceptionalism, the German desire for order and efficiency, the English stoicism and the French romanticism, to name only a few. These

---

[549] I am using this as an example and should be viewed as such. The roles of father and mother and what is masculine and feminine is currently being blurred and at some odds with our biological reality.

generalisations change over time, but do emphasise a nations' identity and certain characteristics typical of that nation.

This identity leads to projection onto other nations. Countries that feel exceptional fear the loss of that attitude and defend the associated insecurity. The natural reaction is to reinforce the exceptional attitude by force of will. Feeling exceptional is always compensated with a feeling of inferiority. This is how nature balances our attitude with the help of other nations or people. The balance can also be restored through self-criticism and reflection.

Unfortunately, nations are made of many individuals, and the process of differentiation and integration is far slower than that of an individual. It is as if the whole nations' population has to understand the psychological phenomena of the opposites of being 'special' with being 'not so special', before it can be integrated. It is the same reason arrogance and insecurity is a couple. The feeling of insecurity is trying to correct the lofty ideal and bring it into balance.

Individuals and nations alike identify with the idea of themselves, and project the characteristics they don't identify onto other individuals or nations. For example, an exceptional attitude compensated by feelings of inferiority is uncomfortable and hence projected onto others. This makes nations interact with each other as if they were individuals, with a resulting positive or negative attitude to each other through projection. Nations that support the exceptional attitude of a nation share in that exceptionalism, but also become dependent in the process. They do so through fear, identification or admiration, just the same as one would project onto a parent. This type of interaction has positive outcomes for the exceptional nation, as reinforcement by other nations sustains the ideal. On the other hand, if a nation does not feel the need to project a parental authority onto the exceptional nation or simply wants to go their own way and be independent, it risks the wrath of the exceptional nation, resulting in tension and possible conflict.

Identification with a nation is only one of the instances of group dynamic involving projection. Race also plays an important role in the collective functioning of humans. These days, race is a subset group within nations, has great influence on its constituents, and in some instances has more influence on them than national identity. Nations are made of a mixed collective of races, particularly the new states such as the US, Canada and Australia. Races tend to have similar physical and cultural background, grounded in a geographical location. In many instances, races have stronger cohesion than national identity, due to their similar traditions and cultural norms.

I am treading very carefully in this chapter, as contemporary sensitivities to race are acutely present. There are certain facts concerning race that people may not like, but are true. The word 'racism' is used to further political agendas and browbeat dissenting voices. It is with this thought that I attempt tackle this ticklish issue of race and projection. In the end however, race has more to do with a group's behaviour than skin colour or ethnicity.

The idea of race is particularly problematic, in that the characteristics pertaining to it have many and varied influences. The obvious characteristics of race are skin colour, which is based on climatic and nutritional influences. Similarly, eye and hair colour, texture, height, bulk, shape etc., all influenced by the physical environment. In this day of multiculturalism, these characteristics are almost irrelevant as opposed to the behaviour and attitude of the race.

History is full of accounts of conquer, subjugation and slavery of indigenous peoples because they were less powerful, hadn't developed weapons or hadn't pegged the ground and made a claim on the land. It is unfortunate but natural for a race of greater physical strength and lower moral awareness to come to a land and simply take it from its indigenous inhabitants. We see the same functioning in the animal kingdom. The saying 'might is right' still dictates our behaviour as it does animals. We are aware that other races have their own culture, often developed over thousands of years, yet physical strength is still the benchmark for our functioning. We have not made the leap from the physical to the spiritual, even though we have several guides that set the example. The problem is that we have not taken the milestone to heart and our earthly nature still influences our behaviour without criticism and reflection. This is our current level of awareness. We know that other races have a history and culture that binds the people together, yet lack the self-awareness to respect those cultures. Our western history shows a lack of respect and understanding of other races and a feeling of superiority because we have developed one side of our nature over the other. The Australian Aboriginal for example, knew about the unconscious (Dreamtime) thousands of years before Plato and his idea of model and copy.

Our earthly nature[550] is our greatest danger today. If one does not become aware of this earthly nature and this aspect of the human function ignored, we project it onto others. Today we find ourselves in this dangerous situation. We regard ourselves as the good guys, and they are

---

[550] 'Earthly nature' includes all the aspects of our functioning we have in common with other mammals.

the bad guys. This fact is an inevitable consequence of humanity's development from a purely instinctive background to an identification with all that is good and proper[551] and the projection of all that evil onto our neighbours, rather than owning it in ourselves.

Religion forms another group alongside nation and race and has a deep influence on individuals. Generally, religion plays a moral role in a nation and sets the tone of behaviour. The west has established penal codes based on its Judaic Christian background and moral codes. Most western political leaders ignore this fact, are unaware of it or have an alternative agenda. This is true when political leaders are only concerned with the economics of a nation. Individuals have a natural tendency towards their idea of unity and a nation's attitude and moral codes need to incorporate this fact. If groups have disparate ideas of unity, it eventually leads to friction.

The western separation of religion and state is an interesting idea, but less of a reality. With high levels of immigration, this problem becomes acute, particularly when immigrants bring differing moral codes than those of the host nation. Some groups are inclined to seek a unified, holistic society, where religion and state are in harmonious conjunction. This provides them with a secure framework for life and work, but reinforces dependency and projection of parental authorities onto the political and spiritual leaders. The ethics of the individual is thus in harmony with the state and religious codes. This is presumably why nation states in the Middle East have a very close relationship between religion and state, to the point where the final authority in matters of state are the religious leaders, not the political leaders.

This clash is quite evident when two cultures come into contact from very different backgrounds. When the English colonised Australia and encountered the indigenous peoples, the result ranged from genocide to re-education. The Australian Aborigines had a culture with its associated mythology of more than 20,000 years, yet the English landed, claimed the land as their own and progressed to usurp the people and destroy their culture. As westerners, we may feel guilty about the behaviour of our ancestors, but they believed they were righteous and feared the unknown in themselves as a projection onto the aboriginal people.

This begs the question why a culture with a Christian background and associated penal code would deny the indigenous beliefs and take their land. Theft in the English penal code was at that time, dealt with harshly, and people were sent to Australia as punishment, which was set up as a

---

[551] These are relative terms and vary from culture to culture.

penal colony for trivial offenses. The only conclusion we can reach is that the colonisers felt that the indigenous population were so different in culture and had so little power that they regarded them as conquerable. Aboriginal culture is rich in tradition and has a spiritual relationship not only the cosmos, but also the land itself.

Our inclination for theft is still as strong as it ever was, as contemporary events show. We steal land and plunder resources through multinational corporations and control of the banking system. The conflicts of Iraq, Ukraine, Libya and Syria have all had land, resources and regime change as their central concern. They may try to convince the general population that they are liberating the population to empower them through democracy, but this is a lie. It is interesting to note that the oil industry was one of the first infrastructures secured in Iraq after invasion. Likewise, the government planned to pipe gas reserves across Syria to the Mediterranean for European consumption. The conflict in Ukraine was also concerned with Europe's need for Russian gas and fertile land for agriculture. This dependence on Russian gas did not sit well with the US, hence the proposed gas pipeline from the Middle East through Syria. In addition, there is a plan called the 'Greater Israel Project', which expands its territory into Syria, Lebanon, Egypt, Iraq and Saudi Arabia. We can conclude that all these scenarios driven by our basic human need for power, control, wealth, security and survival, is the same as a baby behaves with their parents. It is an example of nations and other groups displaying the simple need to be in control and survive. Unfortunately, the instinct permeates much of the West's foreign policy, with dramatic and murderous consequences.

The goal of nature is complex and prone to unfortunate deviations. In religious language, they call these deviations sin, having gone astray from a set course. For humans, evolution is a journey from instinctive unawareness to awareness of our functions, role and meaning in nature. To believe that we stand outside nature is an unfortunate result of an exceptional attitude that we have grown beyond our own nature. As Nietzsche screamed from the mountaintop "God is dead", but soon after replaced the old idea of God with a similar idea called the "Overman". This was Nietzsche's God replacement, and an obvious attempt by the unconscious to bring him back down to earth and himself. Even though Nietzsche felt he had attained the heights of spiritual enlightenment, his everyday life was that of a wandering vagabond, with illness and lonely isolation. He put aside the natural man for the sake of the spiritual man. His identification with his spirit and inattention to his everyday life contributed to his breakdown and forced him to return to his family in a dissociated state.

e. Possession by the Idea of Unity

For the purpose of this study, as mentioned previously, it is important to understand the difference between unity and the idea of unity. Unity encompasses everything physical and psychic, and those realms are so vast and unknowable and we have limited knowledge and experience of either. The idea of unity, however, can be known by an individual, and is based on personal experience, insight and understanding. The idea is behind all religions, political movements and ideals, and can have varied permutations. Globalism is such an example and its implementation has far reaching consequences.

One world is a noble idea that has only recently included the entire earth. Before, it was limited to communities, cities, regions, nations and continents. As an idea however, it comes from individual minds. It is not something that we can create consciously although we can appreciate and support the idea in others. The very nature of unity perceived in oneself is to some extent beyond our influence. Its representation and interpretation are as personal as the individuals themself.

The idea of Unity in its spiritual form has organised cultures with a common belief. Ancient Egypt for example, organised its population through their leader pharaohs, who believed they had a direct connection to their idea of unity in their Gods as a compliment to their physical reality, and built a ritualistic culture to honour that idea. It organised the population and gave them a connection to the hereafter (unconscious). It was one of the first cultural expressions with little differentiation between the political and spiritual. The pharaohs had ultimate power and control over the population through their all-encompassing system.[552] Subsequent systems differentiated practical matters such as law, order, feeding the population, resource distribution, taxes etc., from the spiritual, and provided a framework for the latter. The Roman Empire, for example, controlled their population through political and physical power, yet allowed free spiritual worship if the population remained peaceful and obedient.

The political idea of unity is practical and down to earth, in that it deals with the physical aspects of life. It leaves the spiritual to the religious institutions, and in most cases accepts and protects them. This does not avoid the problem of what is the same idea from a different point of view. Some ordering systems attempt to remove the spiritual aspect of the idea to form a totalitarian state. The political class takes the place of the

---

[552] See Chapter 6a on Egypt.

spiritual, elevating its leader to demigod status, where both political and spiritual aspects are contained in one practical system. From a teleological point of view, this interpretation of unity encompasses all aspects of the human condition; that is, both physical and spiritual and in that sense, it is a more comprehensive idea of unity. Why then, do these systems have so much opposition and always collapse?

The answer lies in the way the individual perceives unity and the misconception that others share their idea in the same way. It is natural to want to share such a powerful idea because there is an enormous amount of energy behind it. There is a danger however, the idea can overwhelm and possess an individual[553]. Tyrants and spiritual leaders are prone to sacrifice their humanity and well-being to their own personal interpretation of unity. It is important to know one self and to have one's feet firmly planted in the earth because the energy behind the idea has the ability to possess the personality of the individual. Without roots, the danger of possession is high and the natural consequence is projection of the idea onto the world and other people, rather than accepting its unique relationship to oneself.

As an idea, unity brings together all aspects of existence and all functions in a unified and related pattern. Unity brings the physical into relationship with its foundation, the unconscious. Projection is nature's first step in the realisation and differentiation of the opposites. The projection of the idea of unity is the same as any projection, whether it is of evil onto another, or the projection of an individual's contra sexual ideal onto another person. Nature makes us see everything we are unaware of in the physical world yet the idea may be completely different to the object. This is where most of the conflict occurs, when the behaviour of a person or group does not match the idea.

The idea of unity relates to the male/female problem of projection and differentiation, and its realisation unites them. For example, if a man orients himself through thinking (air) and intuition (fire) in an extroverted (towards the physical) way[554], the opposite functions of feeling (water) and sensation (earth), are to some extent below his level of awareness and understanding,[555] and projects them onto other people and objects. In this example, the man's orientation is for him masculine and the undifferentiated functions feminine. This is the reason some individuals

---

[553] There are numerous examples of totalitarian systems such as Nazism, the Bolshevik revolution and Russian communism, all of which collapsed in time. Even the Roman Empire had enough sense to allow some religious freedom to its population.

[554] JUNG C. G., Psychological Types, Routledge and Kegan

[555] This example was selected to emphasise the point of the passage. All the psychic functions can be spread across the wide spectrum of male and female genders.

project what they are not aware of onto the world as a whole. If Nietzsche had turned away from his mythological and psychic exploration back to the practical world of earning a living, wife and family, it may have spared him his tragic end[556].

One world and all its institutions controlled by one government comes from this idea of unity perceived by individuals. Who these individuals are is difficult to answer because they may not be the obvious political leaders, but they would have to be extremely powerful and influential. They would have access to enormous monetary resources to influence people beyond nation state leaders. The idea of unity is the same as any product of the unconscious, and points to an inner and outer component in relationship in the individual. It requires careful differentiation to avoid cross contamination between the opposites and the recognition and understanding of the differences. Similarly, the idea of a one-world government requires all people governed to accept the proposal without loss of identity. Not considering this leads to a reaction and urge to return to the individual through smaller groups and nationalism.

The main problem with the idea of unity is it is not the same for every individual. For example, an introverted thinker will be to some extent be unconscious of his extroverted feeling. Similarly, an extroverted intuitive will be less aware of his or her introverted sensation, and need to integrate this to find their unity. This is why ideas of unity have differing permutations. It is as if unity is the centre of a circle and everyone stands on the perimeter looking at the same thing from a different viewpoint, and therefore has a different idea of unity. This explains why we have so many spiritual and political systems. If one is not aware of the purpose of the idea of unity, it is projected and lived out as such, the same as the projection of the idea of a partner onto an actual partner.

The reaction of people to a projected idea of unity is varied. If they are in tune with the idea, it may be accepted, live by its tenets and help its realization. If not, it is rejected for another idea closer to their nature. Globalists seem to be possessed by the idea of unity and intoxicated by its power. They do not base their ordering system for unity on the individual and the broad spectrum of individual ideas. There are as many permutations of the idea as there are personality types. This is the central problem with all political and religious ordering systems.

The idea of unity is so powerful that it can possess an individual and leads to catastrophic consequences; particularly when the individual lacks

---

[556] Frederick Nietzsche went insane due to physical illness and a lack of relation to the everyday reality.

awareness of his or her own functioning. This is the key to the problem of globalism, in that all systems based on the idea of unity originate in individuals. It is an individual task and journey, and can only interpreted as such. We can no more ask another to live in our personality, as we are the only one that perceives our dreams. This fact shows that ideas of inner characters or systems are personal, even though the idea has a universality and collective attraction. Individuals react adversely when forced into an unsuitable system.

Contemporary events illustrate this reaction. The United Kingdom's referendum to leave the European Union and the election of an outsider president in the United States are a natural reaction to the dilution of identity. Immigrants from the Middle East and Africa into Europe, and Britain, and immigrants from Mexico to the US, leave the existing population in fear of losing their identity, as well as their economic standing and wellbeing.

The globalist agenda is to erode borders of nation states and have no ethical guidelines in achieving this goal. The hallmark of Globalism is possession by their idea that should be an individual accomplishment and not projected onto the wider world. The possession by the idea of unity is so strong that 'false flag' events staged to achieve this goal, and there is growing speculation that the US government was complicit in the attacks on September 11 2001. Indeed, there are numerous anomalies in the event that warrants a closer look at the evidence. Engineers, architects and demolition experts believe Building 7 was 'brought down' on purpose. Other discrepancies include the lack of response to the hijacking by the military, and the anomalous video of what looks like a missile striking the pentagon, and lack of bodies, seats and luggage at the scene. The subsequent invasion of Middle Eastern countries[557] followed this attack, which had little relationship to the attack itself. Invasions of counties like Iraq, Libya etc., had more to do with territorial expansion[558], currency and control, than revenge.

Other more subversive methods of promoting globalism involve cultural change over many years through education, media, finance and politics. It is a slow transformation of the general population into an amendable state for the globalist agenda. This includes the dismantling of the nation states and borders as already mentioned, promoting unrest in nations, mass immigration, diluting the indigenous population, diluting religious

---

[557] See interview with Gen Wesley Clark concerning the plan to invade seven countries in five years. https://www.liveleak.com/view?i=a61_1378358265#wj1odflv7sH0lbPj.01
[558] 'The Zionist Plan for the Middle East' from Oded Yinon's "A Strategy for Israel in the Nineteen Eighties" Published by the Association of Arab-American University Graduates, Inc. Belmont, Massachusetts, 1982 Special Document No. 1(ISBN 0-937694-56-8)

belief systems, the blurring of gender, the weakening of the family unit, population reduction, the weakening of the middle class and climate change[559]. These are just some of the methods used to achieve the globalist agenda. It is no wonder the general population react to this agenda in a forceful and definitive way. The British saw their job prospects diminishing, their safety compromised and their Christian system under threat, in addition to laws created by an external unelected body in Brussels. So too, in the United States with the loss of their manufacturing base to cheaper labour markets, floods of immigrants, lack of border control, general discontent, and the view that political and corporate leaders were enriching themselves at the cost of the general population, and skirting the law to do so.

In addition to the practical and immediate rebellion to the idea of global governance is something much deeper and far-reaching that is often ignored. This is what the psychologists call "the spirit of the land". It includes the climate, landscape, ancestral heritage, deepest collective myths and individual connection to the land. Physically, the 'spirit of the land' results in the typical physiognomy of a culture. It also affects the population's behaviour, in that a sunny climate promotes sports and outdoor activity, and cold climate indoor activities. The appropriate metaphor for such a culture is the 'tree of life'. It has its roots firmly planted in the ground and is drawn out into the atmosphere, its form dependent on type and environmental conditions.

The connection to the land nourishes us physically, emotionally and spiritually, and is an innate part of our makeup. A culture that has this connection is hesitant to relinquish it or have it diluted by others who do not share it. When the connection is not strong, as with the relatively new territories of Australia, United States and New Zealand, a general lack of adaptation can lead to a cultural inflation. We are witnessing this in the United States with its belligerence, arrogance and disconnection from reality. Its belief that it is good and righteous and projects evil onto others that do not agree with them; its targeting of nations for "regime change"; bringing in corporations for resource exploitation and its unwavering protection of Israel and theft of land from the Palestinians. They simply throw their might around when it suites them. These are all characteristics of a bullying teenager with too much power. In time the 'Spirit of the Land' tempers youth and draws its inhabitants down to earth with the corresponding change in psychic behaviour. This is why it is so important to have experience, knowledge and understanding of the indigenous

---

[559] United Nations Conference on Environment & Development, Rio de Janerio, Brazil, 3 to 14 June 1992, AGENDA 21

population of a land and how their culture grew out of the land they inhabit.

The idea of unity is one of humanity's best creative acts, and as with all products from the unconscious, can easily take possession of the individual or group. It is this danger that leads to major conflicts that have plagued humanity throughout history. The idea of unity in particular has enormous possessive power over the individual; over and above the possessive strength of the contra-sexual idea mentioned earlier. Throughout history, the idea had the highest spiritual value, and literally united the individual with all things inner and outer. This is the true nature of the idea, yet its realisation is an individual task. It is a personal exploration of one's own individuality, and the connecting to one's own dream life. This is where the error occurs, particularly when an individual has no eyes for their dreams. Unity has a feeling of universality and it is natural to assume all people feel the same way. Unfortunately, different people have different ideas about unity. The religious and political systems existing in the world today emphasise this fact. When an individual or group try to force their idea of unity onto others, there is a natural reaction.

Is it actually possible to get a united world in either a spiritual or political system? This is difficult to answer, and we can only speculate on the way it might look. For any idea of unity to work for all people, they would have to have a say in how it is constructed and who runs the system. The system would have to be flexible enough to accommodate individual freedom of choice, expression, morality and understanding of our true nature. This is the difficulty of a united world system in that our current level of understanding of human nature is poor. Some governments are actually attempting to outlaw hate, which is the same as trying to outlaw love, its emotional opposite. This would be equivalent to outlawing sexual love from the population, which is impossible without drastic and abhorrent means. This shows a lack of understanding and knowledge of the human condition, and the fact that we have the ability to dream and create the highest forms of culture, yet have the body of a beast with all the functions in between.

As Freud rightly pointed out, our relation to our base instincts is fraught with difficulty. Our species has the same urges and potential modes of behaviour as other mammals and these need incorporating into our lives. Sport is an excellent outlet for aggression, competition and battle, and is preferable to war. Mating rituals are also preferable to rape,[560] and ownership laws preferable to theft. Freedom of expression is important for

---

[560] Rape is quite prevalent in the animal kingdom.

a population's well-being, and restriction hinders the flow of material from the unconscious and retards personal growth. This may be intentional on the part of various governments, as an uneducated population is easier to control, and encourages projection of a parental authority onto the political leaders. This is what the leaders count on in some instances, as it feeds their own power issues. It is easier to control an unaware child than a fully functioning, aware, freethinking and independent adult.

All large movements in history, whether political or spiritual, have the idea of a universal system of order; in other words, an idea of unity. These include political systems such as Communism, Fascism, Liberalism and Conservatism, etc. The same is true for religious systems, and both groups have caused major conflict and unspeakable atrocities. The United Nations, the predecessor to the post World War I League of Nations, grew from the debris of World War II and was set up as a peacekeeping force. As a peaceful organisation however, it lacks the power to reign in the larger nations that have their own agenda,[561] and as such, is ineffectual. The other major problem is the United Nations' own agenda and the lack of connection to the individual.

The main points in this chapter all lead to the same conclusions, and they are that unity is universal, but the idea of it varies considerably.

•All ideas come from the same place[562] that is, the individual, and are expressed individually.
•Projecting one's idea of unity onto others is a mistake, as others have their own idea, whether they are aware of it or not.
•Forcing the idea onto others leads to a natural reaction and rebellion.

If the individual is the vehicle of all advances in growth and awareness, then this is where we have to start. In other words, the species can only grow through the growth of the individual. In some ways, it is recapturing the myth-making of the ancients. It may take centuries or millennia for our species to come close to individual self-awareness. The groundwork exists however, in the works of the ancient philosophers such as Heraclitus and Plato, the undercurrent of Alchemy, and our modern conceptions of psychology by Freud and Jung.

This is why it is important to include art, dream work, mythology, indigenous belief systems (spirit of the land), psychology and philosophy in addition to science and math subjects. More importantly, it is important

---

[561] United States led coalition and invasion of Afghanistan and Iraq.
[562] The same place is the individual unconscious and its varied forms of expression of dreams, fantasies, visions and ideas.

to include daydreaming and play throughout the education system in all years. Our western culture seems to be under the prejudice that play, creativity and daydreaming are for young children, maths, and science for adults. This is a one-sided view of reality, which suits some, but not all.

10. TRANSFORMING PROJECTIONS

a. Objective View of Reality

A scientific fact, as we know it today, is a physical and verifiable truth through observation and experiment. In this context, we perceive facts with the senses and understanding that can be verified by others. It is therefore an observed part of physical reality. This understanding of facts does not explain how humanity's culture grows; our insight and creativity continues and how we evolve as a species. Our physical evolution is very slow and has not changed in aeons. Our psychological capacity has however, and includes knowledge, skills, understanding and technology. It has only been a few hundred years since Jean-Francois pilatre de Rozier first took flight in a balloon in France in 1783 and the first powered flight by the Wright Brothers in 1903. Since then, we have been to the moon, sent probes beyond our solar system and are now planning travel to Mars. The idea of flight is not new. Birds have been around longer than humans, and are an integral part of the natural world, and our ideas of the natural world. Examples include a myriad of mythological creatures like the Sphinx, Pegasus, Dragon, Griffin, and human-bird hybrids such as Horus and Thoth from ancient Egypt; Mercury, Nike and Eros from ancient Greece; Satan and other fallen angels from Christianity: and the Alchemical Mercurius, all have the ability to fly.

The idea of flight has been with us for a long time. This shows how humans, before actual flight, imagined how to fly and projected the idea onto all kinds of creatures and human hybrids. It was not until we actually studied birds in their mechanical detail that we began differentiating the idea of the bird and took flight ourselves. What was originally magical and wondrous, slowly became known in terms of the birds body/wing structure and aerodynamic function. With this knowledge, the bird lost its magical aspect, and taught us how to fly. The idea transformed into a workable and functioning technique for flight. We transformed something magical into something practical. This is an example of how we transform projections. The flight of birds is a fact, as is flight by humans, yet the fact came from an idea that nature had already provided. Are we to call the former a fact because it is physical, and the latter not, because it is psychic?

Facts are not only physical, but also psychic, as exemplified by dreams. No one can verify that you had a dream or that you perceived certain images and feelings attached to the dream. It was personal, and you were the only person to perceive it. The dream is however, a fact. It is not a physical fact, but a psychic fact. You cannot deny having had the dream. You cannot deny that you perceived certain images and had certain feelings towards the images. To the individual, the dream is perceived as an inner reality. It is not a physical reality but a reality nevertheless.

Humanity has only recently learned how to study psychic reality[563] in an objective method of analysis, in addition to the study of physical reality. The confusion comes from the function of projection. In other words, we see the unconscious projected onto the physical world. The phenomenon of projection is part of our nature and pervades all aspects of our lives. If this were not so, we would never fall in love, not have anything in common with others and not learn about the world around us.

This is the natural process of projecting the idea from the inner psychic source onto physical objects. Science as all other disciplines, are totally dependent on this system of projection. Science has the benefit of verification of an idea through experiment and if carried out multiple times becomes a physical fact. Where did the idea come from in the first place? For example, the Big Bang Theory is to some extent still an unverified theory and may never be verified, due to the time it was supposed to have occurred and the vast distances involved. The idea is a projection of how the beginning of the universe may have come about and is at least real as an idea[564]. One has only to consider the creation myths of many peoples to see the truth of the idea, that is the creation of the universe from nothing or something unknown.

When this shift of understanding reality as both physical and psychic occurs, it gives us the opportunity to see both aspects of reality in a new light. Matter suddenly becomes alive, and the underlying unity of the cosmos becomes evident. The new standpoint recognises the differences between physical and psychic and how they relate to each other in a unified system. If we do not identify with our ideas, thoughts and dreams, and view them as objective aspects of reality, we also tend to see the physical aspect of reality in the same objective way.

This is invaluable when it comes to relationships, as the underlying idea of unity depends on the relationship between what is physical and what is psychic. The unconscious (dreams, fantasies, ideas etc.) on one side and consciousness (matter, animals, people etc.) on the other; their

---

[563] See the work on the personal and collective unconscious by the Analytical Psychologists
[564] See the Section on 'Relating to the Cosmos Part 'g'

relationship provides a third viewpoint, which gives objectivity to both sides and shows their underlying unity.

b. Methods of Transforming Projections

Even today, the term 'introversion' has a stigma attached to it that makes people feel that they should be more extroverted. In many ways, introversion is discouraged due its withdrawal from the physical world of commerce and culture. Daydreaming still regarded as mysterious, and to some extent dangerous. Indeed, a withdrawal can become habitual and as one sided as only dealing with the physical world. Nevertheless, introversion is an important standpoint that extroverts find hard to understand. Why would anyone leave this marvellous colourful world for an imaginary intangible world of make-believe, is the usual extroverted response.

On one hand, introverts perceive the stream of images and ideas in the unconscious, have an easier chance to expresses that material, and in some instances, engage in it. On the other hand, extroverts tend to project that material onto the physical environment and mould it to those projections. What one sees inside the other sees outside! If you are not aware of the characters and ideas projected onto the world, you have no hope of integrating them into your own personality. Instead of relating to the inner characters, they own you.

This form of possession by an inner character, is one of the biggest barriers to self-awareness. Possession excludes all other possibilities and viewpoints, and is the essence of dogmatism. Possession is dangerous when it includes the positive and all other viewpoints, negative. The projection of one's shadow onto another avoids us having to own that shadow. It is easier to see your own undeveloped functions in someone else than in yourself. This is the hardest pill to swallow for an extrovert.

We are all animals as long as we have bodies. What we regard as evil is simply nature in the wild. The evidence is all around us, even in our own back yards. A cat tearing apart a bird, a Preying Mantis devouring its mate, a bird eating a beetle alive and a spider trapping a fly, are all nature's realities. We do not regard these facts as 'evil', we regard them as simply 'nature'. We call it evil when a human acts on the same instinct. It is obvious that we need to know something about this nature. If we accept it on a personal level and acknowledge it as part of our true nature, we may be able to transform it into a culturally beneficial form. In the ancient world, anger and conflict had a character behind it, called Mars. Getting to know Mars in our-selves can temper his behaviour with the help of his lovely half-sister, Venus. Possession by Mars means possession by the urge to fight and control. Possession by Venus means we look for love and beauty in life at the exclusion of Mars. Acknowledging both in our personality reduces possession, and helps us see more than one side of an argument.

Unfortunately, our western culture is not supportive of our human nature. Governments believe that we can overcome an instinct by simply outlawing it. As experience shows, this is furthest from the truth. Is it better to accept our nature on an individual and personal level and give it life through sports, computer games, art, or something similar. Is it better to give our instincts some form of personal expression rather than let the energy build to an extreme resulting in an illness or worse still, a collective conflagration such as rebellion or war?

Repression and possession are hallmarks of our Western Culture. The will to overcome our nature and the emphasis on consciousness has led us to this juncture. We may ask how this came about? How did we lose awareness of our natural instincts? The question is difficult to answer, but has its roots in our Christian background and individual leaders outlawing troublesome modes of behaviour. The twentieth century had well ordered civilised societies behave in ways that we still do not understand. The beast and lust for destruction and brutality was freed with horrendous consequences.

Many of our western laws are reactionary impulses to individual events. We do not condone those individuals who steal, yet we blindly follow the elite, who plunder other countries for their resources. This is the unconsciousness in our collective psyches. We are so eager to keep the individual in check; we have lost sight of keeping our countries in check. Individuals run Nation states and have the same fears, anxieties and projections as that of the population. If, by some means, our western culture were able to defeat the enemy we are projecting onto, we would immediately have to find another group to do the same. As long as evil is projected, we will have enemies everywhere. By destroying our enemy, we are destroying that part of ourselves that we saw in them. "Why do you look at the speck of sawdust in your brother's eye and pay no attention to the plank in your own eye?[565]

Another way of seeing and understanding projections is through creative work. The objectification of material expressed by the unconscious is an excellent way to make the material static in a depicted and physical form. Some forms of expression have advantages over others, but all serve the purpose of making the unconscious visible. This allows us to study,

---

[565] Luke 6:41

amplify and associate with the ideas in the material and to form a relationship to the expressed material. It is as if we were to ask, what does this material mean to me and my life?

There are many forms of expression, ranging from painting, sculpture, architecture, music and filmmaking, to name a few. All have their advantages and disadvantages. We can paint quietly in a room with cheap and readily available materials and representation does not have to be literal. It can take on many forms, from realism to complete abstraction. Skill in visual depiction may be an advantage in exploring aesthetic criteria, but not essential in the expression of unconscious material. Art Therapy is a relatively new field where emphasis is made on the expression, rather than aesthetic considerations.

Sculpture has an advantage over painting as it is expressed in three dimensions, thus giving it more physical reality than a flat image. The use of sculptural techniques to express the unconscious does require additional knowledge of materials and skill compared to painting, as we can apply paint to a surface without much technical consideration[566]. Playing with clay for example, can be very pleasurable and satisfying, as it is playing with the earth itself. Stone sculpting is even more specialised, as is metalwork and the use of synthetic materials.

Architecture is possibly the most evolved of the visual arts, in that it requires highly technical knowledge and skills to give it expression. In addition, the constraints placed on architecture by the government and building regulators make it not only a challenge, but fraught with compromise and frustration. Occasionally, with great effort and rare individual accomplishment, we create buildings that express the unconscious in a form that relates to the spiritual epoch of the time. One has only to consider the impact of the Egyptian pyramids and how they were integral to religious life of the day. Similarly, the temples like the Parthenon of ancient Greece also had religious functions.

Music has also the potential to express the unconscious material with an emphasis on the emotional content of inner characters. Gustav Holst's composition, called the 'The Planets', is an excellent interpretation of the emotional qualities of the Roman deities. Mars is angry, threatening and loud, whereas Venus is soft, loving and attracting. Music can encourage a character or idea by connecting to its emotion. Another example of associating types of sound with environments or events is Beethoven's 1812 Overture. The trumpets and cannons bring forth images in oneself

---

[566] I refer to the technique of automatic drawing and painting developed by the Dada Art movement.

of battle and conflict. Similarly, William's victory music at the end of the first Star Wars movie episode VI, conjures a feeling of joy, victory, celebration and glory. The ideas behind the music are universal and common to all.

Transforming projections is difficult at an individual level, and even more so at a societal level. It requires the recognition that what one thinks and feels about an object; person or group is not necessarily the characteristics of that object, person or group. For example, the persecution of indigenous peoples in the new colonies of the United States and Australia was compensation for fear and lack of understanding and the need to alleviate the fear by removing its cause. It must not have dawned on the colonisers that they were the intruders and the fear was their issue, not that of indigenous peoples. In this case, it was the unconscious inferiorities projected onto the indigenous population.

Another example is the founding of Australia as a penal colony, where English, Irish, Welsh and Scottish prisoners were sent for trivial offences. This shows that the prevailing laws of old England were so strict that it was difficult not to break them at some stage. The overdevelopment of law is a natural consequence to the repression of uncomfortable facts about human nature. It also intensifies the projection of rejected contents by a culture onto another group, especially a group that is not technologically developed or organised to defend themselves. It has taken many years, but some of the coloniser's descendants are slowly trying to repair the damage their ancestors carried out on the indigenous peoples.

It is commonplace to project our own inadequacies onto less technologically developed peoples. Why do we not feel the same way about our children? They do not have an adult's education, or have developed skills and knowledge. We do not persecute them because we love them. It is this feeling for our offspring we have in common with most other animals, including reptiles. Why then, is it so difficult to extend this feeling to strangers? This is one of the crucial methods of transforming projection. That is, forming a relationship with the object of one's projection. It not only dispels fear, but also helps differentiate the object, person or group from the projection and changes the idea of them into one aligned more with their reality. Once we learn about something, it reduces the level of misunderstanding and overcomes negative emotions associated with the object, and the idea transforms into one closer to the object.

The guilt some white people are feeling over colonisation is another attempt to transform the previous projections of one's inferiorities onto others. That guilt means that we feel that something is wrong in our previous attitude of superiority and that the abuse we were carrying out led to this realisation. It is yet to be seen if that guilt can be integrated into the wholeness of each individual with the realisation that the opposites are within each of us as a an idea of unity. We cannot be truly free until we liberate our own inferiorities within ourselves and own them. It is a painful exercise to give the inferior aspects of our own nature a life. It is to allow the inner, undeveloped child in us a life, and this is the beginning of our unity.

In the previous section, I briefly touched on the difficult problem of racism. History shows that racism has been part of our makeup for aeons, and only now in the twenty-first century are we questioning its validity and our attitude to it. Understanding racism is a difficult problem but the main aspects seem to be based on fear and insecurity of the 'others' power and differences, coupled with a feeling of superiority. The feeling of superiority can originate from many sources, including upbringing, religious conviction, possession by an inner character and a disconnection from the reality of our species.[567]

Calling someone a racist is the same as being a racist. On one hand, racism is the projection of our inferiority onto another, thus dispensing with the anguish of feeling that inferiority and siding with what we feel is superior. Calling someone a racist is the same functional projection. A typical scenario is as follows: "You are a racist, and I am not. You are inferior to me because you are a racist, which makes me superior to you." It is the same functioning as the projection of the idea of a slave onto another and identifying with the master.

We should not confuse racism with an individual's behaviour. For example, if an individual comes to me and hits me in the face, I do not dislike them for their race, but dislike them and retaliate because of their behaviour. The same applies to groups. We do not disparage Nazis because they were German, but because they brutalised and murdered other people. In the same instance, we cannot accuse somebody of being a racist if they are reacting to our behaviour. This method of slander is quite prevalent in this politically correct age and is used as a 'power word' to reinforce the feeling of superiority. It is the projection of one's shadow and dispensing with uncomfortable feelings of inferiority onto others.

---

[567] All humans share a common genome, the same emotional responses and capacity for love, intelligence and understanding.

As mentioned previously, nation states often have definite characteristics making them like an individual. The same conflicts that occur in individuals also occur in groups of individuals that make up the population of a nation. It is a form of contagion or 'participation mystique', that each individual contributes to the character of the nation. When characters with different values come into contact and the values are different, there may be attraction or repulsion, and there is no way of reconciling this difference without an adjustment of both sets of values. This shows that values are highly subjective and relative to the individual or group.

Projection, as described above, is a natural part of human functioning and the first stage in relationship to the object. The discrepancy between what is projected and the behaviour of the object shows how conflict arises though misunderstanding and the natural urge to make the object comply with the projection. It also arises with possession by an inner character or idea that feels the other side is wrong, and needs conversion or conquering. This is our nature, and the way humanity functions. The unconscious influences our decisions and as we are aware and critical of external input, so too do we need to be aware of internal input. This is the only lasting way that we can come to terms with our own nature as an individual.

Projection and its transformation is a difficult problem and the realisation that values are relative adds to this problem. Values often become the footings for a nation or culture. Challenging a nation's values undermines its footings and destabilises the culture. This is most evident in the new states where the values were brought from the European countries through immigration. This relativity of values is by no means an easy realisation for a nation. It challenges the legal, political and educational institutions, and can leave the population in a state of instability and imbalance.

This is why it is important to know one's personal idea of unity. This above all, is where stability and balance originates; it cannot be found in the physical world of objects, which are in constant motion and decay. We gain stability and balance by relating to the objective products from within, such as dreams, ideas, visions and so on. These reflect our outer lives, rebalance the personality and guide us to our personal idea of unity.

Emotions are also an important function as they bring additional material to consciousness, and behind them are inner characters that have definite personalities. The list of characters is many and varied and is as unique as the individual. Emotions are the same for all people and not limited to the human species. In the initial stage of self analysis, we discover all the insecurities, undeveloped functions, emotions and instincts that we tend to dislike and disparage in others. These traits are part of our nature and belong to the dark side of our personality that has a relationship to our animal ancestry.

This is aptly termed the 'Shadow'[568] by the school of Analytical Psychology. The Shadow is like the dark gateway to an inner group of characters that form our psychological functioning, and the darkness made by the absence of light from the conscious world and our ego[569]. Unfortunately, it is no easy task to integrate the Shadow, as our western culture does not tolerate overt instinctive behaviour. There are ways, however, which I touched on above, which can help give an outlet to that part of our nature.

Team sports are a natural pair of opposites that come together to fight and win. The fervour of the barracking fans is a good way of letting out that energy that belongs to one's instincts. It is an example of the projected unity of Ego and Shadow onto two opposing teams. The Ego identifies with the chosen team and the Shadow with your teams' enemy. They fight it out and one team prevails. We are elated when our team is victorious and demoralised when defeated.

Extreme sports also give an outlet to the natural person. Skydiving, for example, not only strengthens the will of the Ego by overcoming the fear of falling and death, but also relies on eye/body coordination and flight in free-fall. Skydivers practice their manoeuvres on the ground so that it becomes second nature. In free-fall, decisions are instinctive and with practice, become a learned skill. Jumping with others tends towards formations that are stable and balanced in freefall, which viewed from above or the ground are mandala like patterns of unity. The patterns made by the skydivers' bodies tend to be symmetrical and orderly[570]. Skydivers tend to be free-spirited and somewhat wild on the ground at the drop zone where they jump. It is an excellent outlet for the natural person, and complements their restricted behaviour in their weekly jobs.

A less dangerous activity that children enjoy these days is the simulation of life in the form of computer games. They can play individual or team sports, ski, skydive, drive, fly, fight in wars between nations and alien cultures and so on. The list of simulations is extensive and satisfies the Shadow to a certain extent. We can do things forbidden in the world, as

---

[568] JUNG C G, 'Aion, Researches into the Phenomenology of the Self, Princeton University Press 1979
[569] I use the term Ego in its psychological sense, not in its common usage. Ego in this instance means the centre of ones conscious world as differentiated from the unconscious part of our personality.
[570] See the concept of 'Mandalas', which are symbols of unity and wholeness.

there are no consequences for killing someone, and a player can die and be reborn in an instant. In this respect, computer games and simulations are more like the fantasy activity of the unconscious, rather than the physical reality of flight, freefall, war and so on. It is a suitable outlet for an individual's aggression, particular young adults and their aggressive tendencies.

The Internet is also to some extent forming a unity of conscious and unconscious. Computers, tablets and smart-phones are more than communication devices. They actually form a bridge between people and ideas. Information that required painstaking effort at the library is now a click away, other people are in constant contact and has drawn the younger generation into an almost stupefied life of constant electronic interaction. The Internet has also given us insight into the true nature of human instinct with the plethora of what was previously, hidden behaviour.

There are a myriad of other activities people seek to give their Shadow a life and represents the urge to seek and maintain their idea of unity. To give life to one's Shadow is to satisfy that part of us, which is difficult to express freely in a strict culture. Political systems constantly try to suppress certain behaviour, particularly if they are problematic to the functioning of the state. It is a mistake to underestimate our animal nature and political correctness is another nail in the Shadow's coffin. If we cannot express ourselves on a personal level, the energy dams in the unconscious and bursts forth at a later date. Personal expression of our instincts and emotions is also the basis for our mental well-being.

Individuals cope with the urge to give the natural person a life through intoxicants such as drugs and alcohol. Alcohol has a dampening effect on consciousness and a loosening of one's ethical outlook and the instincts have some freedom of expression. It is the Dionysian spirit, liberated from the confines of culture. This leads to displays of instinctive behaviour and a liberation of all the things not compatible with everyday life, particularly when those include, a defined persona of a job or profession. People behave in different ways under the influence of alcohol, depending on their natural disposition. They become either overly aggressive or overly loving. It has the effect of lowering the ethical standards as well as the moral codes of the host culture. Rules are ignored or challenged and more intoxication leads to more unconsciousness of behaviour. Instinct has free to play and all the traits that are hitherto repressed, come to the surface.

It is very difficult to be in the company of drunken people when you yourself are not drunk. The atmosphere is thick with what lies under the surface. People behave not as they behave while sober and are goofy, or overly touchy. Ideas are freely expressed, misunderstandings are frequent, and disputes inevitable. Put simply, the effect of alcohol is to reduce the conscious feeling connections for a freer, uninhibited, instinctive and honest interaction.

This loosening of cultural norms and ethics does, however have some positive aspects. Ideas come more freely, spontaneous behaviour encouraged, the noise and irritating aspects of consciousness reduced and alcohol greases the wheels of commerce. This is a reason alcohol is accepted by western cultures as opposed to other drugs. Drugs such as marijuana and the opiates remove and withdraw people from action in the world, which to the culture is counter-productive. Society does not thrive on people sitting in opium dens or at home watching television.

Intoxicants such as marijuana have a tendency to diminish the strength of consciousness through a heightening of spiritual and imaginative capabilities. It has the effect of lifting the ego out of the here and now and reduces its influence through separation. This only works during intoxication and one comes down to earth once the effect wears off. Prolonged use can lead to psychotic symptoms and a separation from the physical world and other people.

c. Child to Adult

Life created in nature is by far the purest and noblest example of unity. This unity is a constant reminder that nature re-establishes herself repeatedly in regular cycles. Consider the facts surrounding our design and how nature's unity is instilled in us. With few exceptions[571], people are either male or female and we have an 'a priori' instinct for these opposites to regularly unite in what we call sexual union. The inclination to unite is a powerful urge and its goal in nature is to continue the species, in other words, to create the third uniting element between the opposites. This is well known to most people and may sound like a simplistic description, but the symbolic significance is far-reaching.

The system involved in propagation is nature's way of providing us with a biological imperative for life. Men have within them a strong urge to penetrate, and women to accept this penetration. It is rare for a young man to woo a young woman with the idea of propagating. The urge in itself is blind and removed from the hindering aspect of consciousness. In fact, instinct uses consciousness as a tool. This is emphasised by the

---

[571] I do not make any value judgements on sexuality and am discussing traditional forms of conception, as they have always existed.

elaborate courting rituals and preparation for the eventual union. Other species such as Bowerbirds, green Turtles etc., also have elaborate courting rituals and comprise of dances, touching, vocalizations and displays of beauty or power.

In this study I am less concerned with the chemical release of neuro-hormones such as dopamine, oxytocin etc., as I am about the motivating force that initiates the release of these chemicals. In addition, the pleasure often associated with sexual union is incentive enough to reproduce. It would be less appealing if it were associated with pain or displeasure, which would lead to repulsion instead of attraction. This does raise questions concerning the cannibalistic mating habits of some species of arachnids and amphipods.

The cause and effect of human reproduction is obvious, but the instinct is blind so that the cause continually strives for the effect with out necessarily achieving it. If this connection between cause and effect were integral to the reproductive process, we would only have to carry out the sexual union for as many offspring as we need. In other words, the sexual instinct in its 'raw state'[572] is somewhat oblivious to the effect of the union and the force behind the instinct independent of the outcome. It is as if the instinct took into account the random ability of successful reproduction. Young men make all efforts to satisfy this force, but also make efforts to negate the possibility of conception. This fact indicates that the force is in itself a motivation for union, and the completion of the union with or without conception, dispels the force and offers relief from its influence. That is, until it returns the next time.

The above shows how the physical and psychic work together for the goal of unity. The psyche contains the idea of unity with all its associated symbolism. Awareness of the idea is irrelevant to the reality of the idea, for it acts upon us anyway. The idea of union thus employs the physical, as in the body, with the release of neuro-hormones and brings the ego, our awareness, into action. Satisfying the force behind the instinct nullifies it for a time until the energy once again builds and the cycle repeats. This system is a very beautiful arrangement of nature in that the idea of unity works in a cyclic manner much the same as a woman's menstruation cycle.

In a woman, the instinct is similar to a man but generally includes a more differentiated feeling, and therefore idea of unity. The motivating force includes relationship, whereas this can be absent in a man. A woman's

---

[572] I use the term 'raw state' to emphasise the instinct's overwhelming urge to unite with its opposite.

'biological clock' and associated idea, emphasises a timeframe where a woman feels a need to give birth. This is the crucial difference between men and women. For the man, the instinct has a force somewhat independent from the possible outcome, whereas a woman has more connection with the outcome. The reasons for this may come down to the simple psychic and physical differences between men and women. Men have a force to penetrate, whereas women have a force to accept penetration[573]. This is simple biology and shared by other species.

The physical aspects of propagation reinforces this idea, in that a sexual union that results in a fertilization of an ovum remains within the woman, and she becomes a receptacle for new life. The man, on the other hand, has completed his biological duty, which changes to a social duty of support and care for the woman and new uniting life. This is presumably, why some female species of insects devour their male counterpart after he has performed his biological duty. His service is complete, and he is no longer required for the incubation of the offspring and can contribute to the female and offspring with his body and life as nutrients.

Now that the third uniting element is forming, the union of opposites reside within the woman's womb. She contains within her the union of male and female, which is now forming a third with the information contained in the DNA from both parents. This is what Plato refers to as the model, copy of the model and the nurse, who incubates the copy (from a man's point of view). These universal patterns repeat themselves throughout nature.

Birth is the physical separation from the mother and the dark, enclosed, warm, moist and safe environment, to a light, cold, dry and less safe environment. The most beautiful and wondrous aspect of life is that every one of us has lived and been nurtured in the same home in a maternal womb[574]. It is this fact that not only places us with other mammals, but also affects our psychology in the profoundest ways. Symbolically, the womb represents a variety of metaphors, a fiery furnace, an oven, hermetic vessel and the unconscious itself, to name a few. It is not too far a stretch to regard the womb as a precursor and determining factor for the entire built environment.

The child is now out of the woman, but still very dependent on the mother and father for their nutrients, safety and care. What started out as attraction and love of the sexual kind between a man and a woman has

---

[573] The penis is a penetrating organ.
[574] I am concentrating on the natural way humans propagate but acknowledge that our technology is leading us to alternative methods.

now transformed into love of a nurturing kind towards the child. From the child's point of view, everything is new. One of the first things the child learns is how to get what it needs by crying. In a traditional family, the mother provides the child's nutrients through her breasts. A short time after birth the senses activate and the child sees, hears, tastes, smells and senses through their skin their immediate environment.

The disposition or personality of the child is however, debated among many scholars. The 'Nature versus Nurture' argument has more to do with the psychic orientations of introvert and extrovert, in that the extrovert sees the influences on a child from outside, whereas the introvert sees the innate qualities of the child. Experience shows that a child is born with a complete personality in undeveloped form. What they are to be is already present, how they are to achieve this form is dependent on the environment. It is the same as discussed previously, with the propagation and development of plants and animals. The personality is already present in an unconscious state and slowly emerges over the years into consciousness. This includes an overlay of personal relationships mixed with projections of inner characters. Both sides of the argument are thus true. The original personality is present at birth and constitutes the framework or structure of the individual. As they grow, the external influences of relationships and events add layers to the personality.

This is Plato's idea of model (father), nurse (mother) and copy. A child is very dependent on these two larger versions of himself or herself, and the models (parents) can be either benevolent or malevolent. To the child, the parents are Gods, so to speak (parental authorities). They provide all their nutritional needs, love, encouragement, as well as frustration, annoyance and displeasure. Indeed, this projection onto the parents lasts for many years, and only through painstaking awakening do the projections fall away to reveal the earth-bound individuals who happen to be one's parents.

This aspect of awakening and transforming projections is not just the task of the child. The parent can help with this process of awakening by being themselves with their children. If you accept the role of father or mother and this is the only way you behave in front of your children, not only do you restrict your own personal growth but limit your children's ability to see you as you are. In other words, the inner character of parent has possessed us through the role and model of mother or father. This possession denies the other inner characters, including one's own childlike creativity. This reinforces the roles of father and mother as inner characters, thus making it more difficult for the child to transform the projections.

This highlights the difference between an actual father or mother and the idea of a father or mother. The ideas are innate, and based in mythology. Plato was aware of this psychological fact 2,400 years ago, when the foundation of western thought was first established. Basic human nature has not changed since then, what has is our awareness of that nature and ability to make improved tools. This difference between parent and idea causes so much confusion and trouble in the parent/child interaction. The Christian idea of the father as all-loving, forgiving, understanding and compassionate is a good model, but we have to mindful of the child's need for independence and adulthood, in other words, the differentiation of child from parents[575], and balance and unity a parent feels for their children. On one hand, we love them and want them close and attracted to us, on the other hand, we have to push them away and help them grow into adulthood.

The projection of an inner parental authority leads to a complete child-like trust in that authority and being told what to do, how to behave, and in some circumstances, what to think. Obviously, there are differing degrees of intensity in such hierarchies with the armed services on one side and co-operative businesses on the other. The armed services extinguish most individuality for the machine-like function of the hierarchy. It is only through this projection of authority that enables hierarchies to form the basis of societies' structures. Most, if not all such hierarchies could not function if its participants questioned the orders from their superiors. This is the nature of the projection of authority and its use in our society.

As a child grows to teenage years, new sets of problems emerge, and the adult sexual function activates. This period is fraught with difficulties and initiates a phase in the child's development where biological demands change the child's physiology to include the instinct to propagate. The burden and responsibilities the sexual function is expulsion from paradise into adult life. In addition to the physical changes induced by hormones, which affects the sexual organs, hair growth, body changes etc., there are significant psychological changes in interests, ideas and attitudes. This change from child to adult can be traumatic and all the earlier interests of play, fun, uninhibited joy etc., either transformed or discarded altogether.

This change is the second prototype of all future changes of personality and regarded as the prototype of death and rebirth. The old ways shed,

---

[575]Mathew 34 & 35—Do not suppose that I have come to bring peace to the earth. I did not come to bring peace, but a sword. For I have come to turn `a man against his father, a daughter against her mother, a daughter-in-law against her mother-in-law......

and new ways thrust upon the child independent of his or her will. Sexual pursuit in boys and relationship in girls become major concerns and the child thrust into a new realm of early adulthood with all its sexual responsibilities and burdens. The fun-loving days of childhood recede into the unconscious and a new attitude dawns with a view to adult life, work and building one's personality.

For some young adults, the transition from childhood to adult comes easily. For others, the event is a traumatic and a loss of personal wholeness. The wholeness, identification and connections of the parental home replaced by the need to become whole through a sexual partner. The parental projections transfer to a wider community and a soul partner of equal stature and age sought for the sake of personal unity and propagation. It is the yearning and search for one's mate, or at least the idea of a mate. This in turn raises a completely new set of projections, which complicates life even more, which I shall address in the next section.

From a masculine point of view, the young man now belongs to the adult male world. His concerns become more adult-oriented, and the connection to childhood recedes. Indeed, this is where many cultures employ ritualistic behaviour such as circumcision to reinforce the transition. Western culture reinforces masculinity by the repression of emotion and building willpower and strength. Competition between men in various fields becomes the way they interact and relate to each other. Activities such as sports, drinking, drug taking, academic achievement, sexual conquests etc., all become part of the male arena of competitiveness.

One of the big problems that occurs with the transition from boy to man is the loss of connection to the past and to the individual's free and playful attitude. The new paradigm is one of adaptation to the man's world and society in general, as its structures are still based on male ideas of hierarchy and competitiveness. Obviously, there are exceptions to this scenario, as the sensitive and artistic types bring their creativeness to the world through the arts. This is the importance of the arts in that they reflect the society and its systems.

The projection of the personal father transfers to the broader and wider world. This position can either give the individual a sense of awe and excitement full of possibility in a larger arena, or scare the individual to recoil from what they perceive as a hostile world. Generally, extroverts adapt quite well, whereas introverts hesitate, and do not wish to give up their natural inclination for the inner world. This is the hallmark of living in a particularly extroverted western culture, where achievement is measured in external rewards. School gives little time for daydreaming and fantasy and emphasise activity and achievement. Even the art courses at schools emphasise the external nature of the art rather than its inner processes.

Introverts are far more prone to loss of balance when it comes to the transition to the wider world. The problem stems from the over- emphasis and lack of balance in the external world itself. In history, religion has always satisfied the need for individuals to connect back to their origins. The term 'religion' derived from the Latin word 'religare', meaning 'to bind'. Religion, particularly Christianity, has therefore the function of binding us to our origins, much the same as the Australian Aboriginal circumcision and incision ritual.

d. Relating to other People

Our previous discussion of a boy's transition to the man's world at puberty is a communal ritual. The older men have gone through the ritual themselves and can help the child through the transition to manhood with bonding rituals and mateship. Unlike women, men usually require a uniting activity, such as a sport, drinking sessions, building, working on a car etc., for them to enjoy a male relationship. This form of friendship is less prone to the problems of parental projection, as a relative equality exists between friends. It then becomes another projection of equal stature like a brother, and this forms the bond between young men.

It is when the young man enters the hierarchical world of society that parental projections become active as authority figures. Bosses, teachers, mentors, military officers, political and religious leaders all attract father projections from young men. If the young man's father was particularly strict, they will respond to strict bosses, if their father was benevolent and loving, they will respond to such men in the world. Success quite often depends on how well a young man interacts with his authority figures. This is also true for boys at school. When a projection does not fit the person who receives the projection, it quite often leads to conflict. In other words, the idea and the man do not match.

This is where we can learn about our self and our projections through recognising conflict as a mismatch of idea and person, which encourages self-awareness and independence. This approach can have enormous benefits for the well-being and growth of the individual. As mentioned earlier, projection is a natural way of interaction between people and the starting point for relationship. Male interaction is less to do with relationship than it is to do with mateship based on competition[576] and fitting into a hierarchical system. This makes it easier for men to fit into a system, because all they have to do is obey orders without objection.

After the transition from boy to man, adaptation to the world becomes the main concern, which includes career or job, a partner to love, and a nest for propagation. A young man searches for his soul mate in projected form. It is this fascinating arrangement of nature that has affected all men at all times. It is the difference between the idea of 'one's inner woman' and the physical woman herself. The idea originates at birth with the mother and her nurturing role and is the prototype that most men carry into their relationships with women[577]. Other women that a man meets such as sisters, nannies, aunts, cousins, close friends etc., also influence the idea of their 'inner woman'.

The idea of an inner character is sought in the outer world so that the inner and outer halves of reality may come into relationship and unite. In other words, all male and female relationships have the seed of a spiritual awareness contained within them. Unfortunately and too often, the man projects his idea of his woman onto his physical partner and that is where it remains. Living out an inner woman is an affront to a man's masculinity and often misinterpreted as homosexual inclinations. It doesn't dawn on most men that to integrate his inner femininity not only gets them in touch with their feeling function, but makes them more independent and less likely to project that inner character onto and actual women.

There is however, a change afoot where the roles of male and female are slowly evolving. The feminist movement is an example of the liberation of female role from mother and wife. Unfortunately, these movements have more to do with power than actual femininity. It seems to be resulting in the masculinisation of women and the feminisation of men and the blurring of gender beyond the biological determinants. Indeed, gender is to some extent a psychic function, in that we all have the characters of male and female in us. The problem with a sustained identification with a character at the expense of all others is a stagnation of personal growth and possession by that character.

In addition, a possession by an inner character that is contrary to one's biological foundation means a poor relationship to that foundation. In other words, if one denies the biological reality of the body, then one is unrelated to that reality which complicates matters considerably. The

---

[576] I emphasise 'less to do' as there is always a mixture of projection and true feeling for a person.
[577] There are obvious exceptions to this arrangement but it is more prevalent than not.

important aspect of the male and female problem is the eventual differentiation of femininity, masculinity, and their union as opposites. It is far easier and quicker to go through this process as an individual than swept along by a cultural revolution. There is an enormous wealth of information on this process from the ancient teaching of Tao to the modern writings of Analytical Psychology.

To recap, every man has an idea of his woman and every woman, an idea of her man[578]. When the two meet and their inner figures have a close correlation, we call this 'falling in love'. Most of us know the effect and overwhelming psychic force at work when this happens. Our thoughts are distracted, we cannot get the other person out of our mind, and we can't sleep well unless we are together; all kinds of emotions are active and the thought of losing the other person is devastating.

The function of falling in love is a purposeful arrangement of nature in order to bring the male and female individuals together. It also helps the individuals become aware of the idea of their contra-sexual character projected onto the other person. In the first stage, the projection creates the match and there is a symbiotic attractive force making the connection. If this force is the basis for their union the couple live their lives as one, remaining completely unconscious of their projections, and hence their individuality. He becomes dad and she mom, they have lovely children and that is where it stays. They do not fight a lot because they represent each other's ideal.

The second stage involves becoming aware of the inner character behind the projection. This is more likely when the compatibility between individual and idea does not quite fit, or is not quite compatible. He or she behaves in a way that does not fit the desired behaviour of the idea or inner character. This leads to argument and an attempt by either individual to convince the other to behave according to their idea. Arguments between couples are the same all over the world and provide an opportunity to find the differences between the person and projected idea or character. Achieving this to some extent reduces conflict and the relationship becomes more objective. We see the other person as they are, rather than as we would like them to be and the projected idea transformed into an idea closer to the reality of the person.

In some instances, the first stage is not the biological union and the goal of their interaction. The goal is then the spirit for growth of the individual

---

[578] The inner man and woman have always been viewed as 'soul' images. There are many different masculine and feminine characters inside us, and their character traits contaminate each other and change over time.

and personal awareness. Such an interaction occurs when a man with an idealised inner woman falls in love with an overly erotic 'femme fatale'. As the name suggests, the outcome is not the permanent union as a couple, but the fateful opportunity to become aware of the inner idea of the female in the man. It is an interesting and purposeful arrangement of nature to bring two people together for the purpose of growth and awareness of these ideas. The unifying forces in our own nature encourage us to become aware of our functioning, albeit in disastrous form.

Knowledge that our inner character is different to our partner is a starting point to the transformation of the idea of one's partner. This is by no means an easy task, and requires painstaking and drawn-out effort. First, it is a slow and careful observation of the things that irritate us about our partner and the reason for the irritation. Why does she behave differently to how I want her to behave? Arguments are another fertile ground for reflection. Why such opposition, what in me is different to how he or she behaves? If he or she does not behave, as I want them to, then my idea must be different. This path of reflection can enable the transformation of the idea of one's partner to a closer approximation to the actual partner. It is the recognition of the inner character belonging inside and different to what we project onto one's actual partner. The idea of one's partner still exists, but it has transformed into a closer approximation of their reality. Then it becomes an idea based on the reality of one's partner and different to one's own inner soul character. This means we have a partner in the physical world with a corresponding idea of them in the inner world next to the idea of our soul character. Withdrawing projection does not delete the idea of one's partner; it transforms it into an idea closer to their reality. The differentiation of inner character from outer person helps us becoming aware as independent individuals.

Hence, in every male/female relationship there is four-fold system of interaction. This comprises of the man/woman, the projected male/female inner characters, and a contamination of soul and idea of one's partner. Within this crossover lies the unity for each individual. This unity has a force of attraction for both parties and can serve as a crucible for transformation. We are initially dependent on the other person hoping that the feeling reciprocated. Differentiating the character from the other person and seeing it in oneself gives the individual a sense of unity and independence and more importantly, an ability to relate to their partner as a person in their own right. Although this is a goal of relationship, it is a slow life long process of becoming aware of one's own inner contra sexual characters and path towards one's own unity. In other words, recognising the projection as an inner character helps us see the difference between inner and outer and their inherent unity.

One of the ways for a man to become aware of his inner female character is to live alone for a while. In that way, we have to perform all the tasks of independence that include food preparation, household chores, entertaining and so on. Other ways of transforming projection in a relationship include the development of shared household tasks, and not falling into typical roles. Women give birth and it is important to reinforce and support that role. It can however, become habitual and lead to a form of possession by the inner mother character. This form of possession becomes more complicated if there is a daughter in the family. In this instance, the man may project his mother onto his wife and his soul onto his daughter as in the story of Oedipus.

Our contemporary western culture is blurring the roles of male and female. This blurring of role can have negative or positive outcomes. On one hand, it can lead to possession and identification with one's contra-sexual character in contrast to their biologically determined reality. It is the same for a woman who identifies with masculine traits at the expense of her natural femininity. Possession by one's contra-sexual character leads to unusual personal traits, such as irritability and moodiness in a man, and dogmatism and argumentativeness in a woman. This is why it is important to have a good anchor in one's physical biological gender and avoid possession by an inner character. On the other hand, it may provide insight into unconscious processes, and possession may lead to new interests and forms of adaptation. Any long-enduring possession leads to stagnation and putrefaction, and if recognised, leads to the next step in the unfolding process of life.

e. Relating to Society

At the early stage of a person's life, the world stands before them in all its pleasure and horror. It is indeed a daunting task of adaptation to what appears as a jungle full of hidden corridors and dangerous precipices. For those endowed with an extroverted disposition, adaptation may come naturally, but for those who are introverted, society can be a horror of unspeakable chaos full of demons and monsters. In other words, introverts project their extroverted unconscious onto the world with all its contents. Whatever type a person is, adapting to society requires self-sacrifice and obedience. If one becomes a student, they are required to play by the institutions rules, do their work and not make too much trouble. In this instance, it is success or failure in the selected courses. If it is a workplace, one must obey the boss's commands or lose one's employment and income.

Studying and employment are fertile grounds for projection. It is in these arenas that we find mentors, teachers and bosses, with definite modes of behaviour depending on the field of study or work. This hierarchical organisation of society reinforces projection onto superiors. True and equal relationship between student/teacher and employer/employee is rare because it disturbs the hierarchy involved, particularly when an organisation depends on its hierarchy to function. If an individual wishes to climb the hierarchical ladder in a large organisation, then pleasing the boss, showing initiative and performance become the hallmarks of growth. Little does anyone realise that large organisations are soft tyrannies, even in democratic nations. You have to do as the boss tells you or suffer the consequences.

Strict hierarchies such as the Armed Services are fraught with projection. In this instance, it is the projection of authority onto the upper officers and inferiority onto the lower ranks. It is a simple form of priority, based purely on artificial rank rather than skill, knowledge or bravery, although these may be included in the hierarchy. The basis of such a projection is generally the idea of a parental authority. The authority knows more, is more experienced, has more strength of will and is higher in rank. We also find such projections in government and educational institutions, although to a lesser degree. Put simply, such hierarchies are ladders and those higher up on the ladder require respect and authority, those lower on the ladder must give respect and reverence to those higher up. In the first instance, there is a projection of superiority (parental authority) on those higher up, and the second, a projection of the inferiority (shadow) onto those lower down, which is all based on the 'will to power'.

We often refer to these hierarchies as power structures. This power can be independent of the individual's ability, knowledge, intelligence, insight, etc., although these attributes may help climbing the ladder in the structure. It is a very interesting aspect of our nature, particularly of men. In essence, it is the same path that each individual experiences growing up, gaining knowledge, experience and becoming aware of the world around them, and their place in that world. In this instance, a collective structure contains the idea of unity. This is the task of most young adults and their adaptation to one of these structures and the world in general.

It is interesting to note that society's structures can be totally independent of one another. Anyone who has made a change from one such structure like a profession, to another profession knows that it generally requires a new beginning, new skills, learning, and knowledge starting at the bottom of the ladder. This is due to specialised knowledge and skills required from one structure to the next. For example, an architect cannot become a doctor without study, internship, experience etc., and has to go through a complete re-education to do so. These structures permeate all of our lives and take the form of institutions, professions, corporations, belief systems, and nations. Structures provide a sense of belonging and feeling of unity. It is, however a unity based on identification (participation mystique) and collective support, in other words, projection.

What was an instinctive and innate urge to grow and become aware is replaced with a collective structure of known parameters. What was an individual path is now a collective path. What was natural now replaced with a collective mode of behaviour related to the specific structure. This is what the Analytical Psychologists call 'persona'. Behavioural traits accumulated over the life of the structure can be quite specific and strict. For example, a house call by a doctor dressed in board shorts and a t-shirt, raises questions about the doctor's validity. This also applies to his behaviour, in that a doctor is calm, intelligent, knowledgeable and compassionate, which is written into their oath of allegiance. This is one of the major medical objections to the debate on euthanasia and abortion, because a doctor abides by this oath- 'I will take care that they suffer no hurt or damage'[579].

This aspect of human nature to form structures, which guide and control behaviour, has benefits and drawbacks and is not unique in nature. Bees also structure their society with a strict hierarchy with the queen at the centre, supported by drones and workers. They all have their respective roles and functions. The benefits of our societal structures are numerous and our western style of life could not function without them. The structures provide a feeling of belonging and unity with a higher power than our own personalities. These structures are highly beneficial to the functioning of the culture and state. The unfortunate aspect of being involved in these worldly structures is the potential loss of one's own individuality. If we project part of our personality onto an external structure or a parental authority, it makes us dependent, and we have to behave in a way that fits into the structure. It is only a difference of degree between master/slave, boss/employee and officer/private.

A good citizen is therefore the goal of any societal structure, whether it is the state, religion or culture. They reinforce the idea of belonging and build it into the education system and media, which flows into family attitudes. Cultures frown upon ideas that differ from the status quo and are discouraged or dismissed. This is why the church fathers did not include the gospels of Judas and Mary Magdala, even though they were personally closer to Jesus. What they wrote did not serve the rest of the apostles' intentions for a church system. If the followers of Jesus became

---

[579] Hippocratic Oath

introspective and found their own inner God, the church could not establish itself as a religious system of authority. The church had to be an outer reality with access to God through their structure. This gave them the authority and ability to lead millions of people. In this instance, humanity becomes no more than a flock of birds or a school of fish following its leader(s).

The hierarchical structures we create are slow to evolve and somewhat fearful of free and alternative thinking. For example, new ideas have only recently swayed religious dogma because of political pressure. Ideas such as homosexuality have only recently been accepted by the Catholic Church and only because the current Pope regards them as God's children. In this instance, the true message of Christian brotherly love and acceptance usurped centuries of dogma. Previously, the church set the moral codes for the population, now the population sets the moral codes for the church, or at least reminds the church of the true meaning of Christianity.

State structures, such as the education system, rely on an authority over their pupils and set the curriculum to what they deem as suitable and beneficial to the state. Western education is oriented more on externals and good citizenship than the development of the individual. Even courses in the arts are oriented on outcomes rather than ideas. There are exceptions in some private institutions, such as the Steiner and Montessori schools, which encourage individual learning. Generally, daydreaming, fantasy and active imagination are less important than math, science and language. There are however, signs in our popular culture that show a shift to fantasy-oriented drama and stories of gods and demons. Movie franchises such as Lord of the Rings and Star Wars have little or no connection to our earthly existence. Both are set in fictional worlds, with little or no reference to planet earth. This shift in emphasis from fact to fiction is a natural compensation to a materialistic science-based culture. Both have their place and both are part of the overall unity.

Some structures, such as law enforcement authorities are not only oriented towards good citizenship, but exist to enforce it. In this case however, good behaviour is expected, and bad behaviour punished. Individual discretion removed from the officers, and their role to enforce fixed laws. For example, the outlawing of hate speech has more to do with stifling dissent than addressing the root cause. Hate is a natural emotion and is coupled with love. It is wishful thinking to try and outlaw it. It is the same reason western democratic governments shy away from outlawing sexual activity between consenting adults as it cannot be done. Governments often create laws for more control over the population and stifle dissent. We can see these events unfolding in the US and other western countries to a lesser degree. The hallmark of all law enforcement is physical strength and the threat of containment, loss of freedom or fines; in other words the 'law of the jungle', in contrast to the law of mutual consent. Nation-states also interact with each other using the same threat of force. The 'Will to Power' still dictates the terms of interaction between them and laws are created by the strongest nations still set the tone for world politics. Nation-states interact as if they were individuals and show that they have definite and individual personalities.

An example is the United States and its lofty hegemony and powerful war machine. It is a nation separated from the reality of a grounded and reasonable attitude. Americans live in the clouds of superiority and look down upon other nations as weak and less evolved. It is literally a possession by their national symbol, the eagle. It is a predator bird that hunts from the heights and is the ruler of the skies, is a symbol of freedom with excellent vision and hunts in a fast and furious manner. The eagle was an integral part of the American Indian spiritual outlook, with its symbolic representation in their headdress. This is another example of how the 'spirit of the land' permeates the culture over time. Like the eagle, the hallmark of the US power is from the air as shown in World War II, which ended with two atomic bombs dropped from the air. Today, the US conducts war through air campaigns using cruise missiles, drones, fighter jets etc., and is reluctant to send in ground troops because dead soldiers look bad for the politicians. It may be that they do not send in large amounts of ground troops because the eagle lacks confidence on the ground as they have a history of loss in ground wars. The US does not seem to understand that waging war from the air sanitises it, turns it into a computer game, and divorces it from reality. The consequences of this type of war is not felt or seen by its personnel, or only on a screen or from a distance, and becomes a form of extermination rather than warfare.

The Russians, on the other hand, are very hardy, down to earth people with a tough and adapted demeanour. The bear signifies their personality very well with characteristics of power and fearlessness. In addition, the bear spends a great deal of time in hibernation, which indicates a strong relation to the unconscious. In addition, the Russians have had an uninterrupted tradition and culture spanning eons, whereas the US is a relatively new country with a population of immigrants. In behavioural terms, the US is considerably younger emotionally, than the Russians, as exemplified by its bullying attitude and inflated (exceptional) opinion of themselves.

Adapting to the realities of such a world is fraught with difficulties, and young people have to bend, cramp or simply ignore their individuality so they can fit in somewhere. It is literally the biting of one's tongue, so that others accept us in the hierarchical system. Adaptation in this instance becomes an external problem, where the needs of the individual personality are secondary and even neglected, for the sake of a functioning system. Self-knowledge and an inward-viewing eye have little value to an extroverted oriented system and regarded as counterproductive. The outer world has in reality, an equal and opposite inner world, of which the general population is slowly becoming aware through discoveries in depth psychology and other fields.

The practical application of transforming projections on a personal level is difficult and problematic. There are however, signs and indicators that help us become aware of these projections. Conflict for example, can be an indication that what one thinks and feels on an issue is different to what the other person thinks and feels. Having an opinion on an issue that disagrees with another person, means we may not see the whole picture. We expect the other to agree with us, and are dismayed when they do not. The same holds true for interactions between the sexes. The characters differ in relation to the person receiving the projection and help us become aware of the differences. The number of inner characters is varied and numerous and they change to fit different circumstances. Knowing and relating to an inner character makes it less likely to be under their control. This is particularly important for men who seek their inner paternal character in the outer world. Projecting an inner character onto another person blinds us to the individuality of the other personality and their human qualities. For example, we tend in the west to require our political leaders to be above human foibles and have little tolerance for behaviour that does not fit that projection. This is particularly true when the political leaders do not live up to the projected moral standards. We expect our leaders to be parental authorities, and behaviour that does not fit the projection disparaged.

A direct method of withdrawing projections is to actually remove oneself from the projection-attracting environment. Simply put, it is self-isolation and away from other people. In this way, we can reflect on our lives and interactions with others, and how they differ from our ideas of them. Other methods include dream work, which is the notation and analysis of dreams, including the characters and unfolding story therein. Daydreaming, play and creative work also liberate inner characters and ideas for analysis and integration into one's conscious viewpoint.

Nation-states are also prone to collective projection, particularly if the nation is cohesive. A strong national identity gives the clearest indication of the way nations adopt the personality traits of an inner mythological character. We can all tell the difference between a Russian and an American[580], between a Frenchman and a German, and the subtle differences between a Dutchman and a Belgian. These differences are outside of individual control, and are part of the underlying mythological base in that particular region. Leaders are born in a tradition and ethos out of the national zeitgeist. If a leader went against the culture, they would not last long, as the population would feel unrepresented and betrayed. The result is internal turmoil where the leaders have their own political agenda that does not fit the nation's ethos. This very problem is unfolding in the European experiment, where nation-states have less influence over their population than the artificial political union.

As nation-states take on the characteristics of an individual, they are also prone to projection as an individual. It is obvious from an objective viewpoint that projection of evil onto a neighbour while feeling righteous is a psychological problem. Although this attitude may result in conflict, it does show the unity in the projection. Love and hate as opposites make a connection and the beginning of relationship. If projection is the problem of world conflict, then how can a nation transform that projection? This is a very difficult problem and it begins and ends with the individual.

Nations operate on a collective level, where all individuals contribute to the projections. It follows that all individuals have to transform their projections where they are. In other words, know one self as an individual to become aware of our functioning. It is doubtful that a leader, whether political or religious, can achieve the transformation of a projection on a collective level. No one can doubt, however, the influence of a religious movement such as Christianity, but it took centuries to influence the general population. The problem with such a belief system is that it does not have origins in the US, Russia and other western nations. It grew out of the Middle East from a Jewish population under Roman occupation. Jesus was not the fighter, liberator and worldly man the Jews were seeking, but provided another inner world where one felt free and at peace, even under external occupation. His life and work showed the enormous influence a single individual could have on the awareness of the collective and the transformation of projections. He liberated the soul from the bonds of occupation, but had to do it at the cost of his physical humanity.

The Christian story and its teachings is the base of Western nations legal systems. This is due to the overwhelming cultural input of immigrants

---

[580] I use the term 'American' to describe a citizen from the Unites States as used in common language.

from Great Britain and Europe, which are to date, Christian-based cultures[581]. This is a surface layer of civilisation prone to dissolution under certain circumstances, as exemplified by Germany and their possession by the Teutonic god Wotan, and shows that a nation's mythology runs deeper than its religious overlay.

Other ways nations can become aware of the collective myths and the eventual transformation of projections, are through the culture itself. The background mythology of a nation gives it its depth and anchor to the earth. The Christian myth liberated us from earthly concerns through the denial of our natural instincts. Art has always been a reflection and expression of a nation's mythological background, as exemplified by the ancient Greek and Roman nations. Their indigenous Gods were an integral part of their culture and represented elemental forces of nature, but also the forces of their own inner nature. It is a beautiful example of the opposite realms of inner and outer reality given character and purpose.

The underlying culture and traditions set the tone of a nation's individuality. If the Christian myth had ultimate influence over the population, all western nations would lack their individual character, and this is not the case. The problem arises with newly formed nation states such as Australia and the United States. They are young nations, and their traditions imported from other nations. These new nations have indigenous peoples who lived on the land for centuries and have a deep and connected mythology. This mythology is born out of the land and climate and already penetrating the new settlers. Ignoring this fact leads to feelings of uprootedness and disconnection from the spirit of the land. They feel inflated and better than others, because they have a poorly developed connection to the earth, climate, vegetation and hence the lands mythology.

The positive aspect of this inflation is that a nation strives and develops to keep up with their idea of themselves. This leads to abstract innovation in technology and science, breakthroughs in aviation and space exploration and confidence in their own abilities. The compensation of such an attitude is an equal neglect of earthly and practical matters, such as physical infrastructure, relationships to other nations and a moral outlook on life. The arrogance compensated by an equal and opposite insecurity, as shown in the paranoid suspicion that everyone is out to kill them. Indeed, the suspicion is real, as their urge for destruction and control of other nations makes it a reality. The only solution to this problem is

---

[581] I acknowledge the presence of other religious and non-religious groups but in this case refer to the majority belief system that has influenced the presiding penal code.

through the individual. It is here that a nation can eventually come down to earth.

Artists reflect and compensate this exceptional attitude in their work, particularly the architecture of Frank Gehry and Eric Owen Moss. The hallmarks of their work are unusual sculptural shapes, chaotic forms and have little relationship to recognizable objects. Sometimes Frank Gehry verges on the mythological, particularly with his earlier work. His 'Dancing House' in Prague, done in collaboration with Vlado Miluni, looks like two different characters in a supporting embrace, one leaning heavily on the other. Gehry's recurring fish motif hints at a new idea coming forward with great symbolic significance. It appears that art's function of compensation is yet to form a definite style and direction to American exceptionalism. The term 'post'[582] refers to a lack of direction in art, and an unawareness of its true function as compensation to the conscious attitude of a culture.

Identification with an unconscious character or ability, that should belong to a God causes an inflated attitude. It is a form of possession by an inner character or idea. Nietzsche's life is an example of such an inflation, in which he identified with his inner God to such an extent that he had to kill off the old Christian God for the sake of his possession by his new God he called the 'Overman'. People have a distinctive dislike for inflated individuals. It annoys and irritates them and they react with derision and hostility, and the same is true for nations.

Conflict between two individuals is however, less destructive than two nations at war. The problem with an inflated nation is that it takes much longer for the population to realise its imbalance and the way to correct it. The compensation is already present inside, in the form of collective insecurity, and in some cases, feelings of dread and persecution. An inflated nation looks for the cause of the insecurity, and suffers the age-old problem of projecting it onto an enemy. This inner misalignment and projection onto an enemy makes them believe that removal of the enemy will remove the feelings of insecurity. This however, does not occur. The enemy is within and not removed with the destruction of another group of people. Conquering one group of people just moves the projection to another group, and so on. A moral outlook can play a part in the overcoming of possession, but generally, when a nation's population is gripped by an inner character or idea, no amount of moral reflection or reasoned argument can bring about the necessary correction in attitude.

---

[582] I refer to the 'Post-Modernist' style of architecture, which seems to include a variety of styles and approaches.

This is where the young nation like the Unites States finds itself in the world. It has too much physical power for an undeveloped sense of reality. If it were not for the Russian cool-headedness, we would have already fallen into a conflagration of epic proportions. However, if the US continues to provoke the bear, he will muster all his power and swipe the eagle from the sky. This is a sure way to bring the eagle down to its nesting ground and to reality.

We need to become aware of our functioning now, more than ever. The knowledge is available, and always has been. The modern developments of depth psychology bring this knowledge closer to our everyday lives. If we consider reality as purely material, we ignore the subject of that materiality. We live in two worlds which are yet one. To understand the material, we have to understand the function of apprehension of that material. Nothing exists without a subject to perceive that material. As the alchemists indicated, the opposites require differentiation before uniting. When a baby is born, they are in complete unity with their environment, but totally dependent. Everything is projected, and the unity is undifferentiated and all functions are still in their original condition. The world concentrates on outer development, which means that the inner realm is projected onto others, either in individual or collective form.

f. Relating to Nature

A discussion on our relation to nature requires that we go back to the first steps our ancestors took out of the trees and onto the savannah plains of Africa. We cannot underestimate the influence the climate of a particular region has on the individuals and groups in that region. The physical effects on individuals' bodies are obvious, in that colder and wetter climates with lower UV radiation results in paler skin and blue eyes and blonde straight hair, whereas hotter and dryer climates with higher UV radiation result in darker skin, darker eyes and dark curly hair. This is simply a fact of our evolution. During this first step from forest to plain, we lost most of our body hair.

There are several theories proposed for this loss of hair including the need for cooling; increasing movement to hunt; bipedality; reduced sun exposure; the introduction of clothing; Neoteny - the retention of juvenile characteristics in adults; humans as aquatic creatures; and a few other less obvious theories[583]. All these approach the question from a different point of view. The cooling theory explains the loss of hair due to the movement from the forests to the savannah landscape, and that the increased heat load eventually shed the hair. The transition from forest to

---

[583] https://biology.stackexchange.com/questions/23693/why-did-humans-lose-their-fur

savannah and loss of hair set humans apart from the existing savannah animals such as lions, hyenas & wildebeest, which all have fur. The hunting theory is similar, but the other predatory savannah animals also hunt and still have fur. The bipedality theory suggests that the upright stance of early humans reduced overhead exposure to the sun. This in itself does not take into account the ability to move. Early humans, like most other animals, have the ability to avoid direct sun exposure by seeking shade. The heat gain from the sun as a cause for the loss of hair, as with the cooling theory, does not explain why other animals still have their fur. The introduction of clothing as a cause disproved because hair loss predates the use of clothing. In addition, the Australian Aborigines lost most of their hair and wore very little clothing up until a few hundred years ago.

The Neoteny theory proposes that early humans lost their hair as retention of juvenile physical characteristics and a slowing of maturation and development, compared to the great apes. This theory does not give a reason why this would occur over time. Biological changes such as this may explain the hair loss, but then raises another question as to why the change occurred. The aquatic theory proposes that early humans spent much time in water environments, which in turn reduced the need for hair. This does not explain how the ancient Australian Aborigines loss most of their hair in desert regions.

Whatever the cause or causes for the human hair-loss, we can determine some known facts about our evolution. The first is the transition from forest to Savannah lands, and the necessity for protection from large predatory animals. This, coupled with a bipedal stance, increase in speed compared to apes, and climbing ability retained from the forest, gave early humans a distinct advantage over four-legged creatures. To make the evolution from forest to plains complete, it was necessary to defend against larger predatory animals with the use of tools and weapons. Weapons were an observational discovery, in that various plains animals already had weapons as part of their own evolutionary protection and hunting ability. The wildebeest has its horns, the rhino its tusk, the snake its fangs, the hyena its speed and pack abilities, the lion its strength and teeth and so on. These resulted in the use of spears and clubs, thus vastly increasing humans' defending and killing ability compared to other animals. In addition to weapons, early humans hunted in groups, thus increasing their strength through numbers, much the same as the hyenas do.

Another possibility is the harnessing and taming of fire as one of the causes of hair loss. Before its use, early humans experienced wildfires started by lightning strikes that often went through the plains. It was only a matter of time before this divine spark given a central place in the human arsenal. With fire, early humans could stay warm at night, protect themselves from predators, cook their food and create light. They therefore could regulate their body temperature, which in turn reduces the need for hair. They could also move from hot to colder environments, with the knowledge that they would not freeze to death.

The second layer of protection, which gave early humans more mobility and better adaptation to the external environment, was the use of animal skins for clothing. In this case, clothing replaced the lost hair and regulated body temperature by adding or removing clothing when required. This gave early humans another ability to regulate their body temperature in addition to fire. With this reasoning, it seems plausible that many factors caused human hair-loss, but the ability to regulate body temperature stands out. The wearing of animal skins also relates to the symbolic connection between animal and human, as discussed previously.

The third layer of adaptation is dwellings, which gave early humans the ability to not only regulate their body temperature through an internal fire, but also protect them from other aspects, such as rain, snow, insects, predators, and so on. The urge to build stems from the desire to reproduce the security once lost when we came out of the trees. From here on, building became a way to live and protect themselves from the environment. It did pose a new set of problems, in that nomadic or semi-nomadic groups had to learn to obtain food close to their dwellings due to their fixed position or move their dwellings. Remaining in one place as they did in ancient Egypt due to the water resource resulted in animal husbandry and agriculture and enabled early humans to build a civil society.

The progression from trees to savannah, the taming of fire, invention of weapons, use of clothing and dwellings shows that our evolution was an adaptation to the somewhat dangerous external environment and nature. Each new circumstance brought about another problem to solve. What nature had provided on our bodies in the way of protective fur, replaced by fire, clothing and buildings to regulate body temperature and protection. If we view our evolution in this way, we have to acknowledge that our inventions, weapons, tools, clothing, buildings, etc., are all a natural replacement for what used to be part of our bodies. All these things are psychic extensions for what nature had previously provided in rudimentary form. Instead of a fist, we can now use a hammer; a gauging finger is now a knife; fur is now clothing and dwelling; hunting is now animal husbandry and foraging now agriculture.

Our physical evolution shows a distinct ability to solve problems, which to some extent[584] makes us nature's success story. Our psychic nature enabled us to solve these problems but there was a price to pay for our ingeniousness. These changes reduced our physical strength and resilience as our psychic development increased. It is a transformation from an instinctive physical being to a creative and considered psychic being and is the flow of psychic material from idea to outer manifestation. In other words, it is a flow of material from the unconscious to consciousness. It is the same as the growth of a child to an adult, except in this case it is the evolution of our species. It is therefore understandable why we have an insatiable need to control our environment. It is an extension of our physical well-being and rooted deep in our ancestry.

The physical transformation from instinct to idea in order to adapt to the external environment has a corresponding psychic transformation. When early humans tamed fire, they took that energy from a projected unconscious. That is to say, they learned about the quality of fire and how to make it at will. This gave them enormous power and control over their environment including threats to their lives from wild animals and other tribes. Fire, up to that point had been uncontrollable and devastating, and taming it through knowledge, gave humans a leap beyond the animal world. It is the same as the snake example used previously. Before the use of fire, it was unpredictable, seemingly came out of nowhere and devastated the landscape and everything else in its path. This is the reason Plato made fire one of four constituents of his cosmology as it is a little bit of the sun's energy giving light and heat.

The taming and ability to make fire transformed the idea of it into something useful and liberating in addition to its devastating and threatening quality. Fire never loses it qualities and will always be both harmful and out of control, as well as beneficial and controllable. To early humans fire was magical and wondrous and was the spark of civilisation. Today, we control fire efficiently for our use and understand its quantum mechanical properties and how to liberate it as stored solar energy. We have the ability to create the same energy through atomic manipulations as discussed previously. With this knowledge and the transformation of the idea of fire, we still use it in its simplest form. We heat our homes and cook our food with gas flames, less directly through the generation of electricity, as well as capturing the energy from the sun and so on. Uncontrollable house and bushfires still remind us that fire can quickly get out of control.

---

[584] I say 'to some extent' because building is not new in nature. Termites, bees, birds, beavers etc., all have the ability and skill to build very complex and purposeful structures.

The mythology of fire's discovery emphasises its positive and negative qualities. Prometheus, from the ancient Greek tradition, stole fire from the Gods (unconscious), giving it to humanity, which he created from clay. Fire has both physical and psychic qualities. The idea of fire goes beyond its physical nature into its associations. For example, Prometheus created man from clay, but needed the spark of fire to animate him and give him life. The idea of fire extends to energy in general, and includes energy that animates our body and gives it life. The body generates its own heat, and this heat is lost very quickly when the atmospheric temperature drops. In addition, fire also relates to emotion and passion. Anger increases our temperature and gives us energy for action. Similarly, fear over a dangerous situation releases energy to act and avoid the danger.

Passion also releases fire or energy and draws our attention and emotion. We feel alive and vibrant, and the energy released attracts us to the other person. Fire also has an association with intuitions as they flash before our mind like lightning, and give us an idea or insight into a situation. Fire converts one material into another, and as we have seen, has an important place in alchemical transformation. Indeed, fire is the spark of consciousness, and the reason we have come so far in our evolution. If we view fire in this way, it differentiates us from the clay (earth) that Prometheus created.

The use of animal skins for clothing also has a symbolic content. When early humans had the idea of putting on the outside skin of a wild animal, some of that animal's qualities transferred to the human. The practical purpose of regulating body temperature became a symbolic association of becoming that animal. If a person wore the skin of a cheetah, its qualities of speed, agility, stalking and hunting abilities, transferred to the person, because they had outwitted the cheetah and overcome its skills and abilities. The outer skin became a character with definite qualities. We have the same thing today when we wear a suit. We associate it with business or politics and the ability to negotiate and make deals. Similarly, the attire of a legal professional denotes balance and judgment, a lab coat experiment and research, and so on.

A further development of an outer protective layer is the dwelling. It protects us from the climate, predators and provides a safe place to rear our young. In cold climates, we can regulate our body temperature within a larger space, thus freeing us from cumbersome clothing. We do this with a heat source like fire or its derivatives. In hot climates, we can take advantage of the breezes or build so that all external air excluded and cool the interior with water. There is debate about the origins of dwellings and if they originated from practical needs for shelter and protection, or came about by an innate idea for enclosure.

Early human life on the savannah tamed fire for protection, heat and light, yet the biggest and most relentless problem during the day is the sun. Shade is an imperative in hot arid climates, and trees and other natural features provide this shade. A makeshift roof from the surrounding materials could also provide shade. The problem with overhead shade is it only protects from the sun at its highest elevation. The early morning and in particular, the late hot afternoon sun adds to overheating. Walls solve this problem, and from here, we have the beginnings of an enclosure and a dwelling.

The symbolic qualities of dwellings are broad and elaborate. The idea of enclosure stems from our original dwelling we all know as the maternal womb. The associations with the womb are many and varied, and include hermetic vessel, oven, belly of the whale, a cave and the unconscious itself. As an idea, it is the precursor and determining factor for the whole built environment. The womb is indeed a container of incubation and transformation. We grow in there from an egg and sperm cell into a viable embryo and living, breathing human baby. Not only do we all go through this process during our own birth, we can experience it from the outside as parents, and provide the actual container for new life[585].

Its psychic aspect as a container further elaborates the idea of enclosure. That is to say, dwellings are also psychic spaces and all the activities, emotions, intrigues, relationships, etc., have symbolic significance within the container. Consider the cooking of food as a transformation of something raw into something cooked, using fire or its derivative. Similarly, washing one's body is cleansing and purification of the outer worlds grime, the bedroom, our access to dream through sleep and sexual union. Everything we do in the home has an obvious physical and a less obvious, symbolic component. What we take for granted in everyday life has a deeply important meaning.

In summary, what was an animistic and ritualistic attitude of our distant ancestors has not disappeared, but simply sunk below the threshold of awareness. There are however, groups today that show remnants of this ancestral background, contaminated by colonisation and migration of other peoples, but still have their relationship to nature and the land. The Australian Aboriginal has developed over thousands of years in a unique and intriguing way, with little or no influence from other cultures, until

---

[585] It is obvious that only women can contain and incubate life, but a man can share and experience the emotions of the process.

recently. This is mainly due to geographic isolation and a vast continent with virtually unlimited resources. Although predominately semi-nomadic, they developed, a very elaborate mythology and tradition of story telling closely connected to physical nature.[586] Their cultural traditions permeated all of their lives. The practical consideration of survival so integrated with their mythology that one grew out of the other and was expressed in their concept of 'Dreamtime'. This beautiful expression of a period in the distant past, where giant semi-human beings roamed the landscape and performed the tasks of adaptation to the environment, much the same as the aborigines did. When these giants left, where they had camped, made fires etc., became mountain ranges, rock outcrops, rivers and other natural features.

We can see similar ideas of creation all over the world, particularly the ancient Gods of Olympus and Valhalla. The aborigines regarded the sky as the home of the sun, moon and star-people as well as rain, thunder and lightning. The term 'dreamtime' is the same as the myth-making unconscious or concept of the 'collective unconscious' termed by Jung. Their myths evolved in geographic isolation from Europe, Asia and America, which indicates a common foundation to other cultures like the ancient Egyptians and Greeks. This also shows there are common experiences of the environment that permeates our myth-making unconscious and gives us creation stories of the land and climate.

Although our myth-making unconscious has changed over the years[587], we can experience what it means to step outside of our comfort of layers into the harshness of nature and all her varying permeations. Activities such as camping, bushwalking, mountaineering, caving, safari, sailing, etc., link us to simpler and more dangerous times, where we adapted to the environment and used our knowledge and wits to survive. When we subject ourselves to these activities, particularly the extremes of nature, such as storms, rough seas, desert dryness, blizzards, etc., it links us back to what our ancestors had to endure as a normal part of their lives. Extreme sports also give us this connection to nature, which in turn connects us to our own nature. What would drive an individual to throw him or herself out of an aeroplane with a backpack and folded cloth inside? In the beginning, it is facing and overcoming one's fear of death and mortality. In the end, it is the excitement of self-challenge, and doing an activity that makes us feel heroic and godlike.

All these activities teach us the power of nature and how little influence we have in her functions. Awareness of this power gives us respect and

---

[586] Dreamtime Stories, Charles Mountford and Melva Roberts, Rigby Publishers 1983

[587] These days our myths are galactic adventures, aliens and fictitious lands of fantasy.

teaches us our limits in the face of her power. We know that the climate has extremes of temperature, winds, storms, droughts and floods that can easily destroy our structures. Life is a risk, and we can be killed at any moment if reckless. Depending on where we live, we still have a to avoid certain predators. They include the larger animals such as lions, tigers, rhinos, hippos, elephants, sharks, etc., to the smaller creatures like spiders, snakes, scorpions, sea snakes, blue-ringed octopi and even smaller organisms such as bacteria and viruses.

In summary, we are totally dependent on nature for our food, water, light, air, etc. We may feel emboldened that we have progressed to complex forms of agriculture, animal husbandry, and resource recycling, but the main attributes of nature are still far beyond our influence. These include the orbit of the earth around the sun, the earth's rotation, the energy output of the sun, which drives our climate, and so on. In addition to the physical aspects of our existence, we are dependent on our inner nature, including our instincts for survival and love.

The instincts are so powerful, that they use our reasoning capacity to support their influence. If what we are told about the recent wars in the Middle East are true, and that these countries were invaded because they had 'weapons of mass destruction', then the decision was based on fear of a possible threat. Fighting wars for resources or a greater territorial expansion is based on insecurity and greed. These emotions are in themselves a natural part of our functioning, but it seems likely that the individuals were unaware of the instinctive drive behind their decisions. Our inner instinctive nature still dominates much of our behaviour.

g. Relating to the Cosmos

The idea of the cosmos evolves as our knowledge of it evolves, yet our everyday experience of the cosmos has not changed since the ancients. Human curiosity has developed tools and devices that enable us to see the cosmos as never before. We know that there are billions of galaxies, with billions of stars and planets. This is however, not what we see and experience when we walk outside of our homes and look up at the night sky. This remains unchanged and is the difference between knowledge and experience[588]. We know that our sun 'Sol' is but an insignificant star among billions of others. Our instruments can observe UY Scuti[589] a bright red, hyper-giant, pulsating, variable star with a radius 1,700 times that of our sun. We know this through a complex method of observation outside

---

[588] This statement refers to people not involved in astronomy and view the cosmos with their naked eyes and general experience.
[589] https://www.universeguide.com/star/uyscuti

of normal experience. In the night sly, it is a point of light amongst other points of light and its physical affect on us is negligible. We cannot experience its effect in any way, other than what it impresses upon our observation through instruments, knowledge and our imagination. Everyone can experience our star Sol in an immediate way and its physical effect leaves a lasting impression on us. Knowledge always relates to experience through the imagination. If all we can do is observe UY Scuti visually and through calculation, our experience of it as an idea is borrowed from what we can experience of our own star, Sol.

The physical effect of Sol is almost beyond description. It is the enabler of all life on our planet, drives the climate, gives us light, heat and other forms of radiation, enables our motion through the solar system and holds it together. Our star up until a few hundred years ago was the centre of our cosmos. Indeed, it is both physically and symbolically the centre of our immediate cosmos in terms of its overwhelming influence on our everyday lives. Sol has been for many cultures, the ultimate expression of the original idea of the father-God[590], and viewed as the prototype for the idea of a father-God. Sol is both good and bad. He provides all our needs but disrespect is punished with a bad burn, dehydration, headache, skin cancers and many other ailments. Fire is an attribute of the sun and has similar effects on us in its burning ability and provider of heat and light.

The second most significant celestial body, and often regarded as the refection of Sol, is the moon 'Luna'. Sol's cycles are straightforward[591] whereas Luna's cycles less obvious. Sol is visible and present during the day, and not present during the night, whereas Luna is sometimes present both day and night, and changes her appearance throughout the month. She not only affects the ocean tides, but also has a relation to the female menstrual cycle. Unlike Sol, she does not provide heat, but provides reflected light. To the ancient observer, Sol was predictable, regular and his disc remained intact, whereas Luna is sometimes visible and sometimes not, and changes the shape of her disc. It is not hard to see how these characteristics have direct bearing on our own nature and its unity. On one hand, we regard our relationship to these celestial bodies as a projection of inner ideas based on observable behaviour. On the other hand, we regard their behaviour as the prototype of inner ideas. The Goddess Luna was often associated with childbirth, due to the waxing and waning aspect, and its approximate relation to a woman's

---

[590] The sun is generally associated with a male authority but it has also been associated with a female authority. This shows the wondrous variability of our human expression of power and strength.
[591] I am writing this from an observational standpoint of immediate experience. The knowledge that the earth's rotation causes the cycles is not how we perceive the sun's behaviour.

menstrual cycle. This gives Luna a decidedly motherly aspect, and forms a counterpart to predictable Sol, thus forming a parental pair of opposites in relationship.

This is the nature of myth. It unites physical objects, events and experiences to patterns of behaviour, culture and ideas in the human being. We can regard Sol as a ball of gases going through a thermonuclear reaction, as we know it is, but the meaning for us provides relationship to him, but does not detract from his physical reality and his masculine qualities. Likewise, Luna is a sphere comprised of dust and dirt, void of water and life, but also has feminine qualities. These qualities are more than ideas alone, and based on our everyday perception. The mythology of a Sol and Luna has its base in their perceived physical behaviour. When viewed in this way, object and idea are different, but united. Whatever additional ideas are overlayed to this original unity, are like the garments we place on ourselves to denote certain characteristics.

Similarly, the planets have characteristics based on their appearance and behaviour through the night sky. The visual nature of the planets is similar to the stars, in that they are points of light in a black sky, although they have less impact on our everyday lives than Sol, and Luna. Mercury for instance, is the smallest and closet planet to Sol but is almost indiscernible from other points of light in the night sky. The Babylonians called it 'Nabu' and the ancient Greeks called it 'Stilbon', and later 'Hermes', and the Romans called it Mercury. He moves across the night sky faster than the other planets due to his close proximity to Sol. The fact that the Roman God Mercury is swift-footed and a messenger have its roots in the actual behaviour and location of the planet.

Venus is the second planet from Sol and after Luna the second-brightest object in the night sky. Venus, as another inferior[592] planet, does not venture far from Sol, and is known as the morning and evening star. The ancient Greeks thought that Venus was two separate bodies, and named them Phosphorus and Hesperus. Similarly, the Romans named the two aspects of her, Lucifer 'light bringer', for the morning and Vesper for the evening. The Babylonians knew that the morning and evening bodies were the same body, and regarded Venus as the 'bright queen of the sky'. The relationship between the planet and the Roman Goddess is less obvious than Mercury. The characteristics of the planet Venus include its yellowish-white colour; it shines brightly in the morning and evening; and orbits between earth and Sol. The characteristics of Venus, the Roman Goddess are sex, love, beauty, fertility, prosperity and desire. The

---

[592] Inferior planets orbit between the Sun and Earth, whereas superior planets orbit beyond earth

relationship between the mythological and physical aspects of Venus are firstly, the planet is visible early in the morning around dawn before Sol rises. In other words, Venus is the last bright point of light visible before the rising and return of Sol. Likewise, Venus is visible just after Sol has set, and is the first bright point of light visible as darkness approaches. Venus in other words, stands at the threshold between the light of day and the darkness of night and has a position between these opposites, therefore unites them. Venus, as a sexual being, is an appropriate symbol for the union of the light and dark, sex being the union of opposites.

The location of Mars in the Solar system causes its opposition to Sol. This means that earth finds itself in the middle and between Sol on one side and Mars on the other, thus opposing Sol. Ancient Egyptian astronomers regarded him as the wandering planet, and its abundance of iron oxide gave it its distinctive red colour. Mars in Roman mythology is the God of war and guardian of agriculture. The characteristics of Mars are masculine virility, aggression and power, and although he was the force that drives wars, he used war to secure peace. Our everyday experience of Mars is of a wandering red body, with some connection to Venus. Our contemporary knowledge of Mars is growing and he is fourth planet from the sun, has an abundance of iron oxide, may have had water flowing on it at some time, and is the last of the terrestrial planets from Sol. The characteristics the ancients perceived were its colour and movement. Red is of course, the colour of rust and hence iron which is a fitting idea for strength and durability. Red is also the colour of rage and blood spilled during war.

Jupiter is the fifth planet from Sol, a gas giant and the largest planet in the solar system. It is the fourth brightest object in the night sky, and the first recorded sighting was by the Babylonians in the 7th or 8th century BC. Although Venus is brighter, Jupiter is in the night sky longer. Venus is closer to the sun, and therefore generally only visible in the morning and evening, whereas Jupiter is further away and remains visible during the night. With these characteristics, we can see why the ancients called the planet the 'King of Gods', Jupiter (Jove). He is the God of the sky and thunder, and his primary sacred animal was the eagle.

Saturn, the last visible planet to the naked eye, is the sixth planet from Sol, the second-largest planet and a gas giant, with a close association to Jupiter. Approximately every twenty years, Saturn and Jupiter do a retrograde dance across the night sky, which gives them a unique relationship. Jupiter moves across the sky with the less bright and older Saturn behind. Saturn loops back upon its path, Jupiter continues for a time, and does the same and loops back upon its path to follow Saturn. The loop is completed when both return to their original path. The ancients interpreted this unique relationship as a father and son. Jupiter as the young bold son that is younger and brighter, leads the way forward and is called back by his ageing father Saturn, to eventually return to their original path.

Saturn, as the God of agriculture and time, is a perfect example of the wisdom of nature and cycles. Agriculture depends on the seasons more than any other activity, and is the basis of stable and non-nomadic settlement. Other attributes are liberation and time. This, combined with agriculture, shows how the ancients viewed such a God and its dependency on cyclic seasons and correct timing for planting and harvest. With this knowledge, the people liberated themselves from the effort of finding food and bringing it back to their settlements.

I shall only mention the outer planets briefly, as they are not visible to the naked eye, and therefore outside of everyday experience. The ancients were not aware of their existence as they were discovered in the seventeenth century. John Flamsteed first sighted Uranus in 1690, and named it after much wrangling. Johann Bode argued that because Saturn was the father of Jupiter, this new planet should be the father of Saturn, which in mythology is Uranus. Similarly, Neptune discovered by mathematical calculation and anomalies in the orbit of Uranus, thus pointing to another body even further out in the solar system. The naming of Neptune was also controversial and after much argument settled in 1846, although the eventual name is the God of the sea, Neptune's colour was more of a coincidence than a connection to myth. Pluto was also predicted through mathematical analysis and the name proposed by Venetia Burney (1918–2009), an eleven-year-old schoolgirl in Oxford.

The constellations are by far the most difficult and vast expression of our myth-making unconscious. From the beginning of humanity, people looked up at the night sky and saw their Gods in differing situations and relationships. With little or no knowledge of the makeup of the actual constellations, the unconscious had full expression. The ancients perceived the planets moving across the night sky differently from the background constellations, which determined their name as planets (wandering stars). The constellations therefore become background images and stories to the Gods (planets) in the foreground. The patterns and locations of the constellations encouraged imaginative creatures including animals, half-animals and people.

The ancients knew very little about the background stars of the Zodiac constellations as they could only perceive them visually with the naked eye. They moved, as they do today, in unison across the night sky, with the planets moving independently in the foreground. They were therefore free to associate with what they saw. Both the planets and the background constellations have changed very little over time and we can see almost the same things in the night sky as the ancients did. With this knowledge we can differentiate the planets and constellations from the myths associated with them, and look for the elements that reveal their unity. It is as if one were looking into the perception of star patterns, the association to those patterns and the unity between them. We know for example, that Ptolemy related the individual planets to their known behaviour at that time[593]. The following illustration shows how Ptolemy viewed the planets and their locations in the Solar System.

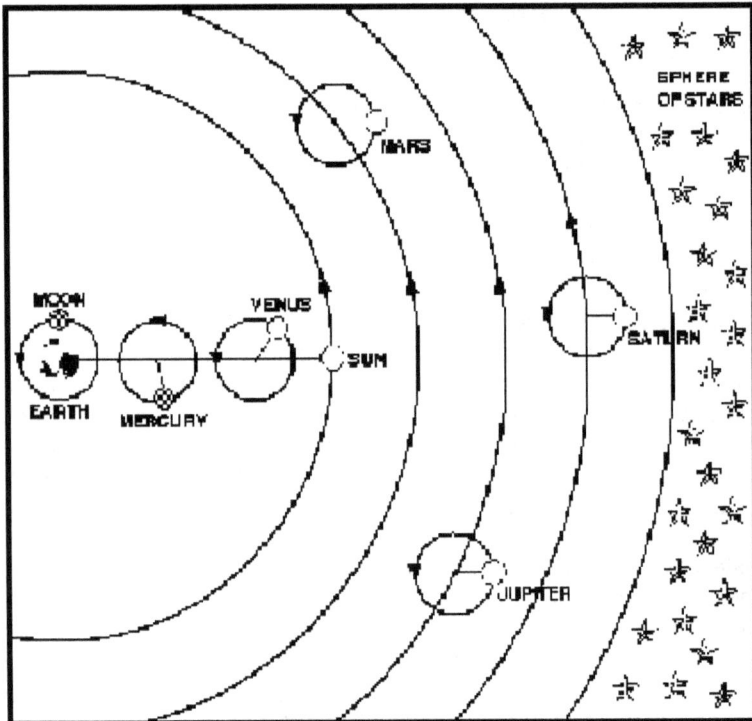

His observations or ideas about the bodies are summarized as follows:

1.   **The Sun**   -Heating and to a certain degree drying,
                         masculine, beneficial and harmful, diurnal
                         -Reason- Size and obvious seasonal changes in

[593] PTOLEMY Claudius, Tetrabiblos Translated from The Greek Paraphrase Of Proclus By J. M. Ashmand , London, Davis And Dickson, 1822

2.	**The Moon**	elevation observed from earth -Humidifying, soften and cause putrefaction, shares moderately in heating due to light from sun, feminine, beneficial, nocturnal -Reason -Close to earth and moist exhalations
3.	**Mercury**	-Drying and absorptive of moisture and humidifying and change quickly from one to the other, masculine and feminine, beneficial and harmful, diurnal and nocturnal -Reason -Close to the sun, next above the sphere of the moon, change due to speed near sun.
4.	**Venus**	-Same temperate nature as Jupiter but acts in opposite way. She warms moderately and humidifies like the moon, is feminine, beneficial, nocturnal -Reason -Nearness to the sun, humidifies because of her femininity
5.	**Mars**	-Dry, burning, masculine, harmful, nocturnal -Reason -Fiery colour and nearness to the sun light and appropriates the exhalations from earth
6.	**Jupiter**	-Temperate active force, both heating and humidifying and produces fertilizing winds, masculine, beneficial, diurnal -Reason-Between cooling of Saturn and burning of Mars
7.	**Saturn**	-Chiefly to cool and dry and rarely moist, masculine, harmful, diurnal[594] -Reason -Furthest removed from sun, exhalations about earth

The way Ptolemy describes the celestial bodies makes it clear that his observations are part physical and part mythological. For example, the sun clearly heats and dries, is definitely diurnal, and can be beneficial and harmful, depending on exposure. We can see the moon during the day, making it both nocturnal and diurnal. The humidifying effect may relate to the effect the moon has on the tides. We know that the physical moon is

---

[594] Ibid, Section 7, "They also assigned to each of the sects the two destructive stars, not however in this instance on the principle of similar natures, but of just the opposite; for when stars of the same kind are joined with those of the good temperament their beneficial influence - is increased, but if dissimilar stars are associated with the destructive Ones the greatest part of their injurious power is broken. Thus they assigned, Saturn, which is cold, to the warmth of day, and Mars, which is dry, to the moisture of night, for in this way each of them - attains good proportion through admixture and becomes a proper member of its sect, which provides moderation. "

a dry, dusty and stony desert, with no obvious moisture. In addition, Ptolemy notes the moon having moist exhalations, because it is close to the earth. We can interpret this as the 'breathing of earth' related to the rising and lowering of the ocean tides (moisture).

The sun and moon have a direct and dramatic effect on the earth. The effect of the other planets is less distinct. In 1852, Swiss astronomer Johann Wolf showed that Jupiter has more gravitational effect on the sun than any other planet. Dr José Abreu from the Institute of Geophysics in Switzerland, recently showed a connection between the other planets and earth and how their gravitational fields had direct relation to sunspot activity and in turn increased levels of cosmic rays hitting earth's atmosphere.

This does not prove the effect the planets have on us, but does point to a physical relationship between them. It may explain how the planet's attributes affect individual's intuitions in astrology. Whether it is direct gravitational and magnetic forces or indirect forces through the sun's activity, it does point to an underlying unity. It is doubtful that Ptolemy knew the physical effects from distant planets but was aware of their associated mythological Gods. In this case, Ptolemy drew conclusions from this knowledge and gave the outer planets their characteristics. It is my task in this book to differentiate between what the ancients could verify visually and what they projected onto them from the myth-making unconscious and find its underlying unity.

Mercury, as we know is the closest planet to the Sun, but to Ptolemy it was the closest planet to Earth. He describes the duality of Mercury and its ability to be either of the opposites with a quick changeability from one to the other. The reason for this viewpoint is due to Mercury's proximity to the sun viewed from earth. This is why we see the planet before sunrise and after sunset. Mercury was originally seen as two planets named Apollo in the morning and Hermes in the evening and in 350BC, the ancients realised it was one planet. This emphasises the physical behaviour of Mercury having a dual nature of a morning and evening aspect. It is from this physical foundation that all the other mythical aspects of Mercury follow. Mercury, the celestial body and its presence in the sky predates human awareness and was therefore always in the night sky for humans to perceive. The behaviour of the planet attracted the projection of a God called Mercury through it behaviour. This forms a connection between an object (Mercury) and an inner character (God) and its behaviour uniting idea and object.

The constellations, which form the background to the planets, are part of our galaxy as seen from earth. There are 88 known constellations, with twelve forming the Zodiac. This was simply a division of the night sky into twelve segments, with each segment dominated by one of the Zodiac constellations. It has not substantially changed since the ancients projected their imaginary animals and characters onto the patterns made by the stars. It is these patterns, and their arbitrary arrangement, that attracted the projections. The patterns in the night sky acted like the Rorschach Inkblot test of the 1960s designed to attract associative projection for psychological analysis. In this case, it was relating visually close stars[595] into an imaginary pattern or mythological scene of animals or characters. The ancients saw the patterns as a background to their Gods, giving them a context for their behaviour.

In addition, the planets are members of the same family with Saturn the patriarch, Jupiter his strong son and Mercury, Venus and Mars, Jupiter's children. Later, when they discovered the outer planets, Uranus became Saturn's father, Pluto and Neptune, Saturn's sons. The relationship between the Zodiac and planets is more complicated and based on behavioural qualities and characteristics that the planet and sign have in common and relate to Plato's cosmological determinants. This gives them their astrological place in the cosmos and relationship to the human myth-making unconscious.

Sol the sun was associated with sign Leo the lion and the element fire. It is also associated with consciousness, spirit, masculinity and Apollo, the sun God. What we know of the sun as thermonuclear reaction and the mythological attributes show how they relate. Leo is the king, and fire the giver of heat and light like the sun. Daylight enables clear perception of the physical world and the spirit of consciousness. Apollo is the personification of those attributes in the form of a deity. In contrast to Sol, Luna is associated with the sign Cancer the crab and the element water. She is also associated with the unconscious, emotion, femininity and Diana, the moon Goddess, who is the twin sister to Apollo. The crab lives in or near the ocean, water is cooling and nourishing and a counterpoint to fire, and thus form a pair of opposites[596].

What we know and imagine about the sun and moon, shows how their relationship originated from their physical characteristics. This is why mythology, and stories in general, resonate with us because they relate to our own inner dream images, ideas and stories. There does not seem to be a positional or mythical relationship between the planets, sun, moon,

---

[595] I say 'visually close' because it depends on our position when viewing the stars. In reality, the stars that look close together in the night sky may be many light years apart.
[596] This interpretation is particular to the western male culture as different cultures have different interpretations. For example the Australian Aborigines regard the sun and feminine and the moon as masculine.

and the star sign constellations. This is presumably because the locations change considerably over time, and the characteristics of each planet and sign relate them to each other. Unlike the sun and moon, the other planets in the solar system are associated with two star signs each, making their relationship more complex and their characteristics more involved.

The relationships between planets and mythology began in ancient times. Today, we have more sophisticated devices to view the cosmos, albeit somewhat removed from everyday life. This is an important fact; the knowledge we are gaining about the cosmos is beyond our everyday perception, and therefore remains knowledge. This is the difference between knowledge and experience as mentioned previously. Knowledge of an object transforms the idea of the object and its projection. Once we know about an object that is observable and verifiable, its projection attracting qualities diminish and the mystery moves further into space. The Hubble telescope has shown us as never before; that we are a very small and insignificant star system among billions of other stars in our galaxy, and our galaxy one of billions of other galaxies.

This has not affected our myth-making ability however. Instead of Mars and Venus, we have a plethora of extra-terrestrial beings superior to us in some way. Some of the aliens are benevolent, and some not. We have developed this movement into space to a fine pitch. Our scientific knowledge of the cosmos has increased and so too, has our mythology. We can see distant star systems with our instruments, and have visited them in our imagination. We can not only travel the great distances faster than the speed of light, but also have friendships and alliances with different species and marvel at their evolution. We have mastered time travel and molecular transportation. The list is as broad as we can imagine and science is finding it difficult to keep up with our myth-making unconscious.

The theory of the Big Bang as discussed previously, shows how we can, with the help of imagination go back to the very beginning of creation, before time, space and matter existed. The only thing missing from that theory is a deity like Ptah or Chaos that gave life to the universe in that instant. I am sure that in time, science will strip away the mystery of creation and reveal the facts involved, and then our imagination will have to move elsewhere for self expression.

11. SYMBOLIC LANGUAGE

a. Associations, Amplification and Objectivity

The language of the unconscious is fraught with difficulty as there is no obvious logic to the images, characters and ideas. We can find ourselves in the most unusual places, flying around without a vehicle, meeting strange people and creatures, doing things that would be immoral to our culture and things that just bewilder us.

Dreams, fantasies, visions, ideas etc., are consistent across all peoples and cultures. This is an important fact, as it has the ability to unite us in a common language beyond political or religious systems. This is why we can find similar stories and behaviours of people with no physical connection on either side of the world. It is the 'sine qua non' of existence. We all emerge from the depths of unconsciousness in childhood, and slowly become aware of ourselves as we grow. The problem with this emergence is that we tend, particularly in the west, to overemphasise the awareness of the outer world and its systems. Obviously, we all need to adapt to the practical circumstances we live in; earn a living, have a family, etc., but the overemphasis on the conscious half of reality stops us from being aware of what the myth-making unconscious has to say about our outer lives, and if we are deviating from our natural path.

This is where the products of the unconscious are important because what the unconscious has to say reflects our conscious lives. It is nature's way of giving an objective viewpoint on our balance in attitude, relationship to the world and other people, and mental and physical health in general. Being natural, the unconscious tends to express itself outside of moral concerns in ways that are often grotesque and brutal. This is where an objective attitude to the images is important. When viewing a lion killing a bison on television, we do not hold ourselves responsible for the act of nature. This is how to view the images and ideas presented to us from inside as objective occurrences given by nature. We may dream of killing someone, but it does not mean that we should kill someone in the physical world. It is generally a reflection of our own attitude and personality. If we recognise this aspect and ask ourselves: What, in my conscious attitude, is killing something in myself? It is a step closer to understanding the dream and its purpose.

The above example illustrates how the unconscious gives us indications of where we are in our lives at that particular moment in time, and reflects our conscious attitude. Initially, the unconscious reflects our personal issues and how we orient ourselves to the physical world. For example, we may prefer thinking, and use that function in our work and life. We are then less aware of the opposite function of feeling. Similarly, the functions of intuition and sensation may be developed and the others remain unconscious. Everyone develops with a natural orientation towards one function, with the other functions emerging as we grow. Three developed functions is rare and four even rarer. This is however, the unity and goal of any personal psychological growth.

At a young age, the unconscious generally[597] produces very personal images and ideas that help the individual adapt and grow in the physical world and culture. It deals with everyday life and reflects that by giving images that one can relate to. The deeper one looks into the unconscious, the more the images become collective representations and mythological. Relationship to these images is simpler and less complex, than the personal unconscious, which requires more insight into the functioning of the individual's psyche. The deeper mythological images and ideas are accessible to all people. In fact, the myth-making unconscious drives everyone and provides the energy to do so.

For example, the most important celestial object in our lives is the sun. Beyond the physical effects and how it provides heat and light for the whole planet, it has a mythological component of dividing the day into light and dark. In other words, it divides the day into consciousness and unconsciousness. It is no coincidence that the celestial bodies such as the sun reflects our own nature.

If we amplify what we know about the sun from our everyday experience, through scientific instrumentality and myths, we can build a comprehensive idea of why the sun is so important to us. Our everyday experience of the sun is not difficult to discern. As mentioned previously, it rises and sets and divides twenty four hours into day and night. To our senses, not enhanced by instrumentality, the sun arcs across the sky around us and we are stationary, which hasn't changed since the ancients. In other words, the sun revolves around us. It is without exception hot and drying and we cannot look at the sun without damaging our eyes. Standing in the sun for too long burns us but enables us to see objects with clarity and distinction by its light. The sun's absence makes objects obscure and indistinct[598]. The sun is predictable and regular to our

---

[597] There are obvious exception to this idea, particularly if the individual is artistic or has a spiritual or philosophical mind.
[598] Artificial light can simulate the sun's light giving properties as a derivative of the sun's energy

senses, yet its elevation in the sky varies throughout the year, giving us the seasons.[599]

Our understanding of the sun is enhanced by our contemporary knowledge of its functioning through observation and measurement. We know that the sun is a star of insignificant importance compared to other stars. It is a 'G' type main-sequence star, with a hot and dense core going through nuclear fusion. The sun's mass is predominately Hydrogen and Helium, with smaller traces of other elements. It is interesting to note that the sun's apparent rotational period at its equator viewed from earth is approximately 28 days, which is the same cycle as the moon.[600]

The sun is middle-aged, with approximately 5 billion years until it turns into a red giant. At that time, the sun will expand in volume engulfing Mercury, Venus, and possibly Earth. The sun is the centre of our solar system, with the planets orbiting it in an approximate flat plane. The sun and our solar system lies close to the inner rim of the Milky Way's Orion Arm and takes 225-250 million years to compete one orbit through the Milky Way at a speed of approximately 792,000 kph.[601] Close observation of the sun's surface through lenses and filters shows it to be volatile and stormy with eruptions of plasma and the ejection of matter into the solar system.

Beyond the everyday experience and knowledge we have of the sun, the mythological background, its projected ideas are many and varied. Many unrelated ancient cultures have worshiped the sun as a deity. These include the ancient Egyptians, Indians, Japanese, Germans and Aztecs, to name a few. Interestingly, not all cultures regard the sun as a masculine God. Some, including German (Sunna), Finns (Beiwe), Arabia (Al-Lat), Australia (Bila, Walo) and Native Americans among the Cherokee (Unelanuhi), Inuit (Malina), associated the sun with a female deity.

A masculine sun generally makes a feminine moon, thus forming a pair of opposites. A feminine sun, switches the role of masculine to the moon, thus preserving the opposites. Why some cultures have a masculine sun and others, a feminine sun is open to conjecture. We know from observation and experience that the sun has a greater influence over our lives than the moon. This may be the key to the male/female projection used to describe the sun's influence. It follows that matriarchal cultures

---

[599] The elevation of the sun is also dependent on location. For example, at the poles the sun arcs low across the sky in summer and below the horizon in winter.
[600] PHILLIPS, K. J. H. (1995). Guide to the Sun. Cambridge University Press. pp. 78–79. ISBN 978-0-521-39788-9.
[601] https://astrosociety.org/edu/publications/tnl/71/howfast.html

regard the sun as feminine and a patriarchal culture, masculine. Whether the sun is male or female is an indication of the cultural background and the people's attitude to the male and female genders. The fact that the sun is both male and female shows that it depends on who perceives the myth, and what the general circumstances are in its creation.

The main point I wish to make is the relationship between the sun's physical qualities and its mythological character perceived by the observer. As a symbol, the sun had a varied but consistent interpretation, based on the sun's actual behaviour. If we dream of the sun, we can use our own personal interpretation to amplify its meaning within the context of our culture. As we have shown, the sun does not mean the same for every culture, yet when coupled with the moon, forms a pair of opposites, which shows that its meaning has common origins.

This is the true nature of symbol and its meaning is never fully understood, as it leads through association to other ideas. As I have shown above, amplifying the meaning of the sun leads to a pair of opposites, with the moon as the sun's counterpart. The sun and moon are the main celestial bodies in our lives, and their influence worshipped as deities by the ancients. Even today, with all our knowledge of the sun and moon as a thermonuclear reaction of hydrogen to helium, and a lifeless and waterless body in orbit around the earth, the influence they have on us is still magical. The sun still guides us with apparent regularity and predictability, illuminates our lives, and gives us comfort in the knowledge that he (or she) will be back again tomorrow to give his (or her) warmth. Similarly, the moon illuminates the dark sky at night, and although less obviously predictable than the sun, still cycles through our lives with regularity.

All physical objects have a corresponding idea in the psyche. For example, the idea of the sun comes from its physical effect on us. It is hot, dry, burning, regular, predictable, gives light, etc. These physical characteristics make up the base idea of the sun. The idea of the sun does not exist in isolation, and draws other ideas to it. In other words, it is our nature to see objects within a pattern of unity. In addition to the energy the object provides, the idea also provides psychic energy. The psyche also puts the object into a context, much the same as the ancients put the planetary Gods in the context of the constellations. As we have seen, they all belonged to a family, and this helps us understand how ideas interact. The family members and relationships between them is the unity of object and idea.

The fact that the sun is dominant in the day and moon at night is obvious. The relationship between sun and moon less obvious. We know that the moon orbits the earth, which in turn orbits the sun. The ancients believed the sun orbited the earth, as did the moon. It is therefore easy to see the association of Sun, Moon and Earth (observer) with the ideas of father, mother and child (observer), or mother, father and child, as the case may be.[602] We all know what it is like to have a sun and moon in our lives. In addition, the light of the moon is a reflection of the sun, putting them into relationship. The essence of unity is the relationship between objects and people and projections onto objects and people, within a given context.

From the above, we can see how one object like the sun leads us to other objects like the moon. It is only with our intellect that we try to isolate one object from another in order to study it. The reality is however, quite different. Nothing exists in isolation, as objects and people always connect to other objects and people. In the cosmic field, the planets orbit around our sun, the sun around our galaxy and it follows that our galaxy orbits around the universe in some way. Our contemporary knowledge has not yet confirmed this possibility. The example of the sun leads us through association to the moon and earth, and on to the other planets and celestial objects, through to the Milky Way galaxy, and so on. One idea leads us to another and another and the chain of ideas leads us to unknown areas of the psyche. Ultimately, this chain of ideas leads to the unity of all things.

When we have chains of ideas such as this, it is our nature to put them into a pattern of relationship. In other words, we connect the ideas with known relationships that are familiar to us. In addition to the sun and moon, the ancients gave names to the planets based on their characteristics and behaviour in the night sky. Mercury, the messenger of the God idea (Sun, father) is due to his proximity to the sun. He therefore appears close to sun at dawn and dusk. Similarly, Venus is the brightest and most beautiful wandering star (planet) in the morning and evening. Saturn is the patriarch of the planets[603]; Jupiter is his son, Mercury, Venus and Mars, Jupiter's sons and daughter. The planets, or more precisely, the projection onto the planets, are an extended family.

As with any family, the ancient mythological characters had definite personality traits. Saturn for example, was the old patriarch and concerned with nature and cycles. If he were a person, he would be sense oriented, practical and earthy. Jupiter his son, a strong and promiscuous leader, having numerous partners, and siring numerous children, including Mercury, Venus and Mars. He is concerned with the

---

[602] See Plato's Cosmology, in 'Ideas of Unity in Philosophy' Chapter 4

[603] Uranus, Neptune and Pluto cannot be seen with the naked eye and were discovered much later with the help of telescopes. However, Uranus is Saturn's father, Neptune, Pluto and Jupiter are Saturn's sons.

light daytime sky (air), state and law, a conscious activity of human order. Mercury a flighty and quick trader, concerned with money (energy) and travel; Venus, a beautiful, loving and sexy woman and Mars, like his grandfather, is a nature (chthonic) character, and a strong and courageous fighter.

What this shows is that the mythological characters are not so different from patterns of behaviour we can experience today. We have all met the down to earth agricultural type, as well as the beautiful, sexy woman and her brother, the fighter. With this in mind, we can conclude that the ancients had developed a rudimentary scheme describing psychological types, and worshipped these types as universal constants. They have not disappeared at all, but simply changed their names. Instead of the Oedipus myth, we now say Oedipus complex, thanks to Freud. Instead of Apollo, we have Luke Skywalker, instead of Artemis, we have Zena, the Warrior Princess.

Mythology is always with us. We can deny it and only look at the world in a rational and sense-oriented way, which removes its soul, or we can acknowledge the brilliance and beauty of a world full of wonder and mystery. The collective ideas of mythology belong to our nature, and denying their existence is to cut one self off from our foundation and nature. Freud and Jung, who were essentially mental health experts recognising the need for a healing connection to the deep myth-making processes we all share.

b. Synchronistic Phenomenon

The term 'Synchronicity' was coined by Carl Jung as early as 1920, and grew out of his personal experiences and interaction with Einstein and Pauli. It is a misnomer to say that Jung discovered this phenomenon, albeit, he gave it a new name. Other terms used for this phenomenon are: 'Serendipity', coined by Horace Walpole (1717-1797), which emphasises the positive aspects of the phenomenon, 'Seriality', by Paul Kammerer (1880-1926) and more recently, 'Simulpathity', By Bernard Beitman, the founder of Coincidence Studies.

As discussed earlier, the mind of our ancestors is based on synchronistic phenomenon, as is the western tradition of Cleromancy and the eastern practices of the I Ching. The connection between synchronicity and miracle is also unmistakeable, as the definition of miracle is 'an event due to supernatural agency'[604], but as with serendipity, its emphasis is on

---

[604] Oxford Dictionary, University Press, Oxford 1969

positive events. Spinoza recognised the unknown aspect of miracles, but suspects that there is a physical cause, yet unknown.

> "miracles are merely law like events whose causes we are ignorant of. We should not treat them as having no cause or of having a cause immediately available."[605]

Hume, on the other hand, regarded miracles as transgressions of natural law, but recognised a supernatural force at work.

> "a transgression of a law of nature by a particular volition of the Deity, or by the interposition of some invisible agent"[606]

Miracles may be the precursor to the concept of synchronicity, but their tendency to be divorced from everyday experience and become part of the mythology, leads us to conclude that the difference between miracles and synchronicity is a matter of degree and relationship. Indeed, as our previous study has shown, projection is the earliest form of synchronicity of a lesser degree. Parting the Red sea, for example, is not possible in our physical reality. Similarly, the resurrection of Jesus as a foundation stone of Christian belief is one of the most important miracles in history.[607] We cannot diminish its mythological importance as part of a great story and psychological reality.

This aspect of miracles shows that their connection to our everyday experience need not be included. This gives the miracle numinosity over our mind, yet a niggling doubt as to their authenticity. One could say that miracles of this calibre are hooks for what is possible in our imagination, but impossible to experience physically in everyday life. Synchronicities, on the other hand, are smaller, closer and personal miracles that most people can experience, particularly if the event moves them inside, or corresponds to an inner idea, fantasy or thought. This is the difference between miracles and synchronistic events, in that the former emphasises the beneficent aspect of the event and fascinates us because it stands outside our physical experience of reality, whereas synchronicity connects us to the physical experience of reality. In some way, it is the miracle coming down to earth, so we can experience it for ourselves.

---

[605] SPINOZA, Benedictus de. 'Chapter 6: Of Miracles'. Thelogico -Political Treatise, translated by Robert Willis.

[606] Miracles on the Stanford Encyclopedia of Philosophy

[607] There are instances in history where people have been pronounced dead and come back to life. This is certainly true with our modern medical procedures. But if someone in AD 33 is tortured, nailed to a cross for days and speared in the chest, the chances of him ever coming back to life is low.

Synchronicity is the name for the connection between physical objects and the corresponding thought, idea or fantasy. It is the connection, or relationship of the inner realm to the object, which makes this phenomenon real. An event without the corresponding inner connection can only be termed a 'coincidence' as the inner thought, idea or fantasy is not connected to the event. More and more people want to bridge the gulf between our scientific knowledge and awareness of the supernatural[608] forces that govern our unity. Synchronistic events are however, unlike miracles not always positive.

We all look for the wonderful event that will lead us to the promise of understanding and awareness. Unfortunately, the myth-making unconscious as part of nature, does not work from moralistic standpoints. Its concern is balance and growth and may take many forms. For example, a man that has lead a righteous and reasonable existence will be lacking instinctive and natural impulses and the unconscious will reflect this in his dreams. If the opposite is denied for too long, the man will experience a personal disaster to correct the imbalance. This may take the form of an accident, broken relationship, or loss of some kind. When an individual is not aware of his inner situation, or the need for growth in a certain area, it happens to him as fate. We all know that fate acts outside of our ethical constructs and does not concern itself with good or evil, it is simply nature. The ancient Greeks personified fate as 'fate spinners', called Moirai, who were three women that spun the thread of our lives. If any man has experienced a love affair with a 'Femme Fatale', and the intense pleasure and beauty of the relationship and its eventual demise, anguish and misery, he will know exactly how fate works.[609]

Milder negative forms of synchronicity occur when objects do not work as they intended. Electronic things break or malfunction when needed. A watch will stop working when you have an important meeting. Your car won't start when you want to meet a new woman, or say the wrong thing in a meeting, or run up the back of the car in front when you are thinking about running away from a responsibility. All of these are meaningful corrections, and happen as everyday experiences. In addition to the small, pleasing and annoying synchronicities that we can experience every day, there are the life-changing positive milestones, such as getting that hard-earned degree, meeting your wife to be, having children, buying your first home. Negative synchronicities are those failures at work, broken relationships, house fires, big accidents, and early death.

---

[608] I use the term supernatural, as we don't understand the forces that cause these phenomena.
[609] JUNG C G, Archetypes of the Collective Unconscious, Routledge and Kegan Paul 1959, page 88 (b) Overdevelopment of Eros

The large positive coincidences that we all experience in life are the ones that connect us to the unity inherent in existence and our path towards that unity. Our education and attainment of qualifications give us the opportunity to gain standing in the community and belonging. Marriage[610] is the union with a partner, and the opportunity to gain knowledge of our own contra-sexual nature[611]. Marriage also gives us the opportunity to have a family and satisfy our biological responsibility. All these aspects of fate generally occur of their own accord, whether we help them or not. A job or profession comes upon us via an idea or a chance encounter or advice from an external source. Meeting one's partner is an event that happens more by synchronicity than it does volition.

On the other hand, personal disasters can be viewed the same as positive events in life. The only difference is that the latter is painful, whereas the former, pleasurable. The goal is the same, and that is the growth and broadening of psychological awareness. It is the meaning of the event, whether positive or negative, that is important for the individual. Relationship breakups are fertile grounds for synchronistic phenomenon. A couple unites to learn something about each other through projection, to bring out something in themself that they needed to know. Once achieved, the relationship may continue, transform, or end.

Jung and Von Franz[612] regard the psyche and matter belonging to a universal 'Acausal Orderedness' that connects both realms through synchronistic phenomena. It is the connection or relationship between the external event and the internal movement of an idea or fantasy that impresses us. These can occur simultaneously in linear time, or at different times, and the connection can take different forms. For example, a connection can be made when an event occurs at the same time and different space. In other words, movement is towards the temporal side of reality and relationship to the physical. We can view the event as an ordered movement towards the physical, analyse the specific aspects of the event as if it were a dream, and apply our knowledge of associative symbol.

Besides the large pronounced events in life as mentioned above, we can miss numerous subtle occurrences due to their low energy level. The little things that may seem insignificant to a third party, but meaningful to the observer. For example, a middle-aged man who had been an aviator and

---

[610] I use the term marriage in its symbolic form as a union of any two people.
[611] Even in a gay marriage it is the masculine component projected onto the partner in order to explore the feminine.
[612] VON FRANZ, Marie Louise, Psyche & Matter. ISBN 978-1-57062-620-3

skydiver in his past had the following experience on a summer Sunday afternoon.

> I was sitting in the sun and noticed a small hovering fly close to the grass. I marvelled at the beauty and magnificence of its flying ability, which seems very precise and co-ordinated. I related it to my own flying experience, and as my thoughts dwelled on that, when the shadow of a predatory bird flew directly over the fly. The meaning of the occurrence was made clear that, although I had fond memories of past experiences of flight and freefall, the experience made me aware that I could not return to my escapist aspect of the past and the danger involved in those activities as symbolised by the shadow of the predatory bird. Trying to relive the past would be negative and not in the best interest of my personal growth.

This is the nature of small synchronistic experiences. These are difficult to convey to other people, because they occur to the individual alone. In this respect, synchronistic phenomenon is similar to dreams, as only the dreamer perceives them. There are instances however, where more than one person perceives the occurrence and the experience is shared.

The goal of synchronistic experiences is to relate the occurrence or event to the unfolding process of one's life and our position on our natural path in life. Unfortunately, or fortunately, depending on which way you look at it, humans have the ability to deviate from their path which makes us prone to instability and imbalance. In religious terms, it is the ability to sin. Deviating from one's path is an individual problem, which has many causes including getting too comfortable, unwilling to change, as well as cultural one sidedness.

For example, the school system provides a broad range of activities so that the students get a taste of as many opportunities available in life. This is a good start to a young person's interests, but too often, the school system emphasises the subjects oriented towards adaptation to the prevailing culture, rather than the individual. Some people do not function that way and we cannot expect an introverted bookworm to do well at athletic sports unless they are so inclined. This is typical of an extroverted culture, in that participation in extroverted activities and subjects are preferred over introversion and daydreaming.

Most extraverts have trouble understanding introversion especially in extraverted countries like the Unites States, and non-participation in society's activities sometimes regarded as an illness. This is where an individual may deviate from their path and forsake their natural orientation, for the sake of external adaptation. Deviation from one's natural path may lead to disturbance if extreme but the imbalance is always addressed in dreams and synchronistic occurrences. Their function is to make us aware of the imbalance and correct our one sided attitude. Many cultures have recognised the importance of synchronistic occurrences, and created methods to encourage its activation. These include: gambling, playing cards and other games, praying, and the eastern I Ching using yarrow sticks, coins, dice, marbles, beads or grains of rice. The idea behind these activities is to encourage chance and patterns that may guide an individual on their path to balance and unity.

Gambling is an interesting form of synchronistic encouragement, in that one bets on a chance event with the hope that the event's outcome will be favourable. Although the reward is monetary, it can help with life's burdens and ease the struggle for survival. The energy behind gambling is the same energy behind a spiritual pursuit. Both look for help from an unknown source to make life easier and less traumatic. There is a character behind every urge to gamble which is expressed in our mood and attitude. In the ancient Greek tradition, the Goddess Tyche (Fortuna in the Roman tradition) was the personification of luck and fate. She is veiled and blind representing life's unpredictability and how fate organises life outside of our will and desire[613].

Unpredictability is uncomfortable for some and governments make every effort to control it. We play games with the hope of a favourable outcome, organise our societies into groups and make laws in order to remove the unpredictability of fate. We create religions and worship deities that represent the unpredictable forces of our nature and prefer positive synchronicities in the form of miracles and serendipity. Yet the negative occurrences move us more, albeit tragically. The ancient Greeks were very aware of this aspect of life.

We pray for life to go smoothly and fate to look upon us favourably, yet the final outcome of life is always a tragedy for those left behind. We build walls between what we know and what we fear to avert disaster and not what lies beyond not to break through the wall. Yet, it is that fear of the unknown that synchronicities, dreams, fantasies and ideas address every day. A wall, law, government, church etc., does not stop the unconscious from its free-flow of material into our conscious minds. Synchronicity helps us become aware of that material, because it connects us to the physical, and encourages us to ask the age-old question, why the inner and outer occurrences coincided.

---

[613] If one is aware of the direction life is flowing, one can see the meaning behind it and synchronistic occurrences, whether positive or negative, are less surprising and destructive.

The meaning of an inner image, fantasy, idea etc., and the physical event or occurrence is the connection or relationship between them. The connection is the third uniting principal which contains its meaning. For example, the story of the fly and its precision flying impressed the aviator emotionally and spiritually. The shadow of the predatory bird that flew over the fly brought the spirit down to earth and made him aware that beauty and savagery unite in nature. The dark bird could eat the skilled fly at any time. The two sides united as one, impressed him through this simple and everyday experience.

c. Components of Synchronicity

Synchronistic events comprise of several components held in unity by the centre of the event. These components pertain to our understanding of idea, space/matter, time, energy and the central component of purpose or meaning, which hold the others together. To begin this study, I shall set the groundwork with a short description of the four components, plus unifying centre mentioned above.

The first component is the psychic material and starting point for such experiences and movement in the unconscious, which can include dreams, visions, fantasies, intuitions, and ideas. Emotions may or may not accompany this phenomenon. It is this psychic material that enables us to experience the synchronistic event. Without this material there is no corresponding inner and outer connection, and therefore no synchronicity. The experience can only occur when a corresponding event in the physical world relates to a corresponding psychic movement.

The definition of space is many and varied. In philosophy, Plato regarded it as the 'Receptacle of being'. Leibniz related space to objects (matter) that occupy it, and could not exist on its own. Kant regarded space as the framework for organising experience. Physics, before relativity, regarded space and time as independent dimensions, as we can move through space in any direction, but can only move through time in one direction. In the myth-making unconscious, however, both space and time are relative and spatial laws of physics do not exist and are relative to the imagery and ideas expressed. Similarly, time loses its temporal and cyclic quality, and becomes eternal for the purpose of the inner expression.

Einstein's general relativity showed that space and time related to each other and explored this concept further in his special relativity. This can be emphasised by the fact that looking at the objects in the night sky, is actually looking into the past, as the light from the observed object is the light that was emitted from that object in the past. This is due to the vast distances in space, the speed of light in a medium, and the time it takes to perceive the light on earth.

Space, at the molecular and atomic level is more intriguing. The scaled distance between the nucleus and electron cloud of an atom is comparable to the distances between our sun and orbiting planets. With this fact, we know that matter is predominately made up of space, and the forces between the nucleus and electron cloud give matter its structure. The Intermolecular (weak) forces (attraction and repulsion) between molecules are easily broken, as previously discussed. They are easily broken with small variations in temperature and pressure. The intramolecular (strong) forces that hold the molecule together require more energy to break. These forces occupy the space between particles over large[614] distances. Space, to our unaided senses, is infinite in its extension and non-existent in matter. Yet, the space within atoms is much larger than the actual size of the particles.

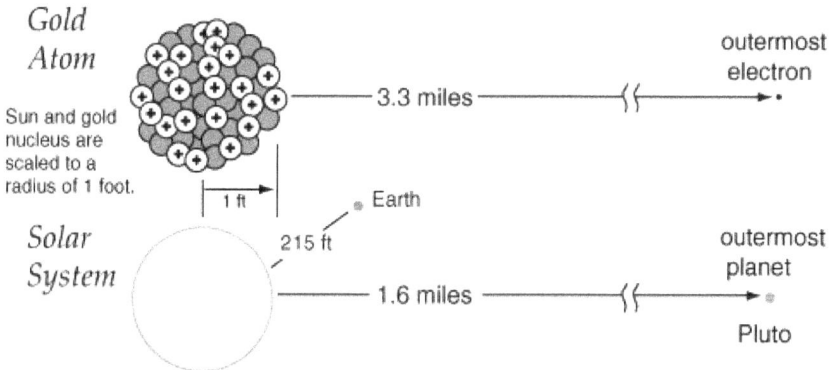

Gold Atom

Sun and gold nucleus are scaled to a radius of 1 foot.

———— 3.3 miles ———— ⟨⟨————→ •

outermost electron

1 ft

• Earth

Solar System

215 ft

———— 1.6 miles ———— ⟨⟨————→ •

outermost planet

Pluto

Matter is therefore a large amount of space between small particles in comparison to the space surrounding them. What we perceive as solid is at this scale more space than solid. Naturally, this knowledge contradicts what we perceive with our unaided senses, for we touch matter and it is solid. When we touch a solid with our fingers, we cannot penetrate it easily due to the forces holding the molecules and atoms together. We can demonstrate this using two magnets where the forces extent beyond their matter into the surrounding space and interact with each other by no visible means.

Time is the measurement of intervals of the earth's rotation in relation to the sun. The cycle is measured, gradated, named and progresses in an

---

[614] Large in this instance is relative to the distance between the particles and the size of the particles.

413

irreversible direction from past, through a conceptual present[615], to the future. We can only move forward through time at a constant rate, depending on the cycle related to it. To our senses, time is an inevitable consequence of life, and presents itself in cycles of day and night. To our feeling, time has some relativity, and felt in different ways. For example, we experience a slow day that seems to drag on and a busy day where time 'flies' at an increased rate. To our intuition, time is even further relativised, and almost loses its linearity into the eternal. The closer we get to the unconscious, the more relative time becomes.

In the immediate world, time has less to do with space than matter. It is possible that Einstein's theory had more to do with his understanding of his feeling and sensation functions. Time, being a symbol for feeling and space for the perception of the physical world. To our immediate experience, we can move through space in any direction, yet we can only move through time in one direction at a predetermined rate. Humans set this rate with reference to celestial cycles. Movement in time, backwards or forwards, is a projection of the relativity of time in the unconscious. Time, as divisions of cycles into regular increments is largely arbitrary, in that it depends on the sun and rotation of the earth. If they were to change, then time would also change. For example, if the rotation of the earth slowed so that the interval of one revolution was now twenty-five hours, our whole concept of time requires adjustment accordingly. If, for argument's sake, we divorced time from the rotation of the earth and related it to an arbitrary reference, we would be moving through time faster or slower than before. It then becomes meaningless to think that time is anything other than a conceptual framework based on natural cycles.

Energy in physics has a mechanical component, in that it has the capacity to perform work. Energy also plays a major role in our psychic system. For example, having a synchronistic experience has a great impression on the psyche releasing energy in the form of emotion. The emotions awe, curiosity, fear, pleasure, guilt, wonder, joy, timidity etc., cause a mechanical movement in our bodies. The list is exhaustive, and depends on the type of experience. These emotions in turn affect the bodily functions with an increased heartbeat and body temperature, etc. We feel liberated and connected to a system much larger than our everyday life.

---

[615] The present has no dimension in time. It is an idea where past and future meet. It does however feel real because it incorporates our immediate memory and prediction of future events. For example if I prepare a meal and sit down in front of it, I remember just preparing the meal and predict (anticipate) that I will soon eat the meal.

The final component in the experience of synchronicity is the purpose of the union of inner and outer movements, and the reason for the event. This is the important aspect of the experience and gives it its meaning. Again, this varies according to the subject's position on their path, and how close they are to becoming aware of their idea of unity. This is the purpose of the experiences, in that they lead the subject to a greater awareness and relationship to their idea.

The purpose of a synchronistic experience is similar to the function of dreams, fantasies, ideas etc., in that they guide us, warn us or help us become aware of the opposites and their relationship to the idea of unity. The biggest difference between the former and the latter is that dreams, fantasies, ideas etc., are unconscious functions and express themselves to the individual alone. Synchronistic experiences express themselves to individuals in the physical world, which makes them perceptible by others. It is impossible to share the impact of a dream with someone else; due to the way we perceive it alone. More than one person can however, share a synchronistic experience, thus help them see the connection between the unconscious and physical world. This aspect of nature brings psychic experiences down to earth for all to see, which were like miracles in the past.

Synchronicities, as with dreams, have degrees of intensity. This depends on the strength of impression and amount of energy released. For example, big synchronicities, like big dreams, leave a lasting impression, and strengthen the idea that there are things within and outside us that orders existence. These experiences happen to all people at some time in their lives. If they do not perceive the inner movement and its relationship to the outer event, it simply becomes a coincidence and the meaning not felt. If the connection made between inner and outer movements, and the experience reaches our feeling, then we realise that there are forces at work in the unconscious as well as the physical world, beyond our control and understanding.

There is a danger however, that all the years of our evolution and hard-won consciousness is overthrown, and the unconscious given the upper hand. This is as one-sided as regarding the conscious world as the only reality. If we throw out our scientific understanding and knowledge and give in to the early human animism, then we achieve nothing, and all of the contents from the unconscious are projected onto the physical world, with a corresponding undifferentiated idea of unity. Everything that occurs then becomes coincident, and one loses the connection to the reality of the object, beyond one's idea of it.

Throughout life, we have opportunities to develop and recognise different parts of our functioning. For example, a new job, partner or moving to a new country with a different culture, requires us to adapt in a different way and develop functions that were previously unconscious. Taking up a new sport also requires new skills and sense adaptations that may have been previously unconscious. The new functions also bring energy and connections to our unity, and this includes synchronicities, which help bring all the functions of our unity into our awareness.

To summarise, synchronicity is the realisation of the connection, or relationship, between an outer event and inner thought or idea, which leaves an emotional impression and has meaning for our personal development. It also reflects our position on life's path and helps us find the natural oscillation from one side to the other along that path. Without recognition of the connection to the inner content, the experience is a coincidence and the impression unrecognised, and the purpose or meaning of the experience missed. The fundamental difference between coincidence and synchronicity is the recognition of the connection or relationship between inner and outer movements, and to know what is inner and outer in itself. It puts the observer in the central position between the two halves of reality and not identical to either.

d. Categories of Synchronicity

The following examples of synchronistic experiences show their relationship and unity in different ways. Sometimes, they coincide in space, sometimes in time, sometimes in matter (objects), or combinations of the three, and on occasion, all three. The following categories are by no means exhaustive, and I regard it as an evolving list. As more and more people experience the unconscious in this way, the categories should grow. Permutations of synchronicity show a complete lack of boundaries, and display a unique form of flexibility and individuality. Synchronicity does not fit into categories very well, and the experiences show a tendency to overlap and be fluid in their expression.

I. Instantaneous Synchronicities

The characteristic of Instantaneous Synchronicity is its immediacy in time and space. For example, the event occurs immediately an inner thought or idea perceived. The hallmark of this type of experience is its instant recognition. In other words, there is no delay in the perception of the synchronicity, and the inner and outer movement coincide in time. For example, we may be thinking about a particular person and the phone rings, and it is that person. Then it opens the door to questions like: why did that person ring? What does the person represent to me? What qualities does the person have and how do I relate and behave with that person?

Another example is the above 'Fly and Bird' experience of the middle-aged man with an aviation past, who instantly realised that his fondness for escapism and excitement was inadvisable at this stage in his life. This experience is a subtle warning to the man that past activities and attitudes should be avoided for the sake of a different form of development, and that he would be avoiding some aspect of his current life for the sake of an old one. In other words, he risked going off his serpentine path of his life. This is quite a common mistake individuals make as they have fond memories of a youthful activity and try to capture that attitude again through the same activity.

Instant synchronicities, as with other unconscious products, can be either positive or negative. They can guide us to the right decision, or detract us from the wrong decision. This is where humans and animals differ. We have a certain amount of free will, and this can lead us into opposition with our own nature. Animals have a weak level of consciousness, and seldom behave outside of their instincts. It is this ability to 'sin'[616], which gives us an opportunity to differentiate the opposites, but also to re-integrate them into a new form.

II.   Series of Synchronicities

Synchronicities that occur in series often link to decision-making and are generally subtle in their expression. They are easy to miss, as they provide subtle hints along a timeline to a goal. The following example from our middle-aged aviator illustrates this path.

> I wanted to buy a new car and didn't know what to get. I went to a local dealer and drove a used Lexus and liked it very much. It wasn't quite the right car but I searched for a similar model to buy. I took my wife to another dealership and test-drove another Lexus. The air conditioner didn't work and for some reason a large truck was backing up towards us at a stoplight and nearly crashed into us. Again, I realised this is not the car. After much searching and disappointment, I found a privately owned car loved by its owner. My wife and I drove to where the car was and I had doubts, as all previous viewings were disappointing. On the way to see the car a Lexus of the same make but opposite colour (it was black and the car we were seeing was white) followed us into the tunnel we had to drive through. This gave me a good feeling about the car I was going to see. Sure enough, the Lexus was in very good condition and we got it for a good price.

---

[616] I use the term 'sin' as our ability to deviate from a set of guidelines. In this instance the guidelines are set by our nature, not a religion.

This set of experiences show his conscious decisions guided by small synchronistic experiences, which were all negative, and positive when the right car came along. Perseverance and the inclusion of his feeling guided him to the right decision. He realised that dealerships just want a sale and did not care about the cars they were selling. On the other hand, the private owner loved and cared for his car which was reflected in its condition. The initial test drive set the scene for the type of car, and through permutations of possibilities, the right car found and purchase reinforced by the final synchronistic event. The car was important to the man because he regarded it as a vehicle to travel into the world and it became part of his persona character.

III. Major Guiding Synchronicities

These types of synchronicities are life changing, and happen to everyone at some time. They include the major positive events such as completing education, finding a career, meeting a future partner, building a home, having children and so on. If we look closely at how these events occur and view them objectively, it generally appears that they come about of their own accord. We meet the right person at the right time, or find a job opportunity just when we needed it, and so on. The following example shows how these life-changing events occur. They are from the life of our aviator meeting his future wife:

> I knew I had to come down to earth and stop trying to escape reality. My first marriage had fallen apart; I was alone and had thoughts about having a family, but didn't know how to go about it. I had a fling with a femme fatale and she made me crash even further down. I was at the end of my jumping and flying activities and needed stability. Having been a bachelor adventurer and athlete most of my life, I thought I should look into doing what everyone else seems to do. I went to visit an old skydiving buddy who told me about this woman who had two kids and was very artistic and had run a café at the local drop zone. I went to the drop zone and she wasn't there, and I didn't think about it again. One Saturday night, the jumpers and I were getting drunk, as was usual, and a car pulled up in front of me. I got in, not knowing where we were going, but was happy to go along for the ride. We ended up at a house in a country estate. Two close female friends were having a party and I eventually married and have a family, with of them.

The above example shows how the unconscious helps an individual on his life's path. Had he rejected this opportunity, his loneliness and lack of connection to the earth would have deepened and possibly led to disaster. His path required a better earthly adaptation, including the responsibility of a wife and children, and he was wise to accept it. Too often, individuals are stuck in a life that they believe they have chosen, and reject change to that life. This is the same as regarding the physical world as the only form of reality.

IV. Major Correcting Synchronicities

These synchronicities occur when one has gone astray from life's path. As mentioned previously, synchronicity is not always positive and can be life changing through disaster. Before such disasters occur, warnings are always given from inside, through dreams, fantasies, subtle synchronicities, etc. Ignoring these inevitably leads to a major correction in attitude through a negative external event or accident. What seems like a disaster on the surface is a correction that was necessary for the balance and well being of the individual.

A 30-year-old man was in a rut and experienced the following events. He had had a few romantic flings and did not enjoy his work. He decided to visit some old friends overseas to help him out of his situation. He was not aware that he was about to have an emotional disaster.

> I had to get away and change my stifling life. I quit my job and flat and moved back into my parent's home. From here, I travelled overseas to visit my old friends. On a connecting flight, I was seated next to a woman towards whom I had an instant like. She stirred something in me that I hadn't felt for a long time. It turned out that she lived in the same city as my friends. I visited my friends, made contact with the woman, and spent much time with her. We were like two little kids together and had much fun. We were in love. I had a return ticket and had to leave, but agreed that we should get married when I returned. I went home and sold my car and shipped my belongings overseas. I returned several months later and everything fell apart. I was stopped at immigration and my passport confiscated and told I had to leave the country within a few weeks and retrieve my passport at the local office in the city I was travelling to.

> I landed on her doorstep in shock and her love for me immediately evaporated. She squirmed at every idea of being a couple, and I was an emotional wreck. I had given up my life for a new one that wasn't there. The experience made me realise that I cannot escape a dreary life for an imaginary one, and flew home completely demoralised and had to start building a new life from scratch. I didn't want to go back to my parents, so I stayed in a hotel till I could get a job, rent a flat and get back in order.

Later discussion with the man revealed that he thought that it was probably necessary to go through this disaster and reach rock bottom so that he could start again. He was not aware enough of his process to make the necessary change by will, and fate organised this disastrous love affair to initiate the change. He later confessed that he felt more alive during this episode than ever before. He went from the ecstatic high of falling in love, to the dramatic fall back to earth and reality, with its emotional upheaval and pain. He also said that he would do it all again just to feel those opposites.

The man's experience extended over several months and shows how the unconscious organises a correction to one's life. In this case, he was still tied to his parents, particularly his mother, and he saw this as an opportunity to escape from her influence to a form a paradise with his newfound mate. He also realised that the woman was a 'femme fatale'[617] and that her function in the events was to encourage his separation from his mother. Her interest evaporated once she achieved the separation and she rejected him, due to a lack of maternal instinct. He recalled an auditory vision of his mother knocking on the front door while lying in bed with his mate, which reinforces this conclusion.

The events experienced by this man show that synchronicity need not be an instantaneous experience coinciding with an inner movement, but can be a series of events that all lead to one conclusion. In this instance, there was an urge for a new life, or at least, a renewal of life. For him it was a sacrifice of his old stifling existence for something new, fresh and different. He lacked an emotional life, and sought it away from his current situation. The fact that he said that he would 'do it all again' just for the emotional experience of high and low, shows that what he needed was given to him in a roundabout way. He needed an upheaval to put him back on track, and this is exactly what happened to him. What, on the surface seemed like a disaster, later turned out to be exactly what he needed at that time in his life.

V. Convergence Synchronicities

This type of synchronicity has the hallmark of a dual series of events that flow together to form a powerful experience, and hence leave a strong impression on the subject. The following is an experience by a young artist who had very interesting ideas about the contemporary morality of his culture.

> I had an idea for a painting of a naked woman coming out of the ocean with pubic hair that had grown into the shape of a bikini bottom. I hunted

---

[617] The femme fatale is written about in C.G. Jung, The Archetypes of the Collective Unconscious, Routledge London, 1955, Page 94. He uses the term 'overdeveloped Eros' and regards this type as a purposeful arrangement of nature and their function is to help males liberate themselves from their mothers.

around for an image to copy and found one in a magazine and proceeded to paint the picture. The painting was almost finished when a friend suggested we visit an old friend of his in the same city. We were sitting in a group around an outdoor setting, and some neighbors' (a couple) came over to join us. They sat down I looked at the woman, and a chill went up and down my spine. She was the woman from the magazine that I was painting. Later in the evening, I had the painting delivered to where we were so that all could see that it was true.

The above example shows how an experience can bring two streams of unrelated events through a series of random movements of the individual in time and space. Firstly, the artist had the 'idea' for the painting. This was uppermost in his mind. He searched for an image to copy and found an image in a magazine. The woman was simply a model posing for a shot in that particular magazine. The artist studied the image and looked at her form, colour, contour and beauty to reproduce her on his canvas. We can safely assume that the image drew much of his attention and concentration. He went through a series of unrelated events to get to his friend's associates house, and through another unrelated event of the neighbours visiting his friend's associate. This is where the convergence of inner psychic material and outer coincidence occurs. The woman he was painting had materialised in front of his eyes, and the synchronistic experience completed. The woman indeed confirmed that she had posed for the magazine picture years ago when she was a model.

Firstly, we have the initial idea for the painting, then the search for a physical image in the form of a photograph of a real person. In other words, matter in space to satisfy the idea. It is not quite the physical person as it is an image of a physical person. This is typical of this individual's creative process using images of real people for his work. The next step in the event is the almost completed painting. Now we have a series of unrelated occurrences of a friend who had an associate that he was visiting and the friend's associate had a neighbour visiting. It only required one of the chains of events to break down and the experience would not have occurred. The final experience of convergence was realised when the artist became aware that the woman he was painting was sitting in front of him in the flesh.

The following breakdown of the experience in terms of the components shows how the sequence unfolded:

Idea	-Unrelated in time & space to experience
Magazine image	-Unrelated in time & space to experience but a physical manifestation (matter) of the idea
Friends neighbour	-Unrelated in time, yet related in space to object (matter) a convergence

Connection	-The process has gone from idea to image of idea to real person.
Impression/Energy	-The artist experienced awe and wonder and realised that other forces were in control of reality and a corresponding increase in personal energy and incentive to explore these experiences further
Purpose	-Movement from inner idea to outer reality, as an artist, his inner images were very important but his relation to outer reality weak. This experience helped him get closer to this aspect of things

The next experience was from the same artist many years later. He had adapted to the outer world, had a wife and children, built a home for them, and was thriving in his profession. At this time, he was doing a depth analysis and tackling the relativity of good and evil[618].

> "I just had the most amazing experience. I was driving my pearl white car to buy a can of white paint for the house. I saw on the road ahead a black snake about 5 feet long. I didn't want to run over it so I stopped, and the snake came up alongside my car. I opened the window and fumbled with my phone to take a picture. It hung around next to the car at my door for a while and then went under the car. I didn't know what to do because I didn't want to run it over. There were cars behind me wondering what I was doing, so I moved forward hoping not to squash the snake and pulled over the side. I got out and expected the snake to be there on the road, but it was nowhere to be seen. My immediate thought was that it climbed into the underside of the car. I walked around the car in a bewildered state, wondering what to do. I rang my wife and one of my colleagues said to drive and brake suddenly to dislodge it. After getting the courage to get back in the car I did that a few times and proceeded to the paint shop. They thought it was amusing. Again, I mustered the courage to get back in the car and drove to the car dealer to ask if they could put the car on a hoist to see if the snake was there. They refused on occupational health and safety grounds. Fair enough. I drove home and left the car in the paddock next to our house."

This example shows how the unconscious presented an event to show the artist what he needed to integrate and understand about himself as a unified, integrated man. This was a difficult process for him, as he had to acknowledge that all the instincts others have are in him too. He could not

---

[618] Good and evil are ways of describing what is beneficial to one or other persons and is highly relative. When we look at animal behaviour and its sometimes grotesque and horrific expression, we don't say that it is evil; we simply say that it is nature. We do not however extend the same courtesy to the human animal.

identify with good alone from this point on. It became a moral question, and a realisation that all good and evil were contained within himself. This urged him to integrate the idea with the help of this experience. In this instance, the unconscious connected the white paint (covers & makes clean) with the blackness of raw instinct.

Idea	-Relativity of good/evil before event in time and not related in space
Event	-Occurred in space, time and matter, not in idea
Impression/Energy	-Fear, wonder, curiosity with a release of energy and attracted attention
Connection	-After event in time, no connection in space, connection found from idea and memory of event
Purpose	-Realisation that one's body has all the base instincts we share with the animal kingdom (snake) and the need to incorporate it for unity.

In this instance, it is not a convergence and flow from idea to matter as the first example, but a realisation of the opposites contained within himself, which occurred after the event. The event was very powerful for the artist, as it threatened his safety with the belief that the black snake was under his car. The fact that he thought the snake had crawled into his car is a good simile for bringing a psychic aspect into his personality, understanding it, and finding a place for it within his wholeness. As an addendum to this example, he came home and sat in his spot on the sofa in the living room. Before he sat down, he noticed a white feather on the seat, which completed the synchronicity. White bird and black snake are a classical pair of opposites.

VI. Shared Synchronicities

Shared experiences have the tendency not only to impress the individual, but reinforce the relationship between individuals. It makes them aware that a greater force is involved in their lives and that they are witnessing that force first hand. Shortly after the snake and car experience of our artist discussed above, he and his eldest teenage son drove to a local hardware store, which was on the same road where he experienced the snake. His son had a milder and connected version of his father's original experience.

The boys have adopted a current Internet app called Pokemon Go. The app actually encourages them to get out of the house and find Pokemon characters to capture. The images of these characters are superimposed on the phone cameras view in real time. Yesterday, my eldest actually wanted to come to Bunning's (hardware store) with me, to see if he could get some of these characters, which can be found in any location. As we drove, I pointed out the corner where a black snake had crawled under my car. As we turned the corner, his app had a snake on it at that particular spot, which he captured. We both looked at each other, amazed at what had just happened.

In this instance, he shared the original experience with his son at a different time. It is important, in that it not only reinforced the original experience, but he shared it with his son. This brought them closer together in their relationship and shared what can only be termed "a magical moment".

Idea	-Snake experience still fresh and on the artist's mind, he told his son about the experience as he was driving to the same corner
Event	-As we turned the corner there appeared a snake on his son's Screen
Impression	-It reinforced the original experience of the artists and it was shared with his son
Connection	-Instant simultaneity in space and time, reinforced experience for father & new experience for son
Purpose	-Reinforcement for father, shared experience for son and his father's connection to the unconscious

VII. Shared Synchronicities in Memory

The next example is from a 36-year-old female financial adviser at a large institution. She has, however, a spiritual side that she had neglected until she met her new male friend.

"I had lunch with a male friend yesterday and as usual, it was very pleasant. He mentioned planning a holiday for his family and I recommended the Gold Coast, because the kids love the amusement parks, especially Dreamworld. In the evening, I learned that 4 people had died, 2 women and 2 men on the rapids ride at Dreamworld."

The event at Dreamworld had impressed her enough to look at the circumstances, and found that it had occurred at the same time she and her friend had discussed taking his family to the resort. Further investigation showed that there were two children on the ride that survived and were thrown clear. There were six people on the ride in total and all the adults died. The event had inspired and gave her a lot of positive energy. Her job at the institution weighed heavily on her and she did not have much childish fun in her life. She was very responsible, worked hard and took care of two children and her husband.

Idea	-Fun times on physical rides, no connection at time when idea perceived, separate space
Event	-A ride on a channel of fast moving water fails, 6 people on the ride, 4 people, all adults drown, 2 children survive
Connection	-Idea and event unrelated until later in time when reported on news. Idea & event coincided in time not space all in memory
Impression	-Connection made after event in memory & still released energy, emotion- awe, curiosity, fear & guilt
Purpose	-Union of opposites- tragedy & joy

In this case her job and family responsibilities burdened her. She yearned for freeness and joy from what she described as a 'joyless childhood'. Her new friend encouraged this aspect in herself, and that life was not just about the practicality of adaptation. After this experience, she was curious about such experiences and actively looked for them.

e. Unity of Idea and Object

We can now draw conclusions concerning the relationship between a symbol as a psychic expression and its connection to the physical. Firstly, it is very rare for a symbol not to have its roots in the physical as we have seen in our study of ancient myths. This is why dreams always draw their imagery, sounds, feelings etc., from the physical world and something that we can relate to in some way. The 'world tree', for example is a worldwide idea that connects the human personality with the natural growth of a tree[619]. A tree starts as a seed that drops to the ground, and if conditions are favourable, sprouts into the earth and sky to make a stable connection to water, nutrients and the sun. As the tree grows, it develops a root system below ground as well as a branch system above ground. This happens simultaneously for the stability and balance of the tree so that it can spread it fruits and seeds for the next generation.

---

[619] I use the example of a tree to emphasise the relation to an ideal form of human growth. There will always be anomalies to the ideal such as the Saguaro cactus where the above structure is much larger than the root structure. In this case however the above ground structure has adapted to an environment where water is obtained from the atmosphere rather than the soil and its above ground structure reflects this adaptation. We see this analogy in brilliant yet tragic individuals like Nietzsche who had a great awareness (spirit) yet lacked the roots (family, relations, profession etc.) and paid the price for his rootlessness with madness and early death.

Similarly, people are born from a seed/egg into a family where they receive water (feeling, belonging, roots, career, family, home) and nutrients (food to grow). They grow towards the sun (awareness, education, knowledge etc.), and sprout fruit, acorns, seedpods etc., (having children and the continuation of the species). The biological cycle completed and continuation of life above and below ground (conscious/unconscious, reflecting on life) eventually succumbs to disease, decay and death.

The above example of the tree is an excellent and universal symbol showing how above and below unite in one living entity. Symbols, particularly when dreamt, lead us to the fullness and unity of life and give us the objective feedback on where we may be going off our serpentine path. This fact is not popular in our western culture yet we live our fantasy and see the latest adventure of our heroes and heroines at cinemas, television or on the Internet. Movies are different to dreams as most are made logical, whereas dreams are sometimes incoherent and in an obscure language. Characters such as Superman make an effort to explain how he can simply take off and fly, whereas if we find ourselves flying in a dream, there is no explanation as to how this came about and why it happened.

This is where a different approach comes in. In the physical world, we know that it is impossible to simply take off and fly. We can simulate flight through devices such as aeroplanes, rockets, etc., and can even simulate flight without vehicles through free-fall and wing suits coupled with a parachute. We can associate flight with leaps of imagination, or the ability to see beyond the physical. This is how symbols communicate. They are not literal expressions, and what belongs to the physical half of reality is not the same as what belongs to the inner unconscious half of reality, although they do complement each other. The differentiation of these halves of reality is life's task and the goal always in the future and not achieved until death.

We can never fully know the physical world, as knowledge of every aspect is impossible for one individual. There will always be unknowns filled with the projecting unconscious. This is a psychological fact that will never change, and as the ancients saw human behaviour and types in the planets, so too, will we see alien cultures and races on planets orbiting other stars in our galaxy, and other galaxies in the universe. It will be a long time before we find life on other planets in our own galaxy, let alone distant galaxies, due to the overwhelming distances involved.[620]

---

[620] That is, unless we are visited by a superior species that have travelled the great distances.

The ideas of wormholes and folding space etc., are at this stage, fantasies of what may be possible. Ideas like this and others, such as the Big Bang theory are just that, theories and not proven physical facts. Even the term 'Black Hole' is an apt description of the unconscious rather than a known fact. The unconscious is the realm of darkness, the darkness of night and dreams. At most, we can say that we do not know what is out there in the universe, except for what we can see. We can say that ideas are as real as physical facts and can lead to the discovery of the unity of the inner and outer halves of the cosmos. To the ancients, the night sky was the myth-making unconscious, and for us it has moved further into space beyond our current scientific knowledge.

With the above limitations in mind and the impossibility of complete knowledge of both inner and outer realms, the best we can do is approximate a standpoint that acknowledges both realms and differentiates inner products from outer realities. Our current level of knowledge of the physical universe is increasing all the time, as is our knowledge of inner psychological processes. As humans, we have the wonderful ability to perceive in either direction, and although this may seem like a linear arrangement, it turns out to be circular. This is where the underlying unity to the existence manifests itself.

f.   Symbol of Meaning and Unity

With a slow and tedious differentiation of the opposites of inner psychic material from the physical world, we realise that both realms are complementary and objective. The consequence of this differentiation is to realise that the inner part of reality is as objective as the outer. No one creates their own dreams; they come to us from inside.   Similarly, fantasies, ideas and thoughts are objective products of the myth-making unconscious. The effect of this shift in attitude makes what the psychologists call the ego, quite small compared to the information from either side. This attitude not only requires an artistic openness, but a scientific objectivity so that we have an open mind, are curious but do not identify with either side.

The idea of the unity of all things is by no means new. In fact, it is an age-old awareness that what is within is without and visa-versa. People from all parts of the world have recognised the inherent unity in existence, and the strong, innate connection we have to this unity. As mentioned previously, awareness of the unconscious requires a transformation of projection. Our earliest ancestors projected a great deal of the unconscious onto the physical world. As we evolved and grew, these projections became fewer, and coalesced into a central figure that encompassed all projections and became a unifying force, which contains everything. This force is essentially unknown to us in its makeup and how it operates. With every advance in evolution and the transformation of projections, comes an increase in awareness of what is physical and what is psychic.

The ancients knew that the night sky was another world full of Gods and demons.

> Astronomy compels the soul to look upwards and leads us from this world to another.[621]

Our knowledge of the cosmos has increased since then, and we know more about the orbits of the planets in our solar system. We know that our system is in a galaxy, and there are billions of systems with billions of planets in this galaxy. Our galaxy is one of billions of other galaxies with billions of systems and planets. Beyond this, we know very little. We have no clue about life on other planets in our galaxy, let alone other galaxies. On the other hand, our popular imagination (unconscious) has given us other species, cultures and life on other planets in our own galaxy and others[622].

This is the nature of projection. The void created at the limits of knowledge fills with mythology. Mythology permeates our lives every day through television, cinema, books, and so on. All this information comes from individual writers and from their own myth-making unconscious. Jung rightly identified this trend in our myth-making in his essay 'Flying saucers: A Modern Myth of Things Seen in the Skies[623]' where he looks at the phenomenon from both sides, the physically real and the imaginative musings of people. His conclusion was fraught with difficulty. On the one hand, he recognised that "something was seen" by people yet there has not been a definitive meeting with the occupants of these flying saucers. If they exist, why not say hello. Why do they fly around without acknowledging the main species on our planet? On the other hand, the creative arts gives full expression to the idea of flying saucers.

This difference between the ancients projecting their Gods onto the local planets and star systems and our contemporary projection of aliens and far off civilisations is a matter of degree. As long as something is unknown, information fills it from the 'other world', as Plato terms it. Once we can form a relationship to an object, we have a chance to transform

---

[621] PLATO (c.427 - 347 BC), The Republic. Book VII. 529
[622] I refer to the popular TV and movie franchises of Star Trek, Battlestar Galactica, Star Wars etc.
[623] JUNG C G, Civilization in Transition, Routledge and Kegan Paul, 1970, Page 307

the projection and see that 'something' as it is, not as we imagine it to be. In other words, the idea of the object transforms to resemble the object more closely when we learn more about it.

The symbolic nature of unconscious material is always ahead of us. On a personal level, the ideas, opportunities and encouragement, all help us grow, develop and become aware of our potential unity. On a collective level, the myth-making of individuals encourages us to explore, develop new technologies, prove scientific theories, and as Einstein explained, "The true sign of intelligence is not knowledge but imagination". Further, I would add the importance of knowing the difference between imagination and knowledge as equal and opposite. Neither should detract from the other. If knowledge of something dispels the idea of that something, then nothing is gained. When knowledge changes, so too does the symbol. As mentioned above, the ancients believed their Gods had direct influence over their lives and so they did. We now know that the planets have minimal effect on our physical lives, but enormous effect on our symbolic lives. Our symbol-making unconscious evolves as our knowledge evolves.

What does all this mean to everyday life? This is a difficult question to answer, as every individual has a unique viewpoint of themselves, and the inner and outer halves of reality. The common experience that seems to bind all humanity together is access to their myth-making unconscious. Although some people claim never to dream, it may simply be a lack of interest, or total rejection of what they find uncomfortable to deal with. Cultures both ancient and modern have always had their myths. These take the form of Gods and their trials, written and verbal stories of adventures far and wide, to our contemporary stories of far-flung planets and cultures on the other side of the galaxy.

The symbol connects us to the unknown in ourselves, and is a potential for growth. It leads us to the underlying unity that has always existed and always will exist. Our personal symbols lead us to the unity we all desire and it may not always be moving forward in the linear sense of time. If an individual has developed himself or herself very well in the world, the urge for unity will try to make that outer world cold and lacking in life. The unconscious will try to compensate the imbalance by leading the individual towards themselves, their lost childhood and creative potential. If an individual is too one-sided, the other side will make its presence felt, one way or another. This is the underlying unity of all things.

g. Three Dimensional Mandala

Mandalas, as described in the preceding text, are abstract symbols of wholeness or a pattern of unity. These patterns are prevalent throughout nature, and have the function of uniting opposites. Their characteristics are stability, order, balance, symmetry, regular shape, occasionally colourful, and above all, attracting. They can be undifferentiated, as exemplified by the wholeness of a baby, or highly differentiated, as that of a wise old man. They are not static expressions, and evolve as the individual evolves. In humans, they reflect the state of psychic and physical development and level of differentiation. If they appear distorted, they can show areas that need attention and neglected quarters not part of the group.

Mandalas appear in the natural world and serve the same function. The flower for example, attracts birds and insects by its colour, beauty, aroma and nectar for the purpose of propagation. Its unity depends on the attractive force of its flower and nectar, and is highly dependent on that force and the presence of insects to help with pollination. It makes them highly dependent on their environment for survival. Another example of mandala-type shapes is the intricate pattern the Puffer fish makes of the sea floor to attract a mate. They spend hours swimming over the sand to make a complicated circular shape with ridges and ripples, all to attract a mate, thus uniting them with their opposite. The image below shows the size difference between the fish and the pattern they are creating. It also shows an innate ability to measure and see a shape far larger than their body. The middle arena has converging ripples to the centre, where mating takes place.

There are numerous examples of mandala shapes in nature that show an organised and ordered pattern-making ability that comes from the molecular structure of the object. These include how plants grow from the centre out, how the spiders weave their webs into a circular shape and sit and wait in the centre for prey, bird's nests, snowflakes, minute scales of crystalline structures to the massive scale of cyclones, hurricanes, tornadoes, planets, solar systems and galaxies. They all display an ordered shape with a centre that they emerge from or revolve around. The common attribute of these natural phenomena is their undifferentiated quadrants. Humans seem to be the only species that can differentiate the four orienting functions of the psyche.

The one thing that all mandalas have in common is they all begin and end, from or to the centre. This centre co-ordinates the arms, perimeter, radials etc., and holds the pattern together. The centre contains the original stalk, as in plants and trees, the stamen, ovary and nectar in flowers, the mating arena for the male and female puffer fish, the eyes of storms, the star at the centre of solar systems, and whatever is at the centre of galaxies and the universe. The centre is either the revolving point, or place for unity. Human mandalas are simple and undifferentiated at birth and approach a differentiated state at death. Individuals tend to circumnavigate the centre and develop the four orienting functions to a certain extent as they move through life. To what extent depends on the individual and how open they are to the demands of the life process. It is natural to stay with what is familiar in one corner, and not move to the next because of fear, or cling to a life that feels comfortable.

Depiction of human mandalas can either be two-dimensional, as in a picture, or three-dimensional as in a sculpture or building. In the first instance, the mandala is flat and abstract in representation. The three-dimensional mandala is tangible, and has a better relationship to the physical world. It is as if that unity had crystallised to form a tangibly real object in the world. As a representation of a stage of personal development, a three-dimensional mandala has more stability than a flat image, and therefore is closet to our everyday life.

12. UNITY IN EVERYDAY LIFE

a. Seeing Unity Everywhere

The unity of existence surrounds us on all sides, from the smallest and largest permutations of nature to the personal myths and events that happen in one's life. The waterfall unites upper and lower, the sun and moon as father and mother, the sky above and the ocean below. They relate through their interactive play. The moon reflects the sun's light and gives us illumination at night. It is the fire and water we cook our food, the activity of day and sleep of night and so on.

It is the third standpoint that unites the opposites. This has to do with the relationship between the opposites and how they unite through the third component of understanding and insight. The most immediate and accessible example of the unity in life is the opposites of male and female. This is somewhat complicated in our contemporary culture as the definitions of what is male and female has become blurred. There are however, indisputable biological facts that place male and female in a relationship that is common to all mammals. For example, men cannot give birth or breastfeed; women have a receptacle and men the delivery appendage for fertilization. All humans begin as females and either stay female or develop into males. This is the reason men have nipples that serve no purpose. The genital tubercle develops into either the clitoris or penis, depending on the presence of the Y chromosome. It is these facts that give us the beginning of what is male and what is female.

If we are biologically male, then what happens to the female we could have been? It does not disappear, it simply moves into the background, where it leads an alternative and unconscious existence as potential. For a man aware of his own masculinity, his unconscious is decidedly female. For a woman aware of her femininity, her unconscious is male. Obviously, these are generalities and what is male and female is open to interpretation, although we can take certain cues from nature. The important thing to know is the difference between male and female in the individual. If you know this difference, you have differentiated between the opposites in yourself and only through differentiation that one can unite them in new form. We are all born in unity and it is only through differentiation of the opposites can they be united again in known and understood form.

Without this fundamental knowledge and understanding, the opposites mix in ways that are unpredictable and chaotic. We cannot separate physical reality and fantasy, as they are unified but undifferentiated. Myth and fact are mixed together and the opposites blur into each other. This is also true in relationships between men and women. She makes demands on him to change into how she feels he should behave and he makes demands on her to behave in a way that would suite him. Conflict always ensues, with collisions such as this. This is a worldwide problem and common to all people. In the initial stages, it is better to consider four entities in the relationship as discussed previously.[624]

This is the recognition and differentiation of inner ideal character with one's outer partner. If you know your inner character, there is less chance of projecting that character onto your partner. An idea closer to the partner's reality based on their behaviour, likes, dislikes etc., takes its place. Projection of contra-sexual characters works unconsciously, in other words, we are not aware it is happening. We only know that our partner does not behave, as we would like them to behave. The overwhelming indication of projection in this instance is emotion.

Emotions bring forth unconscious products, and behind every emotion are symbolic images and characters. This is how we learn to transform projection, for within those images and characters lie the hints of self-awareness. This process of becoming aware of one's own projections is a life-long task. There are no easy or quick fixes in relationship, particularly with a strong projection such as love at first sight. It is an emotional upheaval where the attractive forces of projection are the strongest. She or he are the one, and in the beginning nothing else matters. Everything that is female in him is projected onto her and everything male in her projected onto him. They live in relative harmony because they complement each other so well. They even call each other their "better halves'. Little do they realise that on the surface, their relationship may look ideal, underneath they are totally dependent on each other and do not behave as individuals. A good match may actually be detrimental to personal growth.

When we project an undeveloped aspect of our personality onto another, it is fraught with emotion. In a neagtive instance, one sees in the other person something disliked, hated, regarded as an enemy, or the devil itself. The intensity of the projection indicates the depth of what is projected. The more an individual does not know himself or herself, the more is projected onto their neighbour to the point where individuality does not exist, and they are collective like fish within a school where the

---

[624] There is an enormous amount of psychological research carried out by C. G. Jung and the school of Analytical Psychology. See the concepts of Anima/Animus and concepts of Ying/Yang in Taoist philosophy.

slightest movement turns the whole group in this or that direction. This also holds true for cultural identity and nations themselves.

We elect political leaders in the west to represent the will of the people, but does a large group of people such as a nation actually have a will? Do individuals choose their leaders based on facts, or easily swayed by clever talk and the promise of benefits? On the other hand, inner daemons[625] choose spiritual leaders and not the people. Rarely do we encounter an individual who has both spiritual and political aspirations, and when we do, they tend to be of the ruthless and dictatorial kind as experienced in Germany in the twentieth century.[626]

Areas of mal-adaptation also invoke emotion when circumstances require particular behaviour that is undeveloped in the individual. One feels inferior and not quite up to the task. The feeling of superiority generally compensates this feeling of inferiority. This natural process gives one the courage to take on a task that is new and holds much dread. Arrogance is the precursor to ability, and a natural form of boldness and confidence, and promotes growth. Insecurity compensates the arrogance after the task completed to restore the balance and inner unity. Without the idea we can achieve something, there would be no growth and we are overwhelmed by doubt and lack the energy to carry out the task.

Under normal circumstances, this imbalance subsides once the task achieved and the balance restored. There is a danger, however, that the arrogance, with its usual inflation, becomes habitual and one identifies with the feeling of superiority, which in turn leads to all sorts of conflicts and mal-adaptations. As mentioned above, the identification with one's developed qualities leads to the projection of the undeveloped qualities onto our neighbours. It is like hovering above the world and looking down upon the poor souls rolling in the mud. The truth of the matter is that as long as we have bodies, we all roll around in the same mud of humanity. To be unaware of this fact and to identify with spiritual matters alone denies the individual the unity inherent in life.

The projection of unconscious contents onto others is a purposeful and interesting arrangement of nature. When we project part of ourselves onto another, and this happens automatically, we have a positive or negative emotional connection with that person. This is the starting point for emotional differentiation. When we project an unconscious character

---

[625] By spiritual leaders I mean the leaders that mark the milestones in a populations psychic evolution, not the leaders of established systems such as the Catholic Church
[626] It is believed that Hitler led his country like a shaman and was possessed by the ancient Teutonic god Wotan. Leaders of this kind would be lead themselves by these inner daemons.

onto another person, it not only creates an emotional attachment of a positive or negative kind, it makes us dependent on that attachment. Part of us is outside of ourselves and thus out of our influence. This is why so many conflicts happen between individuals, groups and nations. It is one of the hardest aspects of our nature to understand and deal with.

This conflict has many variables but in essence is the same all over the world. On the national level, we can see a very interesting striving for unity, although its interpretation is misguided. We find ourselves at a very interesting time in history. Humanity is considering the idea of unity in the form of 'One World Government'. The idea in itself is noble and seeks to unify humanity into a peaceful and harmonious existence. Unfortunately, all parties involved have to agree how to implement this idea of unity. Unity cannot occur if one side believes their particular form of wholeness is different to the other side's idea. Wholeness cannot occur if there is no equality and relationship. To destroy, or believe that you can destroy one side is an illusion and cannot be done. It is like trying to destroy the colour orange for the sake of blue, or trying to outlaw hate for the sake of love. We can make as many laws as we like, but it does not change the nature of our being.

The opposites are integral to humans and everything we know in the cosmos. Consider the everyday aspects of water and fire. Water is integral to life as we know it. It nourishes us, sustains us, grows our food, keeps us hydrated; is a precious resource and can create wonderful landscapes and reflections. Water is also tenacious and relentless in its ability to erode, devastate entire regions and cause dramatic destruction.

Fire, on the other hand, is the cause of civilisation. Without it, we would have no heating or light, no cooking, no electricity and no technology. On the planetary scale, the sun as a thermonuclear reaction sustains our lives through heat and light, and drives the climate. Fire also destroys our environment. It can easily get out of control and devastate our landscape, burn our houses and used to torture and kill. Too much sun burns our crops, dries our landscapes and turns them into deserts.

Water and Fire are an everyday example of the importance of the opposites existing in balance. Too much water destroys, as does too much fire. Water can temper and extinguish fire. Fire can evaporate and boil off water. The interaction between them is how we learn to unite the opposites. For example, we can use fire to heat our water, but only if we have an intermediary that protects the integrity of both. We can heat water with the use of a metal pan, which is made of earth,[627] thus letting the opposites affect each other in a beneficial way. Earth is integral in the existence of fire and water. Fire cannot exist without earth to consume in the form of organic matter such as wood, coal, hydrocarbons such as petroleum and gas, and various other earth elements. Fire in its simplest form, cannot exist without oxygen (air), which is part of the water molecule. Water has not only the oxygen atom, but also two atoms of hydrogen, which as we know, is a very combustible gas (air) on its own. This puts fire and water into a relationship at the atomic level.

Without the differentiated opposites, there is no unity and the danger of falling into one-sidedness is all too evident in this epoch. Life is a myriad of opposites and relationships, and for every high, there is an equal and opposite low. The opposites are obvious, and form united pairs when differentiated. Examples are good/bad, smart/dumb, love/hate, blue/orange, red/green, sun/moon, male/female, east/west, north/south, day/night and so on. With these simple opposites, a third and fourth aspect holds the opposites together and sustains their unity. Unity is thus a system of interrelationship of opposites held in a stable and unified pattern.

b. Becoming One of Many - Inner and Outer Figures

Recognising the inherent unity that underlies existence and the relationship between the opposites is an important value. In other words, we cannot perceive one side without the other. We instinctively know that one side means the other side is close by and their relationship binds them together. Both sides then attain an equal and opposite value, and as such gain a respect for their role in the system. For example, the meaning of day, with its clarity and abundance of light has no meaning without the opposite of night, with its lack of light and visual clarity. This fact has always existed on earth and reflected in our own nature.

For everything we know about the physical world, there is an opposite, which dwells in darkness. Yet, it is from this darkness that all culture and civilisation emanates in the form of ideas, dreams, myths, inventions, buildings etc. All it takes is for us to stand still long enough to acknowledge that we do not fully understand how we evolve and build culture. Unconscious contents just pop into our minds, and from here, we mould and develop them into something useful. The myth-making unconscious and its contents, are associated with the darkness of night and the moon, whereas consciousness is associated with daylight and

---

[627] Metal is essentially made from bauxite if aluminium or iron ore if steel, which are all earth minerals

the sun. Our nature is the same as is all of nature, in that we are made of opposites held together in a unified system.

The way we can see the opposites in ourselves is to study their products. The study of the physical world needs little explanation, as humanity has categorised numerous fields for this endeavour. All the branches of science study the physical world of matter, life and the cosmos. The advancement humanity has made in the last 200 years is astounding. We invented flight in the early twentieth century, and have since landed on the moon and are planning to send people to Mars. We also made great inroads into understanding unconscious processes with the advent of the schools of psychology, born around the same time. I say this with a caveat, as numerous philosophers, as shown in the previous chapters, looked into themselves to find the answer to age-old questions of existence and meaning.

In addition to the study of unconscious processes, I must mention the contribution the arts have made to the expression of the myth-making unconscious. Without them, we would have no leaps into the unknown and new ways of seeing the physical world. How impoverished would our lives be without the wonderful creations, inventions and stories of the modern myths of galaxy exploration and adventure? This is also an excellent example of where the physical sciences end and imagination extends that knowledge into myth.

These two expressions of life are both essential for mental health and unity. Too often, we like identifying with one side or the other, but find ourselves with interests that compensate this one-sidedness. For example, to study science does not preclude the belief in a religious doctrine. In the beginning the modern era, art was concerned with new ways of seeing the physical world, rather than its mythological depiction. The container of the arts is architecture, defined as the art and science of building. Its art is the imagination and idea to create a building and science to bring order and build the idea. The more unusual the idea, the harder it is to engineer and build.

The Sydney Opera House is such an idea. Segments of a single sphere form its shells and structure of the building and its engineering was difficult as its shape unusual. The shells are part of the whole, and building it great engineering challenge. Aside from political problems involved in its construction, the Opera House shows how the opposites combine to bring about a unity in an impressive and inspiring building.

Awareness of the unity of the opposites in an individual requires an exploration of those opposites at some time or other. Identification with one side leads to an atrophy of the other. For example, in our contemporary culture with its defined professions and behavioural attitudes, it is encouraged to identify with one's profession and all other attitudes kept in the dark. Men in particular, fall into this problem of identifying with their job and behaving as such without the slightest notion that they are possessed within their group by an inner character. If we look at the example of a Medical Practitioner, we can see how their professional behaviour corresponds to an idea, rather than a real person.

Doctors always dress smartly; strive to be caring with a cordial bedside manner and their oath of behaviour forms part of their character. With all these positive behavioural traits based on love rather than power, where do all the naturally human traits of hate, derision, envy etc., belong? As they do not belong within the behaviour of a doctor, they come out in their private lives, or are repressed completely. This is the problem of identifying with your job. If we look at these behavioural traits and compare them to traditional behaviour of men and women, we would have to say that caring, healing and love belong more to the idea of the feminine than the masculine, and closer to the idea of mother than father[628].

That is to say, those behavioural traits of a profession have an inner character as their origin. We may speculate on how this scenario originated and how it established over time, but conclude that all such behavioural traits begin with individuals. These individuals set the tone and mode of behaviour for a profession. The inner figure has such influence that others recognise its value and it becomes the guiding principal for that profession. Some professions document their ideas, such as Hippocrates and the 'Hippocratic Oath', written between the fifth and third centuries BC. On a national level, a country's constitution and Bill of Rights, laws, etc., set the character of national behaviour over individual behaviour.

Possession by an inner character is as natural as identifying with a group and its associated behavioural traits. The belonging and feeling of security associated with group identity is a powerful force for the individual. It alleviates the pain of being alone or regarded as odd for not belonging or agreeing with the group's behaviour. This is where the danger of group identity lies as it depends on a leader's idea of how the group should behave reinforced by their followers. It may have a great tradition behind it like the US and France basing their behaviour on the Roman Goddess 'Libertas' and its associated freedom. A nation may

---

[628] These analogies are based on traditional ideas of male and female behaviour and should be regarded as schematic and not apply to individual cases.

base their behaviour on another character such as the Teutonic God 'Wotan' that possessed Germany in the twentieth century. There is no way to predict where a group and its behaviour will go. Even in a mental asylum, crazy becomes the norm.

These inner characters, or what Jung calls 'archetypes', are the motivating forces within us all. For example, the sexual instinct in a heterosexual man is naturally the idea of a woman. She is the ideal woman for him, and he looks for her in the world and the inner character provides the overwhelming urge and energy to find her copy in the world so that he can live out his biological responsibility. This is just a starting point. Inner work of any substance which includes the analysis of one's dreams, fantasies, ideas, projections etc., reveals that men have many inner female characters, and women many male characters. It is as if we were filled with a whole crowd of people, all wanting to have their say, just as we have a whole crowd of family and friends who all want to have their say.

The ancients knew this fact, and gave their inner characters elaborate names and traits. Power represents the inner character of father, or strong leader like Zeus, which sets the tone for achievement and striving for standing in the community. Phthonus, the God of envy, Aries the God of anger, fighting and war, Eros, the God of love, or more specifically, how a man feels when he has fallen in love; Dionysus, the God of intoxication and ecstatic vision, The Algea were the spirits of grief, sorrow and distress, and so on. Recognising the inner characters behind our motivations gives us an insight into human behaviour as never before. The ancients knew that each urge had a corresponding character, and that there was a danger of possession, so they worshiped them to allay that fear. Some of these inner characters projected into the night sky in the form of wandering stars we now know as planets.

To avoid possession by an inner character requires an open, objective and differentiating attitude towards them. It does not help that our culture promotes the identification with an inner character as exemplified by professional behavioural attitudes. However, just because the world demands certain behaviours, does not mean that we have to live that behaviour in our private lives. Most people avoid the possession by an inner character by broadening their interests into other fields like sport, hobbies, political and religious groups, artistic endeavours, etc.

If we can stand back and look at these inner characters when they activate in us with the associated urge or emotion, we can form a relationship to them as we would another person. This is exactly what is required for any long enduring and beneficial knowledge of oneself. For example, an over-developed sexual instinct can mask a deeper need for relationship to a female character like a mother. Likewise, an over developed 'will to power', a deeper need for approval and acceptance from a male figure like a father[629] and the corresponding world the father lives in.

Knowing what urges and emotions correspond to what inner characters liberates us from their collective grip. A slow and sure awareness of these characters also gives us a perspective like no other. It is literally the 'fountain of youth', and we have conquered death. We no longer are the age of our body[630]. We can be a child and an old person and anything in between. We can be heroic and timid, male and female, wise or stupid, smart or dumb, sober or drunken, fast or slow, etc. All opposites are contained within one system of unity with their corresponding characters. This also means that you know yourself separate from the inner characters. This includes all your knowledge, experiences, understanding, skills, likes and dislikes, and so on.

Differentiation of the inner characters brings about other benefits that correspond to our relationship to the outer world. When we do not identify with them, we also do not identify with outer characters, in other words, people. If you know your inner woman, you are less likely to be searching for her in the world. If you know your inner father, you are less likely to want a father to tell you what to do or how to behave in the outer world.

Independence from our inner characters gives us independence from real people. This is a liberation of the first order. We cannot depend anymore on others to make us happy, provide for us, to lead us, etc. Finding this level of awareness of inner characters is one of the hardest things humans can achieve, and takes a lifetime. These inner characters are in a constant state of flux and change as we become aware of them. They can be positive and negative and continually challenge our perception and sense of reality. This is why we continually dream, for every nuance of life is reflected, commented on and a solution offered for balance and a guide on one's path. All these inner characters are different aspects of our personality; all answer to one central character, that is the character and idea of unity. Jung calls this central figure the 'Self', others call it their God, others money, power, love, and so on.

This is why it is important to know your inner characters and not identify with any of them. Relationship with them is the important factor. An

---

[629] Again, these are schematic inferences and depend on the definition of male and female. None can deny that some women have enormous power in the world.
[630] This doesn't mean that we should forget the age of our body but we don't have to be possessed by it.

example of this is a parent identifying with their role as a parent. Being a father is a rewarding role, and must be lived to understand that role. However, all the stages in one's life, beginning with childhood to the present are still alive and well in an unconscious state. Becoming a father does not mean that all the experiences; modes of behaviour and creativity from the past disappear. It simply means that another role is being integrated and added to the pantheon of inner characters. To be in that role for a time is natural, to identify with that role to the exclusion of all else, stultifying.

c. Relating to the Unconscious in Others

Awareness and relationship to one's inner characters brings with it an increase in understanding of the inner characters in other people. It is as if you know where they are at, and where they are coming from. It requires a scientific approach and the reservation of judgement until the facts known, as well as an artistic openness to possibilities. If we do not project an inner character onto another person, it frees that person to be themselves, and puts any interaction onto to an equal footing. This does not mean that we interact with our intellect alone, but feel with the other person and understand their process. The whole problem with relationships is lack of understanding between people. This is particularly problematic when one identifies with an inner character.

For example, if we identify with a position in a hierarchy, then all those below in the hierarchy will attract your undeveloped or inferior qualities in the form of projection. If an individual has high rank, he has the final say in matters and gives orders to those of lower rank. Advancement in this situation depends on agreeability and obedience. Men are particularly prone to this scenario, as large organisations such as the military, governments, universities, and corporations etc., are all designed with strict linear progressions of advancement (climbing the ladder). Linear thinking is the basis of the majority of hierarchies with the exclusion of feeling, which is a web of connections. In the worst case, demotion or stripping of one's rank is associated with failure, shame and contempt.

The benefits of becoming aware of one's inner characters, and the subsequent withdrawal of projections, enable us to see other people in a new light. We cannot look down upon others for an inferiority that we may have as well, because we know what it is like. We understand a killer because we too are capable of killing under certain circumstances.[631] We know what it is like to be an animal, and a human at the same time. We

---

[631] I challenge anyone not to feel the impulse to kill if someone hurts a member of your family.

have the same basic drives as other mammals; yet have a thin and vulnerable layer of civilisation that can come apart at any time. Being instinctive is sure and decisive. Making conscious decisions requires evaluation, differentiation and weighing variables. I do not have to emphasise which of the two methods is easier. In instances where immediate action is required like emergencies, the latter is ineffective.

Knowing the opposites in oneself also gives one an insight into where others are in their life process. Either a person leans toward instinct and is less dependent on rules and regulations, or they are part of a culture's establishment, are good citizens and never question the structure in the world they live. "Too much of the animal distorts the civilized man, too much civilization makes sick animals."[632] It is a balance of opposites, and their relationship promotes good health.

Inner characters in one self connect to inner characters in others. In other words, every interaction between individuals has inner characters that cross over and interact with each other. The obvious instance, as mentioned previously, is the love quarternity. Relating objectively helps you see the opposites in other people and gives the opportunity to point out connections, synchronicities and behaviour that seek union of the opposites. Again, the simple and little things point to the path of unity. A ladybug lands on your shoulder when you are depressed. Getting angry with someone for letting you down when you should not be depending too much on that other person. It is also pointing out the meaning of a black dog when it bites you in a dream, or getting that new project just when you needed it. There are numerous things that happen to us every day that point toward the underlying unity in our lives.

Knowing one self and inner characters does give you a broader personality that includes behaviour that does not belong to you alone. We have to be in charge of that behaviour, but not stifle it too much so that the inner character has no form of expression. For example, it is wise not to reveal one's inner child in serious adult company that may not understand such behaviour. We can, however listen to the input the child wishes to make and allow some aspects into the gathering with jokes or changing the subject of conversation. On occasion, the opposites of serious work and play are built into the culture. For example the Dutch are very serious in their professions, but after work they make time for a social feeling called 'gezelligheid', which means congenial warm friendliness and amicability, in other words, fun.

---

[632] C G Jung

Families are fertile ground for projections, especially between children and parents. Sons generally have an affectionate love for their mothers, especially if the mother accepts everything the son does without criticism, which complicates the projection more. They naturally look for such a partner in their adult life. An engaging father can balance the son's projection and guide him to a soul partner rather than a mother figure as a partner. Sisters also help in this balance of parent and child. These parental projections go with us into the world and are found in other environments outside of the home.[633]

Projections between friends are a good place to view how they work on an equal footing. In other words, it is a projection of equality in nature, like a brother or sister, rather than a parent. We choose friendships, unlike family members, for their comfort and compatibility. We are attracted to friends because they have qualities we enjoy which we may not be aware of in ourselves. In this instance, the projections are similar to those in a love quaternity and are generally of an equal type, rather than a parental type. We can learn much about the qualities we lack in ourselves if we can recognise the attraction to those qualities in another person.

When we do our inner work and know our own inner characters, we are less likely to project those on to people. It does not stop other people projecting inner characters onto us. When we recognise projections from other people, it puts and enormous responsibility and complication on one's shoulders and gives us power over the other person and challenges our moral standpoint. With a balance of power and love we can help the other person find their own path if they so desire. This is particularly relevant for parents and children. On the other hand, we can dispel projections by avoiding possession by the character projected from the other person. Our own fluid movement from one to another character easily achieves this goal. For example, behaving like a child can dispel a father projection.

Creativity[634] is an excellent way to perceive and relate to our inner characters. Encouraging creativity in others is simpler than accepting projections as it has a direct orientation to the inner products of fantasy, vision, dreams etc. Creativity can be very contagious and require no more effort than being oneself and showing our childlike character that plays and creates. When we create, we objectify the myth-making unconscious and give it form. The form can be any medium, as long as we give it a

---

[633] There is an enormous amount of research carried out by psychologists on the parental projections and myth (complexes). C.G. Jung, The Archetypes of the Collective Unconscious, Routledge London, 1955,

[634] By creativity I mean using ones imagination rather than the skilful process of painting or modelling.

reality that we can reflect on. Fixing a product is important, because the unconscious flows continually like a river, and unless fixed, images and ideas flow away. Giving it physical form by painting, modelling, writing, building,[635] etc., gives it a physical reality that does not change rapidly. This enables us to contemplate, study and reflect on the material in our own time.

d. Creativity

The name creativity was not recognised by the ancient Greeks, and they had no term for it. Art to them, was a form of discovery and imitation, and reflected an objective attitude to their mythological background. If 'to create', means to make something, what then is a dance or a movie? A movie as an object is no more than a reel of plastic with images and sounds, or in our time, a digital record of such. Those images and sounds, when viewed in a theatre, can take us to far off places that are only limited by the imagination of its creators.

For the purposes of this study, I include playing with toys and other objects, acting out characters, dance, music, computer games, film/video-making, etc., as they all engage the imagination. This, in addition to the well-known forms of object-making such as drawing, painting, sculpture, ceramics, photography, inventing, architecture, etc., all belong to the natural forms of unconscious expression.

Creativity is one of the functions that most children enjoy and are encouraged to explore. Children are by nature, closer to their original unity, and therefore enjoy the benefits of its proximity. Their unity is undifferentiated and in a state of flux. As any parent knows, a child's ego is fragile and prone to dissolution into its effective components. This proximity to the wellspring of unconscious material is what makes children creative. In this epoch, with its emphasis on worldly achievement, competition, money and power, we as parents in conjunction with the education system, encourage our children to grow away from what most see as childish endeavours of play and creativity, and become what we interpret as adults.

Cultures evolve through imitation and similar behaviour is regarded as normal, adjusted and healthy. As the saying goes 'In the land of the blind, the one-eyed man is king'. This emphasises the fact that a culture can go

---

[635] All the arts have the same value in that they objectify the material from the unconscious. Some are however dependent on initial forms of creative activity. For example filmmaking is dependent on a written script, buildings on drawn and written documents, music on written notes etc.

off-track from our human nature. This is one of the big dangers we face as a species, in that most people, particularly our political leaders, do not understand human nature and its need for expression. The study of depth psychology shows that repression pushes something down and it gains energy and momentum and bursts into life with increased vigour. It does not seem to dawn on our leaders that this is also true for nation states. History shows what can happen when part of our nature is repressed for the sake of an ideal. It bursts into the world in the form of major and devastating conflicts.

Nevertheless, children are encouraged to be creative with the help of toys, dolls, and electronic gadgets etc., which give them tools to express their creativity. These objects are designed to attract the projection of inner characters. Young girls pretend to care for and nurture a doll as if it was a baby. Similarly, young boys project the inner hero onto an action figure. This encouragement to project, explore and identify with inner characters gives us as humans the beginnings of all future projections. This in itself is natural, as long as the projection does not become habitual. We know what it is like when someone identifies with an inner character. It may work for a while, but eventually, nature demands other aspects be explored. If this demand denied, the wellspring dries and the individual becomes bored, stale and lacklustre.

Childhood is a time of creative fantasy the uninhibited acting out of stories in play. This usually involves more than one inner character, and is the best groundwork for avoiding one-sidedness and possession by one character. In other words, the child is one of many. This is the best opportunity for health in a broad sense and the realisation that we are not the same as one character alone. The ancients knew this very well, and made every effort to differentiate this fact. Acting out fantasy then becomes a game of participation and enjoyment in the natural and unfolding process of play. This process may seem to subside with age, but in fact, transforms from small toys to bigger toys. Instead of playing with toy cars, we buy a real car, instead of a fantasy aeroplane; we can learn to fly a real aeroplane, instead of playing with action figures, we can participate in real action sports, and so on.

Computer and console games give us the ability to become different figures in a simulated environment. My own sons often enjoy being soldiers, skydivers, pilots, criminals and astronauts etc., all in a safe and accessible environment. I would rather they explore the abilities and skills of a soldier in a simulated environment, than be sent to a far-off country as a real soldier for the sake of a spurious and fabricated conflict. The drawback with these simulated environments is their limitations to hand/eye co-ordination and lack of other physical engagement. It is safer to jump out of an aeroplane in a simulation, but far less exciting and lacks the benefit to our physical health. In addition, the typical creative arts have benefits over simulated play, as they require a skill to work with matter, and are more conducive to contemplation and reflection.

Painting images from the unconscious has advantages over other forms of creativity because perception and rendering is immediate. In fact, some schools of painting encourage this immediacy. This is however, a late development in our evolution and a reaction to the materialistic and scientific leanings. For the last two and half thousand years, our art connected us to the collective myth-making unconscious. Its depiction, in the form of painting, sculpture and architecture kept us connected to our ancient myths or our religious beliefs.

Painted images have up until the last hundred and twenty years been visually objective in their depiction, to which we can relate as physically real. The ideas behind the physically real images were abstract. In other words, the idea is abstract, but the depiction is physically real. Since the invention of photography, the depiction of images disconnected mainstream art from the visually real and became visually abstract. In the first instance, we have deep and abstract ideas depicted as visually real. The second, visually real images depicted in abstract form. I would regard most of the art before the twentieth century belonging the first instance, and the art post-1900 belonging to the latter. These include movements such as Impressionism, Expressionism, Cubism, and Dadaism, etc. The disconnection reached its culmination with the advent of 'Abstract Expressionism', when painting became visual pattern making, with no relation to what we see in everyday life.

Abstract depiction shows how our culture disconnected[636] from the physical world at that time[637], and our myth-making foundation based in physical reality. Science made major leaps in exploration, discovery and technology, and eclipsed our myths. The moon became a stony desert, the sun a thermonuclear reaction, Jupiter and Saturn, gas giants. The myth projected onto these bodies was regarded as untrue. In fact, the word 'myth' means a traditional story on one hand, and a false belief on the other. Even though our knowledge of the celestial bodies was transformed when the projection withdrawn, the idea based on their behaviour, still exists in the myth-making unconscious.

---

[636] I use the word 'disconnected' as not being related to. In other words if you turn your back to something, it still exists but you are not aware of it any longer.
[637] I say 'at that time' because since then our mythological foundation has been given new life in the film medium. Our ancient heroes and demons have been replaced with characters like Luke Skywalker and Darth Vader.

Painting and sculpture was recently recognised for its ability to connect to the unconscious by the medical and healing professions, which use it as a tool for healing. Art Therapy encourages expression of unconscious contents in order to relate and understand what is going on in one's mind. The method of depiction is less important than the depiction itself. In other words, it leans more to a therapeutic tool than an art form, assuming we regard art by its dictionary definition, as depiction using skill. Diminishing the importance of skill, technique and aesthetic criteria shifts the concern to the ideas that one wishes to depict. Artistic criteria can, in some instances, hinder creativity and block the flow of images and inner characters wishing expression. The true skill of artistic expression requires as much thinking and feeling as it does a sense of reality and imagination.

Painting is an excellent tool for the depiction of unconscious contents. We dream predominately in real and recognizable images and these images, are easily depicted on a flat surface. The creation of art, if the images and ideas are important, does require skill in the painting's depiction. The attitude that skill is unnecessary follows the tenets of the modern artists like, Picasso and Chagall, who originally had skill, and tried to draw and paint in a stylised unskilled manner. I can only conjecture that they were trying to integrate their own inner child through art, but had to disconnect from their skills and physical reality to do so. This is where a form of art like painting is invaluable. It can immerse you in the unconscious world of imagination, fantasy and ideas and put you in touch with the inner characters that guide our lives. Paintings can also be important signposts on one's journey through life and one's own personal myth.

Sculpture has its advantages over painting for relating with the myth-making unconscious. The fact that sculpture is a three-dimensional object, rather than a flat image, makes it more real to our senses.[638] We can see, touch and occasionally hear and smell a sculpture. This engages more of our perceptive faculties, and gives us more sense information about the object. If we perceive an interaction between two people in a dream for example, it is easy to depict them in a drawn or painted image. Even if we can only depict them as stick figures, we can still convey their interaction and what they are doing. To model such a scene would require more skill and effort than drawing. In addition, sculpture requires specialised knowledge of materials and structure.

---

[638] Physical reality is determined by our perception and more senses involved in the perception, the more convincing the reality. Psychic reality on the other hand is also to do with perception, but in this case, perception of images, ideas etc., from an inner realm. It is my intention in this study to show that both sides have a unity that we may or may not be aware of.

Sculpture has the ability to relate to more people, as it is a real object. This is reason we find sculptures in civic places, as we are attracted to an object we can walk around and touch. Scale and material also have a determining factor in expression, as it is easier to model a small amount of clay than chisel an idea into a block of stone. Plasticine and Playdoe are often used for children to encourage creativity, and are an easy way to mould and express ideas. Clay has the advantage of being made of earth, and therefore has a grounding aspect to its use as a modelling material.

The last and possibly noblest expression of the unconscious is building. Unlike sculpture, buildings are designed for us to inhabit, whereas most sculpture is an expression of an object to be viewed from outside; buildings are to be viewed from outside and experienced inside. This fact gives buildings a unique place in our lives, which we share with other species. At its basic and practical level, buildings have the function of shelter, made from combined, arranged and united forms of matter. A building protects us from the external environment and predators. We share the impetus to build with many other creatures in nature, including other mammals, reptiles, birds, fish and insects.

In addition to the practical application of building, the ancients used building as a form of worship to their inner characters. These became the temples of old, and were dedicated to specific Gods and their practices. The dedication the ancients had to their inner characters spawned an elaborate and complex system of building we call Classical Architecture. Building evolved into a high art form, with its complex proportioning geometry (Golden Mean), ordering systems and adornments of sculpture and decoration as a way of communicating an inner character's adventures.

Today, our approach to architectural design and building is humanistic and individual, yet the motivation to build is the same. They have become individual expressions of personal inner characters, rather than collective characters of the past. A great deal of architecture today is the expression of an individual's standing and prestige in the community, and a building of an individual's ego. One has only to look at a modern city from afar to see a group of individuals standing together competing and jockeying for prominence. They even compete to see who can be the tallest. Yet, the expression of an inner character is the driving force behind such building. A recent addition to Sydney's landscape is a very curvaceous and crumpled building, designed by Frank Gehry. In an interview about the building, he explained how the folds in the façade are like the folds of a mother's dress. Whether Gehry understands his urge to build a mother is unknown, but it does show the way, an inner character can manifest itself continually in a man's life.

Architecture is an excellent example of the psychological reflection of a culture's aspirations and ideals. The advent of modern materials such as concrete, steel and glass, gave architects the ability to reduce the separation of inner and outer spaces. In the pre-industrial forms of architecture, building materials were limited to stone and timber, thus limiting the spatial configuration. Spaces had small apertures, punctured into the walls to form windows and doors and therefore enclosed space, commonly referred to as Romantic or introverted space. The opposite came about with the increase in technological methods and the use of others materials, such as concrete and steel. The new technology and the emergence of a new awareness in building developed into the open spaces of Mies Van Der Rohe, and the modern movement in architecture. Space thus became uncontained and flowed freely from inside to outside and called modern space, anti-space, or extroverted space. The removal of the barriers (walls) containing space allowed it free flow into the landscape. This aesthetic gave a new viewpoint on how to live in relationship to the external environment.

In contrast, old Christian churches designed to achieve the opposite aesthetic of contained introverted space. Stained glass depicting pictorial representations from the Christian story filled windows rather than clear glass. This created a visual barrier between inside and outside, thus reinforcing the introspective quality of worship. High-level windows also allowed light to fill the space. The church then, reinforces the myth of an inner character through introspection that is above us, but not in the surrounding world of things outside. Modern space, on the other hand is horizontal, and spreads into the landscape of nature. This change in orientation from in to out exemplifies the changing psychological nature of our epoch.

The Dogon[639] people of central Africa build their homes out of the surrounding earth without windows, thus keeping the house dark and cool inside. When asked why they have no windows, the builder explained that "anyone who wants light can go outside, in the house, it should be dark"[640]. The opposites are in this instance, in their purest form, and space inside totally contained and dark, like night, and outside uncontained and light, like day. The homes were designed to represent the mother (unconscious), and resemble her body lying on her side in plan. We can

---

[639] See my paper 'An Introduction to the Psychology of Architecture' at www.arc-design.com.au

[640] 'The Dogon people' an essay by Paul Parin

450

trace these two types of space back to the mother's womb (unconscious) as the original idea of containment, and out of the womb, uncontained in the environment and part of the wider world (consciousness).

The ideas behind buildings are evolutionary signposts in the culture that created them. Talented individuals such as the American architect Frank Lloyd Wright, show how his building designs reflected his pure architectural vision. His client became a means to an end, as he explains, "I don't build in order to have clients. I have clients in order to build". This shows his urge to build his own personality, and its unfolding process of growth was paramount and above the concerns of his clients. His process evolved over his lifetime, and oscillated between the opposites of freeing contained space to enclosed dark spaces, particularly after his personal tragedies. In his later work, his buildings appeared futuristic and resembled flying saucers and mandalas in plan.

Wright had a transcendental belief that the artistic side of humanity represented its divinity, and led him to insist that a structure and coherent pattern, characterised all life: "Organic architecture feels at home with the ideal of unity," he once remarked. His buildings are pure expressions of his idea of unity. In an interview, he stated that he never lost sight of his youth, and indeed, it was necessary for him to retain that youth, even into old age. The floor plans of his houses express his unity, where the central element is either the kitchen (mother), or the hearth (spirit).

Plans of buildings are by nature an abstract arrangement of lines, circles and other geometric shapes. They are a view from directly above, cut through the building at approximately one metre above the floor level. In other words, a pattern for a house reflects in its purest form, the psychological development of the designer. Plans vary, but some include representations of the human body, as they do in ancient Greek and Roman temples, and use complicated proportioning systems based on the ideal human body. Traditional Christian churches use plans based on the cross, which in turn was designed for the human body. The entry is generally located at the bottom of the cross or the feet, which is our connection to the earth or physical reality. From here, we proceed to the cross (torso), and transepts (arms), which is the junction of one direction to the other, and the location of the upper chest and heart. This leads to the sanctuary (head), and the altar, which is the place of sacrifice and worship.

Plans of homes vary enormously from the Mandala-like[641] pattern of the Palladium Villa Rotunda, with its enclosed central space and small outer spaces surrounding it, to the rectangular unenclosed hovering plane and glass space of Van Der Rohe's Farnsworth House. One thing they all seem to have in common is a centre from which all other shapes emanate. In the Villa Rotunda, it is a central two-storey space, lit from above, surrounded by the upper and lower level spaces. The Farnsworth house has the kitchen and other utility rooms in the centre. This centre provides not only the origin of the spaces, but also the stability of the home.

We find numerous things at the centre of homes, depending on the dynamic of the family and what the family revolves around. If the mother is the central figure and provides food for the family, the centre is often the kitchen. If the family revolves around the father, it may be his study, or an abstract representation of him in the form of a hearth. The possibilities are endless, and do not depend on gender or role in the family. It is also as much to do with the relationships between the individuals in a home, as it is the fabric of the home itself. The fabric may reflect the relationships if the occupants had input into the design of the home. The saturation of identical project homes on the market these days, reduce the personalised expression of homeowners and their psychic space.

Nevertheless, each object and room in the home has particular significance for the individuals and family living in it. For example, the hearth, or heating of the home has particular symbolic significance. As a source of heat and light, the hearth contains a piece of the sun, and radiates this quality throughout the house. The hearth is then a fire contained within non-combustible earth in the form of brick, stone or metal, and tamed for heating the home.

In addition to the hearth, each room in the house has a specific function. The kitchen for example, is where raw food is stored and transformed into edible, cooked food. The process of cooking is not only magical; it is an art form, limited only by the ingredients available and the cook's imagination. The kitchen is where we quite often congregate and socialise; it is full of feeling and good cheer. Similarly, we talk and socialise in the living room, listen to music and view the outer world through our televisions. It may also be where the hearth or heating device is located, enhancing that function.

---

[641] The strict definition is a circular figure representing the universe in Hindu and Buddhist symbolism. For this study I use the term in a broader sense to include any shape or pattern that displays a unified whole, either in nature or manmade.

The toilet is where we remove our bodily wastes. Taking in nutrients is celebrated and social, the expelling of waste private and done in solitude. The bathroom used to cleanse the body from the day-to-day grime of the physical world, and to refresh and renew ourselves. In the dressing room or bedroom, we remove or put on our uniforms[642] for our worldly activities. When we remove these clothes, we relax and can be ourselves again. In the bedroom, we sleep and dream. In other words, we rejuvenate ourselves from the physical world by going back into the myth-making unconscious during sleep. It is also a room for couples to engage in physical union, which in itself is the union of opposites.

In addition to the day-to-day functions of the home, it is also a container for the growth of the individual. This aspect of house building is often reflected in the plan, if the occupier had an input into the design. Too often, design professionals have very strong ideas about their buildings and find it difficult to be objective in the design process. It is a difficult situation, in that design professionals lean towards building as an art form and expression of their own psychic process, rather than the ideas of their clients. This is why a building by a well-known designer can be easily recognised belonging to that designer. In this case, the client, occupier or owner of the building is a means to an end for the designer to express his or her own process. This is particularly evident in commercial buildings, where the client is not one person, but a collective of board members or a committee.

The beauty and wonder of architectural design as an art form, reflects the psychic situation of the designer. The abstract nature of the architectural plan and its pattern-like form attracts psychic contents and expresses the designer's psychic situation. In this case, the architectural plan has advantages over other forms of expression, such as painting and sculpture, because it is a collection of abstract shapes put together to form a coherent structure.

The plan combines the architectural elements of space and form into an arrangement that we can interpret for its psychic content. For example, the corners of a plan are important, in that they set the boundaries of the pattern, and convey position relative to a centre. The function of each corner can indicate the development, or lack of, the four orientating psychic functions of the individual. In Plato's language, they are earth, air, fire and water. In psychological language, sensation (senses), thinking, intuition and feeling respectively. It is this differentiation and the essential relationship between the corners and proximity to the centre that shows

---

[642] By uniform I mean any outfit that belongs to a specific group or activity. These include suites, sports clothes, work clothes, professional clothing, uniforms etc.

the developmental stage of the designer's personal unity at the time of the design.

This observation enables us to interpret architectural plans psychologically. Whether this is of interest to the architectural designer is unknown, but in terms of psychological development, an excellent tool to help individuals find their serpentine path, and a tool to encourage development where needed. This is to some extent, an untapped language more related to the physical world, than the obscure and sometimes ambiguous language of dreams. Projecting onto the cosmos, as the ancients did, is similar to projecting onto the elements in a home.[643] The difference is, elements of a home are familiar things that most people recognise, and a container for inner characters.

Instead of the inner character projected onto a remote celestial body like a planet, a room can attract a projection as a container. For example, in a traditional family, the kitchen/dining room, where people are fed can attract a mother[644] projection. It is also a social room of good feeling, where we enjoy each other's company over dinner. If we associate the function of feeling with mother, there can be attraction and warm feelings, or resistance and uncomfortable emotions, depending on the individual's attitude to their idea of mother. If we use the term kitchen rather than mother, the language is softened and becomes a place where the idea of mother dwells, making it less confronting and easier to understand.

Each room in a home has a different meaning for each individual member of the family. For example, an association survey[645] of individuals showed a variety of responses. The word 'fireplace', elicited the associations 'hot', 'wood', 'cosy' and 'fire' from four individuals. This is the difference between the fireplace as an object, and the idea people have of the fireplace. Some simply describe the physical effect of the fireplace, in that it provides heat. Another associated a fuel (wood) used in the fireplace. Others associated feeling with fireplace, in that it makes one comfortable and warm (cosy), and others associated the idea of a fireplace as a place for fire.

The above shows that every object or space in the built environment has different associations and different ideas attached to them. From the

---

[643] Projecting an inner character onto another person can lead to all sorts of difficulties. Projection onto a planetary body, constellation, building or room has less difficulty.
[644] Biologically, it is the mother that feeds their young. Fathers can attract a mother projection too if they take on the feeding and nurturing role albeit, a secondary one through artificial means.
[645] This survey had the names of many rooms, objects and activities carried out in the home. The participants were asked to associate with each word on the survey.

above examples and other data obtained, we can build a comprehensive idea of the spaces and objects in the home from all points of view. The example of the fireplace is hot, cosy, safe, contains fire, burns wood, gas, oil, brings people together, is contained, beautiful, dangerous, Lucifer, hell, spirit, intuition, yellow, white, blue, made of brick, stone, metal, and so on. This list of characteristics is part of the broad idea of a fireplace and is as varied as the individual associations, and may never be completely defined. This is the nature of ideas. As their boundaries are ever changing and what we would call a scientific definition is impossible. Even if we were to map all the possible associations of an object such as a fireplace, it would still not define it in all its aspects. This is due to the feelings that come with associations, which form part of the idea, as this aspect must be felt to be understood, and cannot be described.

The above example is one of many ideas in the home that include objects as well as spaces. The rooms of living, kitchen, dining, bathroom, bedroom, garage, shed, den, drawing room, etc., and objects such as bookshelves, stove, sink, toilet, washing machine, bed, wardrobe, sofa, table etc., all have specific and unique associations related to them.

The home itself is a vessel for transformation. It is where individuals grow and relate to one another and they can be themselves more than in the world of rule and regulation. All the natural emotions we are born with can have a life in the home. Contrary to the government's urge to eradicate some aspects of our nature, the home is where we have enough freedom to express ourselves, vent our frustrations and be emotional. All opposites and their associated emotions have a place in the home. The emotions need a personal life and expression, as they become problematic when expressed in a one sided culture. The problem then, lies outside the personal, and becomes a collective prejudice and bigotry.

There is no greater experience in life than helping your children transform from small, unaware, dependent babies to grow into adults, with some semblance of independence and unity. The home can provide the container and refuge from the world, with all its restrictions and demands. Our real nature and unity determines our mental health, and not what a culture believes is our nature. To repress part of our nature is to ignore our potential for unity. It seems ultimately more practical to accept our nature than repress some part we do not like or does not fit into the culture in which we live.

The home is also a vessel for parents to transform themselves with their children. Adults without children never have to put up with the childish and demanding needs of another person in such an honest and raw form. Having children challenges the unity of the parent to such an extent that it is easy just to give in and provide whatever the child needs. This is, however detrimental to the growth of the parent. We love our children and wish them the best, but too often they, as do all humans, have a strong urge for survival and control of their environment. The biggest lesson for parents is to achieve a balance between the opposites of love and power.

The home then moves towards a symbol of unity within the family and the fabric of the house. In other words, there is a tendency to seek unity, either consciously or unconsciously. For example, a family may need more feeling through another child or animal to love. Rooms are added to the house, bedrooms reorganised and upgraded for a new child, and a doghouse built and entry flap installed, place found for feeding and waste, for a new pet. The way unity presents itself is many and varied and is expressed by all people in all places. This is the wondrous aspect of unity, in that it permeates our lives in everything we do. We can identify with one side, but the other will continually bother us until we have to give in to the urges coming from inside. Indeed, the home is an untapped language for the expression of unity in our everyday lives.

e. Understanding, the Key to Unity

Inner work, such as dream analysis and observation of synchronicities eventually leads to an awareness of one's current position in one's personal evolution. For example, an introverted thinker has extroverted feeling as the least developed function.[646] Likewise, an introverted intuitive has a least developed extroverted sensation function. Under certain circumstances, an individual jumps across their mandala to an opposite function, without going through the adjacent functions. This happens when they require the opposite function for adaptation, or a dramatic change in life occurs such as a new culture or partner.

The functions mentioned above have an inner character associated with them that depends on the individual's natural orientation. In other words, thinking may be associated with the figure of a father, feeling a mother, intuition, a sister etc. These are simply examples of possibilities. The human psyche is varied, and all are functions distributed amongst all people. The important thing is to understand one's original orientation, and where further development is beneficial. Life unfolds in its own time and we can help the process if we aware of it, or regard it as fate, and passively let it unfold. Either way, life flows as it should for each individual and this fact is the basis for understanding psychic processes.

---

[646] These are schematic outlines of possibilities. Research shows there are exceptions such as judges whom develop thinking and feeling together, for their profession.

Awareness of the inner and outer processes of reality gives one a new perspective on life and a view of the somewhat obscure order and unity in existence, and individuals stand in between two great mysteries, which are one. This is evident in the idea that the darkness before birth and the darkness after death is the same darkness.[647] The same goes for the night sky and space. We look into space and see wondrous phenomena and celestial objects; yet, our knowledge of space is limited and replaced with all kinds of imaginings.

A central character in everyone's personality representing their unity has been with us through our evolution since we emerged from the primordial background and is the spark of life and growth. Its permutations have many ideas, as the many religious belief systems show. These central characters and their associated establishments give people an idea, image and a container, to project their own inner characters. The difference between the characters of the great religions shows that the idea of unity is not the same for all people. It also shows there is a personal aspect to the interpretation of unity. For example, the God of Moses is different to the God of Jesus. In addition, the initial Christian story and writings have many interpretations and subsets, and have a slightly different ideas of unity. This means that every individual has the potential to find his or her own inner God due to his or her unique life experience.

This begs the question; how does one go about finding one's own central inner character? This is both simple and complicated. Simple, in that the material required for inner work is readily at hand in the form of dreams, fantasies, synchronicities, creative work, stories, ideas etc., and part of our everyday lives. There is no limit to the material available, as the myth-making unconscious seems to be inexhaustible. Inner work can to some extent, put one at odds with the prevailing culture, particularly if that culture is restrictive or too one-sided. The idea of unity comes from our nature and as nature, guides us to balance and equilibrium in spite of the culture.

The complicated aspect of inner work is what to do with the material provided by the unconscious. Dreams express images, scenarios and situations from the physical world, and arrange them in obscure and unusual ways. The language used by dreams is also fraught with difficulty, and initially relies on personal experience. For example, the association test carried out on elements and rooms in the home, showed that for the idea of a 'fireplace' gave many different associations.

---

[647] I say darkness because we do not know what is before and after physical life. When we close our eyes it is dark, what we imagine to be beyond is different.

Therefore, the elements of a dream and its interpretation depend on the individual's experiences and psychic orientation. The deeper the symbol, the more universal and collective it becomes, and we see the same thing from different viewpoints. Myths display universal symbols that every individual can relate to in some way.

Research in psychology shows that the myth-making unconscious and the central character compensate the individual's attitude to the physical world, and encourage the necessary balance. In fact, many life-changing events move us by an idea or a synchronistic event. The function of the central character seems to draw us closer to it, and provides us with the necessary understanding of its goal. Just as much as we want to know and relate to our central inner character, the character wants to know, relate and become real in the physical world through us.

f. Honouring Unity

A unique central inner character personifies the idea of unity in every individual. It is up to us to form a relationship with this character. We can project it onto an established figure in a religion and try to emulate that figure's behaviour, or we can try to connect with one's own inner character as an individual. This is by no means an easy task, in that the central character changes over time as we change. Some may try to relate to the masculine aspect of the character, but this simply denies its feminine aspect. The problem with relating to any character in the unconscious is that only the individual themselves, can perceive them unless they share their visions, ideas etc., with others. Jesus had a relationship to his God as a father at the cost of his natural humanity, and eventually his life. This was a necessary sacrifice, so that humanity could differentiate the natural man from the God man. It is now probable that we need to recognise the natural and God aspect of the central character as one. We cannot do our God a service if we cannot unite it with our natural instincts and bring it down to earth.

It is important to stand one's ground when dealing with the central character, because identification with him/her, as it is with other characters, is catastrophic for the individual, and can lead to all sorts of mal-adaptations and inflations. A relationship of any kind must have a certain amount of equality and a sense of partnership. It is useless to obey an inner figure without criticism, and it is up to the individual to differentiate between what is beneficial for themselves and the world, and what is not. A truly unified central character encompasses all of the human being and their potential and includes all of the mammalian traits we inherited from our origins. There is no unity if you side with all that is good in people, and project evil onto one's neighbour. This is a hallmark of the Christian tradition, which is understandable as humanity was in desperate need of differentiation from our animal origins and associated instincts. Unfortunately, all the human functions rejected by Jesus are projected onto a perceived enemy or Satan and banished to the underworld. Thus, the heavens became Godly and the earth the realm of Satan.

A relationship to one's central inner character brings an understanding of its uniqueness to you, as it is your own personal God. It may have universal aspects to its functioning, but it is unique to you. Jesus understood this reality, as described in the Gospel of Judas. The other apostles only saw the universality of the message, and wanted to establish a ministry. Nevertheless, a ministry was established, and it served the population at a time when the central message was an important liberation and differentiation from one's natural instincts that Jesus viewed as negative. A truly unified central character includes all aspects of human functioning, including what we perceive as negative. Human morality is a relative construct and what is good for some, is bad for others. This relativity causes conflict when different values come into contact without the necessary tolerance and understanding.

Working with the central character is an exacting task, particularly where all aspects of the human psyche are included. As morality is a necessity in human culture for us to get on, it is irrelevant when alone. When alone, all we have are our inner characters, and morality turns into personal ethics.[648] This is important, because an ethical attitude is an individual personal judgement, whereas morality is imposed on a group by a governing body. Ethics puts the onus on the individual to behave in a way that does not affect others too badly.

This is the unity of our nature. We have a Godlike mind attached to the body of an animal. We can deny the animal as per the Christian teachings, but to do so denies progeny, a typical family life, and power and standing in the community. To deny our Godlike mind is to live by instinct alone, which is fraught with moral dilemmas and may lead to maladjustment and persecution by the moral authorities. Either way, the extremes that are in our nature belong to a unified whole. The relationship between the animal and spirit mediated by the soul, give us the best chance at a unified and healthy life. Conflict between opposites is an individual task and this is the battleground. Projection of inner conflict means physical death to innocent people.

---

[648] I make the distinction between 'morality' and 'ethics' as a moral system for a group in contrast to the ethics of an individual, which is based on one's conscience.

Experience and knowledge of the central inner character begins with an inner journey of discovery. It requires being alone with your thoughts, being creative and expressing the unconscious, suspending external moral judgement,[649] and viewing the images, fantasies, ideas, as objectively as possible. In other words, the material is like an inner movie that is trying to help us grow if we become one of the characters. It is because the material is in our minds that we identify with it, believe we have created it, and are afraid of following it on its course. When we are among a roomful of people, we do not feel that we created the people. This is the same attitude we should have towards the inner characters, as if they were reflections of the people outside, and not ourselves as Plato suggests.

Artists generally have no problem perceiving and expressing the unconscious and give it form for all to see. It is easy to watch a horror movie and marvel at its macabre imagery and ideas, because we did not create it. The artist does, but generally does not relate the material to them self. Expressing it is sufficient, and this is where it stops. If Stephen King asked himself, why am I creating such horror? He would have to look inside to see why it is so horrific in there, which is similar to the horror of Revelation, as discussed previously.

The material the unconscious provides is not the end goal of inner work. It is above all the transformation of the individual, so they have an equal and opposite relationship to the inner world of myth and the outer world of matter. This is the basis of unity of the individual. It is seeing the complex and varied unity in all things. The beauty and horror all at once, the order and chaos that surrounds us, the love and hate that need each other, the complimentary emotional highs and lows, and so on.

Two thousand years ago, the ancient Greeks knew about the opposites and their relationship and how humans function between the opposites. The west has developed an awareness of physical nature to a high degree through the scientific method, and given us complex technology that changed our lives. It also gave us the ability to destroy ourselves with nuclear weapons. The idea of unity is established in history and part of our evolution and many cultures strive for it. Why is there such an emphasis on science over the arts in the west? In my home country, Australia, the arts are the first group to have their funding cut when the

---

[649] This is important in that one of the biggest barriers to exploring the unconscious is the way it expresses itself. It is pure nature and therefore does not have moral concerns. Every beauty and horror contained within it is expressed in symbolic form. For example if you have a fantasy of killing someone you may stop the fantasy because it is incompatible with your ethics. This is a mistake because the unconscious may be letting you know that you are killing what that person represents in yourself.

government wants to save money. It is typical of an overly extroverted culture to hold scientific and physical achievements over creative and cultural ones.

The transformation of culture is far slower than that of an individual. If an individual removes himself or herself from the culture, it can accelerate their transformation by allowing a different viewpoint to come forward. It is a connection to nature in the individual and a view of reality, usually outside of the status quo. Reflecting on the culture one lives in shows all the deficiencies in that culture, and where balance needs restoration for the culture's growth[650] and well-being. Introversion is needed in an overly extroverted culture, and a culture dominated by science, needs more art.[651]

This problem then becomes one of education, where all aspects of reality are included. Imagine a culture where the introvert has as much status as the extrovert, where daydreaming is encouraged, and dreams discussed with the same interest as the latest football scores. Teachers who respect and tailor teaching to the individual; a healthy respect for the inner and outer forces of nature; psychiatrists and psychologists who regard individual behaviour as unique and stop comparing and judging with an average[652]; and above all, a system that acknowledges the need to separate, differentiate, as well as bring together and unite.

g. Speculations on Unity

Recognition and understanding of the idea of unity and the central inner character, raises more questions concerning its goal. What is its goal and can it be reached in our lifetime? What is its purpose? Does the central inner character have a presence in the physical world? Is there life after death, and how will humanity evolve? All these questions unfortunately move us into the realm of metaphysical speculation, which is very difficult, if not impossible to experience and express.

The end goal of any scenario is important in a competitive result based culture. No one enjoys a soccer or football game that has no conclusion, or is a draw. Designers do not create and partially construct a building unless it is in the plan to stage the construction. We set ourselves financial goals, social goals, educational goals, career goals, and so on.

---

[650] I view growth not in linear terms, but a circular process and what may appear at times to be regression is the need to bring in all aspects of our humanity.

[651] When I use the term art, I refer to expression of the unconscious through imagination, fantasy etc. I do not mean the skill of depicting physical objects through a medium.

[652] Psychosis is not limited to individuals as whole nations can be swallowed by a one sided ideal.

What then, is the goal of a central inner character? It is not power, although some may argue this point. It is not love and again, some may argue this point. It is all things, power and love. It is enlightenment and awareness of the individual and as a consequence, the evolution of the human species. Is it to do the best one can in life and understand how the central inner character guides us and that we have to help it[653] and bring its riches to earth? This may be why God loves humans more than Angels. Angels cannot build bridges and have large families. They have no body to carry out God's wishes; only humans or creatures with a physical presence can do that.

The goal seems to be ongoing, meaning that it does not end at physical death. The reason I say this is not through personal experience, but the overwhelming number of documented dreams of people approaching death, which indicate an ongoing adventure or journey. There are instances of people on the verge of death who have come back to life, having seen visions of themselves on the bed or operating table, and perceiving a bright light above them, with a sense of peace and order surrounding it. Some belief systems regard the goal to be after this life, and not achievable in the temporal realm. Others regard the goal to be an ongoing life and death cycle. There is some evidence in nature pointing to this cycle of death and rebirth. In my opinion, if I cannot remember a previous life, then there is no point saying that I had a previous life. Humans can also go through psychological death and rebirth, which brings about major shifts or changes in their behaviour. We also continue living through our offspring, which makes a parent feel immortal, although this does not have much bearing on the individual psyche of the parent.

The abstract shapes of Mandalas produced in a person's life have bearing on the goal. If we are born complete, yet undifferentiated, it is logical to assume that at the end of life, we will approach the most differentiated stage reflected in a comprehensive and complete Mandala. The centre of the Mandala is an abstract representation of the central inner character, with other characters in its orbit. Everything in one's life orbits this centre and it co-ordinates, modifies and unites the arms and perimeter functions in a stable system. Life orbits around this centre and we continually get closer and closer to it. We better ourselves, correct previous issues, and go over old territories that need more elaboration. It is Nietzsche's concept of the 'Eternal Return', to go from inner and outer halves of reality and back again. Life spirals around the centre, whether you see it as a God or a drain, it is still the centre.

---

[653] I say 'it' so as not to give the figure gender, as a unified figure would be both male and female.

It would go a long way to believe in a life after death, if the central inner character had a tangible personality in the physical world. Unfortunately, the character only works through the individual, which is why we only have individual experiences and writings about it. If God walked amongst us as a person, we would probably have to try to kill him as a danger to national security. God's work is everywhere to be seen and exemplified by what we have accomplished as a species in the physical world. Every building in every city is a testament to an inner character. Designers sit in their studios with an open mind, and set of ideas that they put to paper or on a computer screen. They may borrow ideas from others, but all ideas stem from an unconscious process of revelation. In other words, it is a solution revealed to the designer, documented and built. Some designers even suggest that they are tapping a divine force and that they have a handle on God's creation. This puts them in an esteemed group that includes beavers, turtles, birds, termites, bees, shellfish, and other creatures that build.

Another way of seeing the inner characters in one's life is openness to, and observation of small synchronistic experiences that occur every day. I have known people who do no inner work, but have the most amazing experiences, only to dismiss them of as a coincidence. They see no meaning in the coincidences and discard them as irrelevant. The coincidence of inner material with outer objects and scenarios shows that inner characters do indeed work in the physical world outside of our influence.

Emotion is another sign of an activated inner character. In other words, one of the ancient Gods has paid us a visit and is another form of expression in the physical world. Emotion, depending on type, changes one's body chemistry, and if directed outwards, influences those interacting with the individual experiencing the emotion. The expression of emotion also brings forward ideas and images.

This brings us to the final aspects of life itself, and raises questions about the purpose of the central inner character. Does the character exist when we die, and where will our evolution lead beyond death? These questions are by no means easy to answer, and we cannot understand them by thought alone. Experience is the key to understanding, and this is where the problem lies. The purpose of the central inner character is something that the best minds in history have speculated on, and some even sacrificed their lives to. This figure is so integral to our life that differentiating it from us is a life-long task. Nietzsche identified with his inner character, and as such decried that 'God was dead', thus destroying any possibility of return to a normal, down to earth human life. His identification with his character cut him off from the meaning of the human/God relationship, which in the end destroyed him.

To speculate on the purpose of unity is to ask how aware we can be as an individual, and if there is a limit to awareness and understanding. Throughout history, central inner characters are associated with omnipotence and omniscience, thus belonging to eternity. As such, we can say that if the central figure has no limits or boundaries, then we have no limits or boundaries in our personal level of awareness. This may be one of the reasons why a belief in a deity brings the idea that we exist in eternity as well as in the temporal realm.

With this in mind, we can say that inner characters exist outside the influence of space and time. This is obvious when considering dreams. We can at once be flying through space and jump from scene to scene without the usual temporal restraints. Yet, dreams are dependent on a living physical brain with synaptic activity. How can we say, when activity ceases, dream continues. This is where our understanding of the relationship between inner and outer realm ends. Faith cannot prove anything about an after-life, as people disappear and do not return after dying. There are documented experiences of individuals that hint at the independence of the unconscious from our physical existence. These include people perceiving the recently dead as a vision of that person saying goodbye in dreams as well as in the waking state. What is difficult to differentiate is the idea of the deceased person from the person themself.

This conundrum is at the basis of much philosophical speculation, and the idea that an object does not exist unless a subject perceives it. In other words, the removal of one side removes both sides, its reality and meaning. It is an interesting thought exercise, but just an exercise. Death is a heart-wrenching event for those left behind. Someone is there one minute, and gone the next and are never seen again. The question that comes to mind concerning this fact is, why is there not a stronger relationship between life and a potential after-life? A once strong connection between people is broken and never reactivated. It is final, complete and irreversible[654].

From this study, it should be clear how humanity has evolved over aeons into the present moment. In addition, we can see our children evolve from baby to adulthood and become aware of the world and themselves.

---

[654] This is the current state of our medical abilities. We do not know at this stage if it is possible to reverse cell degradation and their death through medical intervention. We may in the future achieve immortality, which brings us a whole new set of problems.

Adaptation is nowadays reaching the average level of awareness of the general population. What does the future hold for our species if we extrapolate this evolution? We are at a point in time where we know that exploring the myth-making unconscious can be an objective endeavour, and with a simple shift in the definition of fact, can through comparative analysis, be regarded as a science. We still live in a mythical world, as shown by our insatiable need for connection to the stories of heroes and demons, far-off places, aliens, space travel and unifying forces.

The advent of robotics and artificial intelligence[655] shows an urge to create ourselves as a God would create its offspring, although the idea of artificial intelligence seems to lack the necessary connection to the creative, reflective and emotional forces that make us unique. We yearn for knowledge like never before. We dislike unsolved mysteries, and need to dispel ambiguity and the unknown. We want to explore the universe and travel to distant planets. We wish contact with other life forms, so at least we feel satisfied that we are not alone in the universe. Yet, we know that the problems of space travel are insurmountable. The nearest star is four and a half light years from earth, and with our current technology, would take approximately 170,000 years to reach[656]. Time thus becomes irrelevant over these distances, and to contemplate such journeys requires imaginative thought, and therefore a standpoint outside of space and time.

Where is our human evolution on earth moving to? From what we have learned through psychology in the last century, it will take several more centuries to bring our level of awareness back to our nature. It becomes a pedagogical issue and a shift in our viewpoint. Introversion will have as much value as extroversion. The inner world regarded as a complement to the outer, and an awareness that being one-sided leads to illness. No longer can we take the side of good and project evil on to our neighbour. No longer can we believe that we are right and they are wrong. Men and women will find equality not by being the same, but regarding themselves as equal and opposite, and more importantly, individuals. Inner work will be the norm, not the anomaly. We may even get on with each other better. God knows the world could use some enlightenment at this time in our evolution.

---

[655] We will never be able to create a human facsimile unless we know how we actually function which means delving into the realm of dream and myth.
[656] This figure was calculated using the Space Shuttle technology with a speed of 28,150 kph over a distance of four and a half light years which is 4.5 x 9,500,000,000,000 km.

13. BIBLIOGRAPHY

"Radio Power Will Revolutionize the World" in Modern Mechanics and Inventions (July 1934)

AGENDA 21 United Nations Conference on Environment & Development, Rio de Janerio, Brazil

ARISTOTLE, De Anima, Book I

ARISTOTLE, Physics
https://ebooks.adelaide.edu.au/a/aristotle/physics/index.html

ARISTOTLE, Ps., On the World

ARISTOTLE, The Physics, Vol. I, Book I

ARISTOTLE, The Physics, Vol II, Book V

BERKLEY, George, A Treatise Concerning the Principles of Human Knowledge, Hackett Publishing, 1982, ISBN 978-0915145393

BUDGE, E. A. Wallis, Osiris & the Egyptian Resurrection Vol. 1, P.L Warner 1911

BUDGE, E. A. Wallis, Osiris & the Egyptian Resurrection Vol. 2, Dover Publications, 1973, ISBN 0-486-22781-2

CALHOUN, John B. (1962). "Population Density and Social Pathology". *Scientific American*

CALHOUN, John B. (1973). "Death Squared: The Explosive Growth and Demise of a Mouse Population" *Proc. Roy. Soc. Med.* 66: 80–88.

CAMPBELL, Joseph, The Hero with a Thousand Faces, Princeton University Press, 1973, ISBN 0-691-01784-0

DARWIN, Charles, The Power and Movement in Plants, D Appleton and Company 1898

DARWIN, Charles, 'On the Origin of Species' London, John Murray, Albemarle Street 1859

DECARTES, Rene, The Essential Descartes, New American Library, 1983, ISBN 0-452-00864-6

EINSTEIN A, Podolsky B, Rosen N, Podolsky, Rosen (1935). "Can Quantum-Mechanical Description of Physical Reality Be Considered Complete?". Phys. Rev. 47

EINSTEIN, Albert on Quantum Physics 1954

EINSTEIN, Albert: "Ether and the Theory of Relativity" (1920), republished in Sidelights on Relativity (Methuen, London, 1922)

FEYNMAN, Richard, QED: The Strange Theory of Light and Matter, Princeton University Press, 1985, ISBN 978-0691164090

FEYNMAN, Richard P. - 'Fun to Imagine' BBC 1983 – transcript by A. Wojdyla

FEYNMAN, Richard, Feynman's Thesis, A New Approach to Quantum Theory, World Scientific Publishing, 2005, ISBN 981-256-380-6

FINKELSTEIN, Israel and Nadav Naaman, eds. (1994). From Nomadism to Monarchy: Archaeological and Historical Aspects of Early Israel.

FLEMING, Theodore H., Sonoran desert columnar cacti and the evolution of generalized pollination systems. In: Ecological Monographs.

FREUD Sigmund, 'Art and Literature' Stanford University Press 1997

FREUD Sigmund, 'The Interpretation of Dreams' The Macmillan Company, 1913

FREUD Sigmund, 'Totem and Taboo', George Routledge & Sons Ltd, 1919

FRY, B.G.; CASEWELL, N.R.; WUSTER, W.; VIDAL, N.; YOUNG, B.; JACKSON, T. N. W. (2012). "The structural and functional diversification of the Toxicofera reptile venom system". Toxicon.

GEERTZ, Clifford (1973). The Interpretation of Cultures. New York: Basic Books, 1977, ISBN 978-0465097197

GILLIARD, Ernest Thomas (July 1956). "Bower ornamentation versus plumage characters in bower-birds". Auk.

GOSPEL OF JUDAS, Translated by Rodolphe Kasser, Marvin Meyer, and Gregor Wurst

GOSPEL OF MARY OF MAGDALA, Karen L. King, Polebridge Press, 2003, ISBN 0-944344-58-5

GRIMES, Shannon L., Zosimus of Panopolis: Alchemy, Nature and Religion in Late Antiquity, 2006, PHD Dissertation Syracuse University

HARRIS W. V., Termite Mound Building, London S. W. 7

HAUCK, Dennis W. from *The Emerald Tablet of Hermes Trismegistus*

HEGEL G W F, Phenomenology of Spirit, Oxford University Press Translated by A. V. Miller, 1977, ISBN 0-19-824597-1

HEGEL G W F, Philosophy of Mind, Part Three of the Encyclopaedia of The Philosophical Sciences (1830), Clarendon Press, Oxford University Press, 1971, ISBN 0-19-875014-5

HERMES Trismestigustus, The Corpus Hermetica

HESIOD, Theogony, Eighth Century BC

HIPPOLYTUS, Refutation of all heresies, IX

Historical Introduction by P C MAHALANOBIS to "Principle of Relativity Original Papers by A Einstein and H Minkowski, University of Calcutta 1920

HOLY TORAH, Book 1, Jewish Publication Society, http://www.ishwar.com

HOMER, Hymns, The Odyssey, 7th Century BC

http://news.ku.dk/all_news/2009/more_oxygen_colder_climate/

http://www.geocraft.com/WVFossils/greenhouse_data.html

http://www.sheppardsoftware.com/content/animals/animals/breeds/dogto pics/dog_mythology.htm

http://www.snowcrystals.com/science/science.html

https://astrosociety.org/edu/publications/tnl/71/howfast.html

https://biology.stackexchange.com/questions/23693/why-did-humans-lose-their-fur

https://earthobservatory.nasa.gov/Features/BOREASFire/

https://en.oxforddictionaries.com/definition/intuition

https://www.encyclopedia.com/humanities/culture-magazines/egyptian-myths

https://www.encyclopedia.com/science/dictionaries-thesauruses-pictures-and-press-releases/flerov-georgii-nikolaevich

https://en.wikibooks.org/wiki/Cell_Biology/Introduction/The_elements_of_life

https://en.wikipedia.org/wiki/Abrus_precatorius

https://en.wikipedia.org/wiki/Apollo

https://en.wikipedia.org/wiki/Dionysus#Other_parallels

https://en.wikipedia.org/wiki/Fibonacci_number

https://en.wikipedia.org/wiki/Nu_(mythology)

https://en.wikipedia.org/wiki/Oedipus

https://en.wikipedia.org/wiki/Roman_Empire#Geography_and_demography

https://news.stanford.edu/pr/02/jasperplots124.html

https://phys.org/news/2011-10-flat-universe.html

https://www.biology-online.org

http://jewishencyclopedia.com/articles/865-adultery

https://www.liveleak.com/view?i=a61_1378358265#wj1odflv7sH0IbPj.01

https://www.skepticalscience.com/co2-higher-in-past-intermediate.htm

https://www.universeguide.com/star/uyscuti

HUME I, A Treatise of Human Nature' Books One, Two and Three; 2nd Edition; Oxford at the Clarendon Press; First Edition 1888, Oxford 1978, 2nd Edition 1978, ISBN 0-19-824588-2

HUME I, A Treatise of Human Nature' Books One, Two and Three; 2nd Edition, 1978, ISBN 0-00-632744-3

JAMES William, 'Pragmatism', eBooks The University of Adelaide Library

JAMES William, 'Psychology' Macmillan and Co 1892

JAMES William, 'The Will to Believe' Longmans, Green, And Co 1912, Project Gutenberg EBook

JAMES William, 'Varieties of Religious Experience' Longmans, Green, And Co, 1903

JIBU, Mari; YASUE, Kunio. Quantum Brain Dynamics And Consciousness, ISBN 978-1556191831

JOHANSON D. "Origins of Modern Humans: Multiregional or Out of Africa?" Action Bioscience. American Institute of Biological Sciences

JUNG C G, 'Aion, Researches into the Phenomenology of the Self, Princeton University Press, 1979, ISBN 0-691-01826-X

JUNG C G, Archetypes of the Collective Unconscious, Routledge and Kegan Paul 1969, ISBN 7100-6295-8

JUNG C G, Civilization in Transition, Routledge and Kegan Paul, 1970, ISBN 0-7100-1640-9

JUNG C G, Psychological Types, Routledge and Kegan, 1976, ISBN 0-691-01813-8

JUNG C G, The Structure and Dynamics of the Psyche, Routledge London, 1969, ISBN 0-7100-6296-6

JUNG C G, Two Essays In Analytical Psychology, Princeton University Press 1972, ISBN 0-691-01782-4

JUNG, C G, Psychology and Alchemy, Series, Princeton University Press, 1952, ISBN 0-691-01831-6

JUNG, C G, Alchemical, Series, Princeton University Press, 1976, ISBN 0-691-01849-9

JUNG, C G, Mysterium Coniunctionis, Bollingen Series, Princeton University Press, 1977, ISBN 0-691-01816-2

KANT Immanuel, Critique of Pure Reason, Cambridge University Press, 1998, ISBN 0-521-35402-1

KING JAMES BIBLE

KING JAMES BIBLE, from Mobile Reference, Thomas Nelson, Inc 1983

GOSPEL OF THOMAS, from the Scholars Version translation published in The Complete Gospels, Elaine Pagels, Harry Camp Memorial Lecturer, January 26-30, 2004 Stanford Humanities Center

LARMOR, J. (1900), Aether and Matter, Cambridge University Press, 1900

LAROUSSE, New Encyclopedia of Mythology, Hamlyn Publishing, 1968, ISBN 0-600-02351-6

LEIBNIZ Basic Writings, The Open Court Publishing Company, 1962

MARTIN R. Thomas, Ancient Greece, From Prehistoric to Hellenistic Times, Yale University Press, 1996, ISBN 0-300-06767-4

MCFADDEN, Johnjoe, (2002). "The Conscious Electromagnetic Information (Cemi) Field Theory: The Hard Problem Made Easy?". Journal of Consciousness Studies

MOUNTFORD Charles and ROBERTS Melva, Dreamtime Stories, Rigby Publishers, 1983, ISBN 978-0727018373

THE NAG HAMMADI LIBRARY, Edited by J. Robinson, Coptic Gnostic Library project.... Brill, 3rd ed. (1988), ISBN 978-0060669355

New York Herald Tribune (September 11, 1932)

NIETZSCHE, Frederich 'The Birth of Tragedy' Cambridge University Press, 1999, ISBN 978-0-521-63987-3

NIETZSCHE, Frederich, 'The Will to Power' Vintage Books 1968, ISBN 394-70437-1

OVID, Metamorphoses, 8 AD, translated under the direction of Sir Samuel Garth, The University of Adelaide Library 2014

Oxford Dictionary, University Press, Oxford 1969

PARACELSUS, Selected Writings, Edited by Jolande Jacobi, Bollingen Series, Princeton University Press, 1995, ISBN 0-691-01876-6

PARIN Paul 'The Dogon people'

PAULI, Wolfgang; et al. (1996). Wissenschaftlicher Briefwechsel mit Bohr, Einstein, Heisenberg, u.a. vol. 4/I. ed. Karl von Meyenn. Berlin: Springer.

PEIERLS, R. (1960). "Wolfgang Ernst Pauli, 1900-1958". Biographical Memoirs of Fellows of the Royal Society.

PHILLIPS, K. J. H. (1995). Guide to the Sun. Cambridge University Press. ISBN 978-0521397889

PLATO (c.427 - 347 BC), The Republic, Penguin Books 1986, ISBN 0-14-044048-8

PLATO'S Cosmology, The Timaeus, Hackett Publishing Company, 1997, ISBN 0-87220-386-7

PLUTARCH, Moralia Vol. V, translated by Frank C. Babbit, The Loeb Classical Library, Harvard University Press, 2003, ISBN 0-674-99337-3

PLUTARCH, Ps., Consolation to Apollonius, 106 E.

POCKETT, Susan, The Nature of Consciousness. ISBN 0-595-12215-9

PTOLEMY Claudius, Tetrabiblos Translated from The Greek Paraphrase Of Proclus By J. M. Ashmand , London, Davis And Dickson, 1822

ROUSSEAU J J, The Reveries of a Solitary, First Promenade

RUSSELL, Bertrand., History of Western Philosophy, p 181, Allen & Unwin Aust P/L 1990, ISBN 0-04-100045-5

SCHOPENHAUER A, The World as Will and Idea, Edited by David Berman, Translated by Jill Berman, Everyman 1997, ISBN 0-460-87505-1

Source for figures: Carbon dioxide, NOAA Earth System Research Laboratory, (updated 2013). Methane, IPCC TAR table 6.1 Archived 2007-06-15 at the Wayback Machine.(updated to 1998)

SPINOZA B, The Ethics and Other Works, Princeton University Press, 1994, ISBN 0-691-03363-3

SPINOZA B, Ethics, Nature and Origin of the Mind, Heron Books

SPINOZA, Benedictus de. 'Chapter 6: Of Miracles'. Thelogico -Political Treatise, translated by Robert Willis

SCHOLZ, Piotr O. (2001). Eunuchs and Castrati: A Cultural History. Markus Wiener Publishers. ASIN B01K2K4CQK

Thirty Years That Shook Physics: The Story of Quantum Theory, 1966, Dover Publications, ISBN 0-486-24895-X

TRISMESTIGUSTUS, Hermes, The Corpus Hermetica, 2nd Century AD

TYLER, E. B., 'Primitive Culture' Volume 1, John Murray 1920

VIERECK, George Sylvester (1930). Glimpses of the Great. New York: The Macaulay Company

VIGNE JD, GUILAINE J, DEBUE K, HAYE L, GÉRARD P (April 2004). "Early taming of the cat in Cyprus". Science

VON FRANZ, Marie Louise, Psyche & Matter, Shambhala Publications, 1992, ISBN 978-1-57062-620-3

VON FRANZ, Marie-Louise, Creation Myths, Shambhala Publictions, 1995, ISBN 1-57062-018-0

WALLACH, Dr J. 'Dead Doctors Don't Lie'
https://www.youtube.com/watch?v=ejUFB424bhM

WILKINSON, Richard H., The Complete Gods and Goddesses of Ancient Egypt, Thames & Hudson, 2003, ISBN 0-500-05120-8

Xenophanes, Fragments of, http://www.iep.utm.edu/xenoph/

YINON Oded 'The Zionist Plan for the Middle East' from "A Strategy for Israel in the Nineteen Eighties" Published by the Association of Arab-American University Graduates, Inc. Belmont, Massachusetts, 1982 Special Document No. 1

14. INDEX

122; disdain for · 152;
dismemberment of · 123;
dismemberment of Osiris · 29;
dissolution of form · 124;
double · 36; garment of soul
and spirit · 124; generating
heat · 388; gross · 144; hair ·
384; healing of · 153; healthy ·
251; idea of · 179; identify with
· 131; immolate · 143;
knowledge of · 171, 173;
liberation from · 102, 124;
modifications · 93; mother's ·
324, 325; negative aspects of
· 152; neglected · 125; of
animal · 459; of beast · 352;
overcoming · 122, 159; penis
of Osiris · 33; positive and
negative · 114; primordial ·
153; prostitution of · 134;
purified · 125; reality of · 125;
regulating · 388; sacrifice and
reconstitution · 36; sacrifice of
· 114; shadow of · 37; shadow
of spirit · 122; sidereal · 153;
soul separated from · 149;
spirit within · 145; temperature
· 324, 386, 414; to become
spirit · 143; two men in one
body · 155; two natures of ·
155; vile and wretched · 139
Budge E. A · 32

C

Cain · 68, 69, 88, 133
Calhoun J. B. · 338
Moses · 89
Campbell J. · 335
Canaan · 61, 62, 65, 69, 70, 71,
80, 84, 85, 86, 94, 162
Carbon Dioxide · 275, 307, 308,
309, 310, 311, 312, 318; and
animals · 12; and

photosynthesis · 274; and
plants · 307, 311, 317, 318;
and sun · 275, 311; as
essential gas · 12; low level of
· 307
Chaos · 25, 57, 59, 157, 184,
212, 303, 375; and Nun · 52;
as myth-making unconscious ·
59; as original Greek deity ·
400; as unformed matrix · 61;
as void · 64; before Creation
in Mythology · 25; of
primordial water · 25;
primordial · 60; unformed · 65
Children of Israel · 62, 81, 89,
90, 91, 92, 94, 95, 97, 98, 101
Christianity · 101, 215, 259, 355,
371, 378, 381; and Alchemy ·
301; and Nietzsche · 259; as
threat to Roman empire · 56;
forced conversion · 63
Circumcision · 93, 141, 333,
334, 370, 371; and
Subincision · 335; as an
affirmation of spiritualised
masculinity · 81; as liberation
of spirit from instinct · 100; as
transformation rite · 335
Cleisthenes · 42
Compartmentalise · 11
Consciousness · 13, 19, 60, 91,
92, 113, 116, 117, 118, 177,
190, 194, 196, 208, 219, 221,
222, 223, 224, 226, 228, 233,
248, 255, 256, 257, 260, 261,
264, 265, 266, 279, 321, 356,
358, 362, 364, 365, 368, 387,
399, 402, 415, 451, 471; and
animals · 417; and fire · 388;
and God · 173; and Hegel ·
220, 221; and Hume · 202;
and James · 236, 245; and
Jung · 258, 262; and Kant ·
189; and Leibniz · 180; and
marijuana · 365; and Osiris ·

27; and Schopenhauer · 207, 208, 210, 212, 213; and Sun · 248, 437; and Will · 341; as Ante Chamber · 41; as daylight · 25, 170; as Father King · 247; as head · 113; as Heaven · 105; conscious attitudes and beliefs · 14; consolidation of · 121; Creative free-flow into · 112; destruction of · 113, 118; disrupted · 114; Ego · 262; Empirical · 195; evolution of · 101, 102; extinguished in Revelation · 113; Freud's concept of Ego · 250; Freud's view · 14; Hegel's Self-Consciousness · 221; Lion symbol · 111; Spirit of Awareness · 399

Constantine: conversion to Christianity · 56

Cosmic Sympathy: Zosimos idea of unity · 143

Covenant · 70, 71, 72, 73, 76, 78, 79

Creation myth · 17, 64, 356; ancient Egyptian · 24; ancient Greek · 52, 61; as origin of awareness · 303; in Astronomy · 303; in the Torah · 64; Roman · 65

Creativity · 91, 160, 175, 215, 355, 442, 444, 445, 446; and painting · 447; and play · 445; and western culture · 354; childlike · 368; encouragement of · 449; hinderance of · 448; of inner child · 108; of Isis · 31; way to relate to inner characters · 444

E

F

Fire · 22, 58, 97, 107, 114, 115,
119, 120, 124, 132, 143, 149,
150, 156, 161, 291, 294, 327,
385, 386, 387, 389, 399, 436,
452, 454, 455; and air · 148;
and cooking · 389; and dragon
· 118; and early humans · 386,
387; and earth · 437; and fiery
spirit · 143; and heart · 121;
and human evolution · 324,
327; and lead · 301; and
Prometheus · 59, 333, 388;
and Satan · 101; and Sodom
and Gomorrah · 72; and sun ·
275; and the God of Moses ·
97; and transformation · 145;
and Vulcan · 156; and water ·
41, 132, 149, 399, 433, 436,
437; as aether · 291; as
energy · 333; as feet · 116; as
heat source · 388; as intuition
· 159; as main Element · 58;
as quality · 193; as spark of
consciousness · 388; as spirit
· 150; as Vesta · 60;
differentiating opposites
through · 147; Gaia's
grandson · 293; in Alchemy ·
149, 300; in censer · 114; in
Philosophy · 162, 164, 165; in
serpent's eyes · 128; in the
eye of Horus · 34; of Exodus ·
89; of transformation · 142;
Ovid's Metamorphoses · 58;
personified by Hephaestus ·
293; Plato's Elements · 144,
453; psychic function · 348;
purification through · 156;
sacrifice in · 90; sidereal body
from · 153; united with water
through earth · 219
Fountain of Youth · 441
Free will · 13
Freud S. S. · 220, 245, 250,
253, 254, 256, 257, 258, 352,
353, 406; and behaviour · 251;
and childhood neurosis · 248;
and complexes · 55; and
dream interpretation · 252,
254; and Eros · 254; and
human nature · 245; and
incest · 249; and James · 245;
and Oedipus myth · 245; and
Orpheus · 255; and primal sin
· 255; and repression · 259; as
father figure to Jung · 256; as
mental health expert · 406;
dream motifs · 245; dreams
and idea of unity · 251; idea of
unity · 254; liberation of
instincts · 245; personal and
mythological categories · 252;
theory of sexuality · 252; view
of the unconscious · 14

G

Gad · 62, 81, 86, 87, 98
Galaxy · 303, 398, 400, 405,
426, 428; and Andromeda
galaxy · 302; and gravity ·
177, 286, 294; and myth · 429,
438; centre of · 288, 295, 297,
303; gravitational lensing ·
286; gravity and synchronicity
· 298; orbital velocities · 286;
warping space · 285
Gambling · 411
Garden of Eden · 65, 133
Geb · 22, 25, 27, 40
Geertz, Clifford · 19
Genesis · 35, 64, 65, 91, 100
Gnosticism · 121, 122, 129; and
Alchemy · 147; and intuition ·
122; outlawed · 140
God Particle · 11, 17, 299
God's Passover · 89
Gold · 71, 89, 90, 141, 299, 300,
301; and God · 139; as sun ·

the thing-in-itself · 212; of the unconscious · 177; of Toa · 211; of transformation · 301; of upper and lower soul · 179; of Will · 210, 211; of world tree · 425; perfect · 203; possessed by · 223, 362; projected · 273, 300; projection of · 356; reality of · 157; slave and master · 361; Soul as mother · 162; symbolic aspect · 200; that god wants to become man · 133; to create a building · 438; transformation of · 146, 199, 201, 360, 400; united with object · 332

Idea of unity · 11, 12, 14, 122, 125, 174, 175, 183, 188, 196, 204, 207, 227, 230, 239, 241, 242, 244, 251, 259, 260, 275, 293, 345, 347, 348, 349, 350, 352, 353, 361, 362, 364, 366, 415, 427, 457, 458; absolute · 198; and ethics · 259; and relationship · 12; as a sphere and world · 226; as living force · 12; as one world government · 436; as Self · 257; between waking and dream · 228; Difference to Unity · *See* Unity; experience of · 12; in collective structure · 376; in Philosophy · 161; in psychology · 245; in waiting · 205; James · 237; Kant's · 191; Paracelsus · 158; personal · 261; Political Idea of · 347; possessed by · 347, 349; represented by saviour · 125; union of opposites · 203

Imagination · 177, 189, 299, 392, 400, 407, 438, 445, 448; active · 378; and art · 438; and dreams · 177; and flight · 426;

and knowledge · 429; and myth · 400; and reality · 101; and sense · 168; and soul · 167; and time · 290; Aristotle's conception · 167; cook's · 452; evil · 70; of Big Bang Theory · 400; of object · 189; passive viewing · 177; popular · 428; Spinoza's conception · 177; the arts · 445

Individuation · 85, 141, 211, 212, 249, 260, 261, 262, 263; and ancient Egypt · 27; and Oedipus · 249; as regulating spirit · 260; Jung's conception · 263; term · 256

Inner Character(s) · 22, 39, 48, 74, 93, 125, 137, 138, 194, 197, 211, 214, 215, 228, 229, 234, 250, 252, 256, 261, 265, 267, 322, 340, 357, 359, 362, 368, 372, 374, 380, 434, 440, 441, 442, 443, 444, 446, 448, 449, 450, 454, 456, 457, 459, 463; and ancients · 440; and buildings · 449, 454; and Dionysus · 233; and emotions · 279; and human functions · 54; and numbers · 239; and play · 380; and professions · 439; and Projection · 21, 24, 36; androgynous · 128; as archetypes · 55, 241, 440; as gods · 46; as matrix · 154; as models · 163; as reflections · 460; awareness of · 373; central · 110, 152, 168, 457, 458, 459, 460, 461, 462, 463, 464; critical of · 132, 136; feminine and masculine · 374; fluidity of · 127; God · 106, 124; have personalities · 362; identified with · 138; introspection · 108; knowledge of · 374; motivating · 223;

J

K

and noumena · 196; synthetic unity · 194

Khaibit · 38; shadow of the body · 37

Khat · 38; term for Body · 36

Khepri · 23, 26, 211

King David · 62

Kitchen · 156, 451, 452, 454, 455

Knowledge · 29, 32, 42, 165, 167, 175, 288, 302, 317, 319, 327, 330, 355, 359, 376, 384, 386, 387, 392, 395, 396, 405, 409, 415, 426, 447, 457, 465; a priori · 194; adaptation and survival · 390; alchemical · 152; and acceptance · 225; and animism · 15; and experience · 146, 264, 328; and first principles · 167; and flight · 355; and hierarchies · 376; and human body · 173; and intuition · 195; and projection · 201, 213, 331; and reason · 158; and relationship · 154, 201; and science · 307; and sense · 150; and snake · 327; and Socrates · 45; and synchronicity · 267; and understanding · 12, 175, 263, 351; and wisdom · 168; architectural · 359; as DNA · 314; Bee hives · 325; beyond our · 427; boundaries of · 187; children · 360; contradicting senses · 413; Einstein's view · 429; Gnosis · 122; in Revelation · 116; innate · 318, 325; inner · 325, 337; inner character · 374; intuition and insight · 122; lack of · 352; limits of · 201, 303, 347; limits of in physics · 159; looking inside · 250; of ancient myths · 398; of artist · 159; of constellations · 395; of cosmos · 391, 400, 428; of eternal truths · 182; of fire · 387; of God · 175, 176, 183; of good and evil · 91, 133; of human body · 171; of inner psychological processes · 427; of inner world · 220; of Mars · 394; of nature · 175; of object · 264; of oneself · 182, 440; of opposites · 433; of Paracelsus · 157; of Plato · 46; of projection · 264; of sculpture · 448; of sun · 22, 403, 404; of the central inner character · 460; of the moon · 229; of the supernatural · 408; of Unity · 216; of upper heavens · 165; present day knowledge of matter · 180; scientific · 167, 229; snake example · 263; snake idea · 263; spirit · 322; tree of life in Genesis · 65; unlearn · 17

L

Laban · 77, 78, 79

Lamb · 114; and Jesus · 112; and lion · 112; and Passover · 89, 91; as child · 112; as royalty · 114; of Abel · 68; opening seals · 114; positive aspect of · 114; sacrifice of · 112

Lead · 301

Leah · 77, 78, 79

Leibniz G. W. · 11, 178, 179, 180, 182, 183, 186, 289, 292, 412; and matter · 181; and memory · 181; and perception · 181; and reason · 178; body and soul · 179; idea of God · 178, 179; idea of monad · 127,

196; idea of unity · 179, 183; mandala · 180; pre-established harmony · 178; rational soul · 182; unity as monad · 180

Levi · 62, 77, 80, 81, 98; as weapon of violence · 86; sons of · 90, 92, 93

Leviticus · 93

Lion · 18, 19, 30, 35, 111, 115, 118, 246, 253, 266, 328, 401; and constellation Leo · 399; and Horus · 30; and humans · 195; and Judah · 86; and lamb · 112; as Cherubim · 68; as king and consciousness · 111; as royalty · 327; as sphinx · 247; brutal reality of · 178, 186; characteristics · 111, 385; displeasing · 19; idea of · 18, 19, 327; nature · 327

Living room · 423, 452

Lot · 71, 72, 73, 96

Luna: See also Moon · 159, 229, 392, 393, 399

Luther · 109

M

Mamluk Empire · 63

Mandala: and psychological functions · 456; and Self · 261; as Monad · 180, 181; at end of life · 462; home plans · 452; in Alchemy · 299; in nature · 431; of Hegel · 226; of Hume · 205; of personal unity · 92; of Puffer fish · 430; of skydivers · 363; three dimensional · 430, 431; two dimensional · 431

Mark Anthony · 56

Mars · 61, 252, 357, 397, 405; and history of agriculture · 60; and Venus · 60, 359, 400; as

angry inner character · 215; as wandering red body · 394; outward looking · 61; planet · 355, 394, 438; son of Jupiter · 399

Mary Magdala · 102, 108, 122, 149, 377

Mary Magdalene · See Mary Magdala

Mary the Prophetess · 141, 159

Matrix: as Maternal Womb · 154

Matter · 11, 15, 69, 122, 136, 139, 159, 172, 174, 180, 183, 199, 211, 237, 242, 264, 271, 272, 273, 280, 284, 286, 287, 288, 291, 292, 294, 297, 300, 302, 303, 305, 356, 400, 403, 413, 421, 435, 447, 460; ancient conception of · 269; and Alchemy · 299; and Aristotle · 168; and Big bang Theory · 302; and body · 102, 140, 152, 181, 290, 333; and building · 449; and Democritus conception · 140; and DNA · 272; and EME · 265, 293; and Gaia · 291; and God · 183; and gravity · 240, 286, 294, 297, 298; and idea · 150, 241, 269, 423; and inner characters · 137; and intellect · 209; and Leibniz · 178, 179; and mandala · 181; and Monads · 180; and photons · 278; and physics · 282; and projection · 299, 304; and psyche · 12, 159, 265, 273, 274, 278, 279, 281, 282, 295, 298, 301; and psyche unified · 265; and Quantum Mechanics · 285, 299; and Schopenhauer · 208, 209; and soul · 168; and space · 12, 285, 287, 293, 412, 413; and spirit · 302; and sun · 146; and synchronicity ·

265, 298, 409; and time · 294; and Unus Mundus · 267; Aristotle and Plato · 169; attracts ideas · 301; balance of positive and negative forces · 41; characteristics of · 292; cognition of · 187; crystalline structure of · 271; dark · 281, 303; dead · 209, 210; decay of · 288; differentiated from psyche · 299; differentiation of · 121; forces of attraction and repulsion · 228, 272; forces within · 209; gods created from pure · 136; gravity attracts matter to a centre · 297; idea of · 180, 183, 209; liberation from · 102; liberation of spirit · 68; living · 272; non living · 270; of animals and humans · 273; organic · 437; predominately space · 187; projection onto · 141; soul in · 144; space as container for · 289; spirit in · 101, 139, 140, 159, 160, 178, 186, 302, 339; transformation of · 122, 158, 273, 274, 300; unity of matter and spirit through soul · 172

Meaningful coincidences · *See* Synchronicity

Memory · 199; and dreams - James · 236; and feeling · 182; and synchronicity · 424; and the present · 204; and time · 288, 290; as Mnemosyne · 54; Hume's conception · 203; Leibniz's conception · 181; part of opposites · 240; Spinoza's conception · 176, 177; unconscious product · 177

Mercurius · 136, 159, 244, 355; as idea of unity · 159; as soul · 39, 159; as Tinctura · 157; male amd female · 159; union of body and spirit · 160

Mercury · 60, 355, 393, 397, 398, 399, 403, 405

Miracle · 406

Model: of Plato · 19, 46, 124, 162, 163, 164, 173, 279, 281, 291, 341, 342, 344, 367, 368, 369, 417, 421, 448, 449

Monad · 127, 180, 181, 183; and John · 127; and Sophia · 128; as unity · 180; idea of unity · 181, 182; Leibniz's conception · 180, 181, 183; of animals · 183

Moon · 23, 29, 34, 36, 57, 65, 97, 112, 116, 219, 281, 304, 390, 397, 399, 403, 404, 405, 433, 447; above and below · 165; and earth · 281; and EME · 304; and flight · 355, 438; and gravity · 286, 298; and Jupiter · 60; and sun · 22, 23, 300, 398, 400, 404, 405, 433, 437; and tides · 397; and water · 22; as Diana · 399; as Horus · 33; as Luna · 229, 392; as mother · 405; as Osiris · 27; as Thoth · 23; as unconscious · 219, 437; blood red · 113; contained by sky · 23; cycle · 403; effect on humans · 304; feminine · 403; idea of · 332, 333; illuminates night · 404; Jacob's dream · 81; lifeless and waterless · 404; masculine · 23; moist · 398; orbit · 286; personification of · 52; phases · 34; Ptolemy's conception · 397; sky, earth and sun · 23; under woman's feet · 117

Moses · 88, 90, 91, 92, 94, 95, 96, 97, 98, 99, 101, 111, 118, 125, 126, 132, 133, 174, 457;

and Aaron · 93; and family ·
91; and fiery serpents · 96;
and law · 103; and magical
rod · 89; and stone tablets ·
90; and twelve tribes · 94; cast
into river · 88; denied the
Promised Land · 98; five
books of · 61, 64; God of · 90,
91; hears the voice of God
directly · 96; instructed by God
· 88, 90, 94; jealous · 92;
outwits God · 95
Mother Nature · 164, 290
Music · 51, 232, 359
Mycenaean · 42
Mythology · 25, 353, 382, 395,
399, 406; and Freud · 256;
and ideas · 369; and Jung ·
258; and miracles · 407; and
Osiris · 41; and space · 293;
Australian Aborigine · 390;
born from the land · 382;
contemporary · 17; Egyptian ·
23; filling void · 428; Greek ·
28, 44, 47, 48, 169, 291, 292,
329; of cosmos · 400; of fire ·
388; of nations · 382; of
planets · 400; of Sol · 393; of
space · 290; relationship to
object · 304; Roman · 56, 394

N

Nag Hammadi Library · 122, 124
Naphtali · 62, 81, 86, 87, 98
Natural Man · 101; and
enlightened man · 125; and
Satan · 103; aware of · 103;
differentiate from God man ·
458; instinctive · 101, 102; of
Hume · 202; of Nietzsche ·
346; of Rousseau · 183, 184,
185, 186; overcome · 120, 152
Nature versus Nurture · 368

Nephthys · 25, 33
Newton I · 281, 283, 287, 290,
292
Nietzsche F. W. · 54, 230, 234,
235, 250, 258, 259, 346, 349,
463; and Jung · 259; Apollo
and Dionysus · 231, 233;
concept of eternal return ·
222, 462; concept of Overman
· 346; descent into the
unconscious · 250; feeling for
people · 234; fine intuition ·
230; idea of Overman · 290;
identifying with inner character
· 252; inflation of · 383; music
and dance · 230; recognition
of moral opposites · 234;
tragic life · 230; will to power ·
316, 334
Nile River · 21
Noah · 69, 70, 71, 73
Nought: of Descartes · 171
Noumena: of Kant · 197
Nuclear Fission · 276, 277
Nuclear Fusion · 276
Numbers · 93, 95
Nun · 25, 52, 64
Nut · 22, 23, 25, 26, 27, 40

O

Oedipus · 247, 248, 249, 250,
253, 256, 375; and Dionysus ·
255; and Freud · 245, 258;
and self analysis · 249; as
complex · 406; descent into
unconscious · 250; detailed ·
246; heroic life of · 249;
means wounded foot · 247;
riddle of sphinx · 248
Old Testament · 104, 110, 111
Olympic Games · 42
One World Government · 436

Osiris · 24, 25, 27, 28, 29, 30, 31, 32, 33, 34, 35, 36, 37, 40, 41, 48, 71, 77; and brother Set · 41; and Dionysus · 123, 142, 218; and Horus · 35; and rebirth of Jesus · 56; as central deity · 24; civilising aspect of · 27; death and resurrection · 26; dismemberment of · 29; family of · 33; ladder to heaven · 35; myth of · 27; on throne in heaven · 36; Plutarch's analysis · 31; Plutarch's version · 27; resurrection · 30; willing death · 145

Overman: of Nietzsche · 252, 290, 346

Ovid · 57, 59; Publius Ovidius Naso · 57

P

Palladium · 452

Paracelsus · 152, 154, 158, 159, 160; and Arcanum · 157; and nature · 160; and Platonic elements · 153; and third uniting function · 155; and Unity · 158; creative process · 155; differentiation of functions · 158; father of Toxicology · 158; fire of Vulcan · 156; need for a pure heart · 154; on women · 155; spiritual approach · 153

Participation Mystique · 263, 341, 362, 377

Pauli W. · 277

Penis: of Osiris · 33

Pericles · 45

Persephone · 48, 50, 51, 53, 54, 231, 255

Persian Empire · 44, 47

Persians · 45, 46, 62

Phantom · See Shadow

Physics · 11; unified with psychology · 12

Plato · 30, 31, 37, 44, 47, 58, 162, 163, 179, 198, 200, 212, 254, 289, 292, 341, 353, 367, 368, 399, 405, 453; and aether · 291; and archetype · 339; and Aristotle · 165, 168, 169; and Descartes · 173; and Dreamtime · 344; and element of fire · 387; and Gnosticism · 122; and Hegel · 226; and Heraclitus · 162; and immortal soul · 46; and inner characters · 460; and Jung · 192; and Kant · 193, 200; and model · 164; and receptacle of being · 412; and Schopenhauer · 212; and Spinoza · 173; and Unity · 164; father as God · 164; follower of Socrates · 46; idea of father and mother · 369; other world · 428; parents and child · 163; receptacle of becoming · 171; search for universal values · 46

Plato's Cosmology · 133, 164, 294

Pleroma: Gnostic term · 124

Plutarch · 27, 31, 32

Poleis · 42

Possession · 32, 167, 195, 262, 352, 361, 375, 383; and broadening interests · 440; and Jesus · 137; by an idea · 223; by an inner character · 99, 357, 372, 383, 440; by an inner God · 222; by consciousness · 358; by contrasexual character · 375; by instinct · 339; by Mars · 358; by national symbol · 379; by one-sidedness · 446; by positive · 357; by the idea of Unity · 347; by Wotan · 382; danger of · 139, 348, 440; healing of · 233; identification with · 13; national · 339; Nietzsche's · 383; overcoming · 262

Prima Materia: in Alchemy · 141, 155, 157, 301

Principium individuationis · See Individuation

Projection · 16, 17, 18, 21, 22, 34, 198, 199, 208, 213, 225, 229, 250, 252, 266, 277, 281, 300, 302, 304, 337, 341, 343, 345, 348, 356, 375, 376, 380, 405, 409, 427, 429, 435, 444, 446, 447, 454; and Animism · 17; and armed services · 376; and astrology · 304; and chemistry · 299; and conflict · 371; and contrasexual character · 161; and emotion · 434; and friends · 444; and instincts · 333; and Jung · 146, 263, 264; and matter · 299; and mythology · 428; and nations · 380, 381; and outer space · 165; and planets · 304; and race · 344; and racism · 361; and romantic love · 340; and Rorschach Inkblot test · 399; and soul · 264; and stealing · 332; and synchronicity · 273, 274, 407; and tree · 19; and Unity · 267; and values · 362; and world · 341; as initial form of synchronicity · 264; as natural form of connectedness · 263; as natural function · 371; attractive forces of · 434; between master and slave · 336; collective · 341, 342; connecting idea with object ·

331; contemporary · 428; cross contamination · 213; different to object · 264; differentiating · 373; diminishment of · 201; drawing out · 261; enforced · 101; forming relationship with · 360; give initial connection · 200; group identity · 377; idea of a partner · 349; ideas onto matter · 301; identification with good · 102; in physics · 17; inner character onto planets and stars · 24; intensity of · 434; knowledge of object · 264; lessening of · 157; love at first site · 434; male and female · 403; natural function of · 336; natural part of human functioning · 362; of authority · 342; of child onto parent · 342; of contrasexual inner character · 340; of evil · 336, 345; of extroverts · 242; of father · 370, 444; of friends · 371; of idea of unity · 348; of inner character · 229; of inner parental authority · 369; of mother · 444, 454; of nations · 343; of negative · 102; of parental authority · 353; of shadow · 357; of symbolic content · 229; of undeveloped qualities · 435, 442; onto animals · 24; onto celestial bodies · 392; onto enemy · 383; onto matter · 141, 299; onto other cultures · 360; onto outer space · 201; onto parent · 340; onto parents · 345, 368; onto people · 16, 331; onto Satan · 103; onto Saturn · 201; psychic and physical reality · 356; recognition of · 374; relativity of time · 414;

slave and master · 361; study and employment · 376; transformation of · 17, 331, 434; transformed · 146; two shadows · 37; unifying function · 263; withdrawing · 331, 380

Promised Land · 90, 94, 98

Protons · 270, 282

Psychology: ambiguous language of · 454; and Hegel · 230; and inner world · 380; and James · 236; and Kant · 198; and myth-making unconscious · 458; and Paracelsus · 158; depth · 384; Freudian · 258; Jungian · 262; male · 250; modern · 211, 226; of instinct · 339; relation to Physics · 12, 282; repression in · 446; schools of · 219

Ptah · 24, 400

Q

Quantum Mechanics · 11, 265, 275, 285, 299, 301

R

Ra · 23, 24, 25, 26, 27, 34, 35, 37

Rachel · 77, 78, 79, 84

Racism · 361

Rebekah · 75, 76, 77

Red Sea · 62, 89, 96

Reuben · 62, 81, 84, 86, 98

Revelation · 109, 338; and number seven · 109; and opposites · 110; ends on positive note · 120; horror of ·

460; relationship to inner woman · 118

Ritual · 18, 19

Romulus and Remus · 60

Rousseau J. J. · 54, 183, 185, 205, 206, 250, 258; and depraved instinctuality · 186; and isolation · 186; and James · 236; and Leibniz · 186; and natural man · 183, 184, 186; and Nietzsche · 212; descent into the unconscious · 250; description of the unconscious · 187; insanity · 132; journey to underworld · 184

S

Sarah · 72, 73, 74, 75, 76

Sarai · See Sarah

Satan · 117, 120, 121, 355, 382, 459; and Jesus · 339; and lower realm of nature · 110; and matter · 140; and natural man · 101; as dragon · 116, 117; as evil and animalistic · 103; cast out · 102, 117; dark adversary · 104; long lost brother · 119; number six · 110; opposite of Jesus · 121; the natural man · 103; with hint of light · 103

Saturn: equivalent to Chronus · 60, 61, 201, 301, 394, 395, 397, 399, 405, 447

Saturnalia: Festival · 60

Saul · 62

Schopenhauer A. · 37, 207, 216, 230, 251, 257, 317, 320; and Hegel · 216; and ideas · 214; and individuation · 212; and inner characters · 215; and opposites · 208; and projection · 208; and

238, 248, 289, 301, 302, 412, 451; and animal · 459; and body · 131, 145; and body and soul · 131; and circumcision · 99; and dove · 139; and fireplace · 455; and introversion · 146; and jealousy · 94; and love · 132, 339; and Platonic elements · 153; and Sol · 399; and Sophia · 128; and soul · 124; and thinking · 289; and twelve stars · 117; as animal spirits · 171; as eagle · 68, 118; as father · 71; as fire and air · 148, 150; as goal · 122; as God · 179; as good · 85; as idea · 155, 159; as Ka · 36, 39; as Osiris · 29; body and soul united with · 147; connecting to body · 150; creative · 225; differentiation from instinct · 103; differentiation from matter · 69, 121; differentiation from soul · 126; differentiation with political · 347; Dionysian · 364; disconnected from body · 122; dwelling in flesh · 153; embedded in body · 122; eternal · 218; extract from body and matter · 160; extracting from body · 140; extracting from metals · 140; fiery · 143; from body · 142; from earth · 68; from earth to · 101; functions · 120; good · 117; guidance of · 247; healing effect · 153; heavenly · 100; higher · 73, 75, 139; identification with · 346; identify with · 131; in matter · 139, 159; in potentia · 25; incorruptable · 217; innate knowledge · 322; liberate from heaven · 152; liberate from matter · 186; liberate from matter and body · 152; light of · 123; making conscious · 225; of consciousness · 399; of culture · 70; of Gnosticism · 122; of God · 140, 154; of goodness · 152; of grief · 440; of growth · 373; of mind · 264; of the land · 351, 353, 379; of Zosimos · 147; orientation · 120; overcoming physical · 125; purified · 141; regulating · 260; seven · 109; union with body · 160; unity of matter and spirit through soul · 172; upper · 102, 129, 172, 227; values · 352; virginal · 127; wandering · 100; whitening · 147; within · 145; within void · 64

Subincision: and Circumcision · 335

Sun · 23, 24, 27, 34, 36, 54, 57, 64, 65, 80, 97, 109, 112, 115, 116, 117, 151, 209, 232, 233, 255, 256, 261, 276, 286, 297, 300, 301, 307, 313, 384, 385, 387, 390, 391, 394, 397, 398, 399, 402, 403, 404, 405, 413, 414, 425, 426, 433, 436, 438, 447, 452; and agriculture · 22; and angel · 116; and Apollo · 255, 399; and climate · 307, 311; and early humans · 385; and gamma rays · 276; and Garden of Eden · 65; and Jupiter · 60; and Leo · 399; and Mercury · 398; and moon · 22, 23, 219, 398, 400, 403, 404, 405, 433, 437; and natural cycles · 26; and person's life · 26; and plants · 339; and shade · 389; and termites · 326; and time · 413; and Vulcan · 60; and water ·

T

component of synchronicity ·
412, 416, 421; cycles of · 414;
devouring nature of · 291;
distortion of · 285; feeling of ·
290; fundamental aspect of ·
284; idea of · 287, 288; linear
progression of · 285, 288, 290,
409, 412; measurable · 285;
physical reality · 196; related
to Ra · 26; relativity in dreams
· 288, 412; space and matter ·
414; travel · 400
Toa · See Individuation
Torah · 68, 69, 100, 101, 124,
126, 128, 129, 146
Tyler E. B · 15, 16
Typhon: Greek name for Set ·
28, 29, 31, 34

U

Ugliest Man: of Nietzsche · 252
Unconscious · 14, 18, 19, 34,
59, 87, 91, 100, 102, 108, 109,
113, 133, 177, 186, 193, 194,
201, 211, 212, 213, 215, 216,
218, 219, 220, 221, 225, 228,
238, 240, 249, 250, 251, 252,
256, 257, 258, 260, 261, 262,
263, 264, 266, 267, 288, 289,
295, 299, 302, 331, 346, 347,
349, 367, 370, 373, 375, 379,
387, 395, 401, 402, 408, 411,
412, 414, 415, 416, 417, 418,
422, 423, 424, 426, 427, 428,
433, 435, 438, 442, 445, 448,
457, 460, 464; and building ·
359, 449; and computer
games · 364; and Conscious ·
106, 356, 426; and creative
spirit · 225; and creative work
· 358; and Descartes · 169;
and dream · 251; and emotion
· 222, 434; and eternity · 112;
and fish · 30, 69; and floods ·
100; and freedom of
expression · 353; and inner
characters · 265, 458; and
inner god · 101; and internet ·
364; and intoxication · 364;
and introverts · 357; and
intuition · 13, 128, 170; and
Luna · 399; and madness ·
212; and music · 359; and
natural man · 185; and
Nietzsche · 250; and night ·
113; and painting · 447, 448;
and Paracelsus · 153, 156;
and personality · 368; and
Prometheus · 388; and
sculpture · 448; and sea · 91;
and space · 292; and symbol ·
331; and synchronicity · 298;
and time · 292, 414; and unity
· 352; and water of life · 77; as
black hole · 427; as dark cave
· 212; as dark devouring
woman · 248; as death of
night · 248; as Dreamtime ·
344; as epiphenomenon · 245;
as feminine · 433; as
foundation · 348; as Id · 14; as
masculine · 433; as maternal
womb · 324; as moon · 219;
as mother · 223; as natural
expression · 445; as night ·
53; as nought · 173; as ocean
· 205; as sea · 28; as super-
sensible · 220; as underworld
· 184; as water · 104; as
wilderness · 100; associated
with hell · 113; collective ·
193, 257; collective projection
· 342; compensating · 114,
335, 429; correcting role · 420;
creative · 257; Creative free-
flow from · 112; dammed
energy · 364; dark and
destructive aspect · 114;

descent into · 114; emergence of Ego · 41; emerging from · 41; expressing · 359, 460; female for male · 99, 221; guideing principle · 401; home as mother · 450; in projected form · 216; influence of · 225; making visible · 358; mollified · 117; Myth-making · 14, 17, 25, 41, 44, 59, 130, 193, 245, 248, 249, 257, 258, 283, 390, 395, 398, 399, 400, 401, 402, 408, 412, 427, 428, 429, 437, 438, 444, 447, 453, 457, 458, 465; objective reality of inner products · 197; observing · 191; of Joseph · 82; ordering system · 177; overcoming · 117; personal · 14; process of revelation · 463; processes · 375, 438; projection of · 20, 21, 34, 141, 229, 273, 300; projection of inferiorities · 360; projection onto planets · 304; projections · 18; Rousseau's conception · 187; scientific attitude towards · 256; separation from conscious · 120; symbolic nature · 429; symbols for · 389; unity with conscious · 220; yearnings · 118

Understanding · 27, 53, 92, 106, 131, 132, 133, 145, 154, 157, 175, 176, 188, 189, 190, 191, 192, 193, 194, 195, 197, 200, 208, 209, 210, 218, 242, 245, 260, 267, 273, 281, 303, 312, 317, 324, 341, 344, 348, 349, 352, 355, 356, 369, 412, 414, 415, 423, 458, 459, 464; and aesthetic function · 218; and awareness · 408; and chain of thoughts · 218; and enlightenment · 110; and enlightenment and insight · 112; and ethics and reason · 102; and experience · 463; and grace, perception and prudence · 128; and insight · 101, 171, 347; and knowledge · 12, 175, 263, 351; and lapis · 144, 147; and love · 92; and love and idea · 128; and number seven · 109; and sense · 196; and spirit of love · 132; and synthetic unity · 194; and thinking · 188; as third component · 433; beings of · 197; contemporary · 173; different to imagination · 177; dreams · 401; including nature · 227; intellectual · 196; intuitive · 172; lack of · 236, 352, 360, 442; myth-making characters behind · 197; of alchemy · 300; of Aristotle · 167; of creation · 302; of Descartes · 170; of facts · 355; of God · 151; of human nature · 186, 217, 352; of inner characters · 442; of material science · 300; of moral relativity · 227; of nature · 175; of Nietzsche · 290; of opposites · 433; of physical universe · 11; of plant behaviour and physiology · 313; of relationship · 464; of the idea of unity · 258; of the sun · 403; of the unconscious · 250; of unity · 120, 173, 461; projections · 358; psychic processes · 456; scientific · 303, 415; spiritual · 172; the idea of unity · 244; the key to unity · 456; unconscious processes · 438; union of opposites · 143; uniting function · 220

relationship to · 225; Self as symbol of · 261; sense of · 374; single in dreams · 251; speculations of · 461; synthetic · 194, 197; systematic · 200; three dimensional · 226; through separation · 108; transcendental · 194, 195; underlying · 298, 302, 427; undifferentiated · 207, 240, 299, 384; undiscovered · 237; union through soul · 132
Unity of the cosmos · 11, 356
Unus Mundus: Latin for 'one world' · 267
Uroboros · 157, 217

V

Venus · 252, 394, 403, 405; and Mars · 60, 61, 357, 359, 394, 400; as bright queen of the sky · 393; as inner character · 215; as wandering star · 405; daughter of Jupiter · 399; goddess of love, beauty and desire · 61; of Ptolemy · 397; second planet from Sol · 393
Virgin Mary · 71, 102
Von Franz M. L. · 278
Vulcan · 60, 156

W

Wallach J. · 305
Water · 22, 34, 41, 58, 75, 76, 90, 91, 93, 105, 116, 117, 118, 120, 132, 134, 148, 149, 150, 151, 153, 154, 176, 193, 219, 269, 272, 273, 275, 291, 294, 313, 314, 317, 338, 339, 385, 386, 391, 393, 394, 399, 425, 436; and agriculture · 22, 52; and air · 149; and combustion · 275; and dragon · 118; and earth · 58, 148, 149; and fire · 132, 149, 219, 433, 436; and lunacy · 304; and minerals · 271; and Moses · 88; and Prometheus · 59; and Reuben · 86; and space · 285; and sun · 151; and transformation · 145; as aqua permanens · 144; as feeling · 426; as life · 91; as living streams · 59; as milk · 23; as primordial chaos · 25; atomic structure · 272; boiling · 142, 144; Cholla · 316; cooling effect · 388; erodes earth · 149; from rock · 89, 95, 96; glacial · 305; great flood · 70; ice crystals · 271; in Philosophy · 162, 164, 165; in photosynthesis · 275; liquid state · 271; molecule · 270; nourishing · 19; of bitterness · 94; of life · 77, 120; Plato's Elements · 144, 453; psychic function · 348; saltwater to sweet · 89; sparkling · 143; speed of light in · 285; transform into blood · 88; vapor · 275; vaporise into gas · 272; walking on · 104
Wholeness · *See* Unity
Will to Power · 340, 379; and survival · 314, 339; instinct for food and survival · 84; Nietzsche's concept of · 317, 334; school of Adler · 258
Wisdom · 92, 154, 157, 170; and Athena · 51; and Isis · 27; and lamb · 112; and Plato · 46; and snake · 67; and the fourth light · 128; intuition and scientific knowledge · 168; knowledge of good and evil ·

www.ingramcontent.com/pod-product-compliance
Lightning Source LLC
Chambersburg PA
CBHW072058040426
42334CB00040B/1325